IMPACT OF MASS MEDIA

LONGMAN SERIES IN PUBLIC COMMUNICATION
Series Editor: Ray Eldon Hiebert

IMPACT OF MASS MEDIA

Current Issues

edited by

Ray Eldon Hiebert
Carol Reuss

Longman
New York & London

IMPACT OF MASS MEDIA: CURRENT ISSUES

Longman Inc., 95 Church St., White Plains, N.Y. 10601
Associated companies, branches, and representatives throughout the world.

Developmental Editor: Gordon T. R. Anderson
Editorial and Design Supervisor: Barbara Lombardo
Production Supervisor: Karen Lumley
Composition: ComCom
Printing and Binding: Alpine Press

Cover Art: Bas-relief sculpture by Karin Goodlive. It is a Multimedia construction of wood, copper, fired enamel, computer components, electronic circuits, and oil paints. This sculpture, done in the mid 1960s, is an early image of the impact of mass media as a function of "social intelligence."

Library of Congress Cataloging in Publication Data
Main entry under title:

Impact of mass media.

    (Longman series in public communication)
    Includes index.
    1. Mass media—United States—Addresses, essays,
lectures. 2. Mass media—Influence—Addresses, essays,
lectures. I. Hiebert, Ray Eldon. II. Reuss, Carol.
III. Series.
P92.U5I46 1985   302.2'34'0973   84-21333
ISBN 0-582-28555-0 (pbk.)

Manufactured in the United States of America
Printing: 9 8 7 6 5 4 3 2 1   Year: 93 92 91 90 89 88 87 86 85

CONTENTS

PREFACE

It is, perhaps, no small coincidence that the man elected to be president of the United States for most of the decade of the eighties has been called "the great communicator." Ronald Reagan became the most powerful man in the world in the 1980s not as a lawyer or legislator or statesman or diplomat or military leader; these might have been the usual routes to power in earlier times, but not now. President Reagan started his career as a radio sports announcer, and he spent most of his professional life as a motion picture actor. He knew how to perform in front of a camera. He knew how to deal with reporters and editors and producers—the gatekeepers of the media. And he knew how to play to the masses through the mass media.

These may be the most important abilities for a man of power and leadership in our age. For this is an age of mass communication. And Ronald Reagan was uniquely qualified for his time as a "camera" president.

Franklin Delano Roosevelt was also a great communicator. He was probably our first mass media president, for he knew better than most of his predecessors how to use the mass media. But Roosevelt was president during the great radio era. He was a "microphone" president; he knew how to project his booming voice to the masses through their loudspeakers at home. He probably could not have been elected in an age of television. He was confined to a wheelchair, and TV cameras would probably not have been able to project the same image of power on television screens as the microphones did through radios.

This simple example illustrates something of the impact of mass media. We cannot argue with the fact that the mass media have played an important role in shaping politics in America. Today, the dominant mass medium is television, and it has dictated the type of person who can exercise political power in our society.

Yet questions about the precise impact of mass media remain unanswered. We know that the mass media have an impact, but the answers as to just how and why and what remain elusive. Behavioral scientists are examining the effects of mass media; we know that we can predict certain outcomes in certain situations. But the variables are numerous. Two social scientists, Bernard Berelson and Morris Janowitz, once summarized knowledge about the effects of mass media in their book *Reader in Public Opinion and Communication* (Free Press, 1966):

> The effects of communication are many and diverse. They may be short-range or long-run. They may be manifest or latent. They may be strong or weak. They may derive from any number of aspects of the communication content. They may be considered as psychological or political or economic or sociological. They may operate upon opinions, values, information levels, skills, taste, or overt behavior. (p. 379)

In other words, it would be impossible to make any sweeping generalizations about the impact of the mass media, even though we know they have impact. And social scientists in the 1980s have not moved much further beyond Berelson and Janowitz's statement. The effects of the mass media have to be measured and predicted on a case-by-case basis, taking into consideration all the variables in each situation.

This book is not devoted to a scientific examination of the specifics of mass media impact. Instead, it presents the current arguments about the impact of the mass media, by some of the media's leading thinkers, experienced observers and thoughtful critics.

Questions of mass media impact usually bring about a heated debate. The answers are still not agreed to universally, even with increased scientific analysis. This book is about those debates. And the arguments that are raised here may be among the most important questions of our age, because we are all affected by the mass media. And we have all debated these questions ourselves, ever since we emerged from behind the dark glasses of childhood to realize that the TV tube and the silver screen and the printed word may not, after all, represent reality.

When we realize that the illusions we have received from the mass media are not real or accurate or perfectly matched to our perceptions, we become disillusioned. The first time we read a story in the newspaper that describes an event in which we participated or a person we knew, we are likely to say, "Hey, that's not the way it was; I saw it myself and it didn't happen at all the way the newspaper said it did." Or the first time we go to a television station and see the painted sets for the local news show, we say, "Oh, I thought that was the real city skyline behind the anchorman." Or the first time we go to Washington, D.C., and see the White House, we remark how small it is (it had seemed so much bigger on TV).

This book is about the illusions we get from the mass media and our disillusionment when we find out that everything isn't the way we thought it was. Perhaps dispelling these illusions may be one of the most important responsibilities of education. Today in America young people spend more time in front of the television tube than they do in classes. By the time the average American graduates from high school, he or she will have spent about 12,000 hours in class, but about 15,000 hours in front of the TV set. The illusions and disillusionments for young people in our society are greater than they have ever been in any society before.

What can we believe? What is true and what is not? Education must provide a way of answering these questions. We have to be educated about mass media if we want to steer a clear course between illusions on one side and disillusionment on the other.

This book takes up some of the basic issues of the impact of the mass media, issues that are hotly debated; and it examines these issues from several different perspectives. Some of the authors presented here are vigorously in favor of the mass media as they are and set about to defend the media. Others are vigorously opposed to the mass media and criticize their operation. And some try to take a balanced approach. Sixteen different issues are presented here, those that are either the most important or the most often argued about.

What are the effects of the mass media on our society? To what extent are we molded and shaped by the media? Are we informed? Or are we manipulated? Are we in control? Or are we merely dancing at the end of strings pulled by mass communicators?

Should the mass media be as free as they are in our society? What rights should they have? And what limits should be placed on them? Should they be responsible to the government? Or to society? Or to their listeners and viewers and readers? Or to themselves?

Are the mass media ethical institutions? What role should ethics play in mass media operations? Where do the mass media overstep ethical boundaries? And what should be done about it when they do?

What about those of us who are not part of the mass media? What rights do we have to communicate to the masses? How can we get access to the media? Or how can we bring pressure on the media to get them to perform in a manner acceptable to us? How can we exercise some control over the process?

And what about crime and violence in the mass media? Have we become a violent society because we read about crime in our newspapers and see violence on television? Do news stories about rape inspire rapists to action? Do stories about terrorism inspire terrorists? Do stories about airplane hijacking inspire hijackers? Do the mass media create violence in our society by reporting it, or do they merely reflect the violence that is already out there?

Have we become more sexually free because of sexual explicitness in the mass media? Or are we becoming jaded about sex because of its overexposure in the mass media?

What have the mass media done to us politically? Can one be elected to political office without the endorsement of the mass media?

And are the media giving us an accurate picture of our politicians? When we go to the voting booth, can we rely on the information we have received from the mass media?

To what extent does our government control the mass media? And to what extent do the media control our government? To what extent do the media control business, and to what extent does business control the mass media?

Has the nature of war been changed by mass communication? Television certainly was a factor in the war in Vietnam; what will be the place of TV in future wars?

Do the mass media present a fair and accurate picture of minorities and women in our society? And are minorities and women adequately represented in the mass media? What are the results of the media's distortions of minority cultures and viewpoints?

How have the mass media affected religion in our culture? And how are religious groups changing in order to use the mass media?

How have the mass media affected our culture as a whole? Are we becoming a classless society as the result of mass media? And are we becoming a tasteless society? Have the mass media brought about a leveling of our culture to the lowest common denominator?

And finally, as the media are changing because of the new technologies, what impact will this have on our culture and our society? What will satellites and cable television and laser beams and computers do to us? And what can we do about it, if anything?

There are no clear-cut and final answers to most of these questions. Each individual must ultimately answer these questions for himself or herself. But this book does provide a variety of viewpoints on these questions, and it presents facts and ideas that readers can use in reaching their own conclusions.

The age of mass communication has made it possible for us to gain access to far more information than any society ever had. Information is indispensable to a complex and advanced civilization. We are an information-hungry society; we need an ever-increasing amount of facts in order to maintain and increase our standard of living. Information today is a commodity we are willing to pay for. And the mass media today are not only entertaining the masses; they are selling information as well.

We have often been told that information is power. The question is, what do we have to do to ensure that the information we receive from the mass media will serve our needs, not the purposes of someone else?

This last question also must be answered by each one of us individually. This book is designed to help readers formulate their own conclusions about the role of mass media in their lives. Conflicting arguments are often presented here, on purpose. These arguments should be aired and discussed, and new facts and perspectives should be brought to that discussion. Only in this manner will truth emerge from this vast market-place of facts and ideas—the truth for each individual.

Today, the mass media are too important for us not to know where we stand on the issues affected by communication. They are too essential to be ignored. And the issues raised by mass media will no doubt continue to grow in importance in the foreseeable future.

ACKNOWLEDGMENTS

"Media and a Changing America" by Leo Bogart. Reprinted with permission from the March 29, 1982 issue of *Advertising Age*. Copyright © 1984 by Crain Communications.

"The Rise of the Newsocracy" by Louis Banks. Reprinted from *The Atlantic Monthly* issue of January, 1981. Copyright © 1981 Louis Banks. Reprinted with permission of the author.

"What is TV Doing to America?" by James Mann. Reprinted from *U.S. News & World Report* issue of Aug. 2, 1982. Copyright ©, 1982, U.S. News & World Report, Inc.

" 'Right Conduct' for a 'Free Press' " by Michael MacDonald Mooney. Copyright © 1980 by Harper's Magazine. All rights reserved. Reprinted from the March, 1980 issue by special permission.

"Objectivity Precludes Responsibility" by Theodore L. Glasser. Reprinted from *The Quill* issue of February 1984. Copyright © 1984 Theodore L. Glasser. Reprinted with permission of the author.

"The High Cost of Free Speech" by Richard McKenzie. Reprinted from *National Review* issue of September 2, 1983. Copyright © 1983 *National Review*. Reprinted with permission.

"Media Power: On Closer Inspection, It's Not That Threatening" by Albert E. Gollin. Reprinted with permission from *Presstime* issue of February 1984. Copyright © 1984 American Newspaper Publishers Association.

"The Might of the Media: Media Self-Censorship" by Robert P. Picard. Reprinted from *The Press* issue of March 1981. Copyright © 1981 Robert P. Picard. Reprinted with permission of the author.

"Perhaps It's Time to Examine the Sins of the Newspaper Generals" by Melvin Mencher. Reprinted from *ASNE Bulletin* issue of February 1984. Copyright © 1984 American Society of Newspaper Editors. Reprinted with permission.

"The Ethics of Compassion" by Gene Goodwin. Reprinted from *The Quill* issue of November 1983. Copyright © 1983 Gene Goodwin. Reprinted with permission of the author.

"Codes of Ethics" by C. David Rambo. Reprinted from *Presstime* issue of February 1984. Copyright © 1984 American Newspaper Publishers Association. Reprinted with permission.

"The Presidential Press Conference" by Laurence I. Barrett. Reprinted from *Topic* issue number 135. Copyright © Laurence I. Barrett. Reprinted with permission of the author.

"Dealing with the Media" by Griffin B. Bell and Ronald J. Ostrow. Reprinted from *Taking Care of the Law* by Griffin B. Bell with Ronald Ostrow, New York: William Morrow and Company, Inc., 1982. Copyright © 1982 Griffin B. Bell and Ronald Ostrow. Reprinted with permission of the authors.

"The Government Shuts Up" by Jay Peterzell. Reprinted from the *Columbia Journalism Review* issue of July/August 1982. Copyright © 1982 *Columbia Journalism Review.* Reprinted with permission.

"The Press and the President: There They Go Again" by George E. Reedy. Reprinted from the *Columbia Journalism Review* issue of May/June 1983. Copyright © 1983 *Columbia Journalism Review.* Reprinted with permission.

"The 'Imperial' Press Corps" by Michael J. Bennett. Reprinted with permission from the June 1982 issue of the *Public Relations Journal.* Copyright © 1982.

"Fear and Fraternity in the Washington Press Corps" by Stephen Hess. Reprinted from *The Washington Reporters* by Stephen Hess. Ccopyright © 1981 by The Brookings Institution. Reprinted with permission.

"The Media as Shadow Government" by William L. Rivers. Reprinted from *The Quill* issue of March 1982. Copyright © 1982 William L. Rivers. Reprinted with permission of the author.

"The Fourth Branch of Government" by Walter H. Annenberg. Reprinted with permission from *TV Guide* Magazine. Copyright © 1982 by Triangle Publications Inc., Radnor, Pa.

"Business and the Media: Stereotyping Each Other" by Jim Hoge. Reprinted from the *ASNE Bulletin* issue of February 1984. Copyright © 1984 American Society of Newspaper Editors. Reprinted with permission.

"The Corporate Complaint Against the Media" by Peter Dreier. Reprinted from *The Quill* issue of November 1983. Copyright © 1983 Peter Dreier. Reprinted with permission of the author.

"Ninety Seconds over the Economy" by Michael D. Mosettig. Reprinted from *Channels of Communications* issue of December/January, 1981–1982. Copyright © 1981–1982 *Channels of Communications.*

"War Isn't War without TV" by Amnon Rubinstein. Reprinted from *The Washington Post* issue of Sunday, July 18, 1982. Copyright © 1982 Amnon Rubinstein. Reprinted with permission of the author.

"Beirut—and the Press—Under Siege" by Roger Morris. Reprinted from the *Columbia Journalism Review* issue of November/December 1982. Copyright © 1982 *Columbia Journalism Review.* Reprinted with permission.

"How Britain Managed the News" by Leonard Downie. Reprinted from *The Washington Post* issue of August 20, 1984. Copyright © 1984 *The Washington Post.* Reprinted with permission.

"Planning for Future Grenadas" by Lyle Denniston. Reprinted from *The Quill* issue of January 1984. Copyright © 1984 *The Quill.* Reprinted with permission.

"Showdown at Culture Gulch" by Brian Winston. Reprinted from *Channels of Communications* issue of August/September 1981. Copyright © 1981 *Channels of Communications*.

"The Personalized Magazine" by Chip Block. Reprinted from *Folio* issue of May 1981. Copyright © 1981 Chip Block. Reprinted with permission of the author.

"Condominiums in the Global Village" by Richard A. Blake. Reprinted from *America* issue of June 5, 1982. Copyright © 1982 Richard A. Blake, author and Executive Editor of *America*. Reprinted with permission.

"The Second American Revolution" by Benjamin Barber. Reprinted from *Channels of Communications* issue of February/March 1982. Copyright © 1982 *Channels of Communications*.

IMPACT OF MASS MEDIA

I

Impact of Mass Media

I F YOU feel comfortable when information is presented in neat packages, when discussions are definitive and irrefutable, when conclusions
are summarized before you move on to a new topic, you're heading for
trouble in your study of mass media.

The mass media of communication operate in and for and with mass
society, and both are alive and constantly changing. Sometimes the changes
seem to be revolutionary. Most times, though, the changes in the mass media
and in society start slowly and are linked. Early communication researchers
believed there was a direct cause-effect relationship between media messages and their audiences—a person who read a credible article would
do what the article said to do. We're wiser now and admit that the situation is much more complex. People do use mass media for information to
help make decisions important to their lives, but not in a vacuum free of
"impurities"—what some researchers call noise or static.

By the same token, the media—the people who make them tick,
really—have to realize that their relationships or associations with their audiences and potential audiences can be tenuous. They have to know those for
whom they're reporting, writing, editing and producing. They have to be
willing to recognize changes in society or their usefulness will cease and so
will their publications and programs.

The articles in this section should help explain those relationships. Leo
Bogart's article is from the perspective of marketing, which is gaining importance, though sometimes grudgingly, beyond the advertising offices of mass
media. Bogart outlines societal changes that can have profound effects on
what the media do and measuring their success.

Louis Banks is critical of past performance of the news and information
media. His criticism is reasoned, not barbed, and he suggests that the social
consequences of what he calls a "newsocracy" can be beneficial to society.

James Mann concentrates on television, the most pervasive mass medium, the one that can give audiences color and action (even live action and
sound), the one that is "on" in our homes more than six hours a day, often
on multiple sets.

Consider these articles and you'll realize that the mass media have numerous impacts on society—and vice versa. Sometimes we can be comforted

by such thoughts because the media can help us in our daily lives, can entertain us, can draw us together as a society. Sometimes we can and should be disturbed about media-society relationships—the impacts of mass media on society and society on the mass media.

Although only the articles in this section are linked under the title "Impact of Mass Media," actually all the articles in the book address this topic. You are being forewarned: there aren't neat packages when it comes to the study of the mass media.

1 · MEDIA AND A CHANGING AMERICA

BY LEO BOGART

"Changes in society, not changes in American beliefs or values, will change our communication needs," says Leo Bogart, executive vice president and general manager of the Newspaper Advertising Bureau. He explains many of the changes taking place. This article is from *Advertising Age,* March 19, 1982.

"We are now at a depth at which restatement of the obvious is the first duty of intelligent man."

GEORGE ORWELL

Revolutionary changes in technology are transforming mass communications, and will be changing the advertising business. Consider the following:

1) As of March, 1982, an estimated 55% of the 83,531,900 households in the U.S. are "passed" by cable systems, and approximately half of

these passed households—23,219,200—are already cable subscribers.

2) Fifty percent of cable households also subscribe (for an additional fee) to some form of pay television. Moreover, among new cable subscribers a much higher percentage are choosing a pay tv option.

3) Videocassette and videodisc players are being heavily promoted, with the suggestion that "any time can be prime time." At present there are 3,157,000 videocassette recorder/players in U.S. homes and 238,000 disc players, and the sales curve slopes sharply upward.

4) The Federal Communications Commission is in the process of considering more than 6,000 applications for tv stations, which will provide highly localized coverage of small communities and neighborhoods. It is moving to authorize direct satellite-to-home broadcasting (DBS) that would cover the entire nation.

5) Fiber optics promise to lower the cost of data transmission and to expand the choices available to include a wide range of auxilliary services like security, financial and retailing.

6) Personal computers, some of them already selling for less than $1,000, can be used for a rapidly growing number of information and news services. Approximately 1,500,000 are now in U.S. homes, with 450,000 of them being purchased in 1981.

7) The line between data processing and communication is blurring, and the process will be accelerated by the recent Justice Department settlement with AT&T.

Even if no revolution in technology were taking place, mass communications would still undergo important changes in the next 10 years both because of predictable factors like demographic changes and unpredictable ones like inflation.

What marketers want to know is: Which changes are truly important, and which are ephemeral? How can we distinguish between the real long-term trends and the short-run cyclical fluctuations? Here are some reflections on what the guideposts ought to be. They restate the obvious about the changes already under way, but perhaps they add up to some conclusions that are not so obvious.

The conventional wisdom knows all about the generation gap, the "age of me," the demise of the family, the new era of mass transit; about the greening of America, the graying of America, the return to the land, the downtown revival, the "gentrification" of urban slums, the decline of literacy, the rejection of higher education, the return of career women to hearth and home. Some of this shorthand fits the evidence. Most does not. A dramatic journalistic buzzword can give a small ripple in the statistics the appearance of a great new wave.

Actually, in the last two decades there has been very little change in people's over-all sense of personal well-being, their hopefulness about the future or their trust in others.

Values change slowly. Even nations overwhelmed by the upheaval of revolution or the catastrophes of war do not change their national characters overnight, nor their established ways of doing things.

The classic study of American values was made in Muncie, Ind., disguised as "Middletown." In a 1977 survey the religious and patriotic feelings of Muncie high school students were almost the same as those of their grandparents in 1924. Parental discipline turned out to be no less effective than it was half a century ago. There was actually a slight narrowing of the generation gap. That gap is narrower than the gaps within either generation.

People do bend to the pressures of the time. Their sense of optimism and well-being goes up and down with the business cycle. In general, the idea of progress is far less taken for granted today than it was by earlier generations. In national opinion polls 20 years ago, individuals in their 20s were happier than older ones. That is no longer true. The world's bad news is something that more and more people, especially young people, show a tendency to avoid. But who accepts the view that humanity is doomed to get progressively more pessimistic? There are similar ups and downs in the tendency toward egotism or altruism, in political participation or apathy. Such cycles of mood generate attention and even alarm, but we would be more interested in the trends that are deep-seated and not likely to be reversed. Several such trends are worth singling out and elaborating later: Tolerance of diversity, changing sex roles and concern with the quality of life. All have consequences for mass communications. But none suggest any dramatic rearrangement of the demands for information or entertainment.

This means that new communications technology must carve out a place for itself by better serving a society whose needs and interests are not going to be fundamentally different, even though it is undergoing changes in population, social structure and life styles. Yet the new technology requires major capital investments and substantial continuing expenditures both by advertisers and consumers. Can the economy afford it?

The economic appraisal must begin with a global perspective. The health of the American economy depends less and less on what businesses decide or on the actions of our government.

We live in a world of nuclear stalemate where there can be no final victory in war, where madmen rule nations and where good guys don't necessarily win.

It's a world with a steadily expanding population and steadily increasing demands on its resources, with a growing gap between haves and have nots that brings political instability to more and more places.

Thus, national security will take ever more of our gross national product and put new pressures on the federal budget and, when the draft comes back, on our political system. Inflation, the major concern of the American people and the major ailment of our economy, will be hard to control as long as our wealth keeps flowing to the oil cartel. (Rising costs of raw materials and energy affect print media, especially newspapers, more than broadcasting and thus shift competitive advantages among the media.)

Economies are interdependent, caught in a vulnerable chain of imbalances in international trade, currency values and debt. Today, no successful business can remain provincial. In the age of the cheap dollar, more and more of our leading advertisers are non-American: Saks Fifth Avenue, Toyota, Nestle.

In communications, international exchange has accelerated the rate of technical change. The three leading contenders for American home communications systems are the Canadian Telidon, the British Viewdata and the French Antiope. As more channels provide the tv viewer with more choice, more overseas programing will fill the tube to satisfy its insatiable demands. Before too long, direct satellite-to-home television (fiercely opposed by the Soviets) will cross national boundaries.

If our domestic economy will be more dependent on world-wide forces and thus more precarious than in the past, does this mean that it will stagnate or decay?

Between 1973 and 1979, our annual growth in productivity per worker was 0.1%, the lowest of any major non-communist country. (By contrast, Japan's average was 3.4%.) In 1979, 1980 and 1981, productivity actually went down. That doesn't mean that people are working less hard; it means the total economy is less efficient. In the last few years, real family income has failed to show the gains that Americans have come to take for granted. From the trough of the current recession, these conditions may appear to mark the beginnings of a continuing decline. There are at least three reasons, however, to believe that this country is entering a period of renewed economic growth:

• The first is new technology, which whets the national appetite for information. Innovation is the key to greater productivity. It arises from the density of potential linkages among existing ways of doing things, which means that it is likely to proliferate rapidly in our complex industrial society. Of course, the rate of growth would be quickened if we stepped up our much too limited investment in research and development and if we could learn to save more and spend less. (Only one-third of American families save at all.)

• A second reason for optimism is the growth of the labor force and especially of its most productive elements. The postwar baby boom generation has reached maturity and begun to raise families of their own. The over-75s are the fastest growing age group. But more significantly, by 1990 there will be 15,000,000 more people in the "age of acquisition," 35 to 54, than in 1970—or 33% more.

• A third factor promoting economic growth over the long haul is the increased level of education, which is closely linked to productivity. Between 1959 and 1978, the work force increased by about 30,000,000. More than half the increase was in professional, technical and managerial types of jobs.

An important stimulus to marketing demand is the fact that there are more consumption units relative to people. Though households have become smaller, they still require basic furnishings and equipment. In the 1970s, the number of households grew by 25%, population by 8.5%. And this trend will keep going, with an expected growth of more than one-fifth in the 1980s, over 17,000,000 homes.

In the past half-century, U.S. Gross National Product grew 24 times in current dollars and five-fold in real terms. The momentum of that growth is not about to grind to a halt in the next 10 years. Personal consumption expenditures, in real terms, will expand by 22%.

There is an important byproduct of the affluence that permits most Americans to take the necessities for granted: A rising interest in the intangible quality of life. It is demonstrated by a concern with the preservation of the environment, by more involvement with the arts, by new kinds of self-expression and by a new conception of work as a source of satisfaction in itself rather than as a means of survival. This trend is already reflected in the new sections of newspapers and in the experimental cultural aspects of cable tv. It should lead to a general upgrading of media content as time goes on.

The growth of consumer purchasing power will make it possible for both consumers and advertisers to spend more money on mass media, existing and new.

In the 1970s, advertising investments grew 170% in current dollars. Rate increases accounted for 121%, leaving a real growth of 49%—greater than that of the consumer economy. The ratio of advertising to sales was raised in the 1950s by the advent of television, which created advertising budgets where none had existed before. In the 1980s, new forms of telecommunications may very well stimulate a similar spurt in advertising investments at a faster rate than growth in the consumer economy. Total investments in advertising will reach $150 billion in inflated dollars by 1990. Newspapers will be a $44 billion advertising medium, 18% bigger in real terms than today.

The ratio of advertising to sales may be set back by the striking shift from goods to services, which now represent two-thirds of GNP and 46% of consumer spending. (McDonald's employs more people than U.S. Steel.) Over-all, services advertise less, and they generally require more informative advertising—texts rather than demonstrations and images.

Media are affected also by the social consequences of another important economic trend, the trend toward concentration. The big retail chains have steadily increased their share of the market. Twenty-five years ago, the top 100 national advertisers accounted for 35% of the total. Today, they account for 43%. The top 10 agencies had 17% of the billings and have 27% today.

Concentration and conglomeration lead to more formalized and more bureaucratic decision-making and to an insatiable appetite for data. The growth of the computer industry has provided management with the means to realize the efficiencies of size, and in turn that growth has been stimulated by increased business concentration. This feeds the flood of information already loosed by the demands of a steadily more intricate and specialized economy. The fact that people are drowning in paper on their jobs will have an effect on the use of reading matter in their leisure time.

More and more, advertising decisions tend to be directed from a central source. They are more often reduced to formula, more impersonal, more quantitative, less sentimental, less flexible and less imaginative. Media salesmen must contact and confront a larger and more complex hierarchy of corporate "influentials." By the popular criterion of "cost per thousand," the ability of media to maintain their share of advertising will depend on their ability to hold their audiences.

The concept of marketing suggests a national market. We have become a culturally more homogeneous nation, entwined in an intimate web of transportation and communication. This makes it possible to think of market segments made up of drinkers of imported liqueurs, compulsive cleaners of pots and pans, one-time users of razor blades—people scattered across the continent but linked together by common attributes. In a society of greater complexity, affluence and education the citizen-consumer's avocational interests multiply, as well as the means to indulge them.

People have always defined themselves by their media preferences and habits. The more restrictive the medium, the greater the sense of kindred sprit among those who share it. There are half a dozen magazines for joggers alone, and over 10,000 magazines altogether. Radio has become a medium of specialized audiences.

The spread of cable television has been hailed by advertisers as a means of permitting them to zero in more efficiently and selectively on particular interest groups. In Dallas today, Warner Amex offers 100 different channels on its cable system. New applicants for cable franchises are promising to double that choice. Does this mean trouble for media that try to speak to everyone, at least in a definable geographic area? I think not.

Inevitably, the cost efficiency of reaching tiny slivers of the population has to be less than the cost efficiency of placing messages before vast audiences. In addition, serious problems of measurement and evaluation occur when audiences are fractionated as they are in radio today and as they may be for television tomorrow. The advertiser can't be really sure of what he's getting.

One advantage of specialized media for the advertiser is that the audience has already defined itself as interested in the kind of information he wants to give them. And when people are willing to search actively for information, they may be ready to pay to get it in a way that saves their time and adds to its value. This suggests that the public will be required to bear more of the financial burden of mass communication. In 1981, advertisers spent $61 billion on the media, and the public $52 billion, including what they spent to purchase, repair and operate radio and tv sets, to buy books and records, and to go to the movies. With the growth of the new media, the public's contribution of 46% in 1981 should go up substantially and might well reach 55% by 1990.

By 1990, consumer spending (at current dollars worth half what they are today) could be $30 billion for cable, pay tv and satellite-to-home services, including View data; $20 billion for videodiscs and cassettes and players and $10 billion for interactive home computer services and hardware. Although the consumer aspect of the British Prestel experiment seems to have failed, 100,000 American households already have computer terminals. There could be 7,000,000 by 1990.

As for entertainment, even in 1990 when at least half the homes are on the cable (mostly pay cable) and a fifth have disc or cassette players, network television will continue to have the lion's share of prime time viewing, though less than the present 85%. (They get most of the prime time audience in cable homes.) Most people seem to want formula, main line, Broadway-Hollywood entertainment. The networks are uniquely equipped to provide it. Pay television can siphon off substantial audiences for first run movies, major sports attractions and soft pornography. It can't capture a majority every night of the year. But pay tv doesn't need most of the audience to change the economics of present-day commercial television. Home communications systems could similarly shift the delicate economic balance of the current media, both broadcast and print.

The media get about the same percentage of consumer expenditures today as they did 20 years ago. Telecommunications can raise this proportion, not as a substitute for the media we know but by delivering new utilities and functions that now don't exist.

Even in the era of market segmentation, the most significant links among people remain those that connect them to a particular place.

Local markets are changing shape under the pressures of urban change. Forty-four percent of all advertising now is local rather than national, up from 39% in 1960. Although Americans everywhere share the same network television programs and the same brands of soap, soup and corn flakes, their communities continue to be different in character and in shape and volume of consumer preferences.

Among the local media, newspapers are the peculiar embodiment of these differences, and the health of newspapers can be no better than that of the communities whose names they carry. The new 1980 Census documents with statistics what the eye can see: The continuing cancerous destruction of our urban centers. Beyond the glitter of the new malls and civic centers, the grim realities still face us. While the old industrial cities of the Northeast and North Central states have drawn most attention, the same blight has hit cities in the Sunbelt, too. And newspaper readership there is lower than in the rest of the country.

Between 1970 and 1980, cities of 250,000 and over lost 5% of their population. This tells only part of the story. Blacks and Hispanics have become a majority in a number of cities and over 49% of the central city population in all metropolitan areas of over 1,000,000. So here we are, facing the urgent warnings of the 1968 Kerner Commission Report, whose message has receded further and further into the national unconscious.

Social disorganization in America's ghettoes, as measured by family disintegration, illegitimacy, crime and drug use is unmatched anywhere in the world.

How will the bright new possibilities of advanced telecommunication jibe with the unemployment, dependency, incapacity, despair and rage of the black underclass?

Changes in the cities have important consequences for local media. The vitality of downtown shopping areas is essential to maintain their retail advertising base. As the big stores have followed their best customers to the suburbs, some of their daily newspaper budgets have been deflected to shoppers, mail, "doorknobbers," and other pinpointed forms of advertising. Cable and low-powered tv will provide additional opportunity for this kind of concentrated coverage.

Sixty-eight percent of Americans live in the metropolitan areas, and a growing majority of these live in the suburbs. In some parts of the country nonmetropolitan areas have grown more than metropolitan ones, and this trend may well continue in the 1980s. This does not represent a return to the farm or, in today's terminology, the rural commune. It instead reflects the further decentralization of new industry and the expansion of metropolitan regions to farther-reaching exurbia. Since people measure commuting distance in time and not in miles, the interstate highway system allows them to enjoy rural amenities without feeling isolated. The development of more sophisticated communications systems may accelerate this trend.

To what degree can communication substitute for personal movement? Not many Americans can just walk down the village street to their jobs, their shopping, their bank, their dentist and their friends. The result is a vastly increased volume of communications to sustain these widely scattered relationships. In 1980, there were 200 billion telephone calls made in the U.S. and 100 billion pieces of mail handled by the Postal Service.

We think of ourselves as a mobile population, though about the same proportion of us (one in five) move every year as did 20 or 30 years ago. But among young people in their 20s, 68% move in a four-year period, over half to a different locality. All this is making us less provincial in outlook, less rooted in regional customs and parochial loyalties. It has changed the meaning of local news and thus changed the public's expectations of the media.

We are mobile not only over our lifetimes, but day by day. Our reliance on the automobile is as great as it ever was. In the past 30 years, the number of cars has grown 2½ times faster than the number of people, and the car today is typically a personal rather than a family utility. Thus shopping goes on over a wide orbit, affecting the retailer's advertising requirements. Out-of-store shopping of all kinds—by catalog, mail and phone—has shown a steady increase, and the Sears catalog is already on videodisc. (As for business travel, only one-fourth of it is to see customers; most of it is for company and industry meeting.)

But per capita local auto trips went down only 6% during the years of the oil crisis. We have a long way to go before rising fuel costs force Americans to stay at home, relying on telecommunications to do their shopping and their work. We won't go that route completely because shopping and work are social experiences, and a computer keyboard is not a substitute for human contact. But even a minor shift of, say, 10% of general merchandise purchased from the store to the communications systems can have a dramatic impact on retailing and on advertising.

And home itself is a different place than it used to be. That picture book family of a working father, a mother at home and two school age children now accounts for only 7% of all U.S. households. More families have a handicapped child than have two children with a mother at home. Marriage takes place later; the divorce rate has doubled since 1970 and there are fewer children per average household. We all know that there are more singles, up 16% since 1970; more female-headed households, up 49%; more households of two or more unrelated individuals living together. Yet to keep this in perspective, 97,000,000 Americans live as married couples, only 2,700,000 as unmarried ones.

For the time being, we've seen the last of the so-called "youth culture." In 1970, four out of ten Americans were under the age of 21. In 1990, it will be three in ten. The actual numbers of those under 21 dropped from 81,000,000 in 1970 to 75,000,000 today, and that number will not change in the next decade. A lot of radio stations will be looking for new music formulas.

Changes in family structure affect communications media and vice versa. Television intrudes into the time that previous generations spent in conversation, play or common projects. This has weakened the mutual allegiance of family members and the emotional bonds that are the basis of trust and understanding. The impersonal communication of the media substitutes, to a degree, for the close, interpersonal family communication of the past. Members of a household are less likely to share the same reading matter and the same broadcast programing.

Since media activity has become more individual, there is a growing discrepancy between household exposure to a medium and the individual's exposure to it. Television sets have been on for more hours in the '70s, but individual viewing hours have not changed.

Increased education moves people away from broadcasting and toward print. They also move in the direction of more sophisticated and cosmopolitan content and specialized media that meet broader interests. They become information seekers. The rise in the average level of schooling has been phenomenal. In 1957, 45% of the civilian labor force were high school graduates. By 1978, the proportion was 73%.

There are ample causes to complain about the deficiencies of the American school system. In New York, half of the students drop out from the ninth grade on. Our complaints about the schools seem to reflect our higher levels of aspiration for our children. But what is commonly regarded as a decline in reading skills may actually represent a decline of reading interest. The average reading and writing abilities of American students didn't change significantly during the '70s.

The rising level of education and the functional demands of a complex industrial society have fostered secularism and a weakening of the traditional moral code. In spite of the continuing strength of religious institutions and the high visibility of certain right wing political groups masquerading with religious labels, there will be more Sunday store openings, not less.

A related consequence of more education is the increased level of public tolerance for racial minorities, for nonconformity, for idiosyncracy in belief and in personal habits. In an incredibly hetergeneous and urbanized country, there is more room for variety than on Sinclair Lewis' "Main Street."

The shift in attitude is most dramatic when young people are compared with older ones. Tolerance for homosexuals, unmarried couples, people with beards and long hair and employes who wear sneakers to work goes with more tolerance in the realm of ideas and of politics. This augurs well for freedom of the press and for the further spread and public support of diversity in communication.

What used to be a substantial educational gap between men and women has been reduced almost to the vanishing point. This helps explain why so many more women have entered the work force: Sixty percent of those between 18 and 64. By 1990, the figure will be 71%. This represents a truly revolutionary change in the attitude of women toward work and in the way men and women relate to each other.

Today, most young women accept work and a career as the norm and feel that fulltime housework is unsatisfying. As time passes, we will no doubt see some mellowing of today's militant feminism, but there will be no reversal of the moves toward equality of the sexes at work, the redefinition of responsibilities in the home and toward children. Since a substantial part of media content, including advertising, is directed at one sex, much of it may require overhauling.

Changes in sex roles might bring about long-term changes in attitudes toward sex itself. But history shows these have always gone through cycles of conservatism and permissiveness.

Both the psychological and economic consequences of women's work will become even more significant as more move up to higher skilled and better paid jobs. There is a second wage earner in a majority of families of working age, two-thirds of all married couples under 35. The median income of two-earner households will rise 50% faster in the '80s than it will for all households.

The effects of new technology can best be understood in the context of the social changes with which they must interact. Out of this interplay come predictions like these:

- Changes in society, not changes in American beliefs or values, will change our communications needs.

- International communication will become more common.

- There will be no letup in the rising demand for information.

- More information will be sought out actively, not randomly delivered.

- Both consumers and advertisers will spend more on the media, in real dollars.

- Consumers will pay a larger share of the cost of communications, advertisers less.

- Economic growth can sustain both the consumer market for media and greater advertising support.

- New communications technology will boost advertising investments, offsetting the shift of consumption from goods to less well advertised services.

- More advertising decisions will follow formulas.

- Advertisers will seek more efficient concentration on key market segments, but . . .

- Advertisers will continue to want mass coverage of local markets at low cost.

- Urban blight will continue to change the media mix for local advertising.

- Geographic dispersion adds to the demand for communication.

- Shopping at home may change the economics of retailing and thus of local media.

- Working women need more information to save time and motion.

- Media experience will be more individual, less based on the household.

- More education builds demand for better and more specialized media content.

- Media content will no longer be dominated by the "youth culture" as it was in the 1970s.

- The networks will continue to dominate prime time tv.

- The leisure time available for media will not soon be increasing.

- More entertainment choices will not add significantly to viewing time.

- Time spent on new forms of communication will have to come from existing media.

The existing media organizations will inevitably find new electronic channels to transmit the vast quantities of information and to use the vast entertainment talents that are their resource. People will make use of broadcast channels that aim at their own special nerve, but they will still want to be part of the popular mainstream of mass entertainment.

As for print, it won't succumb easily to electronic competition. There are limits on the time that the public at large will be willing to give to alphanumeric information served up on a cathode ray tube. Conveying data line by line, screenful by screenful, will never be a substitute for the satisfying package of paper and print that carries its own unique character and that generates ideas, discussion and action.

2 · THE RISE OF THE NEWSOCRACY

BY LOUIS BANKS

The press is increasingly becoming the arbiter of American life, but the values of the news media aren't always the values of the society they serve, says Louis Banks, formerly senior editor of *Time* and managing editor of *Fortune,* now adjunct professor of management at the Alfred P. Sloan School of Management, Massachusetts Institute of Technology. This article is from *Atlantic Monthly,* January 1981.

Viewers who chanced to switch to Washington's channel 4 (WRC-TV) on the evening of March 28, 1979, found themselves looking down the barrel of an ordinary hand-held hair dryer. "This is not a gun, and it doesn't shoot bullets," said the voice-over. "But what comes out can be just as deadly." The program was the result of nine months' investigation by WRC's "Consumer Action" team, and for the extraordinary span of nearly twenty minutes ("without commercial interruption"), it developed a case that Americans were in considerable peril because many hand-held hair dryers were spewing fibers from asbestos insulation. Making the connection between the ingestion of asbestos fibers and the death rates from various forms of lung cancer, investigator Lea Thompson said gravely, "How many of those [deaths] can be attributed to hair dryers . . . no one knows."

By consumerist standards, the program was a stunning success. Such companies as Hamilton Beach, General Electric, Norelco, Sears, Penney's, and Montgomery Ward, all named as culprits, were besieged by angry customers. Gillette and American Electric, which had long used mica instead of asbestos for insulation, were exonerated on the program, but besieged nonetheless. The Consumer Products Safety

Commission, a federal agency, was stung into confusion and open hearings, subsequently forcing a voluntary recall of asbestos-insulated dryers. A Senate consumer subcommittee opened hearings and called Ms. Thompson as a star witness.

By media standards as well, the program scored high. Reversing the usual practice, print media "picked up" the exposé from a local television station and gave it wide coverage. The UPI accounts were reprinted in hundreds of newspapers. Channel 4 being an NBC affiliate, the story made the NBC evening news. It was subsequently featured on both NBC's *Today* show and ABC's *Good Morning America*. (One manufacturer feared that his business would be destroyed just by David Hartman's silent scowl of disapproval as he looked at a hand-held dryer; it wasn't.) The WRC investigation team won the George Polk Award for Distinguished Journalism. And the "genuine coup" was eulogized in a two-page essay in *People*, which revealed what the TV camera had not: that Lea Thompson, the daughter of a journalist and a University of Wisconsin graduate in journalism and marketing, was eight and a half months pregnant at the time of the story.

The strong combination of action pictures, whirring motors, stern interviews, and authoritative explanations certainly alerted millions of Americans in record time to the asbestos fiber problem. But the consumerist consequences, as important as they were, can be seen as part of a much larger societal point. We are rapidly approaching a situation in which reporting is the arbiter of other institutions in American life; in this microcosmic case we see and hear it imposing its own values, standards, and priorities with irresistible impact on agencies of both government and business.

The point is made more broadly when we review the principal categories of news coverage over the past decade. The media—and particularly television—take credit for turning the public against the Vietnam War ("the living room war") and forcing its termination. "Watergate was the greatest journalistic triumph of the twentieth century," wrote one correspondent for Columbia University's "Survey of Broadcast Journalism," and unrelenting media attention certainly prompted the politics that forced President Nixon's resignation. Journalistic coverage was a prime mover in forcing government agencies and boards of directors to ventilate a series of corporate scandals in the mid-1970s, the most notable investigations of which led to the dismissal of top management at the 3M Corporation and the Gulf Oil Company, and eventually to antibribery legislation. The emergence of President Sadat of Egypt as a folk hero and the constant television posturing of the principals in the Iranian hostage crisis suggest that we have, through media coverage, carried foreign policy into a period of "mass diplomacy," as Flora Lewis of the *New York Times* describes it.

One can pursue the point through the agenda of quality-of-life issues: consumerism, dating back to the elevation of Ralph Nader to national prominence; ecology and environmentalism, ranging from the effect of supersonic transports on the ionosphere to the greenhouse effect to acid rain; energy concerns, from off-shore oil spills to the hazards of coal and nuclear power; safety in the workplace, with latter-day attention to potential carcinogens; toxicity, from Kepone to Love Canal.

Such is merely the stuff of news, one might argue. And to a degree this is true. But to another degree these areas represent coverage by selection, which suggests an imposition of media values and standards in contrast, perhaps, to the values and standards of other institutions. In writing *The Brethren,* their gossipy best seller on the disrobed U.S. Supreme Court, Bob Woodward and Scott Armstrong noted proudly in a preface that they had breached "the authority, traditions and proto-cols" of the Court to subject it to journalistic inspection for the first time. Some critics doubted that this inspection did much for the set of values involved in the American system of justice.

It is becoming clear that the increasingly pervasive power of the media is central to the development of most other American institutions. We are, in fact, becoming what might be called a "newsocracy." The technology and substance of today's newscasting combine for an im-pact greater than that of any other informational force in the history of democratic societies—redirecting even the traditional processes of poli-tics. This is a matter of social consequence, because some aspects of media value judgment might be perceived as being at odds with the general welfare. Accordingly, I would argue that affected "others" (e.g. government agencies, educational institutions, and publicly held corpo-rations) have both a right and a duty to enter the informational competi-tion. This contention should not be interpreted as a challenge to press freedom; rather it is an acceptance of today's news coverage for what it is, and an attempt to broaden its intellectual vision in the interests of the society that the First Amendment serves.

In my view, media dominance has been powerfully abetted by two major trends of the past decade. One is a widening perception of the interaction of one kind of endeavor upon another in the post-industrial society. To a certain extent this integrative process has always been manifested in political reform movements, but it gained a kind of per-sonal relevance in the so-called youth movement of the late sixties and early seventies. It has, loosely, been called "holism." The second is a spreading of public awareness, the sense of direct participation in events, which has loosely been described as "populism." These two trends, combined with video technology, have stepped up the power of journalistic influence.

Recently MIT's *Technology Review* gathered a group of the nation's top science writers from print and television to talk about "Science, Technology and the Press." Science is their beat, but as they contrasted the simpler days of "happy talk" reporting with the multidimensional demands of today's assignments, they could be speaking for almost any group of earnest journalistic specialists. David Perlman of the San Francisco *Chronicle* saw science reporting broadening into "the politics of science or public affairs emerging from science." Mark Dowie of *Mother Jones* spoke of the reader's desire to know about "the interface between science and technology and even more, about the interface between technology and the corporate world because . . . that's where science ceases to be apolitical." Cristine Russell of the Washington *Star* confessed that "coverage of recombinant DNA, for example, was always 'biased' toward its possible impact on the public and not toward special interests—be they science or the government, or whatever." This group, gathered soon after Three Mile Island, was properly humble about the responsibilities involved in the widening media function, yet, by implication, quite confident that nobody else could perform it as well. (As a reflection of this attitude, the cover of *Technology Review* pictured a youthful reporter opening his shirt to show a Superman emblem across his chest.)

But if interrelatedness has inspired complex reportorial judgments, populism inspires a broad simplicity—or a low common denominator. Network news not only has usurped the role of the newspaper as the principal source of information, but has constantly increased the number of people who make news-watching part of their lives. For example, ABC-TV, proud of its recent high news ratings, believes that its audience is drawn mostly from people who never before watched TV news regularly. "I don't think there's any doubt that we've created a heightened consciousness of the news," says a vice president of research. Also, there is no doubt that of the three networks, ABC has the most kinetic and visually stimulating and the least mentally taxing news format.

Nobody is more aware than the network professionals of the lowest-common-denominator aspect of their work. Four years ago, Walter Cronkite expressed concern to the Radio and Television News Directors' Association: "We fall far short of presenting all, or even a goodly part, of the news each day that a citizen would need to intelligently exercise his franchise in this democracy. So as he depends more and more on us, presumably the depth of knowledge of the average man diminishes. This clearly can lead to a disaster in a democracy."

"Disaster" may be too strong a word, but TV news does seem to be changing some meanings of democracy by offering a simplistic kind of interrelatedness. For example, one consequence has been the translation of hitherto abstract or impersonal subjects into people, places, and crises. The administration of justice becomes the judge, the lawyer, or the criminal (and his family). The presidency is words, facial expressions, today's necktie, and Amy and Rosalynn [Carter] in the background. The political convention is almost a plaything of television personalities. A plant closing is people wondering aloud what they will do next—and a congressman sympathizing. A gasoline shortage is angry customers and angry service station operators damning the oil companies—and a congressman sympathizing. A nuclear power accident is pregnant women in tears—and nervous officials trying to cope with a backwash of emotion as well as with unknowns of physics.

In their embrace of holism the media—already under pressure to produce specialists in such areas as science, finance, energy, and business—play an interdisciplinary role. To do so, the "supermen" who take this role seriously apply themselves to continuous learning. Yet we see some television journalism that could lead a long way toward Cronkite's "disaster."

Electronic journalism can claim antecedents in the rich history of radio reporting during and after World War II, and many of the leading figures of television news, including Cronkite, have struggled to keep alive that heritage. But TV news is also the bastard child of the entertainment industry. All commercial media contract in one way or another to deliver a certain audience to advertisers, but in the case of the three major networks, variations in audience size, as measured by the ratings, represent millions of dollars in advertising revenue. That fact is reflected in news selectivity, and leads to an image of the world projected daily, competitively, and with striking homogeneity on the evening news.

Since network news was, by definition, confined to national news (so as not to transgress the domain of a network's local TV affiliates), cameras focused on a minimal number of recognizable characters from Washington and New York; the more they could be translated into villains or heroes, the easier the journalistic assignment and the higher the audience attention. The visual nature of the medium put a premium on color, movement, excitement, sensation, novelty. There has always lurked in modern journalism the knowledge that bad news sells better than good. Witness the proliferation of the "question mark" headline, which suggests a threat to mankind on a speculative basis. Under competitive pressures, this stress on anxiety and negativism came to prominence in television.

Attitudinal researchers have wondered for some time about survey results that showed a discrepancy between the average citizen's dim view of government, business, education, etc., and his/her relative satisfaction with the company that he/she works for, the way local government functions, the schools the kids go to. Assessing the data for the 1970s, Everett Carll Ladd Jr. and Seymour Martin Lipset concluded: "To some considerable degree this contradiction may reflect the difference between the steady dose of disasters which people get from television, and their personal experiences."

It is not difficult to project such rogue trends into a gloomy prospect. "Disaster" would not be far if the nation came to see itself primarily through the lenses of critics with an addiction to novelty or blood and guts, and no responsibility for consequences. Not only would the democratic process suffer from a diminished "depth of knowledge," as Cronkite has it, but something vital could be lost if responsible leaders of other institutions were regularly consumed by the "bite 'em off, chew 'em up, spit 'em out" habits of television news.

Some critics think they see this approach already manifest in the techniques of *60 Minutes,* designed to provide the controversy which keeps that weekly "newsmagazine" at the top of the Nielsen ratings. In 1979 the Illinois Power Company of Decatur allowed *60 Minutes* access to the construction site of its nuclear power plant at Clinton to film a segment on escalating nuclear construction costs. Illinois Power's one condition was that it be allowed to put its own cameras alongside those of *60 Minutes* to film everything seen and said in the interviews. The broadcast *60 Minutes* segment, in fact, found Illinois Power guilty of mismanagement of the power project. But by playing its version of what was said and explained, spliced with excerpts from the *60 Minutes* telecast, Illinois Power made a persuasive case for having been the victim of dramatic and serious distortion.

This and similar examples raise the question of whether, in TV's stress on "populism," corporations exist primarily to provide a ready source of "heavies" in the manufactured dramas that hold those customers and those Nielsen ratings.

Media judgments, of course, do not occur in a vacuum. As Illinois Power found out, the media's stories powerfully affect the "others" who are the objects of their attention, and their composite story defines the society for millions of people. The principal problem in a newsocracy is that there is, at the moment, no force to offset the net range and impact of today's informational technology. Since the constructive and the exploitative forces of journalism are constantly in tension, with no certainty about the outcome, it behooves other affected institutions to recognize the problem and accept the fact that they, too, have a stake in the battle.

The beginning of such counterstrategy is the realization that the "others" have allies within the media. Professional journalists can recognize the short-term, audience-grabbing excesses and know that the long-term test is credibility. One catches the essence of embattled professionalism in a credo voiced by David Perlman during that *Technology Review* forum on science-related reporting.

"There are some things," he said, "that we can properly do. . . . We can look for self-serving statements. We can expose biases that exist. We can expose lies; scientists lie occasionally, like everybody else, and they're going to lie publicly at times. So that's our job. It's not to say whether nuclear power is bad or good. Present the debate and be very careful about ascribing expertise to those who are experts."

Professionalism is at work in the development of such thoughtful interpreters of science as Perlman and his colleagues, and in the training of specialists in business and economic affairs as well. As generations change, more and more business and economic news is being handled by editors and reporters who are educated in business practice, rather than by "general assignment" people. This new sophistication is evident in many regional newspapers, whose healthy intellectual diversity is thinning out the New York- and Washington-centered judgments of the national media. Even the TV networks are learning to give more discretion to their economics editors, who, while constrained to simplisms by time limitations on camera, can sometimes moderate the more sensationalist anti-business onslaughts of their general-assignment colleagues.

The first step for "others," then, is to support and encourage media professionals by providing them with information that makes them better able to report factually and to perform the demanding integrative function. But there is more to it than that. All affected institutions must realize that a newsocracy is a different kind of environment, and that they must engage with that environment in a different way. Perhaps the media's concern with interrelatedness provides a clue. If a firm can come to think of itself not only in economic terms but as a unit in a network of social and political values, then it need have no unreasonable fears about explaining itself to media that seek to understand just those relationships. This requires, first, that a company learn to see and feel itself in the consciousness of its particular publics and infuse that sense of public-relatedness into every level of its operations.

For example, the Mobil Corporation's controversial "op-ed" advocacy campaign, which has been a fixture on the editorial pages of influential newspapers, was developed as a result of Mobil's analysis of the political and social prospects for the company and the oil industry. "We decided more than ten years ago that our problem was literally one of survival in a hostile external climate; it was more political than economic," says Herbert Schmertz, Mobil's vice president for corporate affairs and the principal architect of the campaign. "We decided to enter the argument through the media and thus put our case before people whose opinions count." Not everybody likes Mobil's abrasive style— which on occasion has drawn the wrath of the President of the United States—but critics would be hard put to deny that Mobil's editorial insistence has brought new facts to the public debate on energy, and in the process has influenced editorial thought and political action.

Exxon and Shell, affronted by charges of duplicity in an NBC-TV series in late 1979, eschewed flamboyant counterpunches and took their respective cases to the National News Council. In both situations the council examined the facts and came down hard against NBC, agreeing in the Exxon case that the telecast contained "factual error, the selective use of information, lack of perspective, and the building of effect through innuendo."

The reaction of the Gillette Company in the hand-held hair dryer exposé reflects a more positive, and perhaps more internal, kind of operational public-relatedness. Out of its tradition of precise quality control of razor blades, Gillette long ago gave consumer concern high priority and set up a medical test laboratory for all its products. In 1964, the company named Robert Giovacchini, a Ph.D. in medical science, head of the lab; ten years later, he was made vice president for product integrity and given final review of the medical safety of new products and of marketing and advertising claims relating to medical safety. In addition, his group performs a quality review of new and existing products. In 1973 he directed a redesign for the hand-held hair dryers that substituted mica for asbestos as an insulator, even though asbestos particle emissions from Gillette dryers averaged only 5 percent of the maximum allowable under OSHA standards.

Of all the major hair dryer companies, only Gillette offered to help the producers of the WRC-TV program. David Fausch, vice president of corporate public relations and a former *Business Week* editor, argued internally that the story would be told more accurately if Gillette supplied accurate data. It helped, of course, that Gillette was "clean." It helped, too, that in return the program's producers warned in advance of the screening so that Gillette could alert its sales force and its merchandisers to possible trouble. In the fallout, Gillette did not escape damage—and did not really expect to. The relevant point is that the company's operations had long since been sensitive to public concerns, and it could move smoothly into a media spotlight with a clear understanding of its own objectives, and without fear that the world would end if it did not win all the points in the telecast.

Such an approach, in my view, is far more sophisticated than conventional public relations. It is corporate acceptance of the same long-term values that concern the responsible media, and it reflects the First Amendment premise that everybody benefits when the terms of the debate are broadened. The media, after all, live on information, and "others" can influence the outcome by providing accurate material. It is a corollary, of course, that "others" have a right to keep at arm's length media agents who have a record of distorting facts to fit preconceived notions of high drama. Journalists and their organizations have unfor-giving memories for those who put out misleading or dishonest informa-tion, and corporate public relations departments practice a similar form of "redlining." One of the favorite topics when people from those de-partments gather for a friendly drink is "what to do when Mike Wallace calls."

Should corporations and the "others" resort to end runs around the media to get their stories out? Mobil and Illinois Power suggest varieties of end runs: one through advocacy advertising, and the other through countervideo. In 1978 the Supreme Court, in a 5–4 decision, validated the right of the First National Bank of Boston to advertise in opposition to an income tax referendum in Massachusetts *(First National Bank* v. *Belotti)*. In some quarters this and other related court decisions were perceived as unleashing the mighty economic power of big corporations to influence public opinion unfairly. In fact, in writing for the minority, Justice Byron White saw the majority opinion as opening the door to corporate domination of "not only the economy, but also the very heart of our democracy, the electoral process." But Justice Lewis Powell, Jr., for the majority, said, "The inherent worth of the speech in terms of its capacity for informing the public does not depend upon the identity of its source, whether corporation, association, union or individual." And Chief Justice Warren Burger, in a separate opinion, added that "media conglomerates" pose "a much more realistic threat to valid [political] interests" than other corporations.

In the context of my argument, the issue is one not of unleashing corporate power but rather of prodding media power to think in broader social terms. In a newsocracy, the media's implicit role is to translate the values of our conventional morality—what we really want for our-selves and our world—to the institutions that make it operate. Those institutions, in turn, must be heard and understood before judgment is passed. Conceivably, such media power could lead toward "disaster" if it adheres to a Nielsen-rating value system. Conceivably, though—and I prefer this view—it could prompt a higher order of intellectual per-formance from all components of the society, and especially from the professionals who tell us every day in every way what our world means. Ultimately it might even help a confused society to define its values more clearly.

3 · WHAT IS TV DOING TO AMERICA?

BY JAMES MANN

Television has been praised as a miracle and damned
as a distorter of reality, reports James Mann, an
editor at *U.S. News & World Report*. Some see hope
that the new video age will benefit from past
mistakes and triumphs and do the country more good
than harm. This article is from the August 2, 1982,
issue of *U.S. News & World Report.*

Soon after 28-year-old David Radnis watched the movie "The Deer
Hunter" on TV in his Chicago-area home, he was dead—one of at least
29 viewers in the U.S. who shot themselves imitating the show's Rus-
sian-roulette scene.

When Hoang Bao Trinh fled from Vietnam to Silver Spring, Md., he
spent months baby-sitting his grandchildren in front of the TV set. Soon
the whole family was speaking English, much of it learned by imitating
speech heard on the televised programs.

Such cases reflect TV's increasingly pervasive influence on America, both for good and bad. In a country where television has become
a major—and in some cases primary—force determining how people
work, relax and behave, the consequences are staggering. Recent studies show that the lives of Americans, from their selection of food to their
choice of political leaders, are deeply affected by TV, and that influence
is growing.

In an age when millions of inexperienced young people are growing
up in front of the tube without close guidance of elders, many Americans
worry that the nation could be ruined by a generation that gets its moral
values from "Flamingo Road," its cultural standards from "Laverne &
Shirley" and its sense of family relationships from "Dallas."

Most broadcasters, with support from some researchers, maintain
that TV is unfairly blamed for merely conveying what the public demands and argue that the medium's power is exaggerated. They contend

23

that most people treat television simply as one of many sources of information, and that most homes have basically been unaltered since the first modern home-TV set was marketed in 1939.

Others in the industry are worried that what author and actor Steve Allen calls the "amoral force" of TV and other popular media is helping to weaken old values. "It's horrendous," says Allen. "That our nation, our society, our culture is in some state of moral and ethical collapse is absolutely undeniable. In about 50 years, you could create what we already have a good percentage of—people who think it's perfectly O.K. to grab what they want, to do what they want, and the only bad thing is getting caught."

Linking the Tube and Violence   A report released in May by the National Institute of Mental Health says that "violence on television does lead to aggressive behavior by children and teenagers who watch the programs." In one five-year study of 732 children, "several kinds of aggression—conflicts with parents, fighting and delinquency—were all positively correlated with the total amount of television viewing." Defenders of TV have long held that there is no clear link between viewing and violence.

The findings covered a wide range of topics. In one survey, more than half the parents thought their children learned more about sex from TV than from any other source except the parents themselves. TV also was cited for fostering bad habits by glamorizing highly advertised junk foods and frequent use of alcohol.

The federally sponsored study noted that almost all Americans watch TV, many for hours each day. Some of the most avid watchers are the very young and very old, women and minorities. Heavy viewers are usually less educated.

"Television can no longer be considered as a casual part of daily life, as an electronic toy," the report stated. "Research findings have long since destroyed the illusion that television is merely innocuous entertainment."

TV is also partly blamed for a sharp slide in traditional learning. Since television became nearly universal in the early 1960s, average scores for high-school students taking the Scholastic Aptitude Test, the broadest measure of academic ability, have plunged from 478 to 424 on the verbal exam and from 502 to 466 in mathematics.

A panel of educators appointed to study the decline noted that by age 16 most children have spent 10,000 to 15,000 hours watching television—more time than they have spent in school. The panel's conclusion: "Is television a cause of the SAT-score decline? Yes, we think it is. . . . Television has become surrogate parent, substitute teacher."

As TV's children graduated in the 1960s and '70s, an Adult Performance Level test found that "20 percent of the American population was functionally incompetent, that is, could not perform the basic kinds of reading, writing or computing tasks—such as calculating the change on a small purchase, addressing an envelope, reading a want ad or filling out a job application." The result, says Paul Copperman, president of the Institute of Reading Development in San Francisco, is that "society may be compelled to support an increasing percentage of dysfunctional or only marginally functional citizens."

TV Has Brought Americans Together Even the several critics admit that television has achieved unprecedented results in making the public aware of a huge variety of developments—from war in Lebanon and the Falkland Islands to the plight of migrant workers.

Veteran broadcaster Eric Sevareid argues that television has had an enormously positive influence on America in three main areas: It has brought families together more, it has counteracted the country's tendency toward fragmentation, and it has stayed independent of government.

Says Sevareid: "On balance, TV is better for us than bad for us. When Gutenberg printed the Bible, people thought that invention would put bad ideas in people's heads. They thought the typewriter would destroy the muse, that movies would destroy legitimate theater, that radio would destroy newspapers, and that TV would destroy everything. But it doesn't happen that way."

A main virtue of TV, according to scholars, is that the medium is a powerful force for freedom—a far better source of information and motivation than the party apparatus that used to dominate politics in many sections of the country.

Television's broadening of perspectives also is credited with boosting worthwhile causes and diminishing the ethnic, religious and geographic prejudices that have plagued American history. Cited as a key example are the "freedom marches" that caught the attention of TV viewers in the early 1960s. Laws were then passed guaranteeing civil rights that blacks had sought for more than a century.

Many educators add that television has given Americans a wealth of experience and knowledge that isn't being measured by today's school tests. The National Education Association, the nation's biggest teachers' organization, has called for cultivation of "electronic literacy" and has distributed guides to help teachers solidify what students learn from programs like "Holocaust" and "Shogun."

Millions of young Americans have been led through the alphabet and rudiments of algebra by the educational series "Sesame Street" and "Electric Company" of the Children's Television Workshop. One study suggested that children who watch a lot of TV in their early years tend to read more widely later on than children who were lighter viewers when they were young.

The medium also provides an invaluable window on the world for invalids and the elderly. Steve Allen recalls a series of visits he made to hospitals where Vietnam veterans were being treated: "What was helping to pull them through the day was television. The television set does provide company for lonely people, a voice in the house."

Broadcasters point out that, no matter what sociologists think, the public likes what it is getting on television. The A. C. Nielsen Company, an audience-measuring firm, announced that, despite a decline in network viewing, America's 80 million television households averaged a record level of 6 hours and 44 minutes a day in front of the tube in 1981 —up 9 minutes from 1980. That's three times the average rate of increase during the 1970s.

Observes one network executive: "It's all there, good and bad. All you have to do is change the dial."

How the Brain Reacts to TV   Until recently, there was little research on how the human brain absorbs information from TV. Many scholars long have been convinced that viewers retain less from television than from reading, but evidence was scarce.

Now, a research project by Jacob Jacoby, a Purdue University psychologist, has found that more than 90 percent of 2,700 people tested misunderstood even such simple fare as commercials or the detective series "Barnaby Jones." Only minutes after watching, the typical viewer missed 23 to 36 percent of the questions about what he or she had seen.

One explanation is that TV's compelling pictures stimulate primarily the right half of the brain, which specializes in emotional responses, rather than the left hemisphere, where thinking and analysis are performed. By connecting viewers to instruments that measure brain waves, researcher Herbert Krugman found periods of right-brain activity outnumbering left-brain activity by a ratio of 2 to 1.

Another difficulty is the rapid linear movement of TV images, which gives viewers little chance to pause and reflect on what they have seen. Scientists say this torrent of images also has a numbing effect, as measured electronically by the high proportion of alpha brain waves, normally associated with daydreaming or falling asleep.

Who Watches TV the Most?
Weekly TV Usage

Older women (ages 55 and over)	36 hr., 33 min.
Older men	33 hr., 15 min.
Younger women (ages 18–55)	31 hr., 49 min.
Younger men	28 hr., 3 min.
Teenagers	22 hr., 59 min.
Children (ages 2–11)	25 hr., 10 min.

USN&WR—Basic data: A. C. Nielsen Company

The result is shortened attention spans—a phenomenon increasingly lamented by teachers trying to hold the interest of students accustomed to TV. To measure attention spans, psychophysiologist Thomas Mulholland of the Edith Nourse Rogers Memorial Veterans Hospital in Bedford, Mass., attached 40 young viewers to an instrument that shut off the TV set whenever the children's brains produced mainly alpha waves. Although the children were told to concentrate, only a few could keep the set on for more than 30 seconds.

Other researchers have found unrealistic career expectations among young people who watch a lot of TV. According to "Television and Behavior," the new federal report: "Heavy viewers want high-status jobs but do not intend to spend many years in school. For girls, there is even more potential for conflict between aspirations and plans; the girls who are heavy viewers usually want to get married, have children and stay at home to take care of them, but at the same time they plan to remain in school and have exciting careers."

Frustration of these expectations, according to social scientists, can spill over into communities, helping to fuel destructive outbursts, ranging from disruption of schools to ghetto riots. Once civil disturbances are telecast, they may spread through imitation, as they did from Washington, D.C., to dozens of other cities in 1968.

Fictional shows can have a similar effect. An airplane bomb threat on "Doomsday Flight" was followed by a rash of similar occurrences across the nation.

"Facts" Are Not Always as They Seem   Another concern is the growing number of Americans who rank television as their main source of news and information—more than two thirds, according to the Roper Poll.

Some complain that "facts" on TV are not always what they seem. A new form of program, the "docudrama," is cited as a potential source of confusion. Mixing established facts and conjecture, a docudrama often is accepted as totally accurate. One such program, "King," was criticized by associates of the Rev. Martin Luther King, Jr., for allegedly misrepresenting the personality of the late civil-rights leader.

In his objections to video coverage of budget cutting and poverty, President Reagan joined a long list of politicians who charge that their efforts have been distorted by TV's need for dramatic pictures, rather than factual analysis. The late Chicago Mayor Richard Daley complained that "protesters" against various causes often would show up outside his office door, unknown to him inside, wanting not to present their grievances to him but to get coverage by TV crews whom they had notified in advance.

Television also is blamed for making viewers impatient by distorting their notions of what to expect from life. "TV teaches that all problems can be resolved quickly—within 30 minutes on a sitcom, 30 seconds in a commercial," says Neil Postman, a communications professor at New York University. When that doesn't happen in real life, he adds, "many people become frustrated or depressed."

Author Ben Stein, a speech writer during the Nixon administration, says the fictional creations of TV have tended to make Americans contemptuous and suspicious of their leaders. In his book, *The View From Sunset Boulevard: America as Brought to You by the People Who Make Television*, Stein notes that most "heavies" in TV shows are conservative authority figures such as high-ranking officials and business executives. And a recent study by the Media Institute in Washington, D.C., concludes that two thirds of business leaders in entertainment series are portrayed as foolish, greedy or immoral, and half their actions as illegal.

Helping to Reshape Democracy Scholars have grown increasingly troubled by some of the effects of TV on democratic government.

More than two decades ago, Richard Nixon's sweat during a televised debate with John F. Kennedy weighed heavily against the Republican candidate for President, and apparently became a factor in his defeat. Since then, other TV debates during political campaigns also have been judged as much for cosmetics as for content, and are regarded as having contributed to winning or losing.

Even in the midst of ballot counting, TV's effects are far-reaching. In 1980, networks declared Ronald Reagan the projected winner soon after polls in Eastern states closed but before balloting ended in the West. Experts say some prospective voters never went to the polls in the West, believing their choices would make no difference.

A lesser-known issue that worries many political scientists is the frequent satirizing of public officials by entertainers such as Johnny Carson and Mark Russell.

According to some scholars, widely viewed TV skits poking fun at former President Jerry Ford's occasional clumsiness may have contributed to his defeat in 1976 by popularizing the notion that Ford was too awkward to lead the nation. Subsequent Presidents—Jimmy Carter and Ronald Reagan—also have been the objects of ridicule on TV—not a laughing matter if, as some believe, the satire prejudices a candidate's chance for election. Humorous commentary on politics in this country dates back to colonial times, but the immediacy and pervasiveness of television have given such satire added potency. "Now, one or two comics can start nationwide waves of derision that are almost impossible to overcome," says Robert Orben, a humor consultant to many politicians.

Worries About Morality Concern also is growing about the sexual content of programs flooding cable systems and videocassette machines now installed in more than one third of American homes.

Until recently, X-rated shows made up a heavy majority of the sales of prerecorded videotapes for exhibition on home sets. Among the three-dozen pay-cable networks, at least three—the *Playboy* channel, Eros and Private Screenings—include explicit sexual material. Depending on which channel they select, viewers can find everything from partial nudity to simulated intercourse.

Mainstream-movie channels, such as Home Box Office and Showtime Entertainment, also owe some of their success to occasional airings of unedited theatrical films intended for adults only. Such films often contain obscene language, gore and degrees of undress that would never make it past the in-house censors of conventional TV.

All this has prompted a backlash by communities trying to limit what can be brought into homes via cable. In Manhattan, officials have tried to deny use of the "public access" channel to amateur producers who air programs with footage of people who were persuaded to undress or even engage in sex acts in front of the camera.

Peggy Charren, president of Action for Children's Television, urged Congress to head off a wave of local censorship by requiring cable systems to offer free lock boxes—devices that keep children from watching certain channels.

Others have suggested antiobscenity statutes similar to the rules governing over-the-air television. Many constitutional experts believe, however, that cable will continue to be protected by the First Amendment in the same manner as theatrical movies, books and magazines— especially in light of a recent U.S. district-court ruling that Utah's ban on "indecent" cable programs was unconstitutionally vague.

Some scholars also are concerned about another aspect of moral values that may have been distorted by TV. Lois DeBakey, communications professor and head of a nationwide literacy movement, lists the television industry among "profit-hungry pleasure peddlers" who have created a national tendency to exalt entertainment above crucial needs such as health and education. Noting that highly televised sports stars are paid an average of $250,000 a year and teachers only $20,000, DeBakey asks: "Do we honestly expect to motivate young people to take school seriously when the highest monetary and social rewards are reserved for occupations in which education is often unnecessary?"

Bigger Role for Special Interests?   Many business and political leaders are troubled by recent developments in video communications, including a movement toward deregulation of TV.

In conventional broadcasting, stations have always been licensed by the Federal Communications Commission to use a scarce public commodity, the airwaves. As a result, they are bound by laws and policies that strictly limit obscenity and prohibit any company from owning more than seven stations, as well as by the fairness and equal-time doctrines requiring free time for opposing views and candidates when controversial opinions are aired.

None of those rules applies, however, to the new outlets of cable, videocassettes and pay TV. Moreover, a drive is under way, backed by the Reagan administration, to repeal those rules for all broadcasters and leave ownership and program content up to what FCC Chairman Mark S. Fowler calls the new "competitive pressures of the marketplace." Fowler's proposals have drawn fire from critics, who call the deregulation movement an invitation for companies and organizations with the most money to control what people see on TV.

Already, various ideological groups are rushing to buy their way onto the tube. By raising as much as 70 million dollars a year from viewers and using the money to purchase air time, conservative evangelists such as Jerry Falwell and Pat Robertson have virtually drowned out the broadcasting voices of the major denominations. Falwell's TV operation launched the Moral Majority, cornerstone of a religious right wing that was active in the conservative shift of the last elections. A Falwell ally, Texas-based TV preacher James Robinson, has aired two hour-long specials—"Wake Up, America" and "Attack on the Family" —in more than 50 cities. This spring, producer Norman Lear's liberal group, "People for the American Way," countered with "I Love Liberty," a 3-million-dollar extravaganza.

Local stations have taken the lead in what they call "issue-oriented advertising," commercials espousing political views. Participation so far has mostly been by big firms, such as Mobil Oil, attacking what they regard as excessive government regulation.

Backers of "message programing" maintain that rules of fairness and equal time are no longer needed because the many cable channels, independent stations and networks using relay satellites offer affordable soapboxes to almost anybody.

Opponents, however, say that is wishful thinking, because reaching a large portion of the national audience is too expensive except for a few rich organizations and individuals.

Do Viewers Respond Too Quickly?   Fresh criticism is being leveled at the potential for abuse in two-way cable systems spreading across the country. These systems allow viewers with home computers or push-button consoles to communicate with central computers in requesting data, ordering merchandise, conducting banking transactions and responding to opinion polls.

Because computers can build dossiers from viewers' responses, civil libertarians fear violations of privacy by businesses or government agencies.

"Two-way systems are hitched to computers that scan each household every 6 seconds, recording all manner of information," explains Les Brown, editor of *Channels of Communications* magazine. "They know what we watch, what we buy through television, how we vote in public-opinion polls."

More than 90,000 homes now have two-way systems, and rapid expansion into a fully "wired society" is expected eventually. Already, there are TV alarm systems tied to police stations and customers' homes that can turn on TV sets and record when people enter or leave a home. Although these processes are now aimed solely at detecting intruders, the possibility of other uses is alarming to some observers.

Brown says he discovered one unsettling ramification of the cable age when he was discussing the issue of privacy in two-way-cable systems during an interview on the Cable News Network. Suddenly, the interviewer called for an instant plebiscite on Brown's concern, and an undetermined number of noontime viewers on the Columbus, Ohio, QUBE system pushed response buttons on their sets.

Eighty-five percent rejected Brown's suggestion that there was anything to worry about.

Knowing that daytime audiences are frequently dominated by preschoolers who may not understand what they are doing but who are capable of pushing the response button, Brown comments: "What's frightening to contemplate is that such polls are routinely conducted on every kind of important national issue, and their results cited as public opinion.

"You will never hear a cable newscaster say, 'QUBE took a poll today, and here's what some 4-year-old thinks about the sale of AWACS to Saudi Arabia.' But some poor congressman may think he hears the voice of his constituents" in those results.

Despite the uncertainties, there is widespread hope that the new video age will benefit from the industry's past mistakes and triumphs and do the country far more good than harm.

As Benjamin Barber, a Rutgers University professor of political science, observes: "It is difficult to imagine the Kennedy generation, the '60s, Watergate, the Woodstock generation or even the Moral Majority in the absence of national television."

Now, he adds, those concepts "belong to history, for we stand—prepared or not—on the threshold of a new television age that promises to revolutionize our habits as viewers, as consumers and ultimately as citizens."

FOR FURTHER READING

Elie Abel (ed.), *What's News: The Media in American Society.* San Francisco; Calif.: Institute for Contemporary Studies, 1981.

J. Herbert Altschull, *Agents of Power: The News Media in Human Affairs.* New York: Longman, 1984.

Judee Burgoon, Michael Burgoon and Charles Atkin, *What Is News? Who Decides? And How?* A report of the American Society of Newspaper Editors. Michigan State University, 1982.

John Chancellor and Walter R. Means, *The News Business.* New York: Harper & Row, 1983.

Melvin L. DeFleur and Sandra Ball-Rokeach, *Theories of Mass Communication,* 4th ed. New York: Longman, 1982.

Job Fowles, *Television Viewers vs. Media Snobs: What TV Does for People.* Briarcliff Manor, N.Y.: Day & Stein, 1982.

Herbert Gans, *Deciding What's News.* New York: Pantheon Books, 1979.

Michael Gurevitch, Tony Bennett, James Curran and Janet Woollacott (eds.), *Culture, Society and the Media.* New York: Methuen, 1982.

Elihu Katz and Tamas Szecksko (eds.), *Mass Media and Social Change.* Beverly Hills, Calif.: Sage, 1981.

James B. Lemert, *Does Mass Communication Change Public Opinion After All? A New Approach to Effects Analysis.* Chicago: Nelson-Hall, 1981.

Shearon Lowery and Melvin L. DeFleur, *Milestones in Mass Communication Research: Media Effects.* New York: Longman, 1983.

John P. Murray, *Television & Youth: 25 Years of Research and Controversy.* Boys Town, Neb.: The Boys Town Center for the Study of Youth Development, 1980.

Neil Postman, *The Disappearance of Childhood.* New York: Dell (Delacorte Press), 1982.

Werner J. Severin and James W. Tankard, Jr., *Communication Theories: Origins, Methods, and Uses.* New York: Hastings House, 1979.

Alexis S. Tan, *Mass Communication Theories and Research.* Columbus, Ohio: Grid Publishing Inc., 1981.

II

Freedom vs. Responsibility

I N NO other society do the mass media have as much freedom as they have in the United States. Journalists have frequently argued that the constitutional guarantee of the freedoms of speech and of the press should be absolute. Truth, this argument poses, can only emerge from an open marketplace of ideas. Throughout the last half of the nineteenth century and the first half of the twentieth, American journalism was guided by the notion of objectivity, the objective search for and communication of facts, without regard for feelings or beliefs. Any attempt—on the part of government or any other institution—to object to objective reporting was an infringement on constitutional rights.

In the name of objective reporting and searching for the truth, American news media have brought us sex, crime, violence, gossip about the private lives of our public figures, rumors about the graft and corruption of our public officials, revelations of government secrets that affect our diplomatic relations and our national security and even information on how we can build our own nuclear bombs in our basements. The public, according to the theory, will sort out the truth from the falsehoods and thus be informed so that they can fulfill their responsibilities as citizens at the polling booths.

Some resent the media's freedom to present anything they want. And yet, if the press did not search out all the information that the public will pay for, whether or not some like that information, how would the people know all that is going on, both good and bad? Who should tell the news media what they can and cannot disseminate? Where should the line be drawn between freedom and responsibility? Who should draw the line? And who should enforce it? These questions have plagued democracies as long as they have been in existence. For the most part, we have left it to the courts to determine when and how the press has been irresponsible in individual cases. And most of the time in American history, the courts have ruled in favor of freedom, even when it concerns printing articles about how to build your own nuclear bombs.

As the media have become more powerful, however, the arguments have increased. After World War II, the Commission on Freedom of the Press was established to deal with these questions, and leading philosophers and statesmen were named to the commission to study the problem. Ultimately, the commission produced a document that expressed a new theory about the press in democracy, namely the "social-responsibility" theory. This theory suggests that in a mass society that now has the potential for total self-destruction and with mass media that have become such powerful institutions in that society, the press has an obligation that is larger than a simple search for the truth. In such a society, the commission suggested, if the search for truth should threaten the welfare of the society as a whole, some apparatus needs to be established to step in and protect society from such a threat.

To some extent, the social-responsibility theory operates in the broadcast media in our society, where the Federal Communication Commission can, within limits, protect society from threatening broadcasts. It does not operate on the print media. And as a result, the arguments on both sides of the freedom-versus-responsibility debate continue to grow.

4 · "RIGHT CONDUCT" FOR A "FREE PRESS"

BY MICHAEL MACDONALD MOONEY

Michael Macdonald Mooney uses the controversy over publishing an article about building your own hydrogen bomb as his vehicle to explore the ideas of freedom versus responsibility for the press. As he traces the history of the publication in the *Progressive* magazine and the attempts by government to block the publication, he makes an impassioned case for the news media's rights to make their own final judgment without interference from government authorities. His article is reprinted from *Harper*'s, March 1980.

Less than forty-eight hours before the incident began in the core of the nuclear reactor at Three Mile Island, the Department of Justice obtained an injunction in the Federal District Court in Milwaukee to enjoin by "prior restraint" *The Progressive* magazine from publishing an article by free-lance journalist Howard Morland entitled "The H-Bomb Secret." The preliminary injunction issued March 26 [1979] was the judicial result of a temporary restraining order issued Friday, March 9 [1979], by Judge Robert W. Warren. My curiosity about the *Progressive* case began the next morning, Saturday. Starting at ten o'clock and continuing until six that night a "First Amendment Survival Seminar" was conducted at the National Press Club in Washington, D.C. Teams of lawyers were brought on to brief some 300 members of the press on the journalistic procedures currently necessary as a result of recent court decisions. I learned that in the end I should be prepared to go to jail; that I should routinely destroy all my notes; that I should never express my opinion in writing without consulting a lawyer first. While this nonsense about right conduct for a "free press" was in progress, news of Judge Warren's order gagging *The Progressive* arrived in the National Press Club Ballroom. Television cameras were set up to hear from the distinguished members of the bar present. Not one would comment.

The television crews packed their lights and left. Until the facts of the matter could be studied, counsel had nothing to say. They represented the American Society of Newspaper Editors, the Association of American Publishers, Scripps-Howard Newspapers, United Press International, the American Newspaper Publishers Association, the *Washington Post*, Newhouse Newspapers, the Society of Professional Journalists-Sigma Delta Chi, the Reporters Committee for Freedom of the Press, the *Philadelphia Inquirer*, the Radio-Television News Directors Association, the *Washington Star*, and sixteen other sponsoring organizations. Eventually many newspapers would carry editorials supporting *The Progressive* and condemning Judge Warren's order; but many would not because *The Progressive*, in their opinion, had not brought a "clean case." As Benjamin C. Bradlee, the executive editor of the *Washington Post*, put it, he could only support *The Progressive* reluctantly, "with about as much enthusiasm as I would Larry Flynt and *Hustler*," because he thought the passion Morland brought to the subject of atomic energy was extraneous and confused, and had blinded the editors of *The Progressive* "to the fact that there are some secrets."

What amazed me was that both editors and lawyers seemed to presume that the First Amendment protected nice clean cases, but not awkward disputes; that Ben Bradlee couldn't tell the difference between a virgin and a dynamo; that lawyers would not comment on the meaning of law without studying the facts for their auguries.

The legalities of *The United States of America* vs. *The Progressive, Inc., Erwin Knoll, Samuel Day, Jr., and Howard Morland* were astonishing enough in themselves; the concomitant ethical, political, and cultural implications were astounding. Before March, 1979, no gag order, no prior restraint, no censorship prior to publication had ever been upheld in the history of American law, either in peace or in war, to halt publication of a single word.

At the outset of the *Progressive* case, the legal arguments advanced by the Department of Justice appeared to be merely bizarre, certainly contradictory, often mendacious, and largely nonsense. Because the U.S. Court of Appeals for the Seventh Circuit would apparently decline to play the fool for the sake of Justice's extraordinary claims, Justice was forced at last to abandon its prosecution of *The Progressive,* declaring the issue moot. As censors always do, Justice first appeared to prosecute *The Progressive* as the red-eyed zealot of overriding national interests, then retreated from its declarations of higher moral authority into a sullen lethargy. Whereupon Howard Morland's article about the nonexistence of any H-bomb secret was published in the November issue of *The Progressive.*

The substance and the details of Mr. Morland's article were, as he said, that anyone who takes the trouble can understand the technology of hydrogen bombs from the storehouse of public knowledge, *and therefore* that anyone can become competent to question the national policies that oversee the bomb's manufacture. What Mr. Morland demonstrates is that there are no secrets at all in the principles of H-bomb construction, but nearly total secrecy about the ministries of nuclear weapons and nuclear energy.

Since there are no secrets in Mr. Morland's article, its publication by *The Progressive* left national safety undisturbed, the proliferation of nuclear weapons undiminished, and national defense as secure and unaffected as it was before *The Progressive* was gagged. None of these considerations had ever depended on what Howard Morland knew, or how he learned it. Despite what the Departments of Energy and Justice swore in federal courts, none of these concerns for national security was the proximate cause for prosecution by Justice of *The Progressive*— which explains why Justice was untroubled by any inconsistencies in its legal arguments, no matter how bizarre. What Justice meant to demonstrate was the power to quash any debate of nuclear policies. When Justice had to quit prosecution of *The Progressive* to avoid embarrassment, it announced it had been only "temporarily thwarted." Since then, Justice has proceeded to expand the powers of censorship it had claimed—regardless of law, precedent, or any other limitation.

The sovereignties claimed by Justice in *The Progressive* case appeared at first to be merely silly: inadvertencies by inept, dim-witted, or ignorant government lawyers. Chief Justice Warren Burger had previously explained in careful and lucid language that prior restraint—the so-called gag order—was "presumptively unconstitutional." Yet after the incident provided by Howard Morland's article, the Justice Department announced its continuing defiance of the Supreme Court's opinion and every other U.S. law, custom, or tradition relevant to the case.

Moreover, while Justice maneuvered for six months in federal courts, demanding at the same time that the maneuvers themselves be secret, a de facto gag order on *The Progressive*'s presumed right to free speech was in effect for the first time in well over 200 years. In itself, the incident was unusual, but there was more to it than that: to publish Mr. Morland's article at all, the editors of *The Progressive* had to risk continuance of the magazine itself, and they were required to raise more than $200,000 in legal fees and expenses; whereas the funds for prosecution by Justice were spent without keeping records of the time used by dozens of government lawyers, and spent from the tax moneys in the public treasury. Thereafter, to make clear its radical position, Justice announced that it was prepared to prosecute any case that it alone determined might be similar to that of *The Progressive*, if such an opportunity arose. Justice wanted all those who held independent opinions to know that they might be required to match the public bankroll to defray the legal expenses attendant to private belief—regardless of precedent, law, or fact.

Ministries of Culture   To these extraordinary ideological powers without limit, not unlike those claimed in Berlin as necessities for public order after the Reichstag fire in 1933, the apparatus of national cultural agencies maintained a determined silence. Throughout the prosecution of *The Progressive*, and throughout the revelations provided by national authorities on the incident at Three Mile Island, the White House ministry of culture and its constituent subministries—the National Science Foundation, the Endowments for the Arts and the Humanities, the Smithsonian Institution, the General Services Administration, the National Park Service, the Department of Education, and so forth—without exception were examples of quietism. Passive acceptance was also the rule of all the cooperating foundations and corporations, all the coordinated and cooperating advisory councils, systems of peer-review panels, experts, and consultants. Not one peep was officially heard from a single agency devoted to the advancement of the sciences, arts, or humanities. A search through the records and minutes of these agencies' assemblies will show those meetings entirely silent on the topics of Three Mile Island or the *Progressive* case; it was as if Fort Sumter and the Dred Scott case had occurred in the same week, but were somehow considered irrelevant to public debate. Perhaps the agencies of national culture were dumbfounded; perhaps they were indicating by their determined silence that their enlightened enterprises could not include contradicting the Department of Justice or the Secretary of Energy under any circumstances.

It is marvelous how much *The Progressive* differs from those foundlings of which the various cultural ministries are so fond. To begin with, the ministries of culture frequently express their goodwill toward what they characterize as "alternate media." *The Progressive* is almost exactly the opposite of an "alternative" publication. The magazine is an honored tradition in American letters and can claim a considerable history. Founded in 1909 by Robert N. LaFollette, Sr., *The Progressive* and "Fighting Bob" were for seventy years unrelenting opponents of corporate monopolies, big business, and political bossism. As a continuously published expression of LaFollette's evergreen optimism, *The Progressive* was a stalwart of popular democracy in the traditions of the Grange, the Knights of Labor, and the Populists in all their great variety. Always in the mainstream of community values rather than fleeting national party interests, *The Progressive* helped to achieve many of the great reforms, those hopeful tinkerings of democratic machinery now accepted as commonplaces: for example, direct election of Senators, voting rights for women, referendum and recall, and primary elections for direct expression of party preferences rather than secret nominations by oligarchs in smoke-filled rooms.

In 1979 *The Progressive* continued its optimism, continued to believe in independent thought, in change by tinkering for the sake of community continuities against the claims made by national authorities; and it is precisely this independent tradition that earned *The Progressive* the enmity of the new order of federal overseers. The magazine maintains its offices in Madison, Wisconsin, far from the centers of social connections and personal patronage located in either New York or Washington. For its opinions, *The Progressive* owes little to anyone except its editors and authors; for its influence, the magazine depends on what it has to say rather than who says it; and for its circulation, it enlists those interested in well-argued, well-written, idiosyncratic, and sometimes wrongheaded opinions. Such modesty results in a circulation of no more than 40,000, few and infrequent advertisers, slim finances, and no government subsidies. The article by Howard Morland on the nonsecret principles underlying the construction of H-bombs was begun in what *The Progressive* believed was the public interest for the magnificent sum of $500.

To the extent that *The Progressive* can be characterized as a small but influential journal of informed opinion in the American tradition, the publications endowed by the government's cultural agencies are radical opposites. They are published on tax moneys. They are rich, not poor. Their expressions of national goodwill are expensive. The National Endowment for the Arts (NEA) awards grants, for example, for literary fellowships in amounts of $10,000 each to annual totals of $4 million, without any interest in whether there will eventually be any publishable result. In addition, the NEA supports hundreds of small magazines and publications, provided, of course, that they have rocked no boats. The National Endowment for the Humanities (NEH) awards research fellowships to scholars in amounts of $20,000 each, whether or not publishable results appear; and by various devices, if there happen to be publishable results from these scholarly efforts, the amounts may be matched or exceeded by royalties from university or commercial publishers.

As opposed to *The Progressive*'s contentious habits, the opinions published by the national agencies of culture are inevitably syncretic—reconciliations of differences for the sake of national goodwill, modulations of accepted themes to provide the appearance of consensus. Proof of influence is adduced by producing numbers testifying how many have attended or heard or read whatever it is some project has been busy doing in the name of education. *Accessibility* and *reach* are the accepted buzzwords to demonstrate effectiveness. If 500,000 citizens pass through the turnstiles of a museum show advertised as "The Art of Greece," it makes no difference that the art displayed is not Greek; what is important is the number—500,000. In contrast, to the extent *The Progressive* has any "reach," the magazine attains its influence by being passed from hand to hand. During the course of its opposition to the government's attempt to censor its publication, *The Progressive* lost circulation because the magazine was required to budget its funds for legal defenses instead of direct-mail solicitations for readers.

Every agency of national culture seeks out the gigantic corporations for joint funding of programs of goodwill, much as the magazines they fund look to the large corporate advertisers for support. Not one advertisement for Cadillac, General Electric, Glenlivet Scotch, Steuben Glass, Chrysler, Pan Am, Campari, The Edison Electric Institute, or Gulf Oil, however, decorates the pages of *The Progressive* as they do the pages of the government's *Smithsonian*. Never during the course of events after Three Mile Island or *The Progressive*'s gag order could it be said that the "critical choices" had been studied by *The Progressive*'s editors thanks to a grant from the Exxon Corporation. No editor at *The Progressive* can claim tenure to his office, nor are any of the magazine's authors protected by faculty senates for their opinions in the name of academic freedom.

To suggest how unwelcome Morland is in the plush offices of the government's cultural ministers, it is useful to recount what happened in early May, when Morland toured Washington. He appeared before audiences in the House, paid calls to newspaper editors to explain what he believed was at issue. Despite the court's gag orders, the Administration was always ahead of him. The Secretaries of State, Energy, and Defense had called their editorial contacts to explain how secret the materials really were that *The Progressive* had intended to publish. The *Washington Post* editorial on the case had concluded: "As a press-versus-Government First Amendment contest, this, as far as we can tell, is John Mitchell's dream case—the one the Nixon Administration was never lucky enough to get: a real First Amendment loser."

But as Morland was being interviewed by Richard Cohen of the *Washington Post,* Cohen apparently concluded that what Morland was telling the *Post* was remarkably different from what the *Post* had been told by their top-level sources. Cohen asked Morland to wait for just a moment while Cohen went to get the *Post*'s executive editor, Ben Bradlee. Within a few minutes, Bradlee stood on the newsroom floor, staring through the glass of Cohen's office at Morland. Bradlee actually did look much like Jason Robards in *All the President's Men.* After Bradlee had stared at Morland for awhile, he turned and left. Cohen explained that Bradlee was too busy to talk.

As the author of an article that made him the central actor in an extraordinary historical drama, Howard Morland seems at first to have been ill-cast for the part of an enemy of the people. He would have made an equally poor candidate for a federal grant from the National Science Foundation or the National Endowment for the Humanities: his academic credentials are too skimpy. The independent research he pursued as a result of his own curiosity would be an unlikely proposal to win the necessary approval from the appropriate consultants, peer-review panels, and national councils.

Mr. Morland was thirty-six when he appeared on the evening news as the object of federal fury. He grew up in Chattanooga, Tennessee. After high school, he attended Emory University in Atlanta, where he studied physics. Later, while he was gagged by an order of a federal court, he would recall in *The Progressive* the delights he had found in physics: the aesthetic appeal of Newton's laws of motion, of Einstein's extension of those laws into the relativity of phenomena. As a freshman, Morland said, he had been thrilled by the grace of Clerk Maxwell's four equations of electromagnetism: they explained, Morland believed, electricity, magnetism, heat, and light all at once. "I was dumbfounded for a day when I discovered them."

As a freshman, Mr. Morland underlined his physics text, noting those lessons he believed were significant, those that appealed to his aesthetics, and those that had dumbfounded him by their beauty, and he saved his old physics book. Eighteen years later, in its prosecution of *The Progressive,* the Justice Department declared that his old physics book had become a national secret; that before the freshman text could be declared no longer secret, whatever it was that Mr. Morland believed to be significant, graceful, or appealing must be erased of its underlinings; that arguments about whether an old physics text actually contained any secrets were arguments that could only be conducted in secret. Whatever was secret became secret as soon as Justice said it was secret; whether secrets were actually secret was secret; and arguments over what was secret were secret not only from the community at large, but also from the editors of *The Progressive* and from Mr. Morland.

Howard Morland's moral concerns for disarmament are exactly the same as the ethical and political choices frequently faced by popes, presidents, ministers, ambassadors, study groups, and officially approved publications. With respect to SALT, the neutron bomb, and proliferation treaties, Mr. Morland's questions are exactly the same as those funded at exorbitant expense for conferences initiated by many federal agencies, but Mr. Morland earned the enmity of the cultural ministers because he set off *on his own initiative* to discover who makes nuclear bombs, where they are made, why they are made, and how the whole system fits into the social fabric of American life. "I wanted to know why we are so afraid of this subject."

The federal powers were terrified as much by Mr. Morland's questions as by his answers. Four hundred hydrogen bombs would obliterate half the population of the Soviet Union in an afternoon. In any practical sense, 400 H-bombs would send to certain oblivion whatever could be defined by history or by geography or by any other analysis as Russia. What seemed odd to Mr. Morland was that the United States had an inventory of about 30,000 H-bombs—an excess of some 29,600—and was continuing to produce another doomsday machine every three hours of every working day. Not only did there appear to be a surplus in the manufacture of the devices, the entire procedure was shrouded in secrecy from any public debate about its reasons. Both the strange surplus and its secrecy made community discussion of national administration unintelligible with respect to SALT, or any other life-and-death nuclear question.

Mr. Morland in his inquiry didn't have to look far to discover the secret of the H-bomb—it seemed to be common knowledge. He had prepared a lecture with 134 slides that ran forty minutes, suitable for high-school and college audiences. His topic was "Atomic Power and the Arms Race," and he traced the historical connection between military technology for the nuclear industry and the applications of the same technical information by domestic universities and corporations. The fuel used essentially as a means to boil water is the same fuel used to make the bombs; the cycle by which the fuel is mined, manufactured, used, and stored is operated by the same national and corporate organizations. According to Mr. Morland, his lecture in January, 1978, was strong on atomic power, but weak on the details of weapons proliferation. Toward the end of his slide show in a dormitory at the University of Alabama, he asked whether anyone knew the secret of how the H-bomb works. He explained to his audience that he needed to understand the industry's product in order to understand the industry. To his astonishment, a student raised his hand and gave Morland a straightforward explanation.

The Mousetrap Bomb   Despite assertions to the contrary by the Justice Department, the straightforward explanation of how the H-bomb works is not a secret to a student in a dormitory at the University of Alabama, or anywhere else. Since 1939 it has not been a secret to anyone. The hydrogen bomb required the industrial capacity of at least a medium-sized government, vast quantities of electricity, carloads of blueprints and computer printouts, and something on the order of $1 billion worth of technological equipment. No one could make an H-bomb with a chemistry set in his basement; but the principles of how it works have never been secrets. To begin with, a hydrogen bomb requires an atomic bomb as its trigger. Before the first atomic bomb was ever tested, Prof. Henry D. Smyth of Princeton University described in "The Smyth Report" how the Manhattan Project, under the command of Gen. Leslie Groves, had designed the atomic bomb, tested its possibilities in Chicago, built its factories, and then built the bomb itself. "The Smyth Report" described in detail what the atomic factories did, who ran them, and how the wartime physicists solved each problem that had confronted them. One week after Hiroshima, the U.S. Army published Dr. Smyth's report.

By 1948, any Princeton freshman who attended Dr. Smyth's Physics 201 could not only understand the atomic bomb from Dr. Smyth's syllabus, but could also be hugely entertained by Dr. Smyth's imaginative lectures. His assistants prepared in advance the entire back wall of the lecture hall with about fifty vertical feet of mousetraps. For the finale of his justly famous lecture, Dr. Smyth touched the electric switch to spring the first mousetrap located up near the ceiling. The first trap sprung two more; those two in turn sprung four; those fired eight, and so on, in a sequential clatter illustrating nuclear fission. Then, with courtly bows, the historian of the Manhattan Project acknowledged the whistles, cheers, and standing applause from nearly 1,000 students. Those registered in Physics 201 spent their afternoon laboratory hours recording the half-life of twenty-five-cent pieces turned radioactive in Princeton's tiny cyclotron, but Dr. Smyth's lectures were attended not only by students of physics. Students of history, politics, and literature also audited his course. He told all who would listen what he had concluded in the official "Smyth Report":

> Here is a new tool for mankind, a tool of unimaginable destructive power. Its development raises many questions that must be answered in the near future. These questions are not technical questions; they are political and social questions, and the answers given to them may affect all mankind for generations. In a free country like ours, such questions should be debated by the people.

In 1947, another resident of the School for Advanced Studies at Princeton, Dr. Albert Einstein, signed an appeal for support. He wrote that the facts of atomic energy were simple; that scientists had an inescapable responsibility to explain those facts to their fellow citizens;

that atomic energy could not be fitted into outmoded perceptions of narrow nationalism: "For there is no secret and there is no defense; there is no possibility of control except through the aroused understanding and insistence of the peoples of the world."

Mindful of the responsibilities identified by Dr. Einstein, Gerard Piel, publisher of *Scientific American,* went to press in April, 1950, with an article by Dr. Hans A. Bethe, a professor of physics at Cornell University, about how thermonuclear fusion—the energies of the hydrogen bomb—works. At the time, the question being debated among scientists was whether to attempt to make the H-bomb. Many scientists opposed making Faust's bargain with fusion. The energies of fusion were the same energies that emanated from the sun and the stars. They had been reproduced in the laboratory in 1932; connected by publication of Dr. Bethe's theory in 1938 to stellar energy; discussed by Austrian physicist Hans Thirring in a book published in 1946 as an argument for building the bomb. Because of the wartime concentration necessary to produce the atomic bomb (explosion by fission), development of the H-bomb (explosion by fusion) had been postponed. Yet the materials to be used, and the way to use an atomic bomb as a trigger, were widely known and understood. Only an effective design was missing.

Because the Cold War was also then in progress, the new Atomic Energy Commission arrived at the offices of *Scientific American* while its April, 1950, issue was on press. The AEC ordered the presses stopped, destroyed about 3,000 copies of the magazine and the plates that included Dr. Bethe's article, and insisted that *Scientific American* delete four specific concepts from Dr. Bethe's explanation because the AEC had declared them to be secret. Torn between the prospect of no information with which to form the substance for public debate about testing the H-bomb, and at least some theory from the authoritative article by Dr. Bethe, publisher Gerard Piel consented to the AEC's demanded deletions. What was most obnoxious about the AEC's censorship was that three of the deletions were materials published previously by *Scientific American,* and long since in the public domain; the fourth concept was a deliberately false piece of technical information included to slow Russian development of the bomb. The AEC also deleted what was false. Because the bomb had not yet been tested, Gerard Piel charged the AEC with suppressing exactly the information the American people needed in order to make intelligent judgments. Twenty-nine years later, when one of the AEC's successor agencies, the Department of Energy, through the Department of Justice, moved to gag *The Progressive*'s publication, Gerard Piel wrote the *New York Times* immediately: "In the thirty years since America lost its imagined monopoly on the atomic secret, we should have learned that there never was a secret that could keep another country from making a bomb."

Mr. Piel pointed out that it was not secrets that stopped the manufacture of bombs, but the lack of industrial and technological materials, finances, and personnel—the carloads of computer printouts, the shiploads of materials, the nuclear-fuel-processing facilities with which to proceed. All the technical information needed to make atomic and hydrogen bombs was "in the public domain of the world community of physics in 1939."

The Department of Justice, however, was never concerned about what was actually in the public domain. To prove its intentions and demonstrate its unlimited powers, Justice solicited an affidavit in the *Progressive* case from the same Dr. Bethe who was the author of the censored article in *Scientific American* in 1950. Dr. Bethe had declined to comment on the AEC's censorship in 1950, and he had continued to serve the AEC and its successor, the Department of Energy, as a consultant. In 1979 he read Mr. Morland's manuscript after it was supplied to him by the Justice Department. Although others might not read Morland's article without a "Q" clearance, Dr. Bethe was cleared to keep the nation's secrets.

Dr. Bethe swore by affidavit that there were sizable portions of Morland's text that, in his judgment, should be classified as Restricted Data, "because the processes described in the manuscript, despite a number of technical errors, correctly describe the essential design and operation of thermonuclear weapons." Dr. Bethe's affidavit went on to establish how expert his testimony was: he said that he was familiar with the publicly available literature; that he had attended many meetings and conferences of those scientists who were knowledgeable in physics and thermonuclear design; that based on his experience, familiarity with the subject, and his review of the Morland manuscript, "the design and operational concepts described in the manuscript are not expressed in the public literature nor do I believe they are known to scientists not associated with the government's weapons programs."

Unfortunately, there were a number of oddities to Dr. Bethe's sworn expert testimony as introduced by Justice Department lawyers, including its characterizations of all those ignorant scientists not associated with the government's weapons programs. Far more significant, however, is that Dr. Bethe is the author of an article in the *Merit Student's Encyclopedia,* published by Macmillan and promoted to the school and library markets as suitable for junior high-school and grade-school libraries. Dr. Bethe's article in an eighth-grade encyclopedia, along with its accompanying diagram, is one of the sources in the public domain that Howard Morland used to understand the "secret" of the principles of the bomb that Dr. Bethe subsequently swore are known only to those with "Q" clearances. Moreover, Dr. Bethe's article proposed that students consult "books for further study," including the *Scientific Ameri-*

can Reader, published by Simon and Schuster in 1953, in which the student could read Dr. Bethe's own ten-page article censored by the AEC in 1950.

By comparing Mr. Morland's manuscript with Dr. Bethe's encyclopedia article, differences between the two on the H-bomb secret are readily apparent. Mr. Morland is more specific than Dr. Bethe about how the trigger mechanism works and about the effects of radiation pressure on the shield and pencil-shaped container for the hydrogen isotopes. On the other hand, with formulas Dr. Bethe makes clear even to eighth-grade students how the chemistry and physics of the reaction work—not much of which appears in Morland's article.

What is revealing in Justice's prosecution of *The Progressive* is that Justice declared Mr. Morland's article secret, but also declared Dr. Bethe's article in the eighth-grade encyclopedia retroactively secret. When lawyers for *The Progressive* introduced the Bethe encyclopedia article by affidavit, Justice also declared the affidavit showing the evidence in the public domain to be secret. Justice insisted that any arguments over whether an encyclopedia in the public domain is actually secret are arguments that may be conducted only in secret. These arguments about what was in the public domain were so secret that the editors of *The Progressive* who wished to publish Mr. Morland's article could not hear them, so that they could not know even *after* they had published the article what secrets were in either article; nor could they learn whether the secrets they had published were the same as the secrets introduced by secret affidavit and argued in secret over the Bethe article. In connection with these bizarre arguments, Justice asserted after Morland's article was published in *The Progressive* that anyone who communicates the same secret secrets, either Morland's or those in the eighth-grade encyclopedia, by speech or by writing, would be "acting in concert" with Mr. Morland and *The Progressive,* and thereby violating the *in camera* "protective orders" of the Federal Court, subjecting the violators to criminal prosecution. Since the affidavits are secret, and the judge's decision is secret too, there is no way to know which secrets are secret, or what secrets make up a criminal violation of secrecy. Two bright eighth-graders arguing over the mechanism of a hydrogen bomb and reproducing Dr. Bethe's diagram with a stick in the dirt might be criminals. *Any* discussion of nuclear physics, according to Justice, might constitute a criminal violation. *All* "technical information," according to Justice, is exempt from the guarantees provided by the First Amendment. Any intuition about either the workings of the hydrogen bomb or the nuclear-fuel cycle in a power plant are understandings "classified at birth," according to Justice—"Restricted Data requiring a 'Q' clearance for continuance within a knowing mind." Any communication of what the community knows within the public domain might constitute a criminal violation, in any federal district, at any time at all, retroactively or by prior restraint, whenever the Department of Justice or the Department of Energy deemed it appropriate.

Keepers of the Flame   The censors of energy are, of course, acting as patriots. Having ignored the community's certain knowledge that there is no H-bomb secret and never has been, the lawyers representing the Departments of Energy and Justice embarked on a series of deliberate frauds to prosecute *The Progressive.* Having declared Howard Morland's old physics text secret, and an article in an eighth-grade encyclopedia also secret, the Justice Department and its abettors at the Department of Energy, which passed judgment on details in question, were required also to declare secret articles submitted by affidavit from an encyclopedia describing the energies of the sun and the stars. Since those energies are the same as those released by an H-bomb's fusion, the logic of the Department of Energy's classification as Restricted Data of common knowledge about the sun and the stars is an example of impeccable perversity: those heavenly bodies emit energy, therefore the Department of Energy claims sole jurisdiction; the moon, of course, only reflects energy and is presumably exempt from the authority vested in the Department's Secretary, James R. Schlesinger, Jr. All arguments over whether the sun and the stars could be classified under the provisions of the Atomic Energy Act of 1954 were secret arguments, according to Justice, and any violation of the court's protective orders with respect to the arguments, or the affidavits on the sun and the stars, would be a criminal violation.

Along with encyclopedia articles by Dr. Bethe on the H-bomb and those on the sun and the stars, *The Progressive* in its defense introduced by affidavit more than thirty other articles published in the public domain by scientific and technical journals to demonstrate that there was no secret. All these articles, their affidavits, briefs relating to their introduction, and arguments over their evidence were secrets, Justice said. Howard Morland introduced by affidavit an article from the *Encyclopedia Americana,* along with its diagram, by Dr. Edward Teller, often characterized as the father of the H-bomb. Both Dr. Teller's article and the accompanying diagram bore a remarkable resemblance to the article by Dr. Bethe in the *Merit Student's Encyclopedia,* and to the article and diagram eventually published by *The Progressive.* Presumably Dr. Teller's explanation would be an authoritative one, because Dr. Teller and Dr. Stanislaw M. Ulam were generally credited with solving the bomb's mathematical design problems.

Justice declared that Dr. Teller's article in the *Encyclopedia Americana* was secret, the affidavits by which it was introduced were secret, arguments over whether it was secret were secret, and the court's opinion about these secrets was secret. Moreover, the Restricted

Data declared secret in the *Encyclopedia Americana* and *The Merit Student's Encyclopedia* were retroactively secret, even if those secrets were available in the public domain on approximately 63,000 community-school and library bookshelves. Although the diagrams published by the encyclopedias and *The Progressive* were remarkably similar, they were all secrets, because Justice claimed that Mr. Morland had identified in his article three concepts of hydrogen bombs never published before anywhere else. These three concepts understood by Mr. Morland were declared to be Restricted Data even as they resided in Morland's head, even if they were the same three concepts censored from *Scientific American* in 1950 but previously published by the same magazine. The three concepts were so secret that the editors of *The Progressive* were not allowed to hear arguments over whether the three concepts were secret without security clearance. Since the editors refused security clearance after they had published Morland's article, they still did not know which were the three secrets, nor whether those secrets actually appeared in the encyclopedia articles or *Scientific American*. Only the Department of Energy, Justice said, could determine when secrets were secrets. Mr. Schlesinger swore: "Based upon my review of all affidavits submitted by the government and my review of the manuscript and information supplied to me by my advisers, I have concluded that publication, communication, or disclosure of the Secret Restricted Data portions of the Morland manuscript would irreparably impair the national security of the United States by making available to foreign nations Secret Restricted Data pertaining to the design and operational characteristics of a thermonuclear weapon. Such information would materially aid foreign nations by enabling them to develop such weapons in a shorter period of time than otherwise would be possible."

Secretary Schlesinger cited the nonproliferation policy of the United States, including the Treaty on Nonproliferation of Nuclear Weapons. Secretary of State Cyrus Vance made many of the same points by sworn affidavit. If the Morland article were published, Mr. Vance said, "it would undermine our nonproliferation policy, irreparably impair the national security of the United States, and pose a grave threat to the peace and security of the world." The advice examined by these two distinguished authorities to enable them to make these conclusions was so secret that the names of the experts who provided the advice continued to be secret, according to Justice, after the publication of the Morland article.

To understand the technical implications of fusion production, Howard Morland toured the facilities of Union Carbide's Y-12 plant near Oak Ridge, Tennessee. He interviewed Union Carbide's plant manager. His tours and his interviews were arranged for him by Department of Energy officials. Although the same information might be exported to South Korea, Britain, or Brazil, although the same technical principles might be available in the public domain, whatever Mr. Morland saw or heard was retroactively declared secret by Justice to the extent that Mr. Morland understood it. Similarly, Mr. Morland visited libraries and museums, one maintained by the Department of Energy in Los Alamos, and others in Albuquerque, New Mexico, Livermore, California, and Washington, D.C. He collected a stack of unclassified brochures and books six feet high. In Washington, D.C., he saw replicas on display, or actual casings, for nuclear weapons—displayed for the education of tourists by the Smithsonian. All that Mr. Morland saw and all that he read was declared secret, to the extent that he understood it. An *in camera* document he read in one library was retroactively declared secret. The document was removed from the library; the card catalogue index materials listing the document were removed; and the library was then closed to the public. All such materials in the public domain became secrets; arguments before the courts about whether materials in the public domain were secret were secret arguments; and any discussion that the same technical information was regularly exported by the Department of Energy was also secret. These assertions are identical to those imagined by George Orwell in *Nineteen Eighty-four:* even to understand the term *doublethink* involved the use of doublethink; as soon as the party could thrust its hand into the past and say of an event, it never happened—"that, surely, was more terrifying than mere torture and death."

"Reality Control" consisted of an unending series of victories over the community's memory, Orwell said. There were never any H-bomb secrets at issue in the *Progressive* case. What was at stake was the government's "visible means of control."

The Hydrogen Sweepstakes   While the Department of Energy was censoring *The Progressive*'s affidavits haphazardly, affidavits from four physicists at the Argonne National Laboratory about what was in the public domain were censored, but other references helpful to followers of the case slipped through. The article by Dr. Teller in the *Encyclopedia Americana* slipped into the court's open records. An affidavit submitted by a government witness, Jack Rosengren, a nuclear weapons design specialist, indicated that Mr. Morland's explanation in *The Progressive* described the most efficient H-Bomb in the U.S. stockpile. Since Justice failed to declare its own affidavit secret, the Rosengren affidavit slipped into the public domain. Examining the contradictions in the government's case against *The Progressive,* and noting that Justice had introduced into the public domain materials that *The Progressive* had not, the four Argonne physicists wrote an angry letter to Sen. John Glenn of Ohio. Within a month, Energy responded by declaring *the letter* secret.

Following these astounding events by newspaper in California, another amateur in nuclear matters, Charles Hansen, decided to join the case. Hansen was a computer programmer whose only physics-related education consisted of two years of college-level engineering. Using clues supplied by *Fusion* magazine, others from the government's own affidavits and from the references uncensored by Energy, and clues contained in a copy of the letter sent to Senator Glenn by the four Argonne physicists, Mr. Hansen sponsored an H-bomb contest: the first H-bomb design to be declared secret by the Department of Energy would be the winner. He mailed copies of "the Argonne letter" around the country. The *Daily Californian* at Berkeley printed the letter, and six other college newspapers followed suit.

Mr. Hansen then wrote an eighteen-page single-spaced letter to Sen. Charles H. Percy of Illinois. The letter, he said, was based on the affidavits introduced in the *Progressive* case, particularly a brief of the Fusion Foundation, on copies of *Fusion* magazine, articles in encyclopedias, history books on nuclear weapons available in public libraries, and "pure intuitive reasoning." The Hansen letter included a diagram drawn with the aid of a tuna fish can, and circles traced from tops of jars. Mr. Hansen explained the principles of H-bomb design, saying that if anyone should be charged with revealing the H-bomb "secret" it was the government's own weapons experts: Dr. Edward Teller, Dr. George Rathjens of M.I.T., and Dr. Theodore Taylor of Princeton. In addition to mailing his letter to Senator Percy, Mr. Hansen mailed a copy to the Department of Energy. Agents of public conscience appeared in Senator Percy's suite in the Dirksen Building to demand that Hansen's letter be surrendered. It had been declared secret.

Mr. Hansen also sent copies of his letter to the *Chicago Tribune*, the *Wall Street Journal*, the *Oakland Tribune*, the *Milwaukee Sentinel*, the *San Jose Mercury News*, and the *Daily Californian*, among others, and to his hometown paper in Palo Alto, the *Peninsula Times-Tribune*. As a result, the officers of national security were sent on a merry chase. They demanded that the *Wall Street Journal* surrender Hansen's "secret" letter. The *Wall Street Journal* refused. The *Peninsula Times-Tribune* published a portion of Hansen's explanations, along with what the newspaper's editors described as a diagram so crude that it was little more than a cartoon. Justice announced that it was considering filing criminal charges against the newspaper. At the *Daily Californian*, the editors were considering whether to publish Mr. Hansen's letter or a combination of the letter with the same materials the paper had published from "the Argonne letter" three months earlier when they were informed by Justice that both the Argonne letter they had already published and the Hansen letter were now "Secret/Restricted Data," and that publication would result in criminal charges.

Although declared secret, Mr. Hansen's intuitions were characterized as largely mistaken by scientists at the Livermore Laboratory in California, by others at the Argonne National Laboratory in Illinois, and by others at the Los Alamos Scientific Laboratory in New Mexico. Their published comments characterized Hansen's explanations as "a lot of misinformation or poorly understood information, a hodgepodge of material, and much of it inaccurate." Because of the "security regulations" claimed by the Departments of Energy and Justice, however, the same scientists could not declare whether Mr. Hansen's "hodgepodge" was largely true or false. The "technical information" Justice had retroactively declared secret was all-inclusive: all private intuitions were secret with respect to atomic energy, including those that were mistaken. To such nonsense, and in defiance of Justice, the *Madison Press Connection* published Mr. Hansen's letter anyway, on September 16, 1979. The prestigious *Chicago Tribune* declared its plan to publish, unless taken to court. On Monday, September 17, Justice announced it was abandoning its case against *The Progressive* because the publication of the Hansen letter rendered the case moot, but the reasons Justice gave were not even remotely true.

The Justice Department withdrew from the *Progressive* case after the magazine's appeal had been heard by the U.S. Court of Appeals for the Seventh Circuit. By withdrawing before the case could be judged on its merits, the government preserved its powers of censorship, as the *Chicago Tribune* explained it, "when the facts don't interfere so much with its efforts." By backing down when it did, without a court ruling that a prior restraint that stood for six months was unconstitutional, no ruling was made on the government's radical claim that "technical information" is excluded from the guarantees of the First Amendment.

On the day after the Justice Department withdrew its case, Nat Hentoff, a writer for the *Village Voice*, queried the department on what many were describing as *The Progressive*'s victory for a free society. "Everything is exactly as it was—except for this particular case," an official in the Justice Department answered. "The secrecy provisions of the Atomic Energy Act are intact. And I include that section of the act which empowers us to go after prior restraint of publications that, in our judgment, violate those secrecy provisions. Nor are we inhibited in any way from engaging in criminal prosecutions after publication of those who have printed such information without our first knowing about it."

Although the laws, customs, manners, and traditions of the community could be searched in vain for any such precedents, the regulations of the Atomic Energy Act of 1954 were announced to be sufficient to the government's purposes. The regulations state that anyone who possesses Restricted Data, whether that person obtained the data from the government or by their own private initiatives from nongovernment sources—including the results of study, wonder, or intuition—cannot "communicate" the Restricted Data to anyone else by publication or by talking to his neighbor across the backyard fence. Restricted Data included all information—whether true or false—concerning: "(1) design, manufacture, or utilization of atomic weapons; (2) the production of special nuclear material; or (3) the use of special nuclear material in the production of energy."

The government's radical and extraordinary powers are asserted over *all* nuclear information—weapons, fuels, and the production of energy; and the basis for these powers, according to Justice, is that *all* "technical information" is exempt from the guarantees of the First Amendment. Such claims, of course, cannot be supported by either law or precedent because there are no such laws and no such precedents. Instead, these are claims for social and political powers to determine the character of the national culture regardless of how the meaning of the word *culture* is defined.

5 · OBJECTIVITY PRECLUDES RESPONSIBILITY

BY THEODORE L. GLASSER

Theodore L. Glasser argues that objectivity is not the best basis on which to make responsible journalistic decisions. Glasser teaches journalism at the University of Minnesota. This article is adapted from a lecture prepared for the Second Annual Seminar in Applied Ethics, sponsored by the Minnesota Journalism Center, Augsberg College and the Minnesota Humanities Commission. It is reprinted from *The Quill,* February 1984.

By objectivity I mean a particular view of journalism and the press, a frame of reference used by journalists to orient themselves in the newsroom and in the community. By objectivity I mean, to a degree, ideology; where ideology is defined as a set of beliefs that function as the journalist's "claim to action."

As a set of beliefs, objectivity appears to be rooted in a positivist view of the world, an enduring commitment to the supremacy of observable and retrievable facts. This commitment, in turn, impinges on news organizations' principal commodity—the day's news. Thus my argument, in part, is this: Today's news is indeed biased—as it must inevitably be—and this bias can be best understood by understanding the concept, the conventions, and the ethic of objectivity.

Specifically, objectivity in journalism accounts for—or at least helps us understand—three principal developments in American journalism; each of these developments contributes to the bias or ideology of news. First, objective reporting is biased against what the press typically defines as its role in a democracy—that of a Fourth Estate, the watchdog role, an adversary press. Indeed, objectivity in journalism is biased in favor of the status quo; it is inherently conservative to the extent that it encourages reporters to rely on what sociologist Alvin Gouldner so appropriately describes as the "managers of the status quo"—the prominent and the élite. Second, objective reporting is biased against independent thinking; it emasculates the intellect by treating it as a disinterested spectator. Finally, objective reporting is biased against the very idea of responsibility; the day's news is viewed as something journalists are compelled to report, not something they are responsible for creating.

This last point, I think, is most important. Despite a renewed interest in professional ethics, the discussion continues to evade questions of morality and responsibility. Of course, this doesn't mean that journalists are immoral. Rather, it means that journalists today are largely amoral. Objectivity in journalism effectively erodes the very foundation on which rests a responsible press.

By most any of the many accounts of the history of objectivity in journalism, objective reporting began more as a commercial imperative than as a standard of responsible reporting. With the emergence of a truly popular press in the mid-1800s—the penny press—a press tied neither to the political parties nor the business élite, objectivity provided a presumably disinterested view of the world.

But the penny press was only one of many social, economic, political, and technological forces that converged in the mid- and late-1800s to bring about fundamental and lasting changes in American journalism. There was the advent of the telegraph, which for the first time separated communication from transportation. There were radical changes in printing technology, including the steam-powered press and later the rotary press. There was the formation of the Associated Press, an early effort by publishers to monopolize a new technology—in this case the telegraph. There was, finally, the demise of community and the rise of society; there were now cities, "human settlements" where "strangers are likely to meet."

These are some of the many conditions that created the climate for objective reporting, a climate best understood in terms of the emergence of a new mass medium and the need for that medium to operate efficiently in the marketplace.

Efficiency is the key term here, for efficiency is the central meaning of objective reporting. It was efficient for the Associated Press to distribute only the "bare facts," and leave the opportunity for interpretation to individual members of the cooperative. It was efficient for newspapers not to offend readers and advertisers with partisan prose. It was efficient—perhaps expedient—for reporters to distance themselves from the sense and substance of what they reported.

To survive in the marketplace, and to enhance their status as a new and more democratic press, journalists—principally publishers, who were becoming more and more removed from the editing and writing process—began to transform efficiency into a standard of professional competence, a standard later—several decades later—described as objectivity. This transformation was aided by two important developments in the early twentieth century: first, Oliver Wendell Holmes' effort to employ a marketplace metaphor to define the meaning of the First Amendment; and second, the growing popularity of the scientific method as the proper tool with which to discover and understand an increasingly alien reality.

In a dissenting opinion in 1919, Holmes popularized "the marketplace of ideas," a metaphor introduced by John Milton several centuries earlier. Metaphor or not, publishers took it quite literally. They argued—and continue with essentially the same argument today—that their opportunity to compete and ultimately survive in the marketplace is their First Amendment right, a Constitutional privilege. The American Newspaper Publishers Association, organized in 1887, led the cause of a free press. In the name of freedom of the press, the ANPA fought the Pure Food and Drug Act of 1906 on behalf of its advertisers; it fought the Post Office Act of 1912, which compelled sworn statements of ownership and circulation and thus threatened to reveal too much to advertisers; it fought efforts to regulate child labor, which would interfere with the control and exploitation of paper boys; it fought the collective bargaining provisions of the National Recovery Act in the mid-1930s; for similar reasons, it stood opposed to the American Newspaper Guild, the reporters' union; it tried—unsuccessfully—to prevent wire services from selling news to radio stations until after publication in the nearby newspaper.

Beyond using the First Amendment to shield and protect their economic interests in the marketplace, publishers were also able to use the canons of science to justify—indeed, legitimize—the canons of objective reporting. Here publishers were comforted by Walter Lippmann's writings in the early 1920s, particularly his plea for a new scientific journalism, a new realism; a call for journalists to remain "clear and free" of their irrational, their unexamined, their unacknowledged prejudgments.

By the early 1900s objectivity had become the acceptable way of doing reporting—or at least the respectable way. It was respectable because it was reliable, and it was reliable because it was standardized. In practice, this meant a preoccupation with *how* the news was presented, whether its *form* was reliable. And this concern for reliability quickly overshadowed any concern for the validity of the realities the journalists presented.

Thus emerged the conventions of objective reporting, a set of routine procedures journalists use to objectify their news stories. These are the conventions sociologist Gaye Tuchman describes as a kind of strategy journalists use to deflect criticism, the same kind of strategy social scientists use to defend the quality of their work. For the journalist, this means interviews with sources; and it ordinarily means official sources with impeccable credentials. It means juxtaposing conflicting truth-claims, where truth-claims are reported as "fact" regardless of their validity. It means making a judgment about the news value of a truth-claim even if that judgment serves only to lend authority to what is known to be false or misleading.

As early as 1924 objectivity appeared as an ethic, an ideal subordinate only to truth itself. In his study of the *Ethics of Journalism,* Nelson Crawford devoted three full chapters to the principles of objectivity. Thirty years later, in 1954, Louis Lyons, then curator for the Nieman Fellowship program at Harvard, was describing objectivity as a "rock-bottom" imperative. Apparently unfazed by Wisconsin's Senator Joseph McCarthy, Lyons portrayed objectivity as the ultimate discipline of journalism. "It is at the bottom of all sound reporting—indispensable as the core of the writer's capacity." More recently, in 1973, the Society of Professional Journalists, Sigma Delta Chi formally enshrined the idea of objectivity when it adopted as part of its Code of Ethics a paragraph characterizing objective reporting as an attainable goal and a standard of performance toward which journalists should strive. "We honor those who achieve it," the Society proclaimed.

So well ingrained are the principles of objective reporting that the judiciary is beginning to acknowledge them. In a 1977 federal appellate decision, *Edwards* v. *National Audubon Society,* a case described by media attorney Floyd Abrams as a landmark decision in that it may prove to be the next evolutionary stage in the development of the public law of libel, a new and novel privilege emerged. It was the first time the courts explicitly recognized objective reporting as a standard of journalism worthy of First Amendment protection.

In what appeared to be an inconsequential story published in *The New York Times* in 1972—on page 33—five scientists were accused of being paid liars, men paid by the pesticide industry to lie about the use of DDT and its effect on bird life. True to the form of objective reporting, the accusation was fully attributed—to a fully identified official of the National Audubon Society. The scientists, of course, were given an opportunity to deny the accusation. Only one of the scientists, however, was quoted by name and he described the accusation as "almost libelous." What was newsworthy about the story, obviously, was the accusation; and with the exception of one short paragraph, the reporter more or less provided a forum for the National Audubon Society.

Three of the five scientists filed suit. While denying punitive damages, a jury awarded compensatory damages against the *Times* and one of the Society's officials. The *Times,* in turn, asked a federal District Court to overturn the verdict. The *Times* argued that the "actual malice" standard had not been met; since the scientists were "public figures," they were required to show that the *Times* knowingly published a falsehood or there was, on the part of the *Times,* a reckless disregard for whether the accusation was true or false. The evidence before the court clearly indicated the latter—there was indeed a reckless disregard for whether the accusation was true or false. The reporter made virtually no effort to confirm the validity of the National Audubon Society's accusations. Also the story wasn't the kind of "hot news" (a technical term used by the courts) that required immediate dissemination; in fact ten days before the story was published the *Times* learned that two of the five scientists were not employed by the pesticide industry and thus could not have been "paid liars."

The *Times* appealed to the Second Circuit Court of Appeals, where the lower court's decision was overturned. In reversing the District Court, the Court of Appeals created a new First Amendment right, a new Constitutional defense in libel law—the privilege of "neutral reportage." "We do not believe," the Court of Appeals ruled, "that the press may be required to suppress newsworthy statements merely because it has serious doubts regarding their truth." The First Amendment, the Court said, "protects the accurate and disinterested reporting" of newsworthy accusations "regardless of the reporter's private views regarding their validity."

I mention the details of the *Edwards* case only because it illustrates so well the consequences of the ethic of objectivity. First, it illustrates a very basic tension between objectivity and responsibility. Objective reporting virtually precludes responsible reporting, if by responsible reporting we mean a willingness on the part of the reporter to be accountable for what is reported. Objectivity requires only that reporters be accountable for *how* they report, not what they report. The *Edwards* Court made this very clear: "The public interest in being fully informed," the Court said, demands that the press be afforded the freedom to report newsworthy accusations "without assuming responsibility for them."

Second, the *Edwards* case illustrates the unfortunate bias of objective reporting—a bias in favor of leaders and officials, the prominent and the élite. It is an unfortunate bias because it runs counter to the important democratic assumption that statements made by ordinary citizens are as valuable as statements made by the prominent and the élite. In a democracy, public debate depends on separating individuals from their powers and privileges in the larger society; otherwise debate itself becomes a source of domination. But *Edwards* reinforces prominence as a news value; it reinforces the use of official sources, official records, official channels. Tom Wicker underscored the bias of the *Edwards* case when he observed recently that "objective journalism almost always favors Establishment positions and exists not least to avoid offense to them."

Objectivity also has unfortunate consequences for the reporter, the individual journalist. Objective reporting has stripped reporters of their creativity and their imagination; it has robbed journalists of their passion and their perspective. Objective reporting has transformed journalism into something more technical than intellectual; it has turned the art of story-telling into the technique of report writing. And most unfortunate of all, objective reporting has denied journalists their citizenship; as disinterested observers, as impartial reporters, journalists are expected to be morally disengaged and politically inactive.

Journalists have become—to borrow James Carey's terminology— "professional communicators," a relatively passive link between sources and audiences. With neither the need nor the opportunity to develop a critical perspective from which to assess the events, the issues, and the personalities he or she is assigned to cover, the objective reporter tends to function as a translator—translating the specialized language of sources into a language intelligible to a lay audience.

In his frequently cited study of Washington correspondents—a study published nearly fifty years ago—Leo Rosten found that a "pronounced majority" of the journalists he interviewed considered themselves inadequate to cope with the bewildering complexities of our nation's policies and politics. As Rosten described it, the Washington press corps was a frustrated and exasperated group of prominent journalists more or less resigned to their role as mediators, translators. "To do the job," one reporter told Rosten, "what you know or understand isn't important. You've got to know whom to ask." Even if you don't understand what's being said, Rosten was told, you just take careful notes and write it up verbatim: "Let my readers figure it out. I'm their reporter, not their teacher."

That was fifty years ago. Today, the story is pretty much the same. Two years ago another study of Washington correspondents was published, a book by Stephen Hess called *The Washington Reporters*. For the most part, Hess found, stories coming out of Washington were little more than a "mosaic of facts and quotations from sources" who were participants in an event or who had knowledge of the event. Incredibly, Hess found that for nearly three-quarters of the stories he studied, reporters relied on no documents—only interviews. And when reporters did use documents, those documents were typically press clippings—stories they had written or stories written by their colleagues.

And so what does objectivity mean? It means that sources supply the sense and substance of the day's news. Sources provide the arguments, the rebuttals, the explanations, the criticism. Sources put forth the ideas while other sources challenge those ideas. Journalists, in their role as professional communicators, merely provide a vehicle for these exchanges.

But if objectivity means that reporters must maintain a healthy distance from the world they report, the same standard does not apply to publishers. According to the SPJ,SDX Code of Ethics, "Journalists and their employers should conduct their personal lives in a manner which protects them from conflict of interest, real or apparent." Many journalists do just that—they avoid even an appearance of a conflict of interest. But certainly not their employers.

If it would be a conflict of interest for a reporter to accept, say, an expensive piano from a source at the Steinway Piano Company, it apparently wasn't a conflict of interest when CBS purchased the Steinway Piano Company.

Publishers and broadcasters today are part of a large and growing and increasingly diversified industry. Not only are many newspapers owned by corporations that own a variety of non-media properties, but their boards of directors read like a *Who's Who* of the powerful and the élite. A recent study of the twenty-five largest newspaper companies found that the directors of these companies tend to be linked with "powerful business organizations, not with public interest groups; with management, not with labor; with well established think tanks and charities, not their grassroots counterparts."

But publishers and broadcasters contend that these connections have no bearing on how the day's news is reported—as though the ownership of a newspaper had no bearing on the newspaper's content; as though business decisions have no effect on editorial decisions; as though it wasn't economic considerations in the first place that brought about the incentives for many of the conventions of contemporary journalism.

No doubt the press has responded to many of the more serious consequences of objective reporting. But what is significant is that the response has been to amend the conventions of objectivity, not to abandon them. The press has merely refined the canons of objective reporting; it has not dislodged them.

What remains fundamentally unchanged is the journalist's naïvely empirical view of the world, a belief in the separation of facts and values, a belief in the existence of *a* reality—the reality of empirical facts. Nowhere is this belief more evident than when news is defined as something external to—and independent of—the journalist. The very vocabulary used by journalists when they talk about news underscores their belief that news is "out there," presumably waiting to be *exposed* or *uncovered* or at least *gathered.*

This is the essence of objectivity, and this is precisely why it is so very difficult for journalism to consider questions of ethics and morality. Since news exists "out there"—apparently independent of the reporter—journalists can't be held responsible for it. And since they are not responsible for the news being there, how can we expect journalists to be accountable for the consequences of merely reporting it?

What objectivity has brought about, in short, is a disregard for the consequences of newsmaking. A few years ago Walter Cronkite offered this interpretation of journalism: "I don't think it is any of our business what the moral, political, social, or economic effect of our reporting is. I say let's go with the job of reporting—and let the chips fall where they may."

Contrast that to John Dewey's advice: that "our chief moral business is to become acquainted with consequences."

I am inclined to side with Dewey. Only to the extent that journalists are held accountable for the consequences of their actions can there be said to be a responsible press. But we are not going to be able to hold journalists accountable for the consequences of their actions until they acknowledge that news is their creation, a creation for which they are fully responsible. And we are not going to have much success convincing journalists that news is created, not reported, until we can successfully challenge the conventions of objectivity.

The task, then, is to liberate journalism from the burden of objectivity by demonstrating—as convincingly as we can—that objective reporting is more of a custom than a principle, more a habit of mind than a standard of performance. And by showing that objectivity is largely a matter of efficiency—efficiency that serves, as far as I can tell, only the needs and interest of the owners of the press, not the needs and interests of talented writers and certainly not the needs and interests of the larger society.

6 · THE HIGH COST
OF FREE SPEECH

BY RICHARD MCKENZIE

Richard McKenzie reasons that if you support
absolute freedom of the press, then you must
support the absolute freedom of speech of the
spokespeople of all the other institutions in a
democratic society. But, he argues, the press tends to
deny the freedom of others that it demands so
vigorously for itself. When this article was written,
Mr. McKenzie was a senior fellow at the Heritage
Foundation, on leave from the Economics
Department of Clemson University. The article is
adapted from his book *Bound to Be Free* (Hoover
University Press, 1983). The version reprinted here is
from the *National Review,* September 2, 1983.

People like you and me, though mortal, of
course, like everyone else, do not grow
old no matter how long we live. What I
mean is that we never cease to stand like
curious children before the great Mystery
into which we are born. This interposes a
distance between us and all that is
unsatisfactory in the human sphere—and
this is no small matter. When, in the
mornings, I become nauseated by the
news the New York Times *sets before us,*
I always reflect that it is anyway better
than the Hitlerism that we only barely
managed to finish off.

ALBERT EINSTEIN
LETTER TO JULIUS BERGER

It was one of several political cartoons carried on the editorial page
of a Midwestern paper one Sunday in July 1979. The name of the paper
has been forgotten, but the cartoon is too graphic to forget. Five vultures
were perched in a row on a limb of a denuded tree; the head of a
Supreme Court justice—Burger, Stewart, Stevens, Rehnquist, and Po-

well—topped each avian body. Below them lay the mutilated carcass of what was labeled the First Amendment. The vultures were obviously satisfied with their meal.

The justices caricatured that Sunday had not too many weeks before formed the deciding majority in *Gannett Company, Inc.* v. *De Pasquale.* In that case a lower court had precluded press access to the records of a pretrial hearing. The Supreme Court, in agreeing with the lower court, ruled that the right of a defendant to a fair trial outweighed the constitutional right of the press and public to gain access to the proceedings. The cartoonist, as well as editorial writers around the country, was outraged by the decision, suggesting in his work that once again the Supreme Court had abridged the press' basic First Amendment rights.

Earlier in the year the Supreme Court made another important ruling against the press in *Pennington* v. *Kansas.* In investigating a murder, a newspaper reporter cited an unidentified source who claimed he had heard a third party threaten the murder victim's life. The reporter refused to divulge his source, claiming First Amendment protection under the Constitution. A lower court held the reporter in contempt. Again, the Supreme Court reasoned that the rights of the defendant to a fair trial outweighed, on balance, any rights the press might have to confidentiality. The decision stunned the press.

In reporting on the *Gannett* case for *Newsweek* magazine, Aric Press and Diane Camper wrote with a tempered sense of moral indignation: "Most Americans have assumed that secret trials have no place in their judicial tradition. Evils perpetrated behind the locked doors of the British courts led the Founding Fathers to guarantee public criminal trials in their new Constitution, and a courtroom where every person can be judged openly by his peers has become a symbol of freedom." Their report gave considerable prominence to the comments of Allen Neuharth, president of Gannett, the country's largest newspaper chain, who stated, "I have no hesitancy in saying that the majority of the Supreme Court has indicated that they consider the judiciary to be a private club. They're signaling, 'Your chambers and your courtroom belong to you, not to the public.'" And Press and Camper concluded their article with a cheap shot, "Few journalists can realistically expect the Court to find them privileged characters. For the moment, the press has been put on the same level with the citizenry it seeks to enlighten." We must ask: Did the Founding Fathers intend the press (which is composed of people) to be on a social and legal pedestal separate from the "commoners"?

Again, in mid-1981 the Supreme Court handed down its decision in the case of Philip Agee, who in 1974 began a campaign to damage the CIA and to reveal the names of CIA agents. Cyrus Vance, Secretary of State in the Carter Administration, had in 1979 revoked Agee's passport for violating the contract that Agee had freely signed with the CIA and that restrained Agee from talking about his work. In a 7 to 2 decision the Supreme Court upheld Secretary Vance's revocation of Agee's passport; and "for the next 48 hours," wrote columnist James Jackson Kilpatrick, "a bystander might have believed the sky had fallen. The *New York Times* and the *Washington Post* erupted with moans and groans. A huddle of Harvard professors collapsed in heaves and sighs." According to many in the press, the Supreme Court ruling was a clear violation of the press's First Amendment protection: The ruling would have a chilling effect on the willingness of people to disagree with their government.

The important issue here is not the legal correctness of any particular Supreme Court decision. Rather, it is the dual attitude of much (but not by any means all) of the press (and much of the public) toward government regulation. On the one hand, the press, in general, as evidenced by its predictable reaction to recent Supreme Court decisions, has an obvious disdain for any suggestion that its activities be clipped, restrained, or regulated by government. It clings tenaciously and justifiably to the freedoms articulated for it in the Constitution. The First Amendment is a part of the press's professional armor—deservedly so.

On the other hand, a significant portion of the press is often among the first to point out the need for government regulation of this or that industry. Reporters object strenuously to any requirement that they divulge their sources, open their newsrooms to search by the police, testify before grand juries, turn over their notes to courts, and restrict what they write. But many of these same reporters see no harm in the government's requiring other industries to divulge sensitive information relating to their products, to meet officially established standards, to pay legal minimum wage rates, to design facilities to meet government safety standards, and to charge the prices set by government fiat.

Much of the press assumes that there is a clear philosophical, categorical distinction between its activity and the activities of other industries. But this distinction is completely arbitrary. Such vagaries make a poor foundation for a social philosophy of government.

Most people in the press and in society's intellectual circles who favor freedom of speech and of the press, and at the same time advocate government control of various industries, seem to imagine that the material of their labor differs substantively from the products of other private enterprises. They deal in "ideas," so the argument goes; others produce more mundane goods and services, "material" that appeals to the flesh and the senses, not the cerebrum. They view freedom of speech and of the press, but not freedom of the market, as an extension of freedom of thought. Ideas are ideas: elusive, ephemeral, and difficult to regulate without controlling human thought itself. Goods, on the other hand, are goods: identifiable, tangible, largely distinct from thought itself. Ideas are creations of the human mind (and spirit), and they are important because of the (presumed) uniquely human capacity for thought and reason. Freedom to think and reason, so the argument may be developed, is necessary if people are to be human and not just animal. Goods and services, however, embody real-world resources that other animals share, although in other forms.

This presumed distinction between free speech and the free market is misleading at best and a gross distortion of the facts at worst. The production of goods like furniture requires many resources—land, material, labor, and capital. But the fruits of the press (or any other intellectual discourse) are also products of long and complicated production processes involving the use of many resources like gasoline, textiles, food, electricity, and telephone communications, which are subject to extensive government controls. Indeed, the final product of the press appears to be far more physical than the final product of an electric power company or of a psychological counseling service. Any good reporter understands that it takes time (labor) to gather the facts of a story, to mold them into an article, and to see it through the newsroom to the newsstand. A good deal of capital—real and financial—is involved in making free speech and free press a meaningful social phenomenon. The press is a capitalist enterprise dependent on a capitalist system. How free would the press be if ownership of all press-room facilities were not private? If all property were controlled by the government, the "news" would not be worth the paper it is printed on.

True, the final product of the press incorporates ideas that at times concern the most critical issues of our age. The press provides an invaluable public forum for evaluating these issues. However, so-called material goods and services also embody ideas that are often no less critical to people's welfare than the ideas on the front page of the morning newspaper. Consider the complexity of the ideas incorporated into the design and construction of an automobile, a building, or a toaster. Is there any intrinsic reason why ideas inked on newsprint should qualify for any greater protection from government controls than the ideas incorporated into the structure of a garment, a bicycle, or a home? My purpose in indicating the similarities of "ideas in print and speech" and "ideas in goods" is not to defame freedom of the press and of speech (as well as of religion). Quite the contrary, it is to suggest that freedom of the market should be accorded much the same government protection as our political freedoms—for they also are largely political freedoms.

Advocates of free speech and government control of other production processes sometimes argue that goods and services produced by private industries can be harmful to people's health and general well-being. Indeed, they can kill. Cigarettes and guns are good examples. Hence, government must protect people from these goods and services, from the abuse of those who would use unrestricted market freedom to their own advantage.

As intuitively appealing as the argument sounds, it falls flat as a justification for a dual approach to the control of speech and of markets. Freedom of speech and of the press, like cigarettes, can also be hazardous to people's health—and no less deadly than many mundane material goods and services. People have died because someone stood up in a crowded theater or stadium and yelled "fire," or because the press reported strategic military and intelligence information. (Consider the death of Richard Welch, the CIA agent who was killed shortly after his name was revealed by the press under the constitutional protection of the First Amendment.) The Reverend Jim Jones, through his own exercise of the freedoms of speech, press, and religion, led more than nine hundred of his followers first to Guyana, then (with a little coercion) to their suicidal deaths. Social expressions of freedoms of speech, press, and religion are often deadly. Sometimes, extraordinarily deadly. Hitler and others like him rose to power partly because they were free to speak and to convince others, through print and oratory, that they were the true light and salvation of their times.

One of the strongest arguments of proponents of basic First Amendment rights is: "We do not know which ideas are 'right' when any issue is first discussed. Indeed, we do not even know what issues, out of the whole range of issues, warrant public consideration. People must have the freedom not only to speak their own minds but also to listen to others. They need to hear all competing ideas not only because they will be well informed on the range of issues, but also because they will be in a reasonably good position to evaluate competing issues and choose the best course of action under the circumstances."

If this argument is intended to show that freedom of speech is distinct from freedom of markets, it is, again, seriously flawed. We understandably think of markets as dealing with things because things are readily observable. However, we could just as easily view markets as processes by which ideas, incorporated in things, are traded. Indeed, socially recognized rights to do things are the real substance of trade. Furthermore, as with the freedom of speech or religion, we often cannot identify, beforehand, the particular ideas embodied in goods and services wanted by most people. We must allow an individual the freedom to test his ideas in order that he may learn what goods and services are actually preferred. In short, a free market is, like free speech, a competitive process in ideas. We need both freedoms for essentially similar reasons.

Some seem to think that freedom of speech takes preeminence over other freedoms because freedom of speech is necessary in order to prevent any one person from having control over what ideas are actually considered and what courses of action are actually taken. Freedom of speech, it is argued, gives everyone some power to speak his or her mind, ensuring as best we can that no idea is accepted solely because it is the only alternative available. The freedoms of speech, press, and religion are social means of decentralizing the power that some people have over others. By giving people the freedom to speak, we deny people the freedom to coerce others to think or accept any particular ideas. We deny government the right to restrict the freedom of speech simply because we want to deny some people (those who would govern) the rights to impose their ideas on us. The case for the free market has the same philosophical basis: Free markets limit the power of people to coerce one another; they allow for competition and, therefore, voluntary actions. Free, unregulated markets are a means of delimiting the monopoly power of government to determine which goods and services we will have.

Opponents of the free market suggest that freedom of speech means little if speech cannot be used to influence government to accept a particular policy course, such as restricting the scope of market activities through regulation. They may contend with good intentions that in a democracy everyone has a right to voice an opinion and everyone must accept the verdict of the "competition of ideas" worked out through the political process. This position reveals a gross confusion of basic issues.

In its purest form, freedom of speech is a means of restricting the power of people, of attempting to ensure as much as possible that coercion is minimized. Freedom of speech means the freedom to persuade, not to coerce; to elicit voluntary cooperation, not to impose one's will on another. To make freedom of speech meaningful, the scope of democracy must necessarily be restricted. Otherwise, freedom of speech can easily translate into a coercive power that one person or group, through the state, imposes on others.

Granted, no nation can effectively organize without some government, and some issues must be decided by democratic means. That point is well taken and forms the heart of much that has been written. The point here is relatively simple: As the scope and size of government are extended, the freedom of some people to speak and win in the political arena with less than unanimous agreement translates into government force and a loss to others of freedom from coercion. As government expands, the unanimity of agreement—so necessary to social tranquillity—over government policy must evaporate; disagreement will become the hallmark of social discourse; freedom of speech will take on a coercive quality.

Many factions of society now harbor serious resentment toward the press. Both the political Left and political Right denigrate it for its failure to report the "truth." Its freedom to print what it considers news is interpreted by others, now that government is large and expansive, as the power to influence public events and, thereby, as the power to coerce.

Journalist William Cheshire has written, "The press is powerful—

more powerful than in any previous period in all history—and power and humility are strangers." The unchecked power of the press and public skepticism toward it derive, I suggest, from the unchecked power of the government and the ability of the press to set the national political agenda and, in that way and to that extent, to influence and manipulate the government's power. Surely, the press would have less power than at present, and people would be less concerned about the accuracy of news reporting, if government were small and inconsequential. When government is constrained in what it can do, there are few public policies the press can influence by accurate or inaccurate reporting; there is little the press can do to affect taxes or budget allocations.

Almost all supporters of free speech see its suppression as a denial of valuable information that people need to conduct their daily lives effectively. It can be argued with equal vigor, however, that the suppression of market forces by government controls also muffles valuable information that should be available to the public. It is, in short, a gross form of censorship, as Walter Wriston, chairman of Citicorp, has poignantly observed:

> The American press would not tolerate for one moment an attempt by the government to suppress news of riots or political demonstrations on the grounds that it wants to "ensure domestic tranquillity." The press knows a threat to the First Amendment when it sees one.
>
> There are ten amendments in the Bill of Rights, although sometimes it seems that the press is so busy defending the first one that it is hard to get equal time for the other nine.
>
> Let me recall one of them—the Ninth Amendment—which few people ever read any more, let alone defend. It says: "The enumeration in the Constitution of certain rights shall not be construed to deny or disparage others retained by the people." Is something being disparaged when the [Carter Administration's] chief inflation-fighter tells a group of businessmen that "We will, with a degree of enthusiasm that I suspect many of you may consider unseemly, identify the miscreants [those who violate President Carter's 'voluntary' wage-price guidelines] publicly"?

When the Department of Energy sends out agents with binoculars to spy on filling-station operators to ensure that they are not "overcharging," as it did in 1979, government is engaging in a form of censorship. Would the press not be outraged if similar surveillance were directed at it? When government becomes large and expansive, as it has, does it begin to dominate the flow of information and acquire a de facto power of censorship simply by its prominence in the total production of information?

The problem of government control of information is by no means trivial. In reporting on a General Accounting Office study of government information activities and on the public relations activities of just 48 agencies, *U.S. News & World Report* concluded that "the Federal Government spends more money each year trying to influence the way people think than it spends altogether for disaster relief, foreign military assistance, energy conservation, and cancer research." The Watergate era has led many people to believe that the press is constantly dogging the federal bureaucracy for information that the latter does not want to see the light of day. Solid investigative reporting does occur. However, as columnist Joseph Kraft has pointed out,

> In the typical Washington situation, news is not nosed out by keen reporters and then purveyed to the public. It is manufactured inside government, by various interested parties for purposes of its own, and then put out to the press in ways and at times that suit the sources. That is how it happens that when the President prepares a message on crime, all the leading columnists suddenly become concerned with crime. That is how it happens that when the Air Force budget comes up for consideration, some new plane will streak across the continent in record time.

The freedoms of speech, press, and religion are very important. Nothing said here is intended to deny that. On the contrary, I have attempted to show that the case for the free market is quite similar to that for free speech. In the words of University of Chicago Professor Ronald Coase:

> I do not believe that this distinction between the market for goods and the market for ideas is valid. There is no fundamental difference between these two markets and, in deciding on public policy with regard to them, we need to take into account the same considerations. In all of these markets, producers have some reason for being honest and some for being dishonest; consumers have some information but are not fully informed or even able to digest the information they have; regulators commonly wish to do a good job, and though often incompetent and subject to influence of special interests, they act like this because, like all of us, they are human beings whose strongest motives are not always the highest.

Our rights under freedom of speech and freedom of markets are limited. They must be. In the case of free speech, unlimited freedom for all would make the world resemble a Tower of Babel, with no one able to communicate effectively with anyone else. In the case of free markets, unlimited freedom would mean nonexistent property rights and nonexistent markets. Unlimited freedom, therefore, is a contradiction in terms. Free speech and free markets are both means of socially restricting people to ensure that power is dispersed and that coercion is minimized.

Freedoms everywhere can be and have been abused. We have noted that the Reverend Jim Jones abused, in a sense, the freedom of speech. Abuse, however, is not a sufficient case for abandoning freedom of speech or press or religion as guiding social principles. The press would be the first to admit to abuse of freedom within its own camp—

but it would also be the first to defend vigorously the *principles* on which its activities rest. Freedom of speech is intrinsically valuable—but it is also intrinsically practical. So is freedom of the market. Instances of abuse of market freedoms can easily be recounted. Those of us who seek to defend the market need not—indeed, should not—deny that fact. There are only two relevant questions: Has the free market served us well? And, is freedom of expression in markets just as important as freedom of expression in print?

The case for the free market is not a case for "no government intervention." Any suggestion to the contrary makes about as much sense as the suggestion that there is no circumstance under which freedom of the press needs to be curtailed. Freedoms and rights often collide and trade-offs are required. (Consider the cases of *Gannett* and *Pennington.*) The case for the free market is an argument for a predisposition, a social proclivity, toward freedom and against control; for extraordinary caution in shaping government policy; and for the use of principles in the conduct of public policy. That is the way we interpret First Amendment freedoms; that is the way we need to interpret freedom of the market.

Why is much of the press antipathetic toward the free market? To some extent the answer is baffling. The opposition of some segments of the press to the free market may be due to its inability to understand sweeping social issues. Members of the press are continually pushed to get to the scene of the latest fire and to reduce complex situations to a few inches of newsprint or to sixty-second spots on the nightly television news.

Many members of the press may believe that they were anointed by the Founding Fathers with special privileges and special protection from the coercive powers of government. To assume such an attitude, however, the press must overlook the Fifth and Ninth Amendments, as well as a series of court rulings during the early years of the nation that upheld market freedoms. As Alexander Hamilton wrote in the *Federalist,* expressing his concern about the delineation of rights, "The people surrender nothing; and as they retain everything, they have no need of particular reservations," to which he added:

I go further, and affirm that bills of rights, in the sense and to the extent in which they are contended for, are not only unnecessary in the proposed Constitution, but would even be dangerous. They would contain various exceptions to powers not granted; and, on this very account, would afford a colorful pretext to claim more than were granted. For why declare that things shall not be done which there is no power to do? Why, for instance, should it be said that the liberty of the press shall not be restrained, when no power is given by which restrictions are imposed? I would contend that such a provision would confer a regulatory power; but it is evident that it would furnish, to men disposed to usurp, a plausible pretense for claiming that power.

Perhaps, the press' opposition to the free market may also be due to the realization of reporters and editorial writers that they are indirectly competing with other industries for the attention and spendable income of the general public.

Or maybe the reason for the opposition to free markets among segments of the press is even less benign. Journalists may implicitly recognize that the market represents a bound on government and, hence, a bound on the power of those who would use government. By destroying the predisposition of the general public to respect and rely on market processes, some members of the press may consciously envision the enhancement of their own power. In other words, the press may be antagonistic toward the free market because the market represents a constraint on its own power. If this is the way members of the press think, then the game they are playing is a dangerous one. Journalists and others who live by First Amendment protection may think that government can be used to control every industry except the press. That may not, in the long run, be the case. Power unleashed may be power difficult to contain.

7 · MEDIA POWER

On Closer Inspection, It's Not That Threatening

BY ALBERT E. GOLLIN

Albert E. Gollin argues that the very diversity of our mass media today reduces their power. Even though they are at times guilty of being irresponsible, it doesn't really matter because they are not so powerful as their critics claim and the public is not stupid or gullible enough to fall for the media's excesses. Gollin is vice president/ associate director of research of the Newspaper Advertising Bureau. This article is excerpted from a presentation he made at a public forum in Washington, D.C., on "Can the Mass Media Control Our Thoughts?" The forum was part of the Smithsonian Institution's eighth international symposium on "The Road after 1984: High Technology and Human Freedom." This article is reprinted from *presstime*, February 1984.

There are several key assumptions underlying prevailing beliefs about media power. It is useful to recall that concern about the effects of the mass media is rooted in the seeming success of propaganda efforts conducted during World War I, and by Nazi and Soviet regimes subsequently, to mobilize, coerce or control their own citizens. More recently, the agenda of concerns has broadened, without wholly losing the edge of anxiety that characterized discussions in that earlier era. Here are just a few examples of questions that have been raised.

• Has the graphic treatment of sex and violence by the media contributed to a decline of morality and trivialized or vulgarized significant aspects of human experience?

• Has the aggressive handling and criticism of political and economic elites by the media eroded their leadership mandates and led to a general decline in the perceived legitimacy of social institutions?

• Are the media persistently exploited for political and commercial purposes, selling us candidates and products we otherwise would not buy?

• Have the media created a popular culture that has steadily cheapened public taste—"sitcoms" and soap operas instead of Shakespeare and Verdi, Harlequin romances instead of Hemingway?

• Did the news media drive Richard Nixon from office, and did they cost us victory in Vietnam?

The list goes on and on. It might be noted in this regard that the criticisms and questions raised are far from consistent internally or devoid of special-interest motives.

Evidence from mass communication research provides a basis for commenting on several mistaken assumptions made by media critics and others who believe in the media's power to affect our thoughts and actions and to shape our society in various ways, good and bad.

The first of these assumptions is the equating of media content with media effects. In this view, what people see, read or hear—especially when they are repeatedly exposed to the content—actually has the effects one hopes for, or fears, depending upon one's own assessment of a particular message. Based on this simplified stimulus-response conception, for example, are the following convictions:

• Violence in children's TV programming leads to violence on the playground.

• Sexually permissive norms highlighted in films, on television, or in books and magazines are echoed in the behavior of those exposed to such erotic content.

• Sympathetic portrayals of minorities generate compassion and tolerance.

• Media-based campaigns to reduce energy consumption or to get people to lead healthier lives will yield socially desirable results.

Linked with the equating of content with effects is another assumption: that the *intent* of the communicator is faithfully captured in the responses of those exposed to the message. Thus, according to this view, "M*A*S*H" not only entertains, it also successfully conveys the anti-war intent of its producers. Or Archie Bunker's bigotry, rather than giving sanction to prejudiced attitudes, is perceived as misguided, out of date, and morally reprehensible.

The evidence from communications research, while admittedly uneven and less than conclusive, nevertheless portrays a set of relationships between the content or intent of media messages and their effects that are far more complex and variable in nature. People bring to their encounters with the mass media a formidable array of established habits, motives, social values and perceptual defenses that screen out, derail the intent or limit the force of media messages. The media certainly do affect people in obvious and subtle ways. But no simple 1:1 relationship exists between content or intent and effects.

Moreover, while media audiences are massive in size—a precondition for mass persuasion—they are socially differentiated, self-selective, often inattentive, and in general—to use a term once employed by Raymond Bauer of Harvard University—"obstinate." As targets they are elusive and hard to please or to convince. People actively use the media for a wide variety of shared and individual purposes. People are not readily used *by* the media. Why is it, then, that we believe that others in the viewing or reading public are more gullible or passive than we ourselves?

Another assumption often held is that the mass media now operate in an unrestrained fashion, and that their autonomy is a prime source of their power. But media publics not only are individually resistant to the content offered them, in free societies they also significantly affect content through the operation of various feedback mechanisms. In this connection, one has only to recall the decisive role of broadcast ratings, film box-office receipts, subscription and circulation revenues, and the like as market forces that constrain the predilections of media operators and producers. To these "bottom-line" influences one must add the constant stream of criticism, letters and phone calls, self-criticism based on professional values that include service to the public, legal restraints, and the results of marketing studies that seek to discover public tastes, preferences and needs.

Thus, in various direct and indirect ways, the public acts upon the mass media rather than simply being influenced by them. And with the variety of content choices and exposure opportunities expanding steadily, thanks to new communications technologies, the likelihood of successful mass persuasion by the media diminishes still further.

This last point bears upon the initial reception of new technologies, including each of the mass media. As a new type of technology emerges, it is often met by either or both of two sharply contrasting reactions. The first of these is aptly symbolized by the image of the cornucopia—the horn of plenty. The new technology is hailed for its potential benefits —enriching people's lives, removing burdens and contributing to human progress. The contrasting perspective is symbolized by the image of the juggernaut—the machine that is unstoppable, crippling or constraining human freedom.

Most technologies, the mass media included, rarely fulfill either set of extravagant hopes or fears. As they diffuse and become integrated into societies, they change things in the process of extending human capacities. But so too do new forms of art, law, scientific knowledge, war and modes of social organization. Only with hindsight, and often with great difficulty, does it become possible to assess which of these has affected society more broadly and decisively, especially when it comes to human freedom.

To sum up, while at times unquestionably guilty of harmful excess and error, the mass media are less powerful or autonomous than their critics fear—or than their own agents sometimes like to believe. Media publics are far from compliant or passive, and they are becoming increasingly less so as media choices multiply.

Finally, to contradict Ralph Waldo Emerson, things are not in the saddle, riding humankind. Given the existence of media diversity and continuing feedback from the public, the risks of media-fostered political or cultural hegemony remain small.

In any case, such risks are inseparable from those intrinsic to the functioning of free societies, in which the media now play a variety of indispensable roles.

8 · THE MIGHT OF THE MEDIA

Media Self-Censorship
"The public will never know"

BY ROBERT G. PICARD

In an effort to avoid an increasing number of law
suits caused by irresponsible actions, the media may
actually be causing greater damage to the public by
being more cautious, less investigative, blander and
weaker. So suggests Robert G. Picard, a former
newspaper reporter and editor and, when this was
written, a doctoral candidate in journalism at the
University of Missouri. He has written on media
topics for a variety of journalism publications,
including *The Quill, Editor and Publisher* and
Grassroots Editor. This article is reprinted from *The
Press,* March 1981.

American publishers and broadcasters are increasingly exercising
self-censorship to avoid costly litigation and the result is a decline in
press freedom, say journalists and legal experts.

The self-censorship is denying the public a wide range of information because journalists fear libel and privacy suits, and confrontations
with government attorneys, which can result in legal fees of up to $200
an hour.

The cost of lawyers for the media has spiraled upward in recent
years, as the number of suits filed against the media has increased. The
media themselves have also increased their legal costs because a large
number of papers and broadcasting enterprises have chosen to hire
permanent legal staffs.

The attorneys on media staffs are not only handling legal defenses
for their employers—they have also moved into the editorial decision-
making process and are encouraging self-censorship and making decisions on whether articles will be printed or broadcast, say industry
observers.

"There's a lot of self-censorship by editors unwilling to rock the boat. They fear the heavy court costs that could come from a tough investigative article," says Bruce Sanford, a former *Wall Street Journal* reporter who is now an attorney for United Press International and the Society of Professional Journalists.

His analysis is echoed by Dan Paul, attorney for the *Miami Herald.* "Costs of trying libel suits . . . quashing subpoenas, fending off privacy actions and obtaining news under freedom of information laws are already substantial, and the burden is growing," he says. "Because of this burden the hometown newspaper or small radio station may decide to steer clear of news prone to generate litigation costs or search warrants. That is chilling."

Floyd Abrams, an attorney who has represented *The New York Times* and other major media clients, believes such censorship may increase. "If things develop to the point where large jury verdicts or large counsel fees on a yearly basis are the norm and not the exception, then I don't have any doubt that publications will be obliged to trim their sails . . . The real danger is that the public would never know," he warns.

Many journalists and attorneys believe that libel victories by plaintiffs may be increasing the number of suits in recent years because high damages awarded by juries could be an incentive for many individuals to pursue a case even if it is unwarranted.

"The country is in a litigious mood—everybody sues these days, and even if there are no real grounds, suits are expensive to defend," says Art Spikol, a columnist for *Writer's Digest.*

The cost of defending any suit, with attorney fees averaging $1,000 a day, is enough to scare most media managers, and many news organizations have begun settling even unwarranted suits with out of court payments in order to avoid more costly defense costs and the possibility of large jury verdicts.

In a celebrated case, the *San Francisco Examiner* recently sought to reduce its liability in a libel suit brought against it by two policemen and a prosecuting attorney. The case involved stories in the paper that alleged a police frame-up against a member of a youth gang.

The story was written by a free-lance reporter and a member of the *Examiner* staff. When the suit was filed, the paper chose to cut its litigation costs and attempted to reduce its liability by refusing to defend the free-lance writer and blaming the alleged libel on him. As a result both reporters sought separate counsel because they felt the paper did not have their interests at heart.

A defense committee, composed of horrified colleagues, raised $20,000 to pay the reporters' legal bills for the trial. A finding against the reporters in the trial is now being appealed and their defense costs are expected to double, as will the costs for the *Examiner,* which also lost its case.

Defense costs in libel suits involving other parties have also resulted in high expenditures. Litigation costs of nearly $100,000 were recently encountered by Palm Beach, Florida, and Baton Rouge, Louisiana, newspapers when they lost and appealed sizable libel cases. Although both won their cases on appeal, they still had to bear the costs of their defenses.

John Zollinger, publisher of the *New Mexico Independent*, laments, "It's no joke anymore . . . You win and you still pay."

In addition to litigation costs posed by libel and other suits, the media in America are confronted with significant costs when they attempt to defend press rights and privileges. The high cost of such First Amendment defenses is reportedly keeping many publishers and broadcasters from pursuing such cases and leading some to censor material which might bring them into conflict with the government.

The Progressive magazine recently chose to challenge the government's attempt to restrain publication of an article about the H-bomb, and the litigation costs nearly forced the journal out of business.

The magazine, which had already been losing about $100,000 a year, spent nearly $250,000 pressing its case before the government dropped its efforts.

"Our lawyers said at the outset this was likely to be a protracted and horrendously expensive case that could jeopardize the survival of the magazine," says Editor Erwin Knoll. But he reports supporters have raised much of the money needed to cover the defense costs and that only $60,000 remains unpaid.

"As legal costs go up and legal complications grow ever more ramiferous and Byzantine, publishers may increasingly try to avoid these types of difficulties," warns Knoll. "If we were still bearing the $60,000 debt from the last go around . . . and knowing fully the burdens of pursuing such a case, we would do it again. But we would do it with the knowledge that the magazine would not be likely to survive."

Knoll believes few publishers or publications with circulations the size of his 40,000 circulation magazine would elect to pursue such an expensive and potentially harmful course. "I think the cost has a chilling effect to say the least," he says.

The 1980 U.S. Supreme Court ruling limiting the closure of trial to press and public was also an expensive victory for the press. The costs were borne solely by Richmond Newspapers, Inc., which pursued the case after a Virginia judge closed a murder trial in which the defendant was acquitted.

According to Publisher J. Steward Bryan III, the final costs of the case are not tallied yet, but he expects them to be between $75,000 and $100,000. "I don't think there are many newspaper companies who could afford this kind of case. Even daily newspapers between 20,000 and 25,000 circulation couldn't possibly afford it," he says.

Challenges to broadcast licenses are also proving expensive, and pressure groups are increasingly challenging the licenses in order to force changes by broadcasters. It is estimated that even the simplest challenge requiring legal representation before the Federal Communication Commission can cost a broadcaster between $50,000 and $100,000.

Few broadcast license challenges have proved successful, but many challenges are being made only to force changes in station policy or programming content rather than to take the license away from the broadcaster. Owners, who must pay large fees to defend against the license challenges, are often saddled with the challengers' legal costs as well when they come to an agreement that halts the proceedings.

Such costs have the apparent result of encouraging many broadcasters to avoid controversial subjects which may bring about the need for legal representation.

In the mid 1970s, Richard Schmidt, general legal counsel for the American Society of Newspaper Editors, noted "a subtle but pervasive attitude of self-censorship motivated by fear of libel suits." Today, he still believes the litigious climate is making publishers exercise self-censorship.

"Self-censorship is rather prevalent," he says, "but it can't be proved with empirical evidence. It's something publishers don't like to talk about, but I hear about it in conversations at conferences all the time."

Avoiding litigation by self-censorship adds a raw economic factor to an industry that has claimed to be guided by the interests of society and ethical principles. It is an unfortunate reality that there can be no appeal of this kind of censorship because it is instituted by the media themselves and is usually unseen and undetected by their audiences.

"Self-censorship has always been the most pervasive form of censorship," notes Erwin Knoll, editor of *The Progressive.* "Keeping out of trouble has always been publishers' main interest."

The rising popularity of libel and First Amendment insurance policies may help some media, however.

About half of the 1,750 daily newspaper and 425 weeklies now carry libel insurance, but deductibles of up to $25,000 can pose problems because some cases are settled or ended at costs below that level. The interest in libel insurance has brought about the establishment of First Amendment insurance, which aid media in pursuing or defending cases involving First Amendment issues. About 300 companies, mostly daily newspapers, have purchased policies ranging from $100,000 to $1 million in coverage.

Critics of such policies, however, argue that the insurance will not be effective against self-censorship because they actually encourage more litigation which will only increase the cost of insurance policies. They also point out that the smaller news organizations, which are most prone to self-censorship, often cannot afford the policies.

The litigious spirit in the nation has been heightened by some journalists becoming "First Amendment junkies," who seek legal relief whenever they feel any privileges have been infringed, charges Don Reubens, an attorney who has represented *The Chicago Tribune, The New York Daily News* and Time, Inc.

Reubens recently warned journalists attending an Illinois newspaper association meeting that such a "knee jerk reaction" allows bad cases to be brought to court and that such cases can bring unfavorable rulings that cost fellow journalists existing freedoms. It is ridiculous to see, confrontation and test cases that have no real importance or that could be counterproductive, he said.

Whether the media in the United States will be able to break loose of the bonds of litigation costs, self-imposed censorship and the continued growth of the litigious spirit remains to be seen. But many observers in America believe few efforts by the media seem directed toward those goals.

FOR FURTHER READING

Paul P. Ashley, *Say It Safely: Legal Limits in Publishing, Radio, and Television,* 5th ed. Seattle, Wash.: University of Washington Press, 1976.

Daniel L. Brenner and William L. Rivers, *Free but Regulated: Conflicting Traditions in Media Law.* Ames, Iowa: The Iowa State University Press, 1982.

Bill F. Chamberlin and Charlene J. Brown (eds.), *The First Amendment Reconsidered: New Perspectives on the Meaning of Freedom of Speech and Press.* New York: Longman, 1982.

David G. Clark and Earl R. Hutchison, *Mass Media and the Law: Freedom and Restraint.* New York: Wiley, 1970.

Lyle W. Denniston, *The Reporter and the Law: Techniques of Covering the Courts.* New York: Hastings House, 1980.

John Foley, Robert C. Lobdell and Robert Trounson, *The Media and the Law.* Los Angeles, Calif.: Times Mirror Press, 1977.

Clifton O. Lawhorne, *Defamation and Public Officials: The Evolving Law of Libel.* Carbondale, Ill.: Southern Illinois University Press, 1971.

John Lofton, *The Press as Guardian of the First Amendment.* Columbia, S. Car.: The University of South Carolina Press, 1980.

Abraham H. Miller, *Terrorism: The Media and the Law.* Dobbs Ferry, N.Y.: Transnational Publishers, Inc., 1982.

Lee M. Mitchell, *Openly Arrived At: Report of the Twentieth Century Fund Task Force on Broadcasting and the Legislature.* New York: The Twentieth Century Fund, 1974.

Don R. Pember, *Mass Media Law.* Dubuque, Iowa: William C. Brown Company Publishers, 1977.

Hugh A. Rundell and Thomas H. Heuterman, *The First Amendment and Broadcasting: Press Freedoms and Broadcast Journalism.* Pullman, Wash.: Washington State University, 1978.

Bruce W. Sanford, *Synopsis of the Law of Libel and the Right of Privacy.* Cleveland, Ohio: Scripps-Howard Newspapers, 1977.

Benno C. Schmidt, Jr., *Freedom of the Press vs. Public Access.* New York: Praeger, 1976.

Morton J. Simon, *Public Relations Law.* New York: Meredith Corporation, 1969.

III

Mass Media and Ethics

MELVIN MENCHER'S article, which opens this section, is a most appropriate introduction to the discussion of the mass media and ethics. Indeed, the study of ethics has become journalism's latest growth industry—and it remains a popular topic for nonjournalists, too. Major movies have dissected the news business and especially the conduct of reporters and editors. *Time* published a lengthy cover story in 1984 titled "Journalism under Fire" and subtitled "A growing perception of arrogance threatens the American press." (A few months later, *Time* featured "The Ten Best U.S. Dailies.")

Public figures and citizens have voiced opinions about the ethics of the news media and their personnel; and the media have developed codes and sponsored conferences and books about media ethics.

Certainly, there is interest in the topic even though there is no unanimity on resolving a potential conflict or problem. The *National Observer* was right when it headlined a discussion of journalistic ethics a decade ago, "Not Black, Not White, but a Rainbow of Gray."

The articles in this chapter describe some contemporary views of ethics applied to the mass media and some of the problems the media face. Gene Goodwin discusses the ethics of compassion in a traditionally macho business. Neil D. Swan describes the array of media and nonmedia watchdogs, including some pressure groups formed specifically to monitor media and others that have broadened their activities to include media watching.

The test of time is how individuals in the media do their jobs—how they act. Most act ethically now. The current widespread interest in the topic may help the media improve, or at least listen when critics question media activities. Conversely, it may indicate that the public and various nonmedia organizations are also willing to be impressed when the media operate ethically. That will be a milestone!

9 · "Perhaps It's Time to Examine the Sins of the Newspaper Generals"

By Melvin Mencher

The morality of journalism requires giving readers the information necessary for them to make decisions that will help them lead meaningful lives in their communities. This requires publishers to put money into the news-editorial operation, says Melvin Mencher. Mencher joined the faculty at Columbia's Graduate School of Journalism in 1962. He was a Nieman Fellow and worked for United Press as well as the *Albuquerque* (N.M.) *Journal,* the *Santa Fe New Mexican* and the *Fresno* (Calif.) *Bee.* He's written two textbooks, *News Reporting and Writing* and *Basic News Writing.* This article is from *ASNE Bulletin,* February 1984.

At the same time the press is behaving more responsibly than ever, I see heightened concern over the morality of its practices. Many journalists still feel they haven't done enough. Their readers are even more critical.

The study of ethics has become journalism's latest growth industry. All sorts of journalism groups have explored the problem. Hardly a month goes by that editors, reporters and academicians are not meeting to grapple with journalism ethics.

Despite the inability of journalists—by nature disputatious—to agree on much, and their reluctance to subscribe to anyone's imposition of "responsibility," however defined, much has been accomplished. We have described and agreed upon the unacceptable. No one argues that gifts, free travel, conflicts of interests, special privileges and political servility are acceptable. Meanwhile, journalists increasingly worry about their use of pseudoevents, their contribution to the cascade of disconnected news that bewilders readers, and the elevation of trivia —under the guise of features and graphics—to newsworthiness.

Despite this seemingly estimable accomplishment, we are told much more can be done to eliminate unethical practices. I'm not so sure, for two reasons:

First, we must understand that some moral dilemmas cannot be resolved. No matter how many conferences we hold, we can never achieve more than general guidelines in many areas. "Situational ethics" has a bad name, and so we seek codes and guidelines that will cover many situations. That noble effort is doomed to fail because many of the ethical problems that journalists face require choices between conflicting moral actions:

Poses and disguises are immoral. The reporter, therefore, should not use them to obtain a story.

The reporter's moral obligation is to ferret out the wrongdoers, to provide a range of service to readers.

An abortion mill threatens the lives of the women who seek its services, and a reporter disguises herself as a pregnant woman to gain entrance, the only way she can obtain material about the operation of the clinic.

What should we conclude? That the disguise was unethical, that the newspaper should piece together a story with interviews, report its suspicions to authorities and wait for them to act, or do nothing? What is the moral path to take?

As the philosopher Isaiah Berlin puts it: "The world that we encounter in ordinary experience is one in which we are faced with choices between ends equally ultimate and claims equally absolute . . . If, as I believe, the ends of men are many, and not all of them are in principle compatible with each other, then the possibility of conflict—and of tragedy—can never be wholly eliminated from human life, either personal or social. The necessity of choosing between absolute claims is then an inescapable characteristic of the human condition."

Not all ends are ultimate, nor claims equally absolute. A disguise used to expose a local merchant has less moral justification than does a pose to expose a life-threatening situation.

The simplest action is to declare pose and disguise unethical, to state that removing documents is theft, that theft is immoral as well as illegal, and to say that privacy should always be respected. Such an ethic does relieve the pain of decision making, but as the religion writer Harvey Cox says: "Not to decide is to decide."

We could base our decisions on our function: Our task is to be alert to the institutions and to the people that exercise power. We are concerned with any threat by these power sources that would deny the right of everyone to take part openly, freely and justly in the life of the community. Our job is to hold power accountable.

A second reason, then, for suggesting that we pause before continuing to scrutinize the misdeeds of the troops: Perhaps it's time to examine the sins of the generals.

Perhaps we're spending so much time looking at the errors of commission that we have neglected to point out that the basic moral failure of journalism is the failure of many newspapers to do what they're supposed to do.

Too many newspapers do not give their readers the information necessary for them to make decisions that will help them lead a meaningful life in their community, that will give them and their children access to good schools, adequate health care, safe streets, a voice in running things.

The underpinning for such coverage is absent on too many newspapers: They are understaffed. Reporters and editors are underpaid. Coverage is based on the traditional surveillance points, not at the actual sources of power. Too many newspapers are satisfied with bargain-basement news, the kinds of stories reporters can churn out quickly and often.

My favorite restaurant, the Sanitary Fish Market in Morehead City, N.C., points out on its menu: "Good food is not cheap. Cheap food is not good." High-quality news can't be bought on the cheap. It is the moral responsibility of publishers to put money into the news-editorial operation.

The people who lead newsrooms need to work on those who put out the newspaper, to show them what the morality of journalism requires. One might start with the idea of "adversary journalism." The critics, and some of the brethren, condemn it. The reality, of course, is that most papers rarely question the power sources and interest groups in their communities. They never act on the fact that what these people and organizations do is usually designed to further their own ends. Those who run these papers do not want to understand that their First Amendment protections are handed them so they may be free to hold power accountable.

Adversarial journalism is a moral journalism. The press is duty-bound to be adversary to concentrations of power. Every young reporter needs to understand this.

We could, if we tried hard enough, eliminate the inaccuracies and unfairness in reporting and editing. We might put an end to "ambush reporting" and to intrusions into the lives of our subjects. We could declare that no unnamed sources would ever be used. We might be able to eliminate all the unethical acts of which we are accused and for which we blame ourselves. Even then, we could still produce a journalism lacking moral justification. What we need to do most is to ask ourselves what we are about, and to try to do that, without apologies or regrets.

10 · THE ETHICS OF COMPASSION

BY GENE GOODWIN

Breaking news is so competitive that reporters can too easily forget they are seeking information about and from human beings. Journalists need more compassion and less cynicism, says newsman Gene Goodwin. He was journalist for the *Washington Star* and is now a professor at Pennsylvania State University where he was formally director of the School of Journalism. He is the author of a recent book on journalistic ethics, *Groping for Ethics in Journalism.* This article is from *The Quill,* November 1983.

"Compassion" is a word that makes a lot of journalists squirm. It describes a condition that runs counter to the strong tradition in journalism of detachment, the notion that a journalist must be a neutral observer rather than a participant in life or history.

"Dispassion" is a better word for the professional attitude that newsroom folklore teaches. It meshes with the much maligned but still widely practiced discipline of objective reporting. Reporters are not supposed to get involved in or become part of their stories; they are supposed to remain detached, dispassionate observers.

Diane Benison, managing editor of the Worcester, Massachusetts, *Evening Gazette,* one of scores of working journalists I interviewed for a book on journalism ethics, sees journalists as much like medical doctors during a war who have to "go out on the battlefield and save only those who can be saved." She has trouble seeing a place for compassion in news work because "one of the curses of this business is that you're expected to have your pores open, to be able to feel, to be able to empathize with people, and yet to eviscerate yourself to do your job, just as if you were a machine."

"It might be compassionate to suppress a story reporting the arrest of the publisher for drunken driving," says Louis D. Boccardi, executive editor and vice president of the Associated Press, "but that might be disastrous for the credibility of the newspaper."

Boccardi recalls that when he was a young reporter covering the courts, he was asked many times not to put certain things in the paper. "Compassion might dictate that you not report certain things, but there are other considerations" for journalists, Boccardi holds.

Although he's not ready to embrace "compassion" as a prerequisite for news work, Boccardi believes journalists should "have a regard for human life" and be ready, for example, to delay news of a kidnapping if that might help prevent death or injury.

The virtue of "dispassion" is one of the attitudes that James C. Thomson, Jr., curator of the Nieman foundation, discovered among the journalists who have done sabbatical studies under his care at Harvard University. He wrote in *Nieman Reports* (Winter/Spring, 1978) that his Nieman Fellows often reflect "the stereotypical reporter who embodies some traditional male virtues: toughness, terseness, speed, authority, risk-taking, freebootery."

"What is usually lacking is empathy or compassion for their subjects, those reported about, or even token nods toward those qualities," Thomson adds. "Fairness, accuracy, and speed are up front; compassion is almost never mentioned."

Lack of compassion was, to many observers, the most compelling of the many ethical issues raised when *The Washington Post* published Janet Cooke's moving account of an eight-year-old heroin addict she called "Jimmy." Created on the front page, "Jimmy" lived for almost seven months. He "died" when Cooke confessed that she made him up, that her story was a fabrication. The *Post* returned the 1981 Pulitzer Prize for feature writing her story had won.

The two ethical questions that got the most attention right after the fakery was disclosed had to do with the deception itself and the use of anonymous sources (pseudonyms for fictitious people, as it turned out in this case). But to Charles B. Seib, retired ombudsman for the *Post*, the more serious question was: "Why were the *Post* editors so willing to let Jimmy die?" Seib says the massive postmortem that *Post* ombudsman William L. Green, Jr., did on the Cooke fakery (see *Washington Post* April 19, 1981) mentioned no concern for Jimmy. Green's report had lots to say about "the editors' enthusiasm over the story," Seib wrote in *presstime* (June 1981). "There was deep concern for Cooke's safety" after she claimed that Jimmy's dope-dealing guardian had threatened her life if she identified him. "But not a thought for Jimmy."

Another classic compassion vs. dispassion case in modern journalism occurred a few years ago when *Oregon Journal* photographer William T. Murphy, Jr., faced the dilemma of taking his pictures or trying to help a woman stop her husband from killing himself. He tried to do both—by taking five shots as he attempted to talk the man out of jumping one hundred feet into the Columbia River and as he yelled at another motorist on the bridge to go for help. But the man soon struggled free from the desperate grip of his wife and jumped to his death in the swirling river.

When Murphy's pictures were published in his own paper (now defunct) and in others across the country subscribing to United Press International photo service, many people complained. "Don't the ethics of journalism insist that preservation of human life comes first, news second?" asked a Philadelphia woman. "He let a man die for the sake of a good photograph," a New Yorker wrote.

Murphy agonized over the criticism. "I don't know what I could have done differently," he said. "I am a photographer and I did what I have been trained to do. I did all I could."

Murphy's hurt reaction reflects a convention of news photography: Photojournalists are supposed to take pictures, not judge them. Judgments about whether the scenes photographed are too offensive or vulgar or just not newsworthy are made by editors, not by photographers.

But when human lives are at stake, that convention doesn't fly with many members of the public. When I show Murphy's photos to my journalism ethics class at Penn State, most of the nonjournalism majors criticize the photographer for not dropping his camera and going to the aid of the woman. Many of the journalism majors also take this view, but most, particularly those emphasizing photojournalism, sympathize with the photographer and say they believe he did all he could, that his first obligation had to be getting his pictures. I've also discussed this case with friends outside of journalism; most cannot understand how a photographer can just stand there taking pictures when he could be helping prevent a death.

Public reaction was positive, even laudatory, in a more recent case in which a Florida reporter helped stop a man who was trying to take his own life by leaping from a bridge. Reporter Christine Wolff of the *Bradenton Herald* was driving back to Bradenton from an assignment in Tampa one night in October, 1982 when she had to pull around a van stopped on the high center peak of the five-mile Sunshine Skyway Bridge over Tampa Bay, a bridge that had been a platform for some forty suicide jumps. It occurred to the 28-year-old reporter that someone in the van might be planning to jump to the dark water 150 feet below. So she turned her car around and returned to the parked van to find a bridge tollgate supervisor restraining the van's driver who was indeed threatening to jump.

Wolff and the bridge official, who had clamped his large hand on the van driver's forearm to keep him from leaving the vehicle, talked to the would-be jumper for thirty-five minutes until a Florida state trooper arrived. As the bridge official released his grip to start directing traffic, the van driver, who called himself Virgil, lunged out the door on the passenger's side and started toward the bridge rail only a foot or so away.

Wolff ran around the front of the van and grabbed Virgil's arm just as he threw one leg over the rail. "No, no, please don't, please . . .," she yelled. She held tightly to his arm long enough for the trooper to get there and help pull Virgil back against the van. The two of them—the trooper and the reporter—held onto Virgil for about twenty minutes until more police arrived and took him off to a St. Petersburg hospital.

Although she believes that in general "reporters should stay as objective as possible," Wolff says that "in this situation, I became a person, a citizen responding." She recalls that reader reaction to her story about the episode was mostly positive except for a couple of people who told her she should not have interfered with Virgil's right to kill himself. "I have no qualms about what I did."

Her editors also approved of her getting involved in this particular story. She got a bonus, she says, and her city editor, Dan Stober, told her that if she hadn't helped stop the possible suicide, he would not want her on his staff.

Wolff, of course, had an advantage over Murphy. She could help save Virgil and still do her reporter's job (she says she noticed after she grabbed Virgil and pulled him back from the rail that she had her small reporter's notebook and pen clutched in her left hand). It is more difficult for news photographers to take their photos and do very much about what is going on in front of their lenses.

But many people in and out of journalism thought that two Alabama television photographers should have done more than they did to stop a man who set fire to himself while they filmed him in March 1983. The two photographers for WHMA-TV in Anniston were sent to nearby Jacksonville, Alabama, after a man had called the station four times late one evening to say that he was going to set himself afire to protest unemployment. The station notified Jacksonville police. The caller, who turned out to be a thirty-seven-year-old, out-of-work roofer who had apparently been drinking, asked for a reporter and a photographer to come to the town square. WHMA news director Phillip D. Cox says two photographers were sent instead because none of the station's three full-time reporters was working when the calls came in. One of the photographers, Gary Harris, an eighteen-year-old college student, was only a part-timer. He apparently was to play reporter in accompanying full-time photographer Ronald Simmons, who had four to five years experience in news photography, according to Cox.

When the WHMA camera crew climbed out of their car in Jacksonville, the unemployed roofer approached, doused himself with charcoal-starter fluid, and applied a lighted match. Simmons filmed the horror for several seconds before his young partner, Harris, rushed forward and tried to beat out the flames with his small reporter's notebook. But the flames got stronger and were not put out until the burning man raced across the square where a volunteer firefighter smothered the fire with an extinguisher. The man survived but he spent eight painful weeks in a hospital being treated for serious burns.

Cox says his photographers tried to stop the apparently drunken man from setting himself afire, but he warned them off. "He said 'Stay back!' several times," Cox maintains. "It's very distinguishable on the audio track of the tape." Interviewed by telephone a few months after the incident, Cox was also miffed that much of the criticism of his station was based on the assumption that the station broadcast the full tape taken that night. Actually, no scenes of the man on fire were shown on WHMA, he says, but only scenes of the aftermath of the incident.

The question of whether a TV station should show such shocking scenes is an important one, of course, but it is a small ethical question compared to: Should the photographers have done more to stop the self-immolation even if that meant not getting their pictures? Should the crew have been sent there in the first place—"creating the news," as *The New York Times* put it in a critical editorial (March 13, 1983)?

Cox seems satisfied on both counts. "Our people did what was expected of them," he says. And he has no regrets about dispatching the camera crew that night. The two photographers were not punished and are at this writing still working for WHMA-TV. Cox does say that the incident has caused serious discussion at his station and that a copy of CBS News Standards has been distributed to the staff. Although like most TV stations WHMA does not have its own written code of ethics for its news department, Cox claims that he and his staff have become more aware of the ethical guidelines in the recently acquired CBS code as well as in the codes of the Radio-Television News Directors Association and the National Association of Broadcasters.

Contrast what happened in Jacksonville, Alabama, that March night with a similar situation in Rochester, New York, in 1979. The Rochester *Times-Union* got a lot of flak from some readers for publishing a story and a photo about a woman who had poured gasoline over her clothing and then set fire to herself on the streets of a suburban neighborhood. The Rochester photo, however, was not taken while the woman was ablaze; it showed ambulance crew members treating her before taking her to a hospital where she died a few hours later. And the photo was taken not by a professional news photographer but by an amateur who had, with others in his family and his neighborhood, put out the fire with blankets before going back to his house for his camera and taking the pictures he turned over to the *Times-Union*. The criticism the paper received accused it of poor taste in depicting the woman just before death, even though the photo did not clearly show who she was, and for adding to the grief of her surviving family. The critics did not seem aware of or concerned about how the picture was taken.

Some readers with good memories may be wondering why the Alabama and Rochester incidents aroused so much more criticism than did the photos of Buddhist monks burning themselves to death on the streets of Saigon in 1963 during the Vietnam War. Those shocking photos were taken by photographers who presumably might have stopped the immolations or whose presence may have inspired the protesting acts. One of those photographers, Peter Arnett of the Associated Press, known more today for his reporting than his photography, told a meeting of Pennsylvania journalists in 1971 that he "could have prevented that immolation by rushing at him and kicking the gasoline away. As a human being I wanted to; as a reporter I couldn't."

Judging from the widespread use of such photos in U.S. news media during the Vietnam War, few quarreled with Arnett's rationalization. Shocking pictures of self-immolation and other violence "were important in telling the story of that war and the people's reaction to that war," according to Ralph Otwell, editor of the *Chicago Sun-Times.* News photos of a war are bound to be disturbing because war is disturbing. But Otwell seems to believe that the rules change in more peaceful times. He says, for example, that today if an emotionally unstable woman were to go to the Chicago Civic Center Plaza and set herself on fire, "we would not use that picture."

Arnett's words, in addition to describing the different standards that may apply to journalists in wartime, underline the dispassionate attitude so many journalists prized in 1963 and still do today. Yet the perceived lack of compassion in the way many journalists do their work —getting their stories and photos without regard for the other human beings involved—is one of the reasons that the news business is not more highly regarded by the public. Even though compassion cannot be turned on and off like a faucet, encouraging more of it in news work and presentation might improve the public's perception of the journalistic enterprise. It also might improve the perception of news work by journalists themselves, many of whom seem to get cynical at an early age. The folklore of the news business is mostly hard-nosed and macho, disparaging expressions of pity or empathy, or anything that smacks of softness. Perhaps it's time for journalists to start honoring compassion more and cynicism less.

11 · CODES OF ETHICS

BY C. DAVID RAMBO

The public's concern for press performance is
resulting in more written codes of ethics, reports
C. David Rambo, a staff writer for the American
Newspaper Publishers Association's *presstime*. This
article is reprinted from *presstime*, February 1984.

The resolve of numerous newspapers in the late 1960s and 1970s to
adopt ethics codes continues into the mid-1980s. In fact, some observers
say there is heightened interest nowadays in strengthening newspaper
credibility through written codes of professional conduct.

One indicator of interest is a 1983 survey that found nearly three-
fourths of 902 responding newspapers and broadcast stations had
stated policies for editorial staff members regarding outside work and
acceptance of gifts.

The survey was conducted by journalism professor Ralph S. Izard
for the Society of Professional Journalists, Sigma Delta Chi. A 1974
survey by the Associated Press Managing Editors Association had
found that about 9 percent of responding members had such policies.

It was in the mid-'70s that attention to ethics codes picked up speed.
The APME adopted its first code in 1975. Also that year, the American
Society of Newspaper Editors adopted "A Statement of Principles"
[*presstime*, Feb. 1981, p. 4]. SPJ, SDX in 1973 updated its code, originally
adopted in 1926. (ANPA has no code. The Association leaves the question of whether to adopt one up to member newspapers.)

"It looks like there very definitely is a trend to protect credibility,
and one of the best ways to do that is to set up a code of ethics," says
Earl R. Maucker, managing editor of the *Fort Lauderdale* (Fla.) *News
and Sun-Sentinel*. "It's not so much what the writer might do as much
as what the readers think he might do."

The study for SPJ, SDX also showed there is an "apparent move
toward consensus" on the question of gifts and free travel, according to
Izard, chairman of the graduate program of the E.W. Scripps School of
Journalism at Ohio University. The view of most editors seems to be that

journalists should not accept such favors—once considered by some newspapers as permissible perks for their employees.

"Most of the economic kinds of questions, the 'freebies' kind of questions, have been resolved over the last decade," adds Steven R. Dornfeld, Washington correspondent of Knight-Ridder Newspapers Inc. and immediate past president of SPJ, SDX. "The new battleground in ethics has to do with how we gather the news" and questions of possible conflicts of interest in such areas as outside activities.

Addressing head-on the possibility that outside income might constitute a conflict of interest, the *Chicago Tribune* last year established a policy requiring all professional employees, including reporters, to file annual financial disclosure statements. And Charles W. Bailey, former editor of the *Minneapolis Star and Tribune,* just completed a study for the National News Council on the issue of outside activities of reporters, editors, and owners of newspapers and broadcast stations. The study is scheduled to be released April 1.

In a recent case highlighting the outside-activity situation, a reporter for *The Knoxville* (Tenn.) *News-Sentinel* was fired for insubordination after refusing to give up her elected position of school board member in Alcoa, Tenn. Arbitration proceedings are pending in the case [*presstime,* July 1983, p. 51].

News-Sentinel editor Ralph L. Millett Jr. says the reporter violated the newspaper's code of ethics that restricts news employees' involvement in politics because such activity constitutes an actual conflict of interest or at least the perception of a conflict. He says the newspaper follows Scripps-Howard Newspapers' rules for "Principles and Practices," adopted in 1963.

Lots of Arbitrations   The Knoxville situation is but the latest in a series of cases that have gone to arbitration because of questions about the propriety of editorial employees engaging in certain outside activities. The decisions have come down on all sides of the issue.

For example, arbitrators have held in recent months that:

• A newspaper improperly directed an editorial employee to withdraw as a candidate for a seat on a water commission board.

• A reporter was properly given a disciplinary suspension for writing a free-lance story that appeared in another publication.

• An editorial employee was required to obtain advance permission from the publisher before working as media director for a county fair.

• A photographer either had to divest himself of his interest in a local fashion magazine or resign from the newspaper.

• A newspaper properly refused to allow a photographer to work on his own time as a photographer for a baseball team.

In addition, a U.S. District Court judge has ordered *The Seattle Times* and The Newspaper Guild to arbitrate a dispute over when to resolve differences over the newspaper's code of ethics.

The ANPA Labor and Personnel Relations Department reports that of 115 labor agreements with the Guild, 66 have a provision requiring employer permission for outside work, 87 prohibit working for a directly competitive enterprise, 81 state that employees may not engage in outside work or activity which embarrasses or exploits their position with the company, and 10 prohibit working as a paid representative in public relations for any political group or candidate without the consent of the publisher.

Among the newspapers that have codes of ethics prohibiting involvement in outside activities that could cause a conflict of interest, or the appearance of such conflict, are *The Daily Camera* of Boulder, Colo., *The Courier-Journal* and *The Louisville Times*, *The Washington Post*, *The Florida Times-Union* and *Jacksonville Journal*, and all dailies in the Scripps-Howard group.

A related issue is the activity of journalists' spouses. Last March, Elaine Bowers, wife of Michael R. Fancher, managing editor of *The Seattle Times*, was named press secretary to Seattle Mayor Charles Royer. The *Times* said that to avoid a conflict of interest, Fancher would be transferred out of the newsroom. According to the *Times'* code of ethics, employees may not make editorial decisions about people they are related to "by blood or marriage."

Bowers gave up her job to enable her husband to keep his.

These kinds of issues may not be resolved as easily as the more-common question of accepting a free plane ride, however. "I think we're expecting a lot to try and control somebody's spouse," says James F. McDaniel, managing editor of *The Commercial Appeal* in Memphis. "It bothers me that we would try to control that."

Controversial Still   In fact, it still bothers a lot of editors that newspapers set in print any kind of standards for newsroom personnel. They say written guidelines could backfire if a judge or jury ever decided to use them as standards on which to measure a newspaper's actions, or if there were efforts on the part of the government to make enforcement of codes mandatory.

That is exactly what happened in March 1981, when a Washington state Superior Court judge ordered reporters to abide by "voluntary" bench-bar-press guidelines as a condition of attending a criminal pretrial hearing. Numerous press groups including ANPA appealed Judge Byron L. Swedberg's order to the U.S. Supreme Court, but the Court would not hear the case [*presstime*, June 1982, p. 12].

Individual newspapers' ethics codes so far have been cited in only a few cases by plaintiffs suing the press, media lawyers say. But the codes have not been a deciding factor in any case to date.

In another context, the SPJ, SDX code has been used if not against the press then at least in a scolding of the press. Mobile Corp. said in a November 1982 advertisement appearing in the *New York Times* that the media "should adopt and enforce a Code of Ethics. In this regard, we recently became aware that The Society of Professional Journalists, Sigma Delta Chi, has long had an excellent Code of Ethics. It is clear that enforcement has been lacking."

Mobil said, "We hope that after reading (the SPJ, SDX code), you will agree it is a code journalists should follow and media organizations should enforce, and that you will make your views known to them."

"Any time you set up a code you do furnish the possible opposition with ammunition," observes professor John L. Hulteng, who teaches journalistic ethics at Stanford University and who in 1981 prepared an ASNE guidebook on ethics. That threat of a possible backfire effect "has restrained some editors" from adopting written codes, he adds.

One such editor is John K. Murphy of the *Portland* (Maine) *Press Herald.* "We're very conscious of the dangers of committing a lot of things to writing," and it is one reason the paper does not have a code, he reports.

The *Press Herald* does have a "newsroom policy manual," which Murphy says is nowhere near as formal as an ethics code. The paper also plans to begin conducting staff discussions of ethical issues based on videotapes of Media and Society Seminars purchased from the Columbia University Graduate School of Journalism.

Sue Reisinger, managing editor of *The Miami News,* says the possibility of having written guidelines being turned against the paper is one reason the *News* has not adopted a code of ethics. She says the do's and don'ts of conduct and the reasons behind them "are things that you develop with your staff as you go along."

But as the public's concern over the performance of the press continues to grow, more and more newspapers are abandoning such informal approaches toward getting or keeping their houses in order. Call them codes, guidelines or rules, they're on the rise in the newspaper business.

12 · REPORTING GRIEF

BY C. FRASER SMITH

Some people criticize media personnel, especially
television crews, for intruding on grief-stricken
families. But some mourners, says reporter C. Fraser
Smith, forgive such intrusions as part of the
news-gathering job. Smith, a general assignment and
political reporter for the *Baltimore Sun*, covered the
aftermath in Maryland of the bombing of the Marine
headquarters in Beirut. This article is reprinted from
the *Washington Journalism Review*, March 1984.

When ordinary people are involved in a disaster, they can become
"news" and becoming news can be, in turn, disastrous. The point may
never have been made more clearly than in the aftermath of the Marine
bombing, resulting in the deaths of 241 Americans.

Reporters laid siege to the families of those men. People who had
never been before cameras were suddenly part of a major international
news story.

Because of difficulties in identifying the dead, some of those families
did not know for days whether their sons were among the casualties.
As their agony dragged on, news organizations—print and electronic—
had extended opportunities for dramatic stories in small towns and
cities across the country.

Some critics charged that journalism succumbed to voyeurism, the
"pornography of grief," as columnist George Will called it. Marine public relations officers were appalled that reporters wanted to sit with
families, chronicling the anguish of their wait and the shock of the
ultimate news.

In Berlin, Maryland, a Baltimore television crew arriving to interview the family of one Marine victim was greeted by neighbors shouting, "Here come the ghouls."

Critics were equally appalled that some families consented to the
press requests. Were these people too polite to draw the line? Was their
usual good judgment clouded by shock, fear and dread? Or did they feel

the press requests were legitimate, even the obligation of modern families to the modern media?

Interviews with the subjects of this "grief reporting," the relatives of the dead and wounded Marines, make it clear that reaction to the coverage of the bombing's aftermath was more complicated and less damaging to the press than one might guess. Many survivors received reporters with great patience, accepting their clumsiness and giving them the benefit of the doubt.

There were, nevertheless, gross excesses. In one case, a TV cameraman started filming as Marine officers were delivering news of a death, before consent was given by the Marines or the family. In another, a TV cameraman photographed through a sliding glass door as Marine officers delivered the news of a casualty to family members.

If a family agreed to be interviewed or sit for photographs, it was soon overrun by photographers and reporters—and for many days. Then, press attention ended as abruptly as it had begun. The families discovered that enduring grief is not necessarily enduring news.

According to Major Fred Lash, a Marine Corps public affairs officer in Washington, 75 percent of the families who were assisted by Marine Corps officials decided they wanted press coverage, and some of them called television stations and newspapers themselves to volunteer their reactions when they learned that their sons had been killed.

Some parents who agreed to be interviewed did so with a distinct purpose: to affirm the value of their son's life or to raise questions about U.S. policy in the Middle East.

Some of them supported the Marine generals, Secretary of Defense Weinberger and President Reagan. Others were bitter and angry, incredulous that President Reagan was reaffirming the nation's determination to keep Marines in Beirut: "That's fine for him to say," one mother observed during a television interview. "It's not his son coming home in a coffin."

None of the parents we talked to complained about the intrusion of television, although some said they found the longer interviews they had with print reporters more satisfying.

Reese Cleghorn, former associate editor of the *Detroit Free Press* and now dean of the college of journalism at the University of Maryland, says of grief reporting:

"Obviously, we should be outraged by outrageous acts, by failure to follow usual amenities, normal civilities . . . but there is a value in portraying the human condition, including misery, including grief about the loss of a son. I think there's a value even [in] pursuing into privacy in some cases to showing people what has gone on. It adds a dimension to our understanding of war . . . people come home dead from war."

Some of the parents we interviewed agreed.

James J. Langon III of Lakehurst, New Jersey, the father of Corporal

J.J. Langon, killed in the blast, found reporters polite, sympathetic and accommodating. The interviews, he says, were therapeutic. He did not think it was unfair to be quizzed on such personal or geopolitical matters at such a time.

"In our daily lives, we play mind games with ourselves. But when it's your son's death . . . it's almost like someone calls you in a poker game. Let's see what you've got . . . Here it is in your living room. What do you think?"

Is it fair to be asked at that moment?

"Sure. It's fair because here was my son who, because of a decision he made, was put in a political crucible, was asked in service to our country to perform a difficult task. And here we are in our daily lives —you see some of it on TV, of course, and you're worried about the danger—but suddenly it becomes very real. . . . What does it all mean?"

Langon says he almost feels sorry for those whose sons were killed after the press appetite for grief interviews waned, as it had two weeks later when eight more Marines were killed in Beirut.

"There was a very positive payoff for us. We received condolences from people in Alabama, New York City—phone calls from people in New York City. That would never have happened otherwise," he says.

If the press was criticized for its coverage, Langon suggests, perhaps it is because, "[people] quite naturally do not like sadness and tragedy and resent the press for making them see it."

His own decision to meet with the first wave of reporters was a pragmatic one, he says. At first he thought the story was of no concern to anyone but his own family. But then he learned from local police that reporters were on their way to see him.

"These people will be here, anyway, I thought, so let me deal with it in a way that would carry some sense of our feelings and at the same time give it some dignity," he says. He is now glad he changed his mind.

"You hear a lot of criticism of the press," Langon says. "But in my case, they conducted themselves very well. With no exceptions, at the end of the conversations I had with reporters, they all set their jobs aside and we talked as people. I really appreciated that."

Lewis Picher, a Denver-based clinical psychologist who specializes in grief therapy, says those unable to confront their grief would be likely to refuse interviews. A large number of people, he says, deal with grief by ignoring it. Others, however, who could face the interviews, probably benefitted from the process.

"I would guess they're trying to find a way to justify what has happened," Picher says. "People in our culture are very reasonable. We search for meaning and reason in our lives . . . so we talk about the good of the country—some super-ordinate meaning or feeling to justify it to ourselves."

Major Lash was among those who found reporters professional and helpful.

"When [television] people wanted to have a camera on hand at the moment a family was learning about their son, I was taken aback at first. Then I had to realize that . . . people wanted to know as much as they could grasp," he says.

"The more Americans were told, the more information we could get out, the more the press helped us get the information out, the better off people were. People were grieving. People needed to know who was involved," he says.

Jane Severin of Odenton, Maryland, whose son, Lance Corporal Burnam Matthews, was wounded in the bombing, says the reporters were no more or less rude than most people, including families of other Marines. She gives the edge in sensitivity to women reporters—perhaps, she says, because they have children.

Before Severin knew what had happened to her son, she says, television stations were her only source of information. Reporters went to work to help her, seeking specific information about her son.

When Matthews was en route from West Germany to Andrews Air Force base, TV crews staked out her house, and waited for her to come out so they could follow her and cover the reunion.

"I didn't try to hide anything from anybody," she says. She believes ordinary people have some responsibility in such encounters. "Where does the news come from?" she asks rhetorically. "It's a matter of how much you can stand. I can stand anything, I drive a school bus."

Later, she responded willingly to requests for interviews and became a temporary prisoner of the media. She says there were days when she got 100 calls. When she took the phone off the hook, reporters called her 80-year-old neighbor. Severin remembers coming home to find her 8-year-old daughter, Donna, being interviewed by television reporters. Looking at the 11 o'clock news that week became a personal event.

Television allowed her to watch as her son, lying in a hospital bed in Germany, his face cut and bruised, received a Purple Heart from Marine Corps Commandant Paul X. Kelley.

But on Thanksgiving, she says, "We got four calls from TV stations wanting to film us eating Thanksgiving dinner, although Thanksgiving was not that joyous. We're happy Burnie's back, but we can't forget that so many lost their sons. On Thanksgiving Day, Burnie was sitting with a Marine at Bethesda Naval Hospital."

Matthews turned down one of the requests himself. When he told the reporter the family did not want coverage on Thanksgiving, the reporter answered, "Oh well, we know someone whose baby just survived a liver transplant. We'll try them."

Burnam Matthews' family heard from many strangers. "There was a call from the father of another Marine who wanted Burnie to tell him all about the last six months of his son's life. And there was a homosexual who wanted a Marine pen pal. Burnie's gotten love letters from all over. One girl sent him flowers from Chicago."

Mary Lou Meurer, of Westport, Kentucky, the mother of Lance Corporal Ronald Meurer, killed in Beirut, is bitter, particularly about post-Beirut defenses installed around the White House.

"Reagan doesn't deserve any more security than my son," she says, adding, "I'm angry. We can accept his death as God's will. I do not have to accept the circumstances under which he died.

"I'm a truck driver, coast to coast. My husband and I. Thank God we are. I went back out on the road right after, and across the nation I found out a lot of people didn't know that our boys didn't have loaded guns—didn't have the security the White House has now."

Meurer, who wants the Marines in Lebanon given greater protection, welcomed a Baltimore television station's invitation to appear on an interview program.

Like Severin, Meurer has received many letters—700 in all—from all over the country. "I feel like I'm saying the things the whole nation wants to say," she says.

In the weeks before the bombing, Bill Giblin of North Providence, Rhode Island, tried to get newspaper reporters in Providence to write a story about his two Marine brothers, Corporal Timothy R. Giblin and Lance Corporal Donald Giblin, who were stationed together in Lebanon. Known as the "Beirut Brothers," they had obtained a waiver of the prohibition against two members of one family serving together in a combat unit.

Jack Major, an editor at the *Providence Journal,* says, "The idea may look like a natural—now—but at the time, considering the difficulty of getting interviews with the brothers, it did not seem a promising piece for the paper's magazine." When the truck-bomb went off, there were reporters aplenty in the Giblins' house. Timothy Giblin was killed. Donald Giblin survived.

The Giblins symbolized the sacrifice and suffering of the Beirut bombing. Like most of those young men whose pictures appeared in American newspapers that week, the Beirut Brothers looked well-scrubbed, clear-eyed and altogether too young for war.

Bill Giblin says the coverage his brothers received in those days, while taxing to his family, had some useful aspects. "It made me feel good. I'm very proud of my brothers, of my mother, of my family . . ." he says. The reporters, he says, "did their job. They were deeply touched."

What he remembers most about the press was that it was everywhere. "There were cameras in church, cameras at the funeral home, cameras at the cemetery," he says. "They were here every minute. They all said they were sorry for intruding. We invited them in for food and coffee. Half of them slept outside [in their vans] . . . ."

Occasionally they overdid it. When the Marine casualty reporting team arrived late one night at his mother's apartment, a newspaper reporter was playing with Timothy Giblin's daughter on the living room floor. The reporter was asked to leave and did.

But a television crew outside filmed, through a sliding glass door, the family hearing the news of Timothy's death. "Reporters just seem to thrive on tragedy," he says. "When I went down to Dover, Delaware [where his brother's body was returned], to bring my brother back, they wanted a reporter to escort me!

"But they were all right. They were doing their job."

13 · PRESS TAKES INWARD LOOK AT ITS ETHICS

BY DAVID SHAW

The movie *Absence of Malice* is the springboard for David Shaw's analysis of the increasing attention being paid to ethics and ethical practices by the nation's news media. Shaw is a staff writer for the *Los Angeles Times* who often writes about the news media. This article is reprinted from the September 23, 1981, edition of the *Times*.

She's Sally Field, movie star. In *Absence of Malice*, she's Megan Carter, newspaper reporter. Bright. Feisty. Tenacious. Unethical.

Megan Carter illegally wears a concealed tape recorder during an interview. She plunges into a sexual relationship with a man she's writing about. She betrays the confidence of at least one news source. She invades the privacy of another. She is so eager to rush into print with a story about a murder investigation that she blindly allows herself to be used by a ruthless prosecutor to blacken an innocent man's reputation—without making the slightest effort to investigate the prosecutor's story or to discover his motive (and without making more than a token effort to get the alleged suspect's side of what is actually a phony story).

When Carter is all through—well, almost all through—one innocent person is dead and several others are wretchedly unhappy.

"A lot of damage has been done, and I'm responsible for a lot of it," Carter says near the end of the movie. "I keep thinking there must be rules to tell me what I'm supposed to do now. Maybe not."

But there are rules—journalistic principles—and Carter has violated so many of them that even though Field often makes her seem sympathetic and vulnerable, most viewers will probably empathize with the man she first victimizes. . . . He is portrayed by Paul Newman.

Given the luster of these stars—and the essentially cynical view of the press embodied in this movie (written by a former newspaper editor) —*Absence of Malice* is almost certain to trigger anew both public discussion and private soul-searching about journalistic ethics when it's released late this year.

The film could not come at a more appropriate time.

Several well-publicized breaches of journalistic ethics have so besmirched the journalist's image this year that a *Times* reporter traveling around the country on a story recently was repeatedly greeted, by journalist and non-journalist alike, with the comment:

"Oh, you're writing about journalism ethics, huh? Tell me—have you found any?"

The question was asked only partially in jest.

No wonder:

• In April, a *Washington Post* reporter was forced to resign her job and surrender her Pulitzer Prize when it was discovered that her story about an 8-year-old heroin addict was a piece of fiction.

• In May, a *New York Daily News* columnist was forced to resign when he was accused of having fabricated a story about a clash between a British army patrol and a gang of youths in Belfast.

• In June, a *Toronto Sun* reporter was fired and another was forced to resign when it was revealed that they had no documentation for their story charging that a member of Prime Minister Pierre Elliott Trudeau's Cabinet had benefited from stock manipulations through inside government information.

No wonder several polls in recent years have shown that most people don't rate journalists very high in terms of honesty and ethical standards. No wonder a *Washington Post* poll just last month showed that most people are "sharply critical of the national press"—in large part because of ethical considerations.

"I'm not too sanguine about our profession any more," says Michael J. O'Neill, editor of the *New York Daily News* and president of the American Society of Newspaper Editors.

Widespread evidence of such unethical behavior as bias, carelessness and sensationalism has left O'Neill discouraged, and his discouragement has been deepened, he says, by the refusal of many in journalism to adopt anything other than what he calls "a holier-than-thou attitude" toward their critics.

But most reporters and editors say recent press scandals are just isolated incidents—an unfortunate concatenation of unforgivable *individual* acts that should not be used to indict an entire profession.

In one sense, they may be right.

By virtually any standard of measurement, the press today is more ethical—more responsible—than at any time in history. Most journalists are now well-educated and (at big-city papers) well-paid; they're respectable men and women working in a true "profession," and they generally demand far more of themselves and their peers in terms of ethical behavior than their predecessors ever did.

As syndicated columnist Nicholas Von Hoffman says, in an admitted oversimplification:

"In the old days in the newspaper business, almost everyone accepted free gifts and free trips and other freebies, and no one talked about ethics. Now, no reputable reporter takes anything free, and everyone's talking about ethics."

Indeed they are.

The press is more visible and more influential now, and that—combined with its often controversial coverage of the sociopolitical upheavals of the 1960s and early 1970s—has brought increasing public scrutiny and criticism.

The nightly network news shows—which made Vietnam "the living room war"—now reach more than 40 million people every day. The major daily newspapers and weekly newsmagazines—almost all of them now divisions of massive communications conglomerates—help shape the national social, political and cultural agenda. Robert Redford and Dustin Hoffman (as *Washington Post* reporters Bob Woodward and Carl Bernstein) and Ed Asner (as television's Lou Grant) have helped turn journalists into celebrities, with all the glamour, prestige and potential for self-indulgence and public disenchantment that celebrityhood inevitably brings.

Thus, shocked by some journalists' recent betrayals of both professional obligation and public trust—and acutely aware of the damage this has done to the reputation of the press with an already skeptical public—many reporters and editors throughout the country are re-examining among themselves a whole range of ethical questions:

Are reporters relying too heavily on confidential or unnamed sources? Does the media unnecessarily invade the privacy of the people they write about? Is it fair for a reporter to reduce someone's thoughtful 30-minute speech to one colorful sentence for the evening news or the morning paper?

Are reporters ever justified in lying or misrepresenting themselves to get a story? Are reporters—and editors and publishers—compromised by certain personal relationships, business investments and social or political activities? Is the media ever justified in paying interviewees to cooperate on stories?

Does competition for readers, ratings, advertisers, fame and fortune induce some journalists to behave irresponsibly?

"You run into talk about journalistic ethics everywhere journalists get together these days," says Gene Goodwin, a journalism professor at the University of Pennsylvania. "You go to a bar now just to have a drink with some reporters, and you wind up talking about ethics."

But there is more than just talk going on.

Goodwin, for example, is writing a book on journalism ethics, and another new book on ethics—a 90-page booklet, *Playing It Straight,* by John Hulting, a professor of communications at Stanford University— is already in widespread circulation in many newsrooms around the country.

Other academics are also assisting in the examination of ethical problems in journalism:

• Mark Pastin, a professor of philosophy at Arizona State University and a longtime teacher of business ethics, is planning a November ethics seminar for journalists, focusing in large part on the potential conflict between the social responsibility and the profit incentive of the press.

• Columbia University has taken over sponsorship of a series of Socratic seminars on the media and the law, confronting journalists, attorneys, judges and law enforcement officials with hypothetical ethical problems.

• Professors at Utah State University, Brigham Young University and the University of Kentucky are using psychological tests to study the relationship between an individual journalist's personal belief system and his response to ethical problems on the job.

There are other signs that journalists—long as resistant to self-examination as they are resentful of external criticism—are taking their ethical problems seriously.

There will be a two-day program in Chicago in October, 1981, and a panel discussion in Los Angeles Sept. 24, 1981, on ethics and investigative reporting.

Earlier this year, the Modern Media Institute in St. Petersburg, Fla., began trying to design an interdisciplinary program to guide publishers, editors and reporters in developing ethical standards.

At the *Los Angeles Times,* six specially selected reporters who meet monthly with the paper's four top editors to discuss matters of policy and performance have raised such ethical questions in recent months as:

Was a *Times* story on a new drug-use trend irresponsible in giving a fairly explicit formula for the drug? Were several other *Times* stories insensitive and inflammatory in their depiction of black ghetto youths committing violent crimes in predominantly white suburbs? Are some of the paper's special advertising supplements misleading to readers? Was it appropriate for the publisher and editor of the *Times* to participate in a testimonial dinner given by the Times Mirror Co. for Sen. Howard Baker?

Elsewhere in the media:

- A National News Council in New York, a statewide news council in Minnesota and a community media council in Honolulu investigate public complaints of unethical (and other improper) activity by the media.

- Independent journalism reviews in New York, Washington, San Francisco and St. Louis criticize media performance.

- Ombudsmen at two dozen daily papers across the country now respond to readers' complaints and write both internal memos for their editors and periodic columns for their readers, criticizing their papers for unfair, inaccurate, irresponsible or unethical reporting.

- Several large newspapers (the *Seattle Times* and *Minneapolis Star* among them) regularly mail questionnaires to the subjects of stories in their papers, asking if the subjects think they were treated fairly and accurately.

- Hodding Carter III, former assistant secretary for public affairs in the State Department, is the host of a public television program called "Inside Story," a weekly critique of press performance that examined such ethical issues this year as bias, invasion of privacy, conflict of interest, sensationalism and irresponsibility.

Television journalism has also begun examining its own ethical standards:

- "Sixty Minutes" is scheduled to broadcast a program Sept. 27, 1981, in which several prominent journalists criticize the show's interview and editing techniques.

• ABC in July, 1981, broadcast "Viewpoint," the first of several programs providing critics of television news a public forum.

George Watson, whose duties as an ABC News vice president include supervision of "Viewpoint," says he is so concerned about ethics among journalists that he is trying to write a policy book for the network news division—"a code of conduct (to) define the principal areas of ethical concern."

CBS and NBC already have such codes. So do most major professional journalism organizations—the American Society of Newspaper Editors, the Associated Press Managing Editors, the Society of Professional Journalists (Sigma Delta Chi). An increasing number of individual newspapers, both large and small, also have written codes of ethics.

But there is no widespread agreement among editors that a code of ethics—or an ombudsman or a news council or an academic seminar or anything else—is the best way for the press to resolve ethical questions. These matters are now a subject of considerable, often heated debate in media circles.

The top editors of the *New York Times* and the *Los Angeles Times* don't believe in written codes of ethics, for example, but the top editors of the *Washington Post* and the *Philadelphia Inquirer* do. The *Minneapolis Star* has a written code; the *Minneapolis Tribune* does not.

Of the 88 editors surveyed earlier this year by the Professional Standards Committee of the Associated Press Managing Editors, 58 said they had no written code of ethics.

Why not?

Many editors interviewed by the *Times* insist that a code is useless because it can't possibly cover every contingency a reporter or editor might actually encounter.

"We carry our code of ethics in our hip pocket," is the way one editor phrases his opposition to a formal, written code.

But pockets get frayed. They wear out. They develop holes. Some pants have very small pockets. Or no pockets at all.

"It's not so much the printed word (in a code of ethics) that has an effect as it is the wide participation of the people on the paper in discussing and drawing up the code," says Gene Roberts, executive editor of the *Philadelphia Inquirer.*

"Involving everyone in the process of developing a code has the effect of raising everybody's consciousness about the issues, and I think that's very healthy—and much more important than just getting a formal statement of policy or a written rationale that you can later use as a reason for firing someone who violates it."

Roberts thought this heightened consciousness was essential at the *Inquirer* because in the 1960s, before he and the current ownership took over, unethical behavior was pervasive at the paper; one *Inquirer* reporter was actually jailed for extorting money from his news sources.

But not all editors face such problems, and many editors are convinced that a code of ethics is neither necessary nor practicable.

Most codes are just "a bunch of platitudes" and self-evident prohibitions, says William F. Thomas, editor and executive vice president of the *Los Angeles Times.*

To Thomas, Roberts' argument that the development of a written code makes reporters more aware of ethical concerns is "nonsense . . . stupid."

"We all know we're supposed to be honest," Thomas says. "We all know we're not supposed to take free gifts from people who could be perceived as influencing what we do. . . . If you don't know . . . those things when you come here, then you don't deserve to be here.

"I don't like . . . codes of ethics . . . and other things like that which I think would look like we're denigrating the people we're handing them to," Thomas says. "I don't like to be treated like a child . . . and that's what those codes of ethics seem to say to me. . . . It's insulting.

"I've never seen a written code of ethics that wasn't so damned obvious that it was clear that you were doing it more for its outside PR (public relations) value than for any inward impact."

Although many editors say this view is naive and shortsighted—"a lot of baloney" in the words of *Milwaukee Journal* editor Richard Leonard—many others agree with Thomas. Some of these editors also think an ombudsman is largely a public relations device—and they cite as evidence the 18,000-word report the *Washington Post* ombudsman wrote on the *Post*'s Janet Cooke/Pulitzer Prize scandal in April.

In that report—published in the *Post* four days after the scandal broke—ombudsman Bill Green criticized *Post* editors for a number of errors, including their failure to demand that Cooke identify her sources for them.

For many readers, Green's report helped restore some of the credibility the *Post* lost when Cooke's charade was exposed. But many editors say—with considerable justification—that if the ombudsman system had worked properly, Green would have written about suspicions that Cooke's story was fictitious back when those suspicions were first voiced in the *Post* news room, shortly after her story was published, rather than waiting until the Pulitzer Prize announcement triggered public exposure of the sham.

Other editors have a more fundamental criticism.

"If they (the *Post* editors) had set up a system under which the first time Janet Cooke refused to divulge her sources to an editor, they would have fired her or stopped the story, that would have increased their credibility," says one editor. "But after the fact, if somebody comes along and says, 'I did it,' does that increase their credibility? That's false credibility.

"I do not believe in the ombudsman system," this editor says. "It's a red herring . . . a PR gimmick . . . a great way to get the editor off the hook."

When a *Times* reporter repeated these comments to Benjamin C. Bradlee, executive editor of the *Washington Post,* without naming the man who made them, Bradlee shook his head angrily, then laughed and said, "Terrific. Terrific . . . I'll just tell you, he's the editor of some paper that can't hold the *Post*'s socks."

Wrong.

The man who made those statements about the *Post* is A.M. Rosenthal, executive editor of the *New York Times.* And Rosenthal is not alone in his criticism of the ombudsman as essentially public relations gimmickry.

Eugene Patterson, editor and president of the *St. Petersburg Times* and former president of the American Society of Newspaper Editors, is a longtime advocate of improved ethical standards for journalists. But after having had various ombudsmen over the past 10 years, Patterson fired his latest ombudsman last year and decided not to hire another.

"An ombudsman is just window dressing," Patterson says now. "Any editor who can't make value judgments on his own and make them correctly is in the wrong job."

Isn't that both self-serving and self-deluding, though? Isn't it possible that even an editor as excellent and as ethical as Patterson might make a mistake and not realize he'd made a mistake?

William Rusher, publisher of *National Review* and a charter member of the National News Council, says of Patterson's comments: "Anybody who thinks that about himself is halfway to the loony bin. That is exactly . . . the kind of pride that goes before a fall."

Bradlee also scoffs at Patterson's judgment on this issue.

"I just wish I were as wise as Gene," Bradlee says, grinning. Then he adds, "Every editor has got to be an ombudsman. You can't abdicate your responsibility for ethical judgments . . . but I tell you, I think he's just as wrong as he can be. . . .

"In monopoly situations (and more and more newspapers are in monopoly situations), an independent representative—some public embodiment of ethical judgment—is a useful tool for the public and a useful tool for the paper," Bradlee says.

"Most editors are scared of it (an ombudsman) because . . . as soon as you give somebody independence, you can get zopped."

But newspapers "zop" other institutions; why shouldn't newspapers themselves be "zopped"? Why shouldn't the media wash its own dirty linen in public—just as they wash everyone else's dirty linen in public? Wouldn't that be both fair play *and* good public relations?

"Any editor who says he is his own ombudsman might succeed in fooling himself, but not the readers," says Barry Bingham Jr., editor and publisher of the *Louisville Courier-Journal,* the first paper in the nation to appoint an ombudsman (in 1967).

In fact, many critics say the attitude that Patterson, Rosenthal and most other editors have toward ombudsmen is typical of the arrogance of which the press is often accused.

"To Abe, the *New York Times* is a temple, and he is . . . its high priest and protector," says Lester Bernstein, editor of *Newsweek.* "Criticism of the *New York Times'* motivation . . . or performance . . . just shouldn't be done in Abe's view."

Adds Robert Maynard, editor and publisher of the *Oakland Tribune* and a member of the National News Council:

"Our attitude . . . .is appalling. . . . We have assumed a posture of infallibility, and we are afraid to let anybody ever look at what we're doing critically."

Quite so. And anyone who's written critically about the media knows that Bob Pisor, former press critic for television station WDIV in Detroit, is right when he says, "I doubt that anyone in the whole world is more sensitive to criticism than people in the media . . . especially newspapers."

But the refusal of most journalists to accept criticism gracefully or to acknowledge public accountability as an ethical principle can only intensify the resentment that many increasingly feel toward the press.

Is there a solution to this dilemma?

"We've tried to solve the problem . . . by having a reporter write about the media the way we write about other institutions—and that includes making critical judgments about what we do . . . and talking openly about our mistakes," says *Times* editor Thomas.

"But no other paper has done it that way . . . that comprehensively . . . oh a regular basis."

Thomas insists that a story in the paper's news columns speaks with more authority than "one man's voice" in an ombudsman column on the editorial pages. Some critics say, however, that the *Times'* approach is even more deceptive and cosmetic than the ombudsman concept, giving the illusion of accountability, without the substance of an ombudsman's independent editorial voice.

The most popular approach to editorial accountability these days seems to be in the establishment of new policies on correcting specific errors.

Until relatively recently, most newspapers tried to avoid publicly admitting any errors—or, if they did admit them, they did so in a sentence or two buried amid the advertisements for foot powder and trusses.

Now many newspapers have begun to publish regularly—indeed daily, in a prominent or consistent position in the paper—various corrections and clarifications of (and apologies for) their errors and oversights, whether of omission or commission.

But if an editor doesn't think his paper has made a mistake and he refuses to publish a correction—or if the correction he publishes is inadequate—people who feel they have been wronged by the paper still have no recourse.

Several months ago, for example, the *New York Times* published a financial column listing "some of the wealthiest individuals in the nation"—those who purportedly owned more than $100-million worth of stock in various American companies. The list included the name of William L. Cary, former chairman of the Securities and Exchange Commission.

"Mr. Cary, who now teaches at the Columbia University School of Law, has $130.5-million worth of United States Filter Corp. stock and earns $1.91 million in dividends annually," the story said.

Although the story described Cary's name as "perhaps the most surprising name on the list," the reporter who wrote the story apparently wasn't sufficiently surprised (or curious) to bother calling Cary to ask how he had managed to amass such a fortune.

Big mistake.

Cary never owned that stock. He was only the trustee for it, at a fee of about $25,000 a year, he says. When Cary complained, the *New York Times* published a correction, saying that Cary's stockholdings had been "incorrectly stated" and noting that he was only a trustee for the stock "and therefore does not share in the dividends."

But this brief correction, published amid other corrections resulting from the same story, did not really make clear that Cary had no equity interest in the stock, would not benefit from its sale and is not, in fact, a member of what that first *Times* story called "The $100 Million Club."

Because Cary has children, he says he was worried that the original *New York Times* story might make them seem lucrative kidnap/ransom targets. Because of his SEC service, he was worried that the story might lead some readers to assume that he had illegally enriched himself by using inside information he had gained while he had a sensitive government position.

There was nothing Cary could do about any of this, though.

The *Times'* Rosenthal says he did not know of this incident when it happened, but he concedes that if Cary's account is correct (which it is), the paper "should have had a corrective article."

To Rosenthal, "poor handling" of a correction by the *New York Times* is "not a matter of ethics; it's a matter of somebody not doing a job very well . . . ."

To Cary, however, the incident reflected what he sees as the all-too-common "high-handed" attitude the press takes toward those it covers, as well as toward those who criticize its performance or its ethics.

". . . some kind of sanction beyond retraction may become more and more frequent unless the industry shows a willingness to discipline itself," Cary warns.

Those sanctions, most critics inside and outside the media agree, would probably take two forms—more punitive court rulings in libel cases (several of which have already been made) and more restrictive government regulation (which the press sees as the ultimate threat to its freedom).

Fred Friendly, formerly of CBS and now teaching journalism at Columbia University, says journalists who stubbornly resist self-regulation are behaving in much the same way that many businessmen behaved before passage of the Sherman Antitrust Act—and in so doing, they, too, risk inviting government intervention.

"I care a lot about the First Amendment," Friendly says, "but . . . because they (journalists) are not constitutionally Accountable (with a big 'A') to government, doesn't mean that they are not accountable (with a small 'a') to . . . their readers. . . .

"When newspapers get on their high horse and say, 'We're different from everybody else; we are accountable only to ourselves,' and that's somehow what the Constitution of the United States says, that's almost a blasphemy."

For Further Reading

Clifford G. Christians, Kim B. Rotzoll and Mark Fackler, *Media Ethics: Cases and Moral Reasoning.* New York: Longman, 1983.

H. Eugene Goodwin, *Groping for Ethics in Journalism.* Ames, Iowa: Iowa State University Press, 1983.

John L. Hulteng, *The Messenger's Motives: Ethic Problems of the News Media.* Englewood Cliffs, N.J.: Prentice-Hall, 1976.

John L. Hulteng, *Playing It Straight: A Practical Discussion of the Ethical Principles of the American Society of Newspaper Editors.* Chester, Conn.: Globe Pequot Press, 1981.

John C. Merrill and Ralph D. Barney (eds.), *Ethics and the Press.* New York: Hastings House, 1975.

John C. Merrill and S. Jack Odell, *Philosophy and Journalism.* New York: Longman, 1983.

Philip Meyer, *Editors, Publishers and Newspaper Ethics.* Washington: American Society of Newspaper Editors, 1983.

Lee Thayer (ed.), *Ethics, Morality, and the Media: Reflections on American Culture.* New York: Hastings House, 1980.

IV

Mass Media, Access, and Pressure Groups

W HO HAS a right to communicate with the masses? Only those who are wealthy enough to own newspaper and magazine publishing companies, radio and television stations and national broadcasting networks? Or does the principle of freedom of speech in a democracy imply the rights of all individuals, whether wealthy or not, to access to mass communication?

When our Founding Fathers conceived a free press as a bulwark for democracy, times were different. It was not beyond imagination that an average citizen could acquire the means to get his opinions printed or to have his voice heard in the village square or town meeting. But in our modern mass society, the average citizen's voice, without the megaphone of mass media, has been reduced to a puny whimper that few will ever hear.

With the skyrocketing costs of mass media since World War II, questions about who should have access to mass communication have caused heated debate. An increasing number of citizens and citizens' groups have insisted that laws be passed permitting them to use the media, whether they own or are employed by the media or not. Movements have even been started by reporters' groups to demand a say in the final editorial decision making of editors and publishers and owners.

The most powerful of these groups have sought more than access. They have fought for the right to influence the direction and the content of the media and to "reform" those media they regard as irresponsible. But media reform has often turned into politics, especially liberal versus conservative politics rather than Democratic versus Republican party politics.

A great variety of media reform and media "watchdog" groups have come into existence, so many that they tend to cancel each other out and lose their effectiveness. And yet they are probably needed in some ways to keep watch over the watchdog.

14 · The Citizens Movement Takes a Turn

By Susan Witty

The deregulation of broadcasting that has occurred in the 1980s has significantly altered the media reform movement. The movement is not dead but it has changed. "The electronic media are awesome tools of power," writes Susan Witty. "Whoever can dominate them can determine not only how people spend their money, but also what ideas people are exposed to, the decisions they make based on those ideas, and ultimately the political process." Witty is a writer who has served as an editorial consultant to WNET, New York. Her article is reprinted from *Channels of Communications,* June/July 1981.

The way Howard Symons of *Congress Watch* remembers it, the mark-up of HR3333, Congressman Lionel Van Deerlin's widely publicized rewrite of the Federal Communications Act, was like the madcap stateroom scene in *A Night at the Opera.* Squeezed into a very small room were the fifteen members of the House communications subcommittee, their staffs, and as many lobbyists as could push themselves through the doorway—common-carrier people, church people, labor people, public interest people. The bill, purportedly attempting to bring communications law up to date with technology, had upset nearly everyone.

It dealt with the entire telecommunications industry, but its most controversial feature was the elimination of the public interest standard, which has stood since 1934—the requirement that broadcasters, acting as public trustees, serve "the public interest, convenience, and necessity." Chairman Van Deerlin's rewrite trusted that the public interest would be served by market forces.

Van Deerlin had devoted his last two terms in office to creating the bill, then laying the groundwork for its acceptance, promoting it in the House and in the industry. But the mark-up session went badly. Several days later, the whole project was quietly scrapped. Some mighty industries contributed to its collapse—the American Telephone and Telegraph Company and the broadcast industry had fought certain segments —but a major contributing force was a nationwide coalition of citizens groups determined to preserve the established avenues of public access to radio and television. Each member of the subcommittee had been heavily lobbied in his district and, when it came time for mark-up, Van Deerlin could not enlist the support of his own colleagues. Mobilized as a national lobbying force, the citizen-action groups carried the day.

These groups, which sprouted in the sixties and early seventies, and came to be known collectively as the media-reform movement, had become in the last decade a full-time component of the American broadcasting system. They pressured for minority ownership and employment, for greater sensitivity to the needs of children, and for fair treatment in the licensed media for women, gays, Hispanics, and other segments of society that broadcasters seemed to ignore. They lobbied against discrimination, violence, and excessive commercialism in television programming; they were for localism and against monopoly. Generally, they worked to assure a communications system that would respond and contribute to a pluralistic society. Now they saw Van Deerlin's proposals undermining much of what they had striven for.

"When we heard the House wasn't going to hold local hearings on the bill," said Janice Engsberg, field director for Telecommunications Consumer Coalition (TCC), "we came up with something pretty creative. We decided to hold our own hearings in all the subcommittee members' districts." TCC and its parent, the Office of Communication of the United Church of Christ (OC/UCC), in a joint effort with the National Organization for Women's Media Project, got on the phone to affiliates, sent out mailings, and held workshops to prepare local people for effective action. Meanwhile, the National Citizens Committee for Broadcasting (NCCB) kept interested parties around the country alerted to updates in the bill through articles in its magazine, *access.* Other national groups, like the Media Access Project (MAP), the public interest communications law firm, delivered testimony against the bill in Washington.

When HR3333 breathed its last, media reformers heaved a sigh of relief, but they didn't celebrate. "The bill was like Act Two of a five-act play that may not conclude in this century," comments Kathy Bonk, director of NOW's Media Project. Still, TCC's Engsberg concedes, "we were able to hold our turf." The media-reform movement had managed to preserve the mechanisms for guaranteeing public access to broadcasting and affirming public ownership of the airwaves.

This happened in July 1979. Since then, technology has opened new media frontiers, and the scramble for markets by giant corporations has raised important public interest issues. But just when they might be most active, the media-reform groups appear severely weakened. Some observers claim that on the eve of a communications revolution, the groups are fighting a losing battle with the changing times.

The media-reform movement had flourished in the era of social consciousness bracketed by *Brown v. Board of Education* and the beginning of the end of the Vietnam War. Though occasionally capable of wielding a Mighty-Mouse kind of clout, the media-reform groups were relatively low-budget organizations. They operated with small staffs and meager resources. Like many other holdovers from that not-so-distant past, they aren't faring too well.

"Media reform is not dead per se, but it's a far cry from the movement it once was," says Timothy Haight, assistant professor of communications arts at the University of Wisconsin in Madison. According to Haight, the reform effort was an outgrowth of the civil rights movement, and was ultimately liberal and progressive. But then, "the citizen-action groups got pulled into going to Washington and depending more and more on government, which has become increasingly conservative. Media reform is continuing," Haight explains, "but it's being continued by the right instead of the left. The right wing have become much better grass-roots organizers. In the sixties the liberal churches were very active—now the fundamentalist churches are. The left is still trying but they're not in power."

Being out of fashion makes it difficult to attract money. "We are feeling the same fund-raising pressures other public interest groups are feeling," states Peggy Charren, president of Action for Children's Television (ACT), who admits her 1981 budget of $350,000 is "somewhat less than last year's."

"The funding is following the political climate," observes Engsberg. "In the last year and a half, the Ford Foundation has withdrawn its support for every program working for social change."

When Ford, estimated to have provided 57 percent of all public interest funding, got out of the public interest business, a seismic shock traveled through the media-reform movement. One of the most serious repercussions was the decline of the Citizens Communications Center (CCC), a Washington-based public interest law firm representing media-reform groups before the Federal Communications Commission and the federal courts. For ten years, Ford had sustained CCC at the cost of $220,000 a year, which constituted 99 percent of CCC's annual budget. Early this year, its professional staff down to two, CCC was forced to merge with the Institute for Public Interest Representation, itself affiliated with the Georgetown University Law Center.

While other foundations, such as Rockefeller, Veatch, Markle, Stern, and Carnegie, contribute to public interest activities in communications, they are not rushing to fill the hole left by Ford's exodus. NOW's

Kathy Bonk suggests their caution may be because very few media-reform groups have become self-sustaining. Others feel the foundations may be readjusting their priorities to align with the perceived rightward drift of the national mood; perhaps they too have been bitten by the "new" conservatism.

"We were largely responsible for Henry Ford's blast at the Ford Foundation for the way it was using its money for social upheaval," says Dr. Everett Parker, director of OC/UCC. In 1964, the OC/UCC and two black citizens of Jackson, Mississippi, challenged WLBT's license renewal on grounds that the NBC affiliate's programming and hiring practices discriminated against blacks in its community. Ford supported OC/UCC in this legal battle for ten years, but discontinued its grants three years ago. The foundation's retreat happened in part, Dr. Parker speculates, because some powerful broadcast figure said to Henry Ford, "What the hell are you doing giving out money for people to put me out of business? I don't give out money for people to put you out of business."

A decidedly less personal view of the situation is offered by Sandy Jaffe, a program officer at the Ford Foundation: "Foundations like to give seed money. We had been there for about ten to twelve years. That's long enough for a foundation to stay in." In addition, Jaffe believes some goals were achieved. "What you do," he says, "is open up a process and let a lot of people in that hadn't gotten into it, you improve decision-making, make a society a little more responsive. And that's been accomplished. Public interest law is pretty well recognized today," he says. "I think in some form it will persist."

"I'm sorry to say the prognosis for these groups is not good," says Henry Geller, former director of the National Telecommunications and Information Administration (NTIA). "In the Carter Administration we tried to get bills through to provide some funding for those groups that make a useful contribution to the regulatory hearing process, because their participation served the public interest. But Congress did not want to enact such bills.

"It was hoped," says Geller, who had been CCC's board chairman in the mid-seventies, "that Ford's support [of the movement's legal arm] would be replaced by tithing the bar, by more contributions from settlements, by Congress—and none of these have been forthcoming."

Most groups are currently squeaking by on budgets at the low end of six figures. The exception is Accuracy in Media (AIM). This organization, working to counteract what it views as the frequently left-leaning bias of the media establishment, is riding high on the right-leaning financial tide. AIM's present budget of more than $1 million, far more lavish than that of any other group, is double what it was in 1980. AIM's chairman, Reed Irvine, a former Federal Reserve Board official, sees "nothing but growing support for our activities."

"Money is power," says ACT's Charren, referring to the combined force of advertisers and broadcasters who often band together to oppose her organization's proposals concerning children's television. "Those industry groups all have lots of lawyers, and one of their salaries is practically our whole budget."

Money *is* power. But in a nation of laws, those who don't have recourse to vast wealth still believe they have recourse to justice. In 1966, Judge Warren E. Burger handed down a precedent-setting U.S. Court of Appeals decision in *OC/UCC v. FCC,* which said listeners and viewers of radio and television have a right to participate in FCC proceedings even though they may have no economic interest in the matter. Since Judge Burger's ruling, media-reform groups have worked mainly within the legal and regulatory system. But now that system is threatened by the swelling ranks of "market forces" advocates.

The cry for deregulation is reverberating through Congress more loudly than ever. And the expectation is that the salient features of the defeated Van Deerlin bill—which sought to abolish the license-renewal process, eliminate all forms of program regulation, including the Fairness Doctrine, and strike down such structural means of achieving diversity as limitations on the number of radio stations individual broadcasters could own—will be reintroduced in other bills over the next few years.

The FCC, perhaps in anticipation of a Congressional slashing, has already begun to slit its own throat. Its January decision to release radio broadcasters from some of their legal obligations—such as keeping detailed program records—also stripped the agency of some of its own oversight responsibilities.

The loss of these records, useful to citizens groups, broadcasters, and the FCC when a station's license renewal is being challenged, is a serious one.

Most of the media-reform groups are gamely attempting to make the best of deregulation, but that doesn't mean they have to like it. "When you take the rules away," warns Andrew Schwartzman, executive director of Media Access Project, "you may create a situation in which responses have to be more free-form and perhaps more threatening to the First Amendment."

At the moment, the conventional wisdom among media reformers is that radio deregulation is a stalking horse for what's to come. "There will be changes in TV regulation in the next three years legislatively," predicts Samuel Simon, executive director of the National Citizens Committee for Broadcasting (NCCB). "Our objective," he says, "would be to see that when these rules come out, they significantly increase access opportunities, and do not result in excessive concentration of the media. Teleprompter-Westinghouse is an example of this kind of concentration," Simon explains. *"The New York Times* buying into cable is another. There are going to be information monopolies in this country, and that's very serious for democracy. The stakes are higher than most people are willing to admit, especially the regulators."

A painful irony is that a number of the regulators advocating deregulation were people drafted into government from, of all places, the media-reform movement. In the late seventies the Carter Administration co-opted some of the movement's most articulate and charismatic leaders—lawyers who had hitherto argued persuasively on behalf of the public interest. By 1980 a number had taken jobs with the government agencies before which they used to plead their cases, including the FCC, the FTC, the National Telecommunications and Information Administration, and the Corporation for Public Broadcasting.

The hope among their former clients was that they would further the cause of diversity by working from the inside to strengthen the regulatory process and make it more effective. But in several key instances exactly the opposite happened.

Frank Lloyd, for example, was a former executive director of Citizens Communications Center. But as administrative assistant to the chairman of the FCC during the Carter Administration, he supported the commission's *laissez-faire* deregulatory philosophy.

"The public interest groups have to be very concerned about protecting the First Amendment rights of broadcasters. I'm more and more convinced of the importance of that," Lloyd said, shortly after the commission announced its radio-deregulation decision. "Some groups have thought the FCC should decide what is not good programming, and that's folly. When you see the potentially whimsical or political nature of those decisions, giving the government power over program content is very dangerous."

What is government's proper role? According to Lloyd, it is to define the rules of the game so the largest number of people can play, to create as many outlets as possible, to fashion structural rules that assure a fairly open-entry marketplace—in other words, more business opportunities for more people and less government intervention in business.

"Deregulation will not go away," asserts Henry Geller, another former bulwark of the public interest law community, after having been general counsel at the FCC for close to twenty years. He claims that the public-trustee scheme, under which the broadcaster is considered only a temporary trustee for what is essentially a public property, has been a failure. "The FCC never came to grips with what they meant by the public interest," he says. "They never defined what they meant by being 'an effective local outlet.' Licenses were renewed 99 percent of the time."

An NTIA report issued while Geller was that department's chief calls upon Congress to "drastically" change the 1934 Communications

Act and eliminate the public-trustee programming regulation of radio broadcasting. "The broadcaster should be given a long-term license (e.g., twenty-five years . . .)," the NTIA report recommends, "with no renewal of license within that period and no need to obtain prior approval for an assignment."

"Henry Geller and I are very good friends," says Everett Parker of the OC/UCC, "but he's inconsistent. He didn't have a good experience at the FCC. He was there at a time when nobody would do anything, so he thinks that because they didn't make the law work, the law should be repealed."

Whether they are simply putting up a brave front or are indulging in a self-protective act of psychological denial, the surviving media-reform groups refuse to be disheartened by their co-opted confreres, their depleted ranks, their disappearing legal options, and their uncertain financial future. "Nothing could completely handcuff us, short of giving the broadcasters licenses in perpetuity, with no accountability to the public," says National Black Media Coalition (NBMC) chairman Pluria Marshall.

This kind of outsized determination will carry the wounded media-reform movement forward. It may not be riding the wave of the moment, but one of the things that should buoy the movement in difficult times is the record of its past achievements.

The gains the media-reform groups have made may seem minimal to some, but they cannot be called inconsequential. They cracked open a closed legal system. "The media-reform movement has had a tremendous impact in the FCC," says former commissioner Tyrone Brown. "If it weren't for them the commission would not have included the public in any way in its deliberations."

As he pointed out in a 1979 speech to the NBMC, "The general public needs to be reminded of the major role public interest groups have played. For example, a public interest group (OC/UCC) won the right of listener and viewer groups to petition for denial of broadcast licenses at renewal time, and initiated the proceeding that led to the commission's policy and rules on affirmative-action employment in the broadcast industry."

Pluria Marshall's NBMC spearheaded the drive that led to FCC's adopting tax-certificate and distress-sales policies, which facilitate minority ownership. He believes blacks have made "some progress" in employment in the industry. An increase of about 8 to 9 percent since 1973, he estimates. But "the behind-the-scenes jobs are where we're getting our butts kicked," he says. "In management the least progress has been made in news: news directors, executive producers, assignment editors."

Black progress in employment in the broadcast industry is currently being "somewhat stymied," says Marshall, because white women are being hired instead of blacks. "The women's movement is not helping black folks," he says. "If anything, it's hurting them—in broadcasting that's for sure."

"I can name you a dozen or so women news directors and maybe fifty or so women program managers and a few women owners and a couple of station managers, but it's token," says Kathy Bonk, who doesn't think women have come such a long way since NOW got the FCC to amend its Equal Employment Opportunity rules to include women in 1971. It can't be denied, however, that the gains for women in on-air representation over the past decade have been dramatic.

"When we started this," Bonk says, "there were no women on-air as network reporters, no women in sports anywhere, no news about women. After we filed against NBC, they put on *Police Woman*, the first major prime-time network program that had a woman in a leading, dominant role."

Increased broadcaster sensitivity to stereotyping women and other minority groups can be counted a victory for media reformers. So can a number of improvements in children's television, such as the reduction of advertising on children's weekend television by 40 percent.

For the thirty-three million school-age television viewers in the U.S., many of whom spend more hours in front of the set than in the classroom, Action for Children's Television has been a force for eliminating commercial abuse and encouraging diverse programming. "The genius of Peggy Charren," according to Frank Lloyd, "is that she has evolved a carrot-and-stick strategy. She goes to great lengths to give positive feedback. It has become a source of pride for a broadcaster or cable company to win one of ACT's annual 'Achievement in Children's Television Awards.' "

"People give public television credit for changing children's programming for the better," comments Charren, "but public television only released other broadcasters from the responsibility. If it hadn't been for public pressure nothing would have been done."

Most likely, neither would anything have been done about increasing news and public affairs programming, initiating government funding of public television, opening up public television's board meetings to the public, televising Presidential debates—all of which can be credited to the public interest movement in broadcasting, as can efforts to block mergers that would lead to monopoly.

One such effort, a recent legal action by the National Citizens Committee for Broadcasting to foil a General Electric-Cox merger, precipitated a quarrel within the movement. Because GE and Cox had agreed to spin off some stations into black ownership, National Black Media Coalition was willing to have them merge. In this instance, the goals of NCCB and NBMC were different, but that is not so unusual. From time to time the groups will get together in loose coalitions, but basically, as Media Access Project's Schwartzman phrased it, "we cherish our diversity."

Another NCCB initiative that did not have unanimous support among the disparate groups, due to concerns about censorship, was an attempt to reduce violence on television by monitoring shows, identifying the ten with the most acts of violence, and then putting pressure on the companies whose commercials accompanied these shows. NCCB's strategy, which won the cooperation of national organizations like the Parent-Teachers Association and the American Medical Association, and resulted in the disappearance of some targeted programs, was the brainchild of Nicholas Johnson, chairman of NCCB before it moved under the umbrella of Ralph Nader's organization.

Johnson, a maverick FCC commissioner in the sixties and now head of a group called National Citizens Communications Lobby, is the most unreservedly enthusiastic member of the media-reform movement when it comes to rating the movement's achievements. "In the fifteen years from 1965 to 1980," he says, "we accomplished what we set out to accomplish in that we now have media reform firmly ensconsed right in the center of middle America. We expanded from groups specifically interested in media reform into major organizations like AFL-CIO, the Roman Catholic Church, PTA. You can go all across the country now and find innovative things that have been done in terms of improving children's programming, reducing commercials, or increasing public-affairs programming. People's consciousness has been raised."

Johnson's brand of euphoria is not the dominant mood, however. For most of the groups it is not a time of exuberant self-congratulation. It is, instead, a time of reassessment. It could also be called a time of floundering.

Kathy Bonk categorizes the media-reform groups' current discussions as "positive." "We're trying to get some vision in this movement again," she says. Many veterans would agree with Wisconsin's Timothy Haight that "the movement is on the defensive," struggling to preserve former gains in a hostile environment. They would also agree with Engsberg of the Telecommunications Consumer Coalition that, though the first job of the public interest groups may still be to make sure *all* the rules don't get taken away, the next job is to get into more creative roles.

With its focus on a new technology and grass-roots work in local communities, the National Federation of Local Cable Programmers (NFLCP), formed in 1976 to promote and protect public access to cable around the country, seems to be on the right track. "Fortunately, we did a better propaganda job than we knew," says George Stoney, one of the group's founders and co-director of New York University's Alternate Media Center. "There isn't a city council in the country that would give out a cable-franchise contract that didn't have access written into it."

But cable isn't necessarily the promised land. "Cable is simply a useful rehearsal ground," Stoney says. "We need public access to all electronic media."

In the summer of 1980, Congressman Van Deerlin, sometime opponent of the groups on media issues, urged the movement to come to grips with current realities before it was too late. Pointing·out in *access* that the combining of the telephone with computer, satellite, and broadcast technologies would transform American lives, Van Deerlin wrote: "Technological change and industry reorganization raises a host of vexing policy problems. For example, what public interest responsibilities accrue to a direct satellite-to-home broadcaster? What First Amendment restrictions, if any, should be imposed on an electronic publisher? What common-carrier obligations should be assumed by a cable-television operator who offers data transmission or other information services?

"While the media-reform movement concentrates its effort on blocking radio deregulation and imposing new rules on children's television," Van Deerlin warned, "it is missing an excellent opportunity to shape the new telecommunications industry."

Many of those in and out of government pushing for deregulation believe that the proliferating new media are going to solve all the problems. But the new media will by no means assure diversity. All the electronic media are awesome tools of power. Whoever can dominate them can determine not only how people spend their money, but also what ideas people are exposed to, the decisions they make based on these ideas, and ultimately the political process.

Are the groups of the old media-reform movement capable of leading the fight to assure that all electronic communications truly serve a diverse public, and are not monopolized to serve narrow interests? Can they tackle such a monumental job in their present fragile condition? The corporations interested in shaping the new telecommunications industry are certainly not going to welcome them onto the field of battle. And these corporations seem to have momentum on their side.

The imbalance is tremendous, especially now, between the public interest groups in broadcasting and their opponents, the well-financed, politically influential companies who would gobble up the entire communications pie solely for profit. "It's David and Goliath," says George Stoney. The analogy sounds like an admission of defeat. Until you remember who won that one.

15 · THE CHARGE OF THE RIGHT BRIGADE

BY ROBERT BECKER, JUDY KANTROWITZ, CONRAD
MACKERRON, NICK RAVO AND SUSIE SMITH

Being able to control the mass media has become an
important issue for nearly every institution in our
society, particularly (but not limited to) those with a
political mission. Right-wing political groups have
been extremely active in pressuring the media, as this
essay demonstrates. But they are by no means alone
in their attempts to influence media decision making.
Robert Becker, Judy Kantrowitz, Conrad MacKerron,
Nick Ravo and Susie Smith were graduate students at
the American University School of Communications
when this article was written under the direction of
Professor Richard T. Stout. It is reprinted from the
Washington Journalism Review, November 1981.

For years, politicians and pundits of the right have bemoaned "liberal bias" in the media. From the McCarthy era through Spiro Agnew's attacks on the "nattering nabobs of negativism" to the rise of the Reverend Jerry Falwell, staunch conservatives always felt maligned and under-represented in the press.

In recent years, however, virtually unnoticed by political and media analysts, the New Right has built its own alternative press, moving from newsletters to newspapers, from mimeo to video, as a way of gaining influence and respectability.

Today, the New Right press wields widespread influence in small towns and in Washington. It even has its own tax-exempt school of journalism—the National Journalism Center—located just five blocks from Capitol Hill.

Unseen and unpublicized for the most part, the New Right press played a key role in conservative gains in the 1980 elections. The networks, wire services, news magazines, and major newspapers focused on the extensive fund-raising and virulent anti-Carter commercials of the New Right and Moral Majority, while ignoring or giving short shrift to the unifying thread of New Right publications that constantly reinforced the messages of the more visible campaigns. "By use of their literature, they set the public mind to the point that people will believe that the key issues are those determined by the New Right, no matter what issues the candidate wants to discuss," says George Cunningham, director of George McGovern's Americans for Common Sense, created after the election to combat the New Right.

Cunningham follows the New Right press assiduously, as do a growing number of liberals. At least one major union, the International Association of Machinists and Aerospace Workers, has a staffer who monitors organs of the New Right and other anti-labor groups. Some Iowa liberals this year began issuing a monthly newsletter, "Watch on the Right," to chart budding strategies and developments that may guide future campaigns to unseat moderates and liberals. Wesley McCune, who has monitored conservative publications for the past 19 years as director of the Washington-based Group Research, Inc., says today's proliferation of right-wing publications has never been greater. Even some representatives of the New Right are astounded. "Four years ago, I could count on one hand the newsletters that dealt with social issues from a Christian viewpoint," says William Billings, editor of "Alert," a well-established evangelical New Right newsletter. "Now there are about 160 groups, and many have their own newsletters."

Indeed, the bedrock of the New Right press is the burgeoning number of single and multi-issue letters that unite their readers around social and moral issues in the fervent tones of pre-Revolution pamphleteers.

With names like "Point Blank," "Moral Majority Report," "Roundtable Report," "Family Protection Report," and the "New Right Report," the newsletters are spin-offs of pamphlets, handbills, and direct mail that right-wing zealots in the past typed on kitchen tables and mimeographed in church basements.

Individually, they are not impressive. But collectively, they constitute a potent political force. Their readership is mostly the already committed. "You don't create something out of a vacuum," observes McCune of Group Research. "You've got to have something for the troops to read."

What the troops read in the newsletters, magazines, and newspapers amounts to a steady drumbeat of opposition to certain issues the New Right deems detrimental to society—the decline of the family, women's rights, and gun control. Consider these examples:

• "Family Protection Report," published by Paul Weyrich, director of the Committee for the Survival of a Free Congress, alerts grassroots activists to "family issues" under consideration by Congress, the White

House, or state legislatures. The 12-page monthly newsletter, circulating to 14,000 subscribers, blasts sex education and abortion while applauding prayer in the school and the catch-all bill for the pro-family movement, the Family Protection Act.

- "The Right Woman," published monthly by conservative pro-family activist JoAnn Gasper, reports on government's "intrusion" into family affairs, devoting most attention to the status of congressional legislation. Gasper, considered a prime mover in the pro-family coalition, links "equality" and "women's rights" with feminist attempts to change radically social values and family life.

- "New Right Report," published twice monthly by New Right paterfamilias Richard Viguerie, keeps political activists informed of legislative and political developments. Since the 1980 elections, the 4,000-circulation newsletter has harped on ways to "defund the left" by targeting groups for extinction, such as Legal Services Corp., and by trying to derail Thomas P. ("Tip") O'Neill's (D-Mass.) reelection as House speaker.

- "Political Gun News," another Viguerie publication, boosts the repeal of all gun control laws. A recent "quote of the month" in the 4,000-circulation newsletter came from Senator Strom Thurmond (R-S.C.): "I've got my gun ready if anybody comes to get me in my house."

- *National Educator,* published by James H. Townsend in Fullerton, Calif., is in its thirteenth year of disseminating right-wing views. The 16-page monthly has a worldwide circulation of 65,000, according to Townsend. Public schools and Israel are only two of the publication's frequent targets. Wesley McCune says Townsend is "far, radical right," and that the *Educator* "is a real mish mash of stuff—anti-abortion, anti-pornography, and anti-communist, of course."

Publications of the new Christian Right are also plentiful. Consider these:

- *Moral Majority Report,* the Reverend Falwell's monthly tabloid, reaches 560,000 readers. The 20-plus-page newspaper covers timely political and social issues with more depth than most New Right publications, but also with a dose of extremism. The *Report* recently reprinted a U.S. Labor Party article linking *Playboy* magazine and the National Organization for the Reform of Marijuana Laws to a bizarre conspiracy to return society "to a new dark age."

Dr. Stan Hasty, information director of the Baptist Joint Committee for Public Affairs, calls Falwell's views a "gross distortion of the gospel" and his newspaper a mere "pep sheet" for Falwell's outbursts on the nation's moral agenda.

- "Alert," edited and published by William Billings of the National Christian Action Coalition in Washington, D.C., "protects, preserves, and promotes" the Christian home, school, and church in America. Billings has fashioned a New Right press network of sorts by channeling press releases, newspaper clippings, and other political information to New Right activists' groups across the country. "We are not ridiculed as much as we are ignored, so we have our own underground press to get the word out," Billings says.

- "Roundtable Report," a four-page newsletter published monthly by Ed McAteer, president of the Religious Roundtable in Arlington, Va., reminds its 7,000 subscribers about the "moral" side of issues and teaches them rudimentary political skills, such as how to address letters to legislators or determine the status of bills. "Its purpose is to educate people, not convert them," McAteer contends. A biblical quote hanging on the wall behind his desk reflects that philosophy: " 'My people are destroyed for a lack of knowledge'—Hosea Chapter 4:6."

- "Legislative Alert," a one-page newsletter published by the Christian Voice in California, is distributed to 40,000 ministers throughout the country. The ministers, in turn, are encouraged to crank out mimeographed reprints of the newsletter and distribute them to their flocks each Sunday. While claiming to have helped turn the evangelical vote for Reagan, Phil Sheldon, national field director for the Voice, admits his publication "is just a part of a larger effort to mobilize support for candidates deemed most representative of Christian moral values."

The political message to Christian followers is limited only by Internal Revenue Service restrictions. Since most enjoy a tax-exempt status, the religious wings of the New Right press can lobby only for issues, not specific candidates.

The *Moral Majority Report* typifies how New Right publications can sidestep that limitation. One article may tell what the "moral" side of an issue is, while a companion piece identifies the candidates on the moral side. The decision of whom to vote for is left to the reader, but the implication is obvious.

The flagship of the New Right press is the 70,000 circulation *Conservative Digest*. Edited by former Republican National Committee staffer John Lofton and published by Richard Viguerie, the *Digest* is a glossy, literate magazine that is beginning to compete with mainstream conservative publications such as *National Review* and *Human Events* for influence, prestige, and power. It has also become must-reading for reporters and congressional aides of all political persuasions eager to keep an eye on the New Right.

The *Digest*, a monthly, covers a wide range of national and international issues, and differs from most other New Right publications in its ability to attract commercial advertising. (Among its most faithful advertisers are a manufacturer of orthopedic shoes and a publishing house owned by the John Birch Society.)

The *Digest* also manages to attract the full constellation of New Right political leaders as contributing columnists. In addition to Lofton and Viguerie, the *Digest* regularly features Conservative Caucus director Howard Phillips, National Conservative Political Action Committee (NCPAC) chief John T. (Terry) Dolan, Phyllis Schlafly, Falwell, Gasper, and Weyrich.

What also sets *Conservative Digest* apart is its reach into the White House. Morton Blackwell, a Reagan liaison to special interest groups, and Lyn Nofziger, top presidential political adviser, are both former *Conservative Digest* contributing editors.

The *Digest* exemplifies the differences between the New Right and the William F. Buckley school of mainstream conservatism. The magazine and its New Right allies spearhead the drive for social conservatism, the family protection issues, and the opposition to gun control. *National Review* and *Human Events* more often emphasize foreign and economic issues, and usually shun the rhetoric of proselytizing and goading to action. Most issues of *Conservative Digest* carry a signed Viguerie editorial telling readers how to influence an election or promote a cause.

Though the New Right constantly fumes at the regular news media's "liberal-leftist" bias, the media's lavish coverage of the New Right during and since the presidential campaign has made the task of the New Right press easier.

"To some degree, the New Right was early given a size and influence greater than the facts warranted," admits Conservative Caucus director Howard Phillips.

Phillips's comments may be true about the New Right press as well. Some evidence suggests that these publications are nothing more than the bull horn of conservative political and religious movements. None is a money-making proposition. Some are financed through paid subscriptions, but subscription rates barely cover the cost of production. Interestingly, many New Right publications are wholly or partially subsidized by the fund-raising efforts of larger foundations and politicial organizations. For instance, despite *Conservative Digest*'s $15-a-year subscription fee and substantial advertising revenues, Viguerie still subsidizes a third of the $900,000-a-year cost of producing his magazine by pumping in profits from his multi-million-dollar direct mail house, Viguerie Co. Other Viguerie publications, including the "New Right Report," also lose $40,000 to $50,000 a year and manage to stay in print only because of a hefty transfusion of Viguerie Co. money. Subscriptions to "Political Gun News," another Viguerie offspring, sell for $24. No figures are available on its financial status.

At least two New Right publications have ties, one close, one loose, to Richard Scaife, a prominent sugar daddy to New Right causes and publications. Over the past eight years, both personally and through family foundations and trusts—including Carthage and Sarah Scaife Foundation and the Grandchildren of Sarah Mellon Scaife—Scaife has contributed millions to conservative groups.

Weyrich's Free Congress and Education Foundation is one benefactor of Scaife's generosity, receiving at least $700,000 since 1977. Interestingly, one of the Free Congress Foundation's endeavors is to publish the "Family Protection Report." According to Weyrich, in 1980 the Free Congress Foundation offset $46,000 in paper and printing costs for the "Family Protection Report."

Christian Voice, which publishes "Legislative Alert," also receives financial help from Scaife. According to Sandy Otsby, an executive director for the organization, Scaife's name is among 327,000 Christian Voice contributors who subsidize the cost of reproducing its one-page newsletter. "But he's not a major contributor," Mrs. Otsby points out, saying Scaife has donated no more than $100 or $500 "from time to time." The religious organization spent nearly $15,000 of its $750,000 budget reproducing "Legislative Alert" during the past year.

The "Moral Majority Report" also circulates free of charge. The parent corporation, Moral Majority, Inc., with its 1981 budget of $4 million, pays the full cost of production. Who actually pays is kept secret. Moral Majority, Inc., refuses to publish a list of contributors.

Several other New Right publishers charge a subscription fee that fully covers the cost of production. However, unlike other commercial publications like *Time* and *Newsweek,* they are not in business to turn a profit.

The "Roundtable Report" sells for $15 a year. But "Roundtable Report" editor Ed Rowe stresses, "This is not a money-making thing; the $15 subscription fee covers the cost of publishing it. We are not operating to make a profit. We are operating to inform people. It is information, motivation, and training for responsible citizenship."

William Billings' "Alert" is another publication in this category. "Alert"'s $10 subscription covers the cost of printing and first-class mailing, but little else.

Only one New Right publication, the "Right Woman," which is available for $28 a year, is self-supporting, receiving no financial support from a political or religious organization.

Nonetheless, the expansive credence given the New Right by the establishment press has been a boon especially for the growing number of conservative columnists. R. Emmett Tyrell, Jr., editor of the conservative *American Spectator,* now writes a weekly column for the *Washington Post* and is showing up in an ever-increasing number of other newspapers.

Conservative Digest editor John Lofton's feisty column sells well, as does cohort Patrick Buchanan's. Distributed by the Chicago Tribune-New York News Syndicate, Buchanan's column now appears in 120 newspapers, ten of which picked it up after the 1980 elections.

Phyllis Schlafly's column, which soared in popularity in the 1960s, is holding steady. Copley News Service distributes it as part of a package to about 700 papers. Kevin Phillips, another favorite among New Rightists, currently appears in 100 newspapers, and a column by National Journalism Center headmaster M. Stanton Evans runs in 40 papers, mostly in the Midwest, where he was once editor of the conservative *Indianapolis News.*

In fact, New Right and conservative columnists may now be in oversupply. "There is an absolute glut of conservative columnists out there," says Colman McCarthy, liberal columnist for the *Washington Post.*

In an effort to balance the more heavily conservative tone on many editorial pages, many editors say they are now looking high and low for new liberal commentators. McCarthy, for one, is benefiting; since Ronald Reagan's election the list of newspapers carrying his column has increased significantly.

Not satisfied with gains in taming the supposedly liberal regular media, the American Conservative Union's Education and Research Institute operates the National Journalism Center, headed by Evans. Over a 12-week course, young conservatives learn the "right" way to tell the news.

While the New Right press has yet to develop a television news arm, that medium is not being ignored. NCPAC's Terry Dolan now hosts a weekly *Today-*style program spouting New Right perspectives. He funds it with donations channeled through his National Conservative Foundation.

Pat Robertson's evangelical broadcasting network produces a daily Christian TV soap opera, *Another Life,* which made its debut last June in 37 markets. Paul Weyrich puts his pro-family stamp of approval on the show. "Instead of soap opera characters tripping out on drugs and incest, they find moral solutions to their problems."

But the heart of the New Right press remains its network of newsletters and a few magazines led by *Conservative Digest.* Many editors and publishers of the New Right seem to yearn for even broader respectability than election of a conservative president bequeathed them. Viguerie tried to buy several established, large-circulation, conservative publications, including Reagan-favorite *Human Events,* but failed. At the same time, he has urged a new "positive attitude" toward the rest of the media. Yet Falwell and *New Right Report* editor James Martin declined to be interviewed for this article. Lofton failed to return a dozen calls made to his office.

And Martin's March 13 *New Right Report* warned that the "left will try to choke us off by changing postal rates and tax laws. . . . We must develop our own for-profit publications."

Despite its Reagan-era respectability, the New Right still reflects its old style paranoia. That is a characteristic no amount of growth and success will easily erase from the New Right press.

16 · WHO'S WATCHING THE WATCHDOG?

BY NEIL D. SWAN

Neil D. Swan describes a number of media reformers and pressure groups, including the National News Council (which has since gone out of business because it wasn't having much impact). Are they serving any purpose? In the 1980s, an increasing number of people think they are not and that the best watchdog of the press is the press itself. Swan is a staff writer for *presstime*, the monthly magazine of the American Newspaper Publishers Association. This article is reprinted from *presstime*, February 1984.

Americans have long had a love-hate relationship with their press but, at last look at the scoreboard, hate seemed to be inching up. And, as a result of recent events, more and more people are asking: Who watches the media?

Who even *tries* to keep tabs on the news media, the least regulated of all American institutions?

Recent events underscore the fact that virtually everyone who reads publications, listens to radio or watches TV monitors the performance of newspapers, magazines and broadcasters. But the fact that there is no coordination, no formalization and no enforcement powers in America's many media-monitoring efforts may lead to public frustrations that could prove troublesome for the press, some observers feel.

So who's watching the watchdog of the public interest?

Everyone. And no one.

Everyone's watching, yes, but no one—in or out of the media—appears satisfied with the process.

Many publishers and editors, wire service executives and broadcast journalists admit they were stunned at the anti-media sentiment expressed in the public's reaction to the Grenada news blackout. Countless Americans expressed outright glee at the frustrations of the media.

People in the press say they've heard it all before. The complaints against the media are, to many newspeople, hackneyed cliches. And many print journalists lay a large share of the blame on TV news, with its heavy emotional impact, its graphic view of sometimes-obnoxious reporters pestering people, and its dramatic intrusion into the viewer's home and family life. But to millions of Americans, these complaints are not trite cliches; they are the truth, as they gauge it as viewers, listeners and readers.

Grenada was simply the flashpoint.

And when the smoke had cleared, public opinion polls showed that a large number of Americans supported the blackout.

Although many people opposed the blackout, too, Grenada left a widespread perception that the rift between the press and the people it seeks to serve was very deep, with ominous and serious implications. And it proved that—whether or not the media are aware of it on a day-to-day basis—millions of Americans are watching them, with intense, emotional interest.

"I sometimes think half the American population considers themselves media experts," says Ben H. Bagdikian, writer on media issues and professor at the Graduate School of Journalism at the University of California at Berkeley. "But most of them just don't have the standards for valid criticism of the media."

"Everybody's watching the media, but there is no coordination of the efforts or the criticism," says Norman E. Isaacs, former editor of *The Courier-Journal* in Louisville. "It's scattered and kind of anarchic. But you wouldn't want it to be unified, anyway. That would be un-American. I do think the press is in trouble, though."

"The public is monitoring the press, and that is important," says Charles B. Seib, a retired editor who, like Bagdikian, once served as ombudsman for *The Washington Post*. "People really care about their newspaper. It becomes a part of their lives when it comes into their homes every day. And they become upset when they feel their newspaper is letting them down. But that's a healthy situation."

"Everybody watches us," says Jean H. Otto, editorial page editor of Denver's *Rocky Mountain News* and chairman of the First Amendment Congress, a media group dedicated to defending freedom of the press. "Everybody who watches TV and who reads the paper has views on our performance. But too often those views are not based on actual knowledge. They may be a gut reaction."

"Public opinion is the watchdog of the American media," says *New York Times* media reporter Jonathan Friendly. "The readers know us. Somehow the word gets around, (and) impressions are formed on our credibility.

"Of course, constitutionally, we are not supposed to have a media 'monitor' in this country," Friendly continues. "A monitor implies some sort of power that can be imposed, and it's hard to imagine any institution imposing powers on our media other than through intellectual or economic means."

Within the limitations of the First Amendment, however, there are groups and institutions that have assumed the role of trying, at least, to watch and critique the American media. They include ad-hoc groups, permanent organizations, professors, specialized publications and the media themselves.

Citizen's Choice The latest entry among watchdog watchers is the Citizen's Choice National Commission on Free and Responsible Media, an imposing panel which is holding public hearings in a half-dozen cities and which will issue a report this summer on its findings concerning the relationship between the media and various aspects of society [*presstime,* Jan. 1984, p. 43].

"We have proven to people that this is not a sham job," says Thomas J. Donohue, president of Citizen's Choice, a 75,000-member taxpayers' lobby affiliated with the U.S. Chamber of Commerce. "We have had strong witnesses, and we are getting a body of information that can be the basis for, perhaps, a series of monographs that would include our witnesses' testimony and, separately, our observations on the testimony."

Donohue says the commission's observations on the media will receive extensive distribution through the vast resources of the Chamber of Commerce.

So far, however, the nation's media have not shown a great deal of interest in the commission or in covering its hearings, although prominent representatives of the press are participating in them.

According to staff members, the commission's "basic goal is to channel discussion on the media's role in American society in a constructive direction. The commission is not interested in laws or regulations governing the press, nor does it want to tell the media how to conduct their business. Rather, it intends to provide a forum on the state of the media for some of the best thinkers on the subject today."

The commission will terminate after making its report.

National News Council The organization most frequently cited as an active, self-assigned watchdog of the media is the National News Council. It was created in 1973 to investigate complaints about controversial publishing or broadcasting decisions, and to determine and publicly report on whether those decisions were proper and responsible.

The council is voluntary, with no power of enforcement over the media it watches.

"The National News Council is victimized by the fact that most editors and news directors are so opposed to it that they don't see any news in its findings, and they fail to report those findings," says former Louisville editor Isaacs, who headed the council for six years.

"Most newspapers don't bother to publish News Council findings, and most people outside the profession—and a great many inside it—don't even know it exists," observes *Los Angeles Times* media reporter David Shaw.

"The council has minimal impact, I'm afraid," says Hodding Carter, host of the Public Broadcasting program "Inside Story" that focuses on media issues. Carter, who was a member of the commission that called for the council's creation, adds, "The council has (been) semi-strangulated because the press is not overwhelming in covering it. The first knife stuck in the council was the refusal of the *New York Times* to cooperate."

In an effort to win greater acceptance and cooperation from the media, the News Council is in the process of being restructured.

The 18-member panel, composed of eight news professionals and 10 non-journalists, is being supplanted by a two-level governing structure: a board of perhaps seven trustees, composed primarily of non-journalist "public" members; and a council, composed of 11 to 13 members, primarily journalists. The trustees will focus on management and fundraising matters. The council will review complaints independent of the trustees.

Membership of the new board of trustees and council is not expected to be announced before April.

The News Council's president and chief executive officer, Richard S. Salant, sees this "significant" restructuring as the key to making the council work as it was conceived 10 years ago by the sponsoring Twentieth Century Fund. "It's a response to my own feeling that the press would cooperate much more willingly if it felt it was being reviewed by its peers" instead of outsiders, no matter how respected and independent-minded those outsiders might be, he says. "We'll never get support from news people unless they feel it's their peers judging them."

The council's annual budget, already expanded from $300,000 to $549,000, should be further increased to $750,000 "to get the job done," Salant believes. Plans call for a larger staff and the hiring of "academics and outside consultants" to assist in reviewing complaints in specific localities. Also planned is the preparation of "white papers" on common ethical questions, "but not an effort to set down rules," he says.

Yet even with these changes, the council may still find itself lacking widespread media support.

"Any outside organization that sets itself up as a watchdog of the media is immediately placed in a suspect status by those it is monitoring," explains Isaacs. "The National News Council is looked on with disfavor because it is seen by editors as too independent and because, if it works, its role could be taken over by the government."

In Canada, the news council concept is more firmly established, due largely to the specter of government action. The Trudeau government in 1983 proposed, but recently dropped, the idea of controlling mergers in the newspaper industry through legislation. However, there is still interest in a legislative approach to starting a national press council to deal with complaints about newspapers.

Meanwhile, Canada's voluntary, provincial press councils—which have proliferated in the last couple of years in an effort to head off the possibility of government action—are working to arrange a federation, either formally or informally.

At a meeting in October of representatives of the existing six press councils—including journalists, academics and politicians—it was charged that the voluntary councils are controlled by newspaper publishers and therefore may not fully serve the public's needs in responding to complaints. But supporters of the councils and of the effort to form a federation say voluntary press councils are nevertheless more desirable than a federally appointed and controlled council.

Special Interests   While news councils get some attention within the news business in North America, few self-appointed watchdogs of the media attract more attention from the public than Accuracy in Media, a politically conservative group. Many editors express hostility toward Washington, D.C.-based AIM and its outspoken chairman, Reed Irvine. But the group is sometimes cited as a media watchdog with at least some effectiveness, perhaps because AIM is unique in its status. AIM's conservative political leaning is no secret, and it differs from other interest groups in having a continuing, regularly scheduled voice in scrutinizing actions of the nation's print and broadcast media.

"I think AIM has some impact, and I think its activities are not a bad thing for the press," says Richard Reeves, syndicated columnist and author of the 1982 book *American Journey: Traveling with Toqueville in Search of Democracy in America.*

Some other observers disagree. "The AIM people take themselves so seriously," says Daniel Machalaba, until recently the media reporter of *The Wall Street Journal.* "They don't realize they lose credibility by nitpicking and harping on small points in their criticism."

Comments former *Washington Post* ombudsman Seib: "Reed Irvine is bright, and he works hard at what he does. Sometimes he's effective in spite of himself, but when he does latch onto a legitimate point in his criticism of the press, he tends to distort it."

AIM's criticisms are termed "pernicious" by author-professor Bagdikian, who adds that its "accusations are frequently not a good representation of the facts."

Organizations representing the interests of women, blacks, ethnic groups, Jews, the "Moral Majority" and others also critique the media. But they do so sporadically and largely on matters affecting their limited areas of special interest. Also, their criticism tends to be overwhelmingly focused on TV reporting, not published material.

"I guess we are pretty much alone out there," says AIM's Irvine. "There's room for a lot more of what we do because the media are too big. I don't feel we are doing all that much to keep up with the big media."

According to Irvine, AIM operates on an annual budget of $1.5 million, including donations of about $100,000 a year from the Scaife Family Charitable Trust and $75,000 a year from the Shelby Cullom Davis Foundation. Some 30,000 Americans pay $15 or more a year to subscribe to the *AIM Report,* a twice-monthly newsletter which recently stated that the "knock-American media seem not to understand what . . . hit them" after they "tried to stir up a little public hostility to the government by denouncing the military ban on reporters covering the troops" in Grenada.

AIM also produces a "Media Monitor" radio program that is carried as a public service message by about 65 stations, and a weekly column that is made available to and is published by about 100 newspapers, the largest of which is *The Detroit News.*

Also standing pretty much unique and alone but highly visible as a self-appointed media monitor is the Mobil Corp., which regularly critiques the media in newspaper ads and elsewhere.

"Herb Schmertz (Mobil's vice president for public affairs) is very talented, and he knows how to present an argument forcefully," says *New York Times* media reporter Friendly. "Does he convince people? No more so than an editorial. But he does focus public attention on the issues he selects.

"The Mobil ads certainly are timely, but I don't see anyone else (in the corporate world) joining Mobil in what they're trying to do," Friendly adds. "The (Mobil) ads may have the effect of making the press more careful in what it does," says Isaacs, "but I wish the thrust of the ads was not so antagonistic."

Academia, Reviews, Others   At perhaps the other end of the spectrum from skyscraper scrutiny of the media is the criticism emanating from the halls of ivy—journalism schools and their professors, candidates for advanced degrees and their research efforts, scholars, authors and others. The impact of this academic oversight is limited, however, according to most observers.

"There's so little traffic between academics and working journalists," says Seib. "Sometimes I see good material turned up in journalism reviews which gets very little attention in the real world."

"I wish I felt they (journalism reviews) had a more important role, but I just don't see it," says columnist Reeves.

"The journalism reviews tend to go to people in the journalism schools," notes media reporter Friendly. "The J-schools may take on a local TV station or newspaper for some valid, thoughtful criticism. But I have trouble finding academics who have good sources for criticizing the press in general, not just some limited local example."

A New York colleague has a different view. "I turn to academics and journalism reviews and find them helpful and insightful," says Machalaba of *The Wall Street Journal,* who has just moved to another beat on the paper.

Over the years, journalism reviews have come (*Washington Journalism Review*) and gone (*MORE*), but only a few have stayed for any length of time (*Columbia Journalism Review*).

Dr. Richard A. Schwarzlose, professor at the Medill School of Journalism at Northwestern University, feels J-schools and journalism reviews have lost influence in the last few years because "we seem to have crawled more comfortably into the industry's lap."

Journalism schools should be a major influence in media-watching, he says, but faculties—confronted with large enrollments, decreasing resources and increasing workloads—"get burned out in class." Many of the journalism reviews were established in the late 1960s and early '70s when "journalism education was not ready to rise to the occasion" and, as a result, many of the reviews "got a bad rap early on when they seemed to be the province of radicals," says Schwarzlose.

Although there may be little widespread reading of scholarly reviews, the public does avidly read and learn about the media from such best-selling books as David Halberstam's *The Powers That Be,* Gay Talese's *The Kingdom and the Glory,* Barbara Matusou's *The Evening Stars* and Ben Bagdikian's *The Media Monopoly.*

"The books show that people like to know how we in the media operate, as long as it's presented in an interesting fashion. But then, that often turns the spotlight away from more serious questions like ethics," notes Friendly.

Still another outlet for limited, largely locally focused media criticism is the non-establishment press—including some remnants of what was once called the "underground" press. Some of these, like the *Village Voice,* now plump with advertising, might not fit everyone's idea of non-establishment, but many obviously relish the opportunity to critique the news operations of the big dailies and the TV stations in their cities. "They're always jumping up and down and screaming about 'The Story You Didn't Read in the Daily Newspaper Because It Was Suppressed,' " notes Friendly.

There are those who cite the courts as another institution monitoring, or restraining to some extent, the activities of the media.

"Libel cases, or the threat of them, obviously have a monitoring effect on the press," says Friendly. "But most people in the media can live with the situation. It's only the really bad cases that get punished."

Of course, the First Amendment being what it is, courts, judges and juries do not actively seek a media-watchdog role. Except for occasional actions by prosecutors, courts enter the picture only in response to petitions from the public. But it's also instructive for the press to bear in mind that the public's representatives in the courtroom—the jurors— are the ones who are handing down the huge libel judgments against the press.

Self-Assessment   Most Americans' awareness of media monitoring probably comes from the media themselves. In various ways, from ombudsmen to "media" columns, some news organizations look critically at what they do.

There are many who feel, however, that the various elements of the press and their professional societies should do a great deal more in examining their activities and those of other publications, broadcast stations or networks.

Television, despite its pervasiveness in today's society and the amount of broadcast time it devotes to news and public affairs, is especially lacking in media reporting and criticism. Compared with the enormous amount of space the print media now devote to reporting on and criticizing television, TV coverage of any media is miniscule.

"I'm surprised that TV doesn't do more in this area," notes Carter of PBS, a one-time Mississippi newspaper editor. "I guess it's partly a 'Why rock the boat?' attitude and partly a recognition that media criticism is not exactly a mass audience grabber compared to a lot of other things TV does. And local TV is simply not in a position to take on the print media. It doesn't have the space, and there is just not all that much substance to local TV news. Besides, they (local TV stations) depend on the print media for reviews."

Bagdikian agrees: "Local TV is rather simple-minded. It would be hard to argue its importance as an American institution."

Some of the greatest attention TV has focused on the media recently has been from six shows, two on CBS and four on PBS, produced by Stuart Sucherman, Columbia University communications professor, lawyer and writer, and Fred W. Friendly, also a Columbia professor and former president of CBS News.

The shows were videotapes of Media and Society Seminars produced by the Columbia University Graduate School of Journalism, with Columbia professors serving as moderators and guiding dialogue on hypothetical questions about the print and broadcast media. The seminars involve a large panel of press luminaries—network news anchors and producers, news executives, newspaper editors and publishers—plus First Amendment lawyers and judges.

AIM's Irvine finds the seminars' courtroom-like, cross-examination format an "interesting approach, but (they) deal with hypothetical situations rather than the real world."

Although CBS has broadcast two of the seminars, the biggest complaints have been the devastating scheduling of the shows in what were among the worst possible viewing times.

Irvine points to ABC's "Viewpoint" series as a notable exception in effective self-criticism by network television. "The network puts its stars out there subject to some serious criticism." For example, when the Kaiser Aluminum Co. was unhappy about coverage of it on an ABC "20/20" segment, ABC scheduled an appearance by the reporter involved, Geraldo Rivera. " 'Nightline's' Ted Koppel did some serious questioning of Rivera, and as a result Kaiser was quite pleased it got its day in court," says Irvine.

George Watson, ABC News vice president in charge of the "Viewpoint" series, says he does not consider himself an "ombudsman" or "viewers' advocate," but it is his role to "ride herd on policies of good journalism" at ABC.

CBS News instituted a similar executive-review system after retired Army Gen. William Westmoreland filed a $120-million libel suit against the network. The suit is pending.

A few local TV news operations have tried media-monitoring activities, notably WHAS-TV in Louisville, where former newspaper ombudsman Bob Schulman began in 1981 to serve as media critic. But by and large, local TV avoids critiquing other local media, other than what PBS's Carter terms infrequent "nose-tweaking" by a TV station of the local newspaper for supposed errors or irregularities.

While it's true that ombudsmen are much more prevalent at newspapers than at TV news departments, it's equally true that only a small number of newspapers have such a "readers' advocate" to respond to complaints, look out for readers' rights, and monitor and critique the news operation.

The ombudsman concept is the news media's greatest commitment to self-examination. Its perception by readers as a genuine effort to provide quality news coverage while protecting average people from media abuse—intentional or accidental—is a tremendous source of credibility and respectability for those newspapers embracing the concept.

But the fact is, there just aren't very many papers willing to spend the time and effort to subject themselves to internally generated but publicly disseminated criticism [*presstime*, July, 1983, p. 44]. A recent survey showed only 32 ombudsmen serving 39 North American newspapers, meaning only one daily newspaper in 50 has a readers' advocate.

Shaw of the *Los Angeles Times* says too many editors dismiss suggestions they hire a readers' advocate with this attitude: "Any editor who can't make value judgments on his own—and make them correctly —is in the wrong job."

Some newspapers with ombudsmen, and some without, have reporters who cover the media as a beat. Examples include Shaw, Friendly of the *New York Times*, Machalaba of *The Wall Street Journal* and Tom Collins of *Newsday*. They believe more are needed.

"I wish more newspapers would hire somebody to do what I do," says Shaw. "We (the media) are such a powerful institution. We need desperately to focus more upon ourselves—to explain how news-gathering works."

"Inside Story's" Carter puts it this way: "I would like to see the day when we (in the media) treat each other the way we treat any other institution. The (New York) *Times* and the (Washington) *Post* will not hesitate to go after any other institution. But you don't see them going after each other that way. There's just not an adequate job of public monitoring of the media by its own elements. It's a gentlemen's club."

Benjamin C. Bradlee, executive editor of the *Post*, denies the "gentlemen's club" notion—particularly that the *Post* and the *Times* decline to go after one another.

The *Post*, which has not had a reporter assigned specifically to cover the media, will remedy that situation early this year, says Bradlee. And that reporter will 'damn sure" cover actions of the *New York Times*, he asserts.

At the *Times*, Friendly says that in his several years on the media beat, he has found that "people like to know how we operate." But he is somewhat bothered by the fact that a lot of his reportage "has economic roots rather than informational ones. . . . I'm amazed at how often I wind up quoting John Morton," a securities analyst specializing in newspaper properties.

The *Times* recently hired Greenville, Tenn., newspaper editor Alex S. Jones to cover the media for its business section.

Among the "must" reading for media reporters and ombudsmen alike are newspapers' letters-to-the-editor columns, where people disenchanted with media performance often vent their frustrations.

However, because of the heavy volume of letters and limited space in many metropolitan papers, not all letters make it into print. And those that do usually are edited. This can disappoint and further embitter readers.

At smaller newspapers, the problem is less severe. For example, the *Bluefield* (W. Va.) *Daily Telegraph* prints 95 percent of all signed letters it receives, according to Executive Editor Richard Wesley. "We run a full page of letters every Sunday, and it is very popular," he reports.

Also serving the function of providing readers' views, or reactions to them, are newspapers' corrections and apologies columns.

"People like to read corrections—they look for them—and they are a valuable means of maintaining credibility," comments Friendly.

Shaw of Los Angeles quotes research showing that about three-fourths of dailies over 100,000 circulation now run correction notices, up from only one-fourth 10 years ago. And he points out that papers are not just running more corrections, they are printing them in more prominent locations, often in a space regularly reserved for that purpose.

Owning up to mistakes is one way the media can help to overcome an image of arrogance and isolation. Taking additional steps to relate to readers, such as holding question-and-answer sessions with citizens and upholding standards of professional conduct, also can help.

"The media are not perceived by the public as 'friends' anymore," observes Shaw. "Most media people move in totally different circles than their readers or viewers. As a result, reporters and editors may not even be exposed to media criticism that is rampant right in their own backyard."

As for standards of conduct, a fair number of newspapers have adopted codes of ethics, as have professional organizations including the American Society of Newspaper Editors, the Associated Press Managing Editors Association and the Society of Professional Journalists, Sigma Delta Chi.

Most editors say they enforce their codes, but there is a reluctance to rely on them as hard-and-fast rules of the trade. It is feared that aggrieved parties could use written rules against the press in lawsuits or other action that could lead to government controls. Some editors have avoided codes because of this concern.

In another form of self-monitoring, industry groups like ASNE and APME are continually examining newspapers' editorial products.

"The main watchdog of the press, I suspect—and they don't get a great deal of attention—is the APME," says former editor Isaacs. The association conducts continuing studies and involves hundreds of editors in its committee work. "In the past 15 or 20 years, the APME has done a great deal to broaden and enhance the performance of the press," he says.

Bagdikian of Berkeley agrees and also notes that ASNE does an extensive but unheralded "periodic assessment" of the press that is "reliable and careful."

The *Times'* Friendly calls *The Bulletin* of ASNE one of the more

laudable "internal things" being done to critique newspapers' performance by drawing attention of senior editors to common issues.

More Monitoring?   But is all of this monitoring by people both inside
and outside the news business enough? Where is it leading?

Some journalists say that without adequate monitoring, the stage
could be set for eventual governmental intervention. "There's a definite
tendency around the world toward restricting the press," says media
critic Collins of *Newsday*. "The movement here under Ronald Reagan
is troublesome.

"I don't see a law being passed (limiting press freedoms), but it
could start with an executive order," he said. "That's the way freedom
in general is lost, little by little over a period of time."

Wesley of the 27,805-circulation *Bluefield Daily Telegraph* says that
while future government intervention into media activities is a "possibility," of more pressing concern, he feels, is the "loss of credibility" in
media grown remote from the public. "To a large extent, that loss of
credibility has already happened to the networks," he says.

For this reason, some smaller news organizations like his believe it
is prudent to distance themselves from the major media and their perceived evils.

"We're always editorializing about the left-wing, Eastern bias of the
mass media," says Wesley. "Our readers certainly don't think of us in
the same category as the network news."

Some other smaller dailies, while not editorializing against the
major media, distinctly feel and cherish the hometown support granted
them by their readers.

"They do see us in a different light than the national media," says
James D. Ewing, publisher of the *Keene* (N.H.) *Sentinel* (evening, circulation 13,740). "It's a personal relationship, a feeling of intimacy."

And from one corner of academia, concern has even given rise to
a challenge in the form of a "heresy." William R. Lindley, a one-time
newspaper editor who is now professor of journalism at Idaho State
University, says one way for the press to improve its standing with the
public is to expand upon the concept of an ethical code—perhaps by
adopting some form of certification for professional journalists.

"Professionalism means recognized standards and the disciplining
of unethical conduct," he says. "Licensing is foreign to our tradition; its
ready abuse by authoritarian governments makes it clearly unacceptable.

"But what about a national ANPA/ASNE exam, done by experts,
leading to a certificate which optionally could be used as part of the
hiring process, the certificate subject to suspension for unethical conduct?

"If the idea sounds heretical," he says, "let a (media) task force which can read public opinion as well as Ronald Reagan come up with something better. . . ."

Something better, in the view of SPJ,SDX, is to concentrate its efforts on the public rather than on the press. Disturbed by opinion polls showing that many Americans do not see how a free press is important to them personally, SPJ,SDX is planning an ambitious advertising and education campaign to convince citizens that any effort to place outside controls or limitations on the press is a definite threat to their individual rights.

"The theme will be, 'The watchdog may bark at the burglar but occasionally bite the postman by mistake. But if you put too many restrictions on the watchdog, you don't have any watchdog at all," says R.T. Kingman, chairman of the society's Watchdog Project. The group is seeking the assistance of the influential and powerful Advertising Council in spreading its message, due to peak in 1987, the bicentennial of the Constitution.

So, who's watching the media?

Everyone . . . and no one.

But are the media being *adequately* monitored?

Yes, says Bradlee of *The Washington Post:* "I can't think of another institution that examines itself with anywhere near the thoroughness we do. Where's the ombudsman in medicine or in business?"

No, says Northwestern's Schwarzlose: "We have new-found power and we don't know yet how to handle it. We have not yet found the proper monitoring mechanism. I'd hate to see it be the courts. . . ."

"In the last analysis, it comes down to the publishers, the owners and the directing editors," says Isaacs. "If we want a commitment to quality, that's where it'll come from."

FOR FURTHER READING

Lee Brown, *The Reluctant Reformation: On Criticizing the Press in America.* New York: McKay, 1974.

Commission on Freedom of the Press, *A Free and Responsible Press.* Chicago: University of Chicago Press, 1947.

William E. Hocking, *Freedom of the Press.* Chicago: University of Chicago Press, 1947.

A. J. Liebling, *The Press.* New York: Pantheon Books, 1975.

National News Council, *In the Public Interest.* New York: National News Council Inc., 1975.

Ithiel de Sola Pool, *Talking Back: Citizen Feedback and Cable Technology.* Cambridge, Mass.: The MIT Press, 1973.

William L. Rivers, *Back Talk: Press Councils in America.* San Francisco: Harper & Row (Canfield Press), 1973.

Fredrick Siebert, Theodore Peterson and Wilbur Schramm, *Four Theories of the Press.* Urbana, Ill.: University of Illinois Press, 1963.

V

Crime, Violence
and the Mass Media

THE WORDS *crime* and *violence* can quite easily prompt a variety of conjectures about what can be included in this chapter. Starting with *A*, arson is a crime that's covered by the mass media. So are robberies, murders and rapes; and as you read the words, you are probably picturing some degree or kind of violence you attach to each of them. If there's been a particularly gruesome robbery or murder reported in the news or described in a TV drama, that's what robbery or murder means for you right now. If you've watched a rough football game, perhaps that's violence to you. Or if you've been in that game, violence might be one particular tackle, done in sport but bruising nevertheless. Now that you have your own impression of crime and violence in mind, consider it as a possible issue involving the mass media.

Journalists know that people are interested in reports about crime. Sometimes news reports warn us to be more careful, sometimes they make us fearful or even frightened, sometimes they satisfy our streaks of morbid curiosity. Regardless, we pay attention to crime news; and it is often true that the more gruesome the story, the greater is our interest. So-called "white-collar crimes" don't seem to hold our interest as well. Editors have known this for centuries, so they often "play" crime news prominently, even crimes occurring great distances from our own communities. Playwrights, too, are aware of our interest in crime; and as a result, our television screens often portray gruesome activities in the guise of drama. In this section, authors discuss some of the ways the mass media are involved with crime and violence and why. (The crime and violence described in the articles may not be exactly what you had in mind but you can make the transition.)

Mitchell Stephens examines crime in the news in recent years and in years long past and demonstrates that not just big-city publishers and editors play crime big.

Elise Burroughs describes a type of violence that, unfortunately, is growing in this country as well as abroad. The news media have to be wary of becoming part of terrorist tactics. The potential of terrorism and media participation in it has prompted editors and news directors to develop operating procedures with the hope that they will never be needed.

Daniel Schorr's article looks at still another aspect of crime and violence —the effects of television violence, particularly regular exposure to televised violence, on children.

17 · CRIME DOESN'T PAY EXCEPT ON THE NEWSSTANDS

BY MITCHELL STEPHENS

Editors deny purposely giving greater coverage to crime, but violent crime has increased and readers stay interested in it, reports Mitchell Stephens, who teaches journalism at New York University and is author of *Broadcast News.* This article was published in *Washington Journalism Review,* December 1981.

The words "torture" or "murder" in two-and-a-half inch bold type have helped make Rupert Murdoch's *New York Post* the fastest growing newspaper in the United States.

The *Post* is not the only paper that has been expanding its coverage of crime recently, and it certainly is not the first to fill its pages with reports of execrable behavior.

"Crime's been big news since Cain slew Abel," says Shana Alexander, one of a crowd of authors currently writing books on convicted murderess Jean Harris—whose trial was front-page crime news in newspapers all over the country earlier this year.

Crime has long obsessed journalists, and crime news has obsessed their critics. In 1883, the *New York Evening Post* lambasted Joseph Pulitzer for the *New York World's* emphasis on the sordid and the sinful. Today, critics are still deploring what they argue is the inordinate press attention paid to shootings, stickups, and stabbings.

Despite centuries of scolding, crime news has flourished and today may even be enjoying a gentle boom.

"It may be that we're getting more crime news because the rest of the newspaper is so goddamn dull, filled with energy news, interest rates, and economic problems," suggests William F. Thomas, executive editor of the *Los Angeles Times.*

In Delaware County, Pa., H. L. Schwartz recently turned his *Daily Times* into a tabloid. Schwartz says, admiringly, that the *New York Post* seems to "oscillate" on a newsstand. Since the first modern American tabloid, the *New York Daily News,* was launched in 1919, tabloids have traditionally played up crime news, and Schwartz's *Daily Times* will not be an exception.

"In the past I anguished over having too much crime in the paper," Schwartz explains. "We tried to moderate crime coverage, but we don't do that now. We have taken steps to improve our relations with the police and to get crime news sooner and to get more excited about it."

The *Boston Herald American* was also revamped into a tabloid this year. Although *Herald American* executive editor James Toedtman denies his paper's new format will mean increased crime coverage, he says there had already been an increase in coverage before the switch: "We're running more stories in our display pages that involve crime. People are interested in it. There has been a substantial increase in people's perception that they're affected by crime."

William Giles, executive editor of the *Detroit News* runs a newspaper that, in his words, has been "very fulsome in its coverage of crime. As the economy has been getting worse, particularly in Michigan, there is more crime going on," Giles says. "And I think that's reflected in the paper, but I've made no deliberate decisions to cover more crime."

Most editors deny that they are purposely giving greater coverage to crime, yet most admit that their readers have grown more interested in the subject. If so, readers have good reason for their interest: there was a 60.3 percent jump in violent crime in the United States from 1971 to 1980, according to the FBI.

"There is an increase in public concern about crime," acknowledges *Los Angeles Herald Examiner* editor James G. Bellows. "The public is increasingly concerned about its own safety and security." Thomas of the *Herald American*'s more prosperous rival, the *Los Angeles Times,* agrees: "It's possible that we're covering more crime news simply because of the increased concern on the part of citizens, on the part of commissions, on the part of politicians."

A central issue in the controversy over crime and crime news has been that of race. Black Americans have been among the leading critics of crime coverage by the press, largely because, as one reporter says,

"It seemed the only time blacks were getting into the paper was when somebody killed somebody else."

Black readers remain sensitive to newspaper discussions of crime. Hundreds showed up last summer at a demonstration organized by a black weekly, the *Los Angeles Sentinel,* to protest an article in the *Los Angeles Times* about crime. In the second of a two-part series on the "permanent underclass" in the cities, the *Times* had used its own statistical analysis to demonstrate how members of this underclass increasingly prey on other groups. Maps showed how the "marauders," using the freeways, leap-frogged from core urban areas into the affluent suburbs to commit their crimes.

"It made blacks seem like they were all animals!" charges James H. Cleaver, executive editor of the *Sentinel.* "All they showed was the bad side of the black community. It made it appear that all the bad people in the city are black or Hispanic."

Thomas says he is not surprised at the reaction to the article in his newspaper. "It was not a cheerful article for anyone with a black skin walking through a white suburb," he admits. "There isn't any question that the way the article came out it provides ammunition for bigots and it feeds stereotypes. But the question I have to ask is: What are we supposed to do about that? Nobody is disputing that the article was accurate."

Cleaver protests that there should have been more attempt at balance in the piece. Thomas answers that the first article in the series had provided balance by showing the hopelessness of the permanent underclass, and he adds that his newspaper revisits Watts every five years for a "huge" article on the problems of the community.

Robert Maynard, of the *Oakland Tribune,* is conspicuous among editors who admit their papers are paying more attention to crime. He is the first black to edit a major metropolitan daily. Maynard's decision to place more emphasis on crime reporting in the *Oakland Tribune* might seem surprising. He does not think it should be.

"We are printing more about the causes of crimes, more about the consequences of crimes, and more about the particular human circumstances surrounding individual crimes," Maynard explains. "I think it is a very bad idea to ignore a murder."

Blacks make up a disproportionate share of the victims of crimes. (Of the single-victim, single-offender murders in the United States last year, 47 percent of the victims were black, 50 percent of the offenders were black, according to the FBI.) Maynard is among those who believe the role of blacks as victims has been underemphasized as their role as offenders has been overemphasized.

"We have sensed that one of the problems in coverage of crime is a tendency to consider that some murders are 'quality' murders and some are 'ordinary' murders," Maynard says. "We find that one of the reasons for the misunderstanding of our crime rate is the mistaken belief that most of the victims of crime are upper middle-class whites, when in fact most of the victims are poor minorities."

A reporter for the old *Newark News* recalls being advised in the early 1950s that the newspaper was not interested in crimes committed by blacks against blacks, dismissed by some editors as "nigger cuttings." Such overt racism is rare in news rooms today, but some observers claim the murder of a white person is more likely to get into most papers than the murder of a black person.

The *Washington Post,* for instance, pays a significant amount of attention to the problem of crime in poorer areas, but its crime coverage raises some interesting questions.

Of the 52 black and Hispanic people murdered in Washington from June 1 to August 31 this year, only one was considered significant enough to make the front page of the *Post*'s "Metro" section. Of three Washington murders with white victims during that period, one was considered newsworthy enough for the front of "Metro."

Although these statistics are far from conclusive—the sample is small and homicides in suburban areas are not considered—the imbalance is interesting—but not surprising.

Speaking of newspapers in general, Roger Wilkins, former associate editor of the *Washington Star,* says, "There is no question that there is more reporting of certain white murders than of certain black murders. And when you get to the issue of black murders in family fights, you don't get that at all. Absolutely nothing."

Washington Post "Metro" editor Bob Woodward defends *Post* crime coverage, saying, "I am not aware at all that we sit around and look at addresses, and if it's not in the Northwest district [where the largest percentage of Washington's white population lives] we decide not to cover a murder." Woodward admits that deciding what murders to cover is a "continual problem. If the president of the United States is shot, it's big news. If someone else is shot, it may not be. It's relative, and you're asking big questions about news judgment."

The *New York Times,* which gave heavy coverage to the murder of Dr. Herman Tarnower, a white, and the murder of Helen Hagnes, a musician at the Metropolitan Opera, a white—is not immune to charges of discrimination in its crime coverage.

"What I've noticed and what some other reporters here have noticed is that it becomes a matter of addresses," asserts one *Times* reporter. "If something comes over the police wire about a murder that has an address in a black neighborhood and it doesn't seem out of the ordinary, it doesn't get checked out, but if it has an address in a fashionable East Side neighborhood, it will be checked out."

Times metropolitan editor Peter Millones dismisses that charge and explains that his newspaper's decisions on what homicides to cover are based simply on news judgment. "Prominent people make more news than people who are not as prominent," Millones notes.

"The attitude may be that some deaths are more important than others," answers the *Times* reporter. "I can certainly understand that from a news judgment point of view, but from a moral perspective it does bother me."

Blacks are not the only critics of crime coverage in the nation's press.

Drew Humphries, a Rutgers University professor, believes news reports give a distorted picture of illegal behavior in our society. The incidence of violent crime is exaggerated, she says, while more subtle crimes—such as the violation of air pollution regulations—are slighted.

Boston communications researcher John Kochevar believes the problem is that crime reporting is usually "without context. There is very little in crime coverage that is of use, that tells why crime occurs, how it can be prevented or how real the danger actually is."

Humphries agrees: "Crime reporting divorces action from its context. It blinds you to both the causes and effects of crime. It's as if the crimes were occurring on an improvisational stage."

By covering one type of crime, a newspaper can give the impression that kind of crime is increasing. Philadelphia's news media are now reporting a wave of crime by "wolf packs"—teenage gangs—but there is no significant statistical increase in youth crime to support the increased coverage, says Humphries.

"Because of the tremendous emphasis on crime and violence in the news and entertainment media, children and adults tend to overestimate the extent to which crime exists in this society, and they tend to become overly cautious," warns Yale psychology professor Jerome L. Singer.

Whether crime coverage causes readers to be paranoid about the danger of crime or to perceive the danger accurately is a matter of debate. Executive editor Roger Wood of the *New York Post* maintains that it is healthy for newspapers to make people cautious: "We live in a very violent city here in New York."

Roger Wilkins has a different perspective. "There is no question that the city is substantially *less* dangerous than white people think it is," Wilkins says about Washington. He claims flawed crime reporting, along with dishonest politicians, create a public debate on crime that is "generally ignorant and ill-informed."

If crime coverage is increasing in today's newspapers, it is also changing. There is a growing realization by many editors that it is necessary to step back from reports of individual crimes to gain perspective on broader trends. Both the *New York Times* and the *Washington Post* have run sociological articles about crime—with information on its causes and effects that have focused on the problems of minorities.

"It's not as bad as it used to be when you sent some old rummy you didn't want around the news room down to the police shack," Wilkins concedes. "But it's still not the place eager young reporters want to go. With crime reporting of any kind you do not get the same consistent and sustained coverage that you get on, for example, economic news or the State Department."

Wilkins believes such a politically charged subject as crime deserves better treatment. "If crime is as important to this society as they say it is, first of all you upgrade the beat. Put your best reporters there. Send them off to study criminal law as the *Times* sends its Supreme Court reporter to Yale Law School."

With all its inadequacies, it is difficult to imagine newspapers without crime stories. The two grew up together; journalism attracted its mass audience in part through the blood, sex, and tears it was able to find in crime.

The last major boom in crime coverage by the press came in the 1920s when new tabloids were courting new readers among the urban poor. The most uninhibited of those tabloids was probably the *Daily Graphic* in New York, which had no peers in its ability to exploit a sexy trial, like the divorce trial in 1926 and 1927 of "Daddy" Browning and his 15-year-old child-wife, "Peaches." *Graphic*'s headlines about the trial included these grabbers: "Peaches on Stand Tells How Daddy Made Love," "Peaches Admits Hiding Names of Boy Lovers," "When Peaches Refused to Parade Nude" and, "Daddy to Enter Cloister."

Joseph Pulitzer helped produce an earlier boom in crime coverage at the turn of the century. The circulation of the *New York World* went from 15,000 to over a million with headlines that would not be out of place in today's *New York Post:* "A Baptism of Blood," "In Prison for His Brother's Crime," "Maddened by Marriage," " 'Let Me Die! Let Me Die!' "

It would be difficult to find any society—going as far back as Rome in 100 A.D.—that did not pass along tales of anti-social behavior.

Why?

"The traditional psychoanalytic explanation is that there is an instinctual tendency to harm and hurt, which we suppress and which tends to be expressed vicariously in reading about crime," Yale's Professor Singer explains.

Singer, however, subscribes to less Gothic explanations for the fascination with crime news: "There is an element of adventure and excitement about it," he says, "We've grown up with stories about crime; Robin Hood is basically a criminal. And there is an element of envy of people who can get away with crime."

The *New York Post*'s Wood prefers to think that his readers identify and sympathize with the victims, not the criminals. Wood thinks crime coverage serves a civic purpose: "You make people more aware. You make them more careful. You make them more responsive."

Woodward of the *Washington Post* believes the fascination of crime is that it can strike anyone at any time—with an enormous impact.

Major crimes are shocking anomalies in otherwise ordinary lives.

"Horror, fear, curiosity, and sympathy are all involved," says Roger Lane, a history professor at Haverford College. "And these are all elemental emotions."

Giles, of the *Detroit News,* says the simplicity of crime stories makes them readable. "All the readership surveys we take find that crime news, per se, is very highly read," Giles reports. "It's simple. It says something to people about the community in which they are living or about a community in which they are glad they are not living."

Horse trainer Buddy Jacobson is arrested in New York for murder, and soon the newspapers are printing details of his steamy East Side life; during the murder trial of Madeira school headmistress Jean Harris, her love letters are printed on the front pages of the most serious-minded newspapers. Crime brings something special to a reader—a chance to peek at the most intimate details of another person's life.

Nothing is too private to reveal if it is relevant to the determination of guilt or innocence—that is the rule in court, and it becomes the rule when criminal trials are reported. Private lives are invaded with less restraint in crime stories than anywhere else in the news; that is what makes them so offensive to critics and so popular with readers.

"Crimes lead to all sorts of other interesting stories," say Bob Woodward. "My favorite example was a burglary some years back." He refers, of course, to Watergate. That burglary is a good example of how much more we can learn about men when they leave their protected roles as government officials and are caught committing a crime. Mitchell, Haldeman, Ehrlichman, and Dean became human only when looked at as potential crooks. Political stories are not peopled by vulnerable human beings; crime stories usually are.

Crime stories may increase racial tension, they may leave readers with a confused view of who is getting away with what in this country, but they provide rare chances to peer into the deepest recesses of other people's private lives.

Crime news is personal and intense—something Joseph Pulitzer undoubtedly realized when he put it on page one. Perhaps that is what H.L. Schwartz of the *Daily Times* means when he says crime news "is just good-reading stuff."

18 · PRESS BATTLES QUESTIONS OVER DOMESTIC TERRORISM

BY ELISE BURROUGHS

An apparent rise in domestic terrorism—kidnappings, takeovers and the like—prompts Elise Burroughs, a *presstime* staff writer, to describe some newsroom decisions that have been established to keep the media from aiding terrorists. This article is from the March 1982 issue of *presstime,* published by the American Newspaper Publishers Association.

When he was U.S. ambassador to the United Nations, Andrew Young touched off a storm of protest by suggesting that something had to be done about the way news media cover incidents of terrorism.

"The First Amendment has got to be clarified by the Supreme Court in the light of the power of the mass media," said Young, currently mayor of Atlanta.

His comments came after some news people went to the brink of propriety, and perhaps beyond, to cover the Hanafi Muslim siege in Washington, D.C., five years ago.

Interest in the press' performance flared following that and other terrorist acts, but as the number of incidents gradually dropped, so too did interest in how the press should cope. Now, however, domestic terrorism again appears to be on the rise. Many believe the press should be preparing now to deal with it.

Following the Hanafi incident, few people agreed with Andrew Young that the situation dictated a new interpretation of the First Amendment. But many, including some journalists, urged the media to study the ramifications of terrorism and to write some guidelines for covering future incidents of kidnappings, bomb threats, hijackings, hostage-taking and other "use of force or threats to demoralize, intimidate and subjugate"—the dictionary definition of terrorism.

Despite the urging, response from the media has been spotty. While all three commercial networks and several broadcast stations now have guidelines, only about a half-dozen newspapers and one wire service, United Press International, do.

Virtually every written guideline dealing with terrorism begins by stressing the right and responsibility of the press to cover and report the news.

"Normal tests of news judgment will determine what to publish despite the dangers of contagion, since the adverse effects of suppression are greater," state the guidelines of the *Chicago Sun-Times.*

[Former] *Sun-Times* publisher James F. Hoge says, "most of the guidelines I've seen from large, reputable organizations, I applaud. I think they're very good."

Proponents say that voluntary guidelines not only can help a news organization deal with terrorism, but also might head off government attempts to impose regulations in this area.

Testimony submitted by ANPA to a 1978 congressional hearing on terrorism strongly opposed any attempts at government regulation. The Association noted that setting up official guidelines "would be attempting to treat all such incidents alike when, in reality, they occur in different places, in different settings, for different reasons, by different people and create widely varying degrees of danger."

Instead of regulations, ANPA suggested disciplined research and study into the conflicts between the press and law enforcement during terrorist incidents. "ANPA and other press organizations will continue to encourage education and understanding in this area," Jerry W. Friedheim, ANPA executive vice president and general manager, told the hearing.

In Lieu of Guidelines   Indeed, just because a news organization lacks a written policy on how to deal with terrorism doesn't necessarily mean its senior executives have ignored the threat altogether. Many have thought long and hard about the issue and feel mentally prepared to make quick decisions when terrorists incidents occur.

Such a person is Jean Alice Small, editor and publisher of *The Daily Journal* (evening, circulation 32,915) in Kankakee, Ill. She is a veteran of numerous seminars and conferences on the media and terrorism, most of which were held in the late 70s, following the Hanafi incident.

Small says the discussions in which she participated have left her in readiness. "If we had a situation here, we would not panic. We would go right into a plan."

Other executives say they rely on their experience and everyday common sense to guide them if a situation arises.

"We just don't like to tie ourselves in knots," says Lawrence S. Connor, managing editor of *The Indianapolis Star* (morning, 223,289).

"Sometimes, a situation will call for something not on that piece of paper," observes Wick Temple, managing editor of the Associated Press.

Another reason for a reluctance to prepare more fully for terrorism is simply logistical.

K. Prescott Low, publisher of *The Patriot Ledger* (evening, 85,879) in Quincy, Mass., puts it this way: "Small newspapers don't plan very well at all, and they have enough trouble dealing with planning for things like personnel policies and budgets. To get beyond that to . . . things like hostages, if one should ever occur, is something most folks just don't have the time for, unless they are really a bug on the subject."

A Resurgence of Terrorism But whether a given news organization does or doesn't have something in writing about how to cover terrorism, one thing is certain: Terrorism is not about to fade from the scene. Nor is the problem of how to deal with it about to disappear.

"In the future, as in the past, the media's role in covering these events will have a significant impact. How these stories are played, what details of terrorist methods are highlighted, what aspects of law enforcement's response are reported, will be important," Anthony C.E. Quainton, then director of the U.S. Office for Combatting Terrorism and recently named ambassador to Nicaragua, told a gathering of the Inter American Press Association in 1980.

In addition to recent kidnappings, murders and attempted murders of U.S. government personnel abroad, terrorism at home is growing. In January, a Turkish diplomat was assassinated on a street in Los Angeles. And last year, according to the FBI, the number of domestic terrorism incidents jumped from 29 in 1980 to 42—a 45-percent increase.

1981 marked the end of a three-year period in which the number of domestic terrorism incidents had declined: from 111 in 1977, to 69 in 1978, to 52 in 1979, to 29 in 1980.

Among the incidents in 1977 was the Hanafi Muslim seizure of three buildings and dozens of hostages in the nation's Capital. A young radio reporter was killed while covering that story, and the actions of some members of the press were criticized by Andrew Young and others.

For example:

- One Washington newspaper reporter gained access to a hotel that police had cordoned off as a command post by booking a room and registering as a guest. He filed a number of reports before police recognized him. Authorities let him remain with the provision that he not quote sources by name.

- A reporter from the *Ft. Worth* (Texas) *Star-Telegram,* looking for a local angle to the drama, called one seized building long-distance, talked to the terrorists and asked if any of the hostages were from Texas. The hostage-takers told him to read the wire services and get off the line in case more important, national media should call.

• A TV reporter noticed a basket being lifted on a rope to the fifth floor of one of the buildings that had been seized. It carried supplies to some people who were barricaded on that floor hiding from the gunmen who had taken over the upper part of the building. The terrorists didn't know those persons were there—until the TV station broadcast its "exclusive story."

The basic questions in the aftermath of the Hanafi siege are: How far should reporters go in gathering the news in a terrorist situation? What activities will conflict with law enforcement efforts? What will endanger innocent lives? Where does enterprising journalism escalate into sensationalism?

Charles Fenyvesi, then editor of the *National Jewish Monthly* and one of the Hanafi hostages, said at a subsequent seminar on media and terrorism that some of the press' actions outraged the captives. After their release, many of them spoke enthusiastically of regulations and news blackouts in tense situations.

"Again and again I hear the view that the press must be curbed, regardless of the First Amendment," Fenyvesi told the seminar.

As a journalist, he defended the right of the press to make its own decisions.

But Fenyvesi did suggest that news people receive special training on how to cope with terrorist crises. "Editors are careful, usually careful, in assigning the right kind of newsmen to cover, say, a White House dinner or new safety measure on automobiles," he said. "They should be at least as careful in assigning a newsman to cover a life-and-death drama of terrorism."

He also urged the media to follow at least one guideline in terrorist situations: "Life over 'scoop.' "

Partly as a result of the Hanafi incident, several newspaper organizations now instruct reporters generally to cooperate and to obey police instructions at the scene and let editors file any protests later.

Also, some—including the *New York Times* and the *Houston Chronicle*—have policies of never trying to contact hostage-takers or kidnappers on their own. The papers' executives explain that they don't want their staffs to interfere with communication and negotiation by law enforcement officials. They also worry that the wrong words or questions—such as asking about demands and deadlines—might trigger action by the terrorists.

But the AP's Temple says his reporters in the past have telephoned those involved in a terrorist incident and might do so again. "That's a (judgment) call that would have to be made at the time," he says, adding, "we wouldn't do it if we were warned it would endanger hostages' lives."

Newsroom Dilemmas   While some newspapers refuse to initiate contact with terrorists, kidnappers and hijackers themselves sometimes turn to journalists as mediators. That happened twice in a little over one year in Indianapolis.

During the first incident in February 1977, a man who was holding a local business executive hostage—the victim had a shotgun wired to his neck—called a radio station to announce his demands. Radio station personnel were thrust into the negotiations.

The second incident involved *The Indianapolis Star*. Just after midnight one night in May 1978, rewrite man Art Drake was telephoned by a man who said he was holding three other men hostage. The caller said he would begin shooting hostages if Drake did not come to the apartment complex where the drama was unfolding and take down the caller's story.

After consulting with law enforcement authorities, Drake went to the apartment, spent more than an hour interviewing the armed man and his hostages, and later briefed officials, who succeeded in negotiating a peaceful end to the incident.

Star Managing Editor Connor says his paper would prefer not to have its personnel become involved in such stories, but where lives are at stake, "we have an obligation."

The media also feel an obligation sometimes to withhold facts at the request of authorities because the information would be of benefit to terrorists.

"We (at the Associated Press) operate on a general principle of not helping the perpetrator," Temple says. In a hijacking, for example, "we may know that 150 police are ringing the airport, but we won't report that." But the decision to withhold information is a rare one, and it is made only by top editors in New York, he reports.

Kankakee's Small says that if faced with a kidnapping or hostage situation, her newspaper would follow a policy of working with law enforcement authorities. She adds that protecting the privacy and emotions of the victims and families would be paramount. "I wouldn't do anything for a scoop. That is no time for grandstanding."

Newspapers must wrestle not only with the question of when to withhold information from readers, but also when to publish items they would rather not print—such as demands, exhortations and explanations by terrorists and kidnappers.

UPI's guideline on demands states: "We will report the demands of terrorists and kidnappers as an essential point of the story but not provide an excessive platform for their demands." But when lives are

threatened, newspapers sometimes find themselves publishing whatever the terrorists demand.

The *New York Times*, the *Washington Post*, the *Los Angeles Times*,
the *Chicago Tribune*, *The Atlanta Constitution* and the *Cleveland Press*
are among the papers that have published the full texts of terrorist
demands.

Perhaps the most extreme case of this occurred during the Patricia
Hearst kidnapping, when the San Francisco newspapers were told to
print page after page of Symbionese Liberation Army material or be
responsible for Hearst's death. The papers complied.

Reg Murphy, former publisher of the Hearst Corp.-owned *San Francisco Examiner,* says that after the Patricia Hearst incident, the newspaper resolved not to print verbatim texts of terrorist demands
again.

Now publisher of the *Baltimore Sun* papers, Murphy acknowledges,
however, that any newspaper policy of not printing demands would
have to bend under the threat of harm to innocent victims.

It Can Happen Here   Murphy himself was touched by terrorism in 1974
when, as editor of *The Atlanta Constitution,* he was kidnapped by a
man who claimed in a ransom note to be "a colonel of the American
Revolutionary Army."

The so-called colonel was seeking to straighten out what he perceived to be a liberal bias in the news media.

After Atlanta newspapers paid a ransom of $700,000, Murphy was
released. The money was later recovered, and the confessed kidnapper
imprisoned.

Murphy's kidnapping was an unusual event in American journalism. Nothing like it has happened since, and the issue of how to avoid
terrorist threats seems far-fetched to many in the news business. Most
newspaper security efforts are aimed mainly at preventing pilferage,
theft and unauthorized visitors of the harmless variety.

Executives say conventional types of crime constitute a bigger
worry than terrorism.

But a few publishers say U.S. journalists could someday face the
kind of violence that has become rather common in Latin America, Italy,
Northern Ireland and Spain.

"What happens elsewhere inevitably, sooner or later, happens
here," says Massachusetts publisher Low. "Newspapers are sitting
ducks for terrorism activities, as institutions as well as individual members of the establishment."

According to Small, publishers who dismiss the threat are shortsighted in not realizing the ripple effect of far-away happenings.

"In this day and age, I would think it (preparation) couldn't do
anything but benefit the paper even if it were no more than an abstract
discussion of principles," she says.

A couple of years ago, Small asked a regional press association to organize a presentation on terrorism.

"I was told terrorism wouldn't be of any interest to our readers," she recalls. "It wasn't very long before every small town in the country had a yellow ribbon around the tree."

19 · Go Get Some Milk and Cookies and Watch the Murders on Television

By Daniel Schorr

Whether the viewer is watching news or dramatic programs, the amount of violence on television and what it can do to people are concerns of Daniel Schorr, senior correspondent of Cable News Network. He explains why in this article. Schorr is a former network correspondent for CBS News. This article is reprinted from *The Washingtonian*, October 1981.

I believe television is going to be the test of the modern world, and that in this new opportunity to see beyond the range of our vision we shall discover a new and unbearable disturbance of the modern peace or a saving radiance in the sky. We shall stand or fall by television—of that I am quite sure.

E.B. White (1938)

John W. Hinckley Jr. causes me to reflect, having recently turned 65, on what the media age has wrought. Hinckley's unhappy lifetime of some 26 years coincides roughly with my life in television. Whatever else made him want to shoot a President, Hinckley epitomizes the perverse effects of our violence-prone culture of entertainment.

Hinckley weaves together strands of media-stimulated fantasy, fan frenzy, and the urge to proclaim identity by starring in a televised event. His success is attested to by everything that has happened since March 30, when he managed to disrupt the regular programs listed in his copy of *TV Guide* to bring on command performances by Dan Rather, Frank Reynolds, Roger Mudd, and the other news superstars. Since November 22, 1963, these electronic special reports—the modern equivalent of the old newspaper extra—have been America's way of certifying a "historic event."

Much has been shown to Hinckley's generation to lower the threshold of resistance to violent acts. When the time came for Hinckley to act—to plug himself into this continuum of television and movie violence—the screenplay was easily written, the roles nearly preassigned. The media-conscious "public" President, Ronald Reagan, attracted the cameras, which attracted the crowds, which provided both the arena and the cover for the assailant. The network cameras routinely assigned, since the Kennedy assassination, to "the presidential watch" recorded the "actuality" and showed it in hypnotic, incessant replays. The audience tingled to the all-too-familiar "special report" emblazoned across the screen.

To nobody's surprise, the celebration of violence stirred would-be imitators. The Secret Service recorded an astonishing number of subsequent threats on the President's life. One of them came from Edward Michael Robinson, 22, who had watched the TV coverage and later told police that Hinckley had appeared to him in a dream, telling him to "bring completion to Hinckley's reality."

Psychiatrist Walter Menninger examined Sara Jane Moore, who tried to kill President Ford in 1975, and found it no coincidence that two weeks earlier a well-publicized attempt on Ford's life had been made by Squeaky Fromme.

"There is no doubt," Dr. Menninger told me, "of the effect of the broad, rapid, and intense dissemination of such an event. The scene in front of the Washington Hilton must have been indelibly coded in everybody's mind with an immediacy that does not happen with the print media. We have learned from the studies of television that people do get influenced by what they experience on television."

The broadcasting industry says it can't help it if occasionally a disturbed person tries to act out depicted violence—fictional or actual. In 1975, a Vietnam veteran in Hyattsville, Maryland, who had told his wife, "I watch television too much," began sniping at passersby in a way he had noted during an episode of *S.W.A.T.*—and, like the fictional sniper, was killed by a police sharpshooter.

The American Medical Association reported in 1977 that physicians were telling of cases of injury from TV imitation showing up in their offices and hospitals. One doctor treated two children who, playing

Batman, had jumped off a roof. Another said a child who had set fire to a house was copying an arson incident viewed on television.

No court has yet held television legally culpable for the violence it is accused of stimulating. In Florida in 1978, fifteen-year-old Ronny Zamora was convicted—after a televised trial—of killing his elderly neighbor despite the novel plea of "involuntary subliminal television intoxication." The parents of a California girl who had been sexually assaulted in 1974 in a manner depicted three days earlier in an NBC television drama lost their suit against the network.

That's as it should be. I support the constitutional right of the broadcasting industry to depict violence, just as I support *Hustler* magazine's right to depict pornography—with distaste. As Jules Feiffer, the cartoonist and civil libertarian, has noted, one sometimes finds oneself in the position of defending people one wouldn't dine with. What troubles me, as I reflect on the case of John Hinckley, is the reluctance of television to acknowledge its contribution to fostering an American culture of violence, not only by the way it presents fantasy but by the way it conveys reality—and by the way it blurs the line between the two.

> Violence is one of the manifestations of the quest for identity. When you've lost your identity, you become a violent person looking for identity.
>
> MARSHALL MCLUHAN (1977)

In 1974 Reg Murphy, then editor of the *Atlanta Constitution* (he is now publisher of the *Baltimore Sun*), was kidnapped. He says his abductors immediately sped to an apartment and turned on a TV set to see whether their act had made the evening news.

In 1971 prison rioters in Attica, New York, listed as a primary demand that their grievances be aired on TV.

In 1977 in Indianapolis, Anthony George Kiritsis wired a sawed-off shotgun to the neck of a mortgage company officer, led him out in front of the police and TV cameras, and yelled: "Get those goddamn cameras on! I'm a goddamn national hero!"

In 1974 in Sarasota, Florida, an anchorwoman on television station WXLT said on the air, "In keeping with Channel 40's policy of bringing you the latest in blood and guts in living color, you're going to see another first—an attempt at suicide." Whereupon she pulled a gun out of a shopping bag and shot herself fatally in the head.

These incidents—the list could go on and on—were all aspects of the phenomenon of the mass media as grand arbiter of identity, validator of existence. Descartes might say today, "I appear on television, therefore I am."

One becomes accustomed, after working a long time in the medium, to hearing strangers remark, without elaboration, "I saw you on television!" One even gets inured to being hauled over to meet somebody's relatives. It is as though the TV personality has an existence of its own. I experienced the other side of this phenomenon in 1976 when I stopped broadcasting for CBS. People asked, solicitously, if everything was all right—as though, being off the air, I had ceased to be in some existential sense.

"Getting on television" has become a preoccupation of people in government, politics, and industry, not to mention all manner of single-issue advocates. Candidates will fashion their campaigns around "photo opportunities." Senators will be drawn by the presence of cameras to legislative hearings they otherwise would skip.

Many people will do almost anything to get on TV. Some will even kill.

Anthony Quainton, former head of the State Department's Office for Combatting Terrorism, associates the increase in casualties during hijackings and hostage-takings with the desire of terrorists to insure news-media attention. Deliberate acts of horror—like the tossing out of slain victims—are planned as media events. On the other hand, the failure of the hijacking of a Turkish plane to Bulgaria in May was at least partly due to the fact that two of the terrorists had left the plane to give a press conference.

Sometimes the aim is to hijack television itself. When the radical Baader-Meinhof gang in West Germany kidnapped a politician in 1975 as hostage for the release of five imprisoned comrades, it forced German television to show each prisoner boarding a plane and to broadcast dictated propaganda statements. "For 72 hours we lost control of our medium," a German television executive later said.

When Arab terrorists seized the Vienna headquarters of OPEC in 1975, killing three persons and taking oil ministers hostage, the terrorists' plan called for them to occupy the building until TV cameras arrived.

A central feature of the plan of the San Francisco "Symbionese Liberation Army," which kidnapped Patricia Hearst, was the exploitation of the media—forcing radio and television to play its tapes and carry its messages.

The Hanafi Muslims' hostage-taking occupation of three locations in Washington in 1976 was a classic case of media-age terrorism. The leader, Hamaas Abdul Khaalis, spent much of his time giving interviews by telephone, while his wife checked on what was being broadcast.

"These crimes are highly contagious," warns Dr. Harold Visotsky, head of the department of psychiatry at Northwestern University. "Deranged persons have a passion for keeping up with the news and imitating it."

It does not seem to matter much if they are keeping up with "the news" or with "entertainment," for more and more the distinction is thinly drawn. A real attempt on the President's life produces a rash of threats. A prime-time drama about a bomb on an airplane produces a rash of reports of bombs on airplanes.

In all of this, television claims to be innocent—a helpless eyewitness, sometimes even a hostage. It's not that simple.

To begin with, television has helped blur the lines between reality and fantasy in the general consciousness.

Television news itself—obliged to co-exist with its entertainment environment, seeking to present facts with the tools of fantasy—ends up with a dramatized version of life. Everything that goes into making a well-paced, smoothly edited "package" subtly changes reality into a more exciting allegory of events. The confusion is compounded by the use of "cinéma réalité" techniques in fictional dramas, and the modern forms of fact-and-fiction "docudramas" and "reenactments" of events.

It began to come home to me that audiences were blurring the distinction between reality and entertainment when I received telephone calls from several persons, during the 1973 Senate Watergate hearings that preempted soap operas, asking that the networks "cancel" a boring witness and "put back John Dean and his nice wife." Moreover, some friends of mine praised a "documentary" shown by NBC, *The Raid at Entebbe,* and had to be reminded that it was a reenactment.

The gradual erosion of the line between fact and fantasy, between news and theater, can have serious consequences. People slow to react to accidents and muggings may be experiencing the existential question of whether these things are really happening. A woman wrote columnist Abigail van Buren of being bound and gagged by a robber who told the victim's four-year-old boy to watch television for a while before calling for help. The child looked at TV for the next three hours, ignoring his mother's desperate efforts to get his attention. Perhaps, to the child, the show was more real than his mother's muffled screams.

Having obscured the difference between fantasy and reality, television offers incentives to people who are seeking emphatic ways of getting recognition. Innocent hand-waving, as an attention-getting device, yields to demonstrations, which in turn yield to riots.

In my own experience, covering urban unrest for CBS in the 1960s, threatening rhetoric tended to overpower moderate rhetoric and be selected for the network's *Evening News* because it made "better television." I have no doubt that television helped to build up militant blacks like Stokely Carmichael and H. Rap Brown within the black community by giving them preferred exposure. Nonviolent leaders found themselves obliged to escalate the militancy of their own rhetoric. When Martin Luther King Jr. came to Washington in 1968 to discuss plans for the "poor people's march" that he did not live to lead, he told me he had to allude to possibilities for disruption as a way of getting media attention.

At a community meeting after the first night of rioting in the Watts area of Los Angeles in 1965, most of those who spoke appealed for calm. But a teenager who seized the microphone and called for "going after the whiteys" was featured on evening TV news programs. A moderate commented, "Look to me like he [the white man] want us to riot." Another said, "If that's the way they read it, that's the way we'll write the book."

In recent years, television news, compelled to come to terms with its own potency, has sought to enforce guidelines for coverage of group violence. Television tries to guard against being an immediate instigator of violence, but its reaction is too little and too late to overcome the cumulative consequences of a generation of depicted violence. It is like trying to control proliferation of nuclear weapons after distributing nuclear reactors over a prolonged period.

> The most important thing is that a causal relationship has been shown between violence viewing and aggression.
>
> DR. JESSE STEINFELD,
> SURGEON GENERAL OF THE UNITED STATES (1972)

For three decades, since the time when there were 10 million TV sets in America, I have watched efforts to determine objectively the effects of televised violence while the TV industry strove to sweep the issue under the carpet.

What television hated most of all to acknowledge was that violence on TV was not incidental or accidental but a consciously fostered element in the ratings race. In 1976 David Rintels, president of the Writers Guild in Los Angeles, where most of the blood-and-guts scripts are spawned, told a congressional committee: "The networks not only approve violence on TV, they have been known to request and inspire it.

"There is so much violence on television," he said, "because the networks want it. They want it because they think they can attract viewers by it. It attracts sponsors. Affiliate stations welcome it."

A personal experience brought home to me the industry's sensitivity to the subject. In January 1969 my report for an *Evening News* telecast, summarizing the interim findings of the National Commission on the Causes and Prevention of Violence, was altered shortly before air time at the direction of Richard N. Salant, president of CBS News, to eliminate a comment about television. The passage cited the commission's view that while "most persons will not kill after seeing a single violent television program. . . . it is possible that many learn some of their attitudes about violence from years of TV exposure and may be likely to engage in violence." For management to override the news judgment of the "Cronkite show" was extremely rare.

Riots and assassinations would bring the issue periodically to the fore, but the research had been going on for a long time. For more than a quarter of a century social scientists have studied the effects of violence-viewing—especially on children.

- At Stanford University, Professor Albert Bandura reported that children three to six years of age whose toys were taken away after they had seen films showing aggression would be more likely to pound an inflated doll in their frustration than children who had not seen such films.

- A Canadian study by R.S. Walters and E. Llewellyn Thomas found that high school students who had viewed aggressive films were more likely than others to administer strong electric shocks to students making errors on an exam.

- An experiment conducted in Maryland for the National Institute of Mental Health found serious fights in school more common among high school students who watched violent TV programs.

- Bradley Greenberg and Joseph Dominick, studying Michigan public-school pupils, found that "higher exposure to television violence in entertainment was associated with greater approval of violence and greater willingness to use it in real life."

- Drs. Dorothy and Jerome Singer of Yale University concluded from an exhaustive series of interviews that the children who watched the most television were likely to act most aggressively in family situations. Although they could not produce a "smoking gun" that would influence the TV industry, they argued that they had eliminated every other factor that could account for the high correlation between aggressive behavior and viewing of "action-oriented" shows.

- Dr. Leonard Berkowitz of the University of Wisconsin, in two experiments ten years apart, found that third-graders watching a great many violent programs were likely to be rated by other pupils as high in aggressive behavior and that, at nineteen, most of them were still described as "aggressive" by their peers. In fact, reported Dr. Berkowitz, the amount of television viewed at the age of nine is "one of the best predictors of whether a person will be found to be aggressive in later life."

Congress took an early interest in the question of violence in TV programs. In 1952 the House Commerce Committee held hearings on excessive sex and violence on television. Senate hearings on TV violence and juvenile deliquency, conducted by Senators Estes Kefauver of Tennessee and Thomas Dodd of Connecticut, stirred episodic public interest. The hearing transcripts make a tall stack, adding up to fifteen years of congressional alarm over television, and industry reassurance that it was addressing the problem.

The controversy over television assumed a new dimension of national concern in the wake of the urban riots and assassinations of the 1960s. In 1968, after the assassination of Robert Kennedy, President Johnson named a commission, headed by Dr. Milton Eisenhower, to inquire into the causes of violence and how it might be prevented.

Between October and December 1968, the Eisenhower Commission held hearings on television, questioning social scientists and industry executives about the extent to which the medium might be the instigator or abettor of violent acts. One commission member, Leon Jaworski, later to be the Watergate prosecutor, expressed the belief that television might have "a tremendous responsibility" for violence in America.

The television networks acknowledged no such responsibility. When Commissioner Albert E. Jenner asked whether "the depiction of violence has an effect upon the viewer," Dr. Frank Stanton, president of CBS, replied: "It may or may not have. That is the question we don't have the answer to."

Nevertheless, the commission decided to formulate an answer. After a long debate—from which Lloyd N. Cutler, the executive director, disqualified himself because of his law firm's TV-industry clients —the panel declared in its final report that it was "deeply troubled by television's constant portrayal of violence . . . pandering to a public preoccupation with violence that television itself has helped to generate."

The panel's report concluded: "A constant diet of violence on TV has an adverse effect on human character and attitudes. Violence on television encourages violent forms of behavior and fosters moral and social values in daily life which are unacceptable in a civilized society. We do not suggest that television is a principal cause of violence in our society. We do suggest that it is a contributing factor."

A two-volume report of the commission's "Task Force on Mass Media and Violence" concluded that, as a short-range effect, those who see violent acts portrayed learn to perform them and may imitate them in a similar situation, and that, as a long-term effect, exposure to media violence "socializes audiences into the norms, attitudes, and values for violence."

The Eisenhower Commission's report on television had little impact —it was overshadowed in the news media by its more headline-making findings about riots, civil disobedience, and police brutality. The networks acted to reduce the violence in animated cartoons for children and killings in adult programs, and the motion-picture industry quickly compensated by increasing the incidence and vividness of its bloodletting.

However, Congress, on the initiative of Rhode Island Senator John O. Pastore, a long-standing critic of television, moved to mandate a completely new investigation, calling on the US Surgeon General for a report on TV and violence that would, in effect, parallel the report associating cigarette smoking with cancer.

Worried about what might emerge from such a study, the television industry lobbied with President Nixon's Secretary of Health, Education, and Welfare, Robert Finch, to influence the organization and conduct of the investigation. It successfully opposed seven candidates for appointment to the committee, including the best-known researchers in the field. The Surgeon General's Committee on Television and Social Behavior, as constituted, comprised five experts affiliated with the broadcasting industry, and four behavioral scientists innocent of mass-media background.

Three years and $1.8 million later, the committee produced its report, "Television and Growing Up: The Impact of Televised Violence," supported by five volumes of technical studies. The full report, read by few, provided telling data on the role of TV violence as instigator of aggression in young people, but the nineteen-page summary that would determine the public perception emerged opaque and ambiguous, after an intense struggle within the committee.

"Under the circumstances," it said, watching violent fare on television could cause a young person to act aggressively, but "children imitate and learn from everything they see." The research studies, it said, indicated "a modest association between viewing of television and violence among at least some children," but "television is only one of the many factors which in time may precede aggressive behavior."

The summary danced around the crucial issue of causation: "Several findings of the survey studied can be cited to sustain the hypothesis that viewing of violent television has a causal relation to aggressive behavior, though neither individually nor collectively are the findings conclusive."

The ambiguity was mirrored in the pages of the *New York Times*. A front-page story on January 12, 1972, based on a leak, was headlined TV VIOLENCE HELD UNHARMFUL TO YOUTH. But when the report was officially released a week later, the *Times* story said, "The study shows for the first time a causal connection between violence shown on television and subsequent behavior by children."

"It is clear to me," said Surgeon General Jesse Steinfeld, presenting his report at a hearing conducted by Senator Pastore, "that the causal relationship between televised violence and antisocial behavior is sufficient to warrant appropriate and remedial action."

There was no significant remedial action. As the decade of urban violence and assassination ebbed, the issue of television violence faded, to come back another day. And another day would bring another report.

Even before the latest incidents of violence, a new inquiry had started. Dr. Eli A. Rubinstein had first come to the Surgeon General's committee as a vice chairman fresh from the National Institute of Mental Health. His experience with the investigation led him to make the study of the mass media his career.

In 1980, Dr. Rubinstein, now professor of psychology at the University of North Carolina, persuaded President Carter's Surgeon General, Dr. Julius Richmond, to assemble an ad hoc committee to prepare an updated version of the 1972 Surgeon General's report on its tenth anniversary. Two volumes of new technical studies have already been compiled. The conclusions are yet to be written, but there is no doubt that they will reinforce and expand the original timidly stated findings.

One thing the new report will do, Dr. Rubinstein said, is to lay to rest the theory that depicted violence can actually decrease aggression by serving as a "cathartic"—the cleansing and purging of an audience's emotions that Aristotle held to be the highest test of tragedy. Advanced by some behavioral scientists studying television, the theory was examined during the 1972 study for the Surgeon General, which concluded that there was "no evidence to support a catharsis interpretation." The updated report, citing new empirical studies, will make that point more strongly.

"A tremendous amount of work has been done over the past ten years, and the volume of literature has probably tripled," Dr. Rubinstein says. "If any mistake was made ten years ago, it was to be too qualified about the relationship between TV violence and aggressiveness. We have a lot of new evidence about causality, and about what constitutes causality. We know much more about how television produces aggressive behavior. We know more about how fantasy can crowd out reality, and the specific influences of television on disturbed minds.

"The fundamental scientific evidence indicates that television affects the viewer in more ways than we realized initially. You will recall that the original smoking-and-health study was limited to the lungs, and later it was learned how smoking affects the heart and other parts of the body. In the same way, we now know that the original emphasis on TV violence was too narrow. Television affects not only a predisposition towards violence, but the whole range of social and psychological development of the younger generation."

The new Surgeon General's report scheduled for release by the

Reagan administration in 1982, is likely to be challenged by the TV industry with all the vigor displayed by the tobacco lobby when opposing the report on smoking and cancer. Inevitably, it will be read for clues to violent behavior of people like John Hinckley.

> In the absence of family, peer, and school relationships, television becomes the most compatible substitute for real-life experience.
> NATIONAL COMMISSION ON THE CAUSES
> AND PREVENTION OF VIOLENCE (1969)

What made Hinckley different, what made him shoot the President are ultimately matters for psychiatry and the law to determine. But the "media factor" played a part.

As Hinckley withdrew from school and family life, he retreated progressively into a waiting world of violent fantasy, spending more and more time alone with television—an exciting companion that made no demands on him.

But television was not the only part of the media working to merge fact and fantasy for Hinckley. He was strongly influenced by *Taxi Driver,* a motion picture about a psychopath who found the answer to his anxieties through his obsession with violence. Like the taxi driver, Hinckley oscillated between wanting to kill a public figure to impress the object of his affections, and wanting to "rescue" her from "evil" surroundings. Paul Schrader, author of the screenplay, tells me that the moment he heard that President Reagan had been shot, his reaction was, "There goes another taxi driver!"

Hinckley was also affected by fan frenzy, a special manifestation of the media culture. It focused not only on Jodie Foster, the female lead in *Taxi Driver,* but also on former Beatle John Lennon, whose music he played on the guitar. Last New Year's Eve, after Lennon's murder, Hinckley taped a monologue, in his motel room near Denver, in which he mourned: "John and Jodie, and now one of 'em's dead.

"Sometimes," he said, "I think I'd rather just see her not . . . not on earth than being with other guys. I wouldn't wanna stay on earth without her on earth. It'd have to be some kind of pact between Jodie and me."

And the influences working on Hinckley extended beyond the visual media. The idea of a suicide pact was apparently drawn from *The Fan,* a novel by Bob Randall that Hinckley had borrowed—along with books about the Kennedy family and Gordon Liddy's *Will*—from a public library in Evergreen, Colorado. In the book, the paranoid fan of a Broadway star, feeling rejected in his advances by mail, kills the actress and himself as she opens in a theater production. Early last March, as Foster was preparing to open in a New Haven stock-company play, Hinckley slipped a letter under her door saying, "After tonight John Lennon and I will have a lot in common."

The plan that finally congealed this welter of media-drawn inspirations and impelled the young misfit to action was a presidential assassination. Before setting out, he—like the fictional fan—left behind a letter to be read posthumously. It was to tell Foster that he intended, through "this historical deed, to gain your respect and love."

As though to document his place in the media hall of fame, he dated and timed the letter and left behind, in his room in the Park Central Hotel, tapes of his guitar playing, his New Year's Eve soliloquy, and a telephone conversation with Foster.

A failure at most things, Hinckley was a spectacular media success who had survived to enjoy his celebrityhood—a lesson that won't be lost on other driven persons.

No one could doubt his importance or challenge his identity as the news cameras clustered around the federal courthouse when he arrived for his arraignment in a presidential-size limousine heralded by police sirens.

In the great made-for-TV drama, participants more "normal" than Hinckley seemed also to play assigned roles, as if caught up in some ineluctable screenplay. The TV anchors were reviewed for smoothness, composure, and factual accuracy under stress. Secretary of State Haig, making a gripping appearance in the White House press room, was panned for gasping and for misreading his lines. President Reagan, with considerable support from White House aides and from the smoothly reassuring Dr. Dennis O'Leary, himself an instant hit, won plaudits for a flawless performance as the wisecracking, death-defying leader of the Free World.

The effect was to reinforce the pervasive sense of unreality engendered by a generation of television shoot-outs—the impression that being shot doesn't really hurt, that everything will turn out all right in time for the final commercial.

One can understand the desire to assure the world that the government is functioning. But Dr. David Hamburg, the psychiatrist and former president of the Institute of Medicine of the National Academy of Sciences, believes it harmful to imply that a shooting can be without apparent physical consequence.

"Getting shot is not like falling off a horse," Dr. Hamburg says. "To sanitize an act of violence is a disservice. It is unwise to minimize the fact that a President can get hurt and that he can bleed."

One more contribution had been made to obscuring the pain and reality of violence, to blurring the critical distinction between fiction and fact. The media President was, in his way, as much a product of the age of unreality as was John Hinckley, the media freak. In the media age, reality had been the first casualty.

How Many Murders Can Your Kids Watch?

The National Coalition on Television Violence says these are the most violent programs on national television. The data was compiled between February and May of 1981, and the scores for each program are in violent acts per hour.

Prime-time Shows	Network	Acts of Violence
Walking Tall	NBC	25
Vegas	ABC	18
Lobo	NBC	18
Greatest American Hero	ABC	18
Incredible Hulk	CBS	14
Magnum P.I.	CBS	14
Hart to Hart	ABC	14
Dukes of Hazzard	CBS	14
B.J. & the Bear	NBC	14
Fantasy Island	ABC	11
Enos	CBS	11

Saturday Morning Cartoons	Network	Acts of Violence
Thundarr the Barbarian	ABC	64
Daffy Duck	NBC	52
Bugs Bunny/Roadrunner	CBS	51
Superfriends	ABC	38
Richie Rich/Scooby Doo	ABC	30
Plasticman, Baby Plas	ABC	28
Heathcliff & Dingbat	ABC	28
Fonz	ABC	28
Tom & Jerry	CBS	27
Popeye	CBS	26
Johnny Quest	NBC	25
Drak Pak	CBS	23
Batman	NBC	19
Godzilla/Hong Kong Phooey	NBC	18
Flintstones	NBC	13
Tarzan/Lone Ranger	CBS	13

FOR FURTHER READING

Doris A. Grabner, *Crime News and the Public.* New York: Praeger, 1980.

Philip Lesly, *Overcoming Opposition: A Survival Manual for Executives.* Englewood Cliffs, N.J.: Prentice-Hall, 1984.

Dan A. Lewis (ed.), *Reactions to Crime.* Beverly Hills, Calif.: Sage, 1981.

VI

Sex and Sensationalism in the Mass Media

S EX SELLS. That notion seems to have become axiomatic in modern
American society. The mass media are business enterprises, not supported by taxpayers or subsidized by government. They need to sell to make
a profit to stay in business. Sex and sensationalism have therefore become
a staple ingredient in much mass communication in order to gain an audience
and earn a profit.

In truth, American newspapers on the whole are not nearly so sexually
blatant or sensationalistic as the tabloids of London's Fleet Street or so titillat-
ing as the photos of scantily clad young ladies that adorn nearly every page
of South Africa's white and otherwise ultraconservative newspapers. But sex
has often sold in America and has increasingly been used by the mass media.
The older, more journalistically conservative and economically well-established media have given up on sex and sensationalism. But if you look at early
editions of the *New York Times, Washington Post, Time, Harper's, Atlantic,*
etc., you will note that in their youth these publications were not loathe to
tempt new audiences with promises of salacious content.

The younger, less well-established magazines and newspapers frequently
turn to sex and sensationalism to build circulation and audience. And it works,
because America still gets turned on by sex. When *Time* magazine put a
nearly nude Cheryl Tiegs on its cover, the issue sold far more copies than
almost any other in its history. *Playboy* and *Penthouse* magazines are the
most widely read magazines on American college campuses. *Hustler,* a
magazine that features excrement and blasphemy, is among the 30 best-
selling magazines in America, far outselling *Harper's, Atlantic, New Yorker*
and thousands of other serious periodicals.

Despite the taboos placed upon it by the National Association of Broadcasters, the FCC and countless citizens' groups, television also has become
candid about sex. It started in 1972 when ABC produced *That Certain
Summer,* about homosexuality. In 1974, *A Case of Rape* was the first major
TV drama to explore that crime from the woman's point of view, and in the

same year, *Born Innocent* portrayed a teenager sexually assaulted with a broom handle. In the early 1980s, this kind of TV drama increased; *Something about Amelia,* a frank treatment of incest, was aired, and *All My Children,* a daytime serial, added a continuing lesbian character.

20 · Sex and Violence

By Joe Saltzman

Sex and violence without accountability and responsibility is the real problem in the mass media, especially television and the movies, argues Joe Saltzman. He is chairman of broadcasting in the school of journalism at the University of Southern California and a writer/producer of films for television. He is also associate mass media editor of *USA Today,* in which this article appeared in the July 1982 issue.

Those who argue that there is too much sex and violence on television and in motion pictures are missing the point. Both are important aspects of any human situation. It is not the coupling of humans or the murders of unfortunate victims *per se* that should concern us. What *should* bother us is that an increasing number of TV and motion picture characters behave irresponsibly and are never held accountable for their actions. Responsibility for what one does is sidestepped completely. Destroy everything in sight; the credits will come up before the day of reckoning.

Particularly offensive is a film genre involving every conceivable kind of vehicle collision. These include such major films as *The French Connection;* Burt Reynolds' *Smokey* films; Steve McQueen's *Bullitt* and his last movie, *The Hunter;* and scores of others, including those vehicle races across the continent (*Cannonball Run* is a typical example). While these films involve various twists of plot and character, all have one thing in common—a series of car chases and devastation. Some others offer a series of little chases leading up to the grand chase-to-end-all-chases (*The Blues Brothers* is one example).

The violence in these films is not the real problem. The violence is usually so beautifully choreographed that it does not necessarily offend (most of the people seem to survive, if not the cars and buildings), or so gross that it is beyond redemption (straining us to remember that everything is make-believe with special-effects geniuses in charge). What is particularly offensive is that these films are peopled with characters who, once in an automobile or truck, never have to answer for the results of their recklessness. No matter how many buildings, trucks, police cars, animals, people, or you-name-it are maimed, the offending driver simply romps along, usually with some country-and-western song cheering him or her on. After all the carnage is over, the principal character walks away—usually whole, occasionally hurt, always headed for the next adventure. Never is there a hint at or mention of compensation for the injured, the offended, the ones who simply, unfortunately, got in the way; people and property are destroyed with wanton disregard.

The question is, what happens to people watching this continual, impersonal destruction who are never made to understand that we are all ultimately responsible for our actions? If you hit a car, even in pursuit of a criminal, the owner of that car has a legitimate grievance; it is up to you (and your insurance company) to make restitution. If, as producers argue, violence is a part of the human condition, then so is responsibility. In real life, you just do not commit mayhem and then go on to the next scene. By not showing us accountability, no matter how that may distract from the action, filmmakers create a moral limbo that is disturbing.

The same situation holds true for sexual relationships shown on both the big and little screens. The innumerable hit-and-run relationships with anonymous females and males are a far more offensive situation than the actual depiction of coupling. It is the degrading of human beings, not the physical relationship, that is the issue here. That is the true horror of most pornography—the individuals are put through their paces like animals. There is seldom any treatment of love and affection and, again, true responsibility.

There is no reason why filmmakers can not show more responsibility. Occasionally, a film or TV series does show a conscience. The producers of "The Rockford Files" turned the usual consequences-be-damned attitude inside out by insisting that Jim Rockford, played by James Garner, always be held responsible for his actions: a ticket if he parked in a red zone to chase some bad guy on foot; repair bills for damage caused. That accountability gave Rockford a reality and a dimension few other TV characters have had. "M*A*S*H" does similar service to its basically non-violent characters caught up in a violent situation out of their control.

It should be clear by now that the money-paying public enjoys naked bodies and naked violence. To try to talk against sex and violence is not unlike talking against alcohol and cigarettes. People still will drink and smoke because they enjoy it. People will go to see sex and violence on the screen because they enjoy it. All the headshaking and censorship won't alter that fact. It is one thing to argue against drink, quite another to ask that people who are drunk not drive; one thing to order people not to smoke, quite another to ask them to smoke in restricted areas. If discussion shifts from prohibition to responsibility, then we will have made some progress.

What parent-teacher associations, the Moral Majority, and countless other concerned groups should argue for is that fictional characters who hurt or kill or destroy or lust should be liable for their deeds. When a truck-driving country boy destroys people and property, he should own up to his actions and pay the price. When a bounty hunter or police officer destroys people and property, each should reimburse the citizens for either bodily injury or property damage. Anyone on the screen who acts irresponsibly in any situation should pay the price.

Producers of films rightfully argue that sex and violence have been a part of our culture since the beginning of art. No one would deny that. There are few bloodier plays than Shakespeare's *Macbeth* and few sexier romps than *Fanny Hill,* but characters in these fictions are held accountable for their actions in one way or another.

The price need not be prohibitive or overly moralistic, neither puritanical nor prurient. Nothing is more sacred in our traditions than proper compensation for property and person. When the current cinema and TV producers realize that, perhaps we will head back toward a moral mainstream that is altogether proper for any serious-minded populace.

21 · Porn on the Fourth of July

By James Traub

With the rise of cable television, pornography on the
tube has proliferated in the 1980s. Even video music,
the rage of the middle 1980s, has been widely
criticized for exploiting explicit sexual scenes to
attract young viewers. As the new medium on the
block, cable has turned to sex and sensationalism to
win its share of the market and the profit, as James
Traub, a contributing writer for *Channels of
Communications,* indicates. His article is reprinted
from *Channels of Communications,*
December/January 1981–1982.

Soft-core pornography was just beginning its migration from seedy
theater interiors to sacrosanct living rooms when Buffalo's cable operator decided to hop on the gravy train. After ten years of supplying the
Buffalo area with the conventional fare of cable television—movies,
sports, out-of-town programming—CableScope Inc. decided last spring
to get in on the trend by selecting Escapade, a new "adult entertainment" programmer, as one of its upcoming offerings.

In order to push this audacious new product to potential subscribers, the company adopted a time-honored technique from the world of
eroticism, the teaser. In March, CableScope offered a brief peek at
Escapade to viewers of its regular channels. "Send your children to bed
early tonight," the item began. It was nothing much, says CableScope
vice president David Kelly, "a little skin, some violence, some foul
language." But the ad didn't have quite the intended effect: Some
Buffalonians, it turned out, considered sex on television an affront to
their morals, an invasion of their privacy and, above all, a shock. Angry
letters were written to members of the Common Council, the Buffalo city
government; angry denunciations were made to the press. Even before
the actual programming began to appear, Escapade became a local
cause célèbre, and its merits were finally debated at an acrimonious
four-hour public hearing. Nothing was resolved. "Maybe the teaser
wasn't such a great idea," concedes Kelly.

CableScope's blithe salesmanship and the furious reaction of some Buffalonians are being echoed in cities across the country, as cable officials discover the bull market in sex programming, and angry citizens arm themselves against what seems to them an assault on traditional values. Both the availability of sex on cable and the protest against it are increasing at a terrific pace. Escapade now has well in excess of 100,000 viewers nationally, as does an even racier competitor, Private Screenings, which offers such titles as *Love, Lust and Ecstasy.* Neither is much more than a year old. And ON TV, another rival operating as a pay service through the ultra-high-frequency broadcast spectrum, has more than 570,000 viewers. Fancy hotels now routinely contract to show their guests films like *Virgin Prize* along with more conventional fare. At least $60 million worth of X-rated video-cassette tapes are expected to be sold this year. And in what is surely the most striking omen yet of the vast market for televised sex, Playboy Enterprises Inc. and Penthouse, the diversified giants of the sex-and-fun industry, each bought into partnerships with adult-entertainment cable programmers last summer; Playboy now owns half of Escapade. "Give people a chance," says Stuart Altshuler of Quality Cable Network, a group that distributes minimally pared-down X-rated films for cable, "and they'll line up in droves to see what we've got. People want sex materials. That's the bottom line."

Is America really ready for sex materials? And beyond its impact on cable, what will be the effect of all this commonplace sex on our lives?

The gathering vehemence of the protest against such institutions as the public school system and network television, and the "progressive" values they appear to embody, is rooted in the argument that the apparent moral revolution of the last fifteen years has outdistanced a great many Americans, who will not line up in droves for sex "materials." As for cable, only a few years ago (in times that now seem prehistoric) it was touted as a revolutionary medium. It seems naïve today to hold cable to its original promise—that it would make technology serve democracy and let a hundred electronic flowers bloom—especially as the industry comes increasingly under the control of established media powers. Yet the sudden apparition of high-gloss sex, along with its palpable trail of euphemism, seems a particularly blunt reminder of the failure of this promise.

Sex has attained legitimacy on cable so swiftly that groups like the Moral Majority have lagged behind in orchestrating an attack upon it, but it seems reasonable to expect that the protest against "cableporn," as opponents call it, will only grow more vociferous in the future. Cities that do not yet have cable—and most do not—may become battlegrounds for this issue. In the upcoming competition for franchises, citizens groups can be expected to challenge would-be franchise owners on the issue of sex programming. A number of cities have been trying to write clauses into the cable contract prohibiting sexually oriented material. And some of the more conservative nationwide cable system operators have been speaking up for virtue, keeping sex programmers off their local systems, and disowning them as best possible where they do in fact appear. Though over at Escapade the optimism is unbounded, it is unclear whether almost all Americans, or almost none, will be able to watch *The Sensuous Nurse* in their living rooms in the near future.

Buffalo has already suffered from the kind of rhetorical and legal skirmishing now developing among municipalities, citizens, and cable operators around the country. Buffalo is not what you would call a liberal town. Like other cities on the Great Lakes, it enjoyed a heyday in the industrial boom of the first half of the century, and has since been in decline. A high percentage of senior citizens live in Buffalo, which is predominantly white, Catholic, and blue-collar. But along Delaware Avenue, just beyond the fringes of downtown, more and more of the dilapidated Victorian homes are being occupied by relatively prosperous young white-collar workers who may ultimately rejuvenate Buffalo.

Prosperous young people, says CableScope's Kelly, form the constituency of Escapade. He should know. At thirty-seven, Kelly is president of the Buffalo school board and a pillar of the local liberal establishment. His views on television, like those of most cable operators, are laissez-faire. Standing up to his accusers on the Common Council during the tumultuous hearing last April, he said, "Are you going to decide what's moral? You want to talk about morality? You want to set standards? You can't set standards, because you don't represent the community." Who does represent the community? Kelly feels that's a moot point, because individuals should be able to watch whatever they want on television. Community standards should not apply.

A lifelong Buffalonian, Kelly knows the citizenry well enough to expect that Escapade might not be able to creep into town on little cat's feet. "I anticipated some bullshit," he says offhandedly. He felt that with an election coming up council members would use the pornography issue for political capital, and that his enemies among local conservatives would use it in their drive to unseat him from the school board. But Kelly refuses to believe that any of Escapade's critics are genuinely offended by its programs.

James Likoudis, on the other hand, has a hard time crediting anybody who watches Escapade with any semblance of morality. As a board member and unofficial theoretician of Morality in Media of Western New York, Likoudis led the campaign against cableporn, speaking to members of the press, writing to council members, helping to build up the pressure that eventually led to the public hearing. Likoudis is middle-aged and conservative, lives in the comfortable Buffalo suburb of Williamsville, and describes himself as "a Catholic, a teacher, and a lecturer."

It seems no accident to Likoudis that Dave Kelly is the head of the school board. The same "subjectivism" that he feels now dominates and undermines the public schools has become the prevailing ideology in the entertainment industry. Sitting amidst a forest of papers scattered on his floor and chairs, Likoudis pictures his struggle against pornography as part of a grander moral battle—between those who hew to the traditional values rooted in the Bible and the American past, and those "change agents" who, like Norman Lear and Phil Donahue, wish to "impose their lower standards on the whole community."

But don't many people enjoy erotic movies? Likoudis, suddenly the implacable Catholic moralist, retorts, "Many people approve of genocide." The same people who approve of pornography? Yes.

Violent rhetoric and intractable opposition have become common in our national discourse, but it seems clear that the issue of sex on cable will make its own special contribution to the widening gulf between those with "progressive" and those with "traditional" values. Though the Moral Majority and the Coalition for Better Television have not yet paid much attention to cable, Morality in Media has taken up the slack. The group has affiliates around the country and has been consulted in efforts to restrict the dissemination of obscene material on cable in Houston, Fort Worth, Milwaukee, St. Louis County, and Pittsburgh. A related group, the National Obscenity Law Center, has worked with state legislators to devise bills that would ban televised sex without, it feels, infringing on legitimate First Amendment freedoms.

While the opposition to adult entertainment has grown better-organized and more self-assertive, the identity of its purveyors has changed altogether. As cable sex has evolved from an act of rebellion to a growth industry, the amateurs and ideologues have been replaced by businessmen for whom the key word is respectability.

The new breed of cable-sex purveyor calls his work "adult entertainment" and is very clear about what is and is not kosher. Ernie Sauer of Private Screenings says, "We go as hard as we can," and offers titles like *Has Anyone Seen My Pants?* as well as *Gas Pump Girls.* But Private Screenings draws the line at those X-rated films that include penetration, and Andrew Fox, Sauer's lieutenant, insists on calling their goods "light entertainment."

The palm of respectability, though, clearly belongs to Escapade. Until recently the channel was offered in a package with Bravo, a highbrow culture channel. Gerard Maglio, president of Rainbow, the parent organization, is at pains to defend Escapade against charges of undue prurience. He is a strong advocate of "parental control boxes" to lock the set away from curious youngsters, and he points out that Escapade does not show its tapes in public at cable conventions. "People who know Rainbow," says Maglio from the edge of his seat, "know that we're not exploiters of anything. And now there can't be any doubt that we'll be within the boundaries of good taste."

Now, in fact, Escapade has just become a part of the Playboy empire, the bastion of good taste in sex. The Playboy Channel will be *Playboy* magazine on the air, presumably competing head-on with the slightly less prestigious *Penthouse* channel. *The Sensuous Nurse* will still appear, but now it will be surrounded by talk shows, all kinds of earnestness, and such whimsical imspirations as a strip-tease game show.

Escapade did its best to persuade, or disarm, its critics in Buffalo. It commissioned a poll that asked cable subscribers, in a suspiciously leading fashion, whether they objected to legal restrictions on their choice of viewing material. It turned out that 96 percent did so object. Escapade also sent a company representative to the public hearing to speak up for its concern about young people and its all-around integrity. The hearing didn't resolve anything, since city attorneys had already pointed out that New York state law prohibited restrictions on material offered through cable. (New York is one of the few states to have such a law.) It did give Morality in Media and other angry citizens an opportunity to air their grievances and to prove that they were not a tiny band of fanatics. James Likoudis claims that "people in Buffalo don't want dirty porno movies." But since there are at least as many subscribers to Escapade as there are members of Morality in Media, this would be a difficult claim to prove.

But the people in Buffalo have said neither "yea" nor "nay" to porno movies. It was the Common Council, presumably their representative body, that discussed the issue and conducted the hearing; in Buffalo as elsewhere, the city council awards and supervises the franchise, and stipulates its terms. Buffalo's Common Council, which consists of whites and blacks, liberals and conservatives, arrived at no clear point of view on Escapade after much discussion. Of the fifteen members, only three seemed to favor some sort of restriction on CableScope. Councilman James Keane was the principal spokesman for the Morality in Media point of view. In the hyperbolic style typical of Escapade's foes, he argued that pornographic movies "encourage rape and all kinds of sexual deviation and deviant behavior." On the other hand James Pitts, a liberal black, defended CableScope stoutly, calling the dispute "a classic struggle of censorship versus choice."

The laws governing programming on cable remain inconsistent and unclear. The Federal Communications Commission, which regulates television and radio, has over the last few years relinquished almost all control over cable practices to states and localities. All media are subject to federal regulations and state laws prohibiting "obscene" material; according to the 1973 Supreme Court decision in *Miller v. California,* material is obscene if it violates "community standards." If a jury says it's obscene, it's obscene. But whether cable should be subject to the stricter standards applied to television and radio remains to be decided. "Indecent" material—for instance, "dirty words" that are not necessarily obscene—is also prohibited on television and radio. Legal precedent exempts cable from this added stricture, which was originally adopted because people cannot easily avoid indecent material on broadcast media such as radio and television. Also, the use of the public airwaves entails a special public responsibility. Cable, on the other hand, does not use the airwaves, and offers potentially unlimited viewing options.

Nobody at present is very happy with the legal state of things. Few disputants wholeheartedly accept the "community standards" concept. Many civil libertarians and cable businessmen consider it an offense to the First Amendment to subject free speech to a popular test; many conservatives consider it an offense to morality to subject ethical standards to a popular test.

Of course, no one knows what most Americans think about "adult entertainment." Indeed, no one knows what most Buffalonians think, the Escapade poll notwithstanding. Random interviews with residents turned up no more definite point of view than one would expect in a large, heterogeneous city. Carol Scharlau, who says she likes "artistic pornography" but mostly likes public television, says of Escapade, "It's mostly B or C movies. There's a great deal of violence. I don't think much of it myself." Richard Woods says, "If I had cable, I'm sure I'd get a program like that. It just costs too much, is all." (Basic cable costs $8.50 a month, the additional thirteen-channel Supercable another $6, and another $10 for Escapade, which is only available to Supercable subscribers. The total cost is $24.50.) Some of those who have Escapade, not surprisingly, think it's just fine. Dorothy Holmes, who says she watches television eight hours a day—it was audible in the background as she spoke—said of the channel, "I have it and I like it. I can see better movies than on any of the networks. It's worth the money I spend on it."

The idea of "community standards" is chimerical. Some approve, some disapprove, most don't care. Cable's many options tend to break the community down into a series of interest groups. Network television is majoritarian, but cable is pluralistic. This "narrowcasting" capacity has always been considered cable's special virtue, both for viewers and programmers. Escapade can reach some 3,000 households in Buffalo, appall everyone else, and still be profitable. Yet paradoxically, the community-standards concept makes cable programming subject to the will of the community at large.

A recent cover of *Cosmopolitan* magazine featured a model with ample cleavage, who was tugging downward with both hands at her already plunging neckline. It seemed as if she wanted to expose her nipples in a gesture of defiance, but knew that if she did, *Cosmo* would no longer be *Cosmo*. This ambiguity is at the heart of contemporary American opinion on sex and nudity. Some beaches have gone nudist, though the idea still deeply offends many people. In movies, of course, nudity and sex are hardly debated issues. But on television the naked body remains an upstart with an uncertain future. Sex seems to be teetering on the edge of respectability; surely television will push it one way or the other, for better or for worse.

Sex therapists point out that Americans, only now emerging from the dark mists of repression inherited from their Puritan ancestors, will be helped over their fears if sex becomes publicly acceptable. Cable has the additional virtue of being the first mass-marketer of sex that seeks to appeal to women as well as men, since it will now be coming into the home. The *Penthouse* channel's Bob Jacobs, especially sensitive on this score, says, "We don't want to denigrate women." Jacobs is planning to have female film director Lee Grant host his racy talk show, *Gods and Goddesses*. Indeed, moral traditionalists' fears that cable sex will lead to homewrecking, rape, and so on, may prove quite unfounded, given the apparently irresistible tendency towards more softcore, sensual, nonviolent sex.

But will all this adult entertainment really be so good for adults?

The sexual revolution as a whole seems to have led to a widespread sense of inadequacy. With traditional restraints to sexual gratification gone, everyone is exposed to the unattainable ideal of high-powered performance, total knowledge, uninhibited bed-hopping. Nowhere is this ideal more thoroughly taken for granted than in erotic movies, where most of the characters are sex machines. Who can be equal to these fantasy-projection characters? Maybe The Playboy Channel will show us movies about overweight people in their forties who can't get it up. But don't hold your breath.

There is a deeper point, though. What happens if and when television pushes sex into the realm of respectability? James Likoudis points out that television "desensitizes" us about sex, as it does about violence. How can sex be all that special if you can sit in your living room and watch it hour after hour? Similarly, a child may wonder how anyone can make a fuss about his smoking a joint when he can buy rolling papers in the local dime store. Television seems to have a unique capacity for turning whatever it touches—sports events, political candidates

—into a commodity, readily available, readily discountable. Many clergymen feel apprehensive about the electronic church, fearing that television worshippers will lose their capacity to appreciate the beauty and mystery of faith. How can sex, whose allure and popularity need not be compared to that of religion, survive such ubiquity? To put it another way, what will instant gratification do to sex?

What, it might also be asked, will sex do to the media? Adult-entertainment programmers like to point to cable's something-for-everyone capacity in vindicating their product; Andrew Fox proclaims gravely that Private Screenings is "meeting the promise of the communications revolution in one additional way." But titillation was not among the local needs that cable was once expected to satisfy. And if sex becomes commonplace on cable, can sex on network television be far behind?

Already the issue of sex on cable has been clothed in the holy garments of the First Amendment, as well as in the more secular dress of the consumer's right to choose. To most cable operators and programmers it is simply a question of giving the public what it wants. John Lack, the executive vice president of Warner Amex Satellite Entertainment Company, puts it succinctly. "If there's a community that says 'we want X-rated programming,' I don't see why the cable system should be the arbiter of taste." These are businessmen, after all, making marketing decisions: If people want it, it can't be bad and shouldn't be prohibited. The other side says it's bad and therefore should be illegal.

Neither side seems willing to consider the possibility that the televising of naked people may gain constitutional, but not moral, sanction. The world of "victimless crimes"—gambling, prostitution, recreational drugs, and even adult entertainment—may occupy precisely such a twilight area. It is possible to regret the appearance of *Caligula* on television without demanding that it be removed. Yet we have become such a legalistic society that we cannot clearly distinguish between rights and responsibilities. The dispute over sex programming on cable is only now beginning to materialize fully, and its capacity for inflicting further harm on a nation already remarkably divided has become clear. Perhaps the cause of rational debate would best be served if opponents recognized that an unpleasant and even dangerous activity may nevertheless be legal, and if advocates considered the possibility that a legal activity may nevertheless be harmful.

22 · THE TWILIGHT ZONE

Sex and sensationalism sell in America's
supermarkets. The rise of the *National Enquirer*
proves this point. The *Enquirer* now has a weekly
circulation larger than the daily circulation of the
New York Times or the *Washington Post* or the
Wall Street Journal.

Discover magazine's anonymous article, "The
Twilight Zone," points out that the sensationalism in
the tabloids is not limited to sex but spills over into
coverage of medical and science news. It appeared in
the September 1983 issue.

No intelligent person could possibly believe them. No supermarket
checkout counter is complete without them. Press critic Hodding Carter
has called them "the twilight zone of American journalism," and the
dozen or so million people who buy them regularly are hopelessly ad-
dicted to them. They are the enormously successful weekly tabloids,
which shamelessly bombard their readers with a mélange of gossip, sex
scandals, and stories about strange people, animals, behavior, and occurrences.

All this is highly entertaining and harmless, of course—except to the
wronged celebrities who occasionally sue for damages. But the tabloids
also extensively cover medical and science news, and their coverage
does not merely border on the irresponsible. It adds new dimensions to
the term.

The proliferating tabloids are all lurid imitations of the pioneer of
the genre, the 57-year-old *National Enquirer,* which has become conservative in its middle age. Conservative, by tabloid standards, means
that the *Enquirer's* "science" stories these days cover subjects no more
remarkable than the mysterious flying stones inside and outside the
house of a truck driver, the rock-hurling Argentine ghost that is impervi-
ous to police bullets, a New York City psychic who has seen John
Lennon's ghost in the Dakota apartment building, and the attempt by a
Catholic priest in Argentina to exorcise a twelve-year-old boy whose
demon has given him incredible strength and x-ray vision.

It is all downhill from there. A recent issue of the *Examiner* chroni-
cled the claim of a Finnish oceanographer that a species of human

goldfish—perhaps descended from survivors of the lost continent of Atlantis—has been discovered living deep beneath the sea. Under the headline "Hot-Blooded Bigfoot Attacks Chinese Peasant," the *Weekly World News* reports that a shortage of male yetis (Asian bigfoots) led one blue-eyed female yeti to ravish a male Chinese peasant. According to the *News,* Chinese scientists suspect that the yeti is now carrying the peasant's child. Harping on a favorite tabloid subject, the *Sun* claims that nine U.S. presidents have met secretly with aliens from UFOs, and that the eruption of a Mexican volcano may have been "triggered by a deadly beam from a huge flying saucer." Not to be outdone, the *Globe* prints a map of the United States showing the locations of recent UFO sightings. "D-day for the long-feared invasion of America by hordes of extraterrestrials is growing near," the *Globe* warns, quoting a UFOlogist who says, "It's just about time for them to make their move."

The tabloid editors also keep up to date on astronomy. Referring to the recently discovered comet, the *Weekly World News* reports: "Now scientists fear that IRAS-Araki-Alcock could very well shower our planet with a contagious rain of death-dealing germs that medical science would be helpless to cope with."

In a crueler vein, the tabloid editors regularly mislead readers suffering from serious diseases. Hardly a week passes without stories on quack cancer cures. This summer alone, readers have been led to believe that they can relieve their arthritis symptoms with the Pill, carrots, sex, vinegar-soaked sponges, injections of lamb cells, and the X-factor (one's attitude). Some cures for herpes: a heart drug and appropriately worded telephone calls. AIDS, too, has received the tabloids' attention. Reports the *Sun:* "Deadly Gay Disease Caused by King Tut's Terrible Curse."

The tabloids often disagree with each other. In reporting that a previously unknown cosmonaut named Tanya had been violated by aliens in space during a secret mission in the 1960s, the *Examiner* assured its readers that both the recent flight of Sally Ride and the 1982 mission of cosmonaut Svetlana Savitskaya had been "incident free." Not according to the *Sun.* In what should be the biggest scoop of the year, that paper claims that Savitskaya conceived a baby while on board Salyut 7. It actually goes on to quote her: "The conception was a physical act performed solely for the sake of science." That is more than can be said for the bizarre conceptions of the American weekly tabloids.

23 · THE BOSS DON'T LIKE ROBBERY MAKE IT SWINDLE

Inside the *National Enquirer*

BY SIMON BARBER

Simon Barber takes an inside look at how a tabloid
like *National Enquirer* is produced. A former
Washington correspondent for the British newsweekly
NOW, Barber worked briefly for the *Enquirer*. His
article is reprinted from the *Washington Journalism
Review*, July/August 1982.

The genial Scot at the National Press Club bar in November painted
a pleasing picture of *National Enquirer* opulence in the Florida sunshine. Winter enhanced his plausibility. My visions of having to invade
Hollywood funeral parlors, sift through mountains of celebrity garbage
or track Senator Kennedy to see whether he broke the speed limit on
the George Washington Parkway were dispelled. "Mythology," he said.
And if there was a touch of the hustler in his broad Glasgow accent, it
was belied by the half-moon reading glasses, professorial tweeds and
Mont Blanc fountain pen.

The *Enquirer*'s recruiter found me at a vulnerable moment. My
previous employer, a British newsweekly, had folded some months
previously; the job hunt was going badly; I was broke. I could scarcely
afford to go to the supermarket, much less scorn the drivel on its checkout counters. Sympathy for Carol Burnett, whose suit against the *Enquirer* I once cheered, had become a luxury.

He suggested I try my hand as articles editor. It started at $1,000
a week, carried the responsibility of creating and running a network of
reporters, and might, in the event of some really spectacular death or
disaster, involve a little travel. Hopelessness, and the rakish idea of
building a Smileyesque Circus dedicated to ferreting out the Untold,
Amazing and Bizarre, were ample stimuli. I bit, and three days later I
was on a prepaid flight to Florida.

The *Enquirer* resides in Lantana, one of those countless ribs of real estate whose primary function is to separate Palm Beach from Fort Lauderdale and I-95 from the Intracoastal Waterway. A bland tract of telegraph poles, tired palm trees and prefabrication, it is remarkable on two counts: it has a large population of Finns and coruscating soulless-ness.

In the midst of this refugee camp for the cold and old, wedged between a railway line and a crumbling sports facility, the *National Enquirer* makes its one stab at irony and keeps a low profile. Once the visitor has given up trying to figure out the Minoan-style bull's horns that mark the entrance, he is pleasantly surprised by the landscaping. The grounds are thick with hibiscus and other fragrant shrubs, each thoughtfully labelled with its botanical name. The building itself lives up to a more squalid expectation. No bastion of multimillion-dollar publishing this, instead a sleepy single-story sprawl that might serviceably house a small electronics factory. Like everything in Lantana, it exudes the grim quality of being *instant.*

It was perhaps my misfortune to be ushered into the presence of executive editor Mike Hoy at lunchtime. The editorial offices were all but empty, and conveyed, in an efficiently pastel way, a sense of inno-cent cheerfulness, like an outsized kindergarten. Indeed, one of the newsroom cubicles was stacked with exotic toys. I began to suspect that the people who worked here might be having fun.

Hoy, thirtyish, Australian and modelled on the lines of a hygienic rock star, encouraged this view by offering me a job, on a trial basis, within 15 minutes of our meeting, and by explaining why the company would not, as had once been its practice, rent a car for me. One of my more exuberant predecessors had driven an *Enquirer* Hertz into the Waterway.

Then he said something rather strange. "I want you to know that we really are looking for editors." Having been tracked down by a recruiter and flown in from Washington to be interviewed for such a slot, and having just been offered a month's trial at it, I thought this scarcely needed saying. That impermanence was an institution at the *Enquirer* did not occur to me, nor, as yet, did the connection between its despera-tion for new blood and whatever had possessed the predecessor to sink his car.

Every aspect of the *Enquirer,* from its management to what it prints, is governed by a surgically precise appreciation of human frailty. This is the great achievement of its owner and publisher, the splendidly named Generoso Pope, Jr., and evidently appreciated by six million supermarket purchasers a week. Pope's relationship with his employees approximates that between the God of the Old Testament and the Chil-dren of Israel minus forgiveness. His control is total and awe-inspiring, his ways mysterious, his retribution swift. When he deals with a man, he likes, to use his own very secular phrase, to "have him by the balls," and usually succeeds. Under Hoy's guidance, it was hoped I would quickly learn to divine his will.

Known simply as The Boss or GP, Pope dominates the waking thoughts, and more than a few sleeping ones as well, of all at the *Enquirer.* An authorized account, published in 1978 by the *Miami Herald,* describes Pope as "a tall man, built like a Bronx precinct captain." Fifty-four years have softened that image somewhat, except for the face. Said an editor, one of the few women in the *Enquirer*'s higher echelons, "There doesn't seem to be anything behind his eyes." The effect is a mask of staring malevolence, which does little to endear.

He is educated. A top of his class graduate in engineering from MIT, according to the authorized account, he served in the CIA's psychological warfare unit. Further glimpses of his life beyond the *Enquirer,* which he purchased in 1952, are virtually nonexistent. His father was the publisher of the New York Italian-language paper *Il Progresso.* Some see murkiness in the fact that since he moved the operation from New Jersey in 1971, Pope has never left south Florida. He says he hates to fly.

There is an eeriness about him enhanced by gun-toting plainclothes security men who haunt the premises, spot checks on reporters' telephone conversations, and the uniformed Lantana patrolman who escorts Pope to and from his car.

My first day should have taught me more, perhaps, than it did. My initial mistake was to turn up in coat and tie. Higher authority wore shirtsleeves and an increasingly familiar pair of pants, a style, admonished Hoy, that I would do well to emulate. I blundered again by trying to strike up a conversation. Apparently one did not talk to colleagues, be they only six feet away, except by internal telephone and with one's back turned. I needed coffee. "Put a top on it," someone hissed as I carried a cup to my desk. "The Boss don't like stains on his carpet." To atone, I worked through lunch, another miscalculation. "The Boss believes in lunch." Next day I ate, grateful for a temporary escape, only to be informed that I'd been seen leaving the office with the wrong people. My companions were said to be under some form of cloud and best avoided. Besides, what was I doing having lunch? I wondered whether Pope ever specified his desires before punishing those who transgressed them.

The arena in which this curious drama was to be played out might have been a newsroom in any large daily before the electronic age. Its open plan layout was symmetrical about a narrow avenue across which two rows of editors, about nine in all, numbers varied, were occasionally polite to one another. Behind them sat their secretaries, each busily pretending to callers that her boss worked in a private office. Next, pinched into lines of narrow, benchlike desks were the 40 or so reporters, each owing allegiance and his job to a particular editor. Finally the writers, who are responsible for the *Enquirer*'s deathless prose and probably the happiest employees. Deemed creative by The Boss, they were left in peace. At the end of the central aisle, rather too close to where I had been stationed, was a series of glass cubicles. Pope had a grander sanctum elsewhere, but it was here he would come when he wished to make his presence felt. Assistants ensured that a pack of Kents and a lighter always awaited his arrival.

As a deracinated Englishman, I should have had some cause to feel at home. A surprising proportion of my new colleagues hailed from Britain and parts of its old empire. A buzz of familiar accents could be heard insinuating charm down various telephones. Having had some success in this department myself, I could imagine the interrogatees being thoroughly disarmed. To their cost.

Pope's predilection for what one American writer has called British Empire Journalists has little to do with the narcotic power of the speech patterns, however, but derives more from their tradition. American reporters tend to take a rather romantic view of their trade, see themselves as somehow in the public service. Their minds are burdened with scruple. Not so the British Empire Journalist. He can report, as in 1978 one imaginative correspondent for the *London Daily Mail* actually did, that President Carter was growing a beard to look more Lincolnesque, and receive a kudogram from his superiors. Rupert Murdoch ranks high in the Pope pantheon, and as publisher of the *Star,* constitutes Pope's most serious opposition.

My first impression was that my fellow editors all looked very ill: exchange their typewriters for oars and they would have made perfect (though, on $60,000 a year and up, very expensive) extras for the sea battle in *Ben Hur.*

Enquirer reporters had the furtive look of kicked and beaten Labrador Retrievers. Foot soldiers, they were at least insulated from The Boss by their editors, whose paranoia-induced savagery was the price of relative security. The reason I had been brought in from outside to be articles editor was that no reporter wanted to risk his neck or his $45,000 a year more than was strictly necessary. Now and then one or two were forcibly promoted—given the option of leaving or climbing—which regularly amounted to the same thing: climbers who failed at editor could expect to be fired, and the chances of making it were no better than those of a World War I subaltern on the Western Front.

One of the luckier ones was the young Englishman sitting to my left. Promoted some months previously, he had begun his career on a small provincial paper outside London, and had been lured to Florida by wealth and warmth. In an earlier age, he might have set out to make his fortune in some tropical outpost of Empire. He seemed to be doing all that was required of him; his file drawer was full of good stories in progress, yet there was an air of doom about him. Colleagues shied away, spoke of him with, of all things in this emotional charnel house, compassion. It turned out he was being executed, *Enquirer*-style.

First they cut his salary, then removed his reporters, forcing him to rely on stringers, finally demanded a massive increase in output. "This is the way Pope always does it," he said one evening towards the end. "They dig you a grave and say climb out if you can. You never can. The grave just gets deeper." Several days later his desk was empty. In this case the editor was allowed to reincarnate himself as a reporter. A rare privilege.

A reason would have been helpful, but my enquiries were about as fruitful as asking a priest to account plausibly for human suffering. The editor's defrocking could be ascribed to no particular commission or omission, it was just the way things worked around here. A sympathetic reporter noticed my puzzlement. "The Boss is a toy train freak," she explained. "I think he likes to see us as a vast toy train set. He throws switches, sets up obstructions, and races us off bridges just for the hell of seeing what happens."

In terms of how they are put together, there is essentially little difference between the *National Enquirer* and, say, *Time.* To the structuralist, anyway. Leads are developed and assigned, reporters and stringers turn in voluminous files, which are rigorously checked for accuracy, boiled down by writers into the house style, and finally, with luck, printed. There, however, the resemblance ends.

Appearances to the contrary, gungho fabulism is not the *Enquirer*'s line of business. Nor indeed is journalism, in any of the accepted senses of the word.

Bear in mind that the *Enquirer* is not designed primarily to inform, amuse, or even, really, to be read. It performs these functions, of course, but they are secondary. It exists to be consumed, much in the same way as premixed peanut butter and jelly. The idea is pretty simple. People enter the supermarket in a buying frame of mind, so let's give them one more brightly packaged object to shove into their shopping bags.

The editorial content addresses itself scientifically to the consuming mood, a condition frequently brought on by boredom, restlessness and unfocused dissatisfaction. The universe depicted is a bright, uncomplicated, unambiguous place where things either are (in this category we may include metempsychosis, UFOs and psychic fork-bending) or are not (unhappy endings, celibate celebrities, wise government). The buyer is told that he is basically good, that the rich and famous are basically miserable, and that the quality of life is improving immeasurably: cancer, obesity and arthritis can be cured.

In short the *Enquirer* is a kind of printed Valium, its editors little more than pharmacists, cutting each other's throats to combine and recombine a limited number of ingredients which Pope, the master chemist, has determined will have the desired effect. It is a mechanical and, the financial aspect apart, unrewarding task.

The process begins with the lead. Each editor is expected to submit 30 or so to The Boss every Friday, of which perhaps half a dozen may be approved. On the rest he scribbles the ubiquitous initials NG (No Good). The ideas come from reporters and stringers (all of whom receive up to $300 if their offering gets into print), other publications (there is always a race for the new *Omni, Cosmopolitan* and *Self*) and the imagination. Memorable specimens from the latter category include "The Junk Food Diet," "How Brooke Shields, Loni Anderson and Farrah Fawcett are Wrecking Your Marriage" and "Let's Get Accredited as a Salvation Army Fundraiser and Go Knocking on Celebrity Doors to See How Generous the Stars Are." A number of celebrity leads are preemptive. I myself proposed "Wedding Bells for Patti Reagan and Peter [Masada] Strauss." The Elizabeth Taylor-John Warner separation was in the works probably before they had even said their vows, and certainly for months before it occurred. At this very moment at least one editor is contemplating marriage between Robert Wagner, widower of Natalie Wood, and his television costar Stephanie Powers.

Often, of course, celebrities do dramatic things that even the *Enquirer* cannot foresee, the deaths of Natalie Wood and William Holden for example. In these instances, leads are rushed through under the rubric of "Untold Story," the logic being that there will always be one. In the Wood case, which occurred a few weeks after I arrived, the editor involved went to extraordinary lengths to find something that the voluble Los Angeles coroner Thomas Noguchi had *not* said. What he came up with was the suggestion, ascribed to Top Doctors, that the actress, rather than drowning, had been asphyxiated by a potent mixture of drugs and alcohol. This on the basis of a well-stocked medicine cabinet and the alleged absence of froth on the victim's lips. What I heard of the interviews went as follows: "Doctor, if after consuming such and such a quantity of alcohol, a person were to take drugs x and y, what would be the result?"

Even the most grizzled veteran cannot second guess Pope's taste with any certainty. His notions of what constitutes a contemporary star are quixotic, but seem to derive from movies of the '50s and '60s (hence Sophia Loren, Princess Grace and, by association, her daughter Caroline) and the top ten Nielsen-rated shows he happens to watch (not *60 Minutes*). Dudley Moore, of *10* and *Arthur* fame, fails to register on the grounds that he is, and I quote, "Not big enough." The currently lionized Tom Selleck *(Magnum, PI)*, did not have the right stuff either, until Pope was persuaded to poll his favorite gauges of gut reaction, the secretaries.

There are, however, some totally predictable NG's, chief among them blacks, except when they practice voodoo, or are child comic Gary Coleman. I presented Hoy with a heart-warming story of a young New Orleans man who had survived a grain elevator explosion and 80 percent burns to become a multimillionaire (a surefire hit under the Rags to Riches category). He immediately asked me what color he was. Black. Kill it. Gays, on the other hand, may be beaten up at will. An outraged account of San Francisco's demographics was headlined "Sick! Sick! Sick!" The *Enquirer*, a self-styled Equal Opportunity Employer, has no minority employees.

Once an approved lead has pleased Story Control, a computer programmed to weed out duplicates, it is ready to be reported, and the ethical mayhem begins.

If celebrities are the potatoes of tabloid journalism, miraculous medicine is the meat. Unfortunately, the medical fraternity likes to be circumspect about describing its advances, and talks of percentages, hopes, possibilities, rarely of anything so definite as a cure. This is too gray for the *Enquirer* which does not recognize the subjunctive mood: a thing either is or it isn't. The trick, therefore, is to get the medical man, who in his right mind would never even talk to the *Enquirer*, to say things that would cost him his shingle if he tried to say them in the *New England Journal of Medicine*, and on tape. This is known in the trade as Burning Docs.

Technically, the reporter's path is strewn with regulations. Not only must his interviews be taped, but he has signed a waiver binding him to identify himself as working for the *Enquirer* and as using a recorder, thus excusing his employers when, as he must, he sidles past the law. If his editor wants him to get a doctor to say something, he is under considerably more pressure to produce than to be an upright citizen. Refusal to carry out an order is treated with military firmness.

There are many ways to ease on-the-record indiscretion from an interviewee, the most popular being the old 20 Questions ploy. The subject is stroked into a state of trust and then hit with a series of convoluted queries, to which he will answer, if the reporter is adroit enough, merely yes or no. These little words can be made to speak volumes. Critical readers may have wondered how it is that supposedly sophisticated professionals, when quoted in the *Enquirer*, always manage to clutter their remarks with an effusion of amazings, incredibles and fantastics.

This method is openly encouraged by Pope. In a memo distributed to all newcomers he commands bluntly: "Ask leading questions." Lest it be carried too far, reporters are then reminded, "Quotes should not only be appropriate but believable. A Japanese carpenter should not sound like Ernest Hemingway, or vice versa."

Add to this Pope's rather confining taste in vocabulary, and the results can be bizarre. Reporter Byron Lutz had worked hard to produce

"The Biggest Swindle in U.S. History," a tale of a computer rip-off within the federal government. He had even persuaded a Justice Department official to agree that it was indeed "the biggest swindle," a questionable assertion by itself. Enter the Evaluator, a character whose task it is to condense finished files into single paragraphs for the benefit of Pope and the writers.

Evaluator: "This won't get through, Lutz. We don't use swindle."

Lutz: "But that's what the guy at the Justice Department called it, it's on the tape."

Eval.: "It's got to be robbery."

Lutz: "But there's a difference."

Editor (intervening): "He's right. Let's look it up in the dictionary."

Eval.: "Hey, I don't care. The Boss don't like swindle make it robbery."

Editor (snapping to what looked suspiciously like attention): "Get on it, Lutz, get your guy to say robbery. Now."

At least doctors and officials can be made to speak. Celebrities are less obliging with their reputations. To reveal the supposed drama of their lives the reporter must resort to an altogether higher order of guile. In compensation, he is required to offer less in the way of proof. Stars are public property, and consequently vulnerable to the First Amendment.

Much of the information on who is bedding whom, whose career is on the skids and who is currently being detoxified from what, emanates from the thriving gossip industry as a whole. I do not pretend to know how this works. Obviously, however, the *Enquirer* has to delve deeper to satisfy what the commercials call its readers' "Enquiring Minds."

What makes the reporter's mission particularly tough is that he is often covering not a set of circumstances his editor knows or believes to exist, but one that the editor *wishes* to have happen. A new TV series has emerged, perhaps, and The Boss wants an exciting story about its participants. Or an editor may conclude that there has been too striking an absence of Farrah Fawcett. A reconciliation with Lee Majors is needed to fill the gap. Thanks to a large array of "insiders," "friends" and "intimate sources," many of whom are in the *Enquirer*'s pay, such things can be arranged.

In some cases, a great deal of old-fashioned shoe-leather reporting does go on, though it has been known to get out of hand. The coffin photographs of Elvis Presley are not an isolated phenomenon. One reporter told me that while tracking the hometown life of a currently popular television actress, he stumbled onto the fact that that she had had had an abortion. Such was the pressure he was under, he lined up a neighborhood hoodlum to steal the records. Getting mixed signals from his editor, he thought better of it.

Celebrity romance stories are frequently the work of reporters whose main activity is to hang around fashionable watering holes. Maitre d's and waiters are also retained. Thus, the *Enquirer* often has a pair of eyes in place when an interesting couple appear in public for the first time, or have a violent quarrel.

Hollywood sex, in the *Enquirer,* is a formulaic affair. The starting assumption is that any physical contact represents romance. At the lower end of the scale, hand holding is described by "insiders," who do not have to be told the *Enquirer* style, as "they looked like a pair of teenagers in love." Any kiss less demure than a peck is evidence that the relationship has turned "hot and heavy."

Equally earnest is the *Enquirer's* attitude towards the paranormal. Cranks are not tolerated, and anyone claiming to have been reborn, sighted UFOs or communicated with the beyond is subjected to hypnotic regression. This is considered sounder evidence than a lie detector because the latter has the unfortunate habit of being accurate.

The reigning exponent of what may be called the "Hey-Martha-Will-You-Get-A-Look-At-This" school is *Enquirer* superstringer Henry Gris, a former UPI correspondent. His latest find is one "Dr. Victor Azhazha," eminent Soviet scientist. Dr. Azhazha claimed, and there is an artist's conception complete with silhouetted Kremlin to back it up, that a mysterious shining cloud had drifted over Moscow one night causing great consternation. A friend of mine, stationed in Moscow for a well-known British daily, commented, "I didn't see this cloud, which was perhaps careless. It might have started World War III."

A cardinal rule of the information trade is that the more bald and unconvincing a story, the greater the machinery needed to lend it verisimilitude. The *Enquirer* is inordinately proud of its Research Department. A copy of a glowing account in *Editor & Publisher* that appeared in 1978 is compulsory reading for all arrivals.

E&P tells us that Research is staffed by probing professionals, headed by Ruth Annan, a 16-year veteran of *Time.* Her team includes "two medical specialists, two lawyers, a linguist who speaks four languages, a geographer, three with master's degrees in library science, one with a master's degree in educational psychology, and an author."

And yet it regularly lets through palpable inanities. The concept of a "4,000-year-old Stone Age statuette" does not bother it, for example, but this is a quibble. Most of what escapes the tireless fact-checkers is on a grander scale, even in cases where the facts can actually be checked.

Researchers are cunningly paid less than reporters whose work they scrutinize, and thus approach their task with the enthusiasm of inquisitors. That the *Enquirer* is published at all is not their fault.

I have no doubt that Research pursues Truth with genuine vigor; but it is hampered by one major defect: literal-mindedness. If the tapes and copy jibe, and sources when contacted agree to what has been reported, the story must, however reluctantly, be granted the imprimatur of accuracy.

One disadvantage of Annan and her staff is that they clog up an already hopelessly slow system—lead time is usually three or four weeks—with haggling that, given the nature of the beast, is utterly unnecessary. On the upside, however, their mere existence enables reporters to tell a suspicious world that, yes, really, the *Enquirer* does strive after fact. As editor Paul Levy told *E&P,* "Today any reporter can say with justifiable pride that he works for the most accurate paper in the country."

FOR FURTHER READING

Stuart Ewen and Elizabeth Ewen, *Channels of Desire: Mass Images and the Shaping of American Consciousness.* New York: McGraw-Hill, 1982.

Wilson Bryan Key, *Media Sexploitation.* New York: New American Library, 1977.

VII

Mass Media and Politics

THE NEWCOMER to the American political scene can note the number and kinds of mass media available for informing the public and conclude that to get full coverage, to become known to the voters, all a candidate has to do is send releases to all the media, give them all statements, and be ready for the reporters and commentators who will call for interviews.

Of course it doesn't work that way. Political candidates and political issues have to pass the test of newsworthiness and the idiosyncracies of the various media and the men and women who work for them in order to get space and time in the news. The candidates and their aides have to understand how the print and broadcast media differ in the ways that help the public decide what and who are important enough to support—even whether to vote. Most important in today's political climate, candidates have to know how to entice the media for time and space, which leads to the accusation of "show biz."

The articles in this chapter concentrate on what television is doing to major political campaigns, because, unless there is a surprise revolution, candidates will continue to "dress" for television, to plan media events that make them look diplomatic or savvy or down-home or whatever their consultants tell them they should look. Print isn't to be forgotten, but the reporters and analysts have to wait until the bright lights and minicams are moved or watch and take notes from behind them.

Many local candidates, running "lesser races," are following the leaders, hoping—often against reality—that local stations and newspapers have staffs large enough and equipment mobile enough to follow them around their districts. They are finding limits to both staffs and equipment. Perhaps they will wisely turn from the proliferation of media events—pseudo events in terms of newsworthiness—to discussions of issues and their positions on them. Perhaps that's wishful thinking.

On the national scene, the 1980 presidential campaign marked the turning point. The "boys on the bus," the predominantly male newspaper reporters who bused around the country with the candidates and the subjects of Timothy Crouse's popular book, *The Boys on the Bus,* got moved because of television. Joel Swerdlow says, "In 1980, print reporters were shoved to the back by television, which took the best seats, provided the amusements and did everything but call the shots. The candidates did that." His article chronicles the move and discusses the meaning.

Daniel Burstein describes in detail the effect of TV on the 1984 presidential candidates and their consultants. Consultants are downplaying their roles in "packaging," he explains, because the public is skeptical of "packaged candidates." That raises new questions, such as "Is the public better served by the known or the unknown in politics?"

Walter Karp agrees that television is important to American politics—meaning the political process, not the political campaigns—and he examines the sometimes subtle undertones of TV news programs and questions their editorial techniques.

24 · THE DECLINE OF THE BOYS ON THE BUS

BY JOEL SWERDLOW

Television dominates political campaigns but the candidates, not the journalists, call the shots, argues Joel Swerdlow. It's a "campaign sham," he says, that reporters resent and the public should, too. Swerdlow is coauthor with Frank Mankiewicz of *Remote Control Television and the Manipulation of American Life* and author of numerous articles. This article is from the *Washington Journalism Review*, January/February 1981.

In mid-October in Elizabeth, New Jersey, John B. Anderson stands waiting in front of a microphone. His perfectly coifed hair, sharply pressed suit, and impeccably shined shoes are silhouetted against graffiti-covered buildings and rat-infested garbage. Winos wander into the edges of the tableau. Beyond lies the decrepit waterfront. The air is foul.

On cue, cameras whir and Anderson opens a press conference. He makes a lengthy statement that includes no new proposals or insights about the urban blight around him. As cameramen maneuver carefully so that none of the winos block their view of the presidential candidate, reporters begin to shout questions—none of which acknowledge the stark evidence of Elizabeth's decay. The press wants to know what Anderson thinks about the coming Carter-Reagan debate. A few reporters drift off to a nearby bar. Ten minutes later, the entourage of reporters and technicians scramble back to their buses and head out for the next media event.

It is a typical campaign stop, 1980 style—cynically staged with little substance, designed for television, and almost comically blatant in its disregard of the real issues.

The cold essence of presidential campaigning has become the television camera lens. Campaigns are organized for pictures, not words or ideas. In fact, the Boys-on-the-Bus—the romantic truth-tellers licensed to lurch from coast to coast with presidents and would-be presidents—have become irrelevant. Reporters for newspapers and magazines have been nudged, literally and figuratively, to the back of the bus by the steady, inexorable encroachment of television.

Television dominates the stage. TV reporters are the stars, but even they are so controlled that some of the nation's highest paid journalistic talent has become a virtual arm of the campaigns. Reporters covering the campaign have become members of a herd, physically as well as professionally, seduced—or at least tamed—with comfort and drugged with food and drink.

Presidential campaigning changed so much that veterans of the 1960s and early 1970s felt like antiques or vestigial remnants. Gone were the days when a candidate's chief goal was meeting people. Gone were pre-dawn handshaking at factory gates and the post-midnight meetings with campaign volunteers in storefront headquarters. Gone were the exhausted, bleary-eyed reporters, struggling to make just one more early morning baggage call before their flesh gave out.

The normal 1980 campaign day permitted plenty of sleep for candidate and reporter alike. "A synthetic campaign is just as successful at getting attention as the 16-event, bust-your-ass type of campaigning," explained a veteran reporter. Furthermore, when the schedule did pick up, as Jimmy Carter's did during the final weeks, it was simply to jam more "media markets" into a single day.

Police cars with flashing red lights rushed candidates from airports to campaign stops in serpentine motorcades made eerie by the absence of onlookers on sidewalks and street corners. Often candidates skipped the motorcade and simply landed at the airport, spoke to a crowd gathered by the runway, hopped back on the plane, and took off again.

At large rallies, the candidate's purpose was not to speak to live people, but to people watching television's evening news. In addition to national network coverage, every stop offered countless opportunities for local and regional exposure.

Beyond focusing on TV coverage, the campaign tried to control and shape the coverage, often in subtle and complicated ways. Reflecting and reinforcing the dissolution of traditional party coalitions, Jimmy Carter, Ronald Reagan, and John Anderson each carefully constructed his own personal coalition of images for the television camera. Each visited factories, truck stops, Chicano colleges, senior citizen centers, suburbs, and ethnic neighborhoods—not to meet people, but to have his picture taken with people of the "right" demographic characteristics.

NBC's Heidi Shulman said she was very conscious of how the campaign tries to manipulate the picture: "Most days it's all so obvious, everybody winds up with substantially the same thing."

"The Regan staff knows that the picture carries an impact no matter what the correspondent says," Shulman explained, "so they give us a picture with a message, 'Reagan likes blue-collar voters.' And even if I say, 'Reagan is out to get the blue-collar vote,' people will remember the picture and not my words."

The networks did not heroically resist manipulation. Their principal problem, in fact, was which of the good footage to broadcast—a decision reached by a curious combination of news judgment and the outright triumph of appearance over substance. Often a shot was aired, not because of what the candidate said, but because of how he looked while he said it. "New York wanted me to lead with something about Iran," said a network correspondent, summarizing his day's work, "but I told them we couldn't because we have such good pictures."

Those TV pictures, however, depicted a different reality from what an onlooker witnessed. Raw footage of a typical Reagan campaign day, for example, revealed that the crowds always seemed much larger than they actually were. To a large degree, this resulted from clever advance work by the media-sophisticated Reagan staff. At almost every stop, it was the same: they positioned a raised camera platform close to the speaker's platform, and roped off a huge "press area," designated off-limits to the public. This forced the crowd to pack tightly into the space between the candidate and the camera, insuring that Reagan always spoke to an impressive-looking mass of humanity. Of course, the networks sometimes were able to get a wider panoramic shot, say, from the top floor of a nearby building. But the minute-by-minute schedules rarely permitted such innovation, and the risk of a camera crew being left behind was great. As a result, viewers back home got the incorrect impression that the candidate continually addressed massive crowds.

The campaign's virtually exclusive preoccupation with the TV audience made print reporters obsolete—and they knew it. "Where do you even find time set aside for us to file our stories?" Rhetorically asked a *Los Angeles Times* veteran, holding up the neatly typed, multipage daily campaign schedule (or "bible"). The Associated Press and United Press International reporters reached tens of millions of readers daily, but they, too, felt like uninvited guests. "The campaign staff couldn't even care if we disappeared," noted one of the nation's leading wire reporters.

Self-pity flowed freely from ostensibly tough political reporters. "We're second-class citizens," one muttered. "We shouldn't even be here," said another. Indeed, many of the trade's most famous names were not. Among the heavies canonized in Timothy Crouse's *Boys on the Bus* (1973) who spent less time on the 1980 campaign buses were David Broder and Haynes Johnson of the *Washington Post,* Jules Witcover, then with the *Los Angeles Times* and now with the *Washington Star,* and syndicated columnists Rowland Evans and Robert Novak.

Although frustrated, those who did show up accepted their lot docilely. In the not-too-distant past, print reporters complained—loudly and effectively—whenever a microphone or camera got in the way. But now, it is the other way around. Print reporters meekly stepped aside as camera crews pushed by with a barely polite "coming through." When their vision was obstructed by the camera stand, some of the nation's toughest reporters stood passively in the background taking notes.

Occasionally, the print people did assert themselves. For example, at a Reagan "press conference" heralding his endorsement by police and firemen's unions, Eleanor Randolph of the *Los Angeles Times* stood up and asked Reagan a question, pointing out that his position on handgun control differed from that taken by the police union.

"This is a photo opportunity," answered a top Reagan staff member.

Randolph repeated her question.

The aide repeated, "This is a photo opportunity."

Reagan continued to stand there quietly.

Once again, Randolph asked the question. This time, Reagan stepped forward and answered. (This incident provided one of the few insights into Reagan. His natural instinct seemed to be toward politeness and answering questions. "What you have here is a nice old man with an overly ambitious wife and a good staff," old-timers explained to the newly arrived. "If you get the question within earshot, he'll answer it because he's a decent guy," said one experienced wire reporter. But this tendency seemed to scare his aides. At one stop, Reagan extemporaneously discussed the Equal Rights Amendment and his staff was visibly upset.)

The "programmed" candidacy, with its rare direct access to the candidate, was first noted by Joe McGinnis in *The Selling of the President,* when, in 1968, Richard Nixon essentially bypassed the press by appearing in public only under carefully controlled circumstances. Then came the Rose Garden campaigns—Nixon's in 1972, Jerry Ford's in 1976, and Carter's in the 1980 primaries. By the fall of 1980, campaign staffs had learned a valuable lesson—a non-traveling candidate gets as much attention as does an indefatigable hustler.

Whatever their personality and policy differences, Carter, Reagan, and Anderson used similar techniques. Ken Cummins of the *Florida Times Union* computed that during a week of travel to nine states, Ronald Reagan spent only 170 minutes speaking in public. Jimmy Carter was somewhat more active, but on a typical campaign day, running from 12 to 18 hours, the traveling press spent no more than 3 hours within 100 feet of him, and of those few hours, barely a second was made available for questions.

All three campaigns herded the press around. When the plane landed, buses were waiting to take them to the "event," where they generally had to walk through a roped-off gauntlet of sign-waving, campaigning partisans. As soon as the candidate finished his speech, reporters then lunged back toward the buses to begin the whole process all over again. The rules were brutally simple: buses waited for no one. So reporters had to forget about wandering off into the crowd for interviews, or seeking out local officials, or finding out how well organized the local Right-to-Life group was. If you indulged in such wanderlust, you might be left behind in Abeline, Texas, with no commercial flights scheduled to leave until the next day. (Once, ABC correspondent Ann Compton left the Anderson campaign in New York City to stop at her office for a chat with her bosses. Catching up with Anderson's caravan in central New Jersey cost her a $70 cab ride.)

Reporters also had to endure the candidates studiously pretending they were not there. The candidates unabashedly played to the cameras, but in public comments, gestures, and eye contact they acted as though the herd of newspeople hanging on every word were invisible, uninvited voyeurs, unworthy of acknowledgement.

Despite the slights and snubs, however, just about every print reporter, just about all the time, dutifully followed along, scribbling down words he or she had heard dozens of times before, hoping against hope for something worth reporting to happen. "I don't know why I'm doing this," one muttered while writing the candidate's words. "No one wants to hear this stuff again." (Many reporters on the Carter plane carried their passports, hoping for a quick flight to West Germany to greet the released Iranian hostages.) The principal duty of reporters—and many regarded it as demeaning—was to be alert in case the candidate became a "textual deviate," one who strays from his prepared text.

Reporters engaged in a daily struggle to find a morsel, an unplanned quote, or a revealing statement. Whenever the candidate was available—generally while entering or leaving his limousine—camera crews and reporters zeroed in with the precision of heat-seeking missiles. This was called "door-stopping," and the press engaged in it as often as a dozen times a day. Shouting, sometimes on the run, reporters pinched and poked in the hope of eliciting a snappy comment to lead their story.

"What do you think of the polls showing you slipping?" one yelled in President Carter's direction.

"Oh, really?" came the response. "I don't think I'll quit."

Back on board the bus, wire service reporters already were writing their stories with tape recorders at their ears, playing back what the candidate had just said. Clusters of reporters sat listening to similar tape recordings. The candidate's latest evasions were played repetitiously, forming a discordant symphony to be carefully dissected in search of one clue, one nuance—*anything* newsworthy. After a while, the process became numbing, and some reporters simply stopped caring. "Do you think we'll ever find out what he just said?" a straggler asked while boarding the bus. "Who cares?" a colleague answered.

Such tight control suited the candidates perfectly and campaign staffs knew they held the traveling press hostage. Television people were content with pictures, but print reporters, whose employers paid up to a thousand dollars each day traveling with the candidates, were reluctant to tell their editors that nothing interesting had happened.

From the candidate's perspective, a major element in planning the day became control over the all-important lead. Campaign strategists determined the day's principal story—a Reagan statement on the economy, a Carter attack on Reagan's judgment—and they constructed a vacuum around that story, forcing reporters to use it.

Most observers agreed that in 1980, the Reagan people were by far the most talented in controlling the day's lead. Carter, for all the technical and logistical sophistication in his traveling press operation, left too much room for reporters to do their own thinking. Rarely did he serve up the daily juicy tidbit around which an entire day's story could be based. On the Friday before the election, Carter finally did provide a morsel—material documenting Ronald Reagan's earlier opposition to socialized medicine. White House staff members played over the plane's PA system a recording of the offending 20-year-old Reagan speech. Sure enough, Carter's attack dominated the next day's newspaper stories.

Under the strict supervision of their media specialists, all three candidates remained cloistered, afraid that an offguard comment might ruin the day's plans. Even John Anderson, who used only one plane and rode all day just a few feet away from the press corps, did not walk back to say hello.

Instead, he, Carter, and Reagan used their isolation to, once again, manipulate the press. "Exclusive" interviews given to strategically selected journalists, bound by carefully agreed upon release times, helped to guarantee a steady flow of controlled news. Reporters who were not "in" gave candidates uncomplimentary nicknames. Reagan was "O 'n'

W" ("Oldest and Wisest"), and Anderson was "the Sage from Rock-ford."

The campaign staffs were candid about their manipulation of the press. "Sure, reporters don't have much access to the president," acknowledged Jody Powell, his expression emphasizing that he considered the topic silly. "But he has stopped a half-dozen or more times during the campaign to discuss a particular issue when it was important."

Lyn Nofziger, Reagan's press secretary, was more explicit. "If we just let him (Reagan) go his own way, we'd have a perpetual press conference." When, by chance, a reporter got close enough to ask Reagan a question, Nofziger would wave his arms and shout, "No, no, no questions," and literally throw his body in the way. Sometimes, the fail-safe Nofziger system failed, and it was those times that Reagan made comments that seemed to threaten his campaign. His "trees cause pollution" remarks, for example, were made at an unguarded moment.

The public was surprisingly sophisticated about this game. At a rally in central Illinois, deep in the heart of Reagan country, a young truck driver held up a homemade sign that said: "Hey, Ron. Don't worry about a slip of the tongue. You won't let America slip."

Compounding the journalists' isolation from the candidate was their isolation from newscasts and newspapers. Campaign staffs encouraged this, presumably because it increased their control over what reporters wrote.

The Reagan campaign, for example, was so well organized that reporters often found name plates on their hotel room doors; but the campaign never managed to have newspapers, TV sets, or radios in the press room. And it did not arrange for hotel newsstands to order extra copies of the local morning paper. Reporters in need of a news fix after waking early often slipped into the hotel lobby and ripped open bundled newspapers stacked by the locked newsstand door. Even Tom Wicker of the *New York Times* sat on the bus reading a day-old *Times*. Later, he gave up and read Jane Austen.

Reporters, however, did have one crucial lifeline: their "desks." At each stop, they rushed to the telephones, not to file a story, but to "call my desk and find out the latest developments." They sounded like investors comparing stock brokers. "I'm trying to clarify this with my desk in New York," one said in hushed tones, "but you should know that (Iranian Prime Minister) Raji said the hostages might be released before election day." These calls cross-fertilized the individual campaigns—"Our guy on the Reagan plane says they're emphasizing the economy"—which, in turn, armed reporters with information needed to write the charge/counter-charge story that works so well on television.

The best source of information, however—in terms of actually witnessing what the candidate said and did—was the press pool. Generally comprised of a print reporter, a still photographer, the wire services, and at least one network crew, the press pool accompanied the candidate everywhere. They traveled on the candidate's plane, rode in every motorcade, and greeted him first thing in the morning. The other reporters traveled in the press plane, rode on the press bus, and often did not stay in the same hotel as the candidate.

Pools were called the "body watch," a public witness in case the candidate admitted he was a Nazi, or an assassin decided to strike (known in shorthand parlance as "the event"). But by real news standards, pools were a meaningless exercise. On the Anderson campaign, pool reports were virtually nonexistent. The Reagan campaign provided only sporadic, written pool reports, and once, when a Sioux Falls crowd was disappointingly small, Reagan's copying machine mysteriously broke and no pool report was prepared until the following day. For the most part, no one covering the Reagan campaign seemed to care: if you were interested, you could seek out one of the pool reporters and ask questions. "Did anyone get what's in the pool report?" someone asked. "It's just crap," came the reply.

Only the Carter campaign raised pooling to a science. Elaborate planning shuffled different pools for each event, and traveling typists and on-board mimeo machines guaranteed freshly minted pool reports within minutes of take-off. Carter pool members provided their colleagues with information reflecting their boredom and cynicism: "Before boarding Air Force One, Carter shook hands with every motorcycle cop in the state." "One large black woman began crying effusively when the president came into her line of sight. He didn't notice." "As he (Carter) bounded up the steps, Mr. (Sam) Donaldson (ABC News) asked him, 'How do you think you're doing?' 'We'll know next Tuesday,' the leader of the Free World replied."

It is no coincidence that most of the stories coming out of the campaign trail—standings in the polls, the effect of the debates, the "mood" of the campaign, possible release of the hostages, Carter's attacks on Reagan—suited this process perfectly. The dominance of television images, lack of access to the candidates, door-stopping, and isolation bred a peculiar form of pack journalism. No pack existed in the sense of everyone copying CBS or the *New York Times*. The process was more insidious. It grew from using the same rules of objectivity and newsworthiness to piece together a story from the day's meager morsels. Joint efforts amounted to nothing more than reporters standing around tape recorders helping each other figure out what, if anything, was new. If the day was particularly slow, these groups congregated around the walking encyclopedias—people who had covered a candidate for so long they could say, "When Carter was here in 1976, there were 5,000 people standing in the areas that were empty today." ("When nothing jumps out at you and says, 'This is the story,' that's when you start to worry what the veterans will file," explained a younger reporter working his way toward one of the oracles.)

The pack was also quick to pick up certain feelings and attitudes about the candidates. During the final weeks, for example, Anderson was considered "dead and gone." ("I've done the Anderson-is-dead story," said one network correspondent. "I put him in his coffin. Then I nailed him in. Then I lowered it. I don't have the imagination to think of anything else to report.") Carter was the object of scorn. ("Oh, Christ. Is he talking about his difficult and lonely decisions again?" one reporter whispered. Another reporter responded, "I almost got mugged by an old lady who thought I was a Carter supporter.")

More significantly, a full week before election day, the pack sensed that Carter was finished, but rules of objectivity prevented them from reporting it. They were too bound—and sometimes blinded—by the polls, by presumed truths emanating from their desks, and by the cynicism bred from isolation and daily repetition of self-serving exaggerations by the candidates. A desperate search for something newsworthy had worn away the fine edges of their political judgment. Many reporters knew they had big stories at their fingertips—Reagan campaigning against big government while promising vested interest groups at each stop that he would increase spending for them; Carter floundering, desperately pulling out quotes of past Democrats while rarely even mentioning his own record—and yet, most of these stories went unwritten.

Only those reporters who dropped off the campaign trail escaped this trap. Ronald Brownstein, a staff writer for *Ralph Nader Reports,* poked around Youngstown, Ohio, after Reagan's entourage left, and discovered that the steel plant whose closing Reagan had blamed on government interference was, in truth, the victim of corporate mismanagement. Another reporter went to a reception with Carter, asked everyone present for a business card, and then stayed in his hotel room the next day, telephoning them to find out the real extent of Carter's support in the community.

But such enterprising stories were rare. Leading reporters took to joining the caravan for a few days and then going their own way. The 1980 campaign was noteworthy for the absence of permanent in-flight stars. Frank Reynolds or Anthony Lewis would pop up and then disappear the next day. Newcomers arrived armed with a tremendous fear that they would miss a nuance that would appear in everyone else's story, or that they would be excited about something which turned out to be old hat. So, instead of thinking—let alone asking—the tough questions, they tagged along, emulating the pack and very quickly disappearing into it.

Campaign travel bred another kind of control: the tight, womb-like, home-away-from-home environment in which television was head of the household.

The first four or five rows of seats on the bus were always saved for camera crews. It made sense: they had heavy equipment (tape recorders, microphones, extra cameras, spare batteries, and cassettes) weighing up to 80 pounds and would have had difficulty fighting through the aisle. But woe to anyone who broke apartheid. "You'd better not sit there," voices from the back of the bus warned. If the crews found an intruder, "Hey, man. We gotta have these seats" was only the beginning of their spirited reaction.

On the plane, chartered from commercial airlines, television crews reserved the last dozen or so rows of seats, so they could enter and leave the rear door more easily. Their area became known as the "zoo."

The "animals" were readily identifiable by their clothing—jeans, wild hats, halloween masks—a sharp contrast to the jackets and ties and three-piece business suits worn by reporters. Their behavior fit the zoo image. If everyone on the plane had acted like the animals, then the presidential campaign would have lived up to its romantic, devil-may-care reputation.

Animal games varied. The most noteworthy was blowing whistles. No one has documented when whistles first joined the zoo, but myth has it that in 1972, camera crews bought a whistle, and for some unremembered reason, blew it at a top network correspondent as he was boarding the press plane. The network star responded unfavorably so the animals bought more whistles and blew them whenever he appeared.

Whistles then mostly disappeared until 1980 when, for reasons nobody seems to know, they turned up again. The unquestioned king was an NBC cameraman, Houston Hall, who covered Anderson. Hanging on Hall's press credentials chain were two policeman's whistles, a siren whistle, a crow call, a British Bobby's whistle, and a boat-swain's whistle. In his hand-luggage he carried an 18-inch Clarabell whistle and a heavy train whistle.

"You gotta have a whistle nobody has," the champ explained. "Without at least a siren, you're nobody."

TV crews set up shops selling whistles "at cost." "Acme Whistle Company," a homemade sign proclaimed. Its proprietors came equipped with special tools to fix whistles that were literally blown out from overuse. For a while, the animals on the Carter plane blew loudly at every take-off and landing. Then, curiously, as Carter's imminent defeat became obvious, whistling virtually disappeared. On the other hand, as Anderson sank in the polls, his press entourage blew their whistles more and more wildly.

Whistles became a way of belonging, and many reporters wore unused whistles throughout the fall. "I don't know how I got it. It was just there one morning when I woke up," explained a network correspondent.

If the animals frayed the nerves of some of the others on board, flight attendants—the on-board mother and lover figures—were there to soothe them. "They're just like kids," a flight attendant muttered as the press trooped back after still another rally. Their warmth provided the traveling group with its cohesion. They greeted new arrivals by first name, and those so desiring got a hug or kiss on the cheek.

Whistles and flight attendants were harmless diversions in the press corps' constant struggle against boredom. Skyball proved to be something else.

In early October, newspapers showed pictures of Nancy Regan bowling oranges down the aisle as her husband's plane was taking off. She was playing skyball, the object of which was to roll an orange, apple, or any other round object down the aisle during takeoff and try to hit the end of the plane. For the press corps, the obvious attraction, as with most activities aboard the plane, was that it flaunted the rules —skyball players actually stood in the aisle during take-off (that's about as naughty as press activity got during the campaign).

A few days after Nancy Reagan's picture appeared, however, a *Los Angeles Times* story called the press planes "a transnational Mardi Gras" in which "the general rules of commercial flights are ignored.... " The next day, UPI reporter Ira Allen filed a story that said: "Lustful innuendo between passengers and the three stewardesses fly faster than the plane itself, and safety regulations are unheard of." (It was one careless, exaggerated sentence in an otherwise accurate, interesting piece.)

For several days, nothing happened. Then, through the curious chemistry that suddenly transforms a forgotten story into an earth-shaker, disaster struck. Editors back home began to ask reporters about the lustful behavior, and an airline official yanked the female flight attendants off the charter plane and replaced them with men.

The press protested—"they helped us relax," one explained—and Reagan reportedly called United Airlines and officials of the flight attendants' union, pleading to get the women back.

At the same time, the plane's press corps turned against reporter Ira Allen. He returned to his seat one time to find a Secret Service man occupying it. Camera crew members issued childish threats. Prominent journalists made nasty, sarcastic comments. Over the PA system came jokes attacking him by name, and immediately after each take-off, a Reagan aide began to intone, "From the office of the press secretary, this flight is off the record." "It's just like they're back in a schoolyard," Allen said.

Then, only a few days after the departure of the much-missed flight attendants, they suddenly appeared back on board, not to work, but to sit among the passengers as "public relations representatives."

Ultimately, though, it was not romance or games that proved to be the main in-flight diversion. It was food. Not simply first-class fare, but meals specially catered by the best restaurants in each city. It was unbelievable. Fresh lobster, lamb chops, Chateaubriand, Eggs Benedict, fresh stone crab—all served on starched table cloths, with personal salt and pepper shakers, your choice of wines, and a hot towel to cleanse the fingers afterward. Between meals came endless snacks, trays of freshly cut vegetables, caviar, hors d'oeuvres, pastry, shish kebab, baskets of candy bars ("What, no Snickers?" cried a spoiled reporter), cookies and milk, and always, from dusk to dawn, the beverage of your choice. "Oh no, not another meal!" was one of the campaign's most frequently heard remarks. Indeed, the hardest working person on board, putting in longer hours than the candidate himself, was the airline catering representative. Pan American's man in charge of the Carter people once checked into his hotel room after 2:00 A.M. "I'd like a three o'clock wake-up call," he told the clerk. "3:00 P.M.?" the clerk asked. "No," came the response, "in forty minutes."

Chided that food on the Carter plane was better than on Reagan's, press secretary Nofziger insisted that "anyone can have a bad day," and promised, with a straight face, that upcoming meals would certainly be top-rate.

It is unlikely that any story was ever slanted because the Chateaubriand was stringy. But the food subtly helped the press forget the basic senselessness that the traveling assignment had become.

Of course, it need not be that way. Nothing in American society, journalistic ethics, or communications technology *demands* that presidential candidates have extraordinary control over the news or that the most important thing left for the press to think about is the next meal.

However, nothing suggests that things are likely to change anytime soon. George McGovern in 1972 and Edward Kennedy in the early part of his 1980 campaign both operated free-wheeling operations filled with real access to the candidates and top staff. Both lost, a lesson that only seems to reaffirm what other presidential candidates want to believe anyway.

The Kennedy-McGovern approach is now widely regarded as antiquated and quaint. In fact, toward the end of the primary campaign, Kennedy's press operation had tightened considerably. To measure just how far things have gone, the control once held up to derision—Nixon's 1968 strategy—is now expected of so-called "smart" politicians. Not all of Nixon's media machinations are admired and emulated, but the practices he introduced have been refined and made respectable. The TV-oriented, tightly controlled, insulated political caravans of 1980 were noteworthy in that few members of the press or the public found them worthy of note.

The campaign sham, like all show business gimmickry, will change when the audience grows restless. Reporters know this, and deep inside, are eager for the public to react.

One day shortly before the end of the campaign, a reporter wanders aimlessly around the press room. He is tired of free coffee and donuts, tired of rereading the local newspaper, tired of calling his office for the latest political gossip, and tired of waiting for the candidate to leave his hotel room and do something.

"I resent this," he says, "Hell, I resent this. It's all show biz. And the public should resent it, too."

25 · Presidential Timbre: Grooming the Candidates

By Daniel Burstein

Along with the television campaign has come the candidates' television image—and a whole new set of advisers and consultants, says Daniel Burnstein, a New York freelancer. Political issues get attention well after the images of candidates do. Burstein is a New York–based freelance writer. This article is from *Advertising Age,* March 12, 1984.

Walter Mondale seemed to appear tired and even lifeless on occasion.

John Glenn lacked a theme for his campaign and was so uninspiring on the stump that "dullness" was becoming his image in the public mind.

Gary Hart had a tendency to be overly intellectual and too complex in answering questions posed to him.

Reubin Askew blinked too much when he was nervous and frequently shouted when giving speeches, a legacy of his early political days in West Florida when he campaigned without a microphone.

Thanks to the advice of media consultants, however, all four candidates have made progress overcoming these and other chinks in their personal armor. And while debate persists over how influential media consultants really are or ought to be, their importance is underscored by the fact that virtually every presidential candidate from Ronald Reagan to Jesse Jackson has one.

There is only a handful of media consultants capable of advising a presidential campaign—but then again, the client list is fairly short and only develops once every four years. Consultants come from diverse backgrounds in advertising, public relations, journalism, film making and even old fashioned organizational politics. Their role in a campaign can vary from simply producing tv spots or advising on time-buys to helping shape policy, write speeches and plan strategy.

For most consultants, working on a presidential campaign is a one-time experience. "Doing a presidential campaign costs any consulting company a fortune in lost business," says Raymond Strother. "Other people don't want you to represent them because they are afraid all your time will be taken up with the presidential campaign."

On the other hand, for top-flight mediamen and image-makers, the chance to have even a small hand in shaping the image of the next president—at least once—is usually too tempting to pass up.

For the most part, the consultants downplay their own role in "packaging" candidates. Says Mr. Mondale's Texas-based consultant Roy Spence (who spends his noncampaign time as a partner with Austin-based ad agency GSD&M, where he is senior vp-account services), "Walter Mondale has a keen sense of who he is and what he wants to do. Unlike some candidates, there is no need to try to turn him into something other than what he is."

Adds Eli Bleich, Beverly Hills-based consultant to the Askew campaign, "You can never create a whole new candidate. To try to do so would be a real disservice. The media consultant's job is more like that of an attorney trying to put his client's best possible argument in the best possible light. That's what we do—but it's still the candidate's argument, not ours."

Many consultants say that 1984 differs from past campaigns because the public is more aware and more skeptical than ever of "packaged candidates." Books like Joe McGinniss' classic *The Selling of the President 1968,* and movies like *The Candidate* showing a vacuous Robert Redford being manipulated by his consultant have focused attention on the tricks used to project a candidate's image over his reality.

"Any time a political commercial goes on the air today, little red flags go up in people's minds, and they start to wonder if someone is trying to manipulate them," says Raymond Strother, a consultant who divides his time between Washington and New Orleans and who has handled 130 Democratic party candidates over the last 18 years. He enthusiastically believes in the cause of his current client, Sen. Hart.

Mr. Strother says that focus groups conducted by his organization revealed that voters today "want substance and specifics. They want more information than ever."

In Mr. Strother's recent efforts in behalf of victorious Kentucky gubernatorial candidate Martha Layne Collins, he found much more positive reaction to commercials in which her position papers were actually shown or quoted from on tv than those that stayed in the realm of political generalities.

Concludes Mr. Strother, "The days of cute, music-studded spots and glib answers are over. A new attention to detail and fact, suitable for the Information Age, is the order of the day in political advertising."

Mr. Strother claims to have been attracted to Sen. Hart's candidacy because of his "genuine intensity over the issues and impassioned, deeply caring personality."

If Sen. Hart's media convey that image, he insists, it's because it is real. Mr. Strother's imprint has come chiefly in the form of getting the camera in tighter on Sen. Hart to allow his intensity to come through more visibly and in showing the candidate how to be more concise and focused in his replies to questions.

"He knows too much about his subject, and his tendency is to answer a question so thoroughly that he may lose the questioner," observes Mr. Strother.

On the other hand, Sen. Hart also has a tendency to appear uninterested if a question asked of him indeed *doesn't* interest him. Mr. Strother has worked to even up Sen. Hart's tone so that he doesn't appear intense one moment and apathetic the next. On the whole, however, Mr. Strother has found that "Hart resists packaging. If he thinks he's being handled in any way, he'll fight back."

Like Sen. Hart, candidates Cranston and Hollings are thought of as coming across sincerely, without the filters of the image makers. Under the tutelage of the Campaign Group, a consultancy in Philadelphia, Sen. Alan Cranston reportedly gained some weight to appear less gaunt and haggard. But by and large, his advisers accept the fact that Sen. Cranston is not the handsomest candidate in the race and clearly is running on issues, not image.

Sen. Ernest Hollings is called "the unpackaged candidate" by one of his speechwriters, Mickey Kaus, who observes that Sen. Hollings may be the only candidate in the race whose public remarks are exclusively on subjects he deems important rather than ones designed to "correct some problem in perceptions of his positions."

Mr. Kaus acknowledges that the senator plays tennis regularly with one of Washington's top media experts and political consultants, Charles Guggenheim. But although Mr. Guggenheim has offered advice to Sen. Hollings, he is not working for the campaign on a paid basis, leaving Sen. Hollings and Sen. George McGovern the only candidates without paid media consultants.

Even the Rev. Jesse Jackson's campaign—by most estimates in the weakest position of the eight Democratic candidates financially—retained the New York advertising agency Mingo-Jones in February to produce commercials and advise on media issues.

Says David Garth, considered perhaps the shrewdest of all the consultants, "Packaged candidates just don't work since Watergate." He advised John Anderson in the 1980 election and has played a major role in victories of New York Mayor Ed Koch and Los Angeles Mayor Tom Bradley.

Mr. Garth is not working for a presidential candidate this year, preferring to stick to regional and local candidates, but he stresses that with the active, adversarial role of the press on the campaign trail, no presidential candidate can be significantly remade overnight.

"No candidate can stand up to all the tv debates, press conferences and public appearances involved in a modern campaign trying to act out drastic changes in his personality dictated by a media consultant," says Mr. Garth.

While some experts may see a trend away from the "packaged candidate," especially in the *au natural* campaigns of Hollings, Hart, Cranston, McGovern and Jackson, they would get a strong argument from *New Republic* political correspondent Sidney Blumenthal, whose 1980 book, *The Permanent Campaign,* profiled more than a dozen top media consultants.

"Sincerity is the ultimate packaging," says Mr. Blumenthal, who will also serve as a roving commentator for the "Today Show" during the campaign.

"To talk about an unpackaged candidate is like talking about a virgin birth. All candidates use polls, all of them use media consultants, all of them advertise. There's this strange notion that somehow all these techniques are artificially grafted onto politics. But this *is* politics," asserts Mr. Blumenthal.

If there is a candidate more packaged than the others in this year's race, Mr. Blumenthal believes it is John Glenn. "Every other candidate has a real message and a real consistituency. Mondale really is very strong among labor. Jesse Jackson exists because there is an underclass. Gary Hart's talk of 'new ideas' is a direct appeal to people under 40. Glenn is the only one who lacks a specific social base and who represents no concrete force within the Democratic Party. The others are all packaged so as to more effectively reach their natural social and electoral base.

"But with Glenn the packaging itself is designed in the hopes of finding a base. This is the ultimate expression of the packaged campaign," he says.

David Sawyer, a New York media consultant working for the Glenn campaign, has been credited with doing a brilliant job of injecting vibrancy into an otherwise lackluster John Glenn. (A year ago, Mr. Sawyer received some unwanted publicity and in fact became a campaign issue himself while he was involved in the unsuccessful re-election campaign of former Chicago mayor Jane Byrne.) David Garth says Mr. Sawyer's commercials for Sen. Glenn are "the best I've seen in this campaign," and other experts agree that the emotional responses generated by commercials, with their outstanding production values and scenes recalling Sen. Glenn in a space capsule and Sen. Glenn with John Kennedy, have a powerful effect.

Mr. Sawyer's associate Mandy Grunwald denies reports that the consultants gave Glenn speech lessons and insists that "the John Glenn you see in commercials is the same John Glenn you would see in person on a campaign day."

But the impression held by correspondents who have watched Sen. Glenn closely is that the tv commercials—with their nostalgic references to the early '60s, the upbeat music and excited talk of "Believe in the Future Again,"—conflict sharply with the reality of Sen. Glenn and many actually hurt him because the candidate can't deliver on the image suggested by the advertising.

"The image-makers are moving in on John Glenn," said James Reston in a recent *New York Times* column entitled "The Wrong Stuff." "Nothing could be sillier than trying to make John Glenn anything but what he is. He's an intelligent, dead-honest character, a middle-of-the-roader, a bit of a 'square' . . . Nothing could be worse . . . than to try, as his media advisers are suggesting, to be clever and fancy."

"The ads are dramatic but the candidate is prosaic," says *New Republic's* Mr. Blumenthal. "In the long run, the ads will hurt because they are so good. At first it sounds very exciting to talk about the future, until you stop to think that the future doesn't exist, the present does, and John Glenn has nothing to say about the present."

Short of trying to recast a candidate in a whole new image, the consultants have put their imprimatur on the campaign in a variety of ways.

Eli Bleich, for example, suggested to the Askew campaign that given the candidate's lack of name recognition, early 30- and 60-second spots wouldn't accomplish much.

Instead, Mr. Bleich produced a more substantive 15-minute videotape on Mr. Askew. Rather than buy expensive media time, the tape was shown in small living room gatherings every night of the campaigns in Iowa and New Hampshire. The film was deliberately produced with close, tight shots of the candidate, and the presentation was right into the camera to accentuate the "personal" feel in the showings.

Roy Spence is credited with having helped turn a somewhat cold and aloof public image of Walter Mondale into a warmer and more friendly one by creating a five-minute piece that aired in December depicting a folksy, outdoorsy Mondale fishing, hiking in the woods in a pullover sweater, playing tennis hard and talking about growing up on a farm.

The latest Spence creation is a spot first shown in Iowa featuring small children with a dramatic narration accusing President Reagan of saddling the next generation with a trillion-dollar debt, cuts in educational spending and a nuclear arms race that is threatening the planet's survival.

Experts agree that because of Mondale's overwhelming lead over the other Democrats, he has a free hand to position himself against Reagan, while the other Democrats are left trying to position themselves against Mr. Mondale.

Perhaps the most innovative tv spots have evolved from Raymond Strother's collaboration with Gary Hart. Long thought of as an "Atari Democrat" espousing economic revival through investment in technology, Sen. Hart is supported in the spots with a variety of dazzling high-tech graphics. "These ads work well not only to galvanize Hart's base among the post-World War II generation," says Mr. Blumenthal, "but in juxtaposition to Mondale who appears as very much the candidate of the Old Guard by contrast."

If the consultants have a general public image of being all-powerful backroom kingmakers, the consultants themselves see more powerful influences.

David Garth evaluates the role of paid media in a campaign as fourth on a list of factors topped by that of the free media, the strength of the campaign organization and budget resources. He believes that the role of the political consultant has been "overestimated" in national campaigns and says that "the guy who runs the budget is probably much more important than the consultant." He adds that media consultants tend to have more influence in local elections—where they *can* tailor an image for a previously unknown candidate—that will withstand the scrutiny of the less inquiring local press.

Observes Mr. Garth, "The images being formed now in the minds of voters are far more the product of the network news than paid media time. Paid messages from Democratic candidates are reaching only a small number of people in and around the early primary states. In both the Carter and McGovern nominations, their successes came about to a large degree because the national media adopted them. If you are going to do Jesse Jackson's paid media how could you possibly get more results than what was gotten with the free media?"

The role of the consultant has itself become a hot topic in Campaign '84. The *New York Times, Wall Street Journal, USA Today* and numerous other publications have done stories on the strategies of the different consultants. Consultants now prescreen tv spots for the media and explain the strategy behind them, taking campaign coverage to the meta-level of covering what the consultants are trying to get voters to think.

David Garth, for one, thinks that approach is less than useful. "I prefer the mystery. Let the voter think what he wants about the commercial. I don't believe in re-screenings." David Sawyer complained in a recent *New York Times* interview about the news media's focus on internal issues of campaign strategy, saying that his polls showed that voters "know two things about John Glenn: He's an astronaut and he's got a disorganized campaign. They don't even know he is a senator."

Roy Spence attracted a good deal of attention—some would say notoriety—when he said in a recent interview that Walter Mondale had the "courage" to be "cautious."

Political analysts have been debating the remark ever since—did it help Mr. Mondale because it was a true characterization that resonates with voters in this chaotic political time—or did it hurt by portraying him as unimaginative and stodgy?

26 · SUBLIMINAL POLITICS
IN THE EVENING NEWS
The Networks from Left to Right

BY WALTER KARP

Walter Karp explains why he believes network news
programs represent the nation's active political forces
and can be "more politically courageous" than the
leading newspapers. Karp is a political writer and
author of *The Politics of War.* This article is from
Channels of Communications, April/May 1982.

At the White House, Lyndon Johnson used to keep three television
sets going at once so he could watch what all three network news
programs were telling the voters about him. The late President, however, left no known record of his opinion of *NBC Nightly News, CBS
Evening News,* and what ABC now calls *World News Tonight.* This is
unfortunate because it might have provided an answer to a question that
exceedingly few Americans are in a position to answer, although some
33 million of us watch network news nightly. The question, quite simply,
is this: Do the three network news shows differ politically from each
other, and if so, in what ways? Or are all three, perhaps, just mass-
media blurs?

It is not a question you can answer by rapidly twisting the dial back
and forth. I tried that once; all you *will* get is a blur. Nor can you answer
the question by watching a different network's news on different nights.
The only way to discover differences is to see how each network treats
the same day's world supply of noteworthy events. Even a video-cas-
sette recorder alone will not do the trick. It only gives you two network
shows: the one you watch and the one you record. You also need access
to a public-television station that broadcasts, as a service to the deaf,
a late-night captioned rerun of the ABC news. Equipped with a recorder
(rented), access to ABC reruns, and an invincible addiction to American
politics, I sat myself down some days before the Polish crisis erupted

to keep running tabs on what most people casually refer to as "the seven o'clock news."

As the three-headed man, figuratively speaking, the first thing I discovered was an intriguing bit of secret knowledge. On any given evening, the network news shows often differ quite sharply from one another, even about major matters. One evening a few weeks before Christmas, for example, CBS offered as its economic news in "this season of recession," a cheery report on price cutting in Chicago department stores. "A bonanza of bargains," chirped the CBS reporter. "The best Christmas present possible" for sufferers from inflation. That same night, NBC's economic news was "The Farm Squeeze," a grim account of hard times for America's small-farm owners, who were being ground down between low commodity prices and mountainous fuel bills. As for ABC, that same night it drew a dramatic contrast between President Reagan's political triumphs in the spring and economic conditions in the winter.

The very next night, however, CBS cast off its rose-colored glasses and came out with a dark, factual account of the deepening recession. "The figures are grim." Since the figures concerned America's falling industrial production—released that day—it was more than a little surprising to discover minutes later that NBC, the previous night's champion of the poor farmer, passed over the figures as if they were scarcely of consequence. ABC fell somewhere in between.

Then there was the President's last press conference of 1981, which took place on December 17. ABC and CBS treated it briefly and uncritically. NBC took an altogether different tack. Toward the end of the program it offered a remarkably severe attack on the President's performance. According to NBC News, he had been evasive and dishonest. He had made a grossly false denial in claiming that he had never promised to balance the budget—NBC showed footage in which the promise was made. He had made an equally false accusation in blaming the press for exaggerating the menace of the evanescing "Libyan hit squad," when, as NBC noted, all the drumbeating had begun at the White House.

In their treatment of the President that evening, the contrast between NBC and its two rivals could not have been sharper—at least for that day. Was NBC anti-Reagan? If so, what was one to make of NBC News on the day when the stock market dropped 17.22 points and Detroit produced its most catastrophic sales figures in a generation? If there was ever a chance to slam Reaganomics, that evening provided it. CBS, which had swallowed whole Reagan's Libyan menace story, plunged into the grim news with a vengeance. "The Agony of Detroit" was the title of its detailed account of America's worst economic disaster area. NBC thought otherwise. Its chief auto industry story was a feature about American cars being safer in a collision than Japanese models. Buy America, as they used to say in the age of Eisenhower.

All these nightly contrasts, I must admit, had me thoroughly baffled for a while. The differences did not seem to add up to any consistent political line. Moreover, each network seemed to differ from one evening to the next quite as much as it differed from its rivals. It took me some time to realize that the inconsistencies of a given network news program merely blurred—deliberately, I suspect—the edges of each network's quite distinctive political character. The blurs began to fade, however, as the network shows began coping with the stunning events in Poland and with the Administration's reaction to them.

The swift imposition of martial law by the Polish army occurred on Saturday, December 12, which gave the network news programs (and myself) some time to consider what was at stake. Since the Reagan Administration, taken by surprise, was almost speechless for days, the massive influence of the White House did not fall at once on the media. They were quite free for a time to follow their own bent. What I intended to look for was the networks' handling of two facts that seemed almost self-evident. First, the Polish crisis threatened no American interest. It was a crisis—and a grave one—for the Soviet Union, which regards a subjugated Communist Poland as the keystone of its security. This fact the Administration tacitly recognized when it later held the Soviets responsible, quite correctly, for the Polish crackdown.

The second fact followed from the first. Any serious American attempt to champion an independent Poland, whether in the name of Solidarity, liberty, or human rights, could have only one political end: to reduce the power and undermine the security of the Soviet Union. It would become yet another round in the imperious struggle with Russia for global supremacy, in other words, the Cold War. The situation in Poland was a critical moment for the U.S.S.R., a Cold War opportunity for the U.S., and a profound tragedy for the Polish people.

Since almost anything to do with America's thirty-five-year-long rivalry with Russia almost invariably gets distorted in the American press, it was with considerable trepidation that I waited for the story of the Polish crackdown to unfold on the three networks.

CBS Evening News at once confirmed my worst fears. In an ominous tone worthy of a Soviet invasion of Western Europe, CBS described the menacing "Soviet-backed Polish army" and its harsh repressions; played up unsubstantiated rumors of bloodshed, brutality, and heavy resistance; virtually concealed from its viewers the astonishing news that Solidarity had apparently collapsed in a trice. The next evening confirmed my sense of CBS's political object. It continued to report as fact any rumor that might arouse popular anger and raise up a cry for American action—"a wave of sitdown strikes" broken by tanks; troops rebelling against their martial-law masters; "Soviet officials working closely" with the Polish junta. In a fervent sermonette delivered a few days later, Bill Moyers (of whom more later) assailed the Reagan Administration for doing nothing to help Poland regain its liberties. Fresh from frothing over the Libyan menace, CBS seemed determined to further the cause of American intervention in Polish affairs.

When the Administration eventually decided to champion liberty in Poland by imposing economic sanctions, CBS News began covering the Polish crisis as if it chiefly feared that its viewers would fail to support the President's initiative with sufficient fervor. It generally played down Allied criticism of the Reagan sanctions and the Polish Catholic Church's fear of their consequences. On the day a British reporter asked Secretary of State Alexander Haig the deadly question, namely why the United States was such a determined foe of military dictatorship in Poland when it aided and abetted military dictatorships elsewhere (from Chile to South Korea), CBS alone failed to feature Haig's fulminating incapacity to supply a convincing answer.

On Tuesday, December 14, when CBS News began whipping its viewers into a Cold War lather, I took it for granted that the network was merely reflecting the national revival of Cold War attitudes and assumptions. I expected the other two network shows to sound like CBS. To my genuine amazement, NBC that night (and thereafter) treated the Polish news with notable calm and detachment. That cosmopolitanism that treats every event in the modern world as if it were happening three blocks from the White House was utterly absent from the NBC view. Instead of reporting inflammatory rumors, it noted at once that solid information about Poland was lacking. It cited, as CBS did not, a White House spokesman who termed the Polish crackdown an "internal matter." Just what NBC's detachment signified I was unable to grasp at once. On the one hand, it was an unspoken assertion of the fact that Poland did not touch upon America's security and consequently was not something to get dangerously excited about. On the other hand, it could merely have reflected NBC's adherence to the Administration's initial view of the situation.

ABC News proved even more surprising. Like NBC, it was calm, detached, and skeptical of rumors. It surpassed NBC, however, in the sharpness of its analysis of the Polish situation. Unlike its two rivals, it seemed to be genuinely interested in Polish politics. It was the first to note, for example, that the Polish army was not a tool of the discredited Communist Party, but in fact had swept it aside in what was, for all practical purposes, a seizure of power, the first military takeover to occur in the Soviet Union's European empire.

As for America's role, ABC, on December 16, made a particularly penetrating observation. It pointed out that the Reagan Administration seemed to fear that the U.S.S.R. would crush Solidarity, the politically insurgent trade union, without having to intervene directly. The implication was obvious: The Reagan Administration would have liked to see the crackdown fail, and thereby compel the Russians to engage in a costly and enormously damaging military invasion of Poland.

This, however, proved to be ABC's high point. At the President's December 17 press conference (the one that NBC lambasted), Reagan made it plain that the United States would soon commit itself to ending martial law in Poland through the use of economic weapons. America was about to become the official guardian of liberty in Poland after a thirty-five-year hiatus. Considering what it had reported on December 16, ABC might have noted just how questionable such a policy was. If the Soviet Union wanted Solidarity crushed, as the Administration itself insisted, then a U.S. commitment to protecting Solidarity might well make invasion the ultimate outcome. America was skirting periously close to combatting Russia with Polish lives. No such comment, or anything resembling it, came from ABC. By the time the Administration had imposed sanctions on the Soviet Union—December 29—ABC was treating the Polish situation as if it somehow menaced America, a topsy-turvy view strongly espoused by Secretary Haig. But while CBS seemed to regard its viewers as untrustworthy "doves," ABC News showed no such fears. Its reporting on other aspects of Poland continued to be sharp, fair, and analytical as it tried hard to follow, for example, the tortuous political moves of the Polish Catholic Church.

Poland supplied me with a political score card: ABC and CBS seemed interventionist-minded; NBC did not. Indeed it was NBC's devotion to the tacit proposition that the Polish situation did not call for any serious American response that supplied the key to its quite precise political character. Despite the steady hardening of the Administration line on Poland, NBC stuck to its last. On the day of the President's December 17 press conference, for example, it offered the results of a poll showing that 50 percent of the American people regarded the Polish crackdown as inevitable, meaning that half the country expected rebellious Soviet satellites to be squashed one way or the other. When the Administration imposed sanctions against Poland on December 23, NBC alone emphasized that our European allies were sharply skeptical of the policy. NBC, too, was the only network to give a high Polish official time to attempt to justify the martial-law regime. On the other hand, NBC's report on the Marxist regime in Nicaragua was so hostile it verged on the inflammatory.

With that apparent contradiction, NBC's politics at last clicked into place. What its coverage of Poland reflected was not the attitude of post-Vietnam "doves," but something far stronger and more abiding in American politics. In its mild, upright way, NBC News still represented something of the old Midwestern "isolationism," with its aversion to overseas involvement combined with a high-handed attitude toward uppity Central American banana republics. The old isolationist senti-ment, unrepresented now by either political party, cropped up in odd ways at NBC News. When winter storms buffeted America and Europe, for example, CBS duly reported the foul weather abroad. Not NBC. During the period I monitored the networks, it took for granted that snowdrifts in Britain held no interest whatever for its viewers.

Old-fashioned Midwestern Republicanism, upright, decent, and cautious; such was the political character of *NBC Nightly News,* which, aptly enough, is the most popular network news show in the Middle West. The network's conservative treatment of economic affairs confirmed this in a dozen ways. The deepening recession NBC duly reported, but true to its political character, it concentrated on the suffer-ings of small-farm owners, small-business men, and laid-off industrial workers rather than those of the poor, the old, and the black victims of hard times. Moreover, like most Republicans, NBC News seemed deter-mined to give Reagan's economic program "a chance"; it made no effort to link the recession to Reagan's policies. In contrast, when the Ad-ministration settled its American Telephone & Telegraph antitrust suit out of court, NBC was far more critical of the terms than either ABC or CBS, reflecting, I have no doubt, some surviving vestige of the Middle West's once formidable hostility toward giant trusts and monopolies. In a sense, *NBC Nightly News* was more traditionally Republican than present-day Republican party leaders, a fact that was to give its treat-ment of President Reagan a surprising and highly revealing turn.

There was no doubt where *CBS Evening News* stood on the reces-sion and Reaganomics. By mid-January its coverage of hard times had grown powerful, persistent, and grimly eloquent. Shadows of the Great Depression haunted CBS News: frightened old people huddling at a hot meal center; poor children deprived of school lunches; unemployed young men crowding soup kitchens; victims of budget cuts; victims of hard times; victims of Reagan. Unlike NBC, CBS made no bones of its conviction that Reagan's economic policies were a failure, and a cruel failure at that. Alarmist abroad, compassionate at home, CBS revealed a political character as clear as NBC's. It represented, with considerable skill and *éclat,* the Cold War liberalism of the Democratic Party—the party of Harry Truman and Dean Acheson, of "The Great Society" and the Vietnam War, of Senator Daniel Patrick Moynihan and the leaders of the AFL-CIO—hawks with a heart. Since the liberal Cold Warriors are back in control of the Democratic Party, CBS News is virtually a party organ, unlike NBC, which represents a political tradition far more than its represents a party organization.

To embody so thoroughly a somewhat discredited political party cannot be a happy situation for CBS News. This is where the much-esteemed Bill Moyers comes in. Since beginning his CBS commentaries last November, he has taken some of the Democratic Party onus off CBS News. Moyers delivers little sermons whose general theme is that one pol is as bad as another, one party as wretched as its rival, and that, taken all in all, American politics is too repellent to think about. When President Reagan began his campaign against leaks, he revealed once again the Administration's extraordinary appetite for governmental secrecy, so sharply at odds with his continual attacks on governmental bureaucracy, which secrecy quite obviously protects. Instead of investigating that apparent contradiction, Moyers told CBS viewers that Lyndon Johnson was even more fanatical about leaks than Reagan. They're all alike, those bums. When it was revealed that Justice William Rehnquist, a conservative, had been temporarily deranged by medication and his condition concealed, Moyers chimed in with the reminder that the ill health of Justice William Douglas, a liberal, had also been concealed. After describing Reagan's economic program as one that may well lead to "collapse," Moyers concluded that the Democrats had nothing better to offer. That the Democrats have virtually disappeared as a political opposition is the beginning of an important political story. To use it as a getaway line is mere cynical posturing. Moyers' skepticism continually ended where serious political thought should begin. Yet there is method in this muddiness. If CBS News represents a tarnished party, it seems Moyers' function is to pander to the cynical disgust that the Democrats' collusion with Reagan has engendered in the party's rank and file.

Given three networks and only two political parties, ABC, an upstart in the news field, has been forced to be something of a maverick, and an opportunist as well. Of the three networks, it is the least consistent from one day to the next. On the whole, however, it has cast its lot with Reagan and the Republican right, which probably goes far toward explaining its day-to-day variability, which included holding up Reagan's Libyan menace to scorn. Compared to the Democratic Party and to traditional Midwestern Republicanism, the Republican right provides a national network with a perilously narrow political base, and one that was not exactly growing larger in our recent winter of discontent. Despite the frequent surprises, ABC's right-wing character eventually comes through, if only because it is the only consistent thing about it. Like most of Reagan's right-wing supporters, for example, ABC News has expressed its disappointment with Reagan's foreign policy: Bellicose words have not been translated into bellicose deeds. He has offered "the rhetoric of a new foreign policy but not the substance," ABC noted in its critical summary of Reagan's first year in office. Alone among the three networks, ABC deplored Reagan's decision not to sell certain advanced fighter planes to Taiwan. "A bow to pressure from

Peking," ABC tartly noted, as if the ghost of the old China Lobby still haunted its purlieus, as indeed it still haunts the Republican right.

On domestic affairs, ABC generally (but not always) drew a mild picture of hard times and saw to it that Reagan's economic program was stoutly defended. On the day when the worst unemployment figures in recent history were published, ABC featured the President denouncing as a liar anyone who dared attribute the recession to any policy of his. When NBC accused the Administration of backing off from antitrust enforcement—more shades of the old anti-monopoly Middle West—ABC that same evening cited without demur the Administration's lame denial that it had done any such thing.

In truth, the most revealing thing about ABC was how sharply it differed from NBC, the other nominally Republican news program, on certain fundamental points. One difference I already noted: ABC favors an assertive foreign policy, and NBC does not—a contrast reflecting the old isolationist/internationalist split that used to torment the Republican Party.

The second difference reveals something far more significant for contemporary American politics. The issue is Ronald Reagan himself. Although ABC does not treat the President as a sacred totem (it is protective but not reverent), it became clear after watching NBC News for several weeks that its old-fashioned Republicanism was deeply offended by the Republican President. ABC most certainly was not. NBC's criticism of the President's December news conference proved to be, in fact, the precursor to a personal indictment of Reagan that NBC began drawing up on January 14. The date is significant. It was two days after the political storm broke over Reagan's granting of tax-exempt status to two professedly racist colleges. That policy had angered a host of eminent Republicans, and so, quite possibly, it strengthened NBC's resolve to attack the President more boldly than it had done in the past.

NBC began with its account of the President's speech to worried business magnates in New York City. He "sounded more like a cheerleader than a chief executive," noted the NBC reporter, sounding the network's basic theme. On the same program, NBC—and NBC alone—offered a devastating example of the cruel mindlessness of Reagan's budget cuts: War veterans who die as paupers will no longer receive a free military funeral. Thanks to an Administration that endlessly prates about patriotism, such veterans will be unceremoniously cremated, their ashes dumped in a common burial hole. American Legionnaires were "outraged," reported NBC News.

The next evening, NBC homed in on the Reaganites' determined hostility to the Freedom of Information Act, another reflection of the Administration's appetite for secret government. According to a special NBC investigation, the Administration's case for securing FBI immunity from the act is based on utterly false arguments. After the President's January 19 press conference, NBC News once again pounced on his lies, evasions, and misleading anecdotes. A few days later, NBC offered a telling example of the President's shortsighted frugality: A $40 million cut in the Coast Guard's budget was hampering its efforts to keep America's harbors safe for maritime commerce.

All in all, in the space of eleven days, NBC News had painted a devastating portrait of a President who lacked the very first requirement of a serious leader—an honest interest in the realities of the world. The network saw him, instead, as a man who wrapped himself in clichés, dogma, and self-delusion, ignoring as best he could the real business of the world.

I have dwelt on NBC's view of Reagan for two reasons: first, because it demonstrates that a network news program—a medium for the masses, for "ratings," for commerce—can be more politically courageous than the so-called leading newspapers of the country; second, and more important, because NBC's critical assessment of a Republican President strongly suggests that Ronald Reagan, dogmatic leader of a dogmatic faction, may well end up shattering his party. This is but another way of saying that the network news shows represent, with considerable fidelity, the active political forces in this country.

FOR FURTHER READING

James David Barber, *The Pulse of Politics: Electing Presidents in the Media Age.* Beverly Hills, Calif.: Sage, 1980.

Gerald Benjamin, *The Communications Revolution in Politics.* New York: The Academy of Political Science, 1982.

Peter Clarke and Susan H. Evans, *Covering Campaigns: Journalism in Congressional Elections.* Stanford, Calif.: Stanford University Press, 1983.

Timothy Crouse, *The Boys on the Bus.* New York: Ballentine Books, 1972.

Vic Gold, *PR as in President: Press Agents, Media, and the 1976 Candidates.* Garden City, N.Y.: Doubleday, 1977.

Doris A. Graber, *Mass Media and American Politics.* Washington, D.C.: Congressional Quarterly Press, 1980.

Donald D. Groff, et al., *The Press and the 1980 Presidential Campaign: In the Shadow of an Economic Crisis.* Washington, D.C.: The American University Press, 1980.

Michael Barush Grossman and Martha Joynt Kumar, *Portraying the President: The White House and the News Media.* Baltimore: Johns Hopkins University Press, 1981.

Stephen Hess, *The Presidential Campaign: The Leadership Selection Process after Watergate.* Washington, D.C.: The Brookings Institution, 1974.

Ray E. Hiebert, Robert F. Jones, John d'Arc Lorenz and Ernest A. Lotito, *The Political Image Merchants: Strategies for the Seventies.* Washington, D.C.: Acropolis Books, 1971.

Gladys Engel Lang and Kurt Lang, *The Battle for Public Opinion: The President, the Press, and the Polls during Watergate.* New York: Columbia University Press, 1983.

Martin Linsky, *Television and the Presidential Elections.* Lexington, Mass.: Lexington Books, 1983.

Myles Martel, *Political Campaign Debates: Images, Strategies, and Tactics.* New York: Longman, 1983.

Dan D. Nimmo and James E. Combs, *Mediated Political Realities.* New York: Longman, 1983.

Dan D. Nimmo and Kenith R. Sanders, *Handbook of Political Communication.* Beverly Hills, Calif.: Sage, 1981.

David L. Paletz and Robert M. Entman, *Media, Power, Politics.* New York: Free Press, 1978.

David L. Paletz and Robert M. Entman, *Media Power Politics: A Timely, Provocative Look at How the Media Affect Public Opinion and Political Power in the United States.* New York: Free Press, 1981.

Thomas E. Patterson, *The Mass Media Election: How Americans Choose Their President.* New York: Praeger, 1980.

Gerald M. Pomper, et al., *The Election of 1980: Reports and Interpretations.* Chatham, N.J.: Chatham House, 1980.

Austin Ranney, *The American Election of 1980.* Washington, D.C.: American Enterprise Institute for Public Policy Research, 1981.

Austin Ranney, *Channels of Power: The Impact of Television on American Politics.* New York: Basic Books, 1983.

Michael J. Robinson and Margaret A. Sheehan, *Over the Wire and on TV: CBS and UPI in Campaign '80.* New York: Russell Sage Foundation, 1983.

Charles W. Roll and Albert H. Cantril, *Polls: Their Use and Misuse in Politics.* Cabin John, Md.: Seven Locks Press, 1980.

Larry J. Sabato, *The Rise of Political Consultants: New Ways of Winning Elections.* New York: Basic Books, 1981.

Paul A. Smith, *Electing a President: Information and Control.* New York: Praeger, 1982.

Judith S. Trent and Robert V. Friedenberg, *Political Campaign Communication: Principles and Practices.* New York: Praeger, 1983.

Jan Pons Vermeer, *"For Immediate Release": Candidate Press Releases in American Political Campaigns.* Westport, Ct.: Greenwood Press, 1982.

VIII

Government Management
of Mass Media

THE MASS media are among the few institutions in our society that can
and do regularly challenge the government. The media can make such
a challenge largely because the First Amendment to the American Constitution says that "Congress shall make no laws abridging freedom of speech or
of the press. . . . " And throughout our history this has usually been interpreted
as an absolute guarantee of freedom for the press from the restraints and
revenge of government.

But as government has come to take a larger and more complete role in
our lives, the mass media, too, have faced increasing government manipulation. In the 1960s, we began to talk about "government management of the
news," as politicians and bureaucrats learned how to use increasingly sophisticated methods of influencing and pressuring the mass media. Perhaps one
could say that leaders and rulers have always known how to bend the press
to their purposes. Few American presidents have not been involved in one
way or another in trying to control the news to further their administration's
own interests.

Yet government cannot exercise many legal constraints over the mass
media. The famous "Pentagon papers" case in the 1970s reaffirmed the
notion, upheld by most court rulings over the years, that the government
cannot exercise prior restraint or censor or block publication of any item, no
matter how damaging, unless the government can prove that grave national
security is involved. To date, there have been very few such cases.

But while government cannot use the law to control the press, it can use
techniques of public relations and persuasion to influence the mass media.
It can censor itself; it can withhold information from the press and the public.
It can stage events, such as presidential press conferences and Congressional
hearings, to capture the spotlight of news. It can shape the news by timing
and orchestrating the staging of events. It can manipulate the flow of information by selectively releasing those facts and figures that give the government's
slant to an issue. And it can influence the coverage of news by persuasive
techniques, which might include intimidation as well as friendly persuasion.
John F. Kennedy was a master at winning the friendship and good will of

225

reporters; Richard Nixon often had to resort to bullying the press to try to get his way.

We have, in fact, come to think of the government and the press as adversaries, battling each other rather than cooperating with each other. The government has played that role just as often and as well as the media. Such management of the mass media by government in our society will probably grow rather than diminish in the years ahead, as the media become more powerful and the issues become more complex.

27 · THE PRESIDENTIAL PRESS CONFERENCE

BY LAURENCE I. BARRETT

Laurence I. Barrett describes the presidential press conference and its historical evolution as it has become the chief communication tool the White House uses to reach the public. Even though reporters ask tough questions, a shrewd president can make the press conference into his forum to get his message across in a most effective way. As the White House correspondent for *Time* magazine, Barrett covered many a presidential press conference himself. He is the author of *Gambling with History: Ronald Reagan in the White House* which revealed the fact that Reagan's political advisers had advance copies of President Jimmy Carter's briefing book prior to the debates during the 1980 presidential campaign. In this article, Barrett is not strongly critical of the press conference, as some reporters have been. It was written for a government publication, *Topic*, produced by the U.S. Information Agency for dissemination in Africa, and is reprinted from issue number 135 (the issues are not dated).

The White House press room is usually quiet and almost deserted on Saturday mornings. Representatives of the two largest news agencies, Associated Press and United Press International, along with a few broadcast network correspondents may be present to cover routine announcements, but they stay on duty more out of habit than necessity.

In recent decades particularly, the presidential press conference has become an increasingly important aspect of the chief executive's communications with the public. As an institution, the press conference has also become the subject of controversy among politicians, journalists and scholars.

At the beginning of 1981, as Ronald Reagan's Administration was settling into office, Professor Robert M. Entman of Duke University completed a critical study called "The Imperial Media," in which he condemned the modern televised press conference as "a ritual of predictable thrust and parry. Reporters give a show of undaunted inquisitiveness; Presidents, of ersatz candor." At the same time, the University of Virginia's Center of Public Affairs produced a report with a contrary conclusion. This document, which had journalists among its authors, pointed out: "There are, of course, many ways in which a President can *exert* leadership. Equally important, a President must *express* leadership. Surely, one of the best means for such expression is the presidential press conference, where the chief executive has the opportunity to answer questions directly, somewhat as a British Prime Minister does during the traditional 'question period' in the House of Commons."

Ronald Reagan, like all of his recent predecessors, has made some changes in the details of arrangements. However, the President and his aides showed clearly from the first that they would ignore the advice of Professor Entman, who argued that dealings between the White House and journalists should be reduced. Reagan held his first formal, televised press conference within two weeks of taking his oath of office and within the first two months participated in a dozen interviews with journalists individually or in small groups. His eclectic press schedule included sessions with some of the country's most prominent editors and columnists as well as a conversation with a 19-year-old university student who writes for the *Harvard Crimson,* the student newspaper of Harvard University.

Despite the variety of encounters with reporters, only one method has become a firm custom as well as the subject of wide attention. When Washingtonians talk about "the press conference," they mean the kind of meeting between press and President that is scheduled in advance and broadcast live by the major television networks as well as by many radio stations. Magazines and newspapers across the country give the event heavy coverage. Some stations broadcast the conference at later times for the convenience of those who may have missed it the first time. A few major newspapers publish the entire transcript.

Why all the attention? The institution is unique. No other leader of a major nation routinely submits to unrehearsed interrogation by a large number of journalists on any subjects the reporters care to raise. The President may occasionally choose to be unresponsive to a particularly sensitive question, but he must do so in full view of the public.

The U.S. constitutional system provides no formal method by which the President personally can be asked to explain or defend his policies. The heads of his cabinet departments frequently do just that when they appear at hearings conducted by committees of the Congress. However, the cabinet officers are appointed to their posts, not elected. The final responsibility rests with the President. While every President confers frequently with leaders of the Congress, those meetings generally are private.

Thus the American press, as it has in certain other situations, fills a void by providing an unofficial check on the activities of the Presidency, which is the centerpiece of the U.S. governmental system. This check is wholly extralegal; no statute requires that the President hold press conferences and none requires that news organizations cover them. Yet the press conference now has the force of tradition behind it. A President would find it very difficult, in political terms, to end the practice. The press would be equally hard put to diminish its role.

Yet the institution is hardly static. It evolved slowly over the decades and not even the press conference's most enthusiastic supporters would argue that it is flawless. Therefore, it continues to change.

During the 19th century, meetings between press and President were rare. But Theodore Roosevelt—the Republican cousin of Franklin Delano Roosevelt, a Democrat—enjoyed innovation. Though Theodore Roosevelt was the scion of an affluent and prominent New York State family, he mingled easily with people from different backgrounds. As a young man, he worked on ranches in the West. During the Spanish-American War [1898], he organized and led a regiment of cavalry called the Rough Riders. As President in the first years of this century [1901–1909], he invited groups of reporters to the White House and conducted animated conversations with them on subjects of interest to him—occasionally while his barber was shaving him.

The reporters did ask questions of Roosevelt, but he dominated most of the sessions with vigorous orations on his pet projects. He loved the outdoors, was something of an amateur naturalist and wanted wilderness areas protected from commercial development. He also wanted consumers protected from business monopolies and often inveighed against the business "trusts." An ebullient and gregarious man, Roosevelt used the prototype press conferences as a megaphone for his strongly held views rather than as an opportunity to be tested by the press.

The next President, William Howard Taft [1909–1913], was far more reserved than Roosevelt; Taft abandoned the practice altogether. But Woodrow Wilson [1913–1921] brought the press conference back to the White House for good. Not only did he allow open questioning, he also established the principle that all reporters accredited to cover the White House were entitled to participate in the question-and-answer sessions. That was a significant change. It meant that participation was among the rights of the press corps and not a special privilege to be bestowed by the White House on individual reporters.

The three Presidents who followed Wilson—Warren Harding [1921–1923], Calvin Coolidge [1923–1929] and Herbert Hoover [1929–1933]—continued to have scheduled meetings with reporters. However, all three required that questions be submitted in writing prior to the meetings. That technique deprived the press conferences of spontaneity and allowed the Presidents a significant advantage. Coolidge, toward the end of his term, did have one informal conversation with newsmen while he was on vacation away from Washington. Asked whether he intended to run for reelection in 1928, the taciturn Coolidge responded that he was not planning to seek the Republican Party's nomination again. News accounts of that remark were widely interpreted as meaning that Coolidge had decided definitely to retire. Historians later speculated that Coolidge might have been misinterpreted—that he merely was saying that he hadn't decided yet whether he would run. But the initial news stories became the governing interpretation as the Republicans turned to other candidates and finally chose Hoover.

Whatever Coolidge's real intent, the incident underscored an important and lasting element concerning presidential conversations that are made public: The words are scrutinized closely. An impression, once created, is difficult to alter. The lesson for Presidents is painfully clear: if they expose themselves to a free give-and-take, they must be well-prepared to answer questions with precision or to say candidly, on occasion, that they are unable to respond to a particular inquiry.

Franklin D. Roosevelt [1933–1945], like his older cousin Theodore, enjoyed dealing with reporters and had great confidence in his ability to handle the exchanges. As Governor of New York State, he had met frequently with journalists in Albany, the state capital, in what he called "very delightful family conferences." Still, Roosevelt was not prepared to allow unrestricted use of his answers. He thought that would be too risky.

Immediately after taking office in March 1933, Roosevelt summoned reporters to his office and laid down new and specific rules for their subsequent meetings. First, he ended the requirement that questions be submitted in advance; in the nearly 50 years since then, no President has attempted to reinstate that restriction. But if Roosevelt was willing to open himself up on any subject, he was unwilling to speak for direct quotation very often. Only if his press secretary, Steve Early, put the President's remarks on paper could they be used verbatim. Roosevelt also wanted to be able to speak "on background" when he chose to do so. As he defined the term, it meant that reporters could use the information "on your own authority and responsibility, not to be attributed to the White House." (Today that practice is called "deep background," while "background" allows the source to be identified in a general way, for example, a "White House source" or a "top administration official.") Finally, Roosevelt told the reporters that on occasion he would wish to speak "off the record." In those situations, the information could not be published at all; rather it was conveyed solely for the guidance of reporters.

While these rules sound confining by the standards of the 1980s, they represented a breakthrough in the 1930s. Not only would the President be available regularly—sometimes once a week—but he would also attempt to comment on a variety of topics. Further, he would use these sessions to discuss particular items in some depth.

Of course there were drawbacks to Roosevelt's approach. The "background" device sometimes put reporters in the position of lending their own authority to the administration's line. The "family" atmosphere Roosevelt sought to achieve helped the intimacy of the situation but gave the public no sense of the interplay between the President and reporters. Nonetheless, Roosevelt's long incumbency—12 years—established the President's obligation to face reporters periodically. The presidential press conference had become permanent.

Harry S. Truman [1945–1952], facing a larger press corps, moved the conferences to a more spacious chamber and generally spoke on the record. Dwight D. Eisenhower [1953–1961] brought in his own innovation: He allowed filming and tape recording of all his press conferences, though broadcast of them was delayed to prevent slips of the tongue from creating false impressions. The most important step in the evolutionary process occurred when John F. Kennedy took office in 1961. A fluent, witty speaker and fast thinker, Kennedy was the first President to allow live television and radio broadcast of his press conferences. They were held in a large auditorium of the U.S. State Department, usually twice a month, and attracted several hundred reporters.

Kennedy's glamor and the presence of live television cameras gave the press conferences a certain element of political theater. More than ever before, the reporters took on, to some extent, the role of performers. Many were eager to be recognized by the President. As he would come to the conclusion of a response, many journalists would rise and seek to get his attention in order to get their question in. The shouts of "Mr. President, Mr. President" struck some observers as undignified.

The nature of press conferences was itself becoming an issue. At one of the early sessions in March 1961, a reporter asked Kennedy, "There are many Americans who believe that in our manner of questioning or seeking your attention that we are subjecting you to some abuse or a lack of respect. . . . Could you tell us generally your feelings about your press conferences to date and your feelings about how they are conducted?" Kennedy smiled as he responded, "Well, you subject me to some abuse, but not to any lack of respect." He added, as his audience laughed, that he saw no reason to change the arrangements.

Kennedy continued to see some reporters and columnists privately and in those meetings he generally spoke on a background basis. But the televised conference became a regular feature of the President's press relations and has remained one ever since. Kennedy was a master of the art form, moving easily from complicated questions about the economy to sensitive inquiries about national security affairs. His performances also revealed to the general public, in a more graphic way than previously, the adversarial aspect of relations between journalists and any President.

In a press conference a few months before he died, he was asked to comment on the press's treatment of his administration. "Well," Kennedy quipped, "I am reading more and enjoying it less." This produced the chuckles he anticipated, and he added, "I have not complained nor do I plan to make any general complaints. I think they [the journalists] are doing their task, as a critical branch. . . . And I am attempting to do mine. And we are going to live together for a period, and then go our separate ways."

Kennedy was so good at the formal press conference that he was a difficult act to follow. Lyndon Johnson, somewhat less facile, did not enjoy the exchanges as much. Frequently he staged impromptu sessions which kept reporters a bit off balance. For instance, Johnson sometimes answered questions while taking a stroll around the South Lawn of the White House. Richard Nixon [1968–1974], though excellent at repartee, seemed to dislike the form and reduced the number of sessions.

Gerald Ford [1974–1977] and Jimmy Carter [1977–1981] stuck to the basic format while making minor changes. Carter, for instance, held some formal press conferences while traveling around the country. In those sessions, half the questions were allotted to reporters from the locality in which the event was being held. The Washington journalists accompanying the President got the other half.

Ronald Reagan came into office with considerable experience in conducting press conferences. As governor for eight years of the largest American state, he had frequently met California reporters as a group. During the 1976 and 1980 presidential campaigns, candidate Reagan held numerous press conferences. Once in the White House, he and his advisers decided on one simple change to deal with the lack of decorum that had become habitual when reporters sought to be called upon. Reagan's press secretary announced that reporters wishing to be recognized should remain in their seats—quietly—and raise their hands instead of their voices.

The suggestion was one of several made in the study conducted by the University of Virginia's Center of Public Affairs. While there was some skepticism initially that the reporters would maintain discipline, they did accede to the request. Afterward, there was general agreement among officials and most reporters that the more dignified atmosphere was an improvement.

Because the televised press conferences run only 30 minutes and the questions tend be diverse, some observers have argued that the exchanges are superficial. One proposed solution to that is to have reporters follow up each other's questions when the President's answers aren't fully responsive. Some of that does occur spontaneously, but systematic follow-up would require advance coordination—and that conflicts with the larger need to keep the events free of contrivance. Also, the reporters function as individuals—and competitors. U.S. journalists do not like to operate as a group or a collective.

Two other alternatives to overcome superficiality seem more attractive. The first is to allow an opportunity to the reporter who asks the original question to follow up if the response seems inadequate. Reagan and his advisers are sympathetic to that approach, and the President usually pauses to take a supplementary question. A second measure is to have the President hold meetings with small groups of reporters between the formal press conferences. At these sessions, television correspondents—but not television cameras—may attend from time to time. There is more opportunity for detailed discussion of specific issues than in the half-hour conferences, which are normally attended by nearly 300 journalists.

Reagan began holding the smaller meetings—half a dozen reporters attended the first one—immediately after his initial press conference. One flaw of this system is that the White House determines who will participate. However, the President's press staff seems determined to give many news organizations a turn at this mini-conference. Further, transcripts of the conversation are made available to the rest of the press corps.

Still another issue is being confronted. Although any reporter, U.S. or foreign, can attend a formal press conference if he or she holds White House accreditation, the questioning has traditionally been dominated by the regulars—the correspondents who cover the President full time. The regulars defend that practice by saying that they follow White House activities closely and thus are equipped to ask the most penetrating questions. Others argue that only a tiny fraction of the 2,660 news organizations represented in Washington can maintain one or more full-time correspondents at the White House and that some subjects never get aired because the regulars are not interested in them. One suggestion to overcome this is to select the 20 to 25 reporters who will ask questions by means of a lottery before the press conference starts. Early in 1981 the Reagan White House—much to the annoyance of the regulars—announced that it would experiment with such a procedure. In March at Reagan's second formal press conference, a lottery was used. The President himself made the first selections, pulling cards out of a large jar.

The rules for the lottery were complicated and still produced a high percentage of regulars among the questioners. Nonetheless, correspondents from some relatively obscure publications did get a chance, as did two foreign journalists. At this session, the President seemed to enjoy himself almost as much as Kennedy had 20 years before. During the give-and-take, Reagan—following the Kennedy example—muted some harsh inquiries with humor.

How long the lottery will last—and how the press and Ronald Reagan will ultimately get along—cannot be predicted. If history is any guide, it could be a year or more before the full nature of the President's relations with the national press corps becomes clear. But several things were clear during his early months. President Reagan certainly favors extensive and diverse dealing with reporters. In the same week in which he held the lottery press conference, for instance, he also gave an hour-long interview to Walter Cronkite on the occasion of Cronkite's retirement as principal announcer of the "CBS Evening News." Reagan will experiment in other ways. But periodically he will expose himself to live, televised press conferences—the Washington show that gets mixed reviews but has survived through two solid, interesting decades.

28 · DEALING WITH THE MEDIA

BY GRIFFIN B. BELL WITH RONALD J. OSTROW

Public officials quickly learn how to deal with the
press. That seems to go with the territory. When
Griffin Bell was appointed attorney general by
President Carter, he was new to Washington and did
not know how to manage "that Hydra-headed giant
known as the Washington press corps." This article
describes how he learned. Bell is now a managing
partner in the Atlanta law firm of King and Spalding.
Ronald Ostrow, Nieman Fellow '65, is a staff writer
with *The Los Angeles Times* in Washington, D.C.
This article is reprinted from the *Nieman Reports,*
Summer 1982.

When President-elect Carter called on me to be his attorney general, I responded with considerable confidence. After all, as a member of the United States Court of Appeals for the Fifth Circuit, I had worked closely with the Department of Justice for fifteen years and had been immersed in the principal legal questions of the era—civil rights, labor disputes, consumerism, government regulation of business and the like. My earlier years in private practice and in Georgia state government had given me more than a nodding acquaintance with the national scene. In short, like most others in Jimmy Carter's circle of Georgians, I came to Washington with no great trepidation, despite my lack of experience there.

And like most of my Georgia brothers, I was to learn all too soon how much I did not know about operations in the nation's capital. Nowhere, however, was my lack of knowledge more acute than in my dealings with that Hydra-headed giant known as the Washington press corps. Fortunately, perhaps, my media baptism in Washington was in the born-again style—total immersion. I got in trouble with the press even before I arrived in Washington and stayed in trouble through my Senate confirmation hearings. And from my swearing-in to the day I left the Justice Department two and a half years later, there was hardly a day when I was not wrestling with a serious media problem of some sort. As a result, I had no choice but to concentrate a good deal of my time and attention on trying to understand the Washington press corps and figuring out how best to deal with it. On balance, I emerged reasonably satisfied with the results, but along the way I made some mistakes, not the least of which occurred in one major case when I forgot my own hard-earned lessons and got involved in a controversy that almost drove me to resigning as an embarrassment to the President.

As every schoolboy knows, the Founding Fathers attached so much importance to what we now call the news media that they made freedom of the press one of the handful of rights guaranteed in the Bill of Rights, along with freedom of religion, the right to assemble and petition for grievances and the right to be secure in our homes from unreasonable searches and seizures. Everyone in public life in America deals with the press—from selectmen in the smallest New England towns to governors of the largest, most populous states. Even judges do, including myself while I was on the bench in Atlanta, though in the comparative isolation of the federal judiciary I was rarely interviewed and never interrogated. Yet no amount of experience anywhere else is adequate preparation for doing business with the news media in Washington.

In large ways and small, the Washington press corps is unique. Politicians cannot escape it: they try to ignore it at their peril. Whether the newly arrived public official likes it or not, the press is, as Edmund Burke called it, "The Fourth Estate"—the fourth branch of government. Like the executive, the legislative and the judicial branches, the press does not possess absolute power: but it has enormous influence and can shape the issues government officials must deal with. It can color the public's perception of individual political leaders and their programs; and, most important of all, it affects the perceptions that officials in Washington have of one another. And the unique qualities—even idiosyncracies—of the Washington press corps make it likely that, no matter how well intentioned a neophyte public official may be, he will often find the press hard to understand and sometimes impossible to handle successfully. As a starting point, though, I found that one of the most useful skills to develop was to be able to put myself in the place of a reporter and see how a particular set of facts or statements would look to one who was observing, not participating.

One thing that sets the Washington press corps apart is its sheer size. There are more reporters in Washington—thousands more—than in any other American city. This means the competition there is keener and the pressures greater. On the whole, the product is better, too. Most Washington reporters had to win their assignments by demonstrating that they had sharply honed the skills of inquiry, analysis and expression. But because of overreaching caused by competition, because of too little expertise in highly technical matters and because of the time pressures, errors are inevitable. Unfortunately, the errors are hard to catch up with. Once in print, they tend to be picked up by other publications as gospel. Despite their supposedly skeptical natures, reporters and editors apparently are the last of the vanishing breed who really think you can believe everything you read. For example, a profile of me done for *The Washington Star* shortly after I arrived was riddled with inaccuracies and distortions, some of which were adopted—without any attempt to check their accuracy—by Washington correspondents for publications that appeared all over the nation. Similarly, when *The Village Voice* reported, falsely, that I had discussed with the U.S. attorney in Atlanta the legal difficulties of Bert Lance, President Carter's budget director and longtime confidant, *The Washington Post* and others published the falsehood, attributing it to the *Voice* without checking with me. At least the *Post* had the grace to publish a correction when we complained.

The fondness of the press for dealing in drama, conflict and inconsistencies—a characteristic of news no matter where in the Free World it is published—is especially pronounced in Washington. This stress on what is wrong or could go wrong—virtually never what is right—reflects a "herd" instinct. Reporters cover events such as news conferences and congressional hearings in groups; and the group, as the late Senator Everett Dirksen of Illinois used to observe as he scanned the press gallery from the Senate floor, too often operates like a pack of wolves or barracuda looking for mistakes on the part of potential prey. Also, Washington reporters are well aware that events in the nation's capital cast shadows across the country, as well as around the world. The result of this sense of being at the center of history's stage can be exaggeration and distortion, "hyping" the story, reporters call it.

The press corps' search for the negative was accentuated by the Watergate scandal. Previously reporters had generally believed that corruption was something politicians left behind when they reached the highest levels. After Watergate, with characteristic vigor, the Washington press corps set out to eliminate the cancer, with reporters seeking to scale ever-new heights of investigative journalism. The ensuing lack of restraint meant that public officials became suspect, virtually guilty, until proven innocent, and this attitude did not leave town with Richard Nixon. How routine the post-Watergate perspective became is illustrated by the fact that *U.S. News and World Report* reported that "not until recently was it disclosed that the attorney general and Senator Eastland reached a secret agreement in December 1976" on using commissions to help pick nominees for federal appellate courts. It is true that Senator James O. Eastland, chairman of the Senate Judiciary Committee, met with President-elect Carter and me in Atlanta a month before the inauguration and agreed to help get senators to accept the commission concept, a step that would reduce their patronage over the important judicial appointments. But there was nothing "secret" about the meeting or the subject matter. It was reported in *The Atlanta Constitution* the day after it happened.

However justified the media's attitude may have been during Watergate, it made things very difficult for officials who came later. And for the neophyte, the lack of previous dealing with the media was complicated by the difficulty of knowing what individual reporters were after from one moment to the next. I remember a day early in my confirmation hearings when the interrogation had grown tense. During a break, a reporter for one of the news magazines approached me as I sat at the witness table grinning and gritting my teeth.

"What did you have for breakfast, Judge, if you can remember?" she asked.

With some difficulty, I shifted my attention and recalled that I had consumed standard southern fare—grits. For a few seconds, as she jotted down my response in her notebook, I thought of telling her how to spell the delicacy and instructing her that the word always took the plural form, but I remained silent for fear of sounding condescending. Later, I learned that such details are the kind of information savored by reporters for a publication that appears only once a week. They use the extra bits of color to add drama and an "insider" aura to accounts of the basic news already published by their daily competitors.

Thus, one minute I was being questioned on a matter of profound legal policy, and the next a reporter wanted to know what I had had for breakfast. These shifts from the sublime to the ridiculous are so quick that it becomes difficult to keep your balance, and the unwary public official may make the mistake of regarding the exchanges with the press as a game rather than as a serious matter.

How serious a matter the Washington media really is I began to learn even before going to the capital. In Washington, the media not only deal in symbols, but have a lot to say about what those symbols will be. Not realizing this, I was taken unawares when, a few days after President-elect Carter announced that I was his nominee as attorney general, a reporter called my Atlanta home—I was still picking up my own phone in those days—to ask what I planned to do about my membership in private clubs. I belonged to several in Atlanta, including the Piedmont Driving Club and the Capital City Club, both of which had no black members. Without pausing for reflection, I told the reporter that I planned to retain my memberships. I viewed membership in private clubs as my private business, not realizing the media would use it as a symbolic clue to the ideology of the new administration. My attitudes were thought to be especially important both because I was viewed as a close friend of the President-elect and because my Cabinet post was responsible for protecting civil rights.

My nomination had already disturbed some traditional Democratic liberal constituencies who had candidates of their own and who were wary of Jimmy Carter and the Georgians around him. From the beginning, these liberals had doubted the new President's commitment to equal rights, even though blacks had given him strong support in the election. Now, in my too hasty defense of the clubs, they thought they saw the old southern bigotry they had feared all along. Using their ready access to the eastern press, they turned the glowing coal of my private club comment into a damaging fire. It did not matter that most federal judges in Atlanta belonged to the same clubs, including my friend Elbert Tuttle, whom the civil rights movement regarded as a hero, or that several of us sought to integrate other clubs such as the Atlanta Lawyers Club.

My wife, Mary, being more attuned to symbols than her husband, helped put out the fire. She recalled that a controversy over club membership had erupted during the Kennedy administration. The question then was how the President's brother and attorney general, Robert F. Kennedy, could maintain his membership in the Metropolitan Club, an English-style men's club in Washington that banned blacks and women. Mary reminded me that Robert Kennedy had resigned his membership, saying it was important symbolically for an official who was responsible for enforcing civil rights laws. Realizing he had set an admirable precedent, I issued a statement that I, too, would resign from the clubs upon becoming attorney general. The statement dulled the club controversy but did not prevent my being scrutinized more closely during the pre-inaugural period than any other Carter appointee, except the President-elect's short-lived selection of Theodore C. Sorensen, the former aide to President John F. Kennedy, as CIA director. My senate hearing was televised live daily by Public Broadcasting, and my confirmation was delayed a week beyond Inauguration Day, when the other Cabinet members were sworn in. I survived the baptism and learned a thing or two about the media and symbolism in the process.

In some ways, the most worrisome characteristic of the Washington press corps to me is its northeastern bias. Former Vice-President Spiro T. Agnew's complaint that the influence of the Northeast dominates what is reported and how it is presented in print and on the air throughout the nation should not be dismissed just because a disgraced officeholder voiced it. I detected the slant immediately, referring to it as the bias of the Northeast Strip, the urban cluster running from Boston in the North through New York City to Washington at its southern end.

It is displayed in the values reporters and editors apply in defining what is important enough to qualify as news. Reflecting the Northeast, Washington journalists are somewhat internationalistic, attaching more importance to events in Europe than in Kansas City; they place a high premium on formal education, preferably at an Ivy League school; they come down on the liberal or left side of civil rights and civil liberties issues; they regard federal programs as a solution for many of the nation's ills; and they see economic questions through the prism of Keynesian training rather than through that of some other theoretical analysis, monetarism, for example, or supply-side economics. They also suffer from a provincial tendency to attach very little importance to what happens west of the Hudson or south of Washington, D.C.

The impact of the prejudice is felt throughout the nation, reflecting the power of such major city dailies as *The New York Times* and *The Washington Post*. The headquarters of the news operations of the television networks are also in the Strip, as are the weekly news magazines and the press or wire associations. These media leaders feed upon each other in determining what is news and how it should be viewed. Their choices are adopted by news outlets throughout the country and, to a lesser extent, the world. *The New York Times* is particularly listened to. I've been told by a reporter for one of the news magazines that fresh, insightful observations of government activities have been rejected when he or a colleague proposed them as stories, because the *Times* had seen the event differently—or not at all.

If you run afoul of a Strip operation, the consequences are likely to be far greater than if your critic is from another sector. The pervasive role in news selection played by one region may partially explain the public distrust of the media that pollsters have been recording in recent years—a lack of faith I find disturbing. The power and population of the nation is heading west, but the news leaders and their values are still firmly implanted in a narrow, unrepresentative corridor of the country.

Despite experiences with newspapers and television that drove me to exasperation and threatened some of the most important work I was trying to accomplish as attorney general, I left Washington convinced that the press is—however imperfectly—a surrogate for the public at large.

In addition to monitoring government for their readers and viewers, the news media have a voice in setting government's agenda. A

President can propose programs and Congress can take them up, but if the news media don't pay attention, both the Congress and the President will find it difficult to make headway against special interests who are in opposition.

It has been written that we live under a government of men and women and morning newspapers, an observation that I found to be on the mark during my service as attorney general. On many days, an examination of the morning newspapers caused my agenda to be reset. A prime example of this took place during the administration's first year in office when *The New York Times Magazine* ran on its cover the photograph of a man wearing a loud suit that complemented the cocksure expression on his face. "Mr. Untouchable," the magazine's cover proclaimed. "This is Nicky Barnes. The police say he may be Harlem's biggest drug dealer. But can they prove it?"

President Carter saw the picture and read the article, and at the next Cabinet meeting asked me why the government couldn't do something about Nicky Barnes. I promised to look into the matter and called Bob Fiske, then the U.S. attorney for the Southern District of New York. Fiske, because of the call, decided to prosecute the case himself. Six months later, Leroy "Nicky" Barnes, Jr., "Mr. Untouchable," was convicted, along with ten codefendants, of conducting a criminal enterprise —what Fiske described as "the largest, most profitable, venal drug ring in the city." He was sentenced to a term of life in prison by U.S. District Court Judge Henry F. Werker on January 19, 1978. I cannot contend that the President's interest in the matter, which spurred my call and Fiske's decision to take charge himself, was solely responsible for the salutary result of taking Nicky Barnes off the streets of New York. But I do know that the prosecution received top priority once the President concluded from reading the newspaper article that Barnes was a national menace and, thanks to *The New York Times,* a widely recognized one.

In a way, the saga of Mr. Untouchable illustrates the power of the press of the Northeast Strip. The story had a visibility in the White House that it would not have if it had been carried only by the *Kansas City Star* or the *Des Moines Register and Tribune,* in part because such an article from Kansas City or Des Moines would probably not have been included in the news summaries of articles of interest that are compiled daily and circulated in the White House and Cabinet departments. The action against Mr. Untouchable was more than the government's responding to a particularly strong newspaper, of course. It also sprang from President Carter's intuitive response to a problem that millions of Americans worry about all over the country—the vulnerability of their children to drugs; but because the article had appeared in *The New York Times,* the case had a symbolic impact, even on the President, that it would not otherwise have enjoyed.

Along with resetting my agenda, the press indirectly helped me stay on top of my job by providing significant information, not just in what I read but also from what I gleaned from reporters' questions and comments in news conferences and interviews. The regularity of these confrontations proved useful in another way. When we traveled outside Washington for speeches and conferences, my practice was to meet with reporters in each area we visited—all part of the effort to rebuild confidence in the integrity and neutrality of the Department of Justice. To prepare for these encounters, Dean St. Dennis, a veteran member of the department's public information office, would compile a briefing book that spelled out in exhaustive detail what the Justice Department, including the FBI, the DEA, the Bureau of Prisons, and the LEAA was doing of interest in each spot we stopped. St. Dennis's briefing papers became a highly useful synopsis of substantive Justice Department activities.

Unfortunately, the press sometimes goes too far in being the public's monitor of the other three branches. It can get carried away by the sheer momentum of a breaking story and be influenced by values, priorities and even fads that prevail inside the corps. During my years in Washington, "Koreagate" was an example of that. Koreagate was the label attached by the press to the government's inquiry into attempts by the South Korean Central Intelligence Agency to buy influence on Capitol Hill. The label implied that the scandal approached or surpassed the scale of Watergate. Story after story speculated on the number and names of members of Congress involved in the Department of Justice's investigation. The numbers ran from seventy to ninety and even to more than a hundred.

The conjecture prompted me to state publicly several times that very few present and former members of Congress were seriously involved in the investigation. In the end, one ex-member, Richard T. Hanna, Democrat of California, was sent to prison on a guilty plea. Another, Otto E. Passman, Democrat of Louisiana, was indicted but acquitted. And three sitting members, Edward R. Roybal, Charles H. Wilson and John J. McFall, all Democrats from California, were reprimanded by the House of Representatives. Hardly worth comparing to Watergate.

Because of the importance of communicating to the public what you are seeking to accomplish as a public official, I never stopped trying to improve my skills in dealing with reporters. At the same time, I must acknowledge that part of presenting a credible case is doing what comes naturally. Making yourself accessible and being open and candid are good starting points. I tried always to speak "on-the-record," a relatively rare way of communicating in Washington in which the reporter is able to attribute to you by name everything you say. Perhaps even rarer is the practice of admitting your mistakes rather than ignoring them or blaming them on subordinates or on the faceless bureaucracy.

Above all, I found the use of one's sense of humor, particularly a self-deprecating one, went a long way.

My standard for candor was set even before the Senate confirmed me. At a hearing, Senator Mathias extracted a pledge from me to post publicly each day a log of my contacts with persons outside the Department of Justice. These included calls or meetings with members of Congress, judges, private attorneys, Cabinet officers and the White House staff—even the President. The log, which did not include people I saw at social receptions outside the office or calls to me at home at night or during the weekend, appeared daily in the Justice Department press room, down the hall from the attorney general's office. Early editions of the log included such significant data as my crossing Pennsylvania Avenue to use the FBI gymnasium, which promptly appeared in *The Washington Post,* and a visit to the barber in the Sheraton Carlton Hotel, which also was published. Occasionally, we would exercise some editing restraint. For example, when I was telephoning prospects to head the FBI, prospects whose names had not yet been made public, we would list on the log "conversation with a possibility for FBI director —name to be supplied later." I am convinced that the log helped persuade reporters who covered the department that we meant to carry out Jimmy Carter's pledge of an open administration. One of Attorney General William French Smith's first official acts during the Reagan administration was to do away with the logs. He contended that because they did not cover contacts over the weekend and away from the office they were not valuable in keeping track of the attorney general. Aides to the new attorney general said his decision reflected the fact that he "is a very private man." I must say that I gave Attorney General Smith my views on the value of the log system, stating that, while it helped me, the Republic would not fall if he discontinued it, especially since no other government official was following the practice.

As attorney general, I held frequent press conferences, gave scores of individual interviews and, particularly during my last year, invited reporters, columnists and television commentators to the attorney general's dining room for lengthy, informal conversations over quail, grits and rooster pepper sausage, a little-known South Georgia delicacy that Charlie Kirbo and I introduced to Washington. Reporters traveled with me on government planes and in commercial airliners, and I spent much of the time in flight responding to their questions.

Before I was confirmed, the Justice Department's Office of Public Information gave me a detailed explanation of the strange jargon that the media and the government use in communicating with one another. Ground rules under which the communication is conducted begin with "on-the-record" and range downward in terms of the official's willingness to be quoted and to be held publicly accountable for his statement through "on-background," to "deep-background" and, of course, "off-the-record." When a Justice Department official speaks "on-background," his comments can be attributed to "a senior Justice Department official," or if the official feels that's too close to home—and the reporter agrees ahead of time—to "an administration source." When a reporter accepts information on "deep-background," he usually is agreeing to write it on his own, attributing it to no source, as if the information came to him from out of the blue. "Off-the-record" means that the reporter will not publish the information being given him and that he is accepting it only for the purpose of helping him to better understand the situation being discussed. Some reporters use off-the-record information as a lead to pry the same details from another official, under less restrictive rules of attribution. Others treat off-the-record the same way as they treat deep-background, reporting the details but giving no hint of their origin.

I found these tiered levels of decreasing responsibility offensive, believing that if something is important enough to be said, it is important enough for someone to say it publicly and take the responsibility for saying it. I must acknowledge, though, that my staff, particularly Terry Adamson, my special assistant and the department's chief spokesman, used all the guidelines of attribution in talking with the press. Adamson contended there were many times he needed to convey facts but that he couldn't do so if they were to be quoted as the official comments of an aide to the attorney general or those of the chief spokesman for the department. I can understand his argument, but I cannot be comfortable with it. When a government official backs away from standing behind what he tells the press, he injects deceit into his relationship with the public that he is supposed to serve.

Admitting mistakes seems so fundamental, especially when you want to convince people of your honesty, that it should not have to be mentioned. But it is apparently something extraordinary in the nation's capital. One of my initial ideas for reorganization was to merge the Drug Enforcement Administration into the FBI, a proposal that caused a stir, especially at DEA headquarters. When we sent a team of FBI experts to study the DEA, their report made clear that the merger would be a mistake. Reporters soon were asking what had happened. I told them it was one of those ideas that sounded good when you first heard it but that further study showed would be impractical. Not all notions for reorganization are good ones, I added, and it's better to consider a whole host of proposals than only advance those you are certain will work out. I gave this explanation several times, and each time reporters reacted as if the emperor were confessing that he had no clothes.

Another example of how unaccustomed the Washington press corps is to confession of error took place at the White House when I announced the President had selected Judge William H. Webster to be FBI director. Implicit in the announcement was the fact that we were not appointing any of the candidates proposed by the prestigious committee we had created to prepare a list of the best-qualified persons. Naturally, when I was making the announcement, a reporter asked about the committee:

Q: Does that mean that the previous system the President instituted is out the window? (Laughter)

Attorney General Bell: I will have to say that, number one, the President didn't institute it. I will have to take the blame for that. That was one of my brainstorms. (Laughter)

Q: He bought it though.

Attorney General Bell: He sometimes has too much confidence in his attorney general. (Laughter) I have seen some sign of that lately. (Laughter) . . . It looked like a good thing to do at the time.

My friend Reg Murphy, now publisher of the *Baltimore Sun,* has a sign behind his desk advising those who would take on the press that it is never wise to do battle with anyone who buys ink by the barrel. But there are times, particularly for the public official, when an erroneous account is so damaging that it must be challenged, and vigorously. For me, *The New York Times* published such a story on December 2, 1977, when its Pulitzer Prize-winning correspondent, Seymour M. Hersh, wrote in a front-page piece that I had delayed a "planned appointment" of a U.S. attorney in Pittsburgh "under pressure from investigators" in the Justice Department. The implication was that I had been about to appoint a man of questionable honesty. Hersh wrote that sources he identified only as "officials of the Federal Bureau of Investigation and the Justice Department" had charged that we "had improperly delayed a full-scale investigation" into payments from the candidate for U.S. Attorney, George E. Schumacher, to Representative Joseph M. Gaydos of Pennsylvania. There were many things in that story that were wrong, including several statements in the first paragraph. First, I was under no pressure. Second, the appointment was not planned but only under consideration. Third, our investigation of whether there had been payments and, if so, whether there was anything improper about them, had been proceeding for several weeks. Hersh had interviewed me and Associate Attorney General Michael J. Egan the previous day and reported correctly that both of us denied the accusations.

I called a press conference within hours after reading the story and denounced the article as "scurrilous, irresponsible and completely out of keeping with anything I thought *The New York Times* stood for." Hersh had reported that "one well-informed government official" told him that everyone in the investigation "is scared." That was too much for me. If there is anything the Justice Department and its investigative arm, the FBI, can do without, it is frightened investigators. I told the press conference I was sending the head of the Justice Department's Office of Professional Responsibility, the department's internal watchdog, Michael E. Shaheen, Jr., "to find out just what the trouble is there." Shaheen, whose reputation for independence later gained national attention through critical reports he issued concerning my successor, Ben Civiletti, and the President's brother, Billy Carter, had already demonstrated that he would report the facts as he found them, no matter how uncomfortable for anyone.

Shaheen's investigation unearthed FBI agents who readily acknowledged talking to Hersh but who insisted they had not told him they felt pressured. In the end, I decided not to recommend the nomination of Schumacher to the President—but not for any reasons Hersh had mentioned. Later, after I left office, Hersh told Terry Adamson that my reaction to the story had surprised him and that upon further investigation he had satisfied himself that I was telling the truth.

That departure from accurate reporting occurred because one of the nation's leading newspapers let its hunger for "investigative" journalism, a field in which it trailed during the Watergate era, overpower its good judgment. U.S. attorneys' posts are sought-after jobs, with rival factions supporting rival candidates. In the Schumacher case, I think *The New York Times* was used by one politically motivated side in the drive to obtain that appointment, which leads to the obvious conclusion that the reasons for providing a reporter with information should be a subject of that reporter's scrutiny before he runs the story.

Lack of restraint would be less of a problem if the press practiced more self-criticism. Our First Amendment's free press guarantee would not be harmed if the media began to hold itself accountable to the media. The increasing use of ombudsmen by newspapers to monitor their own performance is a step in the right direction.

29 · THE GOVERNMENT SHUTS UP

BY JAY PETERZELL

Government management of the news has gone far
beyond the staging of presidential press conferences
and the seemingly benign treatment of reporters by
public officials. Increasingly, the government has
manipulated information by withholding it from the
press and the public. In spite of the Freedom of
Information Act, passed in 1967 to force government
to reveal all but information that would endanger
national security or individual privacy, each
successive administration has closed more doors to
the press.

Jay Peterzell is a research associate at the Center
for National Security Studies, a Washington-based
organization funded by the American Civil Liberties
Union and The Fund for Peace. His article is
reprinted from the *Columbia Journalism Review,*
July/August 1982.

The most rigorous paradox is Epimenides' confession, "I am lying":
if true, it is false; and if false, it is true.

The Reagan paradox is less rigorous but more troubling, at least to
many reporters who cover foreign policy and other beats that frequently
involve access to national security information. The paradox is that the
Reagan administration has placed unprecedented restrictions on press
access to intelligence information but is at least as willing as past
administrations to use leaks and selective declassification to support its
foreign policy. The result is that security-minded officials have released
information—on Libyan threats to assassinate President Reagan, for
example—that reveals intelligence sources and methods but which, like
Epimenides, leaves us dizzy about the truth.

Attempts to use the press to influence policy are, of course, not
limited to the intelligence community. But the CIA or the National Security Council differs from the U.S. Forest Service in that information
obtained from the former often cannot be independently confirmed by

reporters. It may come from an unreliable or unevaluated source; it may be a conclusion based on secret evidence that does not fully support it; it may have been released as part of an intelligence operation of which the press is unaware. As one *Washington Post* reporter who has "dealt fairly extensively with the CIA" put it, intelligence information is difficult for journalists because "it is less exposed to the cut and thrust of public dialogue about its accuracy and its origin, and it's not so readily accessible to checks on its authenticity."

The Libyan hit-squad story is a good case in point. On October 8, 1981, the *New York Post* carried a "Jack Anderson Exclusive" reporting that the National Security Agency had intercepted a phone call between Libya and Ethiopia shortly after the U.S. shot down two Libyan jets over the Gulf of Sidra last August. During the phone call, Libyan leader Muammar Qaddafi threatened to have Reagan assassinated. "It was not an adverse leak [i.e., it was not hostile to the administration]," Anderson associate Dale Van Atta recalled. "The source was an NSA source." The story was also covered by *Newsweek* and *NBC Magazine;* then it disappeared.

On November 23, *Newsweek* breathed new life into the story after State Department correspondent John Walcott learned that officials now thought Qaddafi had dispatched death squads, armed with bazookas, grenade launchers, and SAM-7 missiles, that were gunning for Reagan and other top U.S. officials. For the next three weeks the press was filled with lurid accounts of countersniper teams on the White House roof, nationwide searches for assassination squads, and even the involvement of the dread Venezuelan terrorist "Carlos." The source of the government reports was later learned to be a former Lebanese terrorist who walked into an American embassy in mid-November and claimed to have heard Qaddafi give the "kill" order the preceding month.

It was on December 6, only a few hours after Qaddafi had dismissed the reports as "big lies," that the State Department for the first time went on record as saying that "we have strong evidence that Qaddafi has been plotting the murder of American officials...." The next day Reagan added: "We have the evidence and [Qaddafi] knows it." On December 10, the president called on some 2,000 U.S. oil company employees and other Americans to leave Libya—a request the administration had made repeatedly and unsuccessfully over the past year to clear the way for economic and military actions reportedly designed to culminate in Qaddafi's downfall.

As soon as most Americans had reluctantly agreed to leave Libya, the hit-squad threat evaporated. "The risk is diminished some," Senate majority leader Howard Baker told *The Washington Post* on December 16. FBI Director William Webster, who had been skeptical all along, said in January that as far as he could tell no Libyan assassins had ever entered the United States. Evidence presented at classified briefings during the height of the crisis "got flimsier and flimsier," a member of the Senate Intelligence committee said in a recent interview. "The more credible people in the agency were telling us over and over there was not enough evidence to justify the public outcry." Asked whether any evidence had been presented apart from the NSA intercept and the testimony of the informer, he said: "No. That was it."

"It was by far the most bizarre story I've been involved in," recalled Philip Taubman, who on December 4 had broken *The New York Times'* long—and prudent—silence about the hit squad with a front-page story revealing that the administration had received reports that five terrorists had entered the country. "I don't think we were used initially," Taubman said, "but the administration used the crisis and took advantage of it once it got out."

CBS's Fred Graham, who had covered the story with considerable skepticism, commented: "You know, we all try to learn from things that happen to us and build in safeguards. The fact is that this can happen to us again tomorrow and there's not a damn thing we in the media can do about it, when you have the president of the United States coming out and confirming it. . . . The press is caught and public officials are caught."

Check It Out? How?   Determining the truth is a chronic difficulty for reporters who deal with intelligence information. But traditionally it has been offset to some degree by a network of formal and informal relationships with mid- and lower-level officials that allowed reporters both to check the accuracy of information with people they have come to trust and to gain background information essential to understanding government actions. "There is considerable value in reporters from serious outfits being briefed, as far as it's possible, so they can understand the intelligence background which affects policy decisions," one defense reporter commented. "I just don't think any administration's policies can be properly analysed and understood unless everyone's working on more or less the same background."

It is this network of relationships which, according to interviews with officials and with more than thirty reporters who cover foreign affairs, defense, and intelligence issues, is threatened by measures the Reagan administration has taken to stop unauthorized leaks and to restrict the authorized flow of information to the press. Past administrations have on occasion become apoplectic about leaks, but rarely have they responded with such a public and many-leveled attempt to seal off the bureaucracy.

Last year the CIA, the NSA, and the Defense Intelligence Agency asked Congress to exempt them totally from the Freedom of Information Act. They did not get their wish, but in October President Reagan submitted a package of amendments to the Senate that would have partly accomplished the same thing by authorizing the attorney general to exempt certain classes of intelligence files from disclosure. The proposal would also have stripped courts of the power to determine whether information disputed in FOIA cases is properly classified; instead, they would be limited to deciding, usually on the basis of secret affidavits from the agency itself, whether the decision to classify had been "arbitrary or capricious." (On May 20, the package was defeated in the Judiciary committee, but it is expected to be reintroduced on the Senate floor or in the next Congress.)

While his FOI Improvements Act was proceeding through the Senate, the president lowered the standard for classification with a stroke of the pen so that now virtually only the devil himself can be shown to have made a capricious decision. On April 2 of this year, Reagan signed a new executive order on national security information that eliminates the requirement that information be classified only if its release can reasonably be expected to cause "identifiable" damage to national security. The order also eliminates the need to balance the public interest in disclosure against the possibility of such damage when deciding to classify. Further, it creates a presumption that intelligence sources and methods are classified even when they are not otherwise sensitive, allows officials to reclassify information already released, and does away with provisions for automatically reviewing old records to determine whether they should remain secret.

Although the Justice Department official responsible for information policy recently said that the FOIA is "over-rated" and has not resulted in the release of much valuable information, studies by the Congressional Research Service and by a private Washington research organization have identified some ninety-six books and more than 300 news articles based entirely or in part on documents released under the act, many of them by the various intelligence agencies. What is perhaps more important, the existence of the law and the disclosure provisions of the old executive order created a climate that helped reporters gain access to unclassified information that had not yet been made public. The most important effect of the new provisions may be the signal they send to the bureaucracy. "When you expand the classification system as this administration has," observed veteran *Washington Post* reporter Murrey Marder, "you're telling anyone intelligent in the foreign policy area, 'Buddy, your feet are in the fire!' "

To Chill a Source   A more direct threat to relations between journalists and officials is the Intelligence Identities Protection Act, which has now passed both houses of Congress, and which will soon be signed into law. The bill became controversial because of a section that could make it illegal for reporters to identify undercover intelligence agents even if their source is public or unclassified information. This section was opposed by every major journalistic and civil liberties organization and, to be sure, it raises serious problems. A survey for this article turned up more than 80 major books and news articles, the authors of which could arguably have been indicted under the law. [A representative sample would include *The New York Times'* investigation of ex-CIA agents Wilson and Terpil; revelations that former CIA agents were involved in the Watergate break-in; accounts of illegal domestic spying by the CIA; and disclosures that an agency employee tried to infiltrate the House and Senate intelligence committees in 1980 at the direction of the KGB.] The conference report reconciling House and Senate versions of the bill, however, argued that journalists who identify agents in the course of normal reporting are not necessarily engaged in the requisite "pattern of activities intended to identify" agents and may not be covered by the bill. It called on the Justice Department to respect this interpretation.

Despite this ambiguous protection, the bill will no doubt discourage some news organizations from publishing some information. But the more serious threat posed by the bill is to the *gathering* of information. It stems from sections of the measure, ignored by virtually all those who opposed it, that make it illegal for officials to reveal identities. For example, the new law will make it illegal for an official to tell a reporter asking about guerrilla activity in Guatemala to "go see So-and-so, he was station chief there." Such referrals are commonplace, and in the great majority of cases result in stories that do not name agents and have nothing to do with intelligence agencies. Imposing criminal sanctions on such routine assistance will clearly chill sources.

"That's the real danger of it," commented *Newsweek* reporter David C. Martin, whose book *Wilderness of Mirrors* describes the bitter counterintelligence disputes that have wracked America's intelligence community for decades. "I could never have done that book with that law in effect, because the last question you ask in any interview is, 'Who else should I talk to?'"

One sign that the legislation is explicitly aimed at chilling news sources was CIA Director William J. Casey's mercifully stillborn request that it be amended to permit surprise searches of newsrooms to identify officials who have violated its provisions. Casey's proposal, set forth in an April 29, 1981, letter to the chairman of the House Intelligence committee, was to create a new exemption to a 1980 law which, in response to the Supreme Court's *Zurcher* decision, requires police to serve a subpoena before examining reporters' files for evidence of crimes committed by third parties.

CBS correspondent Ike Pappas recalls meeting Casey at a reception at the Greek Embassy last year and discussing the new director's views on press access to CIA information. "We got into a very active conversation," Pappas said. "Casey said, 'Who elected you to tell the American people what they should know? When we think they should know something we will tell you about it.' He was kind of hot that night." Casey, reached for comment, replied that the remark "doesn't sound like anything I would have said."

The CIA: A New Brief on Briefings   In March 1981 the CIA terminated its traditional practice of providing unclassified, not-for-attribution briefings on foreign events to reporters who request them. "When the new administration came in and looked at the use of manpower," CIA spokesman Dale Peterson explained, "the decision was made that we wouldn't continue them." A few journalists interviewed for this article did not regard this as a great loss; briefings, they said, usually could not be arranged on breaking news because the CIA's analysts were too busy keeping up with events themselves. But many more reporters said that the briefings had been valuable and that stopping them was an important change.

"I was briefed twice in my checkered career," recalled one reporter who asked not to be identified. He said the CIA briefings, in this case on Angola, were "much fuller and better, in the sense of being hard-nosed and not being ideologically biased toward one group or another," than similar sessions at the Pentagon or at the State Department ("bland").

Michael Getler of *The Washington Post* noted that access to the CIA was particularly valuable because, like the National Security Council staff, it is charged with taking into account the information and interests of many different agencies. He called the result "the closest thing you can get to an objective" account in the government.

The briefings were "really done, very truthfully, as a service," recalled Herbert Hetu, who resigned as director of the CIA's Office of Public Affairs after Casey downgraded the office in mid-1981. "The philosophy was that the country was spending a great deal of money" to gather "a great deal of information that was unclassified. We never gave away secrets."

The briefings were resumed last August—but with a catch. The agency now briefs reporters only if their views are of interest to CIA analysts or they are traveling abroad and are willing to be debriefed when they return. Dale Peterson insisted this should not reopen the controversy about the use of journalists for intelligence gathering. "We are very careful to avoid 'tasking' " reporters by asking them to obtain specific information, the CIA spokesman said. The exchange of views, he added, is also purely voluntary. "What we're trying to preclude," said Peterson, "is a reporter coming in here where it's all one-sided." But if the reporter refuses to be debriefed? "That obviously enters into the decision," Peterson replied. "Why should we give him a briefing?"

According to Peterson, most briefings are for general background and not for reporters about to travel overseas. In that sense, official relations between the CIA and the press have not been reduced to a bald quid pro quo. But they have been reduced—from 127 briefings in 1980, to 27 last year, to 13 as of early May this year. "I used to take briefings on a whole bunch of subjects from the agency. . . . They were very good," said *New York Times* reporter Leslie H. Gelb. Under the new arrangement, Gelb said, "I just don't want to get involved."

Gerald F. Seib of *The Wall Street Journal* had similar reservations. Earlier this year he had scheduled a briefing on Central America, but the agency cancelled the meeting after Seib made clear that he had postponed a planned trip to the area. "They felt they should get something back," Seib said. "We discussed it [at the *Journal*] and decided we couldn't do any briefings under those conditions." Seib rescheduled the trip and the agency did eventually brief him without insisting that he agree to be debriefed. But if the CIA is relaxing its information policy it is doing so selectively, and many reporters say their requests continue to be turned down. (The agency, meanwhile, has not resumed publication, halted last year, of unclassified analytical studies, on subjects ranging from Soviet agriculture to international terrorism, which many journalists and scholars considered useful.)

The Sound of Doors Closing   The CIA was always tough. Perhaps more disturbing is the loss of access to agencies that have traditionally been more open—State, Defense, and the National Security Council staff. On January 12 of this year, President Reagan issued a statement requiring all but the most senior officials to obtain advance approval before discussing "classified intelligence information" with reporters, and to prepare a memo immediately afterwards describing the conversation. This clearance and reporting requirement was rescinded in February, but the rest of the policy was left intact: in the event of leaks, the president warned, officials would be "subject to investigation, to include the use of all legal methods"—meaning polygraph tests and, possibly, wiretaps.

Asked how normal relations with the press could continue under the new guidelines, Reagan insisted at a news conference the next week, "What we're doing is simply abiding by existing law. It is against the law to—for those who are not authorized—to declassify, to release, classified information." A White House spokesman was later unable to say what law the president was referring to. This was not surprising, because the only disclosures of information to the press that are clearly illegal are those involving communications intelligence (e.g., electronic intercepts) and atomic energy information.

Former *New York Times* reporter Tad Szulc, now a Washington-based free-lancer covering foreign policy and intelligence issues, described the administration's attempt to limit contacts with reporters as "damaging to the normal operation of journalism in this town." Murrey Marder of *The Washington Post* put the point in stronger terms. "If you literally enforce a rule that you cannot talk about a classified matter in the field of foreign affairs, you cannot have reporting. The process becomes absolutely insane. It is an illusion [to believe] that you can distinguish between classified information and unclassified information and have any kind of intelligent discussion of foreign policy."

William Beecher, *The Boston Globe*'s diplomatic correspondent and a former deputy assistant secretary of defense, agreed that reporters must be able to talk to officials who have access to intelligence information and pointed out that this can be done without damaging national security. "Frequently, what's sensitive in intelligence reports is not the information but the source," he said. An official can discuss the substance of such reports "intelligently and accurately without saying, 'This is from our latest satellite take,'" Beecher concluded.

While a few reporters thought things were gradually returning to normal, nearly all those interviewed said that the leaks policy announced in January had caused a dramatic chill. "There's no question but that it's scared people, and those who tell you otherwise weren't getting much information to begin with," commented Leslie Gelb. The cumulative effect of the policies, he said, is that now reporters have to work "very, very hard" to cover the administration's foreign policy. This comment was heard time after time in other interviews.

"It used to be relatively easy to get people to think aloud on the phone," noted one *Newsweek* correspondent. He said that his calls to the State Department's Bureau of Intelligence and Research often are not returned now and that one official had taken the precaution of calling from a pay telephone. "There is an element of fear very palpable here now," said Robert Pierpoint, who covers the State Department for CBS. "They constantly say, 'You better talk to the press office,' and the press office is useless."

"I called a guy at the Pentagon the day after [the leak policy was announced]," David Martin of *Newsweek* said. "He was just livid that I'd called him. He said, 'Haven't you read the papers?'" A *Times* reporter agreed: "Guys at the Defense Department say, 'The situation is serious here.'" Jack Anderson associate Dale Van Atta noted that the Pentagon is rumored to be "salting" computer-generated documents by varying numbers from one copy to the next in order to trace leaks. "I have lost a source through a lie detector," Van Atta added. "He was caught and said he couldn't talk to me anymore."

National Security Adviser William P. Clark has refused to grant interviews and has continued his predecessor Richard V. Allen's policy of routing all contacts with his staff through the press office. One reporter characterized the staff as "scared shitless" by the threat of lie detector tests, a novelty at the previously accessible National Security

Council staff. Another, more tactfully, called the situation "more difficult than ever before."

"The biggest problem is that right from the start the CIA and the
NSC were basically put off limits," said Michael Getler of *The Washington Post.* "The two places we could go for on-the-record comments, the
daily briefings at the State Department and the Pentagon, had become
worthless. Spokesmen were limited to reading their guidance." The
result, he said, was an unprecedented restriction of the ability of the
press "to explain what was going on in some rather important areas.
And it hasn't helped the administration, because it produced the impression that they don't have a foreign policy or that they haven't been able
to explain it."

When the Government Leaks   That is the other half of the paradox, for
on several issues the administration has taken positions that can be
supported only by releasing classified information normally denied to
the press. In the case of Libya, bizarre leaks took the place of rational
debate in justifying the imposition of U.S. sanctions and the withdrawal
of workers from the country despite their desire to stay. In the case of
Central America, officials came to realize earlier this year that U.S.
involvement there would come under increasing criticism unless they
could persuade Congress and the public of the basic premise that conflicts in the region were being controlled by outside communist powers.
They decided to mount a public relations campaign. It was a fiasco.

On March 2, Secretary of State Haig declared that the U.S. now had
"overwhelming and irrefutable" evidence that the insurgency in El Salvador was being directed from outside the country by non-Salvadorans.
Two days later Haig announced that the Salvadorans had captured a
Nicaraguan "military man" who had been helping to direct guerrilla
forces in their country. The man, apparently a student, escaped into the
Mexican embassy. On March 9, CIA Deputy Director Bobby R. Inman
hosted a rare press briefing at which declassified U-2 photos of Nicaraguan military installations were made public to show that Nicaragua was
building up its armed forces, a fact no one doubted and which Nicaragua
admits. Finally, a second "military man" was located in the person of
José Tardencilla Espinosa. His charge on nationwide television that his
earlier confession had been obtained through torture proved acutely
embarrassing to the administration.

This public attempt to make its case having backfired, the administration turned to a more easily controlled method of disclosure: a leak
of intelligence information so detailed that, according to an account in
The New York Times, the CIA had previously refused a State Department request that it be made public. Three days after the Tardencilla
episode, *Newsweek* reported that "the best evidence is coming from
radio intercepts. Destroyers that have been stationed off the coast of

Nicaragua since early this year have been able to pinpoint the location of several clandestine radios used by Salvadoran guerrillas and fix the location of their central command post on the outskirts of Managua. The intercepts, still a closely guarded secret, show that the guerrillas report their positions and actions to Managua, which in turn sends details of impending arms deliveries."

It was quite a disclosure. "That caused some real flinching," one knowledgeable source said. "NSA has said they are hurt by the disclosures." Even so, congressional sources said in recent interviews, while the administration's evidence may show that Nicaragua is providing a base of operations and some logistical support, it does not show that the conflict is being controlled by non-Salvadorans.

Whatever else it was, the public relations campaign on Central America was a masterpiece of selectively used information. At the photo-intelligence briefing, for example, a government analyst addressed the central issue—whether the Nicaraguan arms build-up is defensive or offensive—by attempting the difficult task of deducing from photographs of a vacant airfield the use to which planes not yet there would be put. "These, of course, are not for the defense of Nicaragua," the analyst said. But alongside its coverage of the briefing the next day, *The Washington Post* reported that late last year the president had approved covert paramilitary operations against Nicaragua. This was clearly relevant to assessing the evidence presented at the briefing.

Reagan, however, was not particularly upset by the play the covert-operations story received, it was reported, because it showed the Nicaraguans that he meant business. Indeed, the administration's sensitivity to leaks seems to vary according to political, rather than security, concerns. As far as could be learned, for example, no investigations have been undertaken to identify the sources of the covert-operations story or of disclosures of electronic intercepts—among the government's most sensitive sources of information—related to Qaddafi's threat against Reagan or to the content of communications with Salvadoran guerrillas.

On the other hand, investigations are known to have been initiated to identify the sources of two stories printed early this year in *The Washington Post,* neither of which involved classified information. The first appeared on January 8, when the *Post* reported that, according to a Joint Chiefs of Staff estimate, the force required by the administration's military strategy would cost up to $750 billion—or 50 percent more —than planned. And on February 19 the *Post* described a State Department staff meeting at which Haig had called British Foreign Secretary Lord Carrington a "duplicitous bastard" and made similarly frank remarks about other world leaders.

In the light of this peculiar pattern of vigilance, it may be wrong to characterize the administration as having an anti-leak policy at all. As

David Martin of *Newsweek* observed: "When there's a political objective at stake, the leaking goes on undeterred. The only difference is that it's a little better organized."

It would seem, then, that the policies of the Reagan administration pose not a paradox involving lying but a riddle involving trust. The riddle is how reporters cut off from adequate information can know when to believe officials who say, "I am telling the truth."

30 · THE PRESS AND THE PRESIDENT
There They Go Again

BY GEORGE E. REEDY

George Reedy attempts to put the adversarial relationship between government and the press into a more philosophical perspective. He shows that the president can and does manipulate the press but that such efforts can backfire, because the president cannot manipulate *all* the press *all* the time. Reedy has personal experience in the matter, since he served as White House press secretary during the early years of the Johnson administration. He is Nieman professor of journalism at Marquette University and author of *Twilight of the Presidency.* His article is reprinted from the *Columbia Journalism Review,* May/June, 1983.

To the leisurely observer of the Washington scene, there is a distinct charm in the startled air of discovery with which the press greets each step in the entirely predictable course of its relationship with the president and the White House staff.

Actually, the patterns are as well-established and as foreseeable as the movements of a Javanese temple dance. The timing will vary as will the alternating degrees of adoration and bitterness. But the sequence of events, at least in modern times, appears to be inexorable. It is only the determination of the press to treat each new day as unprecedented that makes the specific events seem to be news.

Seen from a little distance, cries of outrage from the press over the discovery that Mr. Reagan seeks to "manage the news" have the flavor of an Ed Sullivan rerun show on after-midnight television. They are reminiscent of similar protests in the administrations of Presidents Carter, Nixon, Johnson, Kennedy, Eisenhower, Truman, and Roosevelt. Presidents before that do not offer much material for discussion simply because they served prior to the FDR era, when press-White House relations were put on a daily-contact basis for the first time in history.

The charge of management is a familiar one because it has a strong element of truth. All presidents seek to manage the news and all are successful to a degree. What is not taken into account is that legitimate management of the news from the White House is inescapable and, human nature being what it is, it is hardly surprising that presidents try to bend this necessity for their own ends. Few men will decline an opportunity to recommend themselves highly.

The press would not be happy with a White House that ended all efforts at news management and either threw the mansion wide open for coverage or closed it to outsiders altogether and told journalists to get facts any way they could. Since the early days of the New Deal, reporters have been relying on daily press briefings, prearranged press conferences, and press pools when the president travels. There would be chaos should all this come to an end.

The point is that the White House is covered by journalists through highly developed and formal organizational structures. It is inherent in the nature of such structures that they must be managed by somebody, and the president's office is no exception. Management technique is employed every time the president decides what stories will be released on Monday and what stories will be released on Saturday; every time he decides that some meetings will be open to press coverage and others will not; every time he decides that some visitors will be fed to the press as they walk out of the Oval Office and others will not. Anybody who believes that he will make decisions on the basis of what makes him look bad will believe a hundred impossible things before breakfast.

There are actually times when the press literally does not want news. This became very clear early in the administration of Lyndon Johnson when he inaugurated the custom of unexpected Saturday morning news conferences. This meant disruption of newspaper production schedules all over the United States. Printing pressmen had to be recalled from weekend holidays to work at exorbitant rates; front pages that had been planned in leisurely fashion in the morning had to be scrapped for new layouts; rewrite men who had looked forward to quiet afternoons with their families worked into the evening hours. It was a mess.

After two such conferences, I began getting calls from top bureau chiefs in Washington pleading with me to put an end to them. They made it clear they wanted stories timed so that they would fit conveniently into news slots. It took some doing on my part; Johnson would have enjoyed the discovery that he was putting newspaper publishers to so much expense and trouble. (I think he started these conferences simply because he became lonely on Saturday mornings when there was little to do.) I talked him into dropping the custom by producing figures which showed that the weekend audiences were not large enough to justify the effort.

While it was actually going on, the episode struck me as just another example of the Johnsonian inability to comprehend the press. It was not until later that I realized the deeper significance. The press had not only acquiesced in news management but had actually asked that it be instituted. The fact that nothing was involved except timing was irrelevant. The ability to control the timing of news is the most potent weapon that any would-be news manipulator can have. No absolute line can be drawn between the occasions when he should have it and those when he should not.

This may well account for the indifference of the public to the periodic campaigns against news management. Even to an unsophisticated audience it is apparent that journalists are not objecting to news management per se but only to the kind of news management that makes their professional lives more difficult. However it may look in Washington, at a distance the issue appears as a dispute over control of the news for the convenience of the president or for the convenience of the press. In such a situation, Americans tend to come down on the side of the president.

Of course, if the president is caught in an outright lie—a lie about something in which the public is really concerned—the public will mobilize against him swiftly. But many charges of news management are directed at statements that Americans do not regard as outright lies. Americans have become so accustomed to the kind of exaggeration and misleading facts that are used to sell products on nightly television that a little White House puffery seems quite natural.

There is, of course, another side to the coin. While presidents always try to manipulate the news—and all too often succeed—there is a very real doubt whether the manipulation performs any real service for them, even in the crassest image-building sense. The presidency is a strange institution. The occupant must accept never-ending responsibilities and must act on never-ending problems. It may well be that what a president does speaks so much more loudly than anything he can say that the normal techniques of public relations are completely futile.

In the first place, a president may be able to time his public appearances but he cannot time his acts. He *is* the United States and anything that affects the United States must have a presidential response. He must react to international crises, to domestic disasters, to unemployment, and to inflation; if he chooses to do nothing in any of these instances his inaction will be writ large in the public media.

In the second place, a president may be able to keep his thoughts to himself but he cannot act in any direction without causing waves that sweep through the Washington community. The federal bureaucracy is shot through with holdovers from previous administrations who do not like him; the Congress is loaded with political opponents with whom he must deal; the lobbying offices of the capital are staffed by skilled president-watchers who can interpret his every act and who have sympathetic journalistic listeners.

Finally, there is the overwhelming fact that the president has a direct impact on the lives of every citizen and there is a limit to his capacity to mislead. He cannot convince men and women that there is peace when their sons are dying in a war. He cannot hold up images of prosperity (although he will try) when men and women are out of work. He cannot persuade constituents that there is peace and harmony when there is rioting in the streets. There may be instances when he can escape the blame but only when his political opposition is not on its toes.

Against this background, the efficacy of manipulation is dubious at best. It may have a favorable impact on public opinion in the short run. But I know of no persuasive evidence that it helps to build the long-term support a politician needs. Every instance I have studied bears a close parallel to what happened when Lyndon Johnson held his meaningless meeting with the late Soviet premier Alexei Kosygin at Glassboro, New Jersey, in 1967. He was able to maneuver the press into treating it as a major summit conference for a few days, and his poll ratings rose accordingly. But it soon became clear that the meeting had produced nothing of substance and that there had been no reason to expect that it would. The poll ratings went right back down again.

On the other hand, efforts at manipulation invariably challenge the press to dig deeper than journalists ordinarily would. The stories they write about manipulation have little effect. But the stories they write as a result of the digging may have the kind of substance that does make an impact. The whole exercise can well be merely an invitation to trouble on the part of the president.

The bottom line can be simply stated. The president can, within limits, manipulate that part of the press which covers the White House. But he cannot manipulate the press as a whole, and it is probable that his efforts to do so will always backfire.

FOR FURTHER READING

William O. Chittick, *State Department, Press, and Pressure Groups: A Role Analysis.* New York: Wiley, 1970.

James A. Fosdick, *Public Relations, Politics/Government, and the Public Interest: A Report on the 1968 Midwest Public Relations Conference.* Madison, Wisc.: The Regents of The University of Wisconsin, 1969.

Lewis M. Helm, Ray Eldon Hiebert, Michael R. Naver and Kenneth Rabin, *Informing the People: A Public Affairs Handbook.* New York: Longman, 1981.

Ray Eldon Hiebert and Carlton E. Spitzer, *The Voice of Government.* New York: Wiley, 1968.

Gladys Engel Lang and Kurt Lang, *The Battle for Public Opinion: The President, the Press, and the Polls during Watergate.* New York: Columbia University Press, 1983.

IX

Media Management of Government

A LTHOUGH THE government cannot legally censor the press, the press can and does censor the government. Reporters, editors, correspondents, producers and directors are the people who decide what news about the government gets communicated in the mass media.

Our Founding Fathers gave the press a powerful role when they formed our country, and some of them even felt that the press should be more powerful than government. "That government is best which governs least," was the cry of the day. Thomas Jefferson took the point to the extreme when he wrote: "Were it left to me to decide whether we should have a government without newspapers or newspapers without government, I should not hesitate for a moment to prefer the latter."

In 1828, the English writer Thomas Macaulary wrote, "The gallery in which the reporters sit has become a fourth estate of the realm." Freedom of the press in England had made the newspapers as powerful as the House of Lords, the House of Commons and the Clergy.

In the late 1950s, an American writer, Douglass Cater, wrote a book describing the Washington press corps as the "fourth branch of government," as powerful and as important as the legislative, judicial and executive branches. Yet the press is not government; it is private industry. Often, however, the other three branches of government cannot win the public support necessary to carry out their mandates without the cooperation of the mass media.

The media's role as the fourth branch of government has grown stronger and more powerful through the twentieth century. Many experts say that the manner in which the media covered Vietnam was responsible for the American failure there. Certainly the media, by exposing the Watergate scandal, brought about the first resignation of an American president. Our history is full of many other instances where the press has forced the hand of government.

But the press is not perfect, and it is not all-powerful. The individuals who make up the mass media are small in number, compared to the legions in

261

government. And they are only human, just as those who are the bureau-cracy. Perhaps it is the adversarial struggle which continues between the two that makes the world safe for democracy.

31 · THE "IMPERIAL" PRESS CORPS

BY MICHAEL J. BENNETT

According to Michael J. Bennett, the press in Washington has become so powerful that it is losing touch with the readers, viewers and listeners back home. These are the people, he implies—the voters, the citizens—who should have the power in a democratic society. And the press is abusing its power by its "imperial" attitude. Bennett is a freelance writer and frequent contributor to the op-ed page of the *Boston Globe.* He has covered Washington extensively, and in 1971–1972 he held a Congressional fellowship from the American Political Science Association. This article is reprinted from the *Public Relations Journal,* June 1982.

The Washington press corps has been zealous in reporting the com-plaints of groups and organizations opposed to the policies of a Presi-dent determined to reverse a 50-year trend toward centralization of government within the Federal bureaucracy.

Indeed, the editorial writers and columnists of the *Boston Globe, New York Times, Chicago Tribune, Los Angeles Times,* and, of course, *The Washington Post,* as well as the major networks have decried, vociferously if not eloquently, the efficacy and even the propriety of vesting more governmental responsibilities in the hands of the states and the communities.

And yet, ironically, the media—who have been in the forefront bemoaning the real and potential dangers of the "imperial Presidency" —have been among the first to defend the utility and inherent virtue of an institution that makes the "imperial Presidency" possible, the imperial Federal bureaucracy. No doubt, some of those attitudes are rooted in ideological or philosophical preferences. But much of the opposition also stems from entirely understandable—although completely unexamined—motives of self-interest, personal stakes in the ever-expanding growth and perpetuation of another silent and unwitting partner in the rise of the "imperial Presidency"—the institution of the "imperial press corps."

Unknown to most Americans, the Washington press corps has expanded enormously within the past 20 years. Even at the height of the Kennedy years when Washington attracted attention as a fashion, cultural and financial center, as well as the political hub, newspapers such as *The Boston Globe, Newsday* of Long Island, New York, *The Atlanta Constitution,* even *The Los Angeles Times* were satisfied with one- and two-member bureau offices tucked away in the down-at-the-heels National Press Building on 14th Street. Only *The New York Times,* the late New York *Herald-Tribune* and, perhaps, *The Chicago Tribune* had bureaus with 10 or more members.

The television networks, with only 15-minute newscasts to fill, had a few black-and-white cameramen roaming about, almost indistinguishable from still-news photographers from newspapers and wire services. Television reporters were barely tolerated by their print colleagues on whom they had to rely for tips and leads.

The focus of media attention in those days primarily was on Congress, a convenient and cheap taxi ride from the National Press Building. There, stalwart icons of regional differences and idiosyncrasies, such as Lyndon Johnson, Sam Rayburn, John McCormack, Everett Dirksen, Charles Halleck and "Judge" Smith—chairman of the then all-powerful House Rules Committee—were readily accessible to reporters, even as those Solons presided over and frustrated most of John Kennedy's legislative initiatives.

However, the dramatic and amusing Kennedy press conferences were beginning to slowly, but inexorably, tilt the "perimeters and parameters" of political showmanship toward satisfaction of the instant, visual imperatives of television. The measured, considered print style of Walter Lippmann, James "Scotty" Reston, the Alsop brothers and other columnists and reporters comfortable with the baronial political style of Washington was soon to pass. The confidences exchanged over a drink or dinner at the Cosmos or Army and Navy Clubs were to make way for televised confrontations, mass marches, non-negotiable demands, conflict as theater, all in living color, with the newspapers and newsmagazines scurrying to pick up every stray bit of gossip, every tidbit of scandal the ever-vigilant cameras somehow missed.

Their Numbers Grew   When President Kennedy left Washington for Dallas almost twenty years ago, he was accompanied by a small pool of wire service, network and regional reporters, instead of the literal plane loads that now follow Presidents on their most trifling trips. Before his death, fewer than 300 reporters were accredited to cover the White House. Today, the number is somewhere around 3,000.

In the early 1960s, the networks would assign a cameraman to the White House literally to protect themselves in the unlikely event the President stumbled over a golf ball in the Rose Garden or was attacked by disguised terrorists at a reception in the Dolly Madison Room. Today, each network assigns a dozen cameramen to cover the White House around the clock to photograph every public—and, when possible, private—action of the President.

The expense involved virtually assures network White House correspondents 30-second to minute-and-a half stories on the evening news every night, regardless of the intrinsic news value of whatever emanates from the Oval Office that day. Indeed, Congressional leaders have a far better chance of appearing on the news by making a visit to the White House than by presiding over their co-equal branch of government.

Not only has the focus of media attention shifted to the White House, but so has the locus of news bureau offices. Instead of being jammed into dingy, yellowing cubicles in the National Press Building, the offices of most of the major news organizations are now housed in comfortable, airy, new and expensive buildings on the other side of the White House, one and two doors down from the old and new Executive Office Buildings—right in the middle of the high-rent district. Congress is now a more expensive two-zone cab ride away, and everyone who is anyone in the news business is within walking distance of one another, a stone's throw from the White House and a martini shake from the best restaurants in town.

The Boston Globe, Atlanta Constitution, Newsday, every paper with any pretension to national significance, has at least 10 bureau members. New York's *Herald-Tribune,* is gone, of course, but *The New York Times, Chicago Tribune,* even *The Los Angeles Times* have bureaus with 30 or more reporters and editors. *The Los Angeles Times,* for example, occupies almost all of a floor in a building just across 18th Street from the old Executive Office Building, which, during the height of the New Deal era, housed both the State and War Departments.

The Boston Globe bureau shares back-to-back suites with Art Buchwald and Evans & Novak in the building next to the one accommodating *The Los Angeles Times,* one floor under *Newsweek.* Even the Hearst Corporation, notorious as a chintzy employer, has offices across Pennsylvania Avenue from *The Los Angeles Times* in a new marble edifice boasting a waterfall in the lobby.

But there is nothing chintzy about the imperial news corps in Washington these days. Washington political reporters traditionally have been well paid in a business notorious for offering psychological rewards in lieu of currency. Salaries of $40,000 to $50,000, relatively rare in most newspaper home offices, are commonplace in Washington bureaus. Network TV reporters can command the kind of six-figure incomes anchormen receive in major media markets—not because of their reportorial skills but because of their appeal and success in weaning viewers away from competing stations. Here, at least, substance, relatively speaking, competes with tinsel.

Washington is not only the sole city in the United States in which being a reporter is considered fully as respectable as, say, dentistry or real estate, it is also unique in that some reporters actually make more money, often considerably more, than the people they cover. Much of that, of course, is due to the artificial, market-proof limit placed on Congressional and Cabinet-level positions—$60,000 a year compared to $250,000 to $500,000 for comparable jobs in the private sector. If it is axiomatic that many Presidential appointees do have to make considerable financial sacrifices to serve their government, it is equally true that no journalist has ever suffered a loss of income from criticizing the private sector that finances the government.

And the financial rewards can be quite handsome. Rowland Evans and Robert Novak were reported several years ago to be clearing well in excess of $100,000 a year. Benjamin Bradlee, editor of *The Washington Post*, has an annual income of over $200,000, in addition to stock bonuses and stock options. The highly regarded, and publicly financed, *MacNeil/Lehrer Report* was nearly forced off the air in the late '70s because of Congressional resentment of $70,000 and $80,000 salaries.

Any resentment scribblers for the print media might feel for their less talented but more photogenic brethren in the electronic media is assuaged by the ego gratification—and financial reward—of appearing on one or more of the numerous public affairs programs airing out of Washington. The essential elements of TV confrontations are no longer mass marches and non-negotiable demands. But within today's electronic conflict as theater, reporters can serve as paid surrogates for the poor, the wretched, those yearning to breathe free. It may not be the traditional role of the journalist—but it pays a lot better.

The Way Is Clear   The passage of *The Washington Star* from the scene in the summer of 1981 has removed probably the last impediment to the emergence of the Washington press corps as a truly imperial corps, with its own self-interest vested in an expansion of Federal as opposed to regional power. The *Star* had served for many years as a counterweight, an honorable "conservative" opposition to the "liberal" hegemony, now monopoly, exercised by *The Washington Post* in the District and its suburbs.

As long as the *Star* was around to check the excesses, if not the abuses of the *Post,* Cabinet secretaries and even the White House were more than satisfied by a journalistic tour of the horizon provided by scanning clips from *The New York Times* and perhaps *The Baltimore Sun.* Reading any other paper was considered superfluous, and, as a matter of fact, finding other papers was difficult. Washington might be the capital of the western world, but it doesn't have anything comparable to the out-of-town newstands in Harvard and Times Squares.

All of that began to change before the folding of the *Star* with the opening of Washington's lavishly expensive, but extraordinarily comfortable and convenient subway system, Metro. Coin machine boxes with copies of *The Wall Street Journal, The New York Times* and *Baltimore Sun* began to appear outside such major stations as Capitol South, Smithsonian, Federal Triangle and Farragut West, two blocks from the White House. Then came boxes with *The Atlanta Constitution* (it was, after all, the Carter years), and by the spring and summer of 1981 *The Los Angeles Times,* New York's *Daily News* and *Post,* the *Boston Globe* and *Chicago Tribune* as well as *Newsday.*

To an ever-growing extent, correspondents for these newspapers no longer are writing so much for the folks back home as they are for their peers on *The Washington Post* and *New York Times,* and for their colleagues at ABC, NBC, CBS and PBS. The result has been a massive reduction of complex political and social issues into a grossly simplified newspeak, which is incapable of making classifications other than "liberal" and "conservative"—words used with about as much precision by news commentators as by shoppers at Bloomingdale's to describe the clothes they just purchased.

Indeed, to many veterans of the imperial press corps, such as syndicated columnist Mary McGrory, President Reagan's vision of a new Federalism seems like a sick joke. In a recent column, "The New Federalism and a Ghost Capital," Ms. McGrory conjures up a satiric vision of a future in which journalists are sent "to the heartland, that wonderful place of Ronald Reagan's fantasy where people help one another and make non-deductible charitable contributions. Let some lofty scribbler who has been baiting the noble chief executive be set to writing paeans to the local gas company executive. Cut them down to size, these people who fabricated stories about guerrilla warfare in the Cabinet. Assign them to chronicling important local feuds between say, the local leading Elk and Lion of Minot, ND."

Some time after he had retired from the White House, Lyndon Johnson—the first chief executive to be labeled an "imperial President" by the Washington press corps—was asked by a TV reporter what force or influence has done most to shape the nature of Washington politics in his time.

"You bastards," he snapped. It was the first and still most cogent description of the imperial press corps.

The day may still come when Mary McGrory, retired to Beacon Hill to write her memoirs, may be asked by an inquiring reporter from the

Boston Globe—squeezing in a feature interview between meetings of the Ward 5 Republican Committee and the Roxbury Home Turf Civic Association—what caused the decline of the imperial press corps.

"That bastard Reagan" might well be her reply.

It's an answer that might not cause joy in Minot, North Dakota, but it is sure to evoke a sardonic grin on the protoplasmic face of Ms. McGrory's first editor, George Minot, the legendary editor of the late *Boston Herald.* George could be wrong about some things. After all, he turned down Mary's request, when she was secretary to the book editor, for a job as a reporter on the grounds that she "couldn't write." But then, he also voted against Franklin Delano Roosevelt as many times as Ronald Reagan voted for him. And we all know how that's turned out.

32 · FEAR AND FRATERNITY IN THE WASHINGTON PRESS CORPS

BY STEPHEN HESS

How does the press actually work in Washington?
Stephen Hess finds that fulfilling the role as the fourth
branch of government is neither as complicated nor
as simple as it might seem. Hess is a senior fellow at
Brookings Institution. This article is excerpted from
his book *The Washington Reporters,* published by
Brookings. Based on 150 personal interviews and
survey responses from 38 percent of all Washington
reporters who cover the national government, *The
Washington Reporters* is the first volume of
Newswork, the most detailed study ever undertaken
of the relationship between the press and government.
This article is reprinted from the *Washington
Journalism Review,* January/February 1981.

To listen to many Washington reporters talk about work is to imagine the beleaguered band at the Alamo. They are surrounded by editors
who do not understand their problems, by deadlines that are unrealistic
and assignments that are simplistic, by politicians who are manipulative and bureaucrats who are uncommunicative and consumers who are
either uninterested or cranks. They are employed by penny-pinching
organizations that will not let them travel to the places where news is
being made. They are never given the space or time to do justice to their
stories. They are constantly being badgered by silly requests from the
home office.

"I have a hell of a fight with [my editor] over the 'trivialization' of
news. Editors are getting fed up with serious institutional problems,
with articles on what government should and shouldn't do. It took me
a week to get an article in the paper on government reorganization, then
[the editor] attacked it as 'another story of government glop.' " "Editors
feel they aren't doing their job if they don't screw around with your
copy." "The power center [of my organization] is New York. But it's a

zero news town. We have to call New York before we can go to the bathroom." "Usually I get letters from far-out people who see communists under every hat." "We're being used by publicity-seeking members of Congress." "Reporters are suspicious of bureaucrats; we consider them always ready to hide behind regulations, unbending paper-shufflers." "This is a company town, let's face it. So it's inevitable that they control the news to some extent."

Is this really the world of the Washington reporter? Or are these tales spun to feed a love of complaining? To intensify the pleasures of a difficult job? To create a specialness of us against them?

"We complain because we are quasi-creative workers," contends Albert Hunt of the *Wall Street Journal.* Creative people are supposed to complain. But in contrast to the often amusing, sometimes bitter, comments of reporters, there are more careful ways to calculate job satisfaction, the extent of disagreements with employers, hours worked, travel, who initiates stories, the amount of copy editing, and story placement. When 38 percent of the Washington reporters who cover national government for the American commercial media answered elaborate questionnaires in 1978, their responses portrayed a very different world.

All self-respecting reporters are capable of pleasurably recounting the wrongs committed against them by their editors or producers and by politicians or public officials. But when asked whether they are happy in their work, the overwhelming majority, 84 percent, rate themselves as satisfied. (Forty percent are very satisfied; 44 percent, fairly satisfied; 14 percent, somewhat dissatisfied; and only 2 percent, very dissatisfied.)

Prestige beats usually rate high in satisfaction, among them politics, science, the White House, and diplomacy. Low-satisfaction assignments include regional news, the Supreme Court, regulatory agencies, and domestic departments. Specialized publications, television networks, and magazines have the greatest percentages of satisfied reporters, though reporters for specialized publications do not rate themselves "very" satisfied.

Reporters on influential outlets are not more content as a group than those who work for the non-influentials. Anecdotally, at least, most tensions in Washington journalism are in the premier organizations. Good gossip, of course, is always the tales told of kings—the ups and downs of famous names at a television network or a major newspaper are intrinsically interesting. Yet, the anecdotal evidence of high tension suggests reasons why job satisfaction is not higher at the places where the prestige is greatest: Washington news, being more important in these organizations, is more worth fighting about; and since these organizations are national, and therefore more centrally controlled, reporters have less autonomy. (The power plays at little-known publications may be equally fierce, merely less noticed. Smaller organizations are probably not composed of "nicer" people; they just fight on other grounds—and less in the public eye.)

Specialists are considerably more satisfied than generalists; the older the reporters, the more likely they are satisfied (although there is a slight rise in the dissatisfaction rating for reporters in their forties); conservatives are more satisfied than liberals, and those in the political middle are most satisfied; there are no job satisfaction differences between men and women.

Constant combat is not characteristic of relations between reporters and editors; benign neglect is a better description. For most journalists in Washington, the home office is far away and out of sight. Local editors are consumed with other problems, and their Washington reporters are too experienced to require close supervision and too knowledgeable—even intimidating—to have their judgments overruled. Local editors fume a lot about the Washington staff not knowing what "the people" really want, but rarely try to run the Washington bureau from headquarters. (In those cases where Washington is headquarters, this obviously does not apply.)

Given the overall low level of disagreement between reporters and their bosses, the most revealing information gleaned from this question is what they do fight about. The majority of arguments—56 percent—concerns matters that could be called professional: length of the story, its placement in the publication or broadcast, the time to write, and writing style—in descending order of importance to the reporters.

There is a widely held belief among newspaper reporters that the space devoted to non-advertising—the news-hole—is shrinking. Whether this is true or not, there are other changes that affect how much space each reporter can expect. Page makeup has changed (bigger headlines, more white space, larger photographs, more indexes). And competition from both Washington and non-Washington material is greater (more sports coverage and service features, business market listings, even fiction; larger Washington bureau staffs; more stories from wire services, supplemental news services, syndicates, and free-lancers).

At the same time, Washington reporters say their stories need even more time or space. The federal government makes more news: it is bigger, more complex, and it is assuming more functions in society. Changes in law and in congressional rules make more information available. The definition of news is expanding, as fewer topics are now considered off limits to public comment. Furthermore, in newspaper journalism a form of anecdotal writing (pioneered at the *Wall Street Journal*), which cannot be easily compressed, is gaining in popularity.

The other significant category of disagreements—nearly a third—has to do with autonomy, the reporter resisting home-office requests, assignments, or story angles. "An editor says this should be the lead and I say that's the lead. I want to do it my way." Autonomy causes the greatest conflict in prestigious organizations (which have greater leverage over their reporters) and among prestigious reporters (who expect the most autonomy). This explains, perhaps, the exit from daily print journalism of such luminaries as David Halberstam, Tom Wolfe, and Gay Talese. The late Laurence Stern, an editor of the *Washington Post,* was fond of saying, "When the history of the newspaper business is written, it will be about those who left it." Although one might expect that friction over autonomy would be much more prevalent in network television, where high technology increases organizational control at the same time that the star system increases reporters' demands, this is not so. What may dampen conflict in this medium is that unhappy correspondents can sell their services to only a limited number of networks. (The most autonomous journalist, then, would be a prestigious reporter working for a non-prestigious outlet, such as the late Peter Lisagor of the *Chicago Daily News.*)

Fights over money—for travel and expenses—are modest. Also, only four percent say they ever argue with their editors over politics— the political slant that the home office or the reporter may wish to give a story. This is a major change since 1936, when Leo Rosten asked Washington reporters whether they had "had stories played down, cut, or killed for 'policy' reasons" and 56 percent said *yes.* William Rivers, asking the same questions in 1961, found that seven percent answered in the affirmative. But by 1978, writing to fit the editorial positions of publishers had simply disappeared as an issue for contention. While it is possible that this is because publishers and reporters now agree, the evidence is otherwise: many reporters make a point of noting that they do not share the political ideologies of their publications.

The near absence of disagreements over political slant is a by-product of higher professional standards as well as the passing of the press "lords"—the Robert R. McCormicks and William Randolph Hearsts—publishers of strong political opinions (and sometimes strong political ambitions), who viewed their publications as outlets for their own views. Many have been succeeded by chain operations, which accept "objectivity" as a necessity of doing business in diverse communities, and by the electronic media, which are legally mandated to be "fair."

Disagreements with the home office are greater in broadcast journalism than in print, about both story length and assignments. Money for travel and expenses is more of an issue at small operations, such as local television stations and regional news services. Fights over story angle and political slant most often occur at magazines, which interpret the news. Specialized publications record the fewest disagreements. However, the range of disagreements does not differ very much among the various types of news organizations.

Nor is there much variation by beat, except for the Supreme Court beat, which is above average in every disagreement category. Reporters on almost all beats are unhappy about story length, with White House reporters being unhappiest. Class A general assignment reporters have the most disagreements about story placement; White House reporters, about time to write; and class B general assignment reporters, about home-office requests. (For the purposes of this study, general assignment reporters are divided into two categories: the class A general assignment reporter, a senior person, even the bureau chief, picks his or her own stories; the class B general assignment reporter, often a younger person, is sent on a daily basis to those events that may produce news outside the main flow.)

Generalists have more disagreements than specialists; the older the reporter, the fewer the disagreements; there are no differences in the disagreement ratings of women and men; liberals and conservatives are also the same, while those in the political center have the fewest disagreements. Apparently reporters with the most pronounced ideologies are the most argumentative, whether they are of the left or right. The few blacks in the study claim to have few disagreements.

The low level of disagreements between Washington reporters and their home offices need not be because the reporters have been housebroken—sociologists make much of news room "socialization"—but because they so often get their way. It is not necessary to push against an open door. A method of measuring reporters' autonomy is to ask "who was primarily responsible for initiating" their latest stories. In 856 cases, reporters initiated their stories 69 percent of the time, home offices initiated 11 percent, and bureau chiefs, 10 percent.

The editor of a chain newspaper in a western state is highly critical of his operation's Washington bureau. His complaints are unusual in that he does not fault the staff for failing to relate to his community but rather, for lacking enterprise. Looking over the Washington schedule of the day before, he asks, "Is there any story here that couldn't have been written in three hours?" He thinks not. He has lots of ideas about stories that should be written, yet he says he never makes requests and does not offer suggestions at the chain's annual meeting of editors.

The editor of a chain newspaper in a southern state is also critical of the stories he gets from Washington, but his is the more typical comment, that Washington reporters have lost touch with the rest of the country. (Unlike the western editor, he runs a high percentage of the copy he receives.) He, too, does not make his views known to the Washington office. "[The bureau chief] would say I'm very poor about generating ideas, but it's 90 out of a 100 on my list of priorities."

Being very busy is not the only reason that editors give their Washington reporters so much freedom. Editors who have not had Washington experience often seem to hold their Washington reporters in awe ("Who am I to tell them what to write?"). And editors who have had

Washington experience often agree with the views of their Washington bureaus.

Nor are Washington reporters very closely supervised by their bureau chiefs, at least in the matter of story assignments. The bureau chief of a large independent newspaper says, "Reporters generate 65 percent of spot stories . . . and some beats generate up to 85 percent of the stories, such as the State Department." He explains, "Most reporters do a much better job if they generate their own stories. They're the ones who really know what's going on." This may be true, but it also avoids hassles. Most bureau chiefs are themselves reporters or columnists; supervising a staff is not high on their list of satisfactions.

Autonomy is very different at the more highly centralized television networks and weekly news magazines. Network correspondents claim to initiate only half of their stories. Since television networks and news magazines are counted among the influentials of journalism, these reporters, it might appear, have chosen to exchange autonomy for other rewards. The reverse exchange could be said to be the case of top journalists who work for less illustrious operations. But, of course, the play of fortuity is such that few reporters are actually presented with this choice. Moreover, it is instructive to note that the Washington reporters of such tightly controlled organizations as *Time* and CBS do at least as many stories of their own initiation as stories thought up by others.

The amount of editing relates importantly to the type of news organization. Television network news can be thought of as pre-edited— carefully constructed to fit time segments before they go to New York. Network correspondents report that there is no home-office editing 93 percent of the time, minor editing 7 percent of the time. In magazine writing, on the other hand, the home office is expected to play a more significant role, and here some editing is reported 62 percent of the time. "It's a myth," says a news magazine editor, "that reporters file beautiful, finished copy that the editors then butcher." Newspapers fall between television and magazines on the editing scale.

What is most important in gauging the freedom of Washington reporters from home-office control is how few respondents—even those who work for magazines—indicate that their work is substantially edited; no stories of regional news service reporters and radio reporters are substantially edited. How much editing is done relates most to the age of the reporter, the youngest being the most edited. Only one of the substantially edited stories is from a high-prestige beat, but this too is age-related, since these are the places where young reporters are seldom located.

In terms of the placement of stories, a bureau chief says, "Our papers understand that we represent an investment. The return of the investment is the stories we do. They want to give us good treatment."

When Washington reporters were asked to indicate placement of 561 major stories that they had just written, 51 percent rate them "prominent" (for television networks, this means the stories appeared on the evening news), 48 percent get "secondary" treatment, and 1 percent are not used. Above-average display of stories is registered by reporters for television networks, radio, and chain newspaper bureaus.

Stories by reporters on high-prestige beats, as expected, are more prominently displayed and less edited. There reporters initiate somewhat fewer stories than their colleagues on the low-prestige beats, reflecting, possibly, bureau chiefs' and home-office editors' interest in the coverage of major events and institutions. Reporters appear to pay a slight price in independence for assignment to the beats that are most important to their supervisors.

Some of the pleasures of Washington reporting are generic to journalism—minimal routine office work, for example. Some satisfactions derive from being far from the home office—such as little editorial supervision. Other satisfactions come from covering the nation's capital —being eyewitness to important events. And there are satisfactions that are a product of having achieved prominence in the profession, including exotic travel. Yet, there are also special problems and stresses that are part of newswork in Washington.

The reporters' isolation from their consumers and their organizations is often considerable. For some, this lack of connection is the dark side of freedom. It can make the workplace a little more unsettling. A fourth of Washington reporters receive no letters or calls from readers or listeners: wire service and radio reporters almost never hear from their consumers; two-thirds of the press corps get three or fewer letters or phone calls in a week. "I consider more than six letters a month a landslide," says a member of a chain bureau. Of those in the mass media, only television network correspondents get an appreciable response from their audience.

"The public is very supine" except on a few highly emotional issues, such as abortion and the Equal Rights Amendment, and this mail is often generated by organized groups. In general, reporters give low marks to their letter writers. "We get some pretty bizarre reactions, especially the reporter covering psychology" (from a specialized news service); "half are from crackpots, a lot from convicts saying their rights are being violated on something" (from a chain newspaper bureau); "some want pictures" (from a television network); "I get a lot from John Birchers and Ku Kluxers" (from an influential newspaper). Mail that expresses an opinion of the reporters' work tends to be heavily unfavorable, particularly of those covering diplomacy. Only journalists on specialized publications, and a few specialists at other news outlets, get mostly favorable reactions; they talk of a sense of community with their consumers.

Says a radio reporter, "It doesn't bother me not hearing from listeners. I realize I'm just a voice. However, I hate getting no feedback from my organization. This lack of guidance is terribly frustrating." Fifteen percent of all Washington reporters claim that they receive no home-office reaction to their stories. Another 46 percent characterize the response as minor. Only those who work for television networks and specialized publications say that they get substantial reaction from their home offices.

"There's no systematic feedback, no memos or notes," says a reporter on a large independent newspaper. "That's fine with me. The less feedback the better." Yet the radio reporter says, "This lack of guidance is terribly frustrating." Which is the prevailing view? The answer relates partly to age. A 24-year-old specialized publications writer says, "There's not enough feedback for me." On the other hand, a 69-year-old newspaper reporter contends, "I seldom surprise them, they don't surprise me. There's no need to pass reactions back and forth." Another pattern seems to be that those who do not hear regularly complain of no feedback and those who get substantial home-office reaction complain of interference.

The isolation of reporters from both consumers and the management of their own organizations contributes to their seeking rewards from association with (and their standing among) their colleagues. Recalling his days on the *New York Times,* sociologist Robert Darnton says, "We really wrote for one another. Our primary reference group was spread around us in the newsroom." Yet those who claim they receive considerable reaction to their work from their home offices rate themselves more satisfied with their jobs, and, conversely, those getting only minor reaction from headquarters are less satisfied.

Washington journalists feel themselves increasingly out of touch with the nation. Asked to comment on a cluster of statements—"Reporters often miss how government affects people 'out there' " and "Washington reporters have lost touch with their roots"—82 percent of the news corps agree, and 54 percent think the problem is serious.

Radio and newspaper reporters are the most concerned; wire service and magazine reporters are most likely to see no problem. Views differ depending on which end of Pennsylvania Avenue the reporter is located: at the White House, 88 percent of the reporters believe the problem is serious, while the percentage drops to 40 among congressional reporters on Capitol Hill. Almost all black reporters say that the Washington news corps is out of touch; women more than men are apt to call this a serious problem; reporters for the influential outlets are less likely than those on the noninfluentials to see a problem here; and reporters 50 years old and over are least likely to worry about being out of touch.

There is a relationship between reporters saying that they are out of touch with the rest of the country and the degree to which they fraternize with their own kind in Washington. Almost half of reporters' closest friends, in Washington are other journalists. Among their non-journalist friends, at least 55 percent are in government or government-related fields, such as lobbying and political party work. The older the reporter (which assumes a longer working life in Washington), the more likely his or her close friends are other Washington reporters: by the time Washington reporters reach 50 years of age, nearly two-thirds of their closest Washington friends are journalists.

Those in broadcast journalism (radio and network television) are most likely to have friends in the news media. Reporters on beats centered in news rooms and press galleries (Congress, White House, State Department) tend to have more reporter friends than those on beats without a central location (regulatory agencies, economics, science). Reporters who say that none of their closest friends is a journalist think the press corps is more out of touch than those who say that their three closest friends are in journalism.

What can be done to close the gap between Washington reporters and the rest of the country? Travel, say reporters. Eighty-one percent of the press corps think they should have the opportunity to spend more time away from Washington. "Drive across the country," advises a news magazine reporter. "I did it in '67. Nobody believed me afterwards when I said LBJ wouldn't be reelected." A newspaper reporter in a chain bureau says, "I make it a point to travel back to Ohio for extended trips of several weeks, at least twice or three times a year. It almost always improves my perspective on how to treat news out of Washington." The reporters who do the most traveling are the most convinced there is a problem.

The press corps is almost equally divided over whether rotating reporters between Washington and the home office would be a workable solution to the problem of losing touch with consumers. (Fifty-two percent say *yes,* 48 percent say *no.*) Many mention one newspaper that keeps its reporters in Washington for only a few years and, as a result, has lost some of its best people. Sixty-two percent believe that rotation would cause serious staff losses, ranging from 71 percent on magazines down to 54 percent at wire services. "You'd have an armed revolt on your hands," says a newspaper chain reporter.

Arguments against rotation usually revolve around acquired knowledge. "Washington is the kind of city where experience pays off." "Contacts are very important, so it doesn't make sense for a paper to shift reporters around too often." "It's a bloody waste to send someone out to the boondocks after he has learned to cover this city." Of course Washington reporters are hardly the ones to offer a disinterested opinion. "I don't want to live in Baltimore." "Reporters going back to local papers would have to take a huge pay cut." "We can't go back to covering cops and robbers." "It would be hard to move with husband and wife both working in Washington."

On the other hand, there are Washington journalists who believe "it's dangerous to have a reporter here longer than most of the politicians" and "rotation holds out hope for other reporters back home." Others point to existing policies of rotating foreign correspondents that, although on a much smaller scale, have not caused problems. "There'd be a lot of bitching and moaning," says a network correspondent, "but there's so large a supply of reporters that filling the ranks of Washington is not a problem." Rotation, however, would be a messy, unpleasant policy to put into practice, and organizations do not do things that are messy and unpleasant unless forced to by necessity.

Washington reporters need not suffer from job insecurity; few reporters get fired. Still, they live in a world of competition and uncertainty. Events seem to happen faster now; actions are more complex. As their stories become more important, so, too, do the stakes. The reporter is alone, except for other reporters—friends, but also rivals. The reporter's work is exposed; there it is on the front page or the network evenings news. Yet, it can never be the whole story, and it may be proved wrong tomorrow. Moreover, reporters think of themselves as serious people, and they take their work seriously.

A paradox of journalism is that the work of journalists remains highly competitive at a time when the news business is becoming less competitive. Fewer and fewer cities have more than one newspaper or different owners for morning and afternoon papers. There are two domestic wire services (there used to be three) and three commercial television networks (there used to be four). But competition between reporters is not economic. This attitude depresses salaries while increasing time and money spent on a story. Competition is "more professional than real," says a veteran writer for a news magazine, who means that the primary object of his labors is not to sell more magazines.

In a sense, every Washington reporter is in competition with every other reporter. Nor is the competition merely for exclusive stories. A news magazine reporter, part of a two-person team at the White House, speaks of tensions when competing "against the person you're working with." Newspaper reporters compete for space with those in their own organization, with wire service reporters, and with reporters whose copy is transmitted through a supplemental news service. Many editors have four versions of the same story to choose from. There is competition between reporters on the same beat, even when they have no readers or listeners in common; reporters from morning and afternoon papers in the same city are in competition, even though their papers have the same ownership and modest overlapping circulations; the *Washington Post* and the *New York Times* compete, although they are·

in different cities. News work attracts highly competitive people, and if no direct competition exists, reporters invent it.

Yet, to describe the Washington press corps exclusively in terms of competition is to picture a human jungle that does not exist. Reporters also cooperate with each other, and cooperation gives way to competition only as information becomes valuable. Cooperating is a product of friendship, fraternity, and self-protection. Journalism has a tradition of fraternal sharing, of exchanging information of routine nature, and of older reporters helping newcomers. An old-timer tells of a day with President Harry Truman at Key West when one of the regular reporters was too drunk to file a story. Independently, three of his colleagues sent their "blacks" (the carbons of their own stories) to the inebriated friend's editor. "I liked the second version of your story best," wired the editor.

In a business that does not rely on documents research, "other reporters are our best information bank," says a reporter for a major newspaper. "When I was doing a story on Mondale, I went to reporters who had covered him in Minnesota." The historical memory of the press corps, however, is limited by the modest number of elders in its ranks.

Cooperation that grows out of friendships and fraternity exists wherever there are journalists; cooperation for self-protection, based on the need to limit uncertainty, is most often evident where reporters work at a distance from the home office. Here one finds an us-against-them attitude, Washington reporters versus home offices. Self-protective cooperation is found most among reporters on beats that have covered major events, where editors are likely to notice differences between rival stories. These are the beats given to older reporters, who are most apt to have known each other for years, and the beats on which reporters work in the closest proximity, in a pressroom or on a press bus. These reporters are also more likely than those on other beats to switch employers, so that over time a competitor may become a colleague.

A newcomer to the political press corps tells of hearing a reporter for an influential newspaper calling in his story in a voice much louder than necessary. Was he cuing his friends about the lead he had chosen? The young man notes with bitterness that such survival techniques lend a hand to lazy colleagues, carrying along the least conscientious. It is also a way that reporters minimize the threat of an uneasy environment and the control of their bosses.

33 · THE MEDIA AS SHADOW GOVERNMENT

BY WILLIAM L. RIVERS

William L. Rivers feels that the press has become so
powerful in influencing government that it might be
going far beyond what the Founding Fathers
originally had in mind. Rivers is a former Washington
correspondent who has written widely about the
press and government. He is now a professor of
communication at Stanford University. This article is
reprinted from *The Quill*, March 1982.

The capital city of the United States of America, like the federal
government it houses, was constructed according to plan. The original
city, most of which still stands, is the physical equivalent of Jefferson's
Declaration of Independence, of Madison's Constitution, and, in general, of the whole assortment of utopian notions that Carl Becker has
called "the heavenly city of the 18th-century philosophers." As London's Crystal Palace symbolized, for all the world, the progressivism,
utilitarianism, and scientism of the 19th century, so the Washington of
L'Enfant, at least in certain kinds of weather, is an artwork of the
Enlightenment—a perfect emblem of the 18th century's spacious, optimistic, slightly naive view of man.

As with any good work of art, every feature of official Washington
has a meaning. The various presidential monuments, the Supreme Court
building, and the Capitol itself reflect, massively, the founding fathers'
dream of resurrecting the Roman Republic (there even are fasci beside
the speaker's platform in the House of Representatives). A tall, cigar-
store Indian perched atop the Capitol's great dome can render the general effect, for the finicky observer, less classical than kitschy. But this
touch of the frontier serves to remind us that the city of Washington was
designed to be the set piece of a continental empire.

By contrast, the executive mansion, at 1600 Pennsylvania Avenue,
is a structure so austere and virginal that posterity has named it, simply,

the White House. Beside the White House, and housing its senior functionaries, is the EOB—the old Executive Office Building—a Victorian ostentation of *nouveau riche* power in which Walt Disney might have felt more at home than Queen Victoria.

Official Washington is majestic and orderly, erratic and tasteless. Its architecture represents the impossible simplicity and systematic character of the U.S. Constitution. It also reflects the labyrinthine complications and overelaboration that were the inevitable products of the Industrial Revolution, of Manifest Destiny, of one civil and two world wars, of bread-and-circus electioneering—the inevitable products, in other words, of two centuries of human foible.

But there is another side to Washington—another government. In a high-rise building on Pennsylvania Avenue, near the old Executive Office Building, is a floor of small offices whose windows overlook governmental Washington—the White House, the Capitol, the great monuments and museums along the mall, and the gargoyled mug of the EOB.

"Here. Look. This is the best view of Washington," says Mel Elfin, capital bureau chief of *Newsweek* magazine. If you can appreciate the incongruous, Elfin is doubly right. These windowed cubicles of one significant organ of that other government reflect not only a different organization from that of official Washington, but a distinct view of man.

Just outside Elfin's office window is a little balcony with a few chairs and a low-slung rail to keep one (barely) from becoming hamburger on the pavement below. The balcony is covered with screaming green Astroturf, which provides a startling emphasis in the foreground to the classical travertine and brownstone edifices beyond. Some old potted petunias and a couple of tomato plants struggle to cope with what appears to be constant neglect.

Somehow, the bedraggled pots fit the scene. Everywhere in the *Newsweek* offices are similar images of an eccentricity that is born of hard-nosed realism. Everywhere, there is also awesome disorder; for although the *Newsweek* offices are fairly plush by press standards, this week they are being renovated—new carpets, some rearranged partitions, and the addition of a kitchen and conference room.

Also being renovated is the National Press Building, some three blocks from the EOB and *Newsweek* offices, and fourteen blocks from the Capitol. Since 1908, this venerable structure has been the focal point for most Washington news operations. It was definitely showing its age. Its brickwork was crumbling, its hallways were yellowed and dingy. In the ornately plastered lobby, elevators chugged up and down like old mules about to give up the ghost, while reporters and editors muttered disagreeably about how long it took them to get up to their offices.

The National Press Building was in an advanced state of decay. It is certain that the Washington press headquarters is getting a face lift. The Other Government—the Washington news corps—has come to consciousness of its power and is gradually moving into larger, more official, less eccentric structures.

Richard Rovere once suggested that our attitudes toward national politics—and, indeed, our national politics—might have been profoundly different if the founding fathers, instead of creating the nation's capital on the mud flats of the Potomac, had set it down in the center of 18th-century Manhattan. Our federal politicians and public servants would not now be jousting in the limiting and incestuous environment of a municipality given over entirely to government. With the national government as but one sector of a complex city, officials could not have avoided rubbing elbows and shaking hands with the nation's literati and its social critics. The condition that resulted might have rendered American politics less peripheral and vague in the national literature, and American social criticism less divorced from the political realities.

Rovere made this point most authoritatively. In order to write about national affairs for *The New Yorker,* Rovere himself commuted to Washington from his work in New York City. He often lamented that "very few reflective, literary intelligences deal with public affairs in this country," and he attributed this problem to the singularity of concerns and the cultural remoteness of Washington, D.C. For political man, no city is more exciting, more electric, than Washington. But for those with other or broader passions, no city is so stultifying. Among the intellectual and creative elite who have been honored in Washington, few have been willing to linger longer than it took them to finish their dinners at the White House.

The result of Washington's cultural estrangement from the nation has been the elevation of Washington's journalists to a kind of academy of national sages and prognosticators. In most other world capitals—which, usually, are also highly cosmopolitan cities—the journalist must vie with the novelist, with the playwright, with the artist, and with the critic in reporting, in analyzing, and in interpreting national public affairs. In Washington, news correspondents win by default. As a result, they have acquired the authority and sometimes even the power of a shadow government.

The Washington press corps has certainly acquired the trappings of power. Privileged as no other citizens are, the correspondents are listed in the *Congressional Directory;* they receive advance copies of governmental speeches and announcements; they are frequently shown documents forbidden even to high officials; and they meet and work in special quarters set aside for them in all major government buildings, including the White House. Fantastic quantities of government time and money are devoted to their needs, their desires, and their whims. Some

White House correspondents talk with the president more often than his own party leaders in the House and in the Senate, and there are Capitol correspondents who see more of the congressional leaders than do most other congressmen.

No wonder, then, that Washington correspondents feel what one presidential assistant has termed an "acute sense of involvement in the churning process that is government in America." A close view of this involvement so impressed Patrick O'Donovan, a former Washington correspondent for the London *Observer,* that he said, "The American press fulfills almost a constitutional function."

Indeed, in Washington today, correspondents who report for the news media possess a power beyond even their own dreams and fears. They are only beginning to become aware that their work now shapes and colors the beliefs of nearly everyone, not only in the United States but throughout most of the world.

For the American public, full acceptance of the media's new authority and responsibility came at the end of the Watergate crisis, when the president of the United States posed his word against that of the press and lost. But Watergate was less coup d'état than it was climax. It was the end of a long evolution that was first observed by a newsman nearly fifty years ago, during the trial of the Lindbergh baby's kidnapper and killer. At that time, Walter Lippmann commented that in our democracy "there are two processes of justice, the one official, the other popular. They are carried on side by side, the one in the courts of law, the other in the press, over the radio, on the screen, at public meetings."

Lippmann's observation remains true today, yet those who would end this discussion on the question of the court verdict versus the popular verdict are missing a much greater issue. For the basic question is not just whether we have two parallel systems of justice in this country, but whether we have two governments. Do we have a second, adversarial government that acts as a check on the first and controls public access to it? Indeed we do—and this Other Government is made up primarily of the more than two thousand news correspondents stationed in Washington.

In our daily lives, we trace a path from home to work and back. Without the news media, we would know almost nothing beyond our own sphere of activity. The public's knowledge of national government depends not on direct experience and observation, but on the news media; and it is the media that set the agenda for public discussion and decision.

To a large degree, the employees of the government—including the president himself—must also depend on the reports of the news media for information about some of their most important concerns. In government, as elsewhere, each worker is circumscribed, and his sphere is small. A congressional assistant may spend much or all of one day absorbing details about the religious leaders of Iran and learning much more than is published or broadcast about the imminence of all-out war in the Middle East. But he hasn't the time to inform all of his colleagues about his new knowledge, and he is likely to know less about House debate that day than any tired tourist from North Carolina who wandered into the public gallery to give his feet a rest. Both the tired tourist and the congressional assistant must depend on the newspapers to find out what happened that day in the Senate.

In an article for a journal of political science, former Senator H. Alexander Smith of New Jersey made it clear that members of Congress are not Olympians who learn what they know in closed-door hearings and secret communiqués. They, too, must depend on the media. Senator Smith listed thirteen different sources of information for congressmen; but the news media, he wrote, "are basic and form the general groundwork upon which the congressman builds his knowledge of current events. The other sources . . . are all supplements to these media."

Even presidents, with their vast and powerful apparatus of information, often end up relying as much on the press as on their own informational systems. John Kennedy admitted that he acquired new information from *The New York Times* about his own secret sponsorship of the Bay of Pigs invasion. Eleven days before the invasion that the CIA had been shepherding so carefully, the editors of the *Times* informed Kennedy that their correspondent, Tad Szulc, had discovered the secret and that a detailed news report was imminent. Kennedy persuaded the publisher to postpone publication until after the landing in Cuba. But, during the discussions with the *Times* editors, the president picked up new information about the mounting of the invasion.

Afterward, in regret at the fiasco, Kennedy said to Turner Catledge, the executive editor of the *Times,* "If you had printed more about the operation, you would have saved us from a colossal mistake."

Even the strongest and most capable president requires such reporting; for he is *always* insulated from the realities of his administration by the fears and ambitions of his subordinates. He cannot possibly sort and absorb all of the vital information that is produced by governmental agencies and activities. Many believe that the fall of Richard Nixon was foreordained by his hatred of and isolation from the media.

The influence of the Washington press corps is also recognized in the third branch of the federal government. Justice Potter Stewart said in 1975, with something like wonder: "Only in the two short years that culminated last summer in the resignation of the president did we fully realize the enormous power that an investigative and adversary press can exert."

The courts have long been suspicious of that power, and over the years, they have waged a largely silent battle with trial reporters over the reporters' access to and publication of courtroom proceedings. Moving ponderously, the courts have attempted to close off much of the access of the news media. Moving quickly and sometimes deviously, the media have anticipated and occasionally foreclosed these efforts, very often using one judge against another.

The Other Government wins some, loses some. During the fifty years since Walter Lippmann's observation about public and private trials, legal maneuvers between the federal government and its courts and the national news media have resembled a very intricate and symmetrical minuet. The courts move to gag orders and to secret trials. The media, stalemated, take the issues to higher courts and begin to employ attorneys as reporters.

But the dance does not always include willing partners, and the Other Government is usually less effective than official Washington at some of the more subtle steps. Often the official government will make the news media an unwitting participant in the never-ceasing warfare among its various branches and agencies.

Twenty years ago, a young reporter was writing an article about the powerful Brooklyn congressman, John J. Rooney, who headed the House of Representatives subcommittee that controlled the State Department budget. Every year, Congressman Rooney savaged the State Department budget request by speaking against "booze money for those striped-pants cookie-pushers." He alarmed the young reporter by exclaiming angrily, "I want to keep an open mind and be fair, but if you people in the press keep harping on it, I'm afraid you'll make me whack the budget too much."

The reporter then interviewed the assistant secretary of state who had the task of arguing in Congress for whatever budget the department thought was reasonable. The reporter asked him how badly Rooney's attacks crippled the budget request. "Why, not at all," the assistant secretary answered. In fact, he explained, Congressman Rooney was "the best friend the Department of State ever had." By berating Old Foggy Bottom on the floor of the House, even as he was pushing a generous budget, Rooney persuaded the representatives who abhorred striped pants that he had the State Department's number. Rooney's strong words were a facade that enabled the congressman to sneak more into the budget than Congress would otherwise have granted.

That sounded to the reporter like doubletalk, but no matter how many people the reporter interviewed, they were almost evenly split on the question. In the end, the reporter decided that Congressman Rooney was not a friend of the State Department; that he was, in fact, an irresponsible budget slasher. But even as the reporter was typing his article, he worried: It *could be* that Rooney is a clever ally of the

Department. Any Washington reporter can be convinced at times that Machiavelli is alive and advising congressmen.

A few months later, in 1961, the same young reporter was feeling the impact of the new Kennedy administration. Like other Washington correspondents, he was invited for the first time in history to share with a president both the crushing responsibility and the glittering aura of the greatest center of leadership in the Western world. Before 1961, the White House had been a closed preserve. Information was channeled through the president's press secretary, and some news correspondents never so much as met the White House advisers and chief assistants. A reporter who had arranged an interview with an Eisenhower assistant without going through Jim Hagerty, the press secretary, was so elated that he telephoned his editor in New York to say, "I broke around behind Hagerty!" The important news was not the substance of the interview but the fact that he got one.

When Kennedy took over, correspondents wandered through the White House offices in such numbers that they created a traffic problem. President Kennedy was his own most effective promoter. He practiced personal salesmanship with the élan of one accustomed to establishing the rules of the game. Kennedy made such a fetish of giving exclusive interviews that his press secretary, Pierre Salinger, once observed that he had to go to the Oval Office to find the White House correspondents.

The heady effect of this unaccustomed presidential attention is demonstrated by the behavior of our young reporter on the morning he received a call from the White House that the president wanted to talk to him. It was a snowy, miserable day. With a studied show of nonchalance, the reporter announced his coup to his colleagues, drew on his topcoat and one of his galoshes, and clumped out the door toward the elevator, leaving the other galosh on his desk.

The reporter who wrote the article about Congressman Rooney and who interviewed President Kennedy was me. I was then working for the now-defunct magazine *The Reporter*. Although I quit being a Washington correspondent near the end of 1961, I remained fascinated by the profession and by the sharpening power struggle between the Washington press corps and the federal government. Through secrecy, through the courts, through its press representatives, the government has awesome control over the public image of itself. Only the news media can exert an effective counterbalancing influence on the public's perception of government. Surely, if the government closes off freedom of access in any area, a balanced picture of government will give way to government propaganda.

Yet, there is another side to this issue. In 1978, philosopher-novelist Aleksandr Solzhenitsyn—an outsider, a Russian—observed, with considerable disapproval, that "The press has become the greatest power within Western countries, more powerful than the legislature, the executive, and the judiciary." How could he believe that? What of the overwhelming power of an attractive and canny president? What of the sheer size of the bureaucracy and its countless daily actions and decisions, which can vitally affect the course of society? Is it possible, despite the odds, that Solzhenitsyn is on to something?

We must remind ourselves periodically that the American republic's founders granted to the press, alone among private business institutions, the task of protecting the U.S. Constitution. Contemporary Washington correspondents are well aware of this responsibility and are proud of their independence from the official government and from the biases of their editors, publishers and station owners back home.

This independence marks the sharpest difference between Washington correspondents and their local brethren and between the Washington press corps today and that of previous generations. In 1936, Leo Rosten made this statement to a group of newspaper correspondents and asked whether it was true in their experience: "My orders are to be objective, but I *know* how my paper wants stories played." Slightly more than sixty percent of the correspondents replied yes, that they felt at least subtle pressure from their editors and publishers. In 1960, the mark came down dramatically; only 9.5 percent replied yes to the same question.

That difference is so dramatic that one may think there was a misunderstanding or a mistake. Another statement, which also tested freedom from home-office pressure, drew a similar response, however. Rosten asked the correspondents in 1936 whether this could be said of their work: "In my experience I've had stories played down, cut or killed for 'policy' reasons." Slightly more than fifty-five percent of the correspondents answered yes. In 1960, only 7.3 percent affirmed the same statement. During the twenty years since 1960, that downward trend has continued.

Yet, as my own experiences with President Kennedy and Congressman Rooney indicate, the independence of the contemporary Washington correspondents may be something of a mirage. In any event, what counts is not so much the independence of the reporters as it is their service of the public interest. How well do the news media serve our interests? How much do they show us of official Washington?

Learning about the national government from the news media is like watching a tightly-directed play. The director features the president at some length, the leading congressmen as secondary players, and the cabinet and justices of the Supreme Court as cameos and walk-ons. There are seldom any other entries in the dramatis personae, although there are *three million* employees of the national government. Any effort to move beyond the stage to see the undirected reality is useless.

We must understand this: that the *reality* of government is often quite different from that reported by the two thousand news correspondents who help to create that image.

The public and the government are awash in a torrent of media reports. Yet, inquiring into how the news media actually serve the public yields a different perspective. Radio and television are mainly useful in signaling news events, providing the immediate—and sketchy—reports that announce happenings. More and more, we depend on television, despite the fact that our understanding is distorted by the brevity of the news reports. Broadcast journalists skim the top of the news, working with headlines, leads, and the bulletins that alert the public. Only occasionally does a documentary flesh out the news. Av Westin, a news executive of the American Broadcasting Company, has said: "I think television news is an illustrated service that can function best when it is regarded as an important yet fast adjunct to the newspapers. I know what we have to leave out; and if people do not read newspapers, news magazines, and books, they are desperately misinformed."

Newspapers cannot compete with radio and television for rapid transmission, and they cannot compete with television for the sheer impact of seeing and hearing news in the making. But a newspaper is available at any time, and it can provide a vast range of information on many subjects. The importance of the newspaper has been described best by a man who was interviewed during a newspaper strike: "I don't have the details now; I just have the result. It's almost like reading the headlines of the newspaper without following up the story. I miss the detail and the explanation of events leading up to the news."

Most magazines can treat their subject in greater depth than newspapers, but they generally cannot cover as many *different* subjects. Even the news magazines, which attempt to cover a wide range of subjects in some depth, do not publish as much information in their weekly issues as can be found in a single issue of a large daily newspaper. Like people who write books, those who write for magazines can seek out the unreported, flesh out the information that has been presented only in silhouette in broadcasts and newspapers, and report matters that the faster media have missed in the rush to meet deadlines.

It would seem that such a division of labor would help us to learn about *everything* that goes on in the government: radio and television rapidly reporting the action; newspapers putting most of the stories into context; and the magazine writers and book authors reporting the major stories more fully, and with more grace and flavor. But this range of public-affairs reports, however carefully some may be fashioned, often seems the reflection of a faulty mirror. The mirror is first held this way, then that way, but how narrowly it is focused! The presidency, the congressional leaders, the State Department, and the Department of Defense are in view. Only occasionally is mention made of such bureaus as the Departments of Energy, of Transportation, or Agriculture, or of such agencies as the Federal Communications Commission, the Food and Drug Administration, the Interstate Commerce Commission, and the many other agencies that figure so importantly in our everyday lives. Only a few such agencies ever make it to the front page, to the television screen, to the radio interview.

Protesting the narrow focus of the Washington press corps, Derick Daniels, former executive editor of one of the Knight-Ridder newspapers, argued that journalists must recognize the reader's needs and desires:

> Yes, yes, we understand that the poor slob in the kitchen is interested in the price of soap when she *ought* to be interested in Congress. But I mean recognizing squarely, as a matter of intellectual honesty, that the kitchen is really, *in fact,* just as important. . . . the amount of knowledge and information collected, and the studies available through the U.S. government, are nearly limitless. A single document—the yearbook of the Department of Agriculture—contains more useful information in its pages than most newspapers report in a year.

The media are thus confronted with a dilemma. It is impossible for any news organization, no matter how large, to cover fully the entire federal government every day. And even if it were possible, no one would want to sift through such reports. So the real question is not whether the media are at fault for not covering the entire government all the time, or for printing only a small portion of what is knowable about the government. The more appropriate questions are: How good is the judgment of the Washington press corps as to what parts of the government to watch and which of its actions to record or investigate? And how good is the judgment of the Washington news bureaus and their outlets in deciding what information to print and to broadcast every day?

These are two important questions—as important as any questions we can ask about our official government in Washington; for, in a sense, the two governments—the official government and the national news media—increasingly form part of a single, symbiotic unit. The major difference between the real government and the media government begins with the conscious and deliberate action by most officials to insert the image they desire into the media process. The government nearly always attempts to create an image of itself. Whether this will be successful depends on the reporter. In some cases, the image of the officials vies with the reporter's own concept of those officials. In other cases, the images are a match.

Ben Bagdikian, one of the most powerful media critics in the United States, commented on the interrelationships between government image-making and press image-making when he made a study of newspaper columnists. He talked to many federal assistant secretaries for public affairs about how they briefed their bosses and how they preferred to break government news. Bagdikian found the secretaries were heavily influenced by what they saw in the news media, that they accepted this as what the media would respond to, and that, as a result, they fashioned their output to serve what they perceived to be the media interest. Thus, the work of the Washington columnists, Bagdikian speculated, "includes guessing what the government is doing." This produces a double-mirror effect, in which each side responds to what the other is doing, while at the same time adjusting itself to the other side's anticipated needs.

Thinking about the mirrors of politics, John Kenneth Galbraith commented wryly: "Nearly all of our political comment originates in Washington. Washington politicians, after talking things over with each other, relay misinformation to Washington journalists who, after further intramural discussion, print it where it is thoughtfully read by the same politicians. It is the only completely successful closed system for the recycling of garbage that has yet been devised."

Viewed in the rawness of this circus of political reporting, government news seems very complicated—and dangerous. It is true that since the Vietnam War and the Watergate crisis, Washington correspondents are much more suspicious of the announcements of government officials. More and more correspondents every year are asking sharp questions of officials.

The questions are important because there have been times in the past fifteen years when *no one* in the official government knew what was true. Phil Goulding, assistant secretary of defense for public affairs in the second Nixon administration, once said: "In our office, the secretary's office, or the White House, we never knew how much we did not know." Again, in reference to the Nixon years and the Watergate scandal, Senator Charles Mathias has said: "The more a president sits surrounded by his own views and those of his personal advisers, the more he lives in a house of mirrors in which all the views and ideas tend to reflect and reinforce his own."

When it became evident in 1973 that Nixon had been living in a world of mirrors—that he saw only the image that he had manipulated—Dr. Edward Teller, who had developed the hydrogen bomb in strict secrecy twenty years earlier, wrote ruefully, "Secrecy, once accepted, becomes an addiction." He might also have noted that secrecy, once the routine practice and defense of the official government, had, by 1973, finally given way to the angry probings of the Other Government.

By the time the Watergate case had brought an end to the presidency of Richard Nixon, the Other Government was firmly in control.

Contemplating the Washington cityscapes from the barely contained chaos of the *Newsweek* offices, one wonders if this is what the founding fathers had in mind.

34 · THE FOURTH BRANCH OF GOVERNMENT

BY WALTER H. ANNENBERG

Walter Annenberg feels that as the "fourth branch of government," the mass media have an obligation to be aware of their power and to use it with responsibility. He has been both a public official and a journalist, ambassador and confidant of presidents and publisher of the most widely circulated periodical in America, *TV Guide,* where this article appeared in the May 15, 1982, issue.

Journalistic coverage of events in Washington during the past two or three decades removes any doubt that we now have, in effect, four branches of Government, not three, and that the fourth—the press—exercises at least as much power in determining the course of the republic as the executive, legislative and judicial branches set forth in the Constitution.

Sheltered by the First Amendment from accountability for what it reports, the press alone has the ability to reach the electorate directly and consistently. Its power lies in reporting and interpreting what the Administration does and how the opposition—and the public—react.

Throughout American history, newspapers have acted as gadfly and watchdog, sometimes defaming honest officials with false charges of misdeeds, sometimes courageously exposing corruption in high places. Some of our greatest Presidents—Washington, Jefferson, Lincoln, Theodore Roosevelt—were moved to anger when the press of the day accused them of everything from ignorance and incompetence to venality.

Lincoln, a mild-mannered man, complained, "If I were to try to read, much less answer, all the attacks made on me, this shop might as well be closed for any other business."

The Presidency survived the attacks and so did the Nation. And most Americans agree that despite its excesses, in the main the press has served us well through the years, has been a constructive factor in our growth and prosperity by keeping our citizenry informed.

In recent years the word "press" has come to include the electronic news media, radio and television, which have the advantage of immediate access to the public. Because television can show events as they happen and can present the words of public officials and their critics as they are spoken, that medium of communication has become by far our most important source of news information and the one Americans trust most.

Considering the press's immunity from the checks and balances that control the other branches of Government, it has tremendous power, power that should be exercised sensitively, especially by those engaged in the dissemination of television news. Certainly the majority of commentators and correspondents are dedicated to reporting the news as objectively as is humanly possible, and they strive to overcome the time limitations of television news that make it all but impossible to offer a well-balanced presentation of complex Governmental issues.

Unfortunately we also find some practicing adversary journalism, placing themselves in what seems to be reflex-action opposition to Government leaders, including the President himself. Although they cannot possibly have access to the same quantity or quality of background information as those in Government, these newspaper and television personalities frequently not only are skeptical—always healthy for a reporter—but question the officials' motives. Others scarcely conceal their advocacy, presenting arguments favoring or opposing Government policies, interviewing members of the public who support their ideas. They also bring before their cameras officials and others who either deliberately or because of lack of information distort the Administration's position and mislead viewers.

When the President makes a major speech or holds a press conference that is covered by the networks, it is usually followed by one or more commentators explaining which points made by the Chief Executive were important, what they really meant, what the opposing arguments are and whether the course he advocates might come to pass. All this in the interest of better informing the public and usually with an effort, not always successful, to be impartial.

As a result, as Theodore White observed some years ago, the President and the press have become the principal rivals in setting the national agenda. The difference is that the President has power with responsibility; the press has power without responsibility.

Far more important than the press's influence on the success or failure of one President's program is the matter of its effect on the Presidency itself. Is it possible for any President to govern effectively under the circumstances that prevail today: when secret international negotiations fast become public knowledge, when Presidential actions are relayed to the public along with uninformed or misleading conjecture as to their possible success, when Presidential efforts to bolster confidence in the economy (because public attitudes have a great deal to do with the strength of the economy) are immediately countered by gratuitously pessimistic reports?

Is it possible, any more, for a President to win a second term when every day in a majority of homes there is heard doubt about his wisdom and his motives? Indeed, is it possible for any President—in the face of the widely publicized criticism that is prompted by innovative programs —to change the course of our country? Can he do other than continue to increase welfare rather than emphasize private-sector job programs, continue to increase taxes, continue to permit the Soviets to maintain nuclear superiority in Europe and extend their influence in our hemisphere?

It certainly is not the place of the press to endorse or support, except in clearly identified editorial comment, the actions or policies of a President. Its job is to report the news, good and bad, fairly and impartially. Our argument is with adversary journalism and advocacy journalism, which are by their very nature biased. We believe there is no place on television news programs for such journalism, that it serves only to confuse the public and weaken the Nation.

More than ratings are at stake here; it is the effectiveness of the Presidency itself. Well-intentioned, patriotic men and women head network and station news operations. They must be more aware of their power and how they use it, of the responsibility that should accompany their influence and of their obligation as the fourth branch of Government to all the people of the Nation.

For Further Reading

Douglass Cater, *The Fourth Branch of Government.* Boston: Houghton Mifflin, 1959.

Michael Baruch Grossman and Martha Joynt Kumar, *Portraying the President: The White House and the News Media.* Baltimore, Md.: Johns Hopkins University Press, 1981.

Stephen Hess, *The Washington Reporters.* Washington, D.C.: Brookings Institute, 1981.

Ray Eldon Hiebert, *The Press in Washington: Sixteen Top Newsmen Tell How the News Is Collected, Written and Communicated from the World's Most Important Capital.* New York: Dodd, Mead, 1966.

Richard W. Lee, *Politics and the Press.* Washington, D.C.: Acropolis Books, 1970.

Michael Bruce MacKuen and Steven Lane Coombs, *More Than News: Media Power in Public Affairs.* Beverly Hills, Calif.: Sage, 1981.

James Reston, *The Artillery of the Press.* New York: Harper & Row, 1967.

William L. Rivers, *The Other Government: Power and the Washington Media.* New York: Universe, 1982.

Steve Weinberg, *Trade Secrets of Washington Journalists: How to Get the Facts about What's Going On in Washington.* Washington, D.C.: Acropolis Books, 1981.

X

Business and the Mass Media

WHEN A representative of a college or university explains the tradition of academic garb, there's often a chuckle when he or she describes the color that designates graduates of business departments and schools. "The academic hood is trimmed in a drab brownish color," the speaker will say, and invariably someone in the audience will comment, "Just like business."

That hasn't been the case with business and the mass media in recent years, however. Business coverage has increased and the quality has improved. Many, though not all, business pages and programs have sparked controversy and moved away from being repositories of dull news releases. Readers and listeners and viewers have expressed interest in business news, and media management has begun to give staff support to business sections in return for the advertising revenues they are generating.

Lest it appear idyllic, healthy tensions remain; reporters and editors worth their paychecks continue to question the motives and activities of business, and businessmen and -women respect hard-hitting staffers who are fair and accurate in their assessments of business.

The articles in this section cover a variety of problems associated with business and the mass media. Jim Hoge succinctly describes the two sides of the business-media picture. Persons who have worked on either side can probably recite from memory the stereotypes he offers. Even the most experienced should study the questions, be prepared to respond to them and try to understand them.

Peter Dreier's article, although titled "The Corporate Complaint Against the Media," has enough on and between the lines to merit close study by business and media staffs and by students of both, the audiences of business news. The study cited early in the article is "Media and Business Elites," by Robert Lichter and Stanley Rothman, which was published in 1982 in *Public Opinion* and subsequently received a considerable amount of media coverage and commentary.

Michael D. Mosettig concentrates on a fact of life of all television reporting—the problem of compression that TV reporters have to face even as they try to tell complex stories.

These articles are starting points for better coverage of business in the mass media and for better understanding of business coverage. Business news doesn't have to be drab; it shouldn't be superficial.

35 · BUSINESS AND THE MEDIA: STEREOTYPING EACH OTHER

BY JIM HOGE

The public wants information about the economy, so business and the media have to peel away stereotypes and find ways to present it. Jim Hoge, former publisher of the *Chicago Sun Times* and now of the *New York Post,* succinctly tells how to do it. This article from *ASNE Bulletin,* February 1984, is based on Hoge's remarks during a workshop at Harvard University.

The public isn't particularly interested in the business vs. media imbroglio. What the public wants is more information from business and the media about changes occurring in the economy and society.

Both business and the media need to think more constructively about the public's information needs and about each other.

Here are three major business perceptions of the media:

1. Business sees the media as essentially *getting it all wrong.* The media write about the bad and ignore the good; they are fascinated by corruption, unsafe products, lawsuits and bribery, and run toward sensationalism and conflict. To top it all off, the media are careless, cursory, inaccurate and, for the most part, underqualified.

2. The media are biased and anti-business, tending to depict business as greedy, antisocial and insensitive to social needs. Media favor public interest groups, are pro the government, pro almost anything which is anti-business.

3. The media are too powerful. They are capable of souring the body politic by encouraging irresponsible behavior by politicians. They hide behind First Amendment rights but are quick to trample on the rights of others, particularly their privacy. The media are rather lame in providing space for rebuttals and equal time.

And I see these media perceptions of business:

• Business constantly hides behind a stone wall, covers up its own wrongdoing. Business stalls needed reforms and fights not only unnecessary regulation but necessary regulation.

• Business is manipulative, at times even deceptive, with information about itself. Business uses its public relations arm as a defense mechanism to stall and mislead rather than to facilitate.

• Business has unrealistic expectations about how it should be treated. Business sees itself as different from government because it is primarily responsible to its shareholders; it sees itself as having the right to determine the timing and relevance of information about itself. Further, it ignores its own power and pervasiveness and its impact on society, while hiding behind the cloak of being a "private" institution.

• Business is arrogant and self-deluding. As an oil executive said to a *Los Angeles Times* reporter who inquired about a public relations release that was not all that clear, "Just print it the way I wrote it, Sonny." Business, in the eyes of the media, assumes unfavorable stories are based on deliberate distortion, and overlooks the large quantity of good or neutral coverage which is given to business and business-related stories. Business overemphasizes government restrictions and underestimates government supports, many of which have been sought by business. Business is too quick to show deference to experts and to experts' solutions, and to expect that the rest of us should have the same kind of confidence in the technocratic approach.

What are some of the remedies?

For the media, an effort must be made toward a balanced skepticism —of government as well as business, of critics of business as well as of business.

It always interests me, whether we are talking about business, media or anything else, how long mythologies of institutions and historical events linger to affect us all. An example is the depictions of business that derive from the days of the robber barons. We must all be released from the images of such outdated stereotypes.

We need more self-examination. In the last few years, print journalism's survival-of-the-fittest trend has led to fewer papers in major metropolitan areas. But the survivors are stronger than they were. That's affected the relative power of business vs. the metropolitan press.

In another age, business might have been able to threaten media by withdrawal of advertising. These days, the shoe is on the other foot. Most of our large newspapers can't be threatened by the withdrawal of an individual advertiser, or even of a whole product category. Today, perhaps, it is far more possible for the media to harm business. We ought to recognize this.

We need further education for our reporters. Some in the media—but not enough—have taken this seriously in recent years.

One analogy: A number of years back, when environmentalism was first breaking upon us, we sent one of our reporters to the University of Wisconsin to get a master's in environmental subjects. We need this same kind of attentiveness to business and the economy.

We should also pursue some internal reforms. One of these is the use of ombudsmen. Another is the expansion of access, particularly to our opinion columns, so they represent views and expertise beyond our own. A third is an alertness to the prominence of corrections and clarifications, clearly understanding that to act as if none are necessary is a sign of weakness, not of strength; that weakness undermines our credibility. Finally, we should meet far more frequently than has been the case with various interested parties, including the people we report about; that, of course, includes business.

Business can do some things, too.

There is still too little recognition, and certainly not enough follow-up action, that reflects an understanding of the need for openness. Business indeed lives in an open society, is powerful, and is held accountable by a public which is increasingly of a mind to hold us *all* accountable.

Business must get to know us better and how we work. People in business must drop some of their comfortable assumptions and their self-defeating biases about the media.

Business understands that media can affect it greatly, and yet business people bother very little to know much about us and how we operate. In no other area does business behave similarly. For example, it is a virtue in business to know the customers and their wants and needs. It is a virtue to know about the financial markets.

Business must improve the performance of the corporate communications functions. Timeliness and candor, active rather than reactive postures, must be honed in business to a finer degree than they have been.

Let me move to some very specific issues of process that I think will facilitate media perceptions of business and business perceptions of the media.

The first question is: *Do you talk to the media when we come calling? And to whom should you talk?* Common sense suggests you should make distinctions, reserving your fullest and highest level responses for reporters who are well prepared and have sound credentials.

Well, when to talk? One of our problems is deadlines. You know about them in business, but you have trouble understanding them in ours. News is perishable, particularly for television, so if you decide not to cooperate, it does not mean that we cannot report the story. It does mean that whatever you might have to say is going to be unrepresented.

Reporters will still talk to whomever they can—critics, government agencies, whomever. We will do the story . . . we have to. Our product is perishable.

You cannot satisfy every want we have, and understanding editors and broadcasters know this. They usually know when you are attempting to cooperate, and when you are just stonewalling and attempting to sabotage the story altogether.

What should you talk about? Obviously, you should talk about your own business and what affects it. Beyond that, however, business must be represented by leaders who can talk to the larger issues in the society —what business thinks about them, what business can or cannot do about them. Only a handful of current senior executives have been able to do this effectively. In business, as in other walks of life, real leaders will be speaking out. Consequently, they won't always make the institutions happy with the positions they take. That is part of being a leader.

What to say? Whatever is asked? Certainly not, at least rarely. In part, it seems to me you have to know what you want from an interview when one is scheduled, as well as what you think the reporter is going to want.

Should you lie? Since I am a practical fellow, I never say, "never," so I'll just say, "rarely." You must understand that lies linger on, and they color more deeply than you may know the attitudes of reporters, of newspapers, and of broadcasting stations. Remember how vulnerable *we* are because we go public every day. When misinformation is our fault, we are upset; when we have been deliberately misled, we are angry as hell!

One last piece of advice: Don't let one bad experience seal your lips. Steady engagement with the media is the way to foster better—if not always adoring—public understanding.

36 · The Corporate Complaint
Against the Media

By Peter Dreier

Big business spends big dollars to get its messages
across, and journalists need adequate resources to
cover the economy and corporations. Business writer
Peter Dreier asks if this is too much to expect when
the major national media are themselves big business.
This article is from *The Quill*, November 1983.

In a series of advertisements currently featured in newspaper op-ed
pages and major magazines, Mobil Corporation takes on the bias of the
news media. In one of them, titled "The myth of the crusading reporter,"
Mobil cites a study purporting to show that "leading reporters and
editors of major newspapers and television networks have distinct hostilities toward businessmen." These journalists, utilizing "publicity-hun-
gry critics of business" and anonymous sources, may then "use the press
to 'crusade' on behalf of these [personal] beliefs." Worse yet, Mobil
informs us, the next generation of journalists is even more hostile to
business, if another survey, of Columbia University Graduate School of
Journalism students, is any guide. Only one-quarter of them believe that
the private-enterprise system is fair.

America's business community did not need Mobil's public-relations department to warn it that the media are hostile to business. Since
the late 1960s, when public-opinion polls began to report a dramatic
decline in public confidence in big business, corporate leaders have
discovered a convenient scapegoat—the news media. In speech after
speech, business spokespersons have accused reporters of being
"economically illiterate," of sensationalizing stories to attract (and
frighten) readers and viewers, and of wanting to put business out of
business.

At every turn, they see the wrongdoings of big business—windfall
oil profits, nuclear power-plant accidents, chemical waste-disposal haz-

ards, bribery of public officials, death and injuries from unsafe automobiles—splashed across the front pages and the evening news.

Business leaders worried that in a hostile climate, elected officials would translate what they saw in the polls into anti-business legislation. They viewed the gains of progressive groups—embodied in the activities of such bureaucracies as the Environmental Protection Agency, the Equal Employment Opportunity Commission, the Occupational Safety and Health Administration, and the Federal Trade Commission (all but the latter products of 1960s activism)—as obstacles to corporate profits and a healthy economy.

Corporate captains genuinely felt maligned and misunderstood. And they were firmly convinced that the public's disapproval of their performance was based almost entirely on misunderstanding rather than on corporate behavior. If those responsible for shaping public opinion (particularly journalists) were accurately informed about the benefits of our economic system, they believed, business's standing in the polls and among elected officials would improve.

The study cited by Mobil—conducted by political science professors Stanley Rothman of Smith College and S. Robert Lichter of George Washington University—simply confirms what corporate leaders have long suspected.* Their findings—though not significantly different from those of a decade's worth of academic research on journalists' backgrounds and attitudes—are being widely circulated. Their research has appeared in magazines, been quoted in mainstream newspapers, and summarized in an op-ed page column syndicated by *The Washington Post*. This study should be seen not simply as a fact-filled academic report, but as ammunition in a full-scale propaganda war being waged by the business community to make the news media more sympathetic to corporate America.

Since the mid-1970s, big business has been on the ideological offensive to change the public's perceptions of the profit system, the role of government, and the dangers of alternative ideas and arrangements. *Business Week* sounded the battle cry in 1974:

"It will be a hard pill for many Americans to swallow—the idea of doing with less so that big business can have more . . . Nothing that this nation, or any other nation, has done in modern economic history compares in difficulty with the selling job that must now be done to make people accept this new reality."

The business community began a five-part "selling job" that is still in process, but has already had a significant impact. The campaign has

*The Mobil ad includes Linda Lichter as a third researcher, but the published articles are co-authored by the two males. She headed the study of the Columbia students.

been only loosely coordinated. It is not headquartered in any one board-room or among any one business clique. There has been, however, a common message and common targets.

The most obvious approach has been the emergence of "advocacy advertising" by large corporations, particularly the oil and energy companies that have been under the closest scrutiny by public-interest groups and government. Their expensive ads in major newspapers and magazines (Mobil's are the most visible) extol the virtues of free-enterprise capitalism and decry the dangers of regulation. To deflect their Robber Baron image, they promote themselves as socially responsible corporate citizens—selling the system rather than specific products. Or, they ask people to view them not as impersonal corporate giants but—as reflected in Bob Hope's TV ads for Texaco—as enterprises owned by folks like you and me. Growing corporate sponsorship of public television is designed both to reveal business's civic-mindedness and to divert public TV from controversial (and potentially anti-corporate) programming. Ads for the corporate-sponsored National Right-to-Work Committee, placed in major magazines, depict powerful trade unions trampling on the rights of beleaguered individual workers. Corporate PR departments place ads in major magazines that reach opinion-makers and journalists, urging them to call to get the facts on industry-related public issues.

Second, corporations and corporate-sponsored foundations organized a variety of forums at which corporate executives and media executives could discuss the media's "anti-business" bias. An early effort was a series of exclusive seminars, sponsored by the Ford Foundation in 1977, that brought together high-level corporate executives and lawyers (most of them from Fortune 500 firms), executives of the major national media, and a few reporters, to engage in frank, off-the-record discussion for two days. The results are summarized in *The Media and Business* edited by corporate lawyer Joseph Califano and *The Washington Post*'s Howard Simons. Similar seminars soon followed. Also, corporate executives and media executives increasingly were invited to speak to each other's organizations on the general topic of "détente" between business and the media. Gannett's Allen H. Neuharth addressed the Cincinnati Chamber of Commerce in 1979 on "Business and the press: Why we ought to understand each other." A few months later, Thomas J. Donohue, vice president of the U.S. Chamber of Commerce, told media executives and journalists at the First Amendment Congress that "Business and media must respect each other's First Amendment rights." The American Society of Newspaper Editors chose as its 1976 convention theme, "Is the press giving business the business?"

The corporate executives' message—that the media needed to become more sensitive to business and to improve their business coverage —obviously had an impact. Since 1978, almost every major newspaper in the country has expanded its business pages and added reporting staff to cover business. A few, such as *The New York Times, The Boston Globe, The Washington Post,* the *Chicago Tribune,* and others, have added special business sections. (In contrast, there are only about twenty-five full-time labor reporters on American newspapers). Although news executives justify this trend as a response to the public's demand for more in-depth news about the economy, the timing of the expanded business coverage appears to be more than coincidental. Much of it is simply boosterism—glowing stories of new investment plans, fawning profiles of corporate executives, summaries of quarterly and annual corporate reports. Stories about personal finance—how to start a new business, where to invest your savings, problems of finding a second home—take up much of the remaining space. There is almost no investigative reporting on these pages and little good to say about unions or consumer groups. Their focus is on "upscale" readers, not inflation-pinched working folks.

Third, big business began cultivating current and future journalists directly. Programs in business or economics journalism are among the fastest growing additions to journalism-school curricula. Corporations and their foundations have targeted journalism schools with endowments for undergraduate, graduate, and mid-career programs to improve journalists' understanding of business and economics. The National Association of Manufacturers joined with the American Newspaper Publishers Association and the Association for Education in Journalism to develop a program to "improve business reporting" through workshops at journalism schools. Because most economics departments and business schools communicate a narrow range of ideas, most journalists and students are exposed primarily to mainstream thoughts. They may improve their technical competence in economics, but the hidden curriculum is never identified in the course outlines.

Says Gar Alperovitz, director of the National Center for Economic Alternatives, "In the United States the economics profession is dominated by a debate between moderate conservatives and conservative conservatives. In the business schools and economics departments, they tend not to talk about the social consequences of economic decisions and economic arrangements, so they miss new intellectual ideas. The range of economic debate in the press in Western Europe and Japan is much broader and more sophisticated than in the U.S. There they talk about planning—not whether, but how—and about worker control, industrial strategy, and credit allocation."

Fourth, business realized that as a profession, journalism—highly individualistic and competitive, but with few agreed-upon standards to evaluate performance—equates prizes with excellence. As a result, the number of awards for excellence in some aspect of business reporting has spiraled upward in recent years. Not surprisingly, most of these contests are sponsored by corporations, industry groups, or business schools with a particular view of what constitutes high-level business reporting. The prestigious Loeb Awards—the "Pulitzer Prizes of financial journalism"—are administered by the Graduate School of Management of UCLA. The Media Awards for Economic Understanding program—which annually receives more than one thousand entries from eager journalists—is supported by Champion International Corporation and administered by the business school at Dartmouth College. Westinghouse offers an award for science reporting, Carnation for nutrition reporting, and the National Association of Home Builders for housing reporting. The list of similar prizes fills pages each year in *Editor & Publisher.* Almost all the prizes include cash awards.

The sponsors may claim that they do not meddle in the contest, that winners are chosen by impartial judges, but the invisible hand surely operates. These corporate-backed awards help, subtly, to shape the kinds of stories journalists pursue and the kinds of standards that editors recognize. This is less blatant than the more traditional means of seduction by which businesses finance luxury trips to various conferences revealing the wonders of corporate technology, new food products, new auto models, and so on. But it has the same intention and —to some degree, at least—the same effect.

Finally, big business, convinced that ideas have consequences, launched a massive effort to provide journalists with "research" and to make friendly "experts" more accessible. Best known are the recent activities of the American Enterprise Institute, a well-endowed right-wing think tank, that has a small army of neoconservative social scientists and economists grinding out studies that "prove" the harmful effects of government regulation, corporate taxes, and labor unions; the misguided or subversive motivations of consumer and labor advocates; and the weakness of the United States' current defense posture. Similar think tanks—the Hoover Institution at Stanford, the American Institute for Public Policy Research, the Institute for Contemporary Studies, the Heritage Foundation, among others—provide the same message and ammunition. Their reports, books, magazines, and pamphlets are sent to journalists on newspapers and magazines around the country. Their authors are promoted and made available for interviews and background briefings with reporters. For journalists—always hungry for "informed sources" with the stamp of scholarly legitimacy—these corporate-sponsored, conservative think tanks and intellectuals are a gold mine. Their ideas became the ideological underpinning and policy guidelines of the Reagan administration.

Enter Rothman and Lichter. The two political scientists had earlier conducted research on the New Left (leading to their book, *Roots of Radicalism*), concluding that students' activism was rooted in personality problems, not idealism. Previous studies had found that most sixties activists were bright, emotionally healthy, and dedicated to pragmatic change. Rothman in particular was well known in conservative academic circles for his efforts to discredit this view and thus lend comfort to those who viewed such challenges to the establishment as the work of misguided and selfish malcontents.

Rothman viewed journalists in a similar way. Two years before he began his interviews with reporters and editors, he wrote an essay for a book published by the right-wing Hoover Institution, blaming liberal journalists of the national media for "the decay of traditional political and social institutions." The essay then repeated the familiar litany of criticism against the so-called liberal media.

When the two professors proposed conducting a large-scale study of various leadership groups (including journalists, business executives, TV and film producers, corporate lawyers, clergy, federal judges, government officials, and Pentagon officials), they had little trouble finding support from right-wing foundations. They received grants totalling more than three hundred thousand dollars from several conservative sources, among them the Scaife Foundation, a major funder of New Right organizations. The research project was headquartered at Columbia University's Research Institute on International Change, a Cold War outpost.

Their initial findings, focusing on business-media comparisons, have already found a home in several conservative publications, including *Public Opinion* (sponsored by the American Enterprise Institute), *The Public Interest* (a leading organ of neoconservatism, edited by Irving Kristol), *Across the Board* (the magazine of the business-sponsored Conference Board), and *Business Forum* (a journal of the School of Business at California State University, Los Angeles). Obviously, their agenda went beyond earning academic credits by publishing in limited-circulation scholarly journals.

Rothman and Lichter's study is fairly straightforward. They interviewed 240 reporters and editors at major national media—*The New York Times, The Washington Post, The Wall Street Journal, Time, Newsweek, U.S. News & World Report,* the three commercial TV networks, and public television. They also interviewed 216 top- and middle-level executives at seven Fortune 500 companies. The gist of the study is a comparison of the social backgrounds, personality characteristics, and opinions of these media and business élites.

Their study is grounded in a theory formulated in the 1970s by conservative intellectuals to explain, and to discredit, the growing influence and visibility of the environmental, consumer, women's, and peace movements. Irving Kristol, Daniel Bell, and others began to argue that postwar America has produced a stratum of well-educated, upper-middle-class, cosmopolitan professionals that they label the "new class."

These professionals are products of urban, affluent families. They are based in the universities, government regulatory agencies, legal services offices, public-interest movements, and the media. It is this "new class," they argue, that is responsible for the challenges to business power that emerged in the 1970s—the followers of Barry Commoner, Ralph Nader, Gloria Steinem, Tom Hayden, Helen Caldicott, Daniel Ellsberg, and their counterparts. Despite their claims of altruism, however, this group is actually out for itself; cleaner air, new sexual morality, and expansion of government social programs (but not the Pentagon) mean greater happiness and more jobs for the élite, according to the "new class" thesis.

[The "new class" theory has some merit as an explanation for expansion of a sector of professional employees in certain institutions. But to view this group as a rival "élite" is misleading. The American economy is dominated by a small upper class based in the largest banks and corporations; stock ownership is highly concentrated and income distribution is heavily skewed as well. The capitalist class may be under attack, but it is in no danger of being replaced by this "new class." See *Who Rules America Now?* by G. William Domhoff for a full discussion.]

Spiro Agnew foreshadowed this theory when he attacked the liberal media as "nattering nabobs of negativism." Joseph Kraft lent it credibility in an article for *Commentary,* a neoconservative opinion journal, entitled, "The Imperial Media." Rothman and Lichter have now translated Agnew's rhetoric, Kraft's self-confession, and the neoconservatives' "new class" theory, into social science.

Journalism's élite, they found, consists primarily of highly educated, well-paid white males. They come from educated, high-status families; 40 percent of their fathers were professionals and an equal number were businessmen; only 12 percent of their fathers were blue-collar workers. The business executives, too, are primarily educated, affluent white males. But only 53 percent came from business or professional families while 28 percent had blue-collar fathers. More journalists than businessmen attended prestigious colleges and grad schools. More journalists come from big cities. Business leaders were only slightly better off economically than the journalists. Fifty-seven percent of the businessmen, compared to 48 percent of the journalists, reported annual family incomes of $50,000 or more. (Of course, since more male journalists than businessmen are married to professional women, *family* income may be misleading. Business execs generally make more than even top reporters. And the inclusion of leading network TV newspeople may skew the journalists' income toward the higher end).

[All sociological evidence indicates that corporate directors and top management come overwhelmingly from upper- and upper-middle-class backgrounds. Domhoff's *Who Rules America Now?* is also instructive on this point. Rothman and Lichter's businessman sample must be heavily skewed toward middle-management. Their claim that big business is open to upwardly-mobile blue-collarites is thus misleading.]

Not surprisingly, the journalists' social and political views are to the left of the businessmen's For example, 88 percent of journalists, compared to 65 percent of businessmen, believe that the U.S. legal system favors the wealthy; 48 percent of journalists, but only 29 percent of businessmen, believe that government should guarantee jobs; 68 percent of journalists, compared to 29 percent of business execs, think the government should substantially reduce the income gap between rich and poor. Journalists were more likely to favor government regulation of business, to believe that corporations put profits before the public interest, and to believe that the U.S. is responsible for Third World poverty and gobbles up too much of the world's resources. As Rothman and Lichter acknowledge, journalists are hardly socialists; only 13 percent think large corporations should be publicly owned. (Seven percent of businessmen agreed—these guys should be fired!) Instead, these élite journalists are "welfare state liberals."

In terms of their social orientations, journalists are clearly more influenced by the post-1960s "new morality." Few attend church or synagogue. Ninety percent believe that a woman has a right to an abortion; 80 percent of the business execs share this belief, only a slight difference. But 47 percent of the journalists, compared to 76 percent of the businessmen, think adultery is wrong; 25 percent of journalists, but 60 percent of business execs, believe homosexuality is wrong.

Their social orientations are consistent with the two groups' personality characteristics. Rothman and Lichter administered Thematic Apperception Tests to their respondents. The psychological profiles are fascinating; briefly, the businessmen were straightlaced, achievement-oriented, and more self-controlled. Journalists were more "narcissistic," personally insecure, and thus likely to build themselves up by devaluing other people. They also scored higher on a "fear of power" scale, which the researchers suggest reveals that they want power but are afraid to pursue it directly, so they attack those who already have it.

Rothman and Lichter interpret their findings in terms of a widening conflict between the media and business in American society, and more broadly as part of the growing rift between the "new class" and the traditional establishment. The hostility, Rothman and Lichter report, is real:

"We asked all of them to rate the influence of various groups in our society and to express their preferences for the power that each group should have. Each group rates the other as the most influential group in America; moreover, each wants to reduce substantially the power of the other and to take its place as the most influential."

But what really worries Rothman and Lichter, and their corporate sponsors, is that the ascendancy of the "new class" has not only tainted the public's faith in business, but has also eroded businessmen's confidence in themselves and the system of which they are a part. In the ideology of capitalism, business pursuit of profits was not only compatible with, but helpful to, the public interest. Entrepreneurs had a sense of "calling," and the self-made businessman was a cultural hero. The rise of big business at the end of the Nineteenth Century—and with it the so-called Robber Barons like Rockefeller, Ford, and Carnegie—turned public opinion against corporate leaders, their brutal labor relations, and their giant holdings. The businessmen responded with a concerted public-relations effort to transform their public image. They set up philanthropic foundations, donated money for libraries and colleges, and established other "good works." The campaign was mostly successful, especially after the Depression. With the post-World War II economic expansion, most Americans agreed with Charles Wilson that "what's good for General Motors is good for America." Prosperity not only restored public faith in business, it also gave businessmen themselves a much-needed shot of self-esteem.

How, then, to explain the sharp drop in public confidence in big business since the late 1960s, which accelerated during the past decade? One answer would be to relate it to the sagging performance of the American economy. Simultaneous high inflation and rising unemployment—stagflation in economists' jargon—can certainly shake a family's belief in free enterprise. Business, of course, has a different answer. The "new class" assault not only on business, but on business-oriented values, has undermined public confidence in corporations as institutions and free enterprise as an economic system. The media, they claim, share much of the blame.

Conservatives worry that there is no longer the widespread sharing of key values that helps hold society together. Many divergent "interest groups" are pursuing their own political and economic agendas; the growing pluralism of lifestyles has replaced the mythic churchgoing/nuclear family. As the economic pie stops growing, people begin to compete for slices of what economist Lester Thurow has called a "zero-sum society." These competing values, lifestyles, and interest groups can have a contagious effect, even on top and middle corporate management. If leaders begin to doubt their own role in society, and society's commitment to their business values, the entire social fabric begins to unravel. As Richard Nixon told *The New York Times*'s C.L. Sulzberger in 1974, the trouble with the country is the weakness and division among "the leaders of industry, the bankers, the newspapers. . . . The people as a whole can be led back to some kind of consensus if only the leaders can take hold of themselves."

This, in part, explains why business has devoted so many resources to its ideological mobilization and schizophrenic efforts to both seduce and discredit journalists. The Mobil ad that cited the Rothman/Lichter study, as well as much of business's advocacy advertising, and self-promotion, is designed not only to influence journalists and, through them, the public, but also to reassure business people themselves that they are not to blame for the nation's economic tailspin. It's the fault of ill-informed or hostile journalists, a confused public, and opportunistic or misguided politicians. Without faith in themselves, corporate leaders and conservative intellectuals worry, businessmen and women will be ill-prepared for the challenges of the coming decades.

Still, Rothman and Lichter's survey begs an important question. We have known for a long time that journalists, in general, are more liberal than the general population. The ranks of journalism have always been filled with reformers and crusaders. Recent sociological studies, such as Gan's *Deciding What's News*, Epstein's *News from Nowhere*, and Johnstone, Slawski, and Bowman's *The Newspeople* only confirm what Leo Rosten observed in his 1937 book, *The Washington Correspondents*. If journalists have *always* been reform-minded, then what explains the increase of investigative and muckraking reporting during the past fifteen years? Perhaps reporters and editors used to keep their political views to themselves, but recently have allowed more of their personal beliefs to spill onto the news pages. Some say that the emergence of "interpretative" journalism, replacing the "just the facts" school of reporting, gives journalists greater leeway to introduce their own biases in the selection, editing, and writing of news. The growing acceptance of "advocacy" journalism, since the 1960s, perhaps gave credence to a generation of reporters who wanted to be agents of social change, not simply chroniclers of the passing scene.

These explanations share a common thread: The national media's growing criticism of traditional centers of power, particularly big business, stems from changes within the profession of journalism and journalists themselves. This is clearly the message of the Rothman and Lichter study, even though the authors themselves never explicitly make the leap of saying that the journalists' values influence their reporting and editing. (They are, however, now completing a study of news coverage which, Rothman indicated in an interview, is likely to discover a liberal bias in news coverage on such controversial issues as busing, abortion, human rights in Latin America, nuclear power, and the energy crisis).

A somewhat different explanation, however, emerges out of the past decade's sociological research on how "news" is created. This includes Herbert Gans's *Deciding What's News*, Michael Schudson's *Discovering the News*, Steven Hess's *The Washington Reporters*, Gaye Tuchman's *Making News*, Mark Fishman's *The Manufacture of News*, David Altheide's *Creating Reality*, Leon Sigal's *Reporters and Officials*, Todd Gitlin's *The Whole World is Watching*, and David Paletz and Robert

Entman's *Media Power Politics.* Earlier studies, including Warren Breed's 1955 "Social Control in the Newsroom" and Bernard Cohen's *Press and Foreign Policy,* reached similar conclusions. According to these studies, "news" is a product of the daily organizational habits of journalists and their contact with sources. Most daily news stories originate from *routine* channels—press release, official proceedings (Congressional hearings, courtrooms, regulatory agencies), reports, staged media events such as press conferences, and background briefings. With limited staff, the media station reporters at "beats" where they expect "news" to happen. This, of course, becomes a self-fulfilling prophecy. Under deadline and competitive pressures, reporters file stories from these beats rather than venture off the beaten track. When reporters spent most of their time hanging around at precinct stations, crime stories dominated the news. Today news tends to flow from reporters positioned at city hall, the state house, the White House, Capitol Hill, the Pentagon, and other centers of power. In addition, as a result of their day-to-day routines, reporters develop cooperative relations with regular news sources. The reporter wants a story and the source wants his/her version of reality reported. This reinforces the tendency to promote an establishment-oriented flow of news. Finally, because high-level government, corporate, and foundation officials have greater resources to reach reporters, they are able to initiate and dominate the flow of what becomes "newsworthy." These powerful organizations have the resources not only to stage events and hire public-relations staffs, but also to fund and publish reports and books by "experts" who can become "reliable sources." In contrast, the poor, the powerless, and the unorganized lack the resources to command such routine access to reporters and the media. To make news, they must disrupt "business as usual." Labor relations becomes news only when strikes become violent or inconvenience the public. Ghetto conditions become news only when the poor or tenants riot or boycott. Nuclear power becomes an issue when demonstrators occupy a nuclear construction site. Otherwise, reporters rarely go to union halls, ghettos, or offices of social-movement organizations.

The accumulated findings of these studies indicate that, as Tom Wicker wrote in *On Press,* objective journalism is essentially "establishment" journalism. News tends to flow from powerful sources and reflects their version of reality. Whatever their personal values, journalists tend to adjust to these professional standards and daily routines.

There appears to be a conflict between the angry complaints by conservatives and business leaders that the press is hostile to the establishment and the overwhelming consensus among sociologists that the press serves as a transmission belt for establishment views. The paradox, however, is not difficult to resolve. The press, the sociologists agree, goes to where the power is. During the past fifteen years or so, the political and business establishment has been deeply divided over how best to cope with foreign policy, economic crisis, and social upheaval. In such a context, journalists' high-level sources are telling them different things.

Similarly, the past fifteen years have witnessed a growing upsurge of grassroots political activism. Although the student New Left disappeared, many of its adherents—as well as a new and more heterogeneous group of activists—have built a more sophisticated range of social movements than existed in the 1960s. These include the women's and senior citizens' movements, the consumer and public-interest groups like Common Cause, the nuclear-freeze and peace movements, the community and neighborhood organizing of such groups as Massachusetts Fair Share and ACORN, environmental groups, and even a growing militance among some segments of organized labor, especially among working women (like 9 to 5) and on issues of workplace health and safety. Some of it, for sure, fits the conservatives' stereotype of the "new class" adherents. But much more of the upsurge has been truly a grassroots phenomenon among what we once called "middle America." It has not gotten the headlines of its counterpart on the other end of the spectrum, the "New Right," but it has been a major influence in politicizing average citizens and shaping the political agenda.

In the light of these two trends—a widening split within the establishment and the upsurge of grassroots protest—the press has shown a greater tolerance for controversy and conflict. What some view as the national media's "anti-establishment" bias is, in fact, a reflection of the canons of objective journalism.

In the 1950s and early 1960s, when there was a national bi-partisan consensus around Cold War foreign policy and domestic welfare-state goals, the press mirrored this in a celebration of Pax Americana and Luce's "American Century." The Vietnam War produced a split within the establishment over the conduct of foreign affairs, a split that has not been mended. It is between a conservative wing pushing for greater military strength and tough talk with the Soviets, and a moderate wing, concerned about bloated defense budgets and the potential for global conflict. The conservative wing is best represented by such groups as the Committee on the Present Danger and the Hoover Institution at Stanford, groups favored by the Reagan administration in filling State and Defense Department slots. The moderate wing is best represented by the Council on Foreign Relations and the Trilateral Commission, corporate-sponsored policy groups whose leaders have filled high-level places in every administration since Truman's.

In domestic economic and social policy, there is a conflict between *laissez-faire* advocates like Milton Friedman and his ideological friends at the American Enterprise Institute and the U.S. Chamber of Commerce, and the moderate Keynesians at the Brookings Institution and the Business Roundtable.

These organizations are simply surrogates for ideas and perspectives. In the real world, the lines between competing establishment points of view are blurred and overlapping. But, if anything, the national media still report conflict within very narrow limits. In the entire spectrum of American political and economic thought, the distance between the Committee on the Present Danger and the Council on Foreign Relations on foreign policy, or between the American Enterprise Institute and the Brookings Institution on domestic policy, is relatively short. But it is the views of the experts at CFR or Brookings—and the politicians who take their advice—that the conservatives treat as the left end of the spectrum, and thus harass the press for its "liberal" bias. There is no denying that the major national media are more in tune with these groups. But, in the broad range of political views, these are hardly "anti-business," or even "anti-establishment." They reflect a struggle *within* the American power structure.

It is worth recalling that when currently fashionable conservative ideas were put forward by Barry Goldwater in 1964, they were considered extremist. The right-wing think tanks have benefited from a decade of heavy financial support from friendly business groups and respectful media coverage that have brought them off the fringe and into the mainstream.

The accompanying table indicates what a real spectrum might look like. Obviously the left side of the table is conspicuously absent from the daily flow of national journalism (except, perhaps, among guest contributors to the op-ed pages). Mary McGrory, perhaps the most progressive national columnist, is at most a McGovern-style liberal. Evans and Novak are Henry Jackson Democrats. There are plenty of right-wing opinion-shapers, such as George Will, William Buckley, and James Kilpatrick. But there is not *one* nationally syndicated columnist who is a socialist, or, in European parlance, a "social democrat," such as Michael Harrington or Barry Commoner. When journalists look for experts on foreign policy, they rarely go to the Institute for Policy Studies, a well-respected left-oriented think tank. When it's economic expertise they're looking for, few turn to the new generation of left-oriented academics (such as Samuel Bowles at the University of Massachusetts, David Gordon at the New School for Social Research, Bennett Harrison at MIT, Barry Bluestone at Boston College, or Gar Alperovitz at the National Center for Economic Alternatives.) The farthest to the left they travel is Harvard (to talk to Robert Reich) or MIT (to interview Lester Thurow).

Reporters doing stories about the nation's housing crisis, or issues like rent control, typically talk to groups like the National Association of Realtors, the National Association of Home Builders, or the Mortgage

Bankers Association of America for statistics and analysis. The two most frequently quoted "experts" on the subject are George Sternlieb, a Rutgers University professor, and Anthony Downs of the Brookings Institution, both of whom have close ties to the real-estate industry. Grassroots groups like ACORN, Citizen Action, and National Peoples Action, left-oriented housing experts like Chester Hartman of the Institute for Policy Studies and the Planners Network, Peter Marcuse of Columbia University, Cushing Dolbeare of the National Low Income Housing Coalition, and John Atlas of Shelterforce, are virtually invisible to the National news organs.

The same could be said for any number of issues—food policy, environment, labor relations, health care, welfare, and many others.

This isn't to say that the "left" is totally left out. There are occasional feature stories on "new trends" among intellectuals that note the growing influence of radicals and democratic socialists. And, when a social movement begins to pick up steam and can mount large demonstrations and rallies—such as the nuclear-freeze campaign—the press quotes its leaders and reports its ascendancy. But in the daily routines of journalism, these "left" oriented views don't come into journalists' line of vision, and journalists rarely go out looking for them.

In the past decade, journalists have covered the major issues and events that cast doubt on the wisdom or managerial skill of American business. The Santa Barbara oil spill, Hooker Chemical's Love Canal problems, and the Three Mile Island power plant incident were all technological accidents that became grist for journalists' mills. Questionable business practices may be hard to uncover, but corporations that break the law—J.P. Stevens' labor law violations, companies that knowingly manufacture and sell unsafe products (like the Dalkon Shield or Ford's Pinto) or businesses that violate trade embargoes or bribe foreign officials (like ITT)—find themselves subject to journalistic scrutiny.

What is interesting, however, is that most of the so-called "anti-business" stories were not initially uncovered by the major media, but by either social-movement organizations or politically-oriented publications. Conditions in J.P. Stevens' textile plants were brought to public attention by the union and its national boycott, not a crusading reporter investigating workplace atrocities. The Love Canal episode—which triggered a national concern over toxic chemicals—came to public attention because of a grassroots effort by working-class neighbors (led by Lois Gibbs) concerned about their children's health.

Both the Ford Pinto story, and the exposé of the dumping of unsafe birth control devices (the Dalkon Shield) on Third World nations, were uncovered by the leftist *Mother Jones* magazine.

Most journalistic exposés focus on the public sector—primarily public officials' conflicts-of-interest and primarily with local enter-

According to Whom? . . . .
The spectrum of American politics: a sampling of sources

■ Topic	■ Left	■ Liberal	■ Moderate	■ Conservative
Foreign policy	Institute for Policy Studies Inst. for Food & Devel. Policy Coalition for a New Military and Foreign Policy	Ctr. for Defense Information Jobs with Peace Amnesty International Comm. for SANE Nucl. Policy	Council on Foreign Relations Trilateral Commission Club of Rome	Comm. on Present Danger Hoover Institution Georgetown Center for Strategic & Int'l. Studies
Domestic Economic & Social Policy	Nat'l. Ctr. Econ. Alternatives Council on Econ. Priorities Conf. on Alternative State & Local Policy	Brookings Institution Urban Institute Ctr. for Social Policy	Nat'l. Bur. of Econ. Rsch. Comm. for Econ. Devel. Business Roundtable	U.S. Chamber of Commerce Amer. Enterprise Institute Heritage Foundation
Legal Institutions	Nat'l. Lawyers Guild	Amer. Civil Liberties Union	Amer. Bar Association	Mountain States Legal Fdtn.
Foundations	Stem Fund Field Foundation of N.Y. Haymarket People's Fund	Stewart R. Mott Ford Foundation Rockefeller Family Fund	Rockefeller Bros. Fund Chas. Stewart Mott Fdtn. Twentieth Century Fund	Scaife Foundation Smith Richardson Fdtn. Lilly Endowment

According to Whom? . . . (Continued)

Topic	■ Left	■ Liberal	■ Moderate	■ Conservative
Opinion Journals	The Nation The Progressive In These Times	The New Republic Washington Monthly N.Y. Review of Books	Foreign Affairs Harper's The Atlantic	The Public Interest Commentary National Review
Major New Books	Rebuilding America (Alperovitz & Faux) Beyond the Wasteland (Bowles, Gordon, & Weiskopf) Deindustrialization of Amer. (Bluestone & Harrison) Economic Democracy (Carnoy & Shearer)	The Zero Sum Society (Thurow) The Next Amer. Frontier (Reich) Winning Back America (Green)	The Energy Future (Yergin & Storbaugh) Theory Z (Ouchi) Industrial Renaissance (Abernathy, Clark, Kantrow)	Wealth & Poverty (Gilder) Post-Conservative America (Phillips) The Way the World Works (Wanniski) Amer. Politics: Promise of Disharmony (Huntington)
Political Organizations	Dem. Socialists of America Citizens Party Citizen/Labor Energy Coalition	Democratic Party (liberal wing) Common Cause Americans for Democratic Action	Democratic Party (moderate wing) Republican Party (moderate wing) Ripon Society	Republican Party (conservative wing) Nat'l. Conservative PAC Moral Majority

preneurs, real estate, insurance, and construction firms. This is relatively small-time, low-level corruption. The information is usually dug out of public documents. But unless government regulatory agencies have done the work already—they are frequently the source for investigative reports—documents about wrongdoing by major corporations and industries are hard to come by.

By fighting for legislation that opens up information on both government and corporate practices, reform movements have aided journalists. Common Cause, for example, helped win passage of laws requiring disclosure of campaign financing, enabling journalists to link wealthy individuals and corporations to elected officials and their voting patterns. The neighborhood movement won passage of the Home Mortgage Disclosure Act requiring banks to disclose lending patterns—permitting urban reporters to investigate "redlining" practices. The Freedom of Information Act has been extremely useful in gaining access to information about FBI infiltration of protest groups, government reports about exposure to nuclear radiation, and many other issues. Reporters interested in piercing the corporate veil, however, still face many legal obstacles. Our legal system protects private businesses from having to disclose very much about their inner workings, even though their decisions have significant public consequences.

For many reasons, journalists tend to avoid the hard work required to investigate corporate behavior. Their employing organizations provide few resources, or incentives, to do so. As Mark Dowie, who investigated and wrote the Pinto story for *Mother Jones,* explained, the story was available all along to anyone who knew how and where to look for it.

"Stories like this are very much like photography," Dowie said. "It's not enough to know how to use a camera. You have to know what you're looking for."

What conservatives view as the press's "anti-business" hostility is, in reality, a quite tame form of objective journalism. Journalists report different views *within* the establishment, and they report the views of protest groups when those groups are able to make a stink, but they rarely go beyond exposing what Herbert Gans has called violations of "responsible capitalism." The national press may criticize or expose *particular* corporate or government practices or *particular* corporations or elected officials who violate the public trust. Thus, the Watergate scandal (and its many counterparts at local and state levels), or the Pinto case (and its many parallels), or a Pentagon weapons boondoggle, lends credence to the view that these violations are *exceptions* to an otherwise smoothly-running system. The bad apples are purged, while the good ones remain. Even the so-called "liberal" media view such occurrences from the viewpoint of "situations needing to be managed," not basic flaws in an unjust or inefficient economic and political system.

Business leaders, obviously, have little patience for the "bad apple" theory. Any public exposure of corporate wrongdoing can taint the entire profits system. And when these stories appear in a context of economic hard times, the bad publicity can become contagious. As a result, what some may view as the media's occasional slaps on the wrist, business feels as a punch in the jaw.

If the national media have contributed to the public's distrust of big business, it is not because reformist reporters and editors have waged a war with corporate America. Whatever their personal beliefs (and, to my mind, Rothman and Lichter failed to capture the somewhat muddled, wishy-washy, non-ideological character of journalists' reformism), journalists are constrained by the routines of daily journalism and the conventions of objective reporting from a consistent assault on corporate America.

The United States has many conservative and right-wing newspapers and a host of moderate liberal papers that take their cue from *The New York Times* and *The Washington Post*. But there is no major daily today that is as far to the left as New York's *PM,* the York, Pennsylvania *Gazette,* the Madison, Wisconsin *Capital-Times,* or the Chicago *Sun* were in the 1940s. At that time these papers were hardly out on a political limb. The 1948 Progressive Party campaign of former Vice President Henry Wallace (more progressive, in context, than McGovern's 1972 platform), the stands of the leftist CIO, and even President Truman's call for national health insurance were opposed by most daily papers, but were popular with millions of American citizens. The Cold War consensus and McCarthyism soon set in, and the "left" voices in American life quieted down. Today, with both conservatives and moderate-liberals unable to find any solutions to gnawing political and economic problems, there's a resurgence of protest and intellectual ferment on both the left and right. But while the national news media find it easy to cover the right flank (if with little sympathy), they have all but ignored the left side of the debate.

Moreover, while the media may occasionally expose both government and corporate wrongdoing, they are even less interested in examining possible solutions to chronic social, economic, and political problems. For example, the U.S. is one of only two industrialized nations (the other is South Africa) without a system of national health insurance; but while Americans can read a great deal about the problems of Britain's national health program, they know very little about its effectiveness in reducing major health problems, and much less about the overwhelming success of Canada's, Sweden's, or Germany's health measures. Experiments with consumer cooperatives, worker-owned or publicly owned enterprises, and other "social democratic" reforms—in the U.S. and elsewhere—might help Americans see some possible light at the end of our narrowing economic tunnel, but if, as Rothman and Lichter report, thirteen percent of élite journalists believe that "large corporations should be publicly owned," they certainly aren't getting their ideas into the news. With few exceptions, the national media are blind to reforms that challenge basic economic arrangements.

The series of Mobil ads attacking the media is designed to intimidate journalists into greater caution in reporting the wrongdoings of big business and the flaws of private-enterprise capitalism. By portraying liberal journalists as motivated by irrational subconscious impulses, Rothman and Lichter's study contributes to three objectives on the corporate agenda: It discredits journalists as being politically and socially out of touch with the readers and viewers and advertisers; it shores up the confidence of the business community by identifying an "outside" source of its problems; and it helps make journalists doubt themselves by replacing credo ("Afflict the comfortable and comfort the afflicted") with ego and Rorschach-blots.

If there is room for improvement, and I think there is, the direction must be not toward making journalists more cautious in scrutinizing the workings of our economy and its central institutions, but in giving journalists the resources to do so better. Perhaps this is too much to expect when the major national media are themselves big business, as Ben Bagdikian notes in his recent *The Media Monopoly*. But it would certainly be worth the effort.

37 · NINETY SECONDS OVER THE ECONOMY

BY MICHAEL D. MOSETTIG

Television's brevity does a disservice to complicated subjects like business and the economy. But, says Michael D. Mosettig, former NBC News producer, network coverage of business has increased, it's no longer a bad news beat. He is an associate at the Columbia University graduate school of journalism. This article is reprinted from *Channels of Communications*, December 1981/January 1982.

Hundreds of international reporters and camera crews shuffled restlessly outside a luxury hotel in Geneva, waiting to pounce on any OPEC oil minister bearing even a scrap of information about the closed-door meetings inside. The deliberations of those sultans, sheiks, and ministers would determine how much more money hundreds of millions of Americans, Europeans, and Asians would have to pay to drive their cars and heat their homes.

The minister from Kuwait emerged, said simply "Arabian light at thirty-two," and immediately went back inside.

"What's the *current* price?" shouted a confused American network correspondent covering his first OPEC meeting. "Thirty-four," came back the chorus from his colleagues. The correspondent raced to the phone to tell New York the remarkable news that OPEC was lowering its oil prices. For hours his network had a scoop; the only problem was that it was wrong. "Arabian light at thirty-two" didn't mean that OPEC was *lowering* its price from $34 to $32 a barrel. The other OPEC nations would follow with their own $2 increase and raise the price of most OPEC oil from $34 to $36 per barrel.

The correspondent's crash course in oil economics resembles what the news departments of the American television networks have been undergoing in the last decade, as they have desperately tried to catch up on a story previously ignored, one so obviously vital to the daily lives of their millions of viewers.

As the American and world economies have caromed from crisis to disaster, toppling U.S. and European political leaders in the process, network television news has been confronted with a difficult, if not impossible, job. To a largely untrained audience now receiving most of its news from television, the networks try to report and explain phenomena that even professional economists said would never occur: simultaneously rising prices and rising unemployment, accompanied by the end of cheap energy and by the fading of the American dream of owning a house and a car.

And now the networks are also reporting a revolution in American economic policy-making that matches the New Deal in scope and boldness, a revolution based on a combination of tight money policies and the largely untested theories of conservative Republican "supply side" economics.

How well the networks meet the reporting challenge is one of the more contentious issues in American journalism today. Professional economists, as well as many business and labor leaders, briskly dismiss the networks' economics coverage—despite their growing investment in specialist reporters, producers, and airtime—as too little, too shallow, and too alarmist. To them it is inconceivable that such a complicated subject can be adequately treated in a ninety-second report.

The surprising fact is that the networks perform as well as they do. The story topics—budgets, taxes, money supply, and trade—are complex and abstract, even if their effects on paychecks and prices are immediate. Many professional economists make the subject more baffling, disguising in layers of jargon their inherent inability to agree. And the "dismal science," as Thomas Carlyle labeled economics, does not lend itself to gripping visuals, the staple of much television news. The OPEC blooper was an aberration, especially since the networks have come to realize that economics stories must be covered by specialists. While the evening news programs obviously do not have the sophistication of *Business Week* or the depth of *The Wall Street Journal*, on any given day they can match the economics coverage on the front pages of most U.S. newspapers.

But despite network efforts, troubling questions remain. First, how many viewers are really listening, and does a large percentage of the nightly audience instinctively tune out when it hears the word "economics"? Second, will television in its relatively brief reports be able to describe what some experts see as a fundamental contradiction in the Reagan program—expanding the economy with tax cuts, military spending, and government deficits, while at the same time restraining it with controls on the money supply? Third, will television be able to explain through the fog of emotion and political rhetoric that the United States faces more than a trillion dollars in pension and Social Security claims from an increasingly aging population, and that those obligations now far surpass the money available in trust funds to pay them? Fourth, can television make comprehensible to an audience largely unaware of the problem that the state and local governments have long deferred and must soon pay hundreds of billions to rebuild collapsing roads, bridges, and water systems at the same time they are cutting taxes? And finally, can the networks explain even more than they do now that the U.S. economy is no longer dominant over or insulated from the world economy?

One alarming bit of evidence shows just how hard it is for television to penetrate the audience consciousness on such baffling issues, no matter how many spots it might run: Only two and a half years ago, as gas lines stretched from Larchmont to Laguna Beach, a *New York Times*-CBS News poll disclosed that only 51 percent of the respondents believed the United States had to import oil. This startling display of either ignorance or disbelief followed six years in which the networks had run energy stories almost daily.

For twenty years, Irving R. Levine had been among the most familiar sights on NBC News, reporting on commissars and popes. In January 1971, NBC reassigned Levine to a newly created beat in Washington called economics. Many at NBC News wondered if the viewing public would ever see Levine again. For several months, as the economy sagged in recession and with inflation at the then alarming rate of 4 percent, he tried to persuade producers to put his stories on the air.

Then, in August 1971, President Nixon made a surprise Sunday-night speech to the nation. The supposedly conservative Republican bared his conversion to the liberal economic theories of John Maynard Keynes, and announced a program of wage-price controls and, in effect, a devaluation of the dollar by splitting it from its last links to gold. In one stroke, Nixon guaranteed his reelection. He also gave new life to Levine's career. In the decade since, Levine has probably racked up more *Nightly News* air-time than any other NBC reporter except White House correspondents.

Where Levine led, others soon followed. Economics specialists have status now at all three networks. George Herman, a CBS Washington veteran, took on economics in 1973. The following year, ABC News reached into print journalism and hired Dan Cordtz, a veteran from *The Wall Street Journal* and *Fortune*. ABC News producer Av Westin, perhaps the first network executive to grasp the full import of the economics story, insisted on putting Cordtz on the air almost every night.

In 1978, when *The New York Times* locked out its unions, financial writer Mike Jensen went to NBC in search of temporary work. The result was another breakthrough in economics coverage, an effort to follow the story full time—beyond the Washington policy-makers to industry and finance. When the *Times* lockout ended, Jensen remained at NBC. In the three years since, he has made some six hundred appearances on *Nightly News* and *Today.*

In 1972, an editor at *Dun's Review* named Ray Brady began doing radio commentaries for CBS. In one of his early reports about OPEC, he had to explain what kind of an organization it was. Brady later joined the *CBS Morning News,* and has also become the *Evening News* correspondent responsible for covering the economy, finance, and industry outside Washington.

In television journalism, where a correspondent's personal style is often as important as the content of his stories, economics coverage has taken on distinctive characteristics at each of the three networks. ABC's Cordtz believes that journalism has an educating as well as a reporting role. At NBC, Levine's reports on Washington policy are complemented by Jensen's explanations of what an OPEC price increase or a boost in the prime rate would mean to the viewer at home. At CBS, Brady combines the occasional skepticism of a Wall Streeter with raspy warnings of another jolt to the wallet from oil men, bankers, or milk producers.

These correspondents—and the producers of the news shows—must not only make the news comprehensible, they must also make it interesting. A newspaper reader can skim past a boring story, but a television viewer is likely to head for the refrigerator—or worse, switch to another channel. To overcome what journalists call the MEGO (mine eyes glaze over) factor, they rely on two basic devices. The first is to link a story to an individual family or worker, which increasingly means telling it outside Washington. The second is to employ, in the absence of compelling footage, such electronic graphics as shrinking and expanding boxes and revealing graphs and numbers.

The use of modern video techniques produces much more interesting visuals. Only a few years ago, most economics stories contained stock footage of grocery stores, farm fields, and factories, at best distracting backdrops for voice-over recitations of indigestible statistics. Another common approach was to report economic policy through excerpts from Congressional committee hearings. As Cordtz recalls his early years on the job: "All three of us—Levine, Herman, and I—covered the beat the same way. We tended to spend a lot of time on the Hill, sitting through those damned boring committee hearings and looking for a couple of sound bites. That reinforced my conviction that this was not the way to do it."

Personalizing economics news by relating it to the travail of a factory worker or homeowner is generally more interesting than hearing once again from the commissioner of the Bureau of Labor Statistics. But when overused, this approach trivializes important news. Correspondents and producers must ask themselves whether people watch a national news program to see their neighbors, or whether they want to hear from public officials otherwise inaccessible to them.

Cordtz sums up the difference between covering economics for a specialty publication and presenting it on a network news show: "When I worked for *Fortune*, I had seven or eight thousand words to explain the story to people who already understood it. When I got to ABC, I had 300 words to explain it to people who didn't have a clue. That's still largely the case," he adds, "although we've made some progress on both counts."

Says NBC's Jensen, "You want to report on and interpret economic events in such a way that everyone who watches it can understand it, and yet you don't want to be condescending. When you talk about the prime rate, you have to relate it quickly to the interest people will be paying on auto loans and home mortgages. When you talk about OPEC price increases, you have to translate that into cents-per-gallon."

Jensen argues that television's time restrictions, and the resulting inability to explain nuances, are countered by one major advantage: With interesting pictures and graphics, he can make a point more dramatically than he could in a column of type. He cites as an example a story this summer on his own network's sagging profits. The story first showed graphics depicting the profits of ABC and CBS in the hundreds of millions of dollars. Then NBC's comparatively paltry $75 million figure came up on the screen. "People sort of gasp and say, 'My God.' There is a dramatic effect in that."

Brady takes the iconoclastic view that television's time constraints may actually produce better coverage. "A lot of financial writing is unduly overwritten," he says. "There is a gut issue in almost every economic story, and it is simpler than economists would have you think. No one will read twenty-seven paragraphs in a newspaper to find out what the story is. The graphics on television make it a great medium. In television you smack them in the eye with the story."

More importantly, time limits are beginning to stretch, especially since ABC and NBC incorporated three- to five-minute special-segment features into their evening news programs. These have provided vehicles to explain in detail subjects that would not otherwise have gotten on the air at all—a Levine report on the World Bank, Jensen's story on the changing face of Wall Street, or a report by Cordtz on the insurance industry.

As electronic graphics improved to the point of rudimentary animation, Cordtz was able to tackle that most arcane of economic issues—the money supply. When money is available, Cordtz explained over a cartoon of a factory billowing smoke, business will invest in new machinery. If money is not available, he said as the smoke puffs went away, the economy stagnates and workers are laid off. With another series of cartoon animations, he showed how the Federal Reserve tries to control the money supply by buying or selling Treasury securities with banks and brokerage firms. Had such a story been attempted a few years ago, it would have been illustrated with prosaic, distracting pictures of bank exteriors and clerks shuffling bills.

Yet even in such relatively lengthy reports, the nuances sometimes get lost. *NBC Nightly News* recently did a week-long series of special segments on housing problems without mentioning that for years, the government indirectly channeled billions into the housing industry, keeping it speculatively profitable and ahead of inflation, at the expense of investments in factories, technology, and jobs.

Furthermore, network coverage of industry is still uneven. The auto industry, directly or indirectly responsible for one out of six jobs, receives heavy coverage, but the steel industry, whose woes even more reflect the declining state of old American industries, is hardly covered. To the extent they're covered at all, the computer and chip technology industries, which will soon revolutionize offices and factories, are largely covered as science stories. Correspondents are more likely to illustrate agriculture stories with Farmer Brown or amber waves of grain than to delve into multi-billion dollar surpluses, subsidies, and exports.

And despite the buildup of the economics beat, inconsistencies remain. On the day DuPont made its merger bid with Conoco—the largest in U.S. corporate history—it was described in a one-minute-and-forty-second spot with Jensen in the third block of *Nightly News,* and led the second block of CBS news with a one minute-and-twenty-five-second spot by Brady. ABC treated it as an anchorman copy item. Jensen has been covering OPEC meetings regularly for almost three years, but when the oil ministers went to Bali last winter NBC sent an Asian correspondent instead. Levine has covered some of the economic summits of Western leaders but not others, depending on whether the executives thought the sessions were a political story or an economic one. Brady has just begun to cover OPEC meetings, and reported the most recent summit. Cordtz covers the summits but not OPEC meetings. Labor-union coverage is particularly erratic. Especially on NBC, unions are as likely to be covered by its crime reporter as by its economics reporter.

Bolstered network coverage has done little to stifle academic, business, and labor critics of television economics reporting.

"Terrible" is the description offered by Robert Heilbroner, a professor at New York's New School for Social Research. He cites as an example the "shallow and alarmist" reports in July on the threatened bankruptcy of the Social Security system. Treating the story in a minute or so only worried pensioners and would-be pensioners, he argues.

Robert Lekachman of the City University of New York complains that even on hour-long specials the networks reach out only for conventional opinions. "You won't find anyone really on the left or even the far right," he says. "A contrast between Milton Friedman and an orthodox Keynesian really adds little to public enlightenment."

MIT's Paul Samuelson, whose textbook has helped millions of college students struggle through introductory economics, thinks network coverage has improved. But, he adds, "It has a long way to go. Perhaps there are limits in the nature of the task that preclude [correspondents] from doing any deeper coverage. If you want to be informed on the American economy, you would do better reading *The Wall Street Journal* or *The New York Times* than watching television twenty-four hours a day."

The business-sponsored Media Institute in Washington voices another frequent complaint—that network economics reporting too frequently follows the line set forth by Administration spokesmen. (Business makes that complaint when a Democrat is in the White House, labor when a Republican is in power.) The Institute report, prepared by *Harper's* Washington editor Tom Bethell in 1980, says the networks usually repeat the statements of government officials that rising prices or wages are the cause of inflation. Very rarely, the report adds, do the news reports cite government spending and easy-money policies as contributors.

Complicating television's economics coverage are the sometimes strained relations between network economics reporters and the economic leaders they are covering. Most business executives react to a television camera as they would to an unmuzzled Doberman pinscher. Says Cordtz, "The business community doesn't make it easier for us to do these stories."

Reporting on the Reagan economic program—a reversal of fifty years of government policy accomplished with only a handful of major votes by each house of Congress—dramatically shows what television is up against in covering economic policy.

Recently, the *Washington Journalism Review* questioned a number of economists about print and television coverage of the Reagan Administration's policies. Nearly all of the economists replied that the media, with few exceptions, did an inadequate job of explaining the new theories of supply-side economics. Economists of both the left and the right complained, for example, that reporters failed to make distinctions between all the different kinds of tax cuts and investments.

All three network evening news shows did special reports after the election on the fundamentals of supply-side economics, the attempt to encourage investment and production rather than consumer demand. The programs explained how different the untested theories were from the programs of Roosevelt, Johnson, or Carter—or even from those of Nixon and Ford.

But on a day-to-day basis, coverage is obviously more limited: reports on the progress of budget-cutting and tax bills, or statements from the President's team and from the floundering Democratic opposition. Washington coverage invariably focuses on political maneuverings involved in getting bills passed, rather than on the uncharted new directions in which the bills may lead the economy. The coverage does not —and cannot—go back to basics every night, as the best newspapers can do.

This absence of consistent analysis or skepticism naturally has irritated economists, who argued that the Administration was receiving a free ride. That charge has less validity since the summer slide of the stock market and the first signs of the unraveling of the President's program. The networks were as quick as the newspapers to pick up on the fundamental doubts that some financial experts and Wall Street economists have developed. One reason for television's quick response, interestingly, was that its New York-based business reporters were able to tap doubting Wall Street sources.

Yet even the professional economists missed a more serious problem in the network coverage. In brief news spots, there is no room to explain that Reaganomics consists essentially of two separate sets of programs and philosophies going in opposite directions: expansionary supply-side tax and military-spending programs and government deficits, and contractional "monetarism"—tight controls on the growth of money, reflected in high interest rates. There has been little effort to explain on television that the top economic policy jobs in the Administration are about equally divided between "supply siders" and "monetarists." Some economists are worried that an attempt to compromise these divergent views can bring the worst possible combination of big deficits and high interest rates. Such a policy, says Wall Street economist Sam Nakagama, is the equivalent of strategic bombing—it only works by destroying industry, as it has in Britain.

But whether Reaganomics succeeds or fails, the economics correspondents seem secure in their hold on increasing amounts of network air-time. The success of their work is better measured by the viewing public's current level of sophistication about economic news. Even such professional economists as Samuelson believe the public is more knowledgeable about economics now than it was two or three decades ago. Samuelson says he does not know whether television is responsible. The network correspondents naturally think it is.

They often base their evaluations on the give-and-take issuing from their appearances on the speech-making circuit. "All I know is that from time to time I have had stuff on the air fed back to me as the prevailing knowledge," Jensen says. "Now whether that has anything to do with what we are pitching on television," he modestly adds, "I don't know." As Brady notes, "When I give the price of gold, people now know why we are reporting it. When you say 'OPEC,' everyone knows what it is. There has been a change in the level of economic sophistication, and what did it was television."

Whether viewers want it or not, more economics coverage is in store for them. Both ABC and CBS aired hour-long specials on the Social Security controversy. ABC News president Roone Arledge has raised the possibility of doing a weekly show on finance. NBC specials have tackled such difficult issues as productivity and problems in the labor force. On CBS, Walter Cronkite's *Universe* plans to cover similar economic issues. And with the advent of hour-long evening news programs, which CBS and NBC are eagerly advocating, economics will be a good candidate for the expanded non-hard-news time. The correspondents feel assured, in short, that theirs is no longer a bad-news beat, that it would exist even if the economy should brighten.

For all their efforts, the networks can only hope that the next time an angry oil nation cuts off supplies to the United States and maroons drivers in gas lines, substantially more than 51 percent of the public will believe that this country is dependent on foreign oil. If that percentage shows up in the next crisis, the networks will have to ask themselves if anyone out there is really listening.

FOR FURTHER READING

Benjamin M. Compaine, *Who Owns the Media? Concentration of Ownership in the Mass Communications Industry.* New York: Harmony Books, 1979.

Louis M. Kohlmeier, Jr., Jon G. Udell and Laird B. Anderson, *Reporting on Business and the Economy.* Englewood Cliffs, N.J.: Prentice-Hall, 1981.

A. Kent MacDougall, *Ninety Seconds to Tell It All: Big Business and the News Media.* Homewood, Ill.: Dow Jones-Irwin, 1981.

Nelson Smith and Leonard J. Theberge (eds.), *Energy Coverage—Media Panic: An International Perspective.* New York: Longman, 1983.

Joseph Turow, *Media Industries: The Production of News and Entertainment.* New York: Longman, 1984.

XI

Mass Media and War

I N THIS age of mass media, war has become a media event. Sometimes, in fact, war seems to have become an event staged for mass media, to send a message rather than conquer territory. That is certainly true of the wars of terrorists. Without a doubt, the nature of all warfare has been changed by the emergence of mass media.

The Civil War was the first war in our history to be reported by correspondents on the battlefield. The Spanish-American war was, supposedly, "fanned into flames" by the headlines of the Hearst newspapers. World War I has been called the first real information war, where the battle was fought over people's minds as much as for their lands. During that war, the American government established the Committee on Public Information, to advise the government on how it should persuade the public to support the war effort. And since that time, government propaganda about its wars has become almost as important as military preparation.

By the time World War II started, several new mass media had been developed, namely, radio and motion pictures (with sound and color), which were enlisted for the government's war propaganda. Both the Allies and the Axis gave propaganda in the mass media a priority role. The Nazis were particularly good at using motion pictures to whip up fanatic patriotism in the German people so they would be willing to sacrifice all for the "fatherland." And Hollywood rushed to put its technology and its stars on the line to use film for the American "fatherland."

The war in Korea, in a media sense, was a minor repetition of World War II. After all, television had not yet blossomed through the land. But Vietnam was an entirely new thing. Now television was in place, ubiquitous and omnipotent. Indeed, war, starting with Vietnam, has never been the same since the age of television began.

The war in Vietnam was the first war that was brought directly to the American people—into their living rooms, night after night, in full color. Prior to Vietnam, all dispatches from a war front were passed through the hands of government officials, who "cleaned them up" for public consumption. Americans had never before been given "body counts," never been shown civilian villages being burned by American soldiers or the cruelties and tortures of war.

Media coverage of the war in Vietnam taught governments everywhere lessons about how to deal with the mass media during war. We are now beginning to see the results of those lessons. The wars in the Middle-East, particularly the Israeli invasion of Lebanon in 1982; Britain's war with Argentina over the Falkland Islands that same year; and America's invasion of the island of Grenada in 1983—these wars demonstrate how the media will be managed and manipulated as part of modern warfare. Media, in fact, have become a vital component of all wars.

38 · WAR ISN'T WAR WITHOUT TV

BY AMNON RUBINSTEIN

Israel was the first nation to suffer defeat at the hands of television even while it won its war. TV coverage of Israel's successful invasion of Lebanon in 1982 turned much of American public opinion against Israel, even though many Americans supported the general reasons for the invasion. Amnon Rubenstein, a member of the Israeli Knesset at the time, wrote this article for the *Washington Post* to put the problem into perspective. It is reprinted from the *Post*, July 18, 1982. Rubinstein is now Minister of Communication for Israel.

Jerusalem—The impact of television coverage on reactions to distant wars is being demonstrated again by the differences between Iran's invasion of Iraq, shrouded as it is by a TV blackout, and Israel's invasion of Lebanon, fully exposed by nightly TV coverage [albeit subject to Israeli military censorship].

War without television is an abstract affair, but war on the screen is a vivid experience literally brought home to millions of viewers.

This phenomenon also explains the striking discrepancy today between the self-image of Israel and outside criticism of its actions.

While outside Israel the war in Lebanon is denounced in unprecedented terms—Israel being accused of a Nazi-like action—within the country the army is praised even by the opposition for its humane conduct and consideration for life and property.

While Nicolas von Hoffman, in the *London Spectator,* writes that "incident by incident, atrocity by atrocity, Americans are coming to see the Israeli government as pounding the Star of David into a swastika," Israelis note that this is the first war in which refugees flee into the area occupied by the "enemy."

While the media abound—at least initially—with estimates of 10,-000 dead and 600,000 refugees, Israelis regard these figures as preposterous and point out that precautions taken by the air force have practically emptied the bombed towns of civilians. Indeed, as any visitor to southern Lebanon can attest, Sidon and Tyre—allegedly flattened by the Israelis—have recuperated from the war with amazing speed. The unshuttered shop windows exhibiting expensive wares, as well as the friendly welcoming populace there—Christians and Moslems alike—contradict the image created by the mass media, and especially by television, of a World War II-type havoc.

The denunciation of Israel also stands in contrast to the almost total silence that greets other wars and acts of aggression whose barbarity and cruelty do not attract international reaction.

What is wrong? Many Israelis react to this discrepancy by falling back on the ever-present suspicion of lurking anti-Semitism and see the comparison with Nazi Germany as obscene proof that indeed the "whole world's against us." That some anti-Semitic elements—or, to use Conor Cruise O'Brien's phrase, "anti-Jewists"—have seized upon Israel's action as a respectable vehicle on which to hang their still unrespectable instincts cannot be doubted. But surely there's more to this story than bad old Jew-baiting.

A partial explanation lies in the very nature of the coverage of wars by news media in general and by television in particular. TV and satellite transmission may have reduced the world into a global village, but in this village some streets are inaccessible. Most wars raging at present are not seen on television simply because they cannot be covered. Indeed, because the impact of TV coverage on public consciousness and international opinion is so crucial, one may divide wars into televisable and non-televisable wars.

In the limbo of non-televisable nonevents is not only the Iran-Iraq war, which reportedly has flattened whole cities and whose cost in human lives is rarely even estimated. Ethiopia's two wars, with the Eritreans and the Somalians, the Afghan rebels' battle against the Soviets and the Afghan army, the continuing struggle in Cambodia and the Yemen wars have similarly become nonevents—not because shots are not exchanged but because shots are not taken.

There were two major wars in Southeast Asia. One, America's Indochina war, became synonymous with total exposure to TV coverage. The other, which continues to this day between Vietnam and Cambodians opposing Hanoi's invasion of their country, practically ceased to exist as far as Western audiences are concerned with the withdrawal of camera crews from Vietnam and Cambodia. That struggle was brought back into public attention only because of the flow of refugees that could be seen on the small screen.

Indeed, one may say that in our day and age, war is war only if it is on the nightly news.

Non-televisable wars are generally associated with theaters in which nondemocratic states participate. But there are exceptions to the rule: Great Britain excluded regular TV coverage from its Falklands war and thus rendered its proceedings less real and less painful than the grisly scenes showing the bloody confrontations in El Salvador.

Moreover, not all televisable wars are given equal time. Visuals—to use TV jargon—are of major importance. The *polisario* war in the former Spanish Sahara is a non-visual war, consisting as it does of sporadic desert raids carried out at night, lacking the trappings of modern warfare.

Even in the same war, the actual coverage is often determined by visual considerations. Sidon—where only a small fraction of the city's buildings was hit—was depicted by TV news as a scene of total devastation, mainly because a number of high-rise buildings that collapsed like card houses under Israel's aerial bombing naturally attracted the focus of camera crews. At the same time, the refugee camps—some of them actually flattened by fierce house-to-house fighting—remained largely unnoticed because the damage to the one-story shacks was visually less impressive.

In addition, because of limited time slots, foreign wars make the evening news only if they maintain the public interest. Remote wars lose their interest as they become protracted and repetitive with their daily litany of clashing communiques. The Iran-Iraq war lost its ratings, so to speak, once it became a drawn-out affair, and, being anyway non-televisable, was quickly relegated, until recently, to the inner pages of the quality press.

The civil war in Lebanon—a televisable and occasionally televised event—suffered from a similar fate, although it ravaged the unhappy country since 1976 and has cost an estimated 70,000 lives. The regime of terror, rape and robbery imposed by the PLO on the Lebanese people similarly lacked visual angles.

Lightning wars—such as Israel's blitz in Lebanon—are the very stuff of which TV coverage is made. They also enable the networks to make an extra effort to send in a star-studded team to cover the war from start to finish. Because of this, and because Israel's wars concern a nation about which people have strong feelings one way or another, Israel's campaign in Lebanon was bound to fall victim to the arbitrariness of television coverage.

If the war in Cambodia and the Pol Pot regime—the worst human catastrophe since World War II—is on one end of the spectrum, being non-televisable and non-everything, Israel's wars are on the other end: televisable, visual, dramatic and highly visible.

Israel, which seeks the support of the free world, will have to face these facts of life. It cannot remove TV crews from the front line because of its nature as a democratic society. And even if it were to impose a TV blackout on war coverage, the Arab side would deliver the goods from its point of view. Israel, like other open societies, will have to take into account the adverse impact of TV war reporting when planning its moves or else pay the inevitable price it is now paying in Lebanon.

39 · BEIRUT—AND THE PRESS— UNDER SIEGE

BY ROGER MORRIS

Roger Morris takes a longer look at the Israel-Lebanon war in 1982 and concludes that the media covered it fairly and accurately, although with disastrous results for America's ally, Israel. Morris is the author of, among other books, *Haig: The General's Progress*. His research reported here was assisted by Vanderbilt University's television news archive and by *Columbia Journalism Review* interns Mark Silber and Claudia Weinstein. The article is reprinted from *Columbia Journalism Review*, November/December 1982.

For many American journalists, and much of their viewing or reading public, it was perhaps the most searing and controversial story in a generation. Israel's invasion of Lebanon in early June seemed to begin as one more round in a familiar cycle of violence and reprisal, one more almost routine combat assignment in covering thirty-five years of war in the Middle East. Yet as the fighting wore on, the Israeli attack not only overran the PLO; as never before, it soon engulfed the media as well, leaving newspapers and television under siege in West Beirut, both literally and figuratively.

As correspondents spoke into cameras or filed dispatches against the backdrop of the smoking city, partisans of both sides—and, increasingly, supporters of Israel—attacked the coverage for omission, distortion, or worse. Networks and newspapers were bombarded with letters and protests and besieged by angry delegations. In the heat of conflict at home and abroad, journalists lashed out at officials and at one another; there was a visible end to innocence and illusion among experienced newsmen who had prided themselves on having shed both long ago; and truth often became a casualty in the domestic war over the front-line reporting. When it was over, there was a sense that nothing scarred by the conflict—journalism, public trust, the Middle East, Israel's moral and political standing with Americans—would ever be the same again.

For sheer intensity and breadth, the controversy fueled by coverage of the Israeli invasion seems to have few parallels in recent journalistic history. After relatively brief and meager criticism of the reporting as anti-Arab, the storm centered on what *Boston Globe* editorial-page editor Martin Nolan called "general angst about the media's coverage of Israel." While criticism poured in on major papers such as the *Globe, The Philadelphia Inquirer, The New York Times,* and especially *The Washington Post,* the Anti-Defamation League of B'nai B'rith hired political consultant David Garth to review ABC, CBS, and NBC television news coverage of the entire conflict to document expected inaccuracies. To the *Jerusalem Post,* most American reporting on the invasion was simply "political pornography." Even *Variety* was troubled, in its own idiom, by the "serious short circuits . . . between reps of the international media" and Israeli authorities. Summoning Emile Zola and Colonel Dreyfus to the fray, Norman Podhoretz, editor of *Commentary,* eventually wrote his own "J'Accuse," an ardent defense of Israel's cause in which he strongly implied that a number of Israel's critics, notably *New York Times* columnist Anthony Lewis, were anti-Semitic.

Meanwhile, reporters lodged criticisms of their own. Writing in the *Washington Journalism Review,* for example, Israeli free-lance writer Pnina Ramati and *The Washington Post*'s Jerusalem correspondent, Edward Cody, deplored Israel's censorship and defended fellow writers on the Arab side whose dispatches "tended naturally to fill the vacuum left by Israeli silence." But the profession's varying frustration and concern with the coverage was turned inward as well. There was "some merit" to the charge of anti-Israeli bias in television reporting, NBC's Marvin Kalb was quoted as telling the August convention of the American Bar Association. On August 6 (in an incident discussed further below), Thomas L. Friedman, *The New York Times*'s bureau chief in

Beirut, cabled his Manhattan editors in outrage when he awoke to discover that they had summarily cut the word "indiscriminate" from his lead on the previous day's Israeli bombing of Beirut. The bombing had "the apparent aim of terrorizing its [Beirut's] civilian population," said Friedman's telex. His editors had been "afraid to tell our readers," and the correspondent thought it "thoroughly unprofessional."

Even after the PLO departed and the siege of Beirut was lifted, questions about the quality of U.S. reporting continued to hang over the scene. Unproven by the critics, unanswered by the media, the charges seemed symbolized by an article that appeared in the August 2 *New Republic*, titled "Lebanon Eyewitness," written by the magazine's owner and editor, Martin Peretz. "Much of what you have read in the newspapers and newsmagazines about the war in Lebanon—and even more of what you have seen and heard on television," Peretz wrote, "is simply not true." Railing against "journalists [who] think themselves chosen people" and a "peculiarly American mixture of ignorance, cynicism, and brashness," Peretz's travelogue through the Israeli occupation of southern Lebanon and its official rationalization did not constitute an intellectually serious critique. His attacks on *The Washington Post* and on the major networks were haphazardly documented; his praise for the *Times, The Wall Street Journal,* and other broadcast news was largely unsubstantiated.

But were the charges true? Had journalists, in fact, misrepresented the causes—and exaggerated the extent—of the carnage that dominated the news from Lebanon? Had they, in the process of reporting the invasion, somehow betrayed an American ally, as well as their own standards?

What follows is an effort to answer those questions by assessing not only the massive summer coverage of the invasion provided by *The New York Times* and *The Washington Post,* but also that provided by the nightly TV news broadcasts of the three major networks from June 4 through August 23, the day after the PLO started to pull out of Beirut and three weeks before the massacre in the Palestinian camps. The analysis concentrates, as did the critics, on four main elements of the coverage: Did the networks, the *Times,* the *Post,* and other major papers report fairly the historical context and justification of the Israeli invasion? Did they portray fully the political realities in a divided Lebanon in which many Lebanese welcomed the Israelis as liberators? Were they accurate in describing the human and physical cost of the Israeli attack? And, finally, were they balanced and factual in their nine-week accounts of the siege of West Beirut?

Beyond these issues, what were the crucial *un*reported stories of the invasion and siege? And what are some of the implications of the Lebanon coverage, and of the heated criticism it generated, for both journalists and the public?

The Reasons Why   The invasion broke onto the networks and into the headlines of the *Times* and the *Post* on the weekend of June 4–6. In swift succession there were the shooting of Ambassador Shlomo Argov in London, the Israeli bombing of Beirut, the PLO rocket attacks on northern Israel, and, finally, the massive movement of Israeli troops across the Lebanese border. From the beginning there was nearly uniform reporting of the reasons for the Israeli attack. "Terrorism has led to tragedy," said ABC's Frank Reynolds on June 4, in a broadcast that included Bill Seamans from Israel showing the damage PLO rockets had wreaked, together with segments depicting the Argov shooting and the raid on the Beirut sports stadium. The same day, CBS reported the bombing from Beirut as "retaliation," and from Israel, with scenes of the PLO shelling, as "reprisal," while NBC's Steve Mallory and Paul Miller, in segments that included file footage on guerrilla exercises in the Beirut sports stadium, emphasized that the stadium was a PLO ammunition dump and training site. *Times* and *Post* dispatches the next day likewise led with the "retaliatory" character of the Israeli attacks on PLO "training facilities" *(Post)* and "guerrilla camps" and "strongholds" *(Times).*

After another day's dispatches on how the attacks had been "triggered" by PLO provocation and were aimed at Palestinian "strongholds," both papers reported the Israeli invasion in similar terms. The *Post*'s William Claiborne, filing from Israel, wrote that the "declared objective" was to rid the border area of terrorists. The *Times*'s David K. Shipler told of PLO shelling and of how the guerrillas had become a menacing "army." Television news similarly emphasized that the Israeli aim was to "clear out" the terrorists (NBC) and "eliminate" their bases (ABC), with Seamans providing another vivid report on the PLO "rain of rockets" on Israel.

In those early days of the invasion, the networks repeatedly provided evidence that, in effect, documented Israel's case against the PLO and provided some historical context. On June 8, for example, there were reports by ABC's Seamans on how the fallen Beaufort Castle had been used to direct rocket fire into Israel; by CBS's Don Kladstrup on the Israeli assault on a PLO "stronghold" at Damur; and by NBC's Mallory and Art Kent on the "years of war" in Lebanon before the attack and on PLO artillery positions at the castle. On that same day, NBC's John Chancellor, later to become so controversial, traced the chronology of the outbreak, noting that Israel had been "ready for many months," that Jerusalem had tried before to subdue the PLO in 1978 when the Palestinians "got away . . . only to start a serious buildup again," and that it was "probably useless today to say just who started the fighting." "What can be said," his commentary concluded, "is that Israel is trying to buy a few years of peace at a terrible human and political cost, and incidentally, making American policy in the Middle East a shambles."

As the Israelis swiftly struck against Syrian missiles in the Bekaa valley and drove to the heights around Beirut, on June 9 the *Times*'s Shipler from Jerusalem and Thomas Friedman from Beirut assessed Israel's war aims as twofold: to "destroy" the PLO and to bring about a "restructuring" of chaotic Lebanon. Meanwhile, the *Post*'s Claiborne described Israel's goal as being to free that nation of "the threat of terrorism," and Cody, on June 12, 14, and 15, provided readers of the *Post* with accounts of Galileans who had undergone PLO rocket attacks "rejoicing" as Israeli forces advanced through what had been "unchallenged guerrilla territory," and of the capture of Palestinian weapons caches said to be intended for "the final destruction of Israel." On June 15 Ike Pappas of CBS sent back through Israeli censors his own graphic report on PLO weapon stores, many of them "placed in schools and other public buildings."

Few if any of these early reports and commentaries on Israel's war aims provided a basis for later charges of omission or bias. In mid-June both the *Times* and the *Post* profiled Israeli Defense Minister Sharon in blunt terms. But if the *Post* reported an opinion that Sharon "skates at the edge of psychosis," he was also said to be regarded as "brilliant and inspiring." The *Times* noted that the minister was thought by many to be a "reckless bully" but had "armies of admirers." In short, both papers did no more than reflect faithfully the partisan debate over Sharon inside Israeli democracy.

Similarly, on June 16, Chancellor commented on "the growing feeling that Israel has turned into a warrior state," using "far more force than is necessary" and raising problems of "Israeli credibility." Yet he went on to say that "no one questions Israel's legitimate security problem in Lebanon." A different balance of justification and unease had been struck on CBS the day before. Bill Moyers in his June 15 commentary had told his audience that "more Palestinians are homeless than ever," and that they faced the prospect of a "fraudulent peace in an indifferent world." But Moyers also noted that "civilian casualties were sure to be high" because the PLO "had embedded itself in camps of innocent civilians," and that Israel was rescuing Lebanon from "murderous gangs."

The Lebanon Puzzle—Explained?   Moyers's editorial pointed to a second major area of controversy—whether the press was paying enough attention to the complex realities of Lebanese politics that could explain the Israeli invasion as something other than a simple attack on a neighboring state. Critics would allege that for many weeks the media largely ignored both the historical setting in Lebanon and the favorable Lebanese reaction to the Israelis. Yet a survey shows some twenty *Times* and *Post* stories on just those subjects from late May to the end of July, with nearly the same number on the major networks. In fact, Lebanon's prolonged era of civil strife before the invasion, its chafing under the PLO occupation, the welcome extended to Israeli troops in many areas —all these were major themes of the first weeks of war reporting.

Thus, in early June Cody reported in the *Post* on Lebanon's "impotence" before the PLO, and on the near anarchy of the "disintegrating" nation, while Claiborne on June 16 noted that Damur, the scene of much destruction blamed on Israel, had been "savaged by years of civil war" as well as by the "relentless" Israeli pounding. The *Post's* Jonathan Randal, meanwhile, described a Lebanon "ever more cynical" about its Syrian and Palestinian "guests." At the same time, the *Time's* William E. Farrell was filing on the "seven years of violence and killing" in Lebanon and on the "flowers and cold soda" given to Israeli soldiers being hailed as liberators by Lebanese Christians.

Much the same portrait of Lebanon was drawn on nightly television news. On June 7, co-anchor Peter Jennings led ABC's *World News Tonight* with scenes of Lebanese welcoming Israeli forces who had "flushed out . . . terrorists" and a report on the country's "opposition" to the PLO. Over the following four days, NBC's Art Kent reported from war-torn Nabatiye that the Lebanese were "glad" at the "peace" brought by the Israelis, and Bob Faw, in a moving CBS report on refugees, observed by way of background that "what has been dirty and ugly and painful here will not change" simply because of the added violence of the invasion. For its part, ABC reported that the Lebanese were "simply glad the Syrians are gone" (Chris Harper, June 9), observed that Lebanon had "suffered a nervous breakdown long ago" (Peter Jennings, June 9), and showed one Lebanese civilian saying an emphatic "Never!" when asked if the PLO should return (Bill Seamans, June 10).

Later, as the siege of Beirut tightened, the papers continued their coverage of the Lebanese reaction. Writing in the *Post* June 28 and again July 5, William Branigin described the "terrible" destruction of the war, yet reported also that some Lebanese were "happy" to see the Israelis, and that in Damur the PLO had desecrated churches and used homes for stockpiling missiles. In the same vein, Shipler was reporting to the *Times* on June 21–22 on CHRISTIAN VILLAGERS' HAPPINESS AMID RUBBLE, on the humiliations inflicted on some Lebanese by the Palestinian forces, and on the "smiles and flowers" greeting Israeli troops as they took positions in the Christians' "lush suburbs" around Beirut.

Shipler and the *Times* returned to this theme in a major article on July 25 describing Lebanon's "anguish" under the PLO. Yet that lengthy dispatch, cited by critics as an exception, came not only in the wake of much other print and television reporting but three weeks after an equally impressive and similarly cast CBS feature by Tom Fenton. Illustrating his observations with colorful shots of the old Mediterranean playground, Fenton had noted that Lebanon had been torn apart by the "insertion of a state within a state" in the form of "hordes of armed Palestinians." The PLO, he added, had "destabilized Lebanon," and this had led to civil war, intervention by Syria, and, "eventually," Israel's invasion. Against film of PLO arms stashes, described as "an incredible quantity" of weapons, Fenton told his viewers that Lebanon was "never unified," but warned that the power of politicians like Bashir Gemayel, soon to be elected president of Lebanon, was based on "ruthlessly sectarian use" of the Israeli-armed Christian militia.

The Numbers War Besides being attacked for scanting the politics and the bloody historical background of the invasion, the news media were soon being angrily criticized for their reporting on civilian casualties, refugees, and the destruction of nonmilitary targets. No single subject would more exercise the critics, who accused journalists of vast inflation, if not invention, in the war's war of numbers. "Arabs exaggerate," Peretz quoted "an Arab friend" as saying to him "coyly in Jerusalem." So, too, he and other critics concluded, did the media.

The allegation raised serious questions. Had journalists identified sources, checked independently where possible, attempted to place figures in perspective? With few exceptions, a thorough reading and watching from June through August showed that the *Times*, the *Post*, and the major networks had done just that.

While transmitting sometimes stark scenes of death and devastation, television news from the earliest moments of the invasion seemed almost self-consciously leery of the numbers game. Casualties were simply "unknown," said Steve Mallory in a June 5 NBC segment on the bombing of refugee camps and a school bus, as well as of "Palestinian strongholds." The next day Mallory reported Lebanese casualties "in the hundreds" from his own observation of the bombing and invasion, while anchor Jessica Savitch noted PLO claims of "six hundred" and "no word" from Israel. On June 7, CBS's Bob Faw, against smoking scenes of battle, reported only that "casualty lists climbed." From southern Lebanon the same day, Vic Aicken sent NBC battle scenes from the fight for Tyre, but offered "no figures" on casualties.

On June 8 ABC's Peter Jennings described "mounting casualties" on both sides, reporting that they were "particularly heavy among Palestinians and Lebanese"; again, he gave no numbers. Noting the same night the devastation in Tyre, Dan Rather on CBS reported that "guerrillas" had occupied a Palestinian school and had thus drawn fire. And completing NBC's extensive coverage of battlefield wreckage that Tuesday evening, Chancellor stressed in his commentary that while "civilians are suffering more heavily than units of the PLO . . . Israel is being as precise as it can be"—an assessment with which many Lebanese and Palestinians might reasonably have disagreed.

On June 9, ABC and CBS footage from Damúr described the hard-hit town as a PLO "stronghold" where guerrillas were "entrenched," and NBC's Mallory, reporting a charge by Lebanon's president that the number of Lebanese killed or wounded "is in the thousands," emphasized that Israeli forces were concentrating on "Palestinian strongholds." The PLO "doesn't say how the figures were arrived at," said Jennings the following night in an ABC report on a PLO claim of 10,000 civilian casualties. Amid film of battle and bombs the same night, NBC's Roger Mudd, like his competitor at ABC, reported the figure of 10,000, attributing it to the "Lebanese Red Cross" but noting that it was also being "circulated by the PLO"; it was, he said, a number that "cannot be confirmed."

Twice the networks slipped noticeably. On June 11, Rather concluded the CBS invasion report by noting that unidentified "international relief officials" believed "thousands" of civilians were casualties in the fighting. A week later, Chancellor commented that Lebanese police estimates of 9,000 casualties and "Red Cross" figures of 300,000 homeless "may be high"—like Rather's, a vague and lax reference even with the attributions. But on June 22, NBC's anchor Tom Brokaw led the news with the simpler, more accurate admission that "we don't know" how many civilians had perished in the invasion thus far.

While television news was scrupulously vague about the war statistics, the newspapers dealt much more specifically with the numbers, and occasionally suffered the consequences of their attempted precision. The *Times*'s Farrell, for instance, early in the war reported an estimate of 500,000 homeless—a figure attributed to the International Committee of the Red Cross but later denied by committee authorities in Lebanon. In the same June 12 dispatch, however, Farrell cabled from Beirut that "no one really knows" casualty figures, just as his colleague Friedman had earlier stressed that Beirut casualties were "not known." From Washington, the *Times*'s Bernard Weinraub on June 17 duly reported "no estimate" of casualties, pointing out, however, that U.S. relief officials were planning to provide aid to as many as 350,000.

It was *The Washington Post* that, by reporting extensively on civilian victims of the invasion, particularly refugees, drew most of the critics' fire. Their charges were lent some validity by a June 16 front-page dispatch from Beirut by David B. Ottaway. Attributing the information to a combination of "Red Cross, U.N., Palestinian, and eyewitness accounts," Ottaway filed questionably high or at least unsubstantiated population and refugee numbers for the southern towns of Tyre, Sidon, and Jazzin. As a means of fleshing out a picture of the "devastating impact" on civilians, it was a dubious use of numbers. But higher in the same story, Ottaway had stressed that "figures seem guesses at best," acknowledged that other reports were only "fragmentary," and balanced his piece by quoting both Yasir Arafat's brother and an Israeli colonel who blamed the PLO for the civilian dead. In the end, Ottaway's slippery mid-June figures would be an exception in *Post* coverage, and he would go on to write another major article, on June 25, on the disagreement over casualty totals and the Red Cross denials of statistics printed by the *Times.*

Repeatedly, from June 6 through July, *Post* correspondents Ottaway, Randal, Claiborne, Cody, and Richard Homan told their influential readership that civilian casualties were "difficult" to measure (June 6), had "no independent confirmation" (June 8), and, in the case of one bombed apartment building, were far lower according to Beirut Radio than the PLO was claiming (June 12). They also took pains to make clear that, at a time when the Lebanese army was releasing estimates, "there was no independent confirmation of casualty totals" (June 14). In later dispatches, Claiborne noted the Israeli charge of "exaggerated" figures. Randal, for his part, referred to the "uncounted" dead of Sidon, adding that there was "little that can be confirmed" about alleged Israeli cruelty to local civilians, while Cody wrote about Israeli anger at and denials of the inflated numbers and went on to observe that it was "unclear" how Lebanese police or other authorities got their statistics.

Whatever the huge or shrunken figures ground out officially by the two sides, however ardent or effective the propaganda efforts of the belligerents and their partisans in the U.S., the major reporting from the battle zone itself was remarkably free of the ersatz authority of firm numbers. Even when the raw-nerve issue of civilian losses was hedged about by the plainest qualifications, the networks, the *Times,* and the *Post* also took visible pains to present Israeli doubts or rebuttals.

The Battle of Beirut   On June 11 a *Times* piece from Beirut described the city's "murdered sleep." Before the siege was over, the same term might have been applied to American viewers and readers of reporting from the scene. Day after day, with bombs and shells exploding along the skyline and sirens wailing through the rubble, television and print coverage of the siege shattered an otherwise relatively sleepy news summer. By almost any measure, it was one of the great sustained stories of the decade, and through more than nine weeks it would present nearly all the issues of accuracy and balance that stoked the controversy over alleged anti-Israeli bias in the media.

From the time the first Israeli bombs and shells fell inside the city, reporters and critics alike faced the question of whether a vast yet concentrated urban battleground was being portrayed fairly, and specifically whether journalists as well as Israeli gunners were distinguishing between the noncombatant city and the PLO forces lodged within it. Despite the medium's acknowledged weakness for wreckage and dazed, grieving innocents, despite its vivid reporting on civilian victims, television news for the most part struck the balance carefully. Characteristic of the early siege coverage was a Don Kladstrup report on CBS on June 10 that described the bombing of the city and nearby Palestinian settlements, but emphasized the destruction of PLO ammunition and supply depots, and noted that one of the buildings hit was near Arafat's headquarters. The following evening, NBC's Mallory sent out a somber report on the shelling of "nonmilitary" positions; it showed an old man weeping amid the destruction, and angry, unidentified Lebanese Moslems saying, "There are no military targets here," and "These are American weapons that are destroying our country." Mallory's images were admittedly sharp, but even here a conscientious attempt at balance was evident. Roger Mudd introduced the segment by saying that the Israelis had aimed their artillery at PLO headquarters and had scored a "direct hit," and minutes later, after Mallory, network correspondent Paul Miller reported from Israel on Defense Minister Ariel Sharon's justification for the continuing battle.

In the continual coverage by all three networks from June 4 throughout the month, there were very few questionable siege reports. One such report was aired on June 13. Chris Harper of ABC reported from Beirut on renewed Israeli bombing in which, "as usual, most of the victims were civilians." He then showed footage of the casings of U.S.-made cluster bombs, followed by a shot of a Lebanese woman who had lost her family in the "Israeli onslaught." Plainly an emotional portrayal, it left the then still-unsubstantiated impression, by juxtaposition, that the Israelis were dropping the brutal weapons on civilians. If noncombatants were now dying in the city, ABC at this early stage had an obligation to remind its viewers pointedly that the PLO had retreated into the heart of West Beirut, bringing the war with them like a plague. At the same time, the segment was a rare lapse in the month's network coverage, and in any case was followed on ABC by a Seamans report from Tel Aviv which explained that Israeli bombing was made necessary by the "organized and continuing" fighting by the PLO, and which showed still more captured weapons.

Far more typical was Mallory's graphic segment on NBC two days later showing a city "shelled to death from without and within." A powerful car bomb, its origins unknown, had destroyed a nearby Moslem building, and in the ensuing chaos of bloody victims, sirens, wild firing of guns, hospital confusion, and an old man pounding the rubble in rage, Mallory caught a West Beirut not besieged by partisan images but simply "overwhelmed by yet another disaster here."

Earlier in the month, as Mallory was reporting shelling of "nonmilitary" targets, the *Post*'s Ottaway from another vantage point filed a June 11 dispatch about Israeli vessels firing "indiscriminately" into the city. Either the naval fire or land artillery had taken mainly civilian casualties, including children in a playground, Ottaway wrote. But his article also told of an attack on "Palestinian and Lebanese leftist positions," as well as on the PLO headquarters building, and there was no later dispute about the accuracy of his description of one of the city's bloodier days of investment. Ottaway's account would be typical of the *Post*'s graphic and detailed coverage of the siege, and a mark as well of the growing contrast with the *Times*, whose Beirut reporting generally focused less on the battle in the streets than on the political and diplomatic aspects of the conflict.

Despite their differing thrusts, however, both papers provided admirably balanced reports throughout June. When the *Post*'s Randal wrote (June 14) about cluster bombs hitting a hospital just outside Beirut, he reported "no evidence" that the Israelis had targeted the institution. Syrian troops had indeed been in the area, and the bombing seemed an "accident of war." Later, Ottaway described the encirclement of Beirut as a siege not of civilians but of "remaining Palestinian guerrilla strongholds," while Friedman of the *Times* reported similarly that Israel was after the PLO "nerve center." When a ceasefire was broken on June 23, Randal thought it "impossible" to say who had started shooting, while the *Times*'s Henry Kamm reported from Jerusalem that ISRAEL SAYS SYRIA BROKE CEASE FIRE. At month's end, both Friedman and his *Post* rivals were reporting on the PLO's cynical "waiting game" in the beleaguered city.

The Siege, the Bombings—and an Explosive Telex   In the second and third weeks of June, the lengthening siege of West Beirut and its undeniable human dimension would begin to dominate both print and television coverage. And while the carnage did not produce sudden sympathy for the PLO, it did impel journalists to write about the sheer horror of what was happening. Thus, on June 21 the *Post*'s William Branigin reported the bombing of a hospital said to be "well away from any military targets"— part of the "backlash" of the "dirty war." Eight days later, Randal filed a similar piece on how the Israelis had "mercilessly" bombed Palestinian refugee camps outside Beirut, and shelled a "clearly marked" hospital. Farrell of the *Times* filed a June 26 story on "fierce Israeli strikes" and on mass graves in a Beirut cemetery that included an interview about civilian casualties with Dr. Amal Shamma of Berbir Hospital, an articulate Lebanese doctor often interviewed by television reporters as well. In the same edition, Shipler told the painful story of a twelve-year-old "drafted" by the PLO, which perhaps technically provided textual balance but was no match for Farrell's images. (It was Farrell who, on June 30, brought the story home to New Yorkers, describing the "Gramercy Park" of Beirut as being now "a sunlit horror of dazed people.") However consciously weighed and tempered, reportage coming from inside Beirut took on gathering drama, and a gathering sense of the human cost, much of it inevitably reflecting on Israel's guns and policy.

Throughout July the siege was the daily staple of news coverage, but the overall balance was maintained. On July 5 Bob McNamara of CBS depicted the "war-weary" city, whose "innocent Lebanese civilians living among guerrillas are hostages trapped in the line of fire." Over the next two days Randal of the *Post* recorded, without assigning blame, the demise of the fifth ceasefire, and credited Israeli explanations for the blockade of water and other supplies. On July 10, Branigin's dispatch to the *Post* labeled the PLO and the Syrians as being responsible for the impasse in talks with Habib. Again, two days later, he wrote about Beirut's "mean streets" and concluded that the city "is suffering from the decay that years of civil war and lawlessness have brought at least as much as it is suffering from Israel's shelling." On July 15, ABC's Hal Walker gave a thoughtful report on the Palestinians trapped by the invasion—their homelessness, their support for the PLO, their fear of Lebanese reprisals when the PLO left, their children among whom "hardly a male over 12 [is] not armed." "Where am I to go?" a woman who had come to Beirut thirty-four years before from Galilee asked Walker. His report provided a relatively rare glimpse of the larger human anguish and history behind the battle, yet it concluded with no attack on Israel, but rather with sharp criticism of the refusal of other Arab nations to take in the Palestinians.

In a month of mounting death and destruction, and growing disillusionment with the siege, both in and out of Israel, coverage continued to be careful and fair. A rare exception was a report by NBC's James Compton. Although July 28 was what anchor Brokaw called "another wild day in Lebanon," Compton reported in obvious overstatement that "night and day Israeli bombs rain on this city," that "nowhere is it safe," and that "no neighborhood has been exempt"—this in a city that had yet to feel the far wider Israeli bombings of August 1 and 4. Compton showed the Canadian ambassador, whose official residence had been hit, talking about his "change of heart" and asking, "Where's the Israel that we know . . . where has it disappeared?" The segment, which was followed by an even-handed report from Martin Fletcher in Damur, took no note of a PLO that Friedman described a day later in the *Times* as burrowing into the city with relative impunity while ambassadors and others seemed to deplore Israel alone.

It was in early August, in the last bloody week of bombardment before an agreement on the PLO departure, that the siege coverage itself became most heated. During the first five days of the month, the papers recorded the "fiercest shelling" of the Israeli "onslaught" (*Times,* August 2) and "severe damage in practically every West Beirut neighborhood" in the "heaviest assault yet" (*Post,* August 5). "Where is the American administration?" asked one U.S. citizen trapped in a burning hotel and quoted in a UPI story by Julie Flint carried in the *Post.* "Either your country has changed or you are making the most appalling mistakes in your history," Randal's story on the fifth had a diplomat saying to an Israeli officer, who responded, "Maybe both."

No published comments, however, would be more telling than Friedman's impassioned telex to *Times* editors William Borders and Seymour Topping when the paper deleted the adjective "indiscriminate" from his August 5 lead on the Israeli bombing. He had always been careful, Friedman said (and his dispatches would document the claim), "to note in previous stories that the Israelis were hitting Palestinian positions and if they were hitting residential areas to at least raise the possibility that the Palestinians had a gun there at one time or another." He had used "a strong word" such as "indiscriminate" only after he had taken a hazardous tour of the city with Branigin of the *Post* and had concluded that "what happened yesterday was something fundamentally different from what has happened on the previous 63 days." The "newspaper of record should have told its readers and future historians" about the Israeli terror bombing, Friedman went on. It was the "very essence of what was new yesterday. . . . What can I say?" he concluded. "I am filled with profound sadness by what I have learned in the past afternoon about my newspaper."

Sent over the Reuters open wire and widely read in the profession, Friedman's cable provided a remarkable inside look at the conscientiousness of reporters in Beirut and their awareness of the sensitivity at home of what they were reporting. In a sense, it would be a more eloquent rebuttal to critics of the war coverage than any dispatch from the front. But Friedman's were scarcely the only illusions destroyed that week in Beirut.

Chancellor and Editorial Pages: Unbalanced?   Over the first four days of August, with commentator John Chancellor now in Beirut, NBC aired some of the most provocative segments of the war. They began on August 1 with Rick Davis and James Compton reporting on the barrage. A bloody, bandaged baby, "innocent of any part of all the years of violence here," was shown; shells were described as falling in a "seemingly random way" on civilian targets; and Lebanese leader Saeb Salaam was shown asking Habib, "Will [the Israelis] be finishing us all before they finish?" The next day, Jim Bittermann depicted the bombardment of areas "long abandoned" by the PLO, with doctors saying that there were no military targets near the bombed neighborhoods, and Salaam touring the rubble and making such remarks as, "This was a school." The powerful segments mentioned Israeli claims that the PLO "fired first" that day, and that not only Israeli artillery but Palestinian mortars as well had hit an apartment building. But there was no explanation that Salaam was a prominent Moslem leader opposed to the Israelis (and a principal go-between with the

PLO for Habib), and no independent confirmation of Salaam's description of the scenes.

Perhaps the most controversial moment in the coverage came at the end of the broadcast on August 2, when Chancellor, silhouetted against the Beirut skyline, reflected on "yesterday's savage Israeli attack ... on one of the world's big cities." The area under bombardment was the "length of Manhattan below Central Park," he observed, and of the 500,000 who lived there, only "one in a hundred is a PLO fighter." The Israelis had claimed they were going after military targets with precision, but now "there was also the stench of terror all across the city." Nothing like it had ever happened in this part of the world, Chancellor went on. "I kept thinking yesterday of the bombing of Madrid during the Spanish Civil War. What in the world is going on?" he asked, shaking his head. Israel's security problem was "fifty miles to the south," so "what's an Israeli army doing here in Beirut?" He then concluded: "The answer is that we are now dealing with an imperial Israel which is solving its problems in someone else's country, world opinion be damned. . . . The Israel we saw here yesterday is not the Israel we have seen in the past."

Clearly introduced as editorial comment, Chancellor's words drew a torrent of protest, impelling the network to take the extraordinary step of showing three of the critical letters on the evening news two nights later, though with Brokaw repeating before and after the excerpts that the "very heavy" reaction had been "about evenly divided" between approval and disapproval.

Belatedly, perhaps, Chancellor's August 2 portrayal of Israeli-wrought devastation would be balanced by his remarks, on the next two nights, on the "resiliency" of the Lebanese and on the exploitation of the situation by the PLO as "civilians die and Yasir Arafat stays put." For that matter, the disputed editorial was scarcely fairer game for critics than Brokaw's ostensible news reference on August 4 to "what's left of West Beirut"—as if the entire city had been demolished, which even in the siege carnage was a definite exaggeration. In any case, Chancellor's comment was offset by August 4 and 9 reports on NBC showing the suffering of Israeli soldiers and their evident conviction that their cause was just. It was further offset by a thoughtful Chancellor commentary from a Palestinian refugee camp in which he observed that, although Israel bore "some of the blame" for the homeless people, it had been Arab countries that refused them refuge; the wretched Palestinians were "useful" because they "made Israel look bad."

Nor was Chancellor alone in his visible anguish. In one of the most moving television tapes of the siege, ABC, on August 10, broadcast Jack Smith's story from Beirut's neuropsychiatric hospital with its 500 patients "virtually abandoned," many of them wailing, retarded children without clothes or food. "They are dying," Smith reported of some of the children, because the PLO is "too busy fighting" and the Lebanese government "won't help"; meanwhile, Israeli shells "have killed or wounded nearly eighty patients." But the critics, revealing the same selective perception they charged was warping American journalism, seized on Chancellor's August 2 editorial as conclusive evidence of media bias.

At the same time, the editorial and op-ed pages of the *Times* and the *Post* also came under heavy fire. "According to one estimate of the first 19 pieces on the war in Lebanon to appear on *The New York Times* op-ed page, 17 were hostile to Israel . . . ," Podhoretz wrote in his "J'Accuse." "I have not made a statistical survey of *The Washington Post* op-ed page, but my impression is that the balance there was roughly the same." With its unidentified "one estimate" and "impression," the claim was undercut by the same sloppiness that Podhoretz and other critics deplored in the media.

Even granting the legitimacy in media criticism of faulting a paper's editorial balance as apart from news accuracy, and leaving aside the tricky question of what constituted a view "hostile" to Israel, the reality of the *Times* and *Post* editorial battlegrounds was hardly what the critics reported. Both editorially accepted the invasion—"tragic inevitability," said the *Post;* part of a "tragic spiral," said the *Times*—and proceeded to offset sharp condemnations of Israel by columnists such as Anthony Lewis and Mary McGrory with pieces by the likes of William Safire, William F. Buckley, Jr., and Rowland Evans and Robert Novak, who described the PLO as "permeated by thugs and adventurers."

While the *Post,* on balance, deplored the invasion and ran conspicuous pieces implicitly critical of Israel—former Tel Aviv correspondent Alfred Friendly on how Israel had lost its "unique splendor" and Claiborne on Israel's "wounded soul," for example, and later editorials on the "unforgettably bloody" fighting in Beirut—its editorialists also thought that Israel was doing "a nasty job" which everyone else wanted done. Editorially, the *Times* did less hand-wringing about the invasion, emphasizing the postwar negotiating opportunities in the West Bank and elsewhere that would justify the carnage unfolding on the front page. On August 5, the day "indiscriminate" was cut from Friedman's dispatch, *Times* editors found the worst bombardment of the siege "lamentable" but an "unavoidable way to keep the heat on."

Other Papers, and Scanted Stories A survey of other major newspapers reveals much the same news balance as evidenced by the *Times,* the *Post,* and the networks. While *The Philadelphia Inquirer*'s Richard Ben Cramer prompted protests with moving dispatches from Beirut on the plight of civilians, for example, the *Inquirer* also featured a syndicated piece by the *Los Angeles Times*'s Norman Kempster on how suspect all casualty figures were, as well as reporting from Robert J. Rosenthal on Israeli policy. Alex Efty of The Associated Press filed vivid stories on the siege, such as his June 25 dispatch on the Israeli shelling of a noncombatant area, but more often the AP wire was intent, as on July 30, on listing the PLO "targets" in the city, and on giving a paragraph-by-paragraph alternation of both sides' versions of the battle. *The Wall Street Journal* typically headlined the heavy Israeli shelling of August 1 as AIMED AT SPEEDING WITHDRAWAL OF GUERRILLAS.

Long respected for its Middle East coverage, *The Christian Science Monitor* duly reported "Israel's awesome pounding" of Beirut, yet editorially the paper made plain that "Yasir Arafat is stalling." The *Monitor* also carried an insightful three-part series by Trudy Rubin, beginning August 6, which emphasized the neglected reality that the Lebanese not only "hate the PLO" but feared the Israelis would "start to act the same" and simply install "new armed outsiders to replace the PLO." Meanwhile, the *Los Angeles Times*'s J. Michael Kennedy, Charles T. Powers, and Kempster filed graphic stories on both the siege and the "oppression" by the PLO in Lebanon, while, on the op-ed page, Kennedy wrote about how, with both the Israelis and the PLO locked in battle, a great city was "being destroyed by people who do not seem to care." Editorially, the *Times* observed during the early August bombardment: "Blame the PLO for the torment of West Beirut and blame Israel no less." (Letters printed on the same page accused the paper of both anti-Israeli and anti-Palestinian bias.)

In some cases, however, comparisons among the voluminous coverage only made more conspicuous certain unreported stories of the invasion. The *Inquirer*'s Robert Rosenthal and Ellen Cantarow for *The Village Voice*, for instance, wrote penetrating articles on the West Bank and the connection between the invasion and the stormy Israeli occupation of that area. In a sense, the West Bank was the gallery to which both warring sides played in Lebanon, its politics explaining the passion of the two armies and its territory likely to be the next symbolic if not literal battleground. But this story went largely ignored, especially by television.

So, too, their pens and cameras poised over the devastation of Moslem West Beirut and the PLO-held cities in the south, reporters barely glanced at what one *Times* writer called the "lush suburbs" of the Christians around Beirut, as well as farther south. The middle-class and wealthier Lebanese had survived the PLO occupation and the invasion by making their bargains with both sides. Telling that story would have provided a stark picture of the social and economic dimensions of the conflict.

With the exception of early reporting by Hedrick Smith in the *Times,* coverage was similarly absent on another front of the war—the U.S. Congress. The silence of Capitol Hill politicians on both sides, not to mention the impact of the invasion on close election campaigns starting up as the fighting and the media coverage grew most controversial was striking. But most home-front journalists tended to dive for cover on the issue along with the politicians.

Not least, there was little reporting on the fascinating "story of the story" in Lebanon—the burdens imposed by Israeli censorship, the conditions under which the doubly beleaguered journalists worked in Beirut, the sociology of their knowledge, the inner politics and reaction at papers and networks as the controversy exploded. It would have made vivid and unique firsthand war correspondence in a war in which the news media were a powerful force; but few in either print or television even brushed it, the networks' reporting on censorship being limited, by and large, to explanations of missing visuals.

But perhaps the most significant unreported story was how it all began. There were intriguing shards of the story here and there. In the *New Statesman* of June 25, Amnon Kapeliuk from Jerusalem reported "hundreds" of articles in the Israeli press presaging the invasion and an interview with Sharon saying he had been planning it since the previous August, while Claudia Wright noted that U.S. arms deliveries to Israel for the first quarter of 1982 were almost ten times the amount during the same period in 1980, and almost half again higher than those in 1981. *The Wall Street Journal,* in an August 10 Gerald F. Sieb feature on the propaganda efforts in the U.S. by both sides, noted that Sharon had toured the U.S. earlier in the spring with a booklet that, in effect, justified invasion. On August 1, NBC's Bob Kur showed previously censored film brought out from Israel depicting Israeli troops and equipment poised along the border in May, well before the attempted assassination of Ambassador Argov or any PLO rocket attacks of early June. The *Post* ran fascinating excerpts of interviews with Begin and Secretary of State Alexander Haig, just before the latter's resignation, that suggested that Haig's views on Lebanon might be closer to Begin's than to Ronald Reagan's. Did the U.S.—or at least some officials—know about the invasion long in advance? What had been U.S. policy, or was there more than one policy? Was an American secretary of state one of the casualties of the siege, and was he really a noncombatant?

Lebanon—and the Vietnam Parallel   To Podhoretz and other critics, commentary on the Israeli invasion of Lebanon revealed the same "loss of nerve" that had afflicted the U.S. in Vietnam. Yet the legacy of the Vietnam conflict helped to produce quite the opposite effect on journalists: a plain determination not to be taken in, to question official claims on all sides. Again, while Podhoretz argued that the press should have celebrated the victory of a U.S.-armed conventional force over Soviet-supported guerrillas, the immediate Vietnam parallel for working journalists was the censorship in Jerusalem, which proved no more popular than slanted American press briefings in Saigon (where, ironically, one of the briefers was Philip Habib). Journalists appeared to resent in particular the transparent falsity of the original Israeli claim to be clearing out only a twenty-five-mile buffer zone.

On the other hand, there was also evident trauma for American reporters, many of whom seemed, for the first time, to be seeing the Palestinians in human terms, in the blood and tears of the street and crowded hospital wards, and not simply as "terrorists" and "guerrillas." As "the other side" took on human reality, reporters inevitably became sympathetic to the plight of civilians. Added to that was the shock of journalists like Chancellor and Farrell made evident by their allusions to Beirut in terms of Manhattan. For Americans watching a great urban center under attack, the first since World War II, the image was brutal and obviously close to home. This was no Asian village or Middle East desert fastness, but streets and apartment houses recalling lakefront Chicago or, as Farrell wrote, Gramercy Park. Moreover, the urban intensity gave what was television's war even more concentrated sights and sounds to compress into the medium's limited compass. In the smoldering streets of West Beirut, with its screaming sirens and people, television caught the story with rare fidelity. Altogether, the result was a story that showed genuine empathy for the suffering city, and dismay at the destruction wrought by the encircling army, however understandable its presence might have been.

But was that empathy somehow political? Would the press have been less sensitive to the story of the human suffering if it had been the PLO, not the Israelis, shelling a hostage city? Would John Chancellor have been less inclined to ask "What in the world is going on?" There was nothing in the coverage to suggest that double standard. Although journalists vividly depicted the suffering of civilians, they continued to credit the Israeli justification for the invasion—right up to the gates of Beirut. Indeed, they did so almost to the exclusion of that other history behind the invasion—the Palestinian exodus and suffering since 1947. When the focus of the siege journalism turned perforce in late June to the calamity of West Beirut, the story reflected sympathy not for the entrenched PLO but for the innocent people among whose demolished homes the two sides fought.

When the invasion and the siege story were over, much seemed buried in West Beirut—the old PLO, perhaps the old Israel, perhaps the innocence of the media, something almost certainly too of American foreign policy—but it was a graveyard as well of the critics' charges of unprofessional reporting. In June, American journalism came to a bloody new war in the Middle East, reported what it saw for the most part fairly and accurately and sometimes brilliantly, provided balanced comment, and provoked and absorbed controversy. For performance under fire, readers and viewers could have asked for little more.

40 · HOW BRITAIN MANAGED THE NEWS

BY LEONARD DOWNIE JR.

When Great Britain went to war with Argentina over the Falkland Islands, the British brought with them the lessons learned from Vietnam and Lebanon. They thoroughly managed all the news about the event, much to their benefit, as Leonard Downie Jr. explains. Downey was the national editor of the *Washington Post* who had recently completed a tour as London correspondent for that newspaper. This article is reprinted from the *Washington Post,* August 20, 1982.

Throughout Britain's war with Argentina over the Falkland Islands, the government and media in London reacted indignantly to wildly false claims emanating from Buenos Aires. With Argentine propagandists repeatedly sinking the British aircraft carriers Hermes and Invincible, even though neither was ever hit, frustrated foreign correspondents in Buenos Aires complained about the difficulty of separating fact from fiction in what they came to call "the Bozo zone."

But those of us trying to cover the Falklands war from 8,000 miles away in London felt nearly as far removed from reality, even though we had access to more verifiable information. We also were being denied significant facts and knew, though we could not then prove, that we were being purposely misled in many cases.

In a recent parliamentary inquiry, British officials for the first time acknowledged misleading the media about British intentions, strengths and weaknesses on numerous occasions during the war. They were, however, more subtle than their Argentine counterparts.

"We aimed throughout not to lie," testified Sir Frank Cooper, the civil servant who runs Britain's defense ministry. "But there were occasions when we did not tell the whole truth and did not correct things that were being misread."

Hours before 5,000 British troops were landed at San Carlos Bay on East Falkland Island in a massive amphibious operation, Sir Frank himself had confided to British newsmen in a restricted background briefing that there were "no plans" for a "D-Day-type invasion." This was not really a lie, he recently told the parliamentary inquiry, because the allies' World War II invasion on D-Day was "an opposed landing," while few Argentine defenders were expected or encountered in the British landing at San Carlos.

He and other officials also left uncorrected a number of news reports, based on speculative leaks from inside the British government, that made it appear the Royal Navy had significantly more ships, submarines and aircraft around the Falklands than it actually did at various times. A nuclear-powered hunter-killer submarine widely reported to be enforcing the original British naval blockade around the Falklands was later found in port in Scotland.

Good news was sometimes released prematurely, with the British recapture of Port Darwin and Goose Green announced a half-day before the Argentine defenders actually surrendered. Bad news, from accidental crashes of British warplanes and helicopters to the number of casualties inflicted by Argentine air strikes, often was held up for days.

Some facts, like the large number of British ships hit by Argentine bombs that failed to explode, have still not been officially released in Britain. In fact, the defense ministry in London has yet to provide reliable figures on either the equipment losses suffered by British forces or those inflicted on the Argentinians. Yet, just yesterday, officials of government-owned British Aerospace, Inc., here to promote the sophisticated British-made weapons that proved so efficient during the Falklands conflict, had no difficulty producing their own statistics on the number of Argentine planes downed by British Harrier jets and surface-fired anti-aircraft missiles.

Television networks were prevented from broadcasting live from the Royal Navy's Falklands task force, and their film of events in the South Atlantic took weeks to reach London by ship and plane. So the war was nearly over before Britons saw dramatic scenes of the destruction of some of their warships or heard emotional interviews with survivors. Still photographs of burning British warships, transmitted more quickly to London, were blocked from publication by military censors for days and sometimes weeks.

Among the strongest critics of British censorship and disinformation during the war are many of the British correspondents, photographers and technicians who were allowed to accompany the task force to the South Atlantic. The Royal Navy tried to keep all newsmen off the task force, but was overruled by Prime Minister Margaret Thatcher's press secretary, who interceded personally for most of the 28 successful applicants. Foreign newsmen were completely excluded.

The BBC correspondent with the task force, Brian Hanrahan, testified to the parliamentary inquiry that the British commander, Adm. John Woodward, told reporters he intended to use the media "to cause as much confusion to the enemy as possible." The newsmen reached an agreement with him, according to Hanrahan, "where he was entitled to stop us reporting things, but we were not prepared to report things that were incorrect."

For an American correspondent in London, none of this should be really surprising. In normal times, the British press accepts a far greater amount of government secrecy and news manipulation than American or foreign newsmen would put up with in Washington.

In place of any legal obligation on the government to make information public—such as the U.S. Freedom of Information Act—the pervasive secrecy of Britain's civil service, military and politicians is protected by an arsenal of powerful legal weapons. The sweeping Official Secrets Act, though only selectively enforced, threatens prosecution and imprisonment of anyone from bureaucrats to newsmen involved in making public any unauthorized government information. The "D notice" system, the provisions of which themselves were long an official secret, is used by the British military to routinely notify editors and broadcasters that they cannot report specific items of information that often have already been put on the public record elsewhere by the United States, other governments or international agencies. Wealthy, blue-blooded and prominent Britons, including politicians and government officials, have long used the country's strict, punitive libel laws to prevent publication of information they find uncomplimentary.

More insidious, however, is a practice that most British journalists agree to voluntarily and even help to protect. Most of their contacts with politicians and government officials are kept completely off the record through what is called the "lobby"—named for an area in the House of Commons where many of these contacts take place, although every government agency has its own lobby arrangement with newsmen covering it. Newsmen participating in "lobby" briefings and conversations are obligated to keep secret all their sources, all direct quotes, and even the times and locations of such contacts. They are sometimes forbidden by their sources to publish important information revealed in these contacts.

This system enables the British government to manage much of what is reported by the national newspapers and television and radio networks and to escape responsibility for planting information—true or false—that newsmen must report only on an "it is understood" basis. This was the system used by the British defense ministry to control through the lobby of defense correspondents most information about the Falklands war. Only these correspondents were allowed into secret briefings held throughout the war, while the rest of the large body of newsmen covering the conflict from London were told little in public statements and press conferences.

Few British newsmen sought to find out more from officials or senior politicians outside these government-controlled forums. The leading political correspondent for a respected British Sunday newspaper said he would not even try to contact members of Thatcher's inner "war cabinet" because he doubted they would talk to him and he wanted to avoid "doing anything that might endanger our boys." As a result of such self-censorship, it was left to an American newsman to report from sources in the war cabinet that it had unanimously made the decision to sink the Argentine cruiser General Belgrano, one of the most important military and political events of the war.

Much of this had shocked me when I first arrived in Britain as a correspondent more than three years ago. But by the time the Falklands war brought a large number of fresh American colleagues to London near the end of my tour, I was surprised by their outraged response to a system that I, too, had grown to live with.

Even after the Falklands war ended, only a few British journalists questioned whether such pervasive news management, in peace or war, was good for the country. One of them, Charles Wintour, writing in the Sunday *Observer,* emphasized that "the hidden attitudes of many people in authority toward the media have been exposed. They think the public should be told as little as possible. They don't object to deception on matters both large and small. They dislike reporters. And they prefer that ruling circles should be left to run the state without being bothered by troublesome disclosures and unpleasant truths.

"In fact," Wintour concluded, "some of them don't really care much for democracy either."

41 · PLANNING FOR FUTURE GRENADAS

BY LYLE DENNISTON

When the Reagan administration invaded Grenada, in
1983, it put to good use the successful experiment of
the British in the Falklands. The result was a total
embargo on all media coverage of the Grenada battle.
The media complained bitterly but to no avail, as
Lyle Denniston explains. He regularly covers the
Supreme Court for the *Baltimore Sun* and writes
frequently on legal issues for journalistic publications.
This article is reprinted from *The Quill,* January 1984.

If the nation's press is expecting an apology from the Pentagon for
its management of the news during the invasion of Grenada, it almost
surely will be disappointed. But if it wants a chance to cover similar
military operations in the future, it probably can get that—although at
a price that may be quite high.

The original round of recriminations and harsh accusations played
itself out rather quickly, and in its place has come a somewhat uneasy
but apparently genuine effort to see that the next time—assuming there
is a next time—will be different. By mid-February, if a rather optimistic
Pentagon timetable is met, there may be something of a consensus that
could shape relations between the military and the media for years to
come.

The task of mutual accommodation, however, is far from easy, for
four basic reasons:

First, both sides recognize that the Vietnam experience has altered,
probably for all time, how the press and the military regard each other.
Very deep wounds probably cannot be healed entirely, but they will
have to be treated extensively to give any future "understanding" any
hope of working.

Second, the press—or at least some significant part of it—has grown
a lot bolder in insisting upon access to cover all forms of governmental

activity. What was once merely a privilege, honored by custom, is now being asserted as a constitutional right.

Third, there is a real prospect of a division in the ranks of the press. What the Pentagon may be willing to offer could turn out to be acceptable to the print media, but to fall well short of satisfying the distinctly different needs of the broadcast media.

Fourth, and most important, the press may have to be willing to accept a significant responsibility, shared with the military, to keep the military's secrets—at least for a time. That may not take the form of outright censorship, with dispatches cleared word for word through military channels, but it almost certainly would take the form of restrictions on the time of release and on certain kinds of information—identification of units, troop strength, etc.

One thing seems clear already: There apparently is no way for the press to gain unrestricted opportunity to cover a secret military operation from the very outset. The military very likely will insist upon exacting a price for cooperation if it is to take any members of the press in with the first wave of troops in any future foreign military adventure.

In Grenada, no members of the press went in with the first wave, or even with the second wave. Four reporters—three Americans and a Briton—who had made their own landing were taken off the island by the military, kept out of touch with their offices for eighteen hours, and then returned to the island, still with no opportunity to file.

It is still not entirely clear how the total blackout was decided on. By some Pentagon accounts, there was nothing in writing to say that the press was to be excluded entirely. There was little time for planning, apparently, and what emerged was a more-or-less practical conclusion that it simply would not work to include the press, at least until after the Americans on the island—medical students, primarily—had been made secure by the invading troops.

Michael I. Burch, assistant secretary of defense for public affairs, who was centrally involved, insists that the Grenada incident is unique, and that there is no broader lesson to be learned from it "on either side."

"If we were presented with exactly the same circumstances—the need for surprise, and the need to finish the rescue before beginning the military operation," Burch says, "I'm not really sure I'd do it much differently. I probably would get [press] pools in a little earlier, and in greater numbers."

But, he adds, there has been and will be no official criticism of the way the military commanders—especially Vice Admiral Joseph Metcalf III, who was in charge of the Grenada assault—handled the press situation at the beginning. There are, as yet, no understandings as to what might be done in the future about situations like the unplanned arrival of four journalists, pursuing the invasion on their own, according to Burch.

But if there is to be no apology, there at least is a developing acknowledgement that Grenada has provided the occasion for a serious exploration of the underlying problem. The Pentagon's inclination, Burch says, is to deal with that problem, and to do so right now. "It is very important that we air this issue while it is still fresh in everyone's mind. We are living in a very imprecise world here. I would hate to get into another of these situations, with hard feelings on all sides."

Clearly, the atmosphere surrounding the issue has changed. The press's angry demand for some immediate "reform," including a Pentagon admission of error, has waned. So has the Pentagon's insistence—joined in by some top White House aides—that the apparent public approval of keeping the press out proved that they'd made the correct decision.

Moreover, the very real chance of a serious constitutional confrontation over media access also seems to have eased, if it has not vanished.

In the early days after the blackout, some leaders of the press, enticed by some media lawyers, planned to go to court with a formal demand for assured access. But, as tempers in newsrooms and editorial boardrooms cooled, and as the fear of losing such a lawsuit in a big way became widespread within the ranks of the mainstream press, the plan was dropped. Meanwhile, however, *Hustler* magazine publisher Larry Flynt—again going his own way—had sent his attorneys swiftly into U.S. District Court in Washington with a formal claim of unconstitutional denial of access. As long as that case remains in court, the effort to get a consensus by negotiation and discussion may be complicated. The Flynt case clearly has many press lawyers troubled, for its precedent-setting possibilities.

One of the initial difficulties facing both sides, as confrontation was giving way to conversation, was that each has approached the access issue with a different perspective. The two sides seem to have contrasting, even conflicting interpretations of the history of the press in combat. Moreover, each has grown to distrust the motives of the other.

The problem with history is most acute in the opposing recollections of what happened in Vietnam. The White House—up to and including President Reagan himself—appears to hold firmly to the view that already was deeply set in Pentagon minds: The press not only did not help with the military effort in Vietnam, but actively sought to—and did—frustrate it. The press, so far as it has a collective mind on the subject, is rather embarrassed by the thought that it came to skepticism too late in reporting that conflict, and that too many of its members were cheerleaders rather than hard analysts.

Each side seems to have viewed the other, in the wake of the Grenada operation, as simply repeating the mistakes of Vietnam. The government was sure that the press would have picked apart and criticized the action (and perhaps even given comfort to the foe), and thus should not have been allowed to interfere at the outset. The press was wholly prepared to believe that the government wanted to hide its questionable adventure ashore, and thus resorted to total blackout as the best way to manage the news.

Looking back beyond Vietnam, historical perspectives also conflict. As the Pentagon interprets that history, the press has never been free to go its own way in a combat zone—and certainly was not allowed to cross the battlefield to get "the other side of the story" objectively. But as many journalists interpret history, Grenada stands out as the first American military operation ever to leave the press behind with the explicit aim of assuring that only the "official" picture of combat got out. On both sides, there does seem to be one piece of common ground: Whatever happened in the past, the government and the press now have a very different relationship, and there is no chance that the press will easily or eagerly be brought back "onto the team."

Official controls—especially those sought to be imposed on news about the military—now are suspect, and both sides know that. The Pentagon's Burch, for example, says that controls that amount to censorship "can only be imposed in time of [formally declared] war. Would the press ever again accept censorship? I just don't see how, with the mood of the press today, just the spirit between the press and the government." He adds, somewhat ruefully, "It's hard even to get an embargo around the Pentagon on stuff that is routine."

As times and attitudes have changed, the risk of confrontation over an incident like the Grenada invasion has grown. The risk has grown, too, because both sides have entered a new era of relations strongly influenced by law, and by differing legal perceptions.

It has been true only in the past few years that the press could make a credible claim that it had a "right"—in fact, a right included in the press clause of the First Amendment—to cover (as distinguished from reporting or commenting on) the government. Few issues now shape government-press dealings more significantly than does the right-of-access question, which has become even more problematic during the Reagan administration as controls on official information deemed to be "sensitive" have multiplied.

It would have been an unsettling thought, even to the press, to have suggested a generation ago that the press had *any* right of access to military information. In fact, for a half-century after the Supreme Court's 1931 decision in *Near* v. *Minnesota,* it had been accepted almost as much by the press as by everyone else that there was a "military exception" to the free flow of information under the First Amendment. Only two and a half years ago, in the case of *Haig* v. *Agee,* the Court appeared to have extended that exception to protect covert intelligence operations abroad from public disclosure.

In recent years, especially since Vietnam, however, the press has been casting off its past willingness to remain in the joint enterprise of keeping the military's secrets. Journalistic skepticism about all foreign and defense policy—in particular, secret military or para-military operations in other countries—has been deepening. Sooner or later, it was bound to mature into a claimed *right* of access to news not only of traditional military operations, but to any use of American forces abroad.

The Grenada incident provided the occasion, and the Supreme Court's 1980 decision in *Richmond Newspapers* v. *Virginia* provided the legal rationale. In *Richmond,* the Court for the first time recognized within the First Amendment press clause at least a limited guarantee of press access to cover some governmental activity. If an official activity —criminal trials, in that case—has been open traditionally to the press, a right to cover it builds up over time, according to that decision.

After Grenada, press lawyers returned to wartime histories, and discovered there what they took to be a common practice of press access to combat zones—in both major wars and limited conflicts.

Jack Landau of the Reporters Committee for Freedom of the Press, for example, concluded from his staff's research: "Since the Revolutionary War, we cannot find a publicly known battle from which the press was excluded, when it was there. It always has been given front-line access as soon as it arrived."

What that seemed to suggest, for the Grenada situation, was that long-standing practice would have supported press inclusion at the outset. "It is the right to observe that is at issue here," according to Landau. In the aftermath of Grenada, he adds, it is inappropriate to focus solely on the conditions for news filing once the press is allowed on the scene. What first must be resolved, he insists, is simply the right to be there to provide non-official observation.

Theories of access based upon that view, buttressed by the *Richmond* precedent, lie at the core of the Larry Flynt lawsuit stirred up by the Grenada blackout. "Traditionally," that lawsuit contends, "the activities of the armed forces of the United States have been covered by war correspondents, accredited to those forces, who have served with the troops and filed their stories from wherever such service took them, including the front lines. No guaranty of their safety was ever asked or given."

The Pentagon, however, has a counter-argument. Directly challenging the theoretical basis of the Flynt lawsuit, government lawyers recalled that the Supreme Court has said repeatedly in recent years (and did not repudiate the idea in the *Richmond* decision) that press access depends first upon access for the public in general. The *Richmond* ruling, according to the Pentagon response, has to do with criminal trials only, and not to military operations in a combat situation. If it is true, as an historical matter, that the general public has not been routinely welcome at the scene of battle (at least, not since the Battle of Bull Run), then the press can claim no historical right of access for itself, the Pentagon contends. The First Amendment would not be offended by total exclusion of the press, it argues.

Assistant Secretary Burch thinks the issue of access to Grenada can be made clear by asking this rhetorical question: "Do firemen have a right to set up fire lines to keep reporters from rushing into burning buildings?" By analogy, he suggests, that was what was done in this military landing.

For Burch, and apparently for military observers generally, the problem of combat news coverage becomes more acute when television is taken into account in the access equation. It takes more seats and more storage space on military press planes to accommodate TV crews, he notes. Operating conditions at the point of combat also may be less than adaptable to TV's needs, he adds. There can be no detachment of crews from the forces with which they are moving. According to Burch, it is inconceivable, for example, that a *60 Minutes* crew would be permitted to travel with American troops and then take off to film opposing forces. And the networks also cannot be left free to operate their own plane charters as often as they like on military airstrips, he says.

As he anticipates possible future arrangements to accommodate the press on military operations, Burch suggests that the most difficult tests will come when both sides face the broadcast-access issues. For the print press, Burch already seems content with an answer to Grenada.

"Ideally, I can see a situation where I would call in the AP and UPI bureau chiefs [in Washington] and tell them we are going to have a conversation that never existed. If they agree to that, then I say to them that I will need two of their reporters—able-bodied people who can be spared for a week to ten days. 'Don't ask me where they are going, and don't expect them to file.' Then, I would take the reporters, walk them out to a plane to somewhere, and send them in, say, with the second wave. When the commander [at the scene] is ready to allow it, they could go out and file."

In that scenario, the wire service reporters would be the only press presence—as pool reporters. From the military point of view, Burch suggests, that would be entirely manageable. Commanders could feel secure about leaks, and thus about protecting their forces from premature disclosure. The press—at least the writing press—would get its story, unfettered by direct censorship of what its reporters write.

In the calmer atmosphere that now appears to prevail over the Grenada situation and the underlying access problem, the Pentagon's civilian and military leaders are setting out to test just what the press wants in the way of access, and how much it is willing to cooperate as the price of access to future military operations.

The original idea of a formal joint commission of press and military representatives—an idea floated by General John W. Vessey, Jr., chairman of the Joint Chiefs of Staff, reportedly without advance concurrence by Pentagon civilian leaders—has been dropped. In its place will be a less formal study panel.

It will be headed by a one-time American military spokesman during the Vietnam conflict, retired General Winant "Si" Sidle, who is now public-relations director for a defense contractor, Martin Marietta Corp.

The Sidle group—including Burch—is now preparing to solicit the views of the nation's major press organizations and of former war correspondents about the fundamental press issues posed by the Grenada episode.

Those organizations will be asked to make up their minds about a very basic legal question: What rights, under the First Amendment, do they believe the media have in connection with military operations? Depending upon how that is answered, the exploration of the remainder of the issues at stake could be made harder or much easier.

Beyond that, the groups will be asked to take positions on the kind of access they believe they need, the use of press pools and how those are to be selected, the kinds of military operations they wish to cover, the kinds of communications they would need, what the military would be expected to do if complications arose for the press during an operation, and censorship—at least as a short-term essential.

It is the Pentagon's hope that each group will work out its own answers, and then send one representative to a Washington seminar, to be held early in the new year. The seminar would also be attended by senior military leaders and civilian information officials from Burch's office.

The seminar's basic assignment would be to work up a consensus, if it can, and to offer explicit recommendations for access standards. Those would then go to Sidle who, in turn, would determine what to recommend to the top echelon of the Pentagon. All of that, it was anticipated in November, could be done by mid-February.

Before the seminar assembles, Burch's staff expects to try to work out some proposed standards of access on its own. In the meantime, however, no temporary arrangement or understanding will be put in place, even should there be another operation raising issues of press access, according to Burch.

He seems not to have many illusions about the "rather cumbersome" process that he and the military leaders have set in motion. "We are dealing with a very competitive press corps—and just the sheer numbers involved add to the problem."

Recalling the experience of Grenada, when some four hundred reporters, by Pentagon count, wanted to move in with the two thousand troops on the island, Burch has little expectation that the problems that became evident there will vanish on their own. Even a small-scale operation in the future, he assumes, would draw another crowd, and the same complex issues would come up all over again.

42 · TOO BAD FOR OUR SIDE: WAR IS A VIDEO GAME

BY BEN J. WATTENBERG

> The lesson we have learned from recent wars, says Ben J. Wattenberg, is that the most important new weapons of modern warfare are "light-weight television cameras and television satellites. They have unwittingly made it more difficult for free nations to operate in the real world." Wattenberg is an editor of *Public Opinion* and longtime observer of American public attitudes and behavior. This article is reprinted from *Public Opinion*, August/September 1982.

Suppose you were a young military officer or a young diplomat. What would be the right lessons to learn from the recent wars?

It has been said that what's new about these wars has something to do with the devastating French missiles used by Argentina, or with the ingenious Israeli adaptation of American smartware, or with the deficiency of Soviet anti-aircraft technology used by Syria.

But I fear that the real lessons to be taught at West Point or the Fletcher School of Diplomacy will be very different. The most important new weapons are light-weight television cameras and television satellites. They have unwittingly made it more difficult for free nations to operate in the real world.

Consider the string of recent wars: Afghanistan, Iraq-Iran, El Salvador and, more recently, the Falklands and Lebanon. And consider some new rules of the road that every geopolitician and military tactician must now teach.

First Rule: Communist countries can wage long, brutal wars and pay very little for them. It is two and a half years since the Soviets rolled into Afghanistan. The Afghans continue to fight well, but the U.S. grain embargo has been lifted, sanctions were never imposed and the nightly news all over the world ignores the conflict. After all, if you can't get television cameras into a country to witness the poison gas, the dead civilians, the maimed children—then what can you show on television? No access; no horror.

Second Rule: Roughly the same guidelines hold for non-free, non-Communist countries. The Iran-Iraq war began almost two years ago; 100,000 people have been killed, including many civilians. The Iranians developed a new mine detector: young boys run across the battlefield to explode the mines. But there are no television cameras to record the battered bits of young life blown sky high. No cameras; no news. No news; no outrage. No outrage; no penalty. And so, Iraq still hoped to host the Conference of Non-aligned Nations; the United States buys oil from Iran.

Third Rule: A democracy can wage a quick war if it is on an isolated, faraway island—which enables it to control the news. There was plenty of television coverage of the ships leaving England to the tune of "Don't Cry for Me, Argentina." But there was no contemporaneous television film of the deaths of the British sailors in the icy sea or in melting aluminum ships. No foreign correspondents were allowed with the fleet; censorship was tight. In many ways, it now comes out, the British public was purposefully misled. Question: if English television had shown the gore of the war while it was happening, could Mrs. Thatcher have kept the political support necessary to finish the war?

Fourth Rule: Only at great cost can democracies get involved—even minimally—if the battlefield is an open country. America provided military aid and fifty advisers to the civil war in El Salvador. They were outnumbered by television folks; the coverage made us appear at times like conspiratorial, lying butchers. It sometimes seemed as if the war was about four dead nuns. Another big story revealed that an American adviser actually carried a rifle. Television coverage helped to turn the American public sour on a limited, moral enterprise; now U.S. political support for El Salvador is fraying.

Fifth Rule: On non-islands, democracies can wage only short wars, telling the whole truth, all at once and immediately. If the war goes on, if goals change as targets of opportunity arise, if the government says something that is not so—beware of the wrath of the world. Because both Israel and Lebanon host plenty of television crews, because a television journalist can get to the front quickly in a Hertz rent-a-car, because the censorship is porous—every bit of the horror that any war produces is in everybody's living room the next day. In war, access equals horror.

The Israelis are complaining bitterly that Israel is unfairly held up to a double standard. Actually, it is more serious than that. The new rules of media warfare establish a double standard for all open societies. Television will show blood in El Salvador, in Lebanon—in any open country—and civilized people will be shocked and exert political pressure to make it stop.

This is important. The use of force and, more important, the threat of the use of force are still key parts of the global geopolitical equation. That is sad, but true.

The nature of television news demands that it show whatever horror is available. Our horror is available; our adversaries' horror is not. That process unwittingly presents our adversaries with a great gift. They can credibly use the threat of force in a harsh world; it is much more difficult for us. They know that; we know that; they know that we know that. Accordingly, they can be more adventuresome than they might ordinarily be. That is not the fault of television; it is the burden of the glory of a free press.

Of course, all this is not brand new. The same phenomenon was apparent in Vietnam, when only our half of a bloody war was shown in the living rooms of the world. Now it is apparent that it was no accident; it will keep on happening that way. That may be a tough lesson for would-be generals and diplomats to swallow, but it is a more important one than which side has the smarter missiles.

43 · WAR COVERAGE IN A TV AGE

BY NICK THIMMESCH

In response to Ben Wattenberg, Nick Thimmesch
suggests that the answer is not less coverage of war
by the media, but more. Television, he says, has been
a force to reduce slaughter, "and perhaps has given
many poor souls a chance to live a few more precious
years." Thimmesch is a former Washington
correspondent for the *Los Angeles Times*, now a
journalist in residence at the American Enterprise
Institute. This article is reprinted from *Public
Opinion*, October/November 1982.

Ben J. Wattenberg warns young military officers and diplomats in
"Too Bad for Our Side: War Is a Video Game" that the television camera
is the most important new weapon in modern war, and that TV technology "unwittingly" makes it "more difficult for free nations to operate in
the real world."

Well, no question that television can bring war's gore into living
rooms, and quickly affect, even change, public opinion about any nation,
free or otherwise. The dramatic shift in American public opinion about
Israel, following its invasion of Lebanon and the siege of Beirut, is the
most recent case in point.

Wattenberg's lament that Communist and other non-"free" nations
can escape such unfavorable exposure because they don't provide access when they wage war, also has some validity. Our sense of fairness
is offended when the Soviets brutalize Afghanistan, *sans* camera, or
when the Syrians kill their own people with artillery, with vengeance,
in a television-free environment.

But Wattenberg's complaints push the reader toward the chore of
trying to determine what the so-called good guys should do about the
media when "our side" lets loose with bombs, shells, rockets, and other
lethal devices. In citing El Salvador and Israel, Wattenberg implies that
"our side" suffered because television captured the violence of these
nations in unpleasant terms.

Does this mean that the U.S. government should follow General

Westmoreland's advice, and impose censorship in any future military action involving U.S. forces? Or should nations presumed to be on "our side"—because they get huge amounts of foreign and military aid—restrict or even bar the cameras from witnessing the killing of war because that might reflect on the nobleness of our "cause"? Or should the media, after stern warning, practice self-censorship, turn cameras away, or perhaps not take them to the scene of carnage at all?

The presence of TV cameras is a risk to the reputation of a combatant, but the price a free nation pays for that presence is worth it. While Wattenberg remarks that television made the war in El Salvador sometimes seem as if it "was about four dead nuns," I want to know if the government we fund is responsible for the killing of those four nuns.

I also want to know about the My Lai massacre, the execution, by handgun, of a Viet Cong killer by a South Vietnamese police chief, and what Israel did in Lebanon, because I helped pay for it, and I am loyal to the U.S. government which had a hand in this violence.

It is to be hoped that the media are intelligent enough to put this sort of activity in perspective, and that we can make judgments on whether the American connection is worth it. Perhaps it is. But let us see it and then decide.

When a free nation's survival is at stake, as was the case in World War II, military censorship is justified on the grounds that the enemy can use freely dispensed information to hurt us. When the United States takes sides in El Salvador, ostensibly we are seeking to stabilize the region in our national interest, but the most hawkish advocate can't argue that our survival is at stake. There is a difference.

The loudest complaints about recent television coverage of military violence come from Israel and its supporters in the United States. Observers agree that since Israel was founded it enjoyed extraordinarily good treatment in the news and entertainment media, to the obvious disadvantage of the Arabs. In recent years, Arabs got better treatment, and the media turned away from showing Israel in romantic terms. Israel's high-technology military machine, superior to that of any Middle East nation, caused the media to cease portraying Israel as David vs. the Arab Goliath.

With all those TV crews in Beirut and Israel, it wasn't surprising that this invasion was seen on our TV screens for months. After all, an invasion is an invasion, and Israel's relentless bombing of Palestinian camps and Beirut neighborhoods, with the inevitable shots of wounded children and stunned elderly people staggering around—well, that's TV footage.

True, only a fraction of similar mayhem was shown a few years back when PLO and leftist forces fought Phalangists in a quite violent civil war which took upwards of 60,000 lives. Nor was there much television footage of the casualties and destruction resulting from Israel's bombing attacks on Palestinian camps and of Beirut itself, in the period of years before last June's invasion.

Television cameras had access to this earlier violence, but news editors in New York expressed only occasional interest in coverage. During this 1975–1982 period, the PLO learned how to cultivate the media, so when Israel invaded, the cameras were ready. Israel's censorship of the invasion in its early stages only heightened the interest of TV correspondents to get the story.

But Israel's press and public is fiercely protective of its freedom, and these tactics backfired, particularly when the massacre story broke. People in a free society expect their media to show what their government and military are up to. The media can't be stifled.

The American media correctly react to their news instincts about the deportment of nations using the lethal power of American-supplied weapons. Our media are right to show what both sides are doing in El Salvador. They should show more of the violence on the West Bank where rock-throwing Arab students have been killed—a score this year by last count—by Israeli soldiers.

Had there only been television cameras to penetrate and expose the persecution of Jews and other "enemies" of the state in the first years of Hitler's Nazi Germany, before he got a head start on the greatest human tragedy of this century, the cruelty may not have taken place. I am glad that TV cameras show the brutality of the Communist regime in Poland toward Solidarity.

We should televise more of the violence inflicted by nations and armies, not less. My hunch is that in a world loaded down with enormous quantities of conventional and highly sophisticated weapons— many supplied by the United States—television has been a force to reduce slaughter, and perhaps has given many poor souls a chance to live a few more precious years.

44 · In Defense of Casualty Pictures on TV

By Ellen Goodman

Ellen Goodman says there is some therapeutic value
to the blood and gore of war on television. She agrees
with Thimmesch that war on television may be our
greatest hope for ending war altogether. She is a
nationally syndicated columnist working in Boston.
This article is reprinted from the *Boston Globe*,
September 14, 1982.

Now that the heavy fighting in Beirut is over and the PLO has been
shipped off to live in assorted nations, I am left with one lingering image
of this war. No, for once, it's not an image I saw on television. It's an
image I saw *of* television.

In my lifetime, I've watched a lot of wars in prime time. Usually
there are good guys and bad guys. Usually, those wars are resolved
before the commercial.

But in the news, it's different. In the news, wars go on and on. In the
news, we see less glory and more gore. In the news, the sides are not
divided into good guys and bad guys, but aggressors and victims.

It was true in Vietnam, it was true in Iran and Iraq, Afghanistan and
El Salvador, and now in Lebanon. We beam home the pictures of the
wounded, the innocent bystanders, the casualties. And the war lovers
don't like that.

Ever since Vietnam, we've heard complaints that television news
was somehow biased. There were angry accusations that the nightly
news fomented the protest movement in the '70s. Now we hear that the
camera, simply by filming the uprooted of Beirut, the refuse of war,
made a statement against the Israeli artillery.

There were suggestions that it wasn't quite cricket to offer up "features" on the effects of the war on a family, a street, a building, a
neighborhood. I even heard that there was something unfair about
"human interest" stories on the wounded of the militarized zone, stories
giving them names and faces and titles: aunt, son, father.

Well, I agree that television is biased. To the degree that TV does its job well, tells us the facts of life in a conflict, it is intrinsically anti-war.

It's anti-war because the average person sitting in the living room responds to another human being. However immunized by years of war movies, we know, as Eliot said in "E.T.": "This is reality." War may be impersonal. But introduce us to a single person, tell us what she thinks, tell us what he feels, tell us what happened to his or her life—and we will care. It is our saving grace.

In our war-sophisticated world, we have learned that before we can kill people, we have to dehumanize them. They are no longer human beings but gooks or kikes or animals. The Japanese who experimented on human guinea pigs in World War II called them "maruta": logs of wood.

It is even easier when we lob missiles from an invisible distance or drop bombs from 15,000 feet at "targets." It's more like an Atari game than a murder. Conversely, the more we humanize people, the more we personalize war, the harder it is to commit.

Our ability to make war impersonal is scariest when we think of nuclear war games. Some years ago, Roger Fisher, a Harvard Law School professor, made a radical proposal for bringing nuclear war home to the man who could actually wage it. We would implant the code needed to fire the first missiles in a capsule near the heart of a volunteer. The president would have to kill one human being before he could kill millions.

"I made the suggestion," says Fisher now, "to demonstrate the difference between the abstract question of saying that I am prepared to kill 20 million people in the defense of freedom and the personal human question saying I am prepared to kill somebody I know, in order to do this.

"There's a difference between saying, we'll exercise Plan A, Option 6B and saying, 'Uh, George, I'm afraid I have to kill you in order to exercise the nuclear option. Shall we do it right here on the White House carpet or in the bathroom?' It brings home what it's about."

In conventional warfare, television does the same sort of thing. It brings home what war is all about: killing, wounding, destroying. It doesn't film ideals, but realities. TV isn't in the war room or the computer room, but the hospital room.

This is not unabashed praise of TV. There are enormous risks in slanted war coverage. It's easy to make yesterday's villain into today's victim. It's easy to portray self-defense as aggression, and be manipulated into sympathy for terrorists.

But if we can't solve problems by confrontations that are resolved before the commercial, if war usually produces victims, not answers, then we have to see this in human terms and witness the personal edge of devastation.

There are people who worry that humanizing war will undermine our resolve to wage it. I say, that is our greatest hope.

FOR FURTHER READING

Michael J. Arlen, *Livingroom War.* New York: Viking Press and Tower Publications, 1969.

James Aronson, *The Press and the Cold War.* Boston: Beacon Press, 1970.

Peter Braestrup, *Big Story: How the American Press and Television Reported and Interpreted the Crisis of TET 1968 in Vietnam and Washington,* two volumes. Boulder, Colo.: Westview Press, 1977.

Gladys D. Ganley and Oswald H. Ganley, *Unexpected War in the Information Age: Communications and Information in the Falklands Conflict.* Cambridge, Mass.: Center for Information Policy, Harvard University, 1984.

David M. Johnson, *Korean Airlines Incident: U.S. Intelligence Disclosure.* Cambridge, Mass.: Center for Information Policy, Harvard University, 1984.

XII

Mass Media and Minorities

THE COLLECTION of articles about the mass media and minorities represents a "mix" of viewpoints to prompt thinking and discussion and to challenge readers to go beyond thinking and discussing. The articles don't include all the minorities in the United States, and some readers will correctly complain. What about Orientals, Latinos, Chicanos . . . ? The editors take responsibility for the selections and for bowing to space limitations.

Two of the articles in this section quote from *The Report of the National Advisory Commission on Civil Disorders,* the Kerner Commission Report that, for the first time, officially chastized the mass media for failing to warn the nation that festering inequities would result in rioting and burning in many U.S. cities. The report was published in 1968, though the conditions that prompted the violence had been seething for decades. It is worthy of consideration again, in the light of contemporary conditions of people in our cities and towns.

Moving from the premise that there are and will be minorities in a society, the bigger questions involve how minorities are included—even whether they are included—in the mass media, which attempt to serve the society. Are there individuals from these ethnic and racial groups employed in the media and, if so, how? Are they decision makers? Are they seen and heard? Or are they hired and forgotten? Are there articles and programs about minorities in the media? Are they accurate and perceptive, or do they espouse stereotypes that are false and misleading? These are some basic questions for any consideration of the mass media and minorities. The articles in this section should prompt many more questions. Each should be followed with "Why?" and "What should be done now?"

45 · AMERICAN INDIANS AND THE MEDIA: NEGLECT AND STEREOTYPE

BY JAMES E. MURPHY AND SHARON M. MURPHY

The article by James and Sharon Murphy discusses the minority probably least portrayed in the mass media. It should also remind readers that neglect and stereotype are too often the media response to all minorities. Why? What can be done now?

The authors trace the history of media treatment of American Indians. Their conclusion: Media neglect and stereotyping has been so thorough that Indians are forgotten people even in an era of civil rights accomplishments. The late James E. Murphy was associate professor of journalism at Southern Illinois University. Sharon M. Murphy is dean of the college of journalism at Marquette University. This article is from *Let My People Know: American Indian Journalism: 1828–1978*, published in 1981.

The mass media of the United States have historically followed a policy of not-so-benign neglect of this country's native peoples. Media coverage is also marked by a fair amount of cynicism about Indians, a prime manifestation of which has been the portrayal of Indians as stereotypes. This chapter traces nearly two centuries of such neglect and stereotyping.

When one thinks of such mistreatment, images of the Indian in Hollywood westerns come immediately to mind. Yet portrayals of the savage Indian of the Old West are limited neither to film nor to the twentieth century. Long before television and films, printed accounts did their part to foster inaccurate images of Indians. In fact, much news reporting about Indians was done in such a fashion that it encouraged or at least condoned savage treatment of Indians. One scholar, Elmo Scott Watson, wrote:

Depending mainly on volunteer correspondents more gifted in imagination than in accurate reporting, [eastern newspapers] spread before their readers the kind of highly-colored accounts of Indian raids and "massacres" that the most sensational yellow journalism of a latter period would have envied.[1]

Watson saw in the press performance of the 1860s a reflection of the strong, sometimes violent anti-Indian sentiment of the frontier. What the frontier readership wanted, the newspaper supplied, including hair-raising accounts of alleged Indian "uprisings."

According to historian William Blankenburg, before the Camp Grant (Arizona) massacre of 1871, for example, the three English-language newspapers in Tucson made every effort to arouse the white settlers, and the rest of the country, against the Indians of the region. Referring to the Apaches, the *Weekly Arizonan* recommended, as an appropriate Indian policy, "to receive them when they apply for peace, and have them grouped together and slaughtered as though they were as many nests of rattlesnakes."[2]

The papers continued to encourage white settlers to kill Apaches who raided livestock and who sometimes killed white persons in retaliation against white slaughter of Indians. They actively supported recruitment of volunteer whites and mercenary Papago Indians for the purpose of raiding the tiny Apache settlement at Camp Grant. The *Arizonan* urged: "Would it not be well for the citizens of Tucson to give the Camp Grant wards a slight entertainment to the music of about a hundred double-barrelled shotguns. We are positive that such a course would produce the best results."[3]

A week later, just before dawn, a hundred Apaches, mostly women and children, were slain in their wickiups.[4] Although the massacre might have occurred without encouragement from the press, it is hard to ignore the effect of unremittingly negative images of Indians. One would probably be justified in expecting something better of the journalists. Blankenburg, however, concludes his study with a commentary that is descriptive of much media treatment of Indians even today: "It's probably wishful thinking to suppose that those editors might have risked iconoclasm in those agonizing times."[5]

In 1876, as the United States prepared to celebrate its Centennial, the Oglala Sioux and the Northern Cheyennes successfully defended their women and children and old people against Colonel George A. Custer and his cavalry. The Sioux and Cheyennes fought with little advance warning and without the superior weapons available to the cavalry. But accounts in the eastern press called the Custer debacle at the Little Bighorn a slaughter of brave soldiers by the red devils. The *Bismark* (Dakota Territory) *Tribune* printed an extra edition on July 6, 1876, with such headlines as "Massacred," "General Custer and 261

Men the Victims," "Squaws Mutilate and Rob the Dead," and "Victims Captured Alive Tortured in a Most Fiendish Manner."

The report, pieced together from various accounts, spoke of the death of one soldier, Lieutenant McIntosh, who "though a half-breed, was a gentleman of culture and esteemed by all who knew him." McIntosh, the account reads, was

> pulled from his horse, tortured and finally murdered at the pleasure of the red devils. It was here that Fred Girard (another soldier) was separated from the command and lay all night with the screeching fiends dealing death and destruction to his comrades within a few feet of him, and, but time will not permit us to relate the story, through some means succeeded in saving his fine black stallion in which he took so much pride.[6]

Throughout the account, the Indians were pictured as marauding savages who were inhumanly cruel to the "gallant defendants" of the embankments thrown up by the cavalry. No acknowledgement was made that Custer's attack, unprovoked by the Indians, was part of a government campaign to steal the territory from its original inhabitants. Neither was there mention of the brilliant strategies employed by Crazy Horse and Sitting Bull at the Little Bighorn, leaders of its rightful defenders. Instead, the day was lost for Custer, and "of those brave men who followed Custer, all perished; no one lives to tell the story of the battle." The writer adds, however, that "we said of those who went into battle with Custer none are living. One Crow scout hid himself in the field and witnessed and survived the battle. His story is plausible, and is accepted, but we have not the room for it now."[7] It is curious that the journalist had no room for the only eyewitness account of the battle.

The tale of brave Custer and his band of heroes was carried in papers from east to west. It strengthened the whites' fears of the Indians. It also fed its readers' curiosity and sold newspapers.

Less than fifteen years later, fears were again fanned by reports of the dangers posed by the growth of the Ghost Dance religion, a messianic, pan-Indian religion of hope and peace. Its doctrine of nonviolence and brotherly love called only for dancing and singing. The Messiah, who had the appearance of an Indian, would bring about the resurrection of the land and of the many Indians slain by white soldiers. Newspaper coverage of the Ghost Dance movement and subsequent hostilities in 1890 and 1891 was inaccurate, sensational, and inflammatory. As one writer put it, the accounts "foreshadowed the 'yellow journalism' that was soon to stampede the nation into a real war. But that was not to happen until the seeds of journalistic jingoism, sowed on the bleak prairies of South Dakota, had borne their first bitter fruit in an 'Indian massacre' in which red men, instead of white, were the victims."[8]

One reason for this comparison to "yellow journalism" was the outright lying by reporters who were "space writers," free-lancers who sold gore by the column inch. They faked "reliable sources" and "eye-witness accounts" and wrote propaganda disguised as news that sent waves of alarm, preceded by vicious rumor, across Nebraska, the Dakotas, and Iowa. The stories, although repudiated by a few serious journalists near the scene, convinced the frontiersmen that Red Cloud's Oglala Sioux were preparing to go on the warpath. They also convinced the federal government that more troops must be sent to the South Dakota towns that were eager for the business that troops would bring to their merchants.

As soldiers began arriving, the Indians fled. The press interpreted and trumpeted their flight as an outbreak of hostilities. Big-city papers began preparing to cover the new Indian "war."[9] Correspondents on the scene were under pressure to send exciting stories. When Chief Big Foot's band was massacred at Wounded Knee as the Indians were being disarmed by the cavalry, the media again ignored the story of the Indians, outnumbered five to one and fighting for their existence. The story was rather one of the protection of innocent white settlers by soldiers who were finally putting an end to Indian treachery.

Only rarely did coverage of the Ghost Dance religion and the Wounded Knee massacre reflect a more accurate picture. One such better-informed account was that of reporter Teresa Howard Dean, who was sent by the *Chicago Herald* to Pine Ridge, South Dakota, in 1871. Before this assignment she had covered weddings, church and social events, and Indian affairs. Douglas C. Jones wrote: "Like a great many other writers who had never been near a Plains Indian, she wrote a number of items deploring the state of Sioux existence, brought on, she indicated, primarily through a native laziness and indolence."[10] She carried a gun and heeded a warning that reporters who were too friendly risked being asked to leave. She filed such tidbits as, "The only incentive to life is this fear of being scalped by red men."[11]

Yet because Teresa Dean boarded at the Indian school while she was in Pine Ridge, she got to know some young Indian students, and she soon became aware of the conditions under which the government forced them to live. Her copy soon reflected her impressions: hunger caused by lack of provisions, education far inferior to that offered by the nearby Catholic mission school for white children, the nonarable lands assigned by the government, and the inability of the local Indian agent to deal with the Ghost Dance religion in any way other than to send for the army, which he had done (his response would be echoed in more contemporary reactions to "Indian problems").

Teresa Dean also met and talked with Indian adults (and brought what she called a "scalping knife," failing to note in her copy that such knives were used by Indians for skinning game and preparing food).[12] Other examples of her work show how even she, like her fellow reporters, failed to see Indians as people. One of her dispatches contained the statement that "the greatest crime for which the government must answer is sending the educated Indian girl back to her tribe where virtue is unknown." Again, after watching a Sioux policeman identify the bodies of his sister and her three children slain near the Wounded Knee battle site, she wrote: "He looked at me with an expression that was unmistakable agony and his lips quivered. For the first time, I realized that the soul of a Sioux might possibly in its primitive state have started out on the same road as did the soul of a white man."[13] The product of white schools and books and a reader of white newspapers written by reporters like herself, Teresa Dean's statements mirror the attitudes and viewpoints in the media of the time, as well as those of a political system that permitted and propagated the atrocities she was witnessing.

From the early years of the twentieth century through the 1960s, during that long period of Indian anguish and tribulation, little coverage of Indian affairs or events was provided by white newspapers.

Then in the 1970s a series of events in Indian country touched off the widespread media coverage that left some wondering if perhaps the earlier policy of media neglect of Indians was not somehow preferable. For the coverage was crisis-activated and did little to further the ongoing story of Indian life and needs in this country. The media gave heavy coverage to the 1973 occupation of Wounded Knee, South Dakota, by the American Indian Movement. One on-the-scene reporter at Pine Ridge said that correspondents "wrote good cowboy and Indian stories because they thought it was what the public wanted. . . . the truth is buried in too many centuries of lies like fossils embedded in layers of shale."[14] The Associated Press, United Press International, *Newsweek, Time,* the *Washington Post* and the *New York Times* were there, as were the three major networks and many foreign press correspondents. The pattern this time was different, however, because the American Indian Movement was in control and was orchestrating the media's sudden curiosity. AIM leaders tried to use Wounded Knee as a stage on which to focus attention on government injustice to Indians. They had only limited success.

Wounded Knee and the events that followed gave birth to several Indian papers, because white-dominated media played the story as they had played the urban unrest in the late 1960s, and Native Americans continued to resent this misinterpretation and other plainly misinformed reporting. One collaborative account about Wounded Knee began:

> The people of the United States, by and large, would rule strongly in favor of native demands at Wounded Knee if they could only find out what happened there. But with the press and television personnel moving along

to bigger and better and more violent headlines, with the U.S. Government managing the news emerging from the Pine Ridge Reservation, and with even the reports on the resulting trials of the participants absent from the media, the people of the United States will not have the information on which to base an intelligent judgment.[15]

One difficulty facing the establishment media was that Wounded Knee did not fit prevailing myths held and taught in the United States regarding Indians. Wounded Knee did not coincide with the belief that America was a democratic country where the courts dispensed justice, government agencies dealt benevolently with Indians, and all people had opportunities to match their ambition and willingness to work hard. As the same source said, "Wounded Knee, people say, must be a bad dream—probably done by 'bad Indians,' influenced by 'outside agitators,' and unrepresentative of native people."[16]

Yet, for many Indians, Wounded Knee represented a last-ditch stand, a final plea in the court of public opinion and the arena of equal rights. Witness these comments by Russell Means, AIM leader, regarding media treatment of the life-and-death issues at stake at Wounded Knee:

> Now, this is our last gasp as a sovereign people. And if we don't get these treaty rights recognized, as equal to the Constitution of the United States—as by law they are—then you might as well kill me, because I have no reason for living. And that's why I'm here in Wounded Knee, because nobody is recognizing the Indian people as human beings.
>
> They're laughing it off in *Time* Magazine and *Newsweek,* and the editors in New York and what have you. They're treating this as a silly matter. We're tired of being treated that way. And we're not going to be treated like that any more.[17]

No matter how distorted the reporting, television coverage of Wounded Knee got "the whole world to watch what is happening to the Indian in America," as one Indian on the scene told the *Washington Post.*[18] Thus the takeover helped inform most Americans about things they had not known before: average per capita reservation income—$1,000; average unemployment rate among Indians—40 percent, with a higher percentage at Pine Ridge; a 900 percent greater incidence of tuberculosis on the reservation than in the white population; and a suicide rate twice that of nonreservation persons.[19] Except for a small number of Indian newspapers, the media had neglected to tell those facts to the American public.

They had also neglected, and continue to neglect, to inform the American public about other Indian grievances: that utility companies are being aided by the government in their attempt to take Indian lands that lie over rich mineral deposits;[20] that dams and waterway reroutings are threatening crop and rangelands upon which whole tribal economies depend;[21] that education available to tribal residents is substandard at best and criminal at worst.[22]

Nor surprisingly, Indian journalists have charged the white media with stereotyping. In May, 1973, the *Navajo Times* quoted Franklin Duchineaux, counsel to the United States Subcommittee on Indian Affairs, who said that the Native American often depicted in the press is a sophisticated and intellectual tribal leader. Yet, the counsel suggested, to call on one person and make him stand for or act as spokesman of all Indians is stereotyping at its worst, perhaps because it is at its least conscious level. *Wassaja,* one of two national Indian publications, frequently charges the establishment press with dishonest coverage of Indian affairs. In one article, the editor wrote:

> Information about Indian affairs is meager and largely inaccurate. People need a vast amount of information in order to make intelligent decisions. We need to know what legislation is being readied for action . . . what programs, educational and economic opportunities and experiences of one or another Indian tribe might help the others.[23]

In June, 1975, another incident at Wounded Knee showed that most journalists were unable or unwilling to probe beneath the surface with their questions. Three men, two of them FBI agents, were shot to death on the Oglala Sioux Reservation in South Dakota. Only hours after the shooting the wires were humming with deadline stories reporting that the shooting "stemmed from" the 1973 Wounded Knee disturbances. The shootings were called an "ambush" and the shots were said to have come from "sophisticated bunkers." The misinformation that emerged from these and other reports both developed from and led to more misinformation and stereotyping.

The exact cause of the FBI agents' deaths was never known. No "bunkers" were found. Trials and accusations failed to bring the incident into clear focus. The deaths of the FBI agents brought a massive siege on houses near the death site, and a search-and-destroy paramilitary occupation by hundreds of FBI agents that lasted for months.[24] Press releases by the FBI and other government agencies resulted in the newspaper headline: "FBI Agents Ambushed, Killed by Indians," although no evidence of "ambushing" had been established.

The Native American press has carried frequent accounts of what happened to Indian activists and "sympathizers" involved in the 1973 Wounded Knee occupation and to those suspected or accused of involvement in the 1975 incident. These stories usually were not picked up by the wire services and consequently did not find their way into the white press. Indian activists were beaten, their homes broken into, their families threatened, one of their spiritual leaders harassed and jailed—and the white press remained largely silent.

According to one source, six "Wounded Knee sympathizers" had been killed on the reservation by winter, 1973. In the winter of 1974 people talked of the "murder of the week" on the reservation. At least twenty killings occurred in the first seven months of 1975; it was "a reign of terror—bad before the occupation, but even worse now."[25] The established media gave scant attention to the deaths.

When the Menominee Warriors Society took over an abandoned abbey near Gresham, Wisconsin, in 1975, the media showed up in force and devoted much time and money to covering the incident. There too, however, Indians frequently protested that white journalists were supplying misinformation to their papers. Part of the problem may have come from the journalists' fear of missing good stories or disappointing their audiences. As one Milwaukee television editor put it:

> On several days, very little happened. . . . The question then became whether to report the fact that basically nothing was happening or ignore the story on those days. We decided nearly every day that we had to carry some word on the situation, for the sake of those viewers who were interested.[26]

But when all was quiet, reporters stayed around in the event that new developments occurred. Menominee leaders, however, claimed that the reporters could have used their time to obtain adequate background information from individuals whose views should have been heard.[27]

Fast on the heels of the Gresham incident came a series of Indian lawsuits aimed at keeping or regaining lands, mineral rights, and fishing rights promised to Indians in treaties but nullified or at least endangered by subsequent and current developments, legal and illegal. Montanans Opposed to Discrimination and the Interstate Congress for Equal Rights and Responsibilities (ICERR) were just two of the groups mounting massive lobbying efforts against Indian tribal interests. By early 1978, ICERR had chapters in twenty states, mainly in the West and Northeast, areas of the greatest activity in Indian rights. In the spring of 1978, Richard La Course, a prominent American Indian journalist, wrote:

> It's a new political epoch American Indian tribes are entering in the late 1970's. Some call it the "backlash period;" some call it a "state of siege." Others view it as the forced Era of Treaty Renegotiation. In any case, it's a new ballgame—with consequent new responsibilities for Indian journalists nationwide.[28]

Some of the responsibilities were directed toward Indian audiences and their education for survival. Others were directed toward the non-Indian public, which had to be reached with or without the cooperation of the white-majority media, either by the printed word or by broadcast. Again a good deal of educating had to be done to break through misunderstandings or biases. Said one director of a Native American studies program: "These people [news reporters and editors] really don't give a damn about Indians. We aren't dangerous enough. They think if they just move in on Indians, we'll be forced to give up. Maybe what we need is violence. That's all they seem to understand."[29]

In addition to newspapers, magazines, and the broadcast medium, the book-publishing industry has done its part to cast Indians in a false or negative light. Indian scholars frequently point to the misinformation and prejudice propagated by textbooks dealing with Indians and Indian affairs. *Wassaja* and the quarterly *Indian Historian* regularly publish reviews of current books about Indians. *Wassaja* editor Rupert Costo published *Textbooks and the American Indian*, a carefully annotated study of books frequently used in Indian schools or as authoritative sources of information about Indians. The book, covering historical, sociological, anthropological, and religious studies, as well as basic materials used daily with young people, pointed to some reasons why journalists write about Indians as they do: One learns patterns of perception from teachers, parents, textbooks, and other environmental elements, and these patterns tend to persist beyond one's school days.[30]

As for film, that medium may have more responsibility for creating the current popular image of Indians in this country than all the print media combined. Writers and dramatists, either intentionally or inadvertently, have propagated the stereotypes: the filthy redskin, the noble savage tamed by white refinement and religion, the headdressed warrior who attacks a wagon train, or the swarming redskins attacking the isolated military outpost to the delight of rerun audiences everywhere.

Especially until about mid-century, films reflected largely hostile and negative attitudes in their representation of Indians, who appeared on the screen as bloodthirsty and treacherous. Since 1950 nostalgia or peaceful coexistence has been reflected in the demeanor of Indians in films. Still, today's screen Indian is often a sullen, broken spirit who drinks cheap wines and lives on the handouts of a sometimes benign, sometimes malicious tribal government, or he is the militant Red Power publicity seeker, burning buildings, taking hostages, stealing government documents, or desecrating church buildings.[31]

One writer points out other images, propagated through film reruns, that are still as convincing to a new generation of viewers. The men were lazy, shiftless, unable to conform to white values, not to be trusted. The women were unusually quiet, loyal, beautiful.[32]

That the Indians portrayed in most films about Indians have been inauthentic relates directly to the fact that in their creation and production American Indians have been largely excluded. Nor were Indians consulted by the film industry regarding authenticity of plots, settings, and characterizations. Consequently, Keshena writes:

Movie makers focused on the tribes of the Sioux and the Apache, who thus became the white man's Indian, molded and cast in the white man's mind as he wanted them to be, but projected before the viewer's eye as convincingly authentic. Indians from all tribes were cast in the image of a prearranged reality.[33]

Some few genuine Indian actors surfaced, playing roles that quickly proved the dominance of white heroes: Jay Silverheels, of "Ugh, Kemo Sabe" fame, first appeared as Tonto in the Lone Ranger movies and series. A Mohawk, he also appeared in *Broken Arrow, Brave Warrior,* and other films. An earlier Tonto was played by Chief Thunder Cloud, an Ottawa Indian, who appeared in films in the 1920s and 1930s. He was also a radio Tonto.[34]

Only in very recent years, with the emergence of strong Indian actors like Will Sampson and Raymond Tracey, has the image of Indians in film begun to turn away from the degrading stereotypes that formed the material of a half century of filmmaking.

In his own powerfully sardonic way Edward R. Murrow commented in 1958 on the image of Indians in the media. Addressing a national convention of the Radio/Television News Directors Association, Murrow said:

If Hollywood were to run out of Indians, the program schedules (for television) would be mangled beyond all recognition. Then, some courageous soul with a small budget might be able to do a documentary telling what, in fact, we have done—and still are doing—to the Indians in this country. But that would be unpleasant. And we must at all costs shield the sensitive citizens from anything that is unpleasant.[35]

Ten years later the National Advisory Commission on Civil Disorders, which published the respected Kerner Report, added its own commentary on the plight of America's minorities. It is interesting that the commission failed to mention American Indians explicitly. That failure is itself a comment on the problem. The call for improvement of media coverage of minorities seemed targeted at blacks and Chicanos. But the same criticism could have easily been applied to the media treatment of Indians.

Chapter 15 of the Kerner Report, supposedly well known to journalists and media critics, charged that the coverage of the 1967 civil disturbances contained "mistakes of fact, exaggeration of events, overplaying of particular stories, or prominent displays of speculation about unfounded rumors of potential trouble."[36]

Another criticism by the Kerner Commission was that white-dominated media have not communicated to the majority of their audience—which is white—a sense of the degradation, misery, and hopelessness of ghetto existence: "They have not communicated to whites a feeling for the difficulties of being a Negro in the United States. They have not shown understanding or appreciation of—and thus have not communicated—a sense of Negro culture, thought or history."[37] The Kerner Report also states that "it is the responsibility of the news media to tell the story of race relations in America, and, with notable exceptions, the media have not turned to the task with the wisdom, sensitivity, and expertise it demands."[38]

If this charge is true for black Americans, it is also true for American Indians. How many Americans know of the conditions on reservations or among urbanized Indians? How many are aware of the true story of how Indians came to be dispossessed of their land? How many have any more than a naïve, misleading vision of eighteenth- and nineteenth-century naked savages running through forests whooping and hollering and making off with the innocent children of equally innocent, brave, and honest white settlers? The story of America's birth and its early nationhood is laced with accounts of how white men tamed the wild land, educated the savages, and gradually assumed benign dictatorship over nomadic peoples unable to control their own destiny and unwilling to rear their children as God-fearing, civilized citizens.

Such are the images of Indians throughout nearly two centuries of media "coverage." The neglect and the stereotyping have served the needs of the majority and so perhaps have been inevitable.

NOTES

1. Elmo Scott Watson, "The Indian Wars and the Press, 1866–67," *Journalism Quarterly* 17 (1940): 302.
2. William Blankenburg, "The Role of the Press in an Indian Massacre," *Journalism Quarterly* 45 (1968):64.
3. Ibid., p. 65.
4. Ibid., p. 61.
5. Ibid., p. 70.
6. *Bismarck Tribune,* extra edition, July 6, 1876, reprinted in *Wassaja,* August, 1975.
7. Ibid.
8. Elmo Scott Watson, "The Last Indian War, 1890–91: A Study of Newspaper Jingoism," *Journalism Quarterly* 20 (1943):205.
9. Ibid., p. 208.
10. Douglas C. Jones, "Teresa Dean: Lady Correspondent Among the Sioux Indians," *Journalism Quarterly* 49 (1972):656–62.
11. *Chicago Herald,* January 20, 1891, in Jones, "Teresa Dean," p. 658.
12. Jones, "Teresa Dean," p. 659.
13. Ibid., p. 662.
14. Terri Schultz, "Bamboozle Me Not at Wounded Knee," *Harper's,* June, 1973, p. 56.

15. Publisher's Introduction to *Voices from Wounded Knee*, p. 1.

16. Ibid.

17. Ibid., p. 136.

18. Neil Hickey, "Our Media Blitz Is Here to Stay," *TV Guide*, December 22, 1973, p. 22.

19. Ibid., pp. 22–23.

20. "An Empty Black Pit," *Akwesasne Notes*, Early Autumn, 1973, p. 4. Almost every issue of *Akwesasne Notes*, *Wassaja*, and other publications carried further developments in the mineral-rights struggle.

21. "Yavapais' Historic Struggle to Keep Fort McDowell," *Wassaja*, October, 1976, p. 10; "Pima Hopes Dashed," *Indian Affairs*, no. 92 (July–November, 1976), p. 2.

22. Estelle Fuchs and Robert J. Havighurst, *To Live on This Earth*.

23. *Wassaja*, January, 1973.

24. *Voices from Wounded Knee*, p. 261; "SD Reservation Ambush: 2 FBI Agents 'Executed,' " *Akwesasne Notes*, Early Winter, 1975, pp. 5–9.

25. *Voices from Wounded Knee*, p. 260.

26. Rick Brown, "The High Cost of Gresham," *Once a Year* 79 (1975):6–8.

27. Ada Deer, head (at the time of the takeover) of the Menominee Restoration Committee, who opposed the action, in conversation with the authors.

28. Richard La Course, " 'Backlash': Indian Media and the 'State of Siege,' " *Red Current*, Spring, 1978, p. 4.

29. Because of possible repercussions, the source remains unnamed. But it was thought appropriate to include this quote because it so effectively mirrors sentiments heard from many quarters.

30. Rupert Costo, ed., *Textbooks and the American Indian*.

31. Philip French, in "The Indian in the Western Movie," *Art in America* 60 (1972):32–39, begins to study this problem, as does Franklin Duchineaux in "The American Indian Today: Beyond the Stereotypes," *Today's Education* 62 (May, 1973):22–23. One is reminded also of Chief Bromden, an Indian character in Ken Kesey's *One Flew over the Cuckoo's Nest*.

32. Anna Lee Stensland, *Literature by and About the American Indian: An Annotated Bibliography*, p. 3.

33. Rita Keshena, "The Role of American Indians in Motion Pictures," *American Indian Culture and Research Journal* 1 (1974):26.

34. Richard La Course, "Image of the Indian," *Air Time*, January, 1975, p. 6.

35. Edward R. Murrow, in an address to the RTNDA convention, Chicago, Ill., October 15, 1958, quoted in Harry J. Skornia, *Television and Society* (New York: McGraw-Hill, 1965), pp. 228–29.

36. *Report of the National Advisory Commission on Civil Disorders* (New York: Bantam Books, 1968), p. 372.

37. Ibid., p. 383.

38. Ibid., p. 384.

46 · THE EMERGENCE OF BLACKS ON TELEVISION

BY REGINA G. SHERARD

In this article, Regina G. Sherard assesses the
emergence of blacks on television. After reading it,
compare her assessments with the current TV
program schedules. Have there been changes even
since this article was written? Are the roles better or
worse? What do viewers know as a result of these
programs? Are there other minorities "emerging" on
television—and how? There's hope for new black
involvement in television, but establishing
independent black television networks will take the
same pioneering spirit that gave birth to the black
press, says Sherard—"We wish to plead our own
cause." Sherard was a doctoral candidate at the
University of Missouri school of journalism when this
article was written. She teaches at the University of
North Carolina school of journalism. This article is
from the *St. Louis Journalism Review,* May 1982.

The political and economic development of blacks over the past two
decades has been both dramatic and superficial. The pattern of the
status of blacks in the media followed a similar motif. While the signs
of progress show evidence of social change and a consistent, if not
concerted, effort by the media to be responsive to the black community,
they also reflect a growing black consensus and a progressing level of
tolerance by a white-dominated field.

America's tendency toward supermarket journalism, where the consumer dictates what is or is not present in the media, has caused the
media to place greater emphasis on the consumers with the largest
amount of economic and social power. Historically, minorities have had
neither the economic nor social power and, therefore, have not played
a terribly important role in the media.

The involvement of blacks in the media has systematically focused
on exposure, broad visibility, the creation of role models and the potential for effecting change in attitudes with respect to positive imaging.

Although these priorities were fostered initially within the upper echelons of the media industry, they were dictated by the aggressive clamor
of blacks for political and economic justice. While the crude reality
bares such a quest to be nothing more than the adoption of an illusion
of power, the black experience in the media derived its momentum from
the "black power" movement of the sixties.

The ideology of black power, which found its support among the
alienated masses of urban residents has faded into the shadow of com-
placency. But during its zenith, the advocacy of black power embraced
the bitter disaffection of the poor with a militant determination.

The powerlessness of blacks had been clearly identified as a lack
of control over the institutions that affect and govern their lives, as well
as the inaccessibility to the "channels of communication, influence and
appeal," as the Kerner Commission reported. The struggle for power and
control requires access to those institutions directly responsible for
disseminating information to the masses and input into the depiction,
whether real or symbolic, of the reformists to the mass audience.

The National Commission on Civil Disorders (the Kerner Commission) charged, "The absence of Negro faces and activities from the
media has an effect on white audiences as well as black. If what the
white American . . . sees on television conditions his expectation of
what is ordinary and normal in the larger society, he will neither understand nor accept the black American. . . . But such attitudes, in an area
as sensitive and inflammatory as this, feed Negro alienation and intensify white prejudices."

The report of the commission, which had been appointed by President Lyndon Johnson to discover the causes of the rioting, remains the
definitive background piece on minority coverage in the media.

The commission stated: "By failing to portray the Negro as a matter
of routine and in the context of the total society, the news media have,
we believe, contributed to the black-white schism in this country."

The commission further emphasized this point by providing statistics concerning the small number of minorities employed in the media
at that time.

As a result, the media reluctantly opened its doors to blacks. What
has been described as a "running sore on the national body" by W.H.
Ferry would have been allowed to fester had the issue of black representation in the media been left solely to the conscience of the industry.

Nevertheless, the response by the media found consolation in the
fact that black people and their fight were big news, and the dictates of
a black agenda for power created a fertile environment for the development of a righteously dichotomous relationship, which continues to this
day.

Blacks are: inferior, lazy, dumb and dishonest; either clowns or
crooks; professional quacks and thieves without adequate skill and
ethics.

Such was the stereotyped portrayal of blacks perpetuated by network television in the CBS series, "Amos 'n' Andy." From 1951 until the network barred syndication and overseas sales of the program in 1966, the presentation of blacks was patently offensive. Although television had inherited "Amos 'n' Andy" from radio, the visual medium was explicit and glaring in its degradation and "black" humor.

The show's creators, Freeman Gosden and Charles Correll, expressed some concern over the visual adaption of the series. However, their concern did not reflect a sensitivity to blacks or the critical objections of the black community; instead the appeasement was in deference to the discomfort that white viewers may have experienced in seeing blacks on the television screen.

The U.S. Civil Rights Commission reports, "Gosden and Correll trained black actors to portray the characters in the nuances of the stereotype with which whites would be comfortable. Apparently, to avoid interaction between blacks and whites, Amos and Andy lived in an all-black world in which all the judges, policemen, shop owners, and city clerks were black."

To avoid affronting the sensibilities of a white audience and thereby risking the wrath of sponsors, network television focused its attention on blacks in roles that exploited the stereotype. As singers and tap dancers, blacks sustained the image of "having rhythm;" as maids, black women were doting "Aunt Jemimas" whose obeisant manner was met with condescension; as handymen, black men were basically slow-witted and recalcitrant misfits. To reinforce the idea of not taking blacks seriously, such "slice of life" programs portrayed them in contextual formats of comedy—situations in which they were ridiculed and laughed at under the guise of entertainment.

The 1950s was a period that saw a tremendous exertion of influence and control by advertisers in television programming.

Sponsors were also leery of having their products associated with blacks. An example is given of Nat King Cole, the first black to star in a network variety show, who experienced great difficulty in obtaining advertising support. When the show first aired on NBC in 1956, it was carried without commercial sponsorship. The popularity and performance in the ratings encouraged the co-sponsorship by Rheingold Beer, but it was not sufficient to sustain "The Nat King Cole Show" beyond a year.

When the networks began to assume control over program production, a ratings war ensued that pivoted around action-oriented entertainment shows. The "audience-flow" concept of television news imposes an entertainment function, which characterized news programming.

After the Supreme Court desegregation decision in 1954 and the acceleration of civil protests, the nation's attention was focused on the highly dramatic elements of the civil rights struggle. The vivid images of ". . . young Negroes dragged out of buildings, grim-jawed sit-ins surrounded by angry whites, hoodlums pouring mustard on the heads of blacks at a lunch counter, and police moving in with brutal swiftness" were brought into the homes of viewers during prime-time, reports William Small.

The television medium became very skilled at covering the "action" of the civil rights movement, with the "good guys and bad guys" clearly identified. Since the movement was for the most part a regional one in the South, the northern-based networks highlighted the atrocities with little recognition of the impending crisis at their own back door.

By 1964 a chain of events had been set in motion that did nothing less than shock an unprepared North and horrify an unsuspecting nation. Sixteen days after President Johnson signed the long-awaited Civil Rights Act, tension erupted in Harlem; after New York came Watts, Chicago, Cleveland, Detroit, Newark, Baltimore and Washington, D.C. As the black movement took a running leap in a direction that gave way to impatience and the assertion of power, the major issue became a question of control.

An idealistic goal at best, control of the community and control of institutions were interpreted as crucial in the decision-making that affects the black community. In the case of the media, the elements of control were realized through attempts to make news and programming relevant to the black community, reflective of the underlying cause of social unrest in the ghettos, a representative of a realistic as well as positive portrayal of blacks.

The dubiousness of some of these interests would cause some to wonder how relevancy is defined, for surely what is relevant to some may not be to all of the black community; and a realistic portrayal of blacks may not necessarily be a positive one. But as the formal news source relied upon in the black community, television was the main object of discontent.

In response to the charge that television coverage of the facts of black unrest had been magnificent in comparison to the underlying grievances, the networks hired a handful of black reporters to cover the riots and tell the story of the black experience. Some of the more noted reporters like Chuck Stone, Mal Goode, Robert Teague, Ted Coleman, William Matney and Wendell Smith achieved national acclaim.

A marriage of television and the black movement was imminent as Molefi Kete Asante described: "For television, the black movement could produce a massive demonstration of singing, chanting blacks, frequently attacked by fierce-looking state troopers and policemen. For blacks, television could cover the grievances and abuses of the black masses and send them nationwide, perhaps world-wide. . . ."

The vast coverage of developments on the civil rights scene served as a visual chronicler of black protest. Television newscasts presented blacks in a sympathetic light and familiarized the public with leaders who were recognized by the black community.

In news and public service programming that did not address the civil rights issue, blacks were conspicuously included to provide the "black perspective." On-the-scene reporters and field interviewers made sure that any representative group of Americans contained at least one black.

CBS broadcast a seven-part series, "Of Black America," in the "hot summer" of '68 that was hosted by black comedian Bill Cosby. But while the series was hailed as a first to address seriously the degradation of blacks by white America, it was severely criticized for employing few blacks in the planning and production of the series.

In the fall of that year, "Julia" made its debut on prime-time television with the recurring proclamation by NBC that it was being presented, "with pride." However, what was labeled as pride over the air may have been a boardroom decision of sublime resignation.

The U.S. Commission on Civil Rights reports, "The previous January NBC had rejected the pilot for the series. In February when the network's programming executives were preparing the fall schedule, they were faced with a half-hour to fill opposite CBS' popular "The Red Skelton Show." Believing that any of their potential choices would fail to be a match against Skeleton, Paul Klein of NBC's audience research department argued that selecting "Julia" to fill the empty time slot would accomplish something of social value."

Klein further argued that while "Julia" might be saccharine, ". . . it had racial importance at a time when television was under heavy criticism as a lily-white medium. With Diahann Carroll in the lead it would be the first situation comedy since the opprobrious "Amos 'n' Andy" to be built around a black person. . . . Although the show was a success by rating standards, the social value of "Julia" as a response is somewhat ludicrous."

The 1960s also saw a sudden recognition of black consumerism. When in 1963 the American Federation of Television and Radio Artists issued a statement promising to ". . . take affirmative steps toward the end that minority group performers are cast in all types of roles so that the American scene may be portrayed realistically," it was met a month later with the NAACP's adopted resolution ". . . calling for selective buying campaigns against the products of those who sponsor offensive motion pictures, television and radio programs or whose programs ignore the presence and achievement of American Negroes, or who refuse to give equal employment opportunity to Negroes."

White-owned businesses discovered that the more than 20 million black consumers of products advertised on television constituted a visible market. Attractive, mulatto-complexioned models were the most frequently seen type in commercials that initially featured blacks. But advertising lagged far behind the news and entertainment areas in utilizing black performers.

A survey conducted in March 1966 by the American Civil Liberties Union showed that blacks had 3.36 percent of the speaking roles and 8.49 percent of the non-speaking roles in regular television programs; less than 1 percent of the roles in television commercials went to black performers.

According to a report issued in 1964 by the Committee on Integration of the New York Society for Ethical Culture, the comparative findings of its monitoring survey conducted in 1962 and 1964 showed an increase from 2 to 36 black appearances in commercials and public service announcements.

In 1965, a television audit by Schmidt for Los Angeles revealed 2 percent of the commercials had black models. By the end of 1969, one audit study showed an increase up to 8 percent of commercials containing blacks. While these figures do not reflect absolute numbers of blacks being used in television commercials and are not necessarily indicative of any particular sensitivity on the part of sponsors, they do reflect a growing trend in the '60s that signaled recognition of the black dollar, if not that of the black problem.

The "Swinging 70s" ushered in a more permissive, youth-oriented era that had been adversely affected by the war at home and the war abroad. In an effort to respond to some of the more salient issues permeating a troubled society, such programs as "Mod Squad," "Storefront Lawyers," "The Man and the City," "The Young Lawyers," and "The Young Rebels" attempted to offer solutions. One element of relevancy common to this new genre of shows was the inclusion of young blacks. With the exception of "Mod Squad," a show built around the premise that young, hip cops could be effective working outside the system and yet maintain the establishment's principle of law and order, all the other shows failed.

Les Brown attributes the failure to their having created a "false aura of relevance" that was unrealistic: ". . . militants were not angry revolutionaries but paranoiacs or agents of hostile countries; . . . bigots, not true haters but merely persons who lived too long in isolation from other races; drug users not the disenchanted but victims of ghoulish weirdos and organized crime. Television faced the gut issues with false characters and instead of shedding light on the ailments of the social system and the divisions within it, the playlets distorted the questions and fudged the answers."

Brown also pointed to the motives of these programs: "For all their genuflections toward social awareness, the networks' intent was not so much to involve themselves with the real issues of the day as patently to exploit them for purposes of delivering up to advertisers more of the young consumers than before without alienating the older habitues of the medium."

An obvious aspect of these and other programs that followed in the '70s was the depiction of blacks in the role of "good guys." To reinforce the down-to-earth quality of these shows, the dialogue was heavily weighted with such black colloquialisms as "right-on," "get down," "brother," "sister," "the man," and "honky." These shows were off-shoots of the black exploitation movies that had been so popular with an element of the black audiences.

The "super-black" period was followed by variety shows and situation comedies that featured blacks as stars in the primary roles. Flip Wilson, Redd Foxx and Bill Cosby capitalized on a style of black humor that forced blacks to laugh at themselves; ghetto jokes and similar travesties on black life were popularized by television. A paradoxical characteristic of such programs was that they projected a positive and negative image of blacks—the black star who exploited the nuances of deprivation and depicted the brutal realities of poverty. For all the subtle implications of the "super-black" stereotype in television, these shows did provide a cushion for the presentation of more serious dramas that explored provocative themes.

One of the most popular and humorous treatments of controversial issues on television may be attributed to Norman Lear, whose realistic approach to contemporary social problems gave us such hits as "Maude," and "All in the Family." The black series, "Good Times" and "The Jeffersons," which were the respective spinoffs from Lear's premier comedies, were a tremendous success during the early '70s. The black shows had antithetical themes: "Good Times" explored the lives of the Evans family whose futile efforts to escape a Chicago ghetto combined equal amounts of pathos and humor, while the Jefferson family was the all-American story of rags-to-riches. Lear's black characters brought bigotry, discrimination and racial inequality into the open.

The style of the new black comedies represented new ground in the TV medium. Viewers were presented with characters who could joke about their miseries and laugh at their ignorance despite a constant array of harassment and insulting innuendo. But the National Black Feminist Organization took opposition to the sophisticated demeaning of blacks in many of the shows during the 1974 television season. In a statement reminiscent of the NAACP's 1951 complaint against "Amos 'n Andy," the organization made the following observations:

1. Black shows are slanted toward the ridiculous with no redeeming counter images;

2. Third World peoples are consistently cast in extremes;

3. When blacks are cast as professional people, the characters they portray generally lack professionalism and give the impression that black people are incapable and inferior in such positions;

4. When older persons are featured, black people are usually cast as shiftless derelicts or nonproductive individuals;

5. Few black women in TV programs are cast as professionals, paraprofessionals or even working people;

6. Black children, by and large, have no worthy role models on television.

The seventies was an impressive decade for blacks on television as their visibility in commercials, comedies, news and other areas of programming increased significantly. However, the critics would question whether this visibility constitutes an improvement from a sociological perspective. Are programs with black performers and so-called black themes merely grafts of the white image of reality; or is the black experience being revealed in its own environment and on its own terms?

Is the "Amos 'n Andy" syndrome being subtly perpetuated to stereotype blacks? Is television still stressing the "bad news" of the black community over its positive aspects? Has the television industry been as responsive in accelerating blacks behind the camera in management positions as it has been in showcasing them in front of the camera?

The questions arise not from a dispute of whether improvements have been made, but from the extent to which progressive advancement of blacks in television has made a positive impact on the social inequities within the medium. These and other concerns have prompted the development in recent years of such groups as the National Black Media Coalition and Black Citizens for Fair Media to monitor programs for their authenticity and fair representation of blacks.

As of 1979, 11 years after the Kerner Commission blasted the media for being ". . . shockingly backward in hiring, training and promoting" blacks, statistics indicated that television had not risen to the challenge:

• While composing 17 percent of the population, only two percent of all media practitioners are black;

• Approximately 99 percent of all news editors and station managers are white. While Detroit had the first black VHF television station in 1975, WHEC-TV in Rochester, New York, became the first black-owned station in 1979;

• Blacks have not been able to control cable television franchises in urban areas with a majority black population;

• Black students in journalism schools comprise less than four percent of the total enrollment.

William Hines of the *Chicago Sun Times* remarks that in a city like Washington, D.C., where the population in the central city is 70 percent black, ". . . there is no real black TV presence (not counting the obligatory black anchorman on every white-controlled station's nightly news show)."

It was a relatively easy move to employ blacks in positions that afforded visibility during a time when the issues of civil rights lent themselves so well to the visual medium. But in the 1980s different issues have emerged, some of which may not be as clearly defined as those during the 1960s: "Today the struggle in journalism is over a second generation of issues; tokenism in employment (as intolerable today to minorities as was exclusion in the sixties), and inaccurate, inadequate portrayal of minority communities (even less excusable than was total neglect years ago)."

An examination of the two popular black shows, "The Jeffersons" and "Different Strokes," points to an exploitation of old stereotypes transposed to atypical environments. George Jefferson is an ignorant, loud-mouthed man who screams at his family, insults his friends and berates his interracial in-laws with one-liners that inevitably focus on the "honky."

Whereas at one time it was considered unthinkable to openly cast aspersions on blacks, it is acceptable for George to be openly hostile to every white character in the show. But George is rich, and he owns a chain of cleaning stores, thereby functioning ostensibly like any other white business executive.

Arnold is an apple-cheeked 8-year-old who lives with his rich white adoptive father and his interracial siblings in a posh apartment. Having come from a ghetto environment, little Arnold has adjusted remarkably to his new family, exhibiting none of the usual trauma that one would expect from a child who had lost his only parent, none of the anticipated identity problems that youngsters under similar circumstances might experience.

Instead, Arnold has made the transition into a predominately white world with humorous ease and precocity. Furthermore, no one seems to notice that Arnold and his brother are black. In fact, neither do they.

Within the past five years, black entrepreneurs have placed an increased emphasis on media ownership. Whereas black-owned and black-oriented radio stations have been relatively common for many years, blacks have traditionally been unsuccessful in making any significant headway in the television industry. The most obvious reason is that with limited frequencies, the three major networks have monopolized ownership and programming, and local markets have been unreceptive.

With the advent of "low power" television, market segmentation will provide opportunities for blacks. On a recent edition of the black news program, the discussion focused on one such service that is currently being developed. Known as the Community Television Network, this low-power television service will offer a variety of minority and children's programming plus a nightly news broadcast. The Community Television Network is coordinated through the efforts of three black lawyers, Dan Winston, Booker Wade and Sam Cooper, all of whom were previously with the Federal Communications Commission. The new television service is being backed financially with $60 million from the Golden West Corporation, an affiliate of Gene Autry Enterprises, Inc. The new service is described as an adaptation of an old technology known as "television translator service," wherein CTN will provide new programming outlets for the black community within a range of 12 to 15 miles, compared to a range of 40 to 60 miles for traditional frequencies. It will also incorporate a subscription television service for pay subscribers who will receive "premium programming," including movies, selected entertainment features and sports.

The new direction of black involvement in the television industry will undoubtedly be at a snail's pace, and without sufficient support and resources, it will remain a goal and not a realization. Although such efforts as those initiated on behalf of the Community Television Network are encouraging, the question of survival becomes paramount in consideration of competition, advertising revenues, and audience appeal. Nevertheless, independent black television networks suggest the same pioneering attitude that gave birth to the black press—an attitude that was built upon the founding words, "We wish to plead our own cause."

47 · THE BLACK PRESS: DOWN BUT NOT OUT

BY PHYL GARLAND

An irony of civil rights and equal employment
opportunities has been the increased strain on black
newspapers to survive. They will survive, possibly as
the urban newspapers of the future, predicts Phyl
Garland, former New York editor of *Ebony* and now
on the faculty at Columbia's graduate school of
journalism. This article is from the *Columbia
Journalism Review,* September/October 1982.

On a dismal midwinter morning earlier this year, managing editor
Lou Ransom sat at the head of an oblong table in the cramped, window-
less conference room of the *New Pittsburgh Courier,* its offices located
on the blighted South Side of a city that once had been the very hub of
northeastern industrial activity but now struggled to stave off the en-
croachments of economic decline. The sporadic clattering of manual
typewriters, an obsolescent newsroom sound in this era of electronic
VDTs, filtered into the room, which was adorned with trophies and
plaques awarded to "America's Best Weekly" by the National Newspaper Publishers Association, an organization comprising most of those
who own the nation's approximately 200 black newspapers.

Ransom, twenty-nine, summarized his analysis of the pressures that
have plunged much of the black press into a state of crisis that has
persisted for more than a decade and shows signs of escalating. "The
way Reaganomics is hitting us, we're in a depression and it's *killing* us.
Not only the *Courier,* but *all* black newspapers," he said. "The first
place Reaganomics hits us is in advertising. Steel mills and other major
businesses are closing down in this area, and firms that used to set aside
a little bit of money to advertise in the *Courier* cut back on us before
they touch the two local dailies [*The Pittsburgh Press* and the *Pittsburgh Post-Gazette*]. They're getting thinner too. It's not just us, but it's
us first. And there has been an almost steady drop in circulation.

"If we're going to survive," Ransom went on to say, "we're going to have to re-evaluate the role we have to play because in the past the black press was everything for everybody. We can't afford to do that today. We must focus on who we want to reach. Most of our readers are older and buy the paper out of habit. But if we want to go for the money, we have to aim for the young professionals, the people advertisers want to reach. We have a lot of black college grads now and they're not being challenged by the *Courier* and other black papers. And they don't buy them either. They read the dailies, *Time*, and *Newsweek*, but they are *starving* for in-depth coverage of black affairs."

In his passion and profound concern for the future of the black press, Lou Ransom reminded me of myself so many years ago when I was an ardent reporter and editor for the old *Pittsburgh Courier*. (The word "New" was added to the name in 1966 when John H. Sengstacke, owner of the *Chicago Defender* chain, purchased the paper's assets in order to rescue it from impending bankruptcy.) One of two blacks to graduate from Northwestern University's School of Journalism in 1957, before student loans, ample scholarships, special programs, and affirmative action policies helped to boost the number of minority journalists, I had worked for the *Courier* during summers and joined the full-time staff in 1958.

Making Change Happen   Like most black journalists of my generation, I had not dreamt of seeing my by-line on the front page of *The New York Times*, *The Washington Post*, or the *Chicago Tribune*. This was not due to a lack of ambition but stemmed from an understanding of the realities that restricted our lives in those days of *de jure* segregation and overt racial hostility. Back then, blacks existed in a shadow world that was seldom, if ever, reflected in the pages of daily newspapers, which were staffed almost exclusively by whites and mirrored their mentality. If blacks were noticed at all, it was in a negative or condescending manner. *The Daily News* in my hometown of McKeesport, Pennsylvania, had carried a weekly back-page two- or three-inch column, headed "Afro-American," listing weddings, births, deaths, and club meetings, compiled from notes sent in by black readers. In white papers generally we were just as invisible as Ralph Ellison said we were.

But a far stronger element in the matter of career choice was the driving sense of commitment that impelled me, and others like me, to cast our lot with the black press. We considered it an effective, if sometimes strident, medium through which we might strike out at the forces that denied us opportunity and respect. This was in the years before the sit-ins, boycotts, freedom marches, mass protests, civil rights laws, and, quite significantly, the urban riots of the sixties had pried open the doors for black journalists, professionals, managers, educators, and skilled workers seeking a place in the mainstream of American life. For us, the black press *was* journalism. The best of our numbers considered ourselves warriors.

In my case, there was another decisive factor. Back in 1943, my mother, Hazel Garland, a housewife with bold aspirations, had liberated herself from the linoleum confines of her kitchen by becoming a stringer for the *Courier,* reporting on weekly events in the network of small towns surrounding Pittsburgh. Three years later when she joined the regular staff, receiving on-the-job training, she became a reporter and later women's and entertainment editor, eventually rising to the position of editor-in-chief in 1974—long after I had left the staff. So I had grown up with the *Courier.* She and her colleagues had been my role models. This was particularly important in a time and place where I had never seen a black sales clerk, bus driver, foreman, or school teacher. For me, journalists always had been special people who not only wrote about what happened but, as advocates of change, helped to make it happen.

The journalistic world that I had entered twenty-five years earlier differed dramatically from the one Lou Ransom was encountering. Though the *Courier,* founded in 1910, had begun its long decline by the fifties, some of the luster of its old glory days remained even then. My co-workers on the national and city desks could recall the boom of the World War II years that spilled over into 1947, when the paper had hit its peak of more than 350,000 copies distributed weekly through twenty-three editions covering all parts of the country. It had set an all-time audited circulation record for black newspapers, and the presses ran daily, from Sunday through Thursday. By contrast, Lou Ransom was presiding over the remains of an enterprise that had shrunk, almost unbelievably, to 10,000 local copies per week, with another 10,000 reached by a skimpy national edition. Even the handsome three-story structure that had housed the *Courier* of my day, set snugly at 2628 Centre Avenue in the heart of Pittsburgh's black Hill District, where folks from the neighborhood could bring their grievances with the guarantee of an immediate hearing, has been demolished. The current rented quarters on South Carson Street are at the edge of a white working-class neighborhood, far from the action.

No less severe had been the decline in prestige. "It was the kind of paper that commanded respect and was widely quoted. If you were running for office on any level, you stopped by the *Courier* to pay homage," recalls Harold L. Keith, who had worked there for eighteen years and was editor when he left in 1963. Now director of publications and information for the Department of Housing and Urban Development and a confirmed, high-level civil servant, Keith eagerly reminisces about the *Courier*'s numerous crusades against Jim Crow, lynching ("seemed there was a lynching or two every week"), segregation in the armed forces, job discrimination, and rampant racial injustices. He remembers the time when Wendell Smith, the sports editor, helped negotiate Jackie Robinson's introduction into major league baseball, breaking that color barrier. "The galvanizing force that made it go was the institution of racism—we were Negroes then. All of us felt involved and it gave us the impetus to work for little money to do the best job we could to fight that institution. We had outstanding reporters in the South, some of them white, who risked their lives to do things like infiltrate the Ku Klux Klan to bring us the news."

And there was the camaraderie. "We had some of the best journalists in the country, trained and highly intelligent people," says Keith, who earned his master's degree in history from the University of Pittsburgh, where he also undertook pre-doctoral studies. "After we had finished our work, we would sit around the desk and discuss every conceivable thing. It was inspirational and informational. You looked forward to going to work because something was always happening. It was really a great place." He adds nostalgically, "I would have been at the *Courier* today if things were right."

But they weren't.

Out of Sync   Many have said that the *Pittsburgh Courier,* like other black newspapers and black institutions as a whole, was a victim of the integration it so doggedly fought for, that providence gave black people an ironic kick in the bottom when they were granted, at least ostensibly, what they had said they wanted. This is a simplistic view and Harold Keith maintains that poor management was a major factor, along with the impact of changing times. "Advertisers pulled out when the paper began covering the movement, though it never had been that successful in getting ads," he notes. When advertising revenue was diminished, management responded "by cutting the staff, getting rid of the people who made it go, while the hangers-on stayed. Management was not willing to invest in newsgathering."

The mistakes of the fifties were considerable and consistent. In an attempt to modernize, the *Courier*'s management invested heavily in a magazine section and color comics featuring black characters, a novelty that did not pay off. It reduced its size from that of a full-scale paper to a tabloid without preparing the public, which felt cheated by the smaller product. In the mid-fifties, when a young minister named Martin Luther King, Jr., led a boycott against segregated bus seating in Montgomery, Alabama, and a civil rights movement that was to alter American history had gotten under way, the *Courier* published a series of articles called "What's Good About the South" by George S. Schuyler, the house conservative and a literary holdover from the Harlem Renaissance. Readers were enraged and circulation dropped. During this critical period, a radical new columnist named Elijah Muhammad appeared in the

Courier's pages, criticizing religious institutions, among other things, as he gained the national exposure necessary to build his Black Muslim organization. This enraged the ministers whose congregations had been the paper's mainstay, and circulation dropped even further. When the column, "Mr. Muhammad Speaks," was discontinued in 1959, followers of the Muslim leader took with them another 25,000 in circulation, for they had been selling the paper in the streets, a method they later used to boost their own publication, *Muhammad Speaks,* to a claimed half-million sales. And, as civil rights became news, mainstream dailies and television began covering stories that once had been the exclusive property of the black press, introducing an unprecedented element of competition.

In spite of these problems, the *Courier* might have continued to prosper had it not been for management's tendency to stand at political odds with its employees and its readership. In 1932, publisher Robert L. Vann had helped to swing the black vote from "The Party of Lincoln" to the Democrats. But Vann, like his successor, Ira F. Lewis, switched parties when he thought black support was being taken for granted, and when Vann died, in 1940, he died a Republican. In 1948 his widow, Jessie L. Vann, emerged from her Oakmont estate to assume leadership of the business. She decided that the paper should remain Republican in its endorsements at a time when blacks were almost solidly Democratic. As Keith recalls, "Their politics weren't right. They were totally out of sync with black aspirations in politics and other activities."

The situation was exacerbated in 1959 when S. B. Fuller, a conservative Chicago cosmetics manufacturer, assumed control. He decided that the *Courier* would no longer be a black paper but an integrated news organ emphasizing "positive" matters and avoiding all controversy, this at a time when blacks were becoming increasingly militant. For those of us who experienced these sieges of mismanagement, the sense of helplessness and frustration—it seemed ridiculous that, due to a lack of correspondents, we should be covering the civil rights movement largely by telephone—was all but unendurable.

Like many of my colleagues, I left the *Courier,* in 1965, moving on to *Ebony,* flagship magazine of the prosperous and soundly managed Johnson Publishing Company. Mainstream publications were beginning to hire blacks, but for some of us that still was not a choice we cared to make. As Harold Keith notes, "I never thought of the white press as a career. I saw no hope there, no future. The rule was that you might get in but you could not enter the boardroom. And it still is. Bob Maynard [editor and publisher of the *Oakland Tribune*] is the exception. The white press represents the same institutions that we used to fight. There was no way that I could do the kind of job I wanted to do there, and I would not be happy."

Of Dreams and Needs   Looking back over the years, those of us who were fortunate enough to pass through the world of the old *Pittsburgh Courier* realize that it was part of a dream that might never again be able to come true for the black press. Many others, throughout the country, shared that dream.

When Robert S. Abbott founded the *Chicago Defender* in 1905 with nothing but a card table, a few pencils, and a tablet as his assets, he foresaw the need for a black publication that would address not only the few educated blacks and their white sympathizers, as had been the case with the early black press, but that would appeal to and perhaps stir the masses. The *Defender,* which is credited with inspiring the great migration of blacks from the South to the North, a trend that has subsided only in recent years, attained a national circulation of more than 200,000 after World War I. Published on a daily basis since 1956, it now claims to reach 35,000 daily and 40,000 with its weekend edition.

A few of the old guard, especially the family-owned *Afro-American* chain of Baltimore, which dates from 1892, have retained a healthy level of respectability, but there are no real circulation giants among today's black newspapers. A 1981 marketing study undertaken for Amalgamated Publishers, Inc., which coordinates national advertising sales for eighty-eight of the largest black newspapers in sixty-eight cities, states that they have a combined readership of 2,537,000—a total arrived at on the basis of a telephone survey rather than circulation figures. This is pitifully small when one considers that a single "white" paper—the Sunday New York *Daily News*—has a circulation of more than 2,000,000. Increasingly, the question arises as to whether black newspapers will survive this period of integration, inflation, and recession.

"Black papers are a miracle in themselves because they have managed to survive on money so minimal that white publishers wouldn't even consider existing on that level," says Raymond H. Boone, who spent sixteen years with the nine-paper *Afro-American* chain and is now a visiting professor of journalism at Howard University. "Those black papers that have survived deserve a lot of credit, though they should be chided for not remaining committed to their basic purpose, which should be to provide leadership in attacking all the dangers that still confront blacks."

A firebrand who, as a Pulitzer juror, spearheaded the successful fight to have blacks and women represented on the Pulitzer board, Boone says that the objective of today's black papers should be to concentrate on "external and internal enemies." Of the "internal" type, he says, "Some of our problems are matters that only *we* can solve—getting out the vote, keeping our kids in school so that they'll be able to compete for jobs, learning how to use our money properly, doing something about black-on-black crime. Black papers need to offer leadership to the community and to encourage greater self-reliance." But he does not downplay the importance of "external" factors, noting, "We are involved in a war of ideas these days and the black community is so greatly underarmed. That's why we need a strong black press. Most owners of white papers are conservative and are concerned about maintaining white power in this country. Their papers are political weapons and *not* simply objective disseminators of the news."

When Boone, forty-four, left the *Afro* chain, he did not seek a job in the mainstream, although he had worked for dailies in Virginia and Massachusetts before earning his journalism degree from Boston University. "It is difficult to go to the so-called enemy when you have been critical of them, and that was the position I was in. But I never have considered the white press the ultimate. My position was, hey, they ought to take a look at what *I'm* doing. I think I did it *better* than they did when it came to covering race relations."

For younger black journalists, who tend to be as concerned about career-building as their white counterparts, there are too many competing lures to keep them long associated with publications that offer limited financial rewards, although they, too, retain a kind of loving loyalty.

"The only thing that distinguishes black newspapers from the others is their lack of resources. The best people are quickly stolen away," says Fletcher Roberts, thirty-five, who was stolen away from the *Baltimore Afro-American* on August 9, 1974. He recalls the date, for it was the day Richard Nixon resigned as president. Roberts and a friend had been drinking champagne in celebration of the event and of the *Afro*'s catchy headline: AMEN in two-inch caps. The phone rang and it was the executive editor of the Annapolis *Capital,* who knew of Roberts's work and offered him a job at the white daily for more money. He accepted. "At the *Afro* I was earning $135 a week, working sometimes fifteen hours a day. This was less than I had been earning as a school teacher, and then I had summers off." Now a staff writer for *The Boston Globe,* Roberts says he enjoyed his days in the black press. "I felt a sense of purpose because I thought that what I was doing was important. What went on there really *mattered* to me." During his eighteen months on the *Afro-American* staff, he shot pictures, worked in the dark room, did layouts, reporting, editing, and "learned the whole operation." But, he warns, the lack of resources is a serious handicap. "How many black papers use offset printing or have VDTs? How many can afford to hire specialists to cover the environment, the law, science, and other complex fields? At the *Afro* we had six reporters. Here at the *Globe* we have eighty-five to a hundred. If you don't have the resources, you can't even get people *to* the story."

Greener Pastures   Roberts is part of the shrinking group of black journalists who entered the field through the black press, once the common route. Far more of the students I meet in my classes these days at Columbia don't consider it a viable option. This translates into a problem for black publishers, who say they cannot upgrade their products because they have difficulty finding qualified people.

Linda Prout, twenty-nine, had worked in New York as a researcher at ABC-TV news, as a reporter-critic at WBAI radio, as an assistant editor at *Us* magazine, and as a general assignment reporter at the Newark *Star-Ledger* before earning her master's degree at Columbia and moving on to her current position as a reporter-researcher at *Newsweek*. Throughout her varied experience, she never considered working for a black publication because "those in the New York area weren't of a very good quality and also didn't pay that well. I didn't want to work for a publication that called itself black but didn't address important black issues or do it with any sense of quality. Besides, money would be a big factor because most of the people I know working in the black press have a hard time making it." She concedes that she would consider it a step backwards to move to a black publication even if the position were much higher than the beginner's spot she holds at *Newsweek*. "I don't even know that many people who, on a continuous basis, read black newspapers. Most of the people I know consider them pretty tacky." In spite of her reservations, Prout affirms there is a strong need for black newspapers, noting, "The white press doesn't address issues from a black perspective. If there were a really *good* paper, I know of a lot of people working in the white press who would contribute to it."

Those who have remained in the black press are not unaware of the criticisms that have been leveled against the papers they produce. And they are quite aware of the greener pastures out there. At the almost inaccessible editorial offices of New York's *Amsterdam News,* located at the top of four steep flights of stairs in the firm's building near Harlem's 125th Street, Melvin Tapley muses wistfully about his options. After more than twenty years on the staff as a cartoonist, writer, and entertainment editor, Tapley has not abandoned the thought of moving into the mainstream. "They used to say that the black press was made up of people who couldn't go anywhere else, and at one time there was no place else we *could* go. But that's not true of most of the people who are here now." Citing the names of some *Amsterdam News* alumni, notably C. Gerald Fraser of *The New York Times,* Tapley says of himself, "I figured that maybe if they thought I was doing something outstanding, they would tap me on the shoulder. But I'm still waiting." His main reason for moving would be "money, no doubt about it!"

Tapley does not flinch when the weekly's flaws are pinpointed, explaining, "I realize that we work under certain handicaps. We have a small staff—about a dozen, plus stringers—and there's a lot of pressure on us. People send in clippings to us circling the typos and grammatical errors, but that's not all bad because we know that at least they're reading the paper. But we don't have any copy editors. We have to proof our own stuff."

Although American life has changed much over the years, Tapley sees few major changes in the paper, the main one being a women's section that no longer focuses on society news. Says Tapley, "The change came in the late sixties when the attitude emerged that there was no black society to compare with white society, and that the demonstrators were protesting not only against whites but also against middle-class blacks who wanted to be white but couldn't quite make it." Social affairs and community events, he says, still get wide coverage because a void is being filled. "Even today, when it comes to matters like weddings, you don't rate the dailies unless you're Whitney Young's daughter or some executive known to the white world. For little black people, we're still the best chance they have. Little white people don't have anything at all."

The *Amsterdam News* has an audited circulation of 41,000, which is hardly impressive considering that New York City has a larger black population than any metropolitan center outside of Africa. Its managing editor, William Egyir, is perhaps even more critical of the paper than are some outsiders. A Ghanaian who studied journalism in his homeland and London before coming to this country ten years ago, Egyir spent four years as an editor at the *Baltimore Afro-American* and helped train young journalists at Brooklyn's minority-based Trans-Urban News Service between two stints as the *Amsterdam*'s m.e.

"The *Afro* is much better run, is a much more disciplined organization than this one," says Egyir with a sardonic grin. "It has been owned by the Murphy family for generations and they have trained their young to handle it, though relatives have been fired when it seemed that they were not doing their job properly. Here, there seems to be no sense of leadership, no direction. If this paper had the sort of direction the *Afro* had, it could be a tremendous success, for we are operating in the largest market in the nation. We have two million blacks in this city. Think of what we could do if we could capture even *half* of them! But we haven't been able to address the issues as they affect black people. That is the most important thing. We need more investigative pieces and more well-written pieces."

Egyir joined the *Amsterdam* staff in the late seventies, after the paper had come under heavy attack for mixing private political concerns with editorial purpose. Founded in 1909, the newspaper had been primarily owned and operated by C. B. Powell, a Harlem physician, from 1936 until 1971, when it was sold, for $2 million, to a consortium of prominent blacks that included then-Manhattan borough president Percy Sutton. Under the editorship of Bryant Rollins, formerly a *Boston Globe* reporter and founding editor of the black-oriented *Bay State Banner*, the *Amsterdam News* abandoned its old sensational mold to emphasize in-depth treatment of pertinent issues and reflective social commentary. The new image was quickly tarnished when the paper increasingly began to reflect Sutton's personal views, its pages liberally sprinkled with encomiums to the politician, his relatives, and his friends. In 1972, worried about compromising his journalistic integrity, Rollins left the paper and it soon reverted to its old blood-and-guts format. But controversy continued to rage as to whose interests the paper was serving, Sutton's or the black community's. Sutton no longer has a financial interest in the paper, but the *Amsterdam News* has not recovered from the loss of stature it suffered during that period.

New Leaders   If the old war-horses of the black press are having such a difficult time merely going through their traditional paces, then where is there any hope of revitalization?

One beam of light seems to be flickering up from Philadelphia, where a new national black weekly newspaper began publication at the end of April. The promise it offers was strong enough to attract Lou Ransom, who left the *Courier* shortly after I interviewed him to join the staff of *The National Leader* as senior editor and production manager. The new paper is the brainchild of Ragan Henry, a Harvard-trained attorney who entered the media investment field in 1972. Two years later, he created Broadcast Enterprises National, Inc., now the largest black-owned radio-television company in the country. To launch the paper, which has an initial $600,000 capitalization, he formed a sister firm called Publishers Enterprises National, Inc., with seven other black investors.

A tabloid-sized publication that incorporates some aspects of both magazines and newspapers, *The National Leader* features long articles focusing on issues of national importance to blacks, such as the plight of the Haitian boat people; the hardships endured by migrant workers; the threat to Meharry, the nation's oldest black medical school; and the NAACP boycott of Hollywood. Separate sections cover topics in education, religion, business, culture, style, and sports, while the paper's editorials are sharply to the point. The columnists are leading black journalists long associated with the mainstream press: Dorothy Butler Gilliam and William Raspberry of *The Washington Post,* syndicated columnist Carl T. Rowan, and Claude Lewis, whose commentary appeared in the Philadelphia *Bulletin* for twelve years before he became publisher of *The National Leader.*

For Lewis, whose journalistic career encompasses ten years at *Newsweek* plus stints at the *New York Herald Tribune,* NBC, and Westinghouse Broadcasting as well as *The Bulletin,* this is an initial venture into the black press and he is starting at the top. It is a challenge he welcomes. When *The Bulletin* folded, Lewis had eleven job offers from the mainstream, but he willingly accepted Ragan Henry's invitation to head up the new enterprise because "this seemed to be the most fun and the most challenging. In any of the other places I would essentially have gone on doing what I already had done, but this was something black and national. We are writing for people who have common interests and we can address them. These are people with whom we can identify. It frees you up to be more open, honest, and direct."

He asserts that this publication, which, unlike the black national papers of the past, does not have a locally based market, is filling a void. "There's a need for a national publication of this sort because events in Boston have implications for people in Berkeley, as those in Selma have implications for people in Seattle. There is a need for black people across the nation to share information so that they might better understand their situation. We are establishing a network that will address problems and keep black Americans informed on major events." The need is pointed up, Lewis says, by a sharp decline in coverage of blacks by the dailies and television. "We are no longer chic. Meanwhile, other organizations and movements have stolen our thunder and our techniques—feminists, the gays, and other groups—and attention has turned toward these others. They do deserve notice and have legitimate claims, but this should not be at the expense of blacks."

The National Leader seems to be off to a healthy start. The operation is streamlined, with a core editorial staff of six in the Philadelphia office; correspondents or stringers file from twenty-eight cities throughout the country. Initial paid circulation was 30,000, but by late July it had grown to 63,000, the bulk of distribution being through subscriptions as efforts are made to develop newsstand sales.

While Claude Lewis is new to the black press, managing editor Pat Patterson brings to the venture a rare breadth of view. The second black to join the staff of *Newsday*—he was hired as a general reporter back in 1963—Patterson has reported for, edited, and published black newspapers and was the founding editor of *Black Enterprise* magazine, where he still holds the title of editor at large.

Evaluating the current conservative drift in society and comparing it with the liberalism of the sixties and early seventies, Patterson says, "In the sixties, we rather blindly fell for an integrationist philosophy without considering the consequences to ourselves. We had the mistaken assumption that there was this great pool of benevolence out there that had been untapped and that, as soon as it was, everything would be all right. There was an awful lot of naiveté. I think we've learned from our mistakes. I think we've learned not to forsake ourselves for something at the end of the rainbow. Enough of us have learned through experience that we must maintain our strong identity with things black, that we must strengthen our institutions, whether they be the press, the schools, the church, or black business. We may make some other mistakes, but I don't think we're going to make that *particular* mistake again."

If *The National Leader* is a promising beam, the virtual beacon of a promise fulfilled beckons from California, where William H. Lee's *Sacramento Observer* might well hold the key to a bright new future for black journalism. Lee, a successful real estate broker, founded the weekly in 1962, when he was only twenty-six. In 1968, he sold his real estate business to become a full-time newspaper publisher with his wife, Kathryn, as managing editor. That was the turning point for a publication that now is widely regarded as the best black newspaper in the United States. In 1973, the National Newspaper Publishers Association first presented it with the John B. Russwurm award. It has earned the award, which commemorates the founder of the first black newspaper, in five out of the last eight years. Based in Sacramento County, where the census says there are 59,000 blacks out of nearly 800,000 residents, the paper claims a circulation of 44,000. Its success has given rise to offshoots, including a San Francisco paper called *The Observer,* which claims a circulation of 48,000; a two-year-old paper in Stockton with 6,000 readers; and an entertainment magazine called *The Happenings,* published in Los Angeles.

A cursory examination of any issue of *The Sacramento Observer* yields ample evidence of the reasons why it is succeeding while so many others are floundering. Its graphics are boldly imaginative. While local stories are played aggressively, it includes neatly encapsulated portions of national news. Major issues are given thorough and thoughtful treatment and special sections provide extensive coverage of a single topic from a variety of perspectives, from black-Jewish relationships to the questions blacks should consider when sending their children to private schools.

Bill Lee approaches publishing with an ebullience that seems to be lacking elsewhere, and his aspirations as to what he might accomplish with his paper apparently know no bounds. In November, he is planning to celebrate the paper's twentieth anniversary by publishing a 500-page edition, to be distributed statewide, that will serve as a major source reference on black life in California.

But what makes Bill Lee go? What does he have to say to other black publishers who seem to be struggling to avoid extinction?

"Creativity in approach," Lee responds. "We don't pretend to have all the answers, but we know that we've got to be more competitive in trying to get readers. We must provide them with something they'll buy because they want it. We can't just give them civil rights news and black news; we've also got to show them how they can survive, how they can buy a house or live happily. In our communities we have acute health problems, acute crime problems, and we must provide some of the answers through our papers."

Good enough, but nothing that has not already been said by others. What distinguishes Lee from other publishers is his conception of a totally different role for black newspapers. "I honestly see us assuming a new role, becoming the urban newspapers of the future," he comments. "Our cities have become increasingly black, and white papers have been unable or unwilling to reach this audience. Some have brought blacks in and tried to incorporate them into the operation, but this still can't give them the kind of credibility we can have. Our papers can fulfill the function of providing urban news and showing people how to cope with the urban environment, a role that white newspapers ultimately may give up. That can be our future."

It is an idea well worth considering.

For Further Reading

David Armstrong, *A Trumpet to Arms: Alternative Media in America.* Los Angeles, Calif.: Tarcher, 1981.

Gordon L. Berry and Claudia Mitchell-Kernan, *Television and the Socialization of the Minority Child.* New York: Academic Press, 1982.

Edmund Ghareeb, *Split Vision: The Portrayal of Arabs in the American Media.* Washington, D.C.: American-Arab Affairs Council, 1983.

James E. Murphy and Sharon M. Murphy, *Let My People Know: American Indian Journalism: 1828–1978.* Norman, Okla.: University of Oklahoma Press, 1981.

Judy E. Pickens, *Without Bias: A Guidebook for Nondiscriminatory Communication,* second edition. New York: Wiley, 1982.

Report of the National Advisory Commission on Civil Disorders. Washington, D.C.: U.S. Government Printing Office, 1968.

Bernard Rubin, *Small Voices and Great Trumpets: Minorities and the Media.* New York: Praeger, 1980.

L. E. Sarbaugh, *Intercultural Communication.* Rochelle Park, N.J.: Hayden, 1979.

XIII

Mass Media and Women

"THE LADIES, bless 'em, have to be protected. No general assignment reporting. No police beat—unless, of course, in disguise to help on an exposé. The desk? Let them read proof because they're good with details. Or let them be in charge of 'Society.' "

Those cliches from the newspaper business are dying out—thanks, in part, to the men and women who are proving them absurd. But across the mass media there are still problems to be solved, goals to be set and achieved. In her 1983 annual survey of women in newsroom management, Dorothy Jurney counted 361 women and 3057 men in directing editorships at U.S. daily newspapers. In 1977 the numbers were 165 and 3025. But, she added, "There are more women policymakers (208) on the under-25,000 papers than on all the other dailies put together."

In terms of recognized leadership roles, women have made it at smaller papers. On magazines and in broadcasting, the situation's much the same, though there hasn't been a Dorothy Jurney to keep track of the numbers.

In this section, Terri Schultz-Brooks gives details on newsroom gains that have been made by women in recent years, often at great cost, she adds, not in great numbers.

Concern about women in the media isn't limited to women in management. There are questions about equal pay for equal work, equal assignments and working conditions. And there are questions about the portrayal of women in news, features, entertainment programs, advertising.

The variety and number of women's magazines, and the advertising that helps support them, have changed in recent years, as Sheila J. Gibbons explains. These developments are because of women's changing roles and changing interests. The new magazines will continue as long as reader interest and advertising support do, which leads to a question: What's next for women?

Lori Kesler describes how marketing to women has changed, how companies are trying to make their products and services more appealing to post-Superwoman women. The article should prompt discussion along several lines: marketing's view of women as conspicuous consumers; how women should react to marketing programs directed to them; the changing view of women, from Superwoman, who can do everything and be glamorous through it all, to 40-with-wrinkles is fine.

Admittedly, the articles in this section just touch the issues involving women and the media. They should start discussion of others.

48 · GETTING THERE: WOMEN IN THE NEWSROOM

BY TERRI SCHULTZ-BROOKS

Terri Schultz-Brooks, a freelance writer who is on the faculty at New York University, recounts the changes in newsrooms since the late 1960s and challenges the media and women journalists to "scale the topmost peaks." This article is from *Columbia Journalism Review,* March/April 1984.

When I walked into the city room of the *Chicago Tribune* my first day on the job, I saw a sea of white male faces above white rumpled shirts; in true *Front Page* tradition, a few reporters puffed on cigars and a few editors wore green eyeshades. That was in 1968. When I left four years later, things hadn't changed much, and I filed a sex discrimination complaint against the paper. Now, twelve years later, 29 percent of the *Tribune*'s general assignment reporters are women. The associate editor is a woman and so is the head of the sports copydesk. "In the old days, women turned on each other; now we turn *to* each other," says Carol Kleiman, associate financial editor and columnist for the paper, and a member of its women's network. "The only place I'm weak is getting women into the higher positions—running the foreign, national, and local desks. But they'll get there," says James Squires, the *Tribune*'s editor.

Gone are the days when women in journalism who wanted to write hard news were condemned to the "soft-news ghettos" of the society, food, or gardening pages, the sections considered second-class journalism by the men who run the papers. Now they not only report on issues of significance to women—from day care to birth control—but also cover the White House and the locker room, the streets of Beirut and the villages of El Salvador. Thirty-six years ago, when Pauline Frederick was hired by ABC as the first woman network news correspondent, she was assigned not only to interview the wives of presidential contenders at a national political convention, but also to apply their on-camera makeup. Today, on most large papers, 30 to 40 percent of the hard-news reporters are women. In television, 97 percent of all local newsrooms had, by 1982, at least one woman on their staffs, as compared to 57 percent in 1972.

Some women have even worked their way into upper management: Mary Anne Dolan is editor of the *Los Angeles Herald Examiner;* Kay Fanning is managing editor of *The Christian Science Monitor;* Sue Ann Wood is managing editor of the *St. Louis Globe-Democrat;* Gloria B. Anderson was managing editor of *The Miami News* until October 1981, when she co-founded the weekly she co-publishes and edits, *Miami Today.* "I remember when there was no such thing as a woman copy editor—the reasoning being that you can't give a woman authority over a man," says Eileen Shanahan, former *New York Times* reporter (one of seven who sued that paper for sex bias) and now senior assistant managing editor of the *Pittsburgh Post-Gazette,* the number-three spot on the paper.

One hundred and twenty newspapers now have women managing editors, according to Dorothy Jurney of Wayne, Pennsylvania, an independent researcher and veteran editor whose annual survey of women in newsroom management appeared in the January issue of the *Bulletin of the American Society of Newspaper Editors.* And about fifty of the country's 1,700 daily papers have women publishers, says Jean Gaddy Wilson, an assistant professor of mass communications at Missouri Valley College who, aided by grants from Gannett, Knight, and other foundations, will release in early summer the first results of what promises to be the most comprehensive study to date of women working in the news media.

The Limits of Change   But serious barriers do remain. "I've seen a lot of change, but it hasn't gone far enough," says Shanahan. Top management jobs in large media corporations are nearly as closed to women now as they were twenty years ago. The situation at *The Washington Post* is fairly typical. The *Post* has beefed up the number of women on its news staff considerably since it reached an out-of-court settlement in 1980 with more than one hundred women there who had filed a complaint of sex discrimination with the Equal Employment Opportunity Commission; it has even appointed a woman, Karen DeYoung, as editor of foreign news, and another, Margot Hornblower, as chief of its coveted New York bureau. "The number of qualified bright female candidates has never been higher," says executive editor Benjamin C. Bradlee. But there are currently no women staff foreign correspondents, and "there aren't many of us in power jobs," says Claudia Levy, editor of the *Post*'s Maryland Weekly section and head of the women's caucus that negotiated the settlement. While Bradlee says he "sure as hell" plans to move women into top editing jobs, they don't include his. "I've seen ten thousand stories on my possible successor, and none has mentioned a woman," he says.

More than half of the women managing editors are at newspapers of less than 25,000 circulation; at large papers, men still hold 90.4 percent of the managing editorships, Jurney has found. Indeed, only 10.6 percent of all jobs at or above the level of assistant managing editor at all daily and Sunday papers are filled by women. And most of those editing jobs are in feature departments, positions generally not considered "on line" for top management slots, which are usually filled from within the newsroom.

In broadcasting, progress is equally mixed. Ten years ago, there were almost no female news directors. Now, women are in charge of 8 percent of television newsrooms and 18 percent of radio newsrooms. More than one-third of all news anchors are women, but there has never been a solo woman anchor—nor, for that matter, a female co-anchor team—assigned permanently to any prime-time weeknight network news program. Nor is there likely to be in the near future.

On local stations, the news team is usually led by a man with a younger woman in a deferential role. Only 3 percent have survived on-camera past the age of forty; nearly half of all male anchors, on the other hand, are over forty. And only three women over age fifty appear regularly in any capacity before network cameras—Marlene Sanders, Barbara Walters, and Betty Furness. (One reason Christine Craft was pulled from her anchor slot at KMBC-TV in Kansas City, Missouri, was because she was "not deferential to men." She was also told that, at age thirty-eight, she was "too old" for the job.)

In top broadcast management jobs, many women feel they are moving backwards. A few years ago, NBC had one female vice-president in the news division: now it has none. CBS had four out of eleven; now it has·one out of fourteen. "There are no women being coached for key positions," says a female former vice-president of the CBS news division, who requested anonymity. "There's no more pressure from Washington, so anything management does for women its views as make-nice, as charity."

"Women feel fairly stuck," concurs CBS correspondent Marlene Sanders, who has broken a number of broadcast barriers—as the first woman TV correspondent in Vietnam, the first woman to anchor a network evening news show (she substituted temporarily for a man), and the first woman vice-president of news at any network. "We may have to wait for another generation—and hope those men in power have daughters whom they are educating, and whom they can learn from."

Resistance—and Revenge   What progress has been made has not come easily. Although Carole Ashkinaze, for example, wanted to be a political reporter, she accepted a position as a feature columnist with *The Atlanta Constitution* in 1976, bringing with her nearly a decade of experience as a hard-news reporter at *Newsday, The Denver Post,* and *Newsweek* (where about fifty women filed a sex-bias complaint in 1972). Her first column—about Jimmy Carter's 51.3 Percent Committee, formed to develop a pool of women for possible political appointment —sent ripples of disapproval through the *Constitution*'s management ranks. "The editors' reaction was: 'We hope you're not going to do that kind of story as a steady diet,' " she recalls. "But women came out of the woodwork, saying 'Please keep writing about this kind of thing.' " Subsequent columns were about battered women, problems in collecting child-support payments, abortion. She wrote about inequality wherever she saw it, and even began a crusade to get a women's bathroom installed near the House and Senate chambers in the state capitol. While male legislators could run to their nearby private bathroom, listen to piped-in debates, and return to their seats in less than a minute, women legislators had to go to the far end of the capitol building and line up behind tourists in the public restroom. "They finally gave the women a restroom, and the women gave me a certificate of commendation," says Ashkinaze.

After about a year, management gave in to her request and she was moved to the city room as a political reporter, but kept her column, in which she now writes about everything from racism to feminism to the environment. In August 1982, she became the first woman ever appointed to the paper's editorial board. "I'm very proud of it, and very humble, because I realize it's a result not only of my talents, but of what women in the South have been fighting for for decades," she says. "It's wonderful for other women at the paper to see more women here in positions of authority. It's something we've never had before." Fifteen women now hold editing and management jobs at the paper. "When I came here," Ashkinaze recalls, "these positions truly weren't open to women. Now, even with the political backlash in Washington, there is a much larger awareness here that women are an extremely valuable resource."

Emily Weiner, a coordinator of the women's caucus at *The New York Times,* was hired by the *Times* as an editorial artist in the traditionally all-male map department in December 1978, shortly after the *Times* had settled its class-action sex discrimination suit. (The *Times* agreed out of court to pay $233,500 and to launch a four-year hiring and promotion program for women.) "I was in the right place at the right time," Weiner says. "There were gold stars out there for *Times* managers who hired women. I am damn good at what I do, but I'm sure there are other good women who wouldn't have gotten this job if they had applied for it earlier."

"The sad part," adds Weiner, "is that the benefits have gone mainly to us younger women, not to those who filed the suits and took the risks, who expended their emotional energy and time and got the wrath of management." As a friend in management told Betsy Wade Boylan, a copy editor on the paper's national news desk who was one of the plaintiffs in the *Time*'s discrimination suit, "The *Times* is not in the business of rewarding people who sue it."

Indeed, more than one woman who has laundered her company's dirty linen in public has found herself writing more obits, working more graveyard shifts, subjected to lateral "promotions," and passed over in favor of women hired from outside. But the same kind of shoddy treatment has been too often dished out to women whether they sue or not.

The Butcher Treatment and Other Games   The story of Mary Lou Butcher is a case in point. A few months after graduating from the University of Michigan in 1965 with a political science degree, Butcher was hired by the *Detroit News* to write wedding announcements—the only kind of position then open to women with no prior reporting experience. (Men were trained in the city room.) Determined to move into hard news, she began writing stories on her own time for the city room and, after a year and a half of "pushing and pleading," was transferred to a suburban bureau, a move that gave her a chance to cover local government.

Three years later, after volunteering to work nights as a general assignment reporter, she finally made it into the city room. But after about six years of covering a wide range of stories—for a while, she was assigned to the Wayne County Circuit Court—she was given a weekend shift, normally reserved for new reporters. Men with less seniority had weekends off, but when Butcher—by now a veteran of eleven years—finally asked for a better shift, she instead found a note on her typewriter saying she was being transferred back to the suburbs.

Other women at the *News* had been similarly exiled. In 1972 there were eight women reporters in the city room. When Butcher was "demoted" to suburbia in 1976, she was the last remaining woman reporter in the newsroom on the day shift; all the others had been moved to the life-style, reader-service, or suburban sections—or had left. When the *News* used its city room to film a TV commercial promoting the paper, it had to recruit women from other departments to pose as reporters.

"When I saw that note, a light finally went on," Butcher says. "I thought: 'Wait. There's something strange going on here.' I had proven myself to be a good hard-news reporter. I saw no reason for being treated like this. It took a long time for it to occur to me that there was something deliberate about what was happening here, that I was the victim of a pattern."

As has been the case with many women reporters, that pattern also appeared in her story assignments. When she volunteered to help report on Jimmy Hoffa's disappearance, she was turned down because, she believes, it was considered "basically a man's story." During United Auto Workers negotiations in the mid–1970s, she—getting much the same treatment as Pauline Frederick thirty years earlier—was assigned to interview the wives of the Ford management team negotiators; the talks themselves were covered by reporters who were male. And when an education official from Washington came to Detroit to talk about how sex stereotyping in schools can lead to stereotyping in jobs, the editor assigned her to cover it because, she recalls, "he said he wanted a light story, and 'we figure we can get away with it by sending you.'" She argued with him and wrote the story straight; it was buried in the paper.

Butcher and three other *News* women eventually sued the paper, which agreed last November in an out-of-court settlement to pay $330,-000, most of which will go to about ninety of its present and former women employees. Butcher decided to leave journalism because, she says, "My advancement opportunities were almost totally blocked at the *News*. And after filing a lawsuit, it wasn't realistic to think that other media in Detroit would be eager to hire me. Management doesn't like wave-makers." She is now account supervisor for the public relations firm of MG and Casey Inc. in Detroit. "Newspapering is my first love, but I think the sacrifice was well worth it," she says. "Now the *News* is recruiting women from around the country, putting them in the newsroom, and giving them highly visible assignments. I feel really pleased; that's what it was all about."

Not all women feel that their complaints against their employers harm their careers in the long run. "Sure, there may be adverse consequences to signing on to these suits. But there are adverse consequences to being a woman working in a man's world. Some managers may punish you for it, but others believe it shows a certain amount of gumption," says Peggy Simpson, one of seven female AP reporters who last September won a $2 million out-of-court settlement of a suit charging sex and race discrimination. (The AP, like other defendants cited in this article who have agreed to out-of-court settlements, has denied the charges of discrimination. "But when a company settles for two million dollars, it suggests they had good reason to want to avoid going to court," says New York attorney Janice Goodman, who represented not only the AP plaintiffs but also sixteen women employees of NBC, who won their own $2 million settlement in 1977. In such settlements, the money is usually divided among the women employees who have allegedly suffered from sex discrimination.)

Still, for various reasons, all the AP plaintiffs have left the wire service for other jobs. Simpson is now economic correspondent for Hearst and Washington political columnist for *The Boston Herald*. Another plaintiff, Shirley Christian, who was on the AP foreign desk in 1973, went to *The Miami Herald* and in 1981 won a Pulitzer for her work in Central America.

It is not only the plaintiffs who may find their jobs on the line. Vocal sympathizers within a company can suffer recriminations as well. When Kenneth Freed, who at the time was the AP's State Department correspondent, won a Nieman Fellowship at Harvard in 1977, he says he was told shortly before his departure that the wire service would not supplement his fellowship money with a portion of his AP salary—a practice it had generally followed up to then. He later learned from friends at AP "that the reason was to punish me for my union activism—especially my role in the suit pressing for women and minority rights. They felt I had betrayed them. After all, I had one of the best beats in Washington and was paid considerably over scale. When I supported the women's suit, it just angered them even more." Thomas F. Pendergast, vice president and director of personnel and labor relations for the AP, says Freed was a victim of circumstance rather than of deliberate ill will. He says AP president and general manager Keith Fuller decided for financial reasons to stop supplementing all fellowships after he took over in October 1976. But unfortunate coincidences did not stop there. When Freed was ready to resume his old job after his year at Harvard, he says he was told by his Washington bureau chief that "there was no longer anything for me at the State Department." He adds, "I told them the only thing I *didn't* want to do was cover foreign policy on the Hill and, after that, it was all they offered me." Freed quickly left AP, and is now Canadian bureau chief for the *Los Angeles Times*.

Newspapers and broadcast stations that have agreed to fill goals for women have often failed to meet them. They blame slow employee turnover, and the general doldrums that have hit the newspaper business, for those failures. *The New York Times*, for instance, agreed in its consent decree to give women 25 percent of its top editorial jobs; in fact, only 16 percent had been so filled by 1983. Out of sixteen job categories in which hiring goals were set for women, the *Times* had met those goals in only eight categories—mainly the less prestigious ones. "We feel it has lived up to neither the spirit nor the letter of the law," says Margaret Hayden, counsel for the *Times*'s women's caucus.

And numbers can be dressed up to look better than they are. Several women at *Newsday* report that, since the out-of-court settlement in 1982 of a suit filed by four women employees, lateral moves by women are sometimes listed as promotions in the house newsletter. And when attorney Janice Goodman inspected the AP's records in 1982, she found that the wire service was giving inflated experience ratings to the men it hired, so that many were starting with salaries higher than those of women with equal experience.

A few years after the Federal Communications Commission started monitoring broadcast stations for their employment practices, the United States Commission on Civil Rights noted in its report, *Window Dressing on the Set,* that the proportion of women listed by stations in the top four FCC categories had risen "a remarkable—and unbelievable" 96.4 percent. In fact, the commission found that, as a result of a shuffling of job descriptions, three-fourths of all broadcast employees at forty major television stations could be classified as "upper level" by 1977, an "artifically inflated job status" that the commission found again in a follow-up report it issued in 1979.

Setting the Pace—and Pushing Hard   Yet even after discounting for such creative manipulation of statistics, the figures do show solid gains for women. At Gannett, the largest newspaper chain in the country, chairman and president Allen H. Neuharth has been a pacesetter at moving women into jobs: its eighty-five dailies now have twelve women publishers, two women executive editors, five women editors, and four-teen women managing editors. Cathleen Black is president of *USA Today* and a member of the Gannett management committee. "For twenty years Neuharth has been working creatively to make it happen," says Christy Bulkeley, editor and publisher of Gannett's *Commercial-News* in Danville, Illinois, and, as vice-president of Gannett Central, in charge of overseeing six of the chain's papers in four states. Neuharth, for instance, sent Bulkeley and another woman to the 1972 Democratic convention, which they saw as an opportunity to "produce enough copy so the all-male staff of the Washington bureau couldn't say we weren't doing our share of the load," Bulkeley recalls. Shortly after, the first woman appeared as a full-time reporter in Gannett's Washington bu-reau.

The AP is now hiring women at a rate equal to men for its domestic news staff. In 1973, when the suit began, only 8 percent of its news staff was female; now it is up to 26 percent, and rising. In 1973, the AP had only two or three women on the foreign desk, a position that prepares reporters for assignments abroad; now six out of seventeen on the foreign desk are women.

At *Newsday,* 41 percent of reporters and writers hired for the news-room over the past nine years have been women. "Before we filed our suit [in 1975] there were no women in the bureaus, no women on the masthead, no women in positions of importance in the composing room," says Sylvia Carter, a *Newsday* writer who was a plaintiff in the suit. "Now, a woman is Albany bureau chief, a woman is White House correspondent; there are lots of women editors, three women on the masthead, and a woman foreman in the composing room."

The most visible gains have been made in cities where women have pushed hardest for them. Take Pittsburgh, for instance. In general, the town "is far and away less than progressive towards women; if someone calls me 'sweetheart' I don't even notice anymore," says the *Post-Gazette*'s Shanahan. But a chapter of the National Organization for Women threatened for several years to challenge local broadcast licenses in FCC proceedings if the city's stations did not improve women's programming and employment. The result: media women are doing very well in Pittsburgh. Today, five women hold top administrative positions at CBS affiliate KDKA-TV, including those of vice-president and general manager. At WTAE-TV, Hearst's flagship station, four women hold top-level jobs. KDKA radio has three women in high executive news jobs, and three women co-anchors. And Madelyn Ross is managing editor of Shanahan's rival paper, the *Pittsburgh Press*.

"When one of the media is a target, it raises other people's consciousness," says ex-*Detroit News* reporter Butcher. "It has a ripple effect." At the *Detroit Free Press*, for example, the managing editor, city editor, business editor, graphics editor, and life-style editor are all female. (At Butcher's former paper the news editor is a woman and women hold about 30 percent of the editorial jobs.) In addition to Butcher's suit against the *News*, the Detroit chapter of NOW and the Office of Communication of the United Church of Christ also negotiated aggressively for women's and minority rights with local broadcasting stations. Today, two major network affiliates—WDIV-TV and WXYZ-TV—have women general managers.

Pressure on broadcasting stations in the form of FCC license challenges has subsided in recent years, in part because improvements have been made in the broadcast industry, and in part because "we don't have the votes anymore at the FCC, which is now controlled by right-wing Republicans," says Kathy Bonk, director of the NOW Legal Defense and Education Fund Media Project in Washington, D.C.

But in many broadcast news organizations a solid groundwork has been laid. "Those women created opportunities for the rest of us, and I will always be grateful for that," says Sharon Sopher, who was hired as a news writer and field producer for NBC in 1973, a few months after several NBC women employees filed a sex-discrimination complaint with the New York City Commission on Human Rights. Sopher became the first network producer to go into the field with an all-woman crew, and has been allowed to do stories previously off-limits to women— from a feature segment on street gangs to a special assignment to cover the Rhodesian war from the guerrilla perspective. Her first independent documentary, *Blood and Sand: War in the Sahara*, aired on WNET in 1982.

Will the Advance Be Halted?   Once at or near the top, women can have significant professional impact on the attitudes of their male colleagues. Richard Salant was president of CBS News in 1975 when Kay Wight was appointed director of administration and assistant to the president. "She made me realize what a rotten job we were doing about hiring and promoting women," Salant says. "She kept at me all the time, in a diplomatic but insistent way, about how few women we had in every department except steno and research." As a result, Salant, who has four granddaughters, began to insist on monthly reports from his subordinates on the numbers of women in each department. "I finally wouldn't approve any openings unless they put in writing what they had done to recruit women and minorities. The paperwork was a pain—but at least it made people conscious of the issues." During his time at the helm (he left CBS in 1979 and is now president and chief executive officer of the National News Council) the number of women in important positions rose dramatically, but not enough to satisfy Salant, who maintains that his greatest disappointment is that "I never got a woman on *60 Minutes.*" (Salant was among the first members to resign from New York's all-male Century Club over its discriminatory policies. Similarly, Arthur Ochs Sulzberger, chairman of the board of *The New York Times,* warned his top executives last year that, as of January, they would no longer be reimbursed for expenses incurred at the club.)

When *Chicago Tribune* editor Squires was Washington bureau chief for the paper, Eileen Shanahan, then with *The New York Times,* and Marlene Cimmons of the *Los Angeles Times* convinced him to join them in a project to eliminate sexism from the AP and UPI stylebooks. They "raised my sensitivity about women's issues above what I ever thought it could be raised," he says. Now, many women at the *Tribune* feel they have an ally in Squires. "The pioneer women in journalism were friends of mine—Nancy Dickerson, Eleanor Randolph, Elizabeth Drew," he says. "A lot of them had a rough time just because they were women. And seeing what has happened to them makes me feel I have to take steps to overcome the problems of the past." But performance can lag far behind promise. Five major editing jobs opened last year at the *Tribune*—managing editor, copydesk chief, metro editor, assistant metro editor, and national editor—and none of them went to a woman.

"The battle isn't over for equal rights in any profession, including journalism," says Helen Thomas, UPI's veteran White House reporter, who has covered six presidents and toted up a number of firsts—first woman president of the White House Correspondents Association, first woman officer of the National Press Club, first woman member of the Gridiron Club. Yet she remains optimistic. "It is impossible for women to lose what we've gained," she says. "We're now secure in our role as journalists—we just have to expand that role."

"We're fighting against enormous odds," says Joan Cooke, metro reporter for *The New York Times,* chair of the *Times* unit of The Newspaper Guild of New York, and a plaintiff in the suit against the *Times.* "Look at the masthead. [Out of seventeen people listed, two are women.] That's where the power is, and they're not going to give up power easily. And most women don't want to devote all their extra energy to equal rights—they want to go home like everybody else, to be with their families or friends. But if the spirit is there, and the will is there, it can be done." Sylvia Carter, a *Newsday* writer who was a plaintiff in the sex discrimination case against her paper, advises women to "be tough, keep your sense of humor, and form a women's caucus—but don't do it on company time."

Slowly, discrimination is easing as men see that women can do the job. The courage, persistence, and sheer hard work of women journalists have made these changes possible. But, at too many news organizations, women have yet to scale the topmost peaks; despite their increasing visibility, they do not have much more power than before. And the important question is: Will they ever? In the past, government pressure in the form of lawsuits and the threat of revoking broadcast licenses forced the news media to give women a chance. Now, in the hands of a conservative administration, the tools by which that pressure is exerted—the EEOC and the FCC—are being allowed to rust. It is up to the news media, then, to spur themselves on toward greater equality in the newsroom and resist the temptation to backslide into the patterns of discrimination that have limited and punished women because of their sex.

49 · WOMEN'S MAGAZINES

BY SHEILA GIBBONS

> Publications for women are changing, according to this article. Women's magazines, like the women they serve, have moved out of the home. Dozens are being published to meet the ever-changing interests of women—and these magazines advertise hundreds of products. Sheila J. Gibbons is the former editor of *Ladycom Magazine,* published especially for women with ties to the military. She is now news editor/consumer for the USA TODAY UPDATE, the on-line news service of the Gannett Company. This article is from *USA Today,* December 7, 1982.

Stand in front of a magazine rack in any town in the United States today and, gazing back at you, you'll find face after beautiful face, each one smiling at you over catchy cover lines. Or you may find yourself wanting to step into the beautiful room arrangements floating just below a magazine's title. What the smiling faces and designer decors have in common is that they sell women's magazines, which have long been among the most successful of American periodicals.

But there are signs that the success so long enjoyed by the established women's magazines is in jeopardy. For one thing, there are more women's publications to choose from than there were a decade ago, so women don't automatically reach for *McCall's* or *Ladies' Home Journal.* Young women are likely to bypass them for *Glamour, Mademoiselle, Self* or *New Woman;* women with children may choose *Working Mother* or *Parents;* career-oriented women have *Savvy* and *Working Woman;* women of color, *Essence.* And "mouseburgers"—Helen Gurley Brown's hard-working, hard-loving disciples—are "having it all" with *Cosmo.*

The ones who are not having it all are the large women's "service" magazines whose circulations, though still in the millions, are eroding and who are having a more difficult time attracting advertisers than they once did. In efforts to sell more ad space, they've slashed their rates, but the rate cut has forced them to compete even more intensely for advertising dollars.

419

And these magazines have also had to bear the indignity of being unfavorably compared to newer women's publications which make the world outside the home seem much more exciting than the one within, and which offer frank, eye-opening discussions of sex, relationships and life in the workplace.

"Too old-fashioned" is a complaint one often hears about the "Seven Sisters" *(McCall's, Ladies' Home Journal, Woman's Day, Family Circle, Good Housekeeping, Better Homes & Gardens* and *Redbook).* "They're all alike," is another and, more specifically, "They still want me to care desperately about the newest jiffy casserole and the quality of the shine on my kitchen floor." Exaggerated as this kind of criticism is, it is common, and it has helped foster an image problem that has been hard for some of these publications to beat.

The readers women's magazines are competing for can no longer be lumped together as "any woman, aged 18-49," whose interests are assumed to be identical. The steady flow of women into the workforce during the 1970s widened the scope of their lives and required them to place affairs of the home into a smaller niche than their mothers did. And if the traditional women's service magazines were slow to make their articles reflect those changes, others wasted no time starting up publications to reach what advertising executive Rena Bartos has called "New Target Opportunity Groups." Women's needs change during their life cycles, writes Bartos in *The Moving Target* (Free Press, 1982), so during their lives they will be members of different target audiences at different times. The titles of the new women's magazines reflect the various life stages that Bartos talks about: *New Woman* (founded in 1976), *Working Woman* (1976), *Working Mother* (1978), *Self* (1979) and *Savvy* (1980).

The combined circulation of these new magazines (3.4 million readers) compared to that of the "Seven Sisters" (43 million) seems minuscule. In truth, these small magazines, by themselves, are not going to put any of the larger ones out of business. But their impact has been felt by everyone in the publishing triangle: readers, editors and advertisers.

Kate Rand Lloyd was the managing editor of *Vogue* when she left to become the editor of *Working Woman.* After 30 years at Conde Nast (publisher of *Glamour, Mademoiselle, Bride's* and *Vogue*), she found herself at a magazine that had just survived a Chapter 11 bankruptcy proceeding.

"You know, when I first came to *Working Woman,* the editors of the older women's magazines had an attitude that was very sweet," Lloyd, now *Working Woman's* editor-at-large, recalls. "They would say wonderful things about the magazine, how good it was that someone had finally done something like *Working Woman.* I think the happiest day of my life, though, was when I was on a panel with one of those editors, and she took off after me, throwing verbal knives. She kept insisting that

50% of *her* readers work, that *she* had the working women's market."
That editor's eagerness to claim Lloyd's readership conferred on *Working Woman* the status of a serious competitor—a moment Lloyd still
savors.

"At about the same time, a big-time publisher said to me, about
working women, 'Don't you think it's just a fad?' At that point, there
were 38 million women in the work force. Now it's closer to 45 million,"
Lloyd says.

Advertisers also had to be convinced that the new magazine was
viable, a process Lloyd says took "quite a while, but which broke new
ground in advertising directed toward women." "One of the reasons that
we're successful is that we've attracted advertising that never used to
appear in women's magazines—office automation equipment, insurance, investments, executive recruiting, automobiles—things that aren't
'normal' for women's magazines." *Working Woman* has its share of
traditional women's advertising, too.

Sy Goldis, senior vice president and director of media services at
Doyle, Dane and Bernbach, has been in the advertising business for 25
years. He has been closely involved with magazines throughout much
of his career.

"Advertisers do believe that women have changed—definitely," he
says. "The fact that these offshoots of the magazine mainstream are
doing well means that advertisers believe in the concept. The trend
appears to be toward specialization of magazines, and advertisers are
acknowledging it.

"It's true that the circulation of these new magazines isn't very big,
but if the money advertisers are spending in them were to flow back into
the older women's service magazines, they would be in better shape,"
Goldis says. "But that's not going to change unless they dramatically
change their editorial direction and"—here comes the Catch-22 of publishing—"that would cause a big decline in circulation." A small decline
in circulation could actually help a troubled publication to cut costs and
stabilize its rate base, but a big drop could be fatal.

McCall's and *Ladies' Home Journal* have suffered the most dramatic shrinkage in circulation in the women's service category, having
lost 1.3 million and 1.5 million readers, respectively, between 1971 and
1981. In 1982 the Charter Co. sold *Ladies' Home Journal* (to Family
Media, Inc.) and an editorially-anemic *Redbook* (to Hearst, which owns
Cosmopolitan, Good Housekeeping and *Harper's Bazaar*). At that time,
Family Media said that no format or circulation changes were planned
for *Ladies' Home Journal.* But Bob Brink, executive vice president and
general manager of the Hearst Magazines Division, quickly announced
that *Redbook* would be returned, editorially, to the "young mamas"
readership with whom *Redbook* enjoyed its greatest success.

It's not just the upstart women's magazines that are enjoying the

favor of advertisers. Fashion magazines led all types of women's magazines in revenues earned during 1981. *Harper's Bazaar, Mademoiselle*
and *Vogue* all had revenue increases ranging from 20 to 30 percent. The
readers' favorite, with the largest circulation of the fashion books, is
Glamour.

But no one can discount the popularity and success of the magazine
with the Plain-Jane name and the reassuring seal of approval. *Good
Housekeeping* has not only held its own in the competitive sorority of
women's service magazines—in 1981 only one other consumer publication made more money in ad revenue than *Good Housekeeping—
Reader's Digest. Good Housekeeping*'s circulation ranks ninth in the
nation. Its editor, John Mack Carter, attributes the magazine's success
to its singularity of purpose: remembering who the GH reader is and
never "graying" the editorial content with material out of *Good
Housekeeping*'s realm.

"I have had a very clear picture of the purpose of *Good
Housekeeping,*" says Carter, who also has been editor of *Better Homes
& Gardens* and *Ladies' Home Journal.* "Our readers do all the same
things other women's magazine readers do—they work outside the
home to the same degree as average, they are married and they have
families—but the purpose of *Good Housekeeping* is to serve that
woman as she is responsible for her family. We have not been deflected
from our purposes as a magazine by trying to serve the reader in her
career. We serve her as a mother and a homemaker.

"Some of the other women's magazines have been confused by the
changes in women's roles and have compromised their purposes by
becoming far more general-interest in scope and less helpful specifically," Carter says. "A woman will read those magazines to be diverted,
to be entertained, to have a little escape. Her expectations of that
magazine are more casual, less precise, so she doesn't have as strong
a link with a magazine like that."

And that type of publication won't make the cut as women choose
from a wide array of information and entertainment technology in the
next decade, Carter predicts. Consequently, he believes there will be
fewer of the same types of magazines in most homes: "The woman
reader of today and tomorrow is not going to be as likely to have
McCall's, Ladies' Home Journal and *Family Circle* in her living room
as, perhaps, *Woman's Day, Ski, Business Week* and *Glamour.*"

There probably will also be television versions of those magazines.
Several of the larger women's magazines have already entered the cable
television arena with programs that range from discussions of issues to
presentations of meal ideas.

Asked what he expects a magazine rack in 1990 to look like, Carter
says: "The really exciting thing, in spite of all these publishing problems,
is that the reader is going to find probably twice as many choices among

women's magazines as she finds today. We'll have a greater variety in many more magazines of smaller circulations. I think there will be fewer of the mass circulation magazines, and not all the same ones we have now."

"I don't believe women's basic impulses are going to change. I think they are going to go right on thinking about men and falling in love and worrying about the kids," Kate Rand Lloyd says. "But I do believe, as everyone else does, that their numbers in the work force will continue to grow and because of that, there'll continue to be a shift in lifestyles. Segmentation will continue also: We'll have more women's magazines, more precisely focused on the type of woman they serve."

50 · BRINGING THE MOVING PICTURE INTO FOCUS

BY LORI KESLER

Changing roles and interests of women are responsible for changing media. It's a marketing situation that can frustrate or enrich advertisers, manufacturers and media, writes Lori Kesler, a St. Louis freelance writer. This article is from *Advertising Age,* April 2, 1984.

"Despite my 30 years of research into the feminine soul, I have not yet been able to answer the great question: What does a woman want?"

SIGMUND FREUD

Freud, poor fellow, wasn't the first person to ask that question. A guy named Adam beat him to it. And ever since it was asked the first time, that question has been on the top 10 hit parade of puzzlers.

The advertiser who answers it correctly stands to reap generous rewards. Likewise, the one who guesses wrong suffers the consequences.

Such is the power of marketing to women.

Experts who watch the trends say advertisers and marketers have made considerable progress during the last few years.

They've learned, for example, that the women's market does not consist of legions of fretful females agonizing over dirty laundry and dirty floors (and probably it never did).

During the 1980s, they also learned that today's woman doesn't claim to be Superwoman. After a short flirtation, advertisers agreed to send that lady packing.

Superwoman, you remember, is that disgustingly perfect specimen who serves her family a bountiful hot breakfast, dashes off to run a corporation all day and then glides in at 6 p.m. to create a lavish gourmet meal while at the same time changing diapers, leading Cub Scouts and carrying on stimulating conversation with her husband. Thank goodness she's gone.

But if today's woman wants to be neither a drudge nor Superwoman, then—as Mr. Freud pondered—what does she want?

Advertisers today seem to be telling us she wants to show off different personalities at different times. In a Jergens commercial, she's soft and cuddly as a kitten. In a Buick commercial, she declares confidently that she bought a car. *Her* car.

Rena Bartos, senior vp-director of communications development at J. Walter Thompson USA in New York, believes advertisers these days are trying harder to understand what women want in products and services.

She works with clients to explore social changes, marriage patterns and trends in life styles "and then we get into the nitty gritty of how all this can be factored into their marketing and product opportunities," she says. "In the last couple of years, we've gone from cocktail conversation to action."

According to Ms. Bartos, the companies that sell big-ticket items—cars, credit cards, financial products, life insurance and investment services—have demonstrated the greatest awareness of women's changed status.

"I think that's because until recently those folks assumed they were dealing only with men. When they began to recognize women as customers, they looked at women who were earning their own money and making their own decisions. Or if the women were married, they were part of an equal household," Ms. Bartos says.

Because the companies didn't have to overcome bad habits *vis-a-vis* their approach to women, "you don't see a condescending approach to women in those product categories."

Household products have made less progress, she says, "but even there we're beginning to see the husband in the kitchen and the family sharing duties."

Judith Langer, who heads her own marketing and social research company in New York, finds the working woman now ranks as an accepted figure in advertising and marketing, not an oddity.

"A few years ago, when the career woman was discovered, she got rather naive treatment," she says. "Advertisers wanted to show high-level achievers, women in nontraditional jobs. Unfortunately, they often did it in ways women couldn't relate to."

Now advertisers tend to take a more subtle approach. "They picture a woman who is out in the world, active and well dressed," she observes. "But we don't really know her job. It's intentionally ambiguous."

A commercial for Comfort-stride pantyhose, for example, shows a woman getting on an elevator. "Is she a secretary or a company president?" asks Ms. Langer. "She could be anybody."

Fulltime homemakers also are demanding more respect, and this attitude, she notes, is beginning to have an impact on advertisers.

For example, many marketers who spent the last few years targeting working women now are broadening their focus to include the active nonworking female. And laundry detergent ads are beginning to show the homemaker pursuing her own interests and hobbies, not simply washing clothes.

Even the Wisk commercials have caught the spirit. Now a man worries about how to wash out his own ring around the collar.

Many women have waited a long time to see that.

With the baby boom generation well into its 30s, advertisers also are having to deal with another emerging trend: The graying of America.

The result? "We're definitely seeing more mature women in ads," Ms. Langer says. "And I think, too, advertisers have come to understand that women want a strong positive image of themselves."

Not too long ago, cosmetics marketers assumed a 40-year-old woman's fondest wish was to look 25. "Now there's the feeling that a woman of 40 just wants to look her best," she says.

"We're not kidding ourselves so much anymore. At one time the ad community played on our fears of getting older. Now they're showing a line now and then. There's more honesty.

"One nice commercial that would never have been done years ago is for Oil of Olay," Ms. Langer says. "It starts out with, 'The first time I saw your face. . . .' What's interesting is you know the woman's in her late 30s or 40s. They shoot it so you do see she's got lines.

"At one time, that would have been an anxiety campaign. Instead, this has been presented in a positive way."

Experts see romanticism and glamor returning to many women's product ads, but this time it's accompanied by a startling new kind of sensuality. "Sex is no longer a taboo subject," Ms. Bartos acknowledges.

She points out, however, that current ads showing women taking an "overt, frank approach to pleasure and sensuality" are different from those of the past which portrayed women as sex objects.

"These new ads show women in a pleasure relationship," she says, "not submitting to a power relationship."

Notes Ms. Langer, "What the new sensuality proves is that women feel comfortable having this as part of their lives. The achievement-oriented woman feels she can relax a little bit. She feels it's okay for her to look feminine on the job and to look sexy in her personal life. She's past the proving stage."

Meanwhile, some kinds of products and services that by-passed women in the past are being recruited in marketers' efforts to catch up. Take automobiles, for example.

Sandy Chumack, an account supervisor for the Ford division at J. Walter Thompson USA, says women represented more than a third of the new car market—fully 38%—in 1983.

That's up from 22% in 1973. And, she adds, "we expect this percentage to increase in the future."

Ms. Chumack is a member of a women's professional review committee, which analyzes and reviews all Ford advertising. She says the committee's research indicates that women want to see some technical information in auto advertising, but not too much.

"If an ad talks about rack-and-pinion steering, it should emphasize the benefits," she says. But above all, a woman wants a safe car, says Ms. Chumack, and that image of reliability should be projected in the advertising.

As examples, she points to two ads for the Thunderbird and the Mustang convertible, which appear in women's magazines.

The ads, headlined "Executive Air" and "Upward Mobility," were designed to appeal to the professional woman's sense of taste and style. But both also include technical details that reinforce the idea of safety and reliability.

Ms. Chumack reports both have received a good response from nonworking as well as working women.

Other industries promoting heavily to women include insurance, financial services and investment companies.

Merrill Lynch regularly conducts educational seminars for women because they make up the largest group of new investors, "and we've known all along they wanted to know more about investing," explains public relations spokeswoman Ellen Golden of Burson-Marsteller, New York.

It all started with fashion and finance seminars in the 1970s when "you still had to sugar coat financing," she says apologetically.

Through the years, though, the seminars have taken on more sophisticated subjects. One series explored investing for the two-income family, and last year Merrill Lynch joined *Working Woman* magazine and several other sponsors to conduct seminars for women entrepreneurs.

Ms. Langer recalls that a few years ago, most of her clients were small package goods companies. Today, it's the insurance companies, computer marketers and financial services companies who are interested in researching the women's market.

"Sometimes," she says, "we find the women's consumers want something different from men. For example, in hotels, they want skirt hangers and good lights. Those things are important to women.

"In many cases, though, we find women don't want different products or services," she says. "They just want to be treated as equals, and the marketers simply have to help them recognize that they need things like pensions, IRA plans and disability insurance—just as men do. There's a dawning awareness of this."

FOR FURTHER READING

Helen Baehr (ed.), *Women and the Media.* New York: Pergamon Press, 1980.

Maurine Beasley and Sheila Silver, *Women in Media: A Documentary Source Book.* Washington, D.C.: Women's Institute for Freedom of the Press, 1977.

Matilda Butler and William Paisley, *Women and the Mass Media: Sourcebook for Research and Action.* New York: Human Sciences Press, 1980.

Laurily Keir Epstein, *Woman and the News.* New York: Hastings House, 1978.

Judith S. Gelfman, *Women in Television News.* New York: Columbia University Press, 1976.

Anita Klever, *Women in Television.* Philadelphia: Westminster Press, 1975.

Marion Marzolf, *Up from the Footnote: A History of Women Journalists.* New York: Hastings House, 1977.

Betsy Covington Smith, *Breakthrough: Women in Television.* New York: Walker and Company, 1981.

Ethel Strainchamps, *Rooms with No View: A Woman's Guide to the Man's World of the Media.* New York: Harper & Row, 1974.

XIV

Mass Media and Religion

TRADITIONALLY, RELIGION in the mass media was restricted to the ceremonies and controversies involving religious denominations. Ceremonies could be reported as simply as a listing of local services in Saturday editions or as elaborately as broadcasting ceremonies live from some distant city. The controversies could involve covering a noisy new splinter group from an established denomination or reporting arguments about changes in the structure of worship services.

Religious beliefs and matters of faith are so intangible, so private, the media seemed to say by their silence, that broader media coverage would be intrusive, inappropriate. In reality, though, religion and religious beliefs permeate the daily lives and activities of millions of people in this country and billions around the globe.

This has become increasingly evident as religious leaders and denominations have taken active roles in U.S. politics. They have rallied support for and against various social, economic and technological movements. They have not stayed confined to pulpits and pews but have reached out, both ecumenically and electronically. The subject begs to be covered in the news media, as David Shaw explains in this section.

From a different perspective, Margaret and Peter Steinfels look at the electronic church, especially the modern revivalism that is controversial when it gets wrapped in show business and big-scale fund raising.

Daniel Cattau describes the extent of religious groups' investment in media and Dennis S. Dobson questions the ways some groups use cable channels.

These articles raise more questions than they answer. Perhaps they'll challenge readers to demand more thorough coverage of the hard questions about religion and society. Perhaps they'll inspire the kinds of study reporters, writers, editors and producers need if religion is to be covered adequately by the mass media.

51 · MEDIA VIEW RELIGION IN A NEWS LIGHT

BY DAVID SHAW

Religion is important to the average American. It is difficult to cover, to get beyond the superficial and the predictable stereotypes, but it is newsworthy, reports David Shaw, a staff writer for the *Los Angeles Times.* This article is from the December 28, 1983, issue of the *Los Angeles Times.*

Kennth Briggs, religion editor of the *New York Times,* is an ordained Methodist minister. Russell Chandler, one of the religion writers at the *Los Angeles Times,* is an ordained Presbyterian minister. Louis Moore, religion editor of the *Houston Chronicle,* is an ordained Baptist minister —an evangelical Christian, in fact, who speaks periodically to church groups, refers colleagues for pastoral counseling when they have problems and, on occasion, officiates at their weddings and funerals.

But Joseph Berger, the religion writer for *Newsday* on New York's suburban Long Island, is a former junior high school English teacher and investigative reporter—and a Yeshiva-educated Jew—who says he attends synagogue only a few times a year and who never considered writing about religion until he failed to get his paper's job as a television reporter and found that religion writing was the next job available.

Virginia Culver, the religion writer for the *Denver Post,* is a self-proclaimed atheist, a woman who writes about religion not out of any personal spiritual conviction but simply because she considers religion the most interesting assignment on the paper, "the one subject that interests almost everyone and touches almost every issue."

Despite their disparate personal beliefs and professional backgrounds, these five journalists have one important common bond: They are among only 15 or 20 religion writers in the entire secular press in the United States who are widely respected in their field, according to a just-completed *Los Angeles Times* study that included almost 100 interviews with editors, religion writers, clergymen, church officials and theologians across the country.

The number of good religion writers on American daily newspapers has begun to grow in the last few years, these experts say, and religion coverage is vastly improved over what it was 20 years or even 10 years ago. Belatedly alerted to the dominant role religion often plays in most wars, civil unrest and social change throughout the world, some newspaper editors are gradually coming to recognize the importance of religion as a field for legitimate journalistic inquiry.

A 1982 survey of 30 newspapers by the Department of Mass Communications at Middle Tennessee State University showed that the percentage of papers devoting more than 100 column inches to religion news each week has more than doubled, from 27% to 59%, in the last decade.

But 100 column inches—less than a full page in most newspapers—is far less than the average paper devotes to sports every day, and it is clear that the newspapers that treat religion seriously and intelligently are still a tiny minority.

Fewer than 200 of the nation's more than 1,700 daily newspapers have religion writers, and only about a third of these 200 cover religion full time. Although some of these full-time religion writers do consistently excellent work, most religion stories that appear in the nation's newspapers are written by general assignment reporters, political reporters, feature writers or others with little understanding of—or interest in—religion.

Most of these reporters are lazy, unwilling to do their basic homework and display "an appalling ignorance" of the traditions and influence of religion, said Msgr. Francis J. Lally, who deals with the press frequently in his role as secretary of the Department of Social Development and World Peace for the United States Catholic Conference.

Thus, most people interviewed for this story said, the vast majority of newspapers—even many of those with full-time religion writers—still do a shamefully inadequate job of covering religion.

Jeanne Pugh, religion writer for the *St. Petersburg* (Fla.) *Times,* said she is "appalled by what I see in religion coverage around the country," and she is far from alone in this judgment.

William P. Thompson, co-stated clerk of the General Assembly of the Presbyterian Church (U.S.A.), said most newspaper stories about religion are "based on incorrect assumptions leading to incorrect conclusions."

"Most reporters just don't understand the subject they're trying to report," Thompson said.

It is widely agreed, for example, that the press was late in recognizing the growth of evangelical Christianity and that it then badly misunderstood and misreported the phenomenon, including its influence on former President Jimmy Carter.

The press was equally delinquent in assessing the role of religion in the social revolutions that have shaken Iran and Latin America and in explaining the relationship between what one editor called "the Muslim psyche" and the recent suicide missions that killed so many Americans, French and Israelis in Lebanon.

Black religious denominations are also widely ignored in most press coverage, as are most Asian denominations—despite the enormous increase in the Asian population in many sections of the United States (and especially in Southern California) since the end of the Vietnam War. In fact, there is little in the press to reflect the findings of a study last year by the National Council of Churches and the Glenmary Research Center in Atlanta showing that almost half the American population is outside the traditional Judeo-Christian denominations, either belonging to other denominations or having no religious affiliation.

In essence, many theologians and spiritual leaders say, the press too often misses (or misinterprets) substantive developments in religion while giving space to "religion" stories that are sensational, superficial, scandalous or stereotypical.

Most major newspapers gave prominent front-page play in October, for example, to stories on the publication by the National Council of Churches of a lectionary of non-sexist Bible readings, but few (if any) papers have written about the significant upsurge in female enrollment in the nation's seminaries.

The percentage of women in seminaries has more than doubled in the last 10 years, and this could have a major impact on those religious denominations that do not permit the ordination of women.

But in covering religion, the press often seems obsessed with conflict, controversy and the kinds of trivial personality stories—or offbeat but ultimately meaningless "religion" stories—that critics (including some religion writers) dismiss scornfully as "Geek of the Week" or "Jocks for Jesus" or "I was a clown for Christ" or what one religion writer called "the old 'nuns playing softball' story."

George Cornell, who has been writing about religion for Associated Press since 1951, said, "There's a tendency (for newspapers) to prefer the silly aspects . . . the circus aspects of religion to serious religion news."

Even when serious issues are covered, they tend to be formal and denominational—mergers, power struggles and policy statements—rather than personal; there is very little in the American press about how religion actually influences people's daily lives.

These same criticisms are often leveled against the press in its coverage of other subjects, of course. Indeed, charges of superficiality, sensationalism and impersonal, institutionally oriented coverage are leveled against the press in its treatment of virtually everything.

"You're basically dealing with a journalistic phenomenon . . . not just religion coverage," said James Wall, editor of *Christian Century* magazine.

Journalists themselves readily admit this.

"We're . . . good at fires, but ideas are a little harder to cover," said Louis D. Boccardi, executive vice president and chief operating officer of Associated Press.

Moreover, it would be impossible for the press to provide either the quality or the quantity of religion coverage most people deeply interested in religion would like to see, just as it would be impossible for the press to fully satisfy those who want comprehensive coverage of the law, science, literature or any other field.

A general-interest daily newspaper is not a journal of religion (or law or science or literature). There is neither the space nor the expertise nor the general reader interest to warrant such comprehensive, detailed treatment of any single subject.

But just as most newspaper editors admit they could do a better job on law, science, literature—and virtually everything else—so they could do a better job on religion. The gap between what they are doing and what they could and should do is perhaps greatest in religion coverage, however, because (1) most do so little, so poorly, (2) religion is so important to so many people and (3) the press could be the best vehicle for furthering religious understanding and tolerance in our society.

William C. Martin, chairman of the sociology department at Rice University in Houston, said he has often been surprised to find out how "biased or ignorant" most of his students are about religions other than their own when he assigns them to review various church services. Many otherwise intelligent adults also know little about other peoples' religions, Martin said, and he worries that the failure of the press to report on religion in a responsible fashion helps to maintain dangerous cultural barriers between people of different religious backgrounds.

Other critics say the failure of the press to cover religion comprehensively denies some believers the public reinforcement they need to sustain their spiritual commitments and thus could contribute to a decline in religious commitment and activity.

Is religion really all that important to the average American in our modern, cynical, technological age?

Yes.

A national survey conducted in 1981 for Connecticut Mutual Life Insurance Co. found that 74% of all Americans consider themselves religious. More recent surveys, conducted by the Gallup and Roper organizations, have found, variously, that 94% of all Americans believe in God or in some universal spirit (and that 67% are members of a church or synagogue); that 65% say they cannot live without religion; that 76% say they pray at least once a week (and 50% said they had prayed within the previous 24 hours); that 54% say they go to religious services at least once a month (and 40% had gone the previous week); that 54% say religion is the solution to today's world problems.

Most surveys show America to be the most religious society in the world today. In one recent study, 58% of Americans said they consider their religious beliefs "very important." In no other industrialized country was the percentage more than 36%. More than 50 million American adults are involved in Bible study, prayer groups or similar activities, and the number is growing.

But there has been little detailed press coverage of this increased religiosity. Nor has the press spent much time examining the seeming contradiction between this increase and the concomitant shift away from traditional denominations and, among some people, away from religion itself.

Many scholars and religious leaders say this neglect occurs because most journalists in America are not themselves religious and are unaware of—or even scornful of—their readers' religious beliefs and commitments.

"Most journalists are simply blind to religion," said Robert Bellah, a professor of sociology at the University of California, Berkeley. "They think it's somehow slightly embarrassing, a holdover from the Dark Ages . . . something only ignorant and backward people really believe in.

"This is not necessarily a conspicuous judgment on their part," Bellah said. "It's just part of their general world view . . . in which religion is seen as an aberrant phenomenon."

Because of this attitude, even newspapers with good religion writers often give the subject too little space.

Many journalists tend to be confirmed in their views of religion by the essentially secular and pluralistic nature of American society. There is no single dominant church in the United States; instead, there are more than 1,000 denominations, no one of which accounts for more than a quarter of the nation's population. Except in certain areas, religion is a fragmented—and to some, invisible—force in American society.

Moreover, because the separation of church and state is mandated by the Constitution, religion is essentially a private matter, largely devoid of political impact, and most American journalists seem ignorant of the enormous influence the church exerts in public policy matters in other countries, with different state-church traditions.

This ignorance, many critics say, helps explain why the American press—like the American government—was so late in assessing the religious aspects of strife in Vietnam and, more recently, in Iran.

"For vast numbers of the world's people, the symbols of religion sum up their highest aspirations," said Mary Catherine Bateson, former dean of social sciences and humanities at the University of Northern Iran. But Bateson said most Western journalists tend to dismiss religion as fanaticism or as a cloak for other political or economic interests.

Bateson is not alone in this judgment.

Peter Steinfels, editor of the liberal Catholic magazine *Commonweal,* said most journalists saw the uprising against Shah Mohammed Reza Pahlavi as "a 'human rights' story or a 'torture' story or a 'U.S.-supporting-dictators' story—all of which it was—but . . . they almost totally overlooked the role of traditional religion forces."

Religious leaders are equally critical of the press's failure to explain early on the role of the Catholic Church and liberation theology in the political unrest in Latin America.

A few newspapers did write about this in the 1970s—and some newspapers have begun publishing such stories recently—but critics say Americans would understand the sensitive, volatile problems of Latin America much better today if the press had provided more intelligent reportage on the church in Latin America a decade ago, or even five years ago.

Even in the United States, religion occasionally plays a public policy role—and that, too, is largely ignored by the press.

In a recent interview with the *Times,* former President Carter said that because the press had "exalted" the Rev. Jerry Falwell as "the spokesman for born-again Christians in the nation," Carter often worried that Falwell was having "an unwarranted impact on members of Congress."

Carter said Falwell was "preaching . . . rather effectively" that anyone who favored his foreign aid legislation or opposed the Panama Canal treaty, SALT II negotiations or the establishment of a Cabinet-level Department of Education "was not a Christian."

Carter said he retaliated by "bringing in Christian leaders by the hundreds to the White House" to solicit their support. Carter asked these clergymen to let Congress know that Falwell did not represent most Christians and to ask members of their congregations to do likewise.

The clergymen "played a very crucial role" in mustering congressional support for Carter on most of these issues, but the press reported virtually nothing of their activities on Carter's behalf, although it would have been a good and important story by any journalistic standards.

Rabbi Marc Tannenbaum, director of interreligious affairs for the American Jewish Committee and a participant in several meetings with Carter, attributes this neglect in part to a "deep-seated bias" in the press, a widespread sense that clergymen are "outsiders," incapable of dealing with serious questions of public policy.

The press assumed that Carter was meeting with clergymen as a public relations exercise, "to put a halo of morality" around his political efforts, Tannenbaum said.

All these criticisms and shortcomings notwithstanding, religion coverage is clearly improving in the American press, no matter how uneven and incomplete that improvement may be.

Until about 20 years ago, newspaper religion coverage was largely limited to Saturday "church pages"—a journalistic ghetto filled with listings of the next day's sermon topics, schedules of church-sponsored rummage sales and pot-luck dinners and press releases from local ministers. Some papers also published Bible verses on their editorial pages and "news" reports on the Sunday sermons in their Monday papers.

Most newspapers assigned their church page duties to their oldest over-the-hill reporters or to the staff alcoholic or, most often, to their youngest, least-experienced reporters. A.M. Rosenthal, executive editor of the *New York Times,* remembers being paid $3 a week to cover Sunday sermons when he was a college correspondent for the paper 40 years ago.

Newspapers had (and many still have) these weekly religion pages largely because the papers "get a lot of (church) ads, and they have to put something around it," said Benjamin C. Bradlee, executive editor of the *Washington Post.*

But the sweeping reforms in the Catholic Church that began with the Second Vatican Council from 1962 to 1965, combined with the active role many clergymen played in the civil rights and anti-war movements, suddenly awakened some editors to the news-making potential of religion and to the need for good, well-trained reporters to cover that news.

In quick succession, other events increased the editors' awareness —and their needs—in this field. The socio-political upheaval of the 1960s—most notably the sexual revolution and the resultant controversies over birth control, abortion, homosexuality and promiscuity—had a strong spiritual component. So, obviously, did the rise of various religious cults. And Carter's presidency. And the emergence of Falwell, the Moral Majority, the New Right and the evangelical movement. And a whole range of issues cutting across the domestic news making spectrum: capital punishment, arms control, genetic engineering, euthanasia.

Most newspapers still do not assign such stories to their religion writers—if they have religion writers—so coverage of these issues often remains inadequate. But some editors are at least aware of their spiritual aspects, and some mention of that aspect is sometimes made; when the best members of the new generation of religion writers— thoughtful, well-educated, many with degrees in theology—report on these subjects, they provide a much-needed extra dimension.

Thus, in several of the best daily newspapers—and, interestingly, in several daily newspapers not otherwise known for their editorial quality—religion has been taken from the church-page ghetto and put on the front page with growing frequency.

Some newspapers—the *New York Times* and the *Detroit Free Press,* for example—have no weekly religion pages. Their editors think religion news should compete with other news for space in the daily paper. Most papers still have weekly religion pages, but the best papers also carry religion news in the regular news pages when the stories warrant that play.

A few small- to medium-size papers—the *St. Petersburg Times, Tampa* (Fla.) *Tribune, Ogden* (Utah) *Standard-Examiner* and *Warren* (Ohio) *Tribune-Chronicle* among them—have weekly tabloid-size religion sections, in addition to daily religion coverage in their news pages.

Are religion stories well-read?

The *Warren Tribune-Chronicle* reported a 10% increase in Saturday circulation—and a quadrupling of its Saturday advertising linage—after it began publishing a community news-oriented tabloid, including eight pages of religion news, in that day's paper.

There are no definitive studies on the readership of religion stories, but because other studies show that the most religious people are also those most likely to vote and to feel a sense of community—both also characteristics of frequent newspaper readers—it seems probable that religion news is widely read, even in large, sophisticated metropolitan areas.

Thus, better religion reporting may be good business as well as good journalism. No wonder then that even the decidedly secular *Wall Street Journal* has been paying increasing attention to religion. In the last two months, the *Journal* has published front-page stories on seminaries, Islam fundamentalism, Chicago's Cardinal Joseph Bernardin, the Mormon Church (a two-part series) and young Mormons working as *au pair* girls for families throughout the United States. The *Journal* also published, on its editorial page, an excerpt from the statement on nuclear arms by the bishops of France.

Earlier this year, most American newspapers also gave thorough coverage to the more strongly worded American bishops' pastoral letter on nuclear arms. Many critics say that much of that coverage was deficient, though—significantly and characteristically so in that it too often failed to place the bishops' apparently unprecedented action in historical perspective. But the press generally did a much better job covering the bishops' pastoral letter than it does on most other religion stories. Indeed, it can be argued that the press routinely covers matters involving the Roman Catholic Church more thoroughly than it does issues involving any other denomination.

A careful examination of major newspapers and news magazines shows that although the best way for a religion story to get good play is, generally, for it to involve the colorful, the controversial, the charismatic, the crooked or the concupiscent, it also helps if the story involves Catholicism.

Over the last two years, for example, about half the religion stories in *Time* and *Newsweek* involved some aspect of Catholicism—the Pope, Jesuits, nuns, the bishops' letter, gays in the church, a new saint, a new cardinal.

Judaism receives far less coverage in the nation's press. It is noteworthy that the Religion Newswriters Assn., to which most of the nation's religion writers belong and which meets annually in conjunction with the meeting of one major religious group or another, has never met in conjunction with a Jewish group, according to several past and present association officers.

Association members select their annual meeting site based on the likelihood that the religious organization meeting there will produce enough news to warrant their editors paying their expenses to attend. Jewish organizations are not thought to be sufficiently productive of such news, they say.

Religion writers admit that their coverage of Judaism is weak, but they insist that is because the most interesting Jewish stories tend not to be "religion" stories per se. Jewish activity on behalf of Israel or various domestic social and civil liberties causes, for example, is generally covered as non-religion news by political or feature or general assignment reporters, not by religion writers.

"The American Jewish community is not sure whether . . . what it does is motivated out of any sense of religious convictions," said Bruce Buursma, religion writer for the *Chicago Tribune.* "It comes sometimes out of a sense of peoplehood . . . a sense of cultural heritage. . . . Religion gets bound up in that, but it's not necessarily the primary or even motivating force."

But that argument ignores the many strictly religious issues that do confront Judaism.

Rabbi Alexander Schindler, president of the Union of American Hebrew Congregations, and other Jewish leaders say that the press largely ignores such Jewish concerns as intermarriage, assimilation, conversion, proselytizing, differences among the Reform, Conservative and Orthodox branches of Judaism and the controversy over whether a child's religion should be determined by the religion of its mother or its father.

Jews make up only about 3% of the nation's population, though. The Roman Catholic Church accounts for almost 25%; its roughly 50 million members make it the single largest religious denomination in the country (it is also the largest in the world, with 606 million members, about 13% of the total population).

But the Catholic Church has more than size. After all, mainline Protestantism still accounts for the largest segment of the American population, and it, too, receives little press coverage.

But Protestantism is fragmented among many denominations. Besides, *Commonweal*'s Steinfels said, "the press pays attention to dramatic events, sharp conflicts and interesting personalities, and . . . the Catholic Church has had a corner on all three of those categories for a while."

Or, as the outspoken priest and novelist, Father Andrew Greeley, put it: "We may not be much as a church just now, but we're splendid theater . . . great copy."

Why? In part because the Catholic Church always seems riven with conflict and controversy: disputes over birth control, abortion and divorce; debates over the church's role in liberation movements abroad; disagreement over the bishops' letter on nuclear arms; changes of financial misconduct in the archdiocese in Chicago. Moreover, the Catholic Church has a large, formal, recognizable hierarchy—headed by the Pope, the most identifiable religious leader in the world.

Michael Novak, a Catholic writer and resident scholar in religion and public policy at the American Enterprise Institute in Washington, D.C., said, only half in jest: "The Pope was invented for a mass communications age; that's what the Lord had in mind in the first place."

Many Catholics think the press spends too much time and space on the Pope, though, and not enough on the less clerical manifestations of daily church life.

When Pope John Paul II visited America in 1980, the press turned out en masse. More than 14,000 journalists were accredited, and most of their coverage was as worshipful as it was voluminous.

Such headlines as "We Loved Him" and "A City Nestles in the Hands of a Gentle Pilgrim" and "A Day of Love and Joy" filled the tops of front pages of major newspapers.

Author (and Catholic) Garry Wills wrote scathingly in the *Columbia Journalism Review* of this "embarrassingly . . . perfervid" journalistic reception and concluded that for the press to have covered the Pope properly "would take a historical consciousness that the press seems unwilling or unable to acquire."

Religion, as embodied for the press in the Pope's visit, is still too often seen by editors as "a big story but soft news," in Wills' words— a story calling for mass coverage, big headlines and big pictures but not necessarily the "hard discipline" that the best papers accord to politics, the economy, law and science.

Greeley, Novak and others say the press too often oversimplifies religion stories, turning every church-related issue into a battle of conservatives against liberals or young against old—writing in predictable stereotypes and "mythic terms," in Novak's words.

52 · THE NEW AWAKENING:

Getting Religion in the Video Age

BY MARGARET O'BRIEN STEINFELS AND PETER STEINFELS

Will the electronic church become so pervasive that it
replaces traditional worship and established
denominations? No, say Margaret O'Brien Steinfels
and Peter Steinfels, as they describe the evolution of
religious programs on television and radio. Margaret
O'Brien Steinfels is an editor, writer and business
manager of *Christianity Crisis.* Peter Steinfels is
executive editor of *Commonweal* and author of *The
Neoconservatives.* This article is reprinted from
Channels of Communications, January/February
1983.

For millions of Americans, Jerry Falwell is not a real person. He is
the symbol of an explosive mixture of fundamentalist faith, right-wing
politics, and modern technology. People who wouldn't know the difference between Rex Humbard and Mother Hubbard, people who might
well assume that Oral Roberts was a toothbrush manufacturer, are
nonetheless worried about the power of the "prime-time preachers."
Not even when Bishop Fulton J. Sheen scored a hit with his prime-time
series in 1952 was there such a furor over religion and television.

The resources—and resourcefulness—of the so-called electronic
church are indeed impressive. Not only have the fundamentalist evangelists on television created a single but effective TV message, they
have mastered the means of delivering it. They produce their own shows
in their own studios with their own production facilities. They own TV
cameras and transmitting equipment, and have begun to acquire transponder time for satellite transmission, enabling their programs to run
on a growing number of cable systems across the country. They pay for
their own broadcast time, and they've developed extensive support
organizations to build their "congregations" and raise funds.

Religious networks are springing up. Pat Robertson, one of the most successful of the TV preachers, has organized the Christian Broadcast Network (CBN), headquartered in Virginia Beach, Virginia, which uses a twenty-four-hour-a-day transponder on Satcom IIIR and computerized production and transmitting facilities. CBN owns four UHF television stations and five FM radio stations, and keeps a staff of more than seven hundred busy. It operates seventy-one regional call-in centers, staffed mainly with volunteers who follow up on financial pledges and provide prayerful counseling. CBN University offers graduate training in communications and theology. Recently Robertson has spun off a secular counterpart, the Continental Broadcasting Network, which will transmit general programming suitable for family viewing.

It is the political potential of establishments like Robertson's that has stirred so much controversy—at least since 1979, when Jerry Falwell used his "Old-Time Gospel Hour" television program as a base for organizing the Moral Majority, and even more so since 1980, when the Religious New Right not only contributed to Ronald Reagan's victory but was widely regarded as a decisive factor in the defeat of several leading liberal Senators. At the same time, the media success of the fundamentalists has posed a direct challenge to the other churches, giving a new urgency to longstanding questions about organized religion's approach to television.

Not that the churches have ever lacked individuals aware of television's power—critics who worry about the medium's destructive or trivializing impact on personal values, enthusiasts who hope to exploit its hold on mass audiences for explicitly religious purposes. But the success of the prime-time preachers, linked as it is to the advent of new technologies, has added fuel to old debates. To some, the electronic church is further evidence of television's distorting effect on authentic religion. To others, it is an implicit call to "go and do likewise."

Swaggart in the Morning   Getting perspective on the electronic church itself is not easy, in view of the political passions it has stirred. In an effort to raise funds to combat TV evangelists, Norman Lear has claimed, "The ability of moral majoritarians to shape public attitudes and to influence the climate of public debate is unprecedented and poses an enormous danger. The leading 'television preachers' alone have an audience approaching 40 million." In sum, says Lear, "The moral majoritarians have overpowered America's airwaves with their messages of hostility, fear, and distrust."

The casual viewer of these programs might be hard pressed to see why Lear was so incensed. For a start, few prime-time preachers actually appear during prime time. In most major markets, they are still likely to be found early in the morning, late at night, or in the Sunday-morning "religious ghetto." Lear also fails to acknowledge the sheer variety of the programming—everything from fire-and-brimstone preaching pitched to stir fear in the backsliding Christian, to staid Bible-study programs sending all but the truly devoted into a stupor.

In the morning, Jimmy Swaggart pedantically explains God's views on first and second marriages; in the evening, he paces the platform, conjuring up pathetic scenes of the alcoholic so wretched that he stole the shoes from his own child's corpse to buy liquor.

Jim Bakker, one of the born-again, gesture-for-gesture imitations of network talk-show hosts, publicly shares the domestic dramas of his marriage to gospel singer Tammy Fay.

Ben Kinchlew, Pat Robertson's athletic-looking black co-host, presides over a slickly produced edition of "The 700 Club," featuring:

• the author of a book claiming that low liquidity among major corporations lies at the root of our economic troubles;

• a reformed workaholic who, but for seeing the light and being saved by Jesus, would have lost his wife and children;

• a clip of a conference on cable television and "narrowcasting," from which *Screw* magazine publisher Al Goldstein's remarks had to be deleted because of his language;

• a woman, once gay, who turned to Jesus and now offers a ministry to homosexuals.

Not to everyone's taste, certainly, and clearly laced with political conservatism. But have the TV evangelists truly "overpowered America's airwaves"?

If audience size is any measure, the evangelists have hardly been a resounding success. During the 1980 elections, normally skeptical journalists were reporting that Jerry Falwell reached anywhere from 18 million to 30 million people each week; by contrast, the Arbitron and Nielsen reports revealed that Falwell was actually reaching fewer than 1.5 million viewers. Contrary to Norman Lear's assertion that the "leading" preachers alone had an audience of 40 million, the 1980 Arbitron figures showed a combined audience of half that size for all sixty-six syndicated religious programs. Furthermore, as Jeffrey Hadden and Charles Swann reminded the readers of their book, *Prime Time Preachers,* not all the top syndicated religious programs were conservative, not all the conservative programs were political, and most of the religious and conservative programs, at least during the greatest public uproar, were losing rather than gaining audience. (More recently, the top programs have recouped their losses, although without any startling growth.)

None of these facts should lead one to underestimate the power of the Religious New Right, but they do suggest that the television component in that power is easily inflated. In this tendency to overrate the influence, critics like Lear mirror the attitude of the right-wingers themselves, who commonly attribute the successes of liberalism to the media power of a small number of established liberals—including Norman Lear. It is easier for all of us to believe that unpopular ideas prosper because their advocates hold some "unfair" technological advantage than it is to think they actually resonate with the experience of large numbers of people.

Quite apart from the appeal of their right-wing ideology, the evangelical programs have more going for them than their willingness to invoke the Lord's name. The talk, the accents, the clothes, the tragedies and comedies of God's people have a touchingly real quality about them —a quality they retain even amidst their studied imitations of "real" television. The electronic church is, if nothing else, one of the few places on television where you encounter genuinely homely people. Neither the stars nor the guests hold back: They exhort, they preach, they laugh, and they cry—oh, do they cry! Not for them the deep-chested authoritativeness of Dan Rather, the cool mien of Barbara Walters, or the impish savior-faire of Johnny Carson and Dick Cavett. These programs remind viewers that most of the country is not, after all, so slick, so professional, so well-dressed, and so damnably *in control.*

Despite the claims of Falwell and others to a truly national audience, the TV congregants are still predominantly female, Southern, small-town or rural, and getting on in years, according to Hadden and Swann. To see people like themselves, or at least like someone they know, confirms their sense of reality. If the guests on some of the shows —ex-alcoholics, former drug addicts, widows with young children, victims of unhappy marriages and miserable childhoods—routinely strike a maudlin note, the viewer can nonetheless identify with these all-too-familiar casualties of ordinary life; this is something every successful soap-opera writer understands. And the casualties are always repaired, with the help of friends, of the church, and above all of Jesus. Though the world's problems can seem insoluble, viewers may take some small comfort in the apparent capacity of individuals and small groups to deal with their own problems.

Obviously the electronic church trades in a kind of unreality of its own. Indeed, it is commonly accused of misleading people about the true nature of the human condition. According to the Reverend James M. Dunn, "The quick, certain, black-and-white theologies so made to order for television are inadequate for life in the real world."

Dunn's criticism is especially interesting because he is a leading staff member of the Baptist Joint Committee on Public Affairs—an agency sponsored in part by churches that many Americans might fail to differentiate from the electronic church itself. Even Carl F. H. Henry, elder statesman of evangelical Protestantism, has echoed this criticism.

The strongest reproof, of course, has come from the mainline Protestant churches, generally those belonging to the National Council of Churches (NCC). Their leading complaint is that electronic churches twist the Gospel into a quick fix, promising a painless life, and aping, rather than questioning, the values of secular culture. If you accept Jesus, you will enjoy immediate relief from suffering. Success, prosperity, and earthly happiness will be yours. This presents an odd contrast to Jesus' message, but it bears more than a faint resemblance to the run of TV commercials.

A Far-flung "Congregation"   The religious critics' second objection is that Jesus called people into a church community—a fellowship of worship and service. The electronic church, however, substitutes for this a pseudo-community of isolated viewers. Finally, TV evangelism fosters the cult-like following of a single leader. In 1979, a habitually measured and good-humored commentator on American Protestantism, University of Chicago church historian (and Lutheran pastor) Martin E. Marty warned that "the electronic church threatens to replace the living congregation with a far-flung clientele of devotees to this or that evangelist. This invisible religion is—or ought to be—the most feared contemporary rival to church religion."

But isn't that rivalry only the latest chapter in an old story? Religious "awakenings" have frequently been tied to new forms of communication—like the printed book in the sixteenth century or the open-air revival in the eighteenth and nineteenth—and on each occasion the established churches have warned that the new techniques were altering the character of the faith. In a sense the established churches were right. Certainly the Protestant emphasis on "scripture alone" derived from both Renaissance humanism and the new power of the printing press. Likewise, the simplified theology and emotional fervor of American Protestantism sprang from the needs of the faithful in the camp meeting. And church structures could no more escape alteration than church doctrine. When so many more people could read and own their own Bibles, the need for a teaching hierarchy diminished. Revivalism put a premium on showmanship and platform oratory, rather than theological training, as a path to religious leadership. The electronic church is not terribly sophisticated about answering the establishment's criticism, seeing it mainly as a reflection of the mainliners' lack of fervor and enterprise. But paradoxically, if it wanted to, it could defend its innovations as nothing new.

To the Electronic Collection Plate   But the tension between independent evangelists and the mainline churches is also part of a larger story—that of broadcasting in America. The early days of radio saw all kinds of religious groups not only buying time but frequently owning stations

—which were often used as weapons against one another. By 1934, however, when the Federal Communications Act established a "public interest" obligation for licensees, a less chaotic pattern began to develop. Led by NBC, most major stations—and eventually the other networks—provided free time to broad, ecumenical groups, which in turn produced religious programming of a nondivisive kind. (NBC, for example, worked in partnership with the Protestant Federal Council of Churches [now the NCC], with the National Council of Catholic Men, and with the Jewish Theological Seminary of America.) As they were providing free time to such mainline groups, NBC, CBS, and ABC actually refused to sell others any time for religious broadcasting, and many local stations followed suit. The Mutual Broadcasting System did sell time, but in 1944 it forbade soliciting funds on the air—a sharp blow to paid-time preachers. In short, the new arrangements left independent evangelicals to fend for themselves—buying time where they could, or owning and operating their own commercial stations.

With the advent of television, a consortium of Protestant, Catholic, and Jewish groups divided free network time on a 3,2,1 basis: Of every 6 hours the networks allotted, the Protestants would receive 3, the Catholics 2, and the Jews 1. The networks subsidized the programming, and local affiliates carried it free. This arrangement allowed the stations to meet their public-interest obligations and avoid sectarian strife, while the major religious groups controlled their allotted time (mostly on Sunday mornings, when audiences were small and advertisers few) and benefited from network expertise and technology.

Richard Walsh, former director of communications for the National Council of Catholic Men and producer of "The Catholic Hour" from 1953 to 1968, remembers the arrangement as highly practical and conducive to good relations between the churches and the networks, as well as among religious groups. "The purpose of network programming for the religious groups was not to convert, and they did little direct preaching à la today's electronic church," says Walsh. In his view, the point was to foster dialogue. 'The Catholic Hour', though addressed to Catholics, was on subjects that might be of interest to others. While financial support varied with each network, Walsh recalls enjoying great independence from the networks in producing a variety of programs—talk shows, operas, plays, documentaries.

Though generally comfortable, the relationship between the networks and mainline religious groups did have its share of ups and downs even before the electronic church hove onto the scene. Some Protestant groups continued to complain that the NCC did not represent the totality of Protestant views—and NBC, for one, provided time to the Southern Baptists. By the end of the sixties, network funds began to shrink and affiliates to be more reluctant about providing free time. Some of this may have been due to a perception, perhaps exaggerated, that religion was no longer, in the cant term of the day, "relevant," a view that declining church attendance figures supported. Bill McClurkin, director of broadcast and film for the NCC, adds another factor: The increase in Sunday sports broadcasting narrowed the time boundaries of the Sunday-morning "religious ghetto." In any case, when enterprising evangelicals proposed to pay for air-time that affiliates had been giving away—why, that was an offer the affiliates could hardly refuse.

More than ideology, program content, or style, money may be the key to the electronic church's rise. As Hadden and Swann point out; 1970 to '75 were years when the costs of video production dropped. They were also the years when the evangelists' audiences doubled, often at the expense of the mainliners' programs. The fact is that mainline and evangelical programs have never gone head-to-head, on the same terms. Would the mainline shows have been dropped by so many stations if they, too, were paying their own way? The TV evangelists, having been forced to wander in the paid-time wilderness for so long, have simply played by the free-market rules and won.

Money may also prove to be the Achilles heel of the TV preachers. Secular critics dwell on the huge sums the electronic church rakes in: the "electronic collection plate," they call it. But the TV ministry not only draws in support; it has to pay it out as well. Television is an expensive habit to maintain, and the TV preachers are hooked. Also, large amounts of money flowing in and out of the coffers are a constant temptation, even to the righteous. With or without scandal, the moderately prosperous lifestyle of most TV evangelists sits uncomfortably with their constant solicitation of funds and the panoply of memberships, pins, study guides, and booklets that they dangle before their followers. Some preachers resolve the incongruity by emphasizing their own versions of Save the Children campaigns—relief and missionary work in impoverished areas of the globe. But that appeal has provoked further demands for accurate accounting of how much money really goes where.

Jerry Falwell has joined with Billy Graham and some other evangelical ministers in establishing an Evangelical Council for Financial Accountability to insure financial self-regulation. Most of the other TV preachers have kept their distance.

Television's Calling   The success of the electronic church has given the established denominations the "feeling of being outflanked, threatened," according to Stewart M. Hoover, TV producer, lecturer on mass communications, and author of *The Electronic Giant,* published by the Church of the Brethren. Why, then, don't they simply start paying their own way too?

The question ignores the important *organizational* consequences of church involvement in television. With the electronic church, what you see is pretty much what there is. Television is at the heart of these ministries. "My specific calling from God," Jim Bakker has written, "is to be a television talk-show host. I love TV. I eat it. I sleep it." Most other church organizations are complex and their activities highly decentralized. Most of their personnel serve local congregations; most of their financial resources are invested in church buildings, community centers, schools, hospitals, and so on. The major churches all have skilled, respected individuals dealing with television. But enlarging their activities would mean switching substantial funds and energies from other areas.

For reasons of theology, propriety, and concern for the effect on other church activities, most of these churches object to soliciting funds on the air. Accordingly, they're not ready to give up on the free-time tradition. In the face of FCC deregulation policies, many church groups have defended the practice of free air-time for public-interest programming, and not just that of a religious nature either.

The cause is not lost. Free air-time does continue to be available. "Insight", a drama program produced by the Paulists, a Catholic order of priests, is shown free by about a hundred stations. In 1980 it was among the top ten religious programs in the Arbitron ratings, and in 1981 it won three Daytime Emmy Awards. "Davey and Goliath", a cartoon series for children produced by the Lutheran Church in America, continues to be re-run in free time slots—and to gain quite respectable ratings.

The networks, however, no longer seem interested in supporting these kinds of shows, so without giving up entirely on free time, the mainline churches know they have to explore other alternatives. Basically there are three:

1. to follow the lead of the electronic church by building their own production and distribution apparatus for religious programming;

2. to concentrate on influencing the effects of non-religious television on public and personal morals;

3. to reject using television entirely.

The last, most radical course has been proposed by Harvey Cox, a noted Harvard theologian. Suppose, he argues, that "all the mass media of all the countries of the world could be turned over to the churches for one whole week, or one whole month, exclusively for making the Gospel known. At the end of the month, do you really think the world would be much better off, or the Kingdom of God be appreciably closer?"

The problem, says Cox, is that the mass media are one-way, hierarchical systems inherently incapable of eliciting the profound belief the Gospel demands. The media "are controlled by the rich and powerful," while "God comes in vulnerability, and powerlessness. The message of the Gospel is essentially incompatible with any coercive form of communication. All 'mass media' are one-way and therefore inherently coercive."

Cox derides Christian "communicators" who want to infuse the networks with "a new and spiritually significant content. The churches should not be wasting their efforts trying to pilfer a few minutes of time from the reigning Caesars of the 'communications industry.' " Instead, "the Christian strategy *vis à vis* mass media is not to try to use them but to try to dismantle them. We need a real revolution in which the control of the media is returned to the people and the technical development of media is turned toward accessibility, two-way communication, and genuine conversation."

Less radical than Cox's approach, but still having something in common with it, are the efforts of some individuals concentrating on influencing non-religious television. Dr. Everett Parker, for example, is director of the United Church of Christ's Office of Communication, a veteran of religious broadcasting, and a leader in struggles to widen access to the airwaves. Under his leadership, the United Church of Christ has tried to influence the values communicated on television by insuring that all community groups are represented on the air. Parker's Office of Communication is a leading critic of FCC deregulation plans, and a sponsor of educational efforts and consulting services. The church-launched Community Telecommunications Service, for instance, has developed a workshop curriculum to teach local churches how to produce cable programs, and another to teach community and church leaders how to negotiate cable contracts, assure public access to cable, and enforce fair employment practices.

Other church programs try to influence the impact of television on values by educating the viewers: The Media Action Research Center, a body sponsored by several denominations and headquartered in the National Council of Churches office in New York, developed television awareness training in the mid-seventies. Its *Viewer's Guide* shows "how we can take command, use TV intelligently and creatively, instead of mindlessly letting TV use us."

Finally there is the first option—getting into the TV business in a big way. There are three outstanding examples of this besides those of the electronic church.

The United States Catholic Conference (USCC) has taken two steps toward keeping its hand in the game. First, an annual Catholic Communications Campaign raises about $5 million a year, 50 percent of which remains in the local dioceses where it is collected; the other half is used to support the USCC Office of Communications and to award grants to a range of communications-related projects.

Second, the USCC has formed the independent, for-profit Catholic Telecommunications Network of America (CTNA) to provide local dioceses with a variety of satellite-transmitted services: news and photo services for diocesan newspapers, electronic mail, videoconferencing for church leaders, administrative and educational materials, and TV program redistribution. The network, which began transmitting last fall, is supported by voluntary affiliation and maintenance fees from local dioceses—and by the sale of its services to commercial users. As of November 1982, 33 out of 172 local dioceses had signed affiliation contracts. Wassyl Lew, head of CTNA, expects that a number of religious orders, Catholic colleges, universities, and hospitals may eventually affiliate with it. Lew emphasizes the word "telecommunications" rather than "television" in describing the network: Its primary purpose is to provide a communications service for the bishops, though TV programming provided by the network will be available for redistribution to local TV stations or cable systems.

The fifteen hours of programming per week that CTNA currently plans to redistribute include programs on marriage counseling and enrichment; an interview program called "Christopher Close-Ups"; several Bible and theology programs; two Spanish-language programs; a missionary program produced by the Maryknoll religious order, and a variety of magazine-format and entertainment shows. All of this will be produced not by CTNA but largely by religious orders and local dioceses. Lew anticipates that as the system becomes fully operational, some of its downlinks will also serve as uplinks, thus allowing dioceses to be senders as well as receivers of TV programming. In the meantime, programs will go out from CTNA's New York transmitter.

CTNA is an attempt to meet the diverse needs of a decentralized church organization with the capacities of the satellite for coast-to-coast transmission. As such, the network might become a model for other church groups. Yet it is unlikely to increase the number of Catholic TV shows available to a large television audience.

One reason that telecommunications will always play a less important role for the Catholic church than for TV evangelists is that it "just doesn't fit with what Catholics think of as a church," argues Richard Hirsch, head of the USCC's Office of Communications. "The electronic church is not a church; it is a pulpit." The point applies to a number of other churches as well—those that consider sacrament and ritual as important to their worship as preaching, in particular the Episcopalians and Lutherans. It is interesting to recall that Bishop Sheen's famous programs had nothing of a church service about them. The bishop was dressed in resplendent episcopal garb, but *not* in his vestments for celebrating mass. The format was one of teaching, not preaching or prayer; a blackboard was the chief prop. Sheen's example suggests the distance that the "ritual" churches are apt to see between effective television and the central acts of their faith.

The Eternal Word Network, another of the three noteworthy efforts by religious groups to build a television base, also depends on satellite technology. Mother Angelica, a Franciscan nun whose convent in Birmingham, Alabama specializes in preparing and printing religious pamphlets and other materials, made the leap from the printing press to a satellite transponder on Satcom IIIR with four hours of programming seven nights a week. From a converted garage, she produces her own show, "Mother Angelica Talks It Over", makes time available to other religious programs, re-runs old favorites, and subleases unused transponder time to the First United Methodist Church in Shreveport, Louisiana. She reports that forty-two cable systems, reaching up to 800,000 homes, carry her programming. The network is supported by direct-mail donations, unsolicited contributions, and foundation grants.

The United Methodists tried a different approach: In 1980, they launched a fund-raising drive to buy a TV station. The church group planned to produce its own religious programs with the projected $1 million profit from the station. But ownership of a commercial station posed conflicts between the values of Methodism and the values the station would be communicating much of the time. The sheer expense of the project has also deterred some church members, who have asked, "How many hungry people can you feed with that money?"

The pitfalls encountered by the United Methodists illustrate the dangers for mainline churches that might be tempted to emulate the fundamentalists. According to Stewart M. Hoover, writing in *The Electronic Giant,* "The mainline churches could probably not 'beat the electronic church at its own game'; they probably would not really want to."

But it should be remembered that the electronic church itself was not born yesterday—which is when it first began getting national attention. It was more than two decades ago that Pat Robertson managed to put back on the air the defunct UHF station he had bought. Jerry Falwell went on the air in Lynchburg, Virginia, six months after he started his church there—in 1956. Oral Roberts first appeared on television in 1954, and his current TV format dates from 1969. At that time, the other churches were comfortably ensconced on the networks; twenty-five years later, they are groping. The outcome of that groping may not be clear for another quarter-century.

53 · Big Bucks Spread the Word of the Lord

By Daniel Cattau

In the 1980s, America has witnessed an explosion of
religious media, both print and electronic, writes
Daniel Cattau. Mass communication has been
discovered by religious groups and they are learning
how to use it. But they are also discovering that mass
communication is an expensive proposition. Cattau is
the news bureau director for the Lutheran Council
USA. His article appeared in *Communicator's
Journal*, July/August 1983.

In October 1979, Pope John Paul II gave religious leaders in the
United States a lesson they have not forgotten: The media, if used
wisely, can be your friend.

The papal trip to Boston, New York, Philadelphia, Des Moines,
Chicago and Washington gave the Roman Catholic Church hundreds of
millions of dollars of free air time and newspaper coverage.

That coverage made the Roman Catholic Church in the United
States even more aware of the need to add to its large network of
diocesan and national newspapers and radio and television broadcasts.

The example of the pope must have impressed Lutherans, Baptists,
Methodists, Mormons, Jews, Moslems, Pentecostals, Seventh-Day Ad-
ventists, Jehovah's Witnesses and others—already with years and hundreds of millions of dollars themselves invested in communications.

"You could not witness the remarkable response of the media in
1979 without drawing some conclusions about the importance of working with the media," says Russell Shaw, secretary for public affairs for
the U.S. Catholic Conference in Washington, D.C.

The communications efforts of the U.S. Roman Catholic Church, like
those of other faiths, are impossible to put a figure on, he added.

"It's more than you think and less than it ought to be," said Shaw.

Even before John Paul II arrived on the scene, however, the post-

Vatican II Roman Catholic Church was already changing its attitudes toward communications.

In 1971, the church published a "Pastoral Instruction on the Means of Social Communications" in response to a Vatican II decree (the council met from 1962-65) to have the church better understand its relationship to communications.

At about the same time, the church was already beginning to show its willingness to be less secret. The twice-a-year meetings of the National Conference of Catholic Bishops were opened to the press.

In an introduction to the pastoral instruction on communications, Archbishop John L. May of St. Louis (then bishop of Mobile, Ala.), says: "The church has not always been quick to understand the implications of modern communications or to put its theoretical understanding into immediate practice. There have been painful episodes in the relationship between the church and media. . . . It is not realistic to think that these difficulties will vanish overnight."

But the pastoral instruction from the Vatican also speaks to the media, says May, and this message goes beyond the boundaries of any faith.

"The message for communicators, as for churchmen, is the centrality of the communications vocation in modern society. The newsman, the broadcaster, the playwright, the filmmaker cannot be considered— or consider themselves—merely as entertainers or technicians," says May.

"They convey information and ideas that are essential to the functioning of society. Even more important, they help to shape the very ethos of the world in which we live.

"Theirs is, then, a calling of high honor—and of heavy responsibility."

The archbishop's comments may set a proper, idealistic tone for a discussion of religious communications. The reality of the communications world and ever-advancing technology may be something totally different, however.

First, something that should be obvious: religious groups are participating in the new communications technology. The strange sounding words like videotext, decoder, satellite receiver dish, floppy disc, interactive, voice-response and user friendliness are making inroads into places where the saints and martyrs used to tread.

For instance, the Church of Jesus Christ of Latter-day Saints (Mormon) is currently buying 500 receiver dishes for its churches, thus establishing the nation's largest single-order satellite network, according to a recent report of the Communication Commission of the National

Council of Churches, an ecumenical organization of more than 30 Christian churches.

The Southern Baptist Convention has signed a contract for the use of two satellite transponders and has applied to the Federal Communications Commission to build and operate a low-power television network.

And television evangelist Pat Robertson, head of the Christian Broadcasting Network, is not merely content with having the nation's second-largest cable network. He is establishing via satellite a complete television network from soap operas to news programs.

Today, Robertson's network is picked up by 3,000 of the 5,500, cable systems.

And the Roman Catholic Church is also in the middle of the telecommunications push by religious groups.

A satellite network developed by the U.S. Conference of Catholic Bishops began programming in late September. About 70 dioceses have signed up for the system and have their own earth stations to receive the satellite signals.

The dioceses will be receiving programs they can distribute by commercial and cable channels and through diocesan newspapers and schools.

The impact of satellite communications on the U.S. Catholic Church may be as significant as the introduction of parochial schools, says Bishop Louis Gelineau of Providence, R.I., and chairman of the Catholic Telecommunications Network of America.

"When the network is fully operational," he says, "services will include television and radio programming, teleconferencing, teleseminars, electronic mail and computer-to-computer communications, all geared to meet the needs of the church's demographics."

And there is more: The 15-month-old National Jewish Television transmits to 92 cable systems with more than 1.9 million homes, mostly in areas where there is a high percentage of Jews in the population.

And more: The United Church of Christ has recently begun offering a program of regional workshops designed to teach religious leaders and others how to use and get the most out of cable television.

The religious leaders behind these efforts know that telecommunications will revolutionize the practice of religion, making even the recent era of the prime-time or not-so-prime-time evangelists obsolete.

Before the "electronic church" of the Jerry Falwells, Jimmy Swaggarts, Oral Robertses and Billy Grahams is placed in a broadcasting museum, there are a few things that need to be said.

The electronic church, like it or not, has changed U.S. religious life.

In a book called *Prime Time Preachers* by Jeffrey K. Hadden and

Charles E. Swann, "televangelism" is viewed a phenomenon of considerable significance.

The televangelists, the authors said, "are destined to play a critical role in the shaping of the balance of the 20th century. They have more undisputed access to the airwaves than any other social movement in American society."

Although they have a potential for doing good, the authors say, the televangelists also might find themselves frustrated "by a system they cannot learn to master."

Quoting Arbitron television audience ratings, the authors say that the combined audience for all syndicated television programs jumped from 10 million in 1970 to 20 million in 1975. But more recent figures show the audience has been decreasing, and when those people who may watch more than one are counted, the total audience for the television evangelists drops to around six to eight million.

Hadden and Swann said that one of the most significant inventions of the electronic church has been "parapersonal communications"—the direct-mail letters, the 800-number phone systems, and the clubs and partnerships that become a surrogate family for the television viewers.

Another positive aspect of the electronic church is that it "has developed an extremely accurate and sensitive diagnosis of the spiritual needs and hunger of persons who are reacting intuitively against the inhuman and un-Christian world of our media culture," says Dr. William F. Fore, assistant general secretary for communications of the National Council of Churches.

"The electronic church understands that people are hurting because they are ignored, they are not needed. . . . Our main-line churches, to our everlasting shame, have tended by and large not to recognize the nature or scope of these new kinds of needs. . . ," says Fore, a frequent critic of the electronic church.

Yet Fore cites two main failings of the electronic church: It has not taken seriously enough the "demonic nature of commercial television" and it has proceeded on "an inadequate understanding the Gospel."

In the quest for large audiences "to pay for even greater audiences," says Fore, the television evangelists could not truly offend or put to the test the hard questions of the Gospel.

So the electronic church at its best helps people and builds certain family ties, though it is done through the airwaves. At its worst, the electronic church undermines the radical call to obedience in the Gospel. What does this mean for the future of telecommunications in the church?

Fore says "labor-saving robots" may help the church communicate faster, farther and more effectively, but "we are in danger of losing sight of the human dimension, the human context, indeed, the human being in the process."

There are a number of groups already attacking cable television systems for non-technological reasons: Cable might have brought more Christian television into homes, but it has also brought more sex on the "adult" channels.

In the long run, however, the benefits of the new telecommunications industry appear to outweigh the problems raised by it.

"It's a rare couple that will read a book together," says Bill Greig, president of Gospel Light Publications, which plans to change its name to Gospel Light Communications. But he added a couple might watch several videotex programs on marriage and family together before reading a book.

The focus on telecommunications and the church is helpful in understanding some of the challenges and problems of the future.

But much of what is going on today in church communications is neither new nor revolutionary.

In my office, the Lutheran Council News Bureau, we send out stories the same way my predecessors did—by mail. It seems almost like riding a buggy at times, but it is still effective. The council represents nearly 8.5 million Lutherans.

Other religious news agencies have a reputation for impartiality and accuracy.

The National Catholic News Service and United Methodists on their voluminous news services also have provided a fair, impartial source of news both for the secular and religious press.

National church magazines and diocesan newspapers still get millions of readers. The quality of these publications is still uneven, but great progress has been made during the past 10 or 15 years in enhancing the journalistic quality.

As much as the telecommunications possibilities in the churches are staggering, so are the figures for religious publications—though continued postal rate hikes have caused some to cut down on their frequency of publication or increase subscription rates.

The Religious Public Relations Council of Chicago estimates there are about 100,000 religious publications (including newsletters) in the United States.

Most of the approximately 170 Roman Catholic dioceses and archdioceses have their own newspaper. *The Chicago Catholic,* the newspaper of the Archdiocese of Chicago (which has 2.5 million Catholics), is the largest with a circulation of 157,000.

Three major Lutheran denominational magazines have a combined circulation of more than 1.6 million. *The Lutheran* (Lutheran Church in America) has a circulation of just under 600,000; *The Lutheran Standard*

(American Lutheran Church) 582,700; and *The Lutheran Witness* (Lutheran Church—Missouri Synod) 440,000.

All these publications, though concerned with denominational matters, increasingly have tackled tough subjects such as the church's involvement in the peace issue, the plight of Cuban, Haitian and Salvadoran refugees, and abortion.

It is difficult to draw the lines between the value of "official" against "unofficial" church publications. In the Episcopal Church, for instance, the official newspaper, the *Episcopalian*, has a circulation of 265,000. In addition, each of the 95 dioceses in the church generally has its own newspaper. And there is *The Living Church*, a semi-independent publication based in Milwaukee, with a more conservative slant and a circulation of 92,000. But it is hard to tell which, if either, is more respected.

In the Roman Catholic Church, the Kansas City-based *National Catholic Reporter* provides an aggressive and independent-minded alternative to the diocesan paper for many Catholics. It has a circulation of 50,000—but its readership is so varied it would be difficult to classify it as exclusively Catholic.

And the slick, *People*-like (in appearance, not content) *U.S. Catholic* has a circulation of 60,509. It tackles subjects that hit Catholics both at home and in the church—homosexuality, divorce, alcoholism and alienation.

For conservative Christians, their equivalent of *Time* or *Newsweek* is *Christianity Today,* a magazine based in the Chicago area with a circulation of 200,000. Its editorial quality has improved dramatically in the last 10 years as has its news coverage of all aspects of religion.

Circulation size is not the only way to judge religiously oriented magazines. *Commentary* (50,000), *The Christian Century* (30,000) and *Commonweal* (19,000), may have small circulations, but they are among those "passed around" publications whose influence far exceeds their circulation numbers.

Tomorrow, church leaders may be able to move into the era of teleconferences with one another without much trouble. But the only way to build trust and respect is in the one-to-one conversations and dialogues. It is worth noting that the National Conference of Catholic Bishops, while moving ahead in the telecommunications field, met this past summer for a week-long retreat for spiritual reflection and education—another first for them.

The church is advancing with technology, but always with one foot touching base with reality, which is serving people for the sake of the Gospel.

"We staunchly resist the image that we are a television network," says Michael Hurley of the Catholic Communications Network.

"We are a telecommunications network, that is, a service organization. We're not in the entertainment business."

Earlier, John Paul II was used as an example of an effective communicator. He appreciates the media and uses it well. Other churches should take heed.

He recognizes that the work of both the church and the media is not easy, and that praise should be given when both turn out well.

At the end of the U.S. papal trip, I was with a group of about 80 reporters who traveled with John Paul II and had a brief meeting with the pope.

He talked about the value of reporting the truth and thanked the media for their work. And then, looking toward the heavens, he thanked God for preserving both him and his media companions in safety throughout the trip.

54 · PRAY TV: A POWERFUL NEW TOOL FOR RELIGIOUS CULTS?

BY DENNIS S. DOBSON

As television is moving toward "narrow-casting," religious programming can and will be directed at smaller and smaller religious sects and cults. That is the prediction of Dennis S. Dobson, who writes frequently on communications systems and is author of a booklet on ways in which business can capitalize on these emerging technologies. He is director of public relations for the Industrial Home for the Blind in Brooklyn, New York. This article appeared in *The Futurist*, August 1983.

Don't be surprised if you turn on your television set in 1985 in search of your favorite sitcom and find instead a group of brightly-clad people chanting and dancing around a steel drum. Religious cults may very well have established outposts on Channel X, weeknights at 9 on your local television station.

"Cultivision" could become a reality if "narrow-casting," a system of telecasting to a specific audience through cable, scrambled signals, or other devices, develops into the popular programming and marketing device that many media experts are predicting.

While advertisers welcome narrow-casting as a way of reaching a specific audience interested in their client's product, this developing aspect of cable television may also be embraced by cults eager to build their own cable networks into stage-door pulpits, to spread the good word while making a profit. We already have all-movie stations and all-sports stations; soon we may also have all-religious networks.

Religious cults that are not wealthy enough to develop their own networks could enter the medium through public-access provisions. Public access is the means by which residents of a local community can make their presence felt and have exposure on their community's local-access station. It is up to the local station operator to grant access on a nondiscriminatory basis, as a public service to the community that grants him the franchise. Under the agreements by which local governments grant cable rights to operators, almost anyone can come in off the street and say, "I want public access." The operator will often give time and studio facilities to these people in order to keep on good terms with the community he is serving.

No longer will wide-eyed, smiling cult members need to stalk Main Street selling records, books, and flowers in an effort to obtain new members. Nor will they need to waste time trying to snare the attention of tourists at airports or bus depots, when they could be in the studio taping their own television show.

The television viewer is under no pressure from either the channel's schedule or the cult's salesman to join forces with the cult. However, relaxed and resting comfortably in his home, he may be much more receptive to the message than when accosted on the street.

Television and Traditional Religious Programming   Just how effective this approach may be in the privacy of one's home is unknown, but established religious programming may give a clue. Traditional religious programming, while appearing heavy-handed at times, attracts huge television audiences because the format is compelling and the evangelical "stars" are charismatic. Video preachers like Billy Graham, Jerry Falwell, Oral Roberts, and Rex Humbard have been on the air a long time and have attracted tremendous followings. The variety-talk show format of the Christian Broadcasting Network's *700 Club* has made it one of the most popular programs on television. Its music, conversation, and Johnny Carson-like monologues capture many people who occasionally flip through the channels to see what's on.

There is a ravenous appetite out there "in television-land" for such an appealing form of preaching, and ambitious cults will likely use these shows as models. Young people may be especially susceptible to such a program as they leisurely turn the channel (especially teenagers, who seem to be constantly trying to find ways to be different from their parents).

With the advent of 50- and 100-channel cable systems, the broadcasting market is open to a greater diversity of voices: news, sports, culture, politics, and community-access programming to local townships. When such cable capacity is universal, virtually anyone will be able to come into your living room. With such freedom for potential programmers, the viewer has only one protection: common sense. Know what cultivision is before you let yourself or your children be taken in by it. In other words, *caveat visor* (viewer beware).

FOR FURTHER READING

Gregor T. Goethals, *The TV Ritual: Worship at the Video Alter.* Boston: Beacon Press, 1981.

Peter G. Horsfield, *Religious Television: The American Experience.* New York: Longman, 1984.

XV

Mass Media and Culture

SOME CRITICS of mass culture have, like Caesar, divided all of the new world into three parts: highbrows, middlebrows and lowbrows.

Highbrows are those who prefer Shakespearean plays, Beethoven string quartets, T. S. Eliot poetry, lithographs by Picasso, movies by Bergmann, chess and tennis, novels by Thomas Mann and Bernard Malamud, the *Christian Science Monitor, Commentary* magazine, and *Foreign Affairs.*

Middlebrows go for Hemingway and Steinbeck, waltzes by Johann Strauss and the Nutcracker Suite by Tchaikovsky, baseball, movies by Steven Spielberg, *Time* and *U.S. News & World Report,* the *Washington Post* or the *Baltimore Sun, Saturday Evening Post* covers by Norman Rockwell, middle-of-the-road radio and easy listening music.

Lowbrows are interested in soap operas, situation comedies, professional football, poker, Michael Jackson, comics in the newspapers, *Reader's Digest* and *TV Guide,* country-western music and detective novels, romance and movie stars.

Of course, critics say that the mass media are reducing us all to the lowest common denominator, degenerating culture into a wasteland of pop art and corn.

On the other side of the argument, however, are those who note that high culture is flourishing as never before. America has more symphony orchestras than ever before, more museums and art galleries, more bookstores and more students seeking a higher education.

In addition, they argue, out of the mass culture of the mass media have frequently come works of high merit that can stand the test of the most exacting criticism and live on in our culture as works of art.

There is probably no end to this argument, except to say that all sides can win.

461

55 · THE GUILT EDGE

BY CLARK WHELTON

One point of view is that we all suffer from guilt
for liking the mass culture of the mass media. It
has become a status thing to be highbrow, but
secretly we sneak off and enjoy our soap operas.
We prefer "M*A*S*H" to Mendelssohn, says Clark
Whelton, but we don't want our neighbors to find
out. Whelton has been a speech writer for the
mayor of New York and is author of a book on
television. This article is reprinted from *Channels
of Communications,* February/March 1982.

Guilt: The small, insistent voice telling you that with a little more
effort you could be having a really miserable time.

Guilt. For me it began on May 9, 1961, in a remote and dusty corner
of Fort Bliss, Texas. I was watching television in the day room of Company D. The rest of my platoon had trudged off to the mess hall after
our evening ritual of watching the cartoon adventures of Huckleberry
Hound, but I had stayed to catch the first few minutes of the evening
news. The army was buzzing with rumors about American involvement
in a place called Vietnam, and I wanted to see if anything was happening that might interfere with my imminent return to civilian life.

But the lead story that night was not about Vietnam, or even about
astronaut Alan Shepard, who had grazed the edge of outer space in a
suborbital rocket shot four days earlier. Instead, the announcer was
talking about someone named Newton Minow. Minow, recently appointed chairman of the Federal Communications Commission by President Kennedy, had delivered a blistering speech to television broadcasters in which he invited them to watch their own programming from
sign-on to sign-off.

"You will see," Minow said, "a procession of game shows, violence,
audience-participation shows, formula comedies about totally unbelievable families, blood and thunder, mayhem, violence, sadism, murder,
western badmen, western good men, private eyes, gangsters, more violence, and cartoons. And, endlessly, commercials—many screaming,
cajoling, and offending. And most of all, boredom."

There was more. Minow acknowledged that a television western draws a larger audience than a symphony, but scolded, "It is not enough to cater to the nation's whims—you must also serve the nation's needs." The thirty-five-year-old former law partner of Adlai Stevenson cut loose with a condemnation that echoed throughout the country. Television, Minow asserted, is a "vast wasteland."

I cringed, besieged by feelings of shame. If television was a vast wasteland, then I, a founding member of the Fort Bliss Huckleberry Hound Society and television fan extraordinaire, was clearly a vast wastrel. I loved it all, the whole Newton Minow hit list. I loved the game shows, the formula comedies, the unbelievable families, the private eyes, gangsters and gunplay, cartoons, cajoling commercials, the works. I can still sing the Mott's applesauce jingle from 1950, and as far as I know I hold the record for continuous contemplation of a test pattern.

But ever since Newton Minow painted a "wasteland" label on my viewing habits, I have been dogged by doubt. Whenever I settle back for a Mary Tyler Moore rerun or another session with *Family Feud,* I hear that small voice telling me I am contributing to the decline of Western Civilization, and I feel guilty. I have spent more than a little time examining this curious exercise in self-condemnation, and I know there are millions of others who suffer from the same affliction.

How did a mechanical contrivance like television get cross-wired into the American conscience? Did it really start with Newton Minow? In fact, the origins of television guilt go back a long way, and are probably as old as the medium itself. *New York Times* critic Jack Gould had already taken a swipe at television as early as 1948, when sets had tubes instead of transistors. Gould wrote that children's shows appeared to be a "narcotic" administered by parents, who had learned that plunking junior down in front of the Philco would keep him out of their hair for an hour or two. By calling television a narcotic instead of something that kids enjoy watching, Gould helped to establish a pattern of overkill in television criticism that would largely be delivered via television's major competitor—newspapers.

Very early in the struggle for media domination, the newspaper business showed its fangs: It was the summer of 1950. At the editorial offices of the *New York Journal-American,* flagship paper of the Hearst publishing empire, a sudden meeting was called. Among the handpicked reporters attending that meeting was Atra Baer, daughter of the well-known humor columnist Bugs Baer.

"The editor came right to the point," Baer recalls. "A message had been received from William Randolph Hearst, the chief himself. It seems that Mr. Hearst was very worried about television, especially about the 'deleterious' effect that it might be having on the American public. So a team of *Journal-American* reporters was assigned to canvass the New York City area and come up with some quotes—particularly from mothers—that would focus on the 'bad effects' of television."

Orders in hand, the reporters fanned out. Atra Baer was sent to a nearby suburb, where she asked the requisite questions in the requisite way: "Madam, are you worried about the harmful effect television is having on your children's eyesight? Are you concerned about the harmful effect television has on your children's reading habits?" The sought-after answers were easily obtained, and a story on the "dangers of television" was easily written. At that time there were Hearst papers in every section of the country.

Merrill Panitt, the editor of *TV Guide,* remembers just how effective anti-television journalism was.

"In our early issues," Panitt says, "we constantly had to answer all the negative stories circulating about television. We ran articles reassuring our readers that no, television is not bad for your eyes; no, television is not bad for your back; no, television does not cause cancer, and it certainly doesn't cause constipation."

Given the newspapers' antipathy toward radio, their alarm at the arrival of television—radio with pictures—can be imagined. The antagonism even extended into press conferences, where newspaper reporters often salted their questions with expletives ("Senator, don't bullshit us, when the hell is Congress going to pass that goddamn tax bill?") so that broadcasters, whose vocabularies are sanitized by their license obligations, couldn't run the footage on the air. When naughty language didn't do the trick, light plugs were pulled, doors were slammed, and coughing epidemics broke out whenever a television reporter asked a question.

"It worked for a while," says a former newspaper reporter who admits to a minor career in sabotage. "But we could see who was winning the war. Politicians wouldn't even let a press conference begin until the cameras arrived."

Newspapers grudgingly accepted the inevitable. The immense popularity of television stars like Milton Berle and Ed Sullivan had helped to sell millions of sets, and the daily papers had to give their readers what they wanted. Bans against television listings were dropped, even though many papers quietly decided that television coverage deserved to be crammed in with the comics or buried deep inside. This snobbery toward television still exists today. A reporter who worked for *The New York Times* in the 1970s recalls an editor saying that the *Times* would not "debase" its culture section with television news. Television reporting was—and still is—relegated to the back pages.

However, it was in the area of television criticism that newspapers made their biggest dent in the competition. Syndicated columnists like John Crosby specialized in scathing reviews of television programs, reviews implying not only that certain shows were inferior, but that television itself was a medium only a lowbrow could love. Although theater critics were expected to love the theater, and dance and movie critics to revere those art forms, television critics were often people who disdained television.

At the center of this conflict between newspapers and television was a life-or-death struggle. Publishers were well aware that someone who gets his nightly news from the tube is less likely to buy an evening paper. Even before television went on the air, newspapers had been fighting for survival. Dozens of double-barreled logotypes *(Post-Dispatch, Herald Tribune)* revealed the many newspaper mergers inspired by the fear of bankruptcy. Fresh competition from television gave newspapers the shudders, especially in large cities where the new medium flourished.

On a national basis, however, there was little reason to fear that television would undermine American literacy. Official figures reveal that the United States had only nine fewer daily papers in 1980 than there were in 1950, and circulation had climbed by more than eight million.

Nevertheless, enemies of television were ever on the alert. In 1963, psychologists claimed to have discovered a "TV Syndrome," which supposedly made kids cranky if they were overexposed to the tube. In the seventies, reports indicated that by the time they reached first grade, television-watching children had spent an average of 5,000 hours in front of the set. A variety of social problems now began to be blamed on television. Low reading scores? College Board scores taking a tumble? Crime and vandalism on the rise? Blame television. And let's not forget the recent news from Tulsa Central Academy in Oklahoma. When English teacher John Zannini's seventh grade class heard that President Reagan had been shot, most of the class cheered. Mr. Zannini blamed it on television.

Television has been subjected to constant scorn and sniping by critics who would have you believe that unless you were watching a show introduced by Alistair Cooke, you had no taste at all. Writer Richard Schickel summed it up this way:

"Television criticism, especially that which aspires to the broad scale and the theoretical, has become, in recent years, little more than a branch of the ecology movement. The brightly glowing box in the corner of the living room is perceived by those who write sober books and Sunday newspaper articles about it as a sort of smoking chimney, spilling God knows what brain-damaging poisons not only into the immediate socio-political environment, but also, it is predicted, loosing agents whose damage may not become apparent to us for decades to come."

In the short run, however, the damage done by snobbish criticism of television is very apparent. America may be the only country in the world where people actually feel guilty about watching. Unfortunately, it is very easy to bully the average American on matters of culture and taste. This vulnerability probably dates back to our colonial past, when most settlers were too busy surviving to give much thought to gracious living. All that was refined and cultured arrived on packet boats from Europe—which to a considerable extent is still true today—and Americans became accustomed to taking orders on questions of taste, anxious to be accepted by the rest of the world. Newton Minow betrayed this anxiety in his "wasteland" speech when he asked: "What will people of other countries think of us when they see our western badmen and good men punching each other in the jaw, in between the shooting?"

I can answer that question. American television is very popular throughout the world, where most people consider it a source of entertainment, not of guilt. I once stayed at a small hotel in Barcelona where the only regulation was: "Never interrupt the manager when he's watching *Sea Hunt* or *Have Gun Will Travel.*" When Americans assigned to a NATO air base in Iceland broadcast old *I Love Lucy* tapes, the show became the number-one hit in nearby Reykjavík. In England, where television is a popular pastime, viewers watch anything and everything without apology. But here at home it's a different story. Americans are plagued by guilt for enjoying television.

There is, for example, the guilt parents impose on children. Michael J. Arlen, television critic for *The New Yorker,* compared this parental harrassment to the guilt-mongering and mythologizing frequently surrounding the subject of masturbation. "Authorities, for example, such as parents and educators, suggest that it may cause vague harm . . . though generally speaking there are rarely any visible signs of ill effects." Instead of encouraging children to develop good judgment about their television habits, parents sometimes taint the whole topic with implications of moral failure by those who watch any television at all. The result is not less television viewing, but subterfuge and feelings of guilt when the set is on.

There is also the vague fear that the tube is wasting your time. You spent all day Saturday watching a *Gilligan's Island* festival, and when you're through you discover that the lawn still isn't mowed. And you feel guilty. Obviously, television offers extraordinary opportunities for wasting time. There is nothing easier than turning on a set, and if television is being used as an excuse for avoiding other duties, then guilt feelings are probably justified.

Then, of course, there is status guilt, the least logical variety of television angst. You prefer *M*A*S*H* to Mendelssohn, but you're afraid the neighbors will find out. You've read critic John Mason Brown's quip that television is "chewing gum for the eyes," and now you deny that you like to chew gum. Status guilt can be a serious problem; however, it will help to know that those who regularly demean television do so out of a need to feel unique. It's easy to be snobbish about the theater, restaurants, clothes, or literature, because status seekers can always claim to have been the first to discover a new play, bistro, fashion, or book. Television, which reaches everyone at the same time, offers little in the way of snob appeal. The viewer can only claim to have done what everyone else in the country could have done if he had turned on his set, and there is no distinction at all in such a boast. Now and then a "cult" show like *Mary Hartman, Mary Hartman* will come along, but as soon as enough people tune in, the snobs tune out and turn up their noses at anyone who doesn't do the same.

The fact that most television guilt has no basis in reality does not mean that television is without flaws. However, it takes more than one generation to shape and refine an innovation so powerful and revolutionary, and we're learning all the time. As for those who agree that television is indeed a vast wasteland, and that those who watch it deserve to be burdened by guilt, I suggest that the world before television was not exactly paradise. Boredom, loneliness, ignorance—these and other social ills have been around for a long time.

From the window of the Company D day room where I watched *Huckleberry Hound,* I could see the distant summit of Guadalupe Peak, ninety miles away across the high plains desert. Ninety miles of sand and chaparral. Ninety miles of nothing. But the Company D television set brought the world a little bit closer. Anybody who has seen a real "vast wasteland" will tell you that television is a vast relief.

56 · ARCHIE BUNKER AND THE LIBERAL MIND

BY CHRISTOPHER LASCH

Archie Bunker is perhaps the most archtypical
lowbrow ever produced by the mass media. Has his
popularity turned us all into Archie Bunkers, making
us tolerant and accepting of his bigotry and
ignorance? Christopher Lasch argues that there are
other, more important aspects to Archie Bunker and
the kinds of material sometimes developed by the
mass media for mass audiences. Lasch is a professor
of history at the University of Rochester and author
of *The Culture of Narcissism*. This article is
reprinted from *Channels of Communications*,
October/November 1981.

In the late sixties, advertisers discovered a new market. Surveys
told them that the most voracious consumers were now affluent, urban,
educated people under the age of thirty-five. In an attempt to reach this
audience, the networks began to experiment with programs slightly
more sophisticated than *The Beverly Hillbillies, The Ed Sullivan Show,*
and *Marcus Welby.* After much hesitation, CBS—which had least to
lose at the time—introduced Norman Lear's *All in the Family* in January
1971. For the first time, a network had dared to confront its audience
with a middle-American antihero who vents the most outrageous opinions, tyrannizes over his wife, and bickers endlessly with his daughter
and her husband, who struggle unsuccessfully to overcome his prejudices against blacks, Jews, women, and other "un-American" minorities. Archie Bunker proved so durable a character that he has been with
us eleven years, now as the hero of *Archie Bunker's Place, All in the
Family's* successor.

From the start, Archie Bunker became the object of passionate controversy. Did the depiction of his bigotry have the therapeutic effect of
dragging a sensitive issue into the open and forcing viewers to confront
their own prejudices? Or did it reinforce bigotry by making it respect-

able? According to Robert Wood, former president of CBS, *All in the Family* helped to "ventilate some of the prejudices and misconceptions in American society today." Many reviewers agreed that *All in the Family* served an "important purpose," even if it offended liberals and other "up-tight viewers." A CBS survey of the show's audience indicated that most viewers took it as a satire, not a vindication, of prejudice. But a somewhat more extensive (though still flawed and simplistic) survey, by sociologists Neil Vidmar and Milton Rokeach, concluded that the program probably reinforced prejudice instead of combatting it.

Laura Z. Hobson, author of *Gentlemen's Agreement,* claimed in a 1971 *New York Times* article that *All in the Family* sanitized prejudice and made it socially acceptable. Her vigorous attack on Archie Bunker and his creators captured the indignation of an older generation of liberals appalled by what they saw as an attempt to make bigotry loveable, "to clean it up, deodorize it, make millions of people more comfy about indulging in it." In reply, Norman Lear accused Hobson of underestimating the intelligence of middle Americans, who could be trusted, he insisted, to recognize his work as satirical in its intention. Yet surveys showing that most viewers identified with Archie (even though many of them thought son-in-law Mike got the better of their arguments) strengthened the fear that the program elicited a "sadistic response," as one educator put it, and served "no constructive purpose." (These views and others were recently collected by Richard P. Adler in a volume entitled *All in the Family: A Critical Appraisal,* published by Praeger.)

Both Archie Bunker and the controversy he has generated tell us a great deal about the liberal mind today. *All in the Family* and *Archie Bunker's Place* implicitly take the position that resistance to social change, failure to "adjust" to change, and fear of change have pathological roots. Lear has argued that Archie Bunker's bigotry rests not on hatred but on the "fear of anything he doesn't understand." Because this fear is irrational, Archie's prejudices cannot be corrected by rational persuasion. Although Mike's arguments always "make sense," according to Lear, while Archie's rebuttals are "totally foolish," Archie can't be decisively defeated by Mike.

Liberals of Laura Hobson's type, convinced that bigotry can be combatted by propaganda depicting it in the most unattractive light, mistakenly see the Archie Bunker programs as a capitulation to popular prejudices. What the programs really seem to say, however, is that prejudice is a disease and that the only way to overcome it, as in psychotherapy, is to bring to light its irrational origins. *All in the Family* "simply airs [prejudice]," according to Lear, "brings it out in the open, has people talking about it."

The series seems to have been influenced, at least indirectly, by the theory of "working-class authoritarianism," which has played an important part in the thinking of social scientists and members of the helping professions ever since the late forties. According to this widely accepted interpretation, prejudice, ethnocentricity, and intolerance of ambiguity originate in the authoritarian child-rearing practices allegedly characteristic of working-class families. Archie Bunker has all the traits commonly attributed to the authoritarian husband and father. Lear's dramatization of Bunker's anti-Semitism, racism, male chauvinism, and xenophobia shares with the sociological literature on authoritarianism a tendency to reinterpret class issues in therapeutic terms and to reduce political conflicts to psychological ones. It ignores the possibility that "middle Americans" have legitimate grievances against society, legitimate misgivings about what is called social progress.

Yet the few gains that have been made in race relations, desegregation, and women's rights have usually been achieved at the expense of the white working-class male. His anger cannot be understood, therefore, as a purely psychological reaction; it has an important political basis. His dislike of liberals, moreover, springs not so much from "anti-intellectualism" or ethnocentricity as from the realistic perception that working-class values are the chief casualties of the "cultural revolution" with which liberalism has increasingly identified itself. With his unsentimental but firm commitment to marriage and family life, his respect for hard work and individual enterprise, and his admittedly old-fashioned belief that people should accept the consequences of their actions, the working-class male rightly regards himself as a forgotten man in a society increasingly dominated by the permissive, therapeutic morality of universal understanding. He sees himself, not without reason, as the victim of bureaucratic interference, welfarism, and sophisticated ridicule. Lacking any real political choices, he sometimes vents his anger in an ill-considered politics of right-wing moralism. But it is well known that many of the same voters who supported George Wallace also supported Robert Kennedy (and in any case the Wallace vote did not by any means come exclusively from the working class).

All in the Family and *Archie Bunker's Place* make no attempt to depict the political basis of working-class prejudice, or even to capture the complexity of the attitudes it dramatizes. The programs reduce a complex historical experience to the single issue of "bigotry," which they then approach as a form of pathology.

But what is true of Norman Lear's famous series is equally true of the commentary they have inspired. Both critics and defenders agree that the "disease" of bigotry is the important issue; they differ only on the question of whether Lear's talking-cure may be worse than the disease itself. Thus historian John Slawson (after stating flatly that "bigotry is sickness") argues that Archie Bunker brings out the worst in his fans. Quoting political sociologist Seymour Martin Lipset on working-class authoritarianism, Arthur Asa Berger (author of *The TV-Guided American*) congratulates *All in the Family* for demolishing the "myth of the common man." But whereas the myth upholds the working man as the salt of the earth, Lipset, and Norman Lear, suggest that he is actually a bigot, endowed with attitudes "to make you shudder." Like many critics, however, Berger would prefer a more straightforward and unambiguous condemnation of Archie Bunker and his kind. Lear's comedy, he thinks, embodies a kind of pornography of prejudice, ridiculing ethnocentric attitudes but at the same time inviting the viewer to find titillation in their frank expression.

There may be some justice in Berger's charge that *All in the Family* delivers a "double payoff": "We enjoy the ethnic humor yet feel superior to it." But instead of asking whether such ridicule serves a useful social purpose, commentators might better ask whether anything of artistic value is served by appealing so consistently to an audience's sense of superiority. Laura Hobson considered the program "elitist" because only well-educated liberal intellectuals would feel superior to Archie Bunker. Lear, noting that Hobson had unwittingly exposed her own elitism, replied in effect that liberal attitudes are now so widely diffused (at least among the younger viewers he was trying to reach) that almost anyone would feel superior to such an antiquated buffoon. When it nevertheless turned out that many viewers do identify with Archie, even though they do not necessarily endorse all his opinions, this fact—instead of prompting speculation about the complexity of the emotional response elicited by the series—simply reinforced the fear that it might have undesirable social effects.

Yet art of any merit to some extent transcends the immediate intentions of its creators. Although *All in the Family* and *Archie Bunker's Place* invite ridicule of their hero, as their defenders contend, the programs also seem to evoke a more complicated response. For one thing, these programs—especially the original series—deal with emotionally resonant themes of family life. In one survey of *All in the Family*'s audience, the children in a working-class family told an interviewer that their mother, like Edith Bunker, mediated generational arguments. Many middle-class mothers could doubtless say the same thing.

Part of the Bunker household's appeal to a more "sophisticated" audience, I suspect, lies in its power to evoke reminders of ethnic neighborhoods and ethnic cultures that the program's upwardly mobile young viewers have left behind in their climb into the "new class." In the conflict between Archie Bunker and his son-in-law, who rises during the course of the series from a Polish working-class background to a university teaching position, *All in the Family* dramatizes experiences central to the formation of a new, liberal, managerial intelligentsia, which has turned its back on the ethnic ghettos, developed a cosmopolitan outlook and cosmopolitan tastes through higher education, and now looks back on its origins with a mixture of superiority and sentimental regret. This experience, repeated now for several generations, has played a formative part in the development of the managerial and professional class. Its ideology of tolerance and anti-authoritarianism puts great emphasis on the ability to outgrow early prejudices. Because the new class has defined itself in opposition to the values of "middle America," it needs to repudiate its own roots, to exaggerate the distance it has traveled, and also to exaggerate the racism and bigotry of those lower down on the social scale. At the same time, it occasionally sheds a sentimental tear over the simpler life it thinks it has left behind.

All this finds almost classic expression in Lear's comedy of popular ignorance and parochialism. In one of the more perceptive commentaries on Lear's work, Michael J. Arlen, television critic of *The New Yorker,* suggests that "modern, psychiatrically inspired or induced ambivalence may indeed be the key dramatic principle behind this new genre of popular entertainment. A step is taken, then a step back. A gesture is made and then withdrawn—blurred into distracting laughter, or somehow forgotten."

America's new managerial elite has not only adopted an official ideology of tolerance, in which it does not yet feel completely secure, it has also developed an "anti-authoritarian" style of personal relations that forbids the expression of anger and violent emotion. *All in the Family* dissolves murderous impulses by foisting them on the father and by depicting this father, moreover, as an opinionated but impotent autocrat crushed by the wheel of historical progress. It helps the viewer not so much to come to terms with anger as to displace it. Beyond that, it reinforces the collective self-esteem of those whose ascendancy rests not on the secure command of an intellectual and political tradition but on their imagined superiority to the average unenlightened American bigot.

57 · SHOWDOWN AT CULTURE GULCH

BY BRIAN WINSTON

With the introduction of cable to the mass media, a
part of television can now go highbrow, catering to
the needs and interests of a smaller group of people
who want better programming than soap operas and
sitcoms and Sunday afternoon football. But Brian
Winston is somewhat cynical, following the premiere
of a new cable service called ARTS. Winston is a
contributing editor of *Channels* magazine and a
professor of film and television at New York
University. This article is reprinted from *Channels of
Communications*, August/September 1981.

Limousines, champagne, searchlights, telegrams, and (if geograph-
ically possible) Sardi's—no industry celebrates new products with the
verve, ballyhoo, and enthusiasm of the entertainment industry. But
nothing of this disturbed the calm in the office of Herb Granath, head
of ABC Video Enterprises, the day following the premiere of its first
cable service, ARTS. The coming of this major endeavor, a "cultural"
service specifically designed for cable distribution, was marked only by
a huge bunch of flowers offered in congratulation by some Japanese
television people Granath was entertaining that morning. How did the
new service go? "The phone isn't ringing," said Granath. "I assume it's
all right."

Narrowcasting culture might be a long way from the excitement of
the 1976 Olympics, Granath's previous major programming task; the
product might consist largely of esoteric material produced by others,
mainly in Europe; the audience, a maximum universe of only four and
a half million homes (most of which were tuned as usual to the networks) might be minuscule—but the seriousness of ABC's cable operation should not be doubted.

Cable, with only a quarter of the nation wired, is a long way from
threatening the existence of broadcasting, but there have been some
small yet ominous signs. In the summer of 1980, for instance, amid the

usual reruns and without the promised Olympic delights from Moscow, pay feature-film services drew greater audiences in cabled homes than any network did during an entire "sweep" period. The cable industry might be somewhat optimistic in projecting an imminent doubling of cabled homes (to 46 million by 1990), but something is clearly going on out there and it would be corporate folly for broadcasters not to be part of it.

ABC, CBS, and NBC's parent, RCA, all intend to test the temperature of the cable water in much the same way—by offering upscale services that rely, albeit in differing proportions, on the arts (mainly in performance) and imported programming.

There is no question the networks are in earnest about cable. But whether or not they are serious about this cultural programming is a moot point. After fifty years of popular—not to say vulgar—programs, their newfound interest in the highbrow is so universal and so sudden as to provoke cynicism in the eye of the beholder. It is widely suggested that corporate strategies, rather than the elevation of the human spirit, lie behind these developments.

In some sense the networks are being forced into culture. Federal Communications Commission rules virtually prohibit them from owning cable systems. And other entrees into the cable business are ancillary. RCA, for example, owns as a common carrier the Satcom I satellite, which transmits some twenty services, among them the most successful of pay channels, Time Inc.'s Home Box Office. But since satellite operations remain too limited a field to be appealing, ABC, CBS, and NBC/RCA have realized that the proliferation of programming services demonstrates a more easily exploited opportunity. With their vast experience as program-makers, they too ought to be able to offer specialized material that can join the galaxy of feature films, sports, fundamentalist preaching, twenty-four-hour news, dirty movies, children's shows, and ethnic services already up on the satellites.

But even here limitations exist. The networks cannot offend their affiliates by offering cable operators any popular forms of programming that would compete with their regular broadcast service. Between the Scylla of FCC regulations and the Charybdis of affiliate relations, very few routes are actually available. Culture is the best network solution. Nothing so clearly fulfills a demonstrated need, looks so good in public-relations terms, and costs so little.

The need is clear. ABC's research reveals that 16 percent of the population, core culture-aficionados, do not watch television very much at all. These elusive folk—"light watchers"—are also better educated and richer than the population generally. A further 24 percent are described as "culturally receptive"—active PTA members and the like, who watch 60 Minutes and network news but give television a low priority. Together these make a sizable, largely untapped universe. The

Public Broadcasting Service currently has some 2.5 million subscribers, each paying an average of about $35 a year. The audience for live ballet, opera, and concerts is increasing by 8 percent a year; non-degree night-school enrollment in arts-related courses is up 23 percent a year, and the success of public television's *Live From Lincoln Center* demonstrates how attractive is television's ability to deliver performances beyond the confines of the great metropolitan houses.

But it is the cheapness of culture as it is currently defined that fosters cynicism. For ABC's ARTS, culture is either performance or documentaries about artists, both of which can be bought from foreign networks or produced by driving remote units into opera houses and concert halls. Each method results in minimal programming costs (by network standards), and these costs can be cut further by running re-peats. HBO has demonstrated that a full-scale service can be main-tained with only twenty-five or so new programs a month. Its audience views the six or seven repeats as a convenience, and all indicators suggest that potential light watchers of culture will do the same. So the basic cheapness of such a service can be yet further reduced by operat-ing with only a few hundred hours of material a year.

So elegant is ABC's ploy with its new service that many are puzzled by CBS's contrasting response. CBS seems to be spending more money than necessary. "We are not packagers but producers, and we will do more than just performance," claims Jack Willis, the seven-time Emmy Award winner who is CBS Cable's programming chief. "*Live From Lin-coln Center* is too narrow." Willis is heading the most distinguished broadcasting team in cable. Relying heavily on small-scale technology, he is promising a daily three hours of programming, repeated three times, beginning October 12. Willis says that despite his expenditure, "the project will be profitable within three years. We'll probably just do it smarter and better, given the talent."

Willis's boss, Dick Cox, the president of CBS Cable, seems to have slightly less ambitious plans. "The economics of cable at this stage require we act as prudently as we can." But Cox explains that original material can be resold, and already an announced jazz series has at-tracted European inquiries. "It is not as loony as it seems," he says. "Since everybody is running off to Europe, exporting programs to Europe is a good way to be distinctive."

ABC's ARTS and CBS Cable will rely on advertising revenue; cable viewers will receive the services as part of their basic subscription. NBC, via RCA's partnership with Rockefeller Center Inc., will offer RCTV, a pay service (one paid for by an extra subscription, as HBO is). The heart of RCTV's strategy is an exclusive deal engineered by its president, Arthur Taylor, with the British Broadcasting Corporation. Arnold Huberman, RCTV's programming consultant, claims a subscrip-tion strategy will help sell the service to cable operators, who could receive as much as 50 percent of each extra subscription. RCTV will not rely on ads, because Huberman does not believe "the ads are there going in."

RCTV's BBC raid is the most flamboyant of the acquisition strategies so far revealed. PBS, which stands to lose an important supplier of its prime-time fare, maintains that RCTV will find the full range of BBC programming simply unappealing to American taste, certainly after the backlog of suitable shows has been used. Public television, says PBS, has been importing all that is appropriate for this market. Huberman disagrees, although he has not tested his conviction scientifically. An ex-movie scheduler for ABC, he has been using showman's intuition rather than audience research to determine whether or not there is enough BBC fare to make up an American schedule. "I sat in London looking at stuff, thinking this is okay. And when I looked at it here, it was still okay. I showed it to the secretaries, and they, with their Bronx accents, confirmed it. It will be entertaining to the U.S. audience." In fact, so far from "culture" is RCTV's material that the service, which will premiere early next year, has been christened "The Entertainment Channel."

In competitor Marc Lustgarten's opinion, "Culture is a defensive term." As the programming executive of Rainbow Programming Services, Lustgarten represents the new breed, his whole career having been in cable. Rainbow's cultural offering, Bravo, began life in tandem with a dirty-movie service, about which Lustgarten is not at all defensive. From December 1980 until July 1981, Bravo (a subscription service) occupied two nights of a schedule that otherwise carried such delights as *Lickerish Quartet, Cheerleaders Beach Party,* and *Part-time Wife* under the generic title of Escapade. (The trade likes to think of these offerings as adult/action.) "We are good smart businessmen," says Lustgarten. "Escapade will help defray Bravo's cost, and there is nothing to be ashamed about." As of mid-1981, a second transponder has allowed both services to operate as separate entities seven nights a week.

Bravo has benefited from what Lustgarten knows about the cable industry's subscribers: "They're almost like your best friends after awhile." But Bravo reveals an equally proper understanding of broadcasting. It's a much better-produced service than ABC Video's ARTS. Like ARTS, it consists basically of performance, but it also offers a television magazine of reasonable quality. Acquisitions are heavily reedited—"Bravo-ized" is Lustgarten's word. This might displease the original producers, but it certainly gives the service a coherence ARTS lacks, despite the latter's attempt to achieve the same effect with thematic "wrap-around" (i.e., Alistair Cooke-type) material. Bravo is more adventurous and entertaining—and, unlike ARTS, not even occasionally embarrassing.

Rainbow's rationale for giving Bravo its frisky bedfellow was that each needed time to get into its stride and develop a seven-day service. But one can be permitted to offer other explanations of this strategy. Escapade is an obvious moneymaker, although cable operators, pressured by the local nature of franchising, might find it difficult to offer. A recent survey shows that 33 percent of cable subscribers would not buy pay cable at all because they would not want their children to see some of the programs. And in some cable communities, voices are being raised against Escapade. Hence Bravo, cynics might suggest, sugars the pill. (The National Christian Network, whose transponder is used for Escapade, keeps its opinions of the service a secret.)

PBS clearly shares the perception that this burst of culture on cable is in some way fueled as much by its own comparative success over the past decade as it is by cable's coming of age. PBS has proposed (somewhat belatedly, in the opinion of many observers) a further service, the Public Subscriber Network (PSN), which would be supported both by subscription and advertiser underwriting. It would involve, in the PBS phrase, "a grand alliance" between itself, the public, and the cultural institutions. Doc Jarden, PBS's director of development, suggests that these cultural institutions would do well to ask whether or not the new competing cable services will still be around in five years. PBS's current 2.5 million subscribers would be the heart of PSN. Persuaded to pay $135 or so a year—almost four times their 1980 average annual donation—they would form a more promising universe of proven loyalty and dedication than the competition could claim.

To PBS's own stations, for whom the scheme looks much like harakiri, Jarden makes this central point: The audience for PBS is now a curious amalgam of minorities and the cultural elite. It would do little harm to give PSN a single—essentially performance—element of primetime PBS programming on a first-run basis, because the stations would carry it afterwards. And, he says, "*Sesame Street* would still be on PBS. So would *Black Journal.*" The stations would be involved in selling PSN, and its profits could be plowed back into PBS programming. Finally, the stations have been promised a veto. "It won't happen without 51 percent of them." It won't happen anyway until 1983, as PBS is mounting an elaborate audience survey and viability study. In the meantime, at least two major PBS stations have established profit-making subsidiaries for the exploitation of cable and other commercial markets. Most observers agree that the whole situation bodes ill for public television.

But how does it bode for the new services? This proliferation of effort should not indicate that the area of cultural programming on television has magically ceased to be problematic. For ABC and CBS, it is likely to be as long a haul finding cable advertisers as it is finding the audience. Madison Avenue has been slow to explore cable as a national advertising medium, spending on cable advertisements less than 1 percent of the amount spent on television. The chances of this changing for culture seem uncertain. Furthermore, there is the strong possibility that the targeted audience might not want commercials. The growth of pay cable, fueled by HBO, is eloquent testimony that a significant number of viewers will spend money to avoid advertisements. The public has shown a startling willingness to pay millions for something it used to get for nothing, but there is resistance to paying yet more for cable services. Nearly half of those who already pay for basic cable said in a recent survey that price was the real reason they were not taking a tier service. Of those who do not have cable, the same survey reported that 49 percent said they did not want to pay for television at all, and 48 percent said it was too expensive. So although major urban areas remain to be wired, it is likely that there are some limits to cable's growth, certainly if the economy in general is not buoyant.

At the moment, most subscribers seem unwilling to contemplate giving the cable company more than about $30 a month. Nearly double the current average national payment, $30 might be stretched to cover all the proffered tier services—two movie channels, sports, dirty movies, and culture. But due to its small potential audience, culture is the most threatened option. It is the cable operator who makes the decisions about tiers of pay services, because a majority of them own systems with very few available channels. In this situation, the operator might sooner satisfy aficionados of the local ice hockey team and lovers of blue movies than the elite of culture buffs.

Cable operators create only one bottleneck in the market. Satellite distribution is crucial in building a universe, but not all satellites are equally efficient at this. Operators wanting the most profitable service but having only one small receiving dish, tend to point it in the direction of HBO, carried on Satcom 1. But satellites have limited capacity and there are fewer spaces (transponders) on Satcom 1 than there are services wanting them. Therefore spare transponders, even on the other two less favored domestic satellites, are worth somewhere around $5 million on the open market. For each of the new culture services, finding a transponder from which to reach a maximum number of cable systems is the single most important factor in getting started.

Bravo was sharing its transponder before Escapade gained its own. ABC Video, jointly with Warner Amex, puts out ARTS at night, on a transponder leased by the latter for its daytime children's service, Nickelodeon.

RCTV, still without a transponder for The Entertainment Channel, claims with admirable insouciance that its relationship with Satcom 1 owner RCA means less than nothing. RCA's allocation of transponders on the satellite in the past has not been without criticism. Now it must rent a transponder from itself or from one of its competitors.

CBS has been forced onto Western Union's Westar III, although the ground dishes of many cable operators are aimed elsewhere. CBS, therefore, goes into operation with a universe markedly smaller than ABC's; that's why it will offer some key cable operators a free dish—so they can receive Westar's signal.

Beyond the questions of audience, operators, and satellites lies the basic problem of production costs. With network prime-time television costing $500,000 or so an hour, and with a cable universe that is as yet very small, all these services must be produced inexpensively. Producing programs at about one fifth of prime-time cost by using the latest light-weight equipment and paying talent at scale, importing programming even more cheaply, and repeating material at an unheard-of rate, are among the techniques being deployed.

Still, the days of buying hours of La Scala opera for pennies will not last long. For one thing, the networks have already begun their competition. (ARTS's Granath scooped CBS by getting on the air first—a deal he initially arranged following an accidental meeting, crossing Sixth Avenue, with Warner Amex's Jack Schneider, an ex-CBS executive.) And for another thing, the Europeans are getting smarter.

Professional opinion in Britain, for instance, is that the BBC has perhaps not shown the greatest acumen at this stage in making an exclusive deal, especially one that ties it down while leaving RCTV free to trade with its British competitors. One leading British commercial-program exporter said, "I think the BBC is nuts, because this is a very flexible market. It is rather potty to be making such a deal, especially when you have no agreement with the artists." (British commercial television is in the middle of negotiations with the unions.)

Theodora Sklover, adviser to a number of American cultural institutions, warns them not to expect "big money up front" from the new culture services, but also advises, "at this stage, don't do exclusive deals."

Even at this experimental stage, the feeling that all is not as it seems —especially with the networks—is unavoidable. Culture programming might be part of the networks' larger strategy to stake out cable territory before it all gets claimed. Some of their major communications-industry competitors are currently having a field day. Warner Amex and Time Inc., for example, are "vertically integrated operations"—that is, they are both major operators *and* providers of programming. They are also among the six users about to control a majority of the available transponders. There are a number of such vertically integrated operations in the industry, but the latest authoritative judicial opinion is that "the extent of vertical integration in the market does not appear to constitute an insurmountable barrier to entry into the market."

But in the cable market, the major urban areas still to be wired require an infusion of capital that only those vertically integrated companies will be able to provide. As their dominance over cable programming threatens the networks ever more seriously, it is difficult to believe that ABC, CBS, and NBC will not put up a fight.

CBS, in a significant move, has petitioned the FCC for a waiver so that it might operate cable systems with a total of up to 90,000 subscribers (the FCC's limit) as a testing ground for programming and technical experiments. The cable industry is not at the moment opposing this. But the Justice Department has made it clear that it regards CBS's entering cable ownership, on however limited a scale, as a threat that would "undercut the cross-ownership rule's goal of promoting economic competition and diversification of control of the channels of mass communication."

With such an uncertain future, and in an already difficult present, culture begins to look like nothing so much as a means of commandeering terrain. The cultural elite is given to sniggers whenever television tries to heighten its brow. And rather than winning that elite over, all the current cavortings are likely to turn the sniggers to guffaws.

There is good reason for the cynicism. These corporations are using the term "culture" as it refers to those court arts taken over in the early nineteenth century by the European haute bourgeoisie. Television as a popular form has never really developed meaningful versions of those arts. And no television service—not PBS here or the BBC in Britain or ZDF in Germany—has created satisfying television from their theatrical incarnations. More television imagination is displayed in covering baseball than is seen in *Live From Lincoln Center.*

It is difficult not to be skeptical about any of the networks' forays into culture. How seriously can ABC be taken as a purveyor of the arts when Granath contends that culture is like the Olympics because the folks doing it are "(a) foreign and (b) largely unknown"? This comment makes sense only in a corporate strategy, one more concerned with dominance and survival than it is with art.

RCTV's attempt at buying American middle-class loyalty to a British middle-class product makes some sense, especially if it can tailor-make some BBC-American co-productions. But Huberman's program choices seem to be avoiding the radical, difficult, and challenging stuff that gives British television its piquant taste. He is certainly avoiding a contentious kids' series because he says the accents are too difficult.

At CBS, Willis seems to understand full well the scope of the task of bringing these refined entertainments to the vulgar little screen. But so far, some of CBS Cable's announced programs look like reruns of the ideas that have already earned the CBS team its many broadcasting awards. The question remains: Will the elusive 16 percent buy this stuff on cable from producers they have already in large part rejected, as it were, over the air?

Huberman says upscale television service "is a baby—but it's going to grow up and go to college." One can only ask—what college? And what grades will it get? Two or three years down the road, all these companies might well have decided to give up and go back to attending the University of Life, just as they always have.

FOR FURTHER READING

Pearl G. Aldrich, *The Impact of Mass Media.* Rochelle Park, N.J.: Hayden, 1975.

Daniel J. Czitrom, *Media and the American Mind: From Morse to McLuhan.* Chapel Hill, N.C.: University of North Carolina Press, 1982.

Stuart Ewen and Elizabeth Ewen, *Channels of Desire: Mass Images and the Shaping of American Consciousness.* New York: McGraw-Hill, 1982.

Thomas M. Inge (ed.), *Concise Histories of American Popular Culture.* Westport, Conn.: Greenwood Press, 1982.

Wilson Bryan Key, *Media Sexploitation.* New York: New American Library, 1977.

David Marc, *Demographic Vistas: Television in American Culture.* Philadelphia, Pa.: University of Pennsylvania Press, 1984.

Gerald Mast, *A Short History of the Movies.* Chicago: University of Chicago Press, 1981.

John M. Phelan, *Media-World: Programming the Public.* New York: Seabury Press, 1977.

Jean-Francois Revel, *Without Marx or Jesus: The New American Revolution Has Begun.* Garden City, N.Y.: Doubleday, 1970.

Bernard Rosenberg and David Manning White, *Mass Culture Revisisted.* New York: Van Nostrand Reinhold, 1971.

Robert Sobel, *The Manipulators: America in the Media Age.* Garden City, N.Y.: Doubleday, 1976.

XVI

Mass Media, Specialized Media, and the New Technology

W HERE WILL the mass media go from here? If the new technologies dictate the future, we will have more specialized media and less mass communication in the years ahead.

The new technologies have made it possible to mass-produce personal-ized messages and media. We can now receive letters in the mail, addressed to us personally, with our names inserted liberally throughout the paragraphs as if some dear, close friend were dropping us a personal note. The letter can be signed at the end in blue ink, with a real person's florid signature. And yet the whole thing can have been produced by machine and never have seen a human hand or eye. We know that such letters are produced by machine, and yet we are still more likely to give them a second glance than we would a letter that doesn't have our name on it. We want personal communication, and the new technologies can mass-produce it for us.

The new technologies have reduced the cost and the complexities of mass communication, bringing about an exploding proliferation of publica-tions and productions and broadcasts. But there will be a price to pay for all this individual attention.

For the first 30 years of the television age, all of us worried about the leveling influence of the mass media, the blandness, the conformity, the uniformity. We felt we would all become puppets, dancing in unison at the end of strings pulled by a few media moguls on Madison Avenue. We would all end up eating the same food, dressing in gray flannel suits, wearing our hair in the same styles, our individuality smashed by mass media. We decried the end of ethnic and racial distinctions and of cultural differences. There was even something fascist about the mass media making us all march to the same tune.

But the world of the specialized media of the future might pose more serious problems in the opposite direction. Instead of becoming acculturated into one nation, we may become polarized into thousands of separate enclaves and tribes—each using its own specialized media and developing its own specialized languages—accentuating all our differences and flaunting our distinctions, until we become a Tower of Babel.

Already we have seen the communication gaps grow—between old and young, between male and female, between children and parents, between teachers and students, between blacks and whites, between English-speaking and Spanish-speaking, between rich and poor, educated and uneducated, and, perhaps most important, between computer types and noncomputer types.

The new mass media brought to us by the new technologies pose a new kind of danger on our horizon, and now is the time to worry about the public policies we need to develop to protect ourselves from the anarchy the new media could well bring.

58 · THE PERSONALIZED MAGAZINE

BY CHIP BLOCK

The mass medium that was the first to become specialized, and is the most specialized today, is the magazine. Indeed, we have now gone beyond the specialized magazine for special groups. We are thinking about the personalized magazine, for individuals. Chip Block is already in the specialized-magazine business, as publisher of *Games*, a Playboy Company publication. This article is reproduced from *Folio*, May 1981.

Publishing is a game of inches. Very often, good management of margins is the difference between profit and loss. However, the inch has shrunk to a millimeter because we are living in a new world—a world of inflation, accelerated change, costly non-renewable resources, expanded video, high technology, and new areas of editorial interest. Thus, any publisher who wants to stay in the game must carefully examine any innovation that might stretch publishing margins, and implement those innovations that are feasible.

Ten years ago, as I began my career in publishing, I learned of an idea that quickly captured my imagination: the personalized magazine. I now believe that the personalized magazine is possibly the greatest technological innovation of the 1980s in terms of its impact on publishing economics. In effect, personalization offers new hope to this game of publishing.

Before examining this concept in depth, however, let's take a look at what doesn't work any longer.

Traditional Leverage Eroded   Publishing margins are to a large degree controlled by a few key leverage points: single-copy sales percentage, ad/edit ratio, subscription renewal percentages, readers-per-copy circulated, and all pricing. Unfortunately, each of these leverage points has been affected negatively by the changes that have taken place both in the economy and in our industry.

Consider the effect of inflation, for example. Consumers today have less discretionary income to spend, and with few exceptions, magazines are discretionary items. Nobody needs a magazine. I often hear people say a magazine failed because it wasn't needed. I can't think of a single consumer magazine the public actually needs.

This lack of discretionary income also means that it will be harder to raise prices. Publishers have been very successful in raising prices to the readers over the last 10 years, partly because they were starting at a very low base price.

Many magazine subscription prices have been raised from, say, $2 a year in 1971 to $10 a year in 1980. Anybody who believes we're going to be able to raise the price to $20 a year by 1990 is in for a surprise, even given the fact of inflation. The same thing is true on the newsstand.

In terms of leverage with the advertiser, the pricing problem is compounded by the fact that we compete not only with each other, but with other media a as well. As the other media expand, especially cable TV, the advertising pie is going to be split up even further. The result is an ever-increasing pressure on publishers to hold down their cost-per-thousand.

In addition, the advertising/editorial ratio can't go much further. If we continue to increase the advertising ratio, the perceived value of the service we provide the reader is undoubtedly going to decline. Furthermore, the advertisers don't like it. Many advertisers are already complaining about clutter in magazines.

One way out of this jam is improved operating efficiency. No doubt we have made some strides, especially in subscription marketing. The use of computers in generating information on promotion effectiveness and in refining direct mail efforts, for example, has enabled many publishers to increase subscription net income even faster than sub prices.

However, such examples are the exception. In other areas, operating efficiency is deteriorating. The total copies sold in retail outlets as a percentage of copies distributed has decreased over the last 10 years. MPA estimates the *absolute* drop at about 10 percent. This, despite increased automation by wholesalers, publisher field forces, and more sophisticated distribution by the national distributors.

The Solution: Personalization   Obviously, if publishers are to survive in this economic climate, they must find new ways to expand operating margins. The key to survival, I believe, is the personalized magazine: an editorial service that offers a range of materials to readers who then buy only those discrete elements that interest them.

To conceptualize the product, think of segments (newsletters or specials) growing out of a base product (the magazine), each one an entity with a constituency of its own.

In 1972, when I first learned of the concept, the technology required was in the development stage. The key element, the computer driven bindery line, was not available. That element—along with the equipment to address copies on line, also crucial to personalization—is now available. I am going to make two major, unverified assumptions about that technology. First, I assume that the technology will work: that is, a system from order entry of subs, to file maintenance, to tape format, to the bindery, ink jet addressing on line, and into the mail. There is no reason why such a process will not work successfully.

Second, I assume that the implementation of such a system will be economically feasible. Actually, the system should eventually cost no more than current methods, given the opportunity for computer-generated promotion material, greater control of the bindery process, and postal savings.

Leverage through Personalization   The personalized magazine has tremendous implications for publishers because it provides several interesting new leverage points.

First, a publisher will be able to charge a premium price to the reader. For example, if *Better Homes and Gardens* were to offer readers the option of subscribing to a special interest signature on indoor gardening, the results—in terms of prices to the reader—could be very favorable because of the reader's special interest in the area.

Second, a publisher need spend virtually nothing on the promotion that goes to the reader. He'll be promoting the magazine's special interest signatures both in the magazine and through the media that he already has to send out—renewal letters for example.

And third, personalization can provide some leverage with advertisers. By providing selectivity, he can charge a higher cost-per-thousand. And although an advertiser who might have purchased a full run might buy only a segment (albeit at a much higher CPM), the benefits will outweigh such effects by far.

Because I believe that the personalized concept has a great potential to expand operating margins, we have begun to implement personalization at *Games.*

Games is a true special interest magazine, so it's probably not the best magazine to be the first one to personalize. However, since I've long been in love with the idea of a personal magazine, I've decided to go ahead and try. The technology is there, nobody else is going to do it, and we think we can make a lot of money.

Our approach is probably unusual. (The only thing I can say about it is that it's safe and that's why we're confident about going ahead.) We're starting simply by offering a series of special sections to our subscribers, narrowing our editorial scope in each case into very special interests.

The first monthly special is called *The Four Star Puzzler,* and it is geared to readers who want more puzzles than the magazine itself offers. Ultimately, we will produce a series of these specials, rated in terms of the difficulty of the puzzles in each newsletter.

We have ideas for three other specials that will be published and tested during 1981. These will be completely different from the puzzler idea, but each one has some tie-in with the magazine. Furthermore, since each special is designed to be profitable as an entity in itself, the program will be profitable even if the personalized magazine concept doesn't work out.

As the system develops, we will offer readers the option of having the specials bound into the magazine. (In fact, some people may want only the specials and not the magazine.) Since several signatures will be available, and since each one will be viable individually, the reader will be able to define for himself what he's interested in.

Expanding Functions   Undoubtedly, the role of editors will change with the advent of such editorial services.

Now, editors produce material they think will interest and entertain readers. Ten years from now, it's entirely possible that editors will be producing material that readers have chosen.

In addition, personalized magazines are going to expand the focus of specialized magazines and narrow the focus of even the most broadbased magazine (*Reader's Digest* or *Better Homes and Gardens,* for example).

This development will result in less waste in publishing because publishers will be targeting their markets a lot better, both in terms of the editorial product and the advertiser's message. And, since advertisers will be closer to the audiences they're looking for, they will pay a premium on a cost-per-thousand basis in order to reach such a highly targeted audience.

In addition, since editors will be forced to communicate with readers, they will get a lot of feedback from them, not in letters to the editor but in terms of marketing information. In fact, readers will be creating new products constantly, and publishers will be obtaining psychographic information about the readers' interests and buying habits.

Implications of Personalization   With such a system in place, a publisher can create a family of mini-magazines around the base product at a low cost, thereby getting pricing leverage. Equally important, if this is done by much of the industry, we will have changed the perceived value of magazines in the minds of the consumer:

•	Base product	=	$12	(per year)
•	Special #1	=	8	" "
•	" #2	=	8	" "
•	" #3	=	6	" "
•	" #4	=	6	" "
*	Total value		$40	" "

(Offer for total package: $30 per year, a 25 percent savings.)

With personalization, a publisher can also segment his audience for ad sales purposes. In the case of *Games,* we will be developing a special signature for people who want a Christmas shopping guide for games. Obviously, any games manufacturer in his right mind would want to reach people who are willing to pay for such information since there will be virtually no waste in that market.

Personalization also makes print a more exciting medium for both the advertiser and the reader. When this technology is used in a creative way, there will be a whole new aura around publishing, especially if it is promoted properly to the ad community and to the consumer.

Another implication: personalization will enable us to compete with the new developments in television which are a tremendous threat to publishing. Advertisers will be attracted to multichannel cable and special interest programming on television and publishers will have to compete with that kind of technology and segmentation.

In spite of these potential benefits, publishers have been rather slow to make moves in the direction of personalized magazines. The obvious candidates for personalization, the large magazines, are most often published by big companies where the decision-making process can be rather cumbersome. Furthermore, most people don't like to take responsibility for doing something that's terribly innovative.

Editorial Franchise Ignored   I also believe that publishers are dead wrong when they persist in seeing personalized magazines as an advertising gold mine. The economic structure of magazines as they exist today is geared toward the advertiser. However, although personalization has great potential benefits for space sales, such benefits should not be the raison d'etre for segmentation.

Publishers who look to advertising income to pay for this kind of program will find problems similar to those of magazines that are designed primarily to deliver an audience segment to advertisers, particularly a demographic segment: a true commonality of interests among readers does not necessarily exist. Therefore, if reader interest is difficult to sustain, circulation becomes costly to maintain. The result: ad revenue must cover most if not all of the publishing nut.

Another fallacious concept has also been promulgated as a framework for personalization: creating an entirely new magazine around the process itself. Some people in Colorado have developed an interesting technology called U-Stat and are trying to promote the idea of a magazine in which the reader can select subject matter he or she desires.

I believe this is an incorrect approach, however, because no editorial franchise exists. Starting a new magazine with a viable editorial foundation is difficult enough. To attempt to do so simply on the basis of a delivery system ignores both the premise and reality of periodical publishing.

The Future Is Now   There are many problems to overcome. However, I believe that publishers must begin to explore the process, to at least attempt to use technology that holds such promise. And, after all, if personalization doesn't work out, a publisher will simply be left with a set of profitable specials (or newsletters) that are mailed separately to subscribers.

I believe that the process will work and will yield excellent margins to publishers. I will report on the results at *Games* as we progress. If I'm right, we will have performed great feats in a world of inches.

59 · CONDOMINIUMS IN THE GLOBAL VILLAGE

BY RICHARD A. BLAKE

Marshall McLuhan's vision of a world more closely
united through communications technologies has been
confounded by the new technologies that have made
listening and viewing into insulated experiences. As
media audiences become more fragmented, writes
Richard A. Blake, communicators spend more time
talking to like-minded people. Blake is the managing
editor of *America,* from which this article is
reprinted, from the June 5, 1982, issue.

Two full decades have passed since *The Gutenberg Galaxy* was
published in 1962 and H. Marshall McLuhan became an academic cult
figure whose writings many thought at the time would create the Coper-
nican revolution of our age. As a professor of literature—and several
other things as well—at the University of Toronto, he published a book
on advertising techniques, *The Mechanical Bride,* as early as 1951 and
had edited with the anthropologist Edmund Carpenter a short-lived
periodical entitled *Explorations,* some of whose essays appeared as an
anthology, *Explorations in Communication,* in 1961.

There is no doubt, even now, that Marshall McLuhan was on to
something important. As a man of many interests, he was able to send
out "probes"—unmanned space probes were the miracles of technology
at the time—in many directions at once. He was aware that the human
environment, even our thought and sense patterns, had been undergoing
enormous changes because of the development of communications technologies, and he had the temerity to ask what these shifts were. If, he
reasoned, historians and anthropologists could chart the change when
a society moves from an oral culture to one with a written language and
then moves from a manuscript tradition to mechanized printing, then he
believed they should be able to discover the changes taking place as
contemporary society moves from a print-dominated society to the age

of radio, television and film. In the 1960's this notion of a generation gap between old breed and new breed was a hot topic, and McLuhan believed it had something to do with the way we communicate to one another.

Despite the importance of his search, Marshall McLuhan was sadly an unwitting assassin of his own ideas. His prose poured out like water from a firehose with knots in it. He had an irrepressible lust for the catch-phrase, which he later mauled into puns that mocked the original concept. From the vantage point of the 1980's these phrases are quaint and oh-so 1960ish, hula hoops for the mind, Mickey Mouse ears for the intellect. For example, in *Understanding Media* (1964), the book that brought McLuhan celebrity and the rest of us headaches trying to understand what he meant by "hot" and "cool" media, he gave one chapter the catch title "The Medium Is the Message." By 1967, the phrase became the title of a book, *The Medium Is the Massage,* which dealt with the importance of tactility in communication—along with many other topics. By 1969, in *Counterblast,* it became an inset heading, "The Medium is The Mess Age," highlighting the proposition that one medium absorbs another, and both become changed or "messed up." People who read, for instance, have speech patterns different from those who do not; people who watch television write differently from those who do not. Our own media-loaded culture is going through the media mixmaster: It is the mess age.

What is regrettable is that some of these ideas, torpedoed by the cleverness of their creator, deserve a better fate. Some of these key concepts should have remained alive so that they could be seriously tested and refined in the light of new data and new trends. After all, McLuhan was dealing with man in confrontation with his rapidly changing technological environment. Even the mustiest, library-bound scholar should be able to admit that technology continues to change and that its ongoing impact on the race should continue to be monitored. What would Marshall McLuhan be able to tell us, if he were still alive, of the meaning of the videogame, the desk-top home computer, the digital alarm wristwatch, or even that computer in Japan that last year stabbed a worker to death on the assembly line? When he was writing, space probes, those unmanned ventures into outer space, were exotic projects. He called his own essays "probes" because he fired them off into space with no idea what they would turn up. The data he uncovered always invited further exploration and refinement; they were rarely the final chapter.

One such probe, still intriguing but clearly in need of revision, is his concept of "the global village." Unlike some of his other aphorisms, like "The medium is the message," the global village keeps a certain ring of currency about it. It is still used by many organizations, especially religious ones, to describe a growing sense of awareness and responsibility for global problems, such as hunger, violence or the need for evangelization. It is a convenient term but a dangerous one, since injecting an old term into a contemporary situation can be misleading. On a practical level such a miscalculation can lead to a misreading of the signs of the times, to oversimplifications, to misdirected strategies and to a great deal of frustration.

The global village, an optimistic projection of the McLuhan era, probably never did exist in fact, and if it was the logical goal of a trend apparent at the time, that trend has long ago hit a detour. Technology, which McLuhan was ever sensitive to, has moved in like a greedy landlord and broken the global village into condominiums. Since the time of McLuhan's initial insight, the world has become less a tribal village and more an urban apartment building, where people in adjacent flats cannot recognize one another.

What kind of change took place? For Marshall McLuhan the notion of the modern postliterate world as a global village was a long time coming. It grew out of his major thesis that people raised in an age of print see reality as segmented and ordered, like letters of the alphabet on a line of type. Preliterate people, coming from an oral tradition, tend to apprehend the whole without awareness of individual components. Literate people rely on vision, and try to see connections between parts as though they were letters in a word; they feel secure in their understanding only when they can objectify something "out-there," even at times reducing reality to an outline or diagram, like a roadmap. Preliterate people make no sense out of maps and diagrams. They are involved with the topography and prefer to think of their environment in terms of hills, stars, ocean currents or dead trees.

Modern man, McLuhan observed, is in the process of returning to the sight and sound world of the preliterate. Even in academia, the clear, precise and diagrammatic answers of scholastic philosophy have become less interesting and less satisfying than the tentative answers based on the empirical data of the sociologist, novelist or psychologist. The age of the electronic media has retribalized us.

By 1967, in *The Medium Is the Massage,* McLuhan pointed out the effects of this new tribalization on a world scale. He announced: "We now live in a global village. . . . We have begun to structure this primordial feeling, these tribal emotions from which a few centuries of literacy have divorced us. . . . Electronic circuitry profoundly involves us with one another." He felt that it is no longer possible for pockets of humanity to remain isolated from one another; electronics was binding the race together. What seemed particularly attractive to religious people was the implication he drew from his observation: "Our new involvement compels commitment and participation." In another place in the same book, he returned to the theme: "Electric circuitry has overthrown the regime of 'time' and 'space' and pours upon us continuously the concerns of other men." Like it or not, electronics has made us, in the words of the Gospel, our "brother's keeper." The signs of the time, another catch phrase of the era, pointed to the social Gospel. Off to the inner city, the picket lines and the demonstrations!

Two of McLuhan's concepts must be distinguished. First, technology was providing more information about remote peoples and places, and, second, our postliterate sensibilities have conditioned us to respond differently. The first is self-evident. There is more news available, and it comes to us more quickly than ever before. As for the second, according to McLuhan, we are more involved with the hungry or the politically repressed because we cannot reduce them to discrete units of reality, separate from our own world, out there, objective and at a distance. When, for example—and this is not an example McLuhan gives, since he rarely gives examples—we see on television a black demonstrator at Selma attacked by guard dogs, we are personally involved and there is a visceral response because our own world is being subjected to the violence and oppression. Thus, the passionate radicalization of thousands of comfortable middle-class students during the civil rights movement was a result of both television information and television sensitivities.

For the religious person reading McLuhan, the one world of peace and harmony was becoming a reality through the miracles of modern technology, God's gift to His creature of intellect. The world of the future would be the ideal forum for extending the world of the Gospel.

Although Marshall McLuhan was a serious Catholic, he did not deal with these religious questions himself. He left such reflections to those who read his essays while they were reading the works of Pierre Teilhard de Chardin, S.J. Between Teilhard's "noösphere" and McLuhan's "global village" there are many congruent notions, but McLuhan chose not to explore in depth the theological implications of his ideas. It is doubtful that he ever thought that the global village, drawn into a tighter and tighter unity by the power of modern communications, would ever lead to the "recapitulation of all things in Christ."

As an interesting parenthesis, McLuhan did, however, include a brief chapter on liturgy in The Gutenberg Galaxy. This was 1962, when liturgical reformers were already stirring in their cocoons, but before Vatican II loosed a stampede of butterflies upon the church. Even then, McLuhan knew that the Tridentine Mass, with its emphasis on the literate person's reliance on the visual, on detachment, fragmentation and solitude would not serve the postliterate generation. After skipping through the works of Louis Bouyer, Thomas Merton and several other liturgical writers, he concludes: "The 'simultaneous field' of electronic information structures today reconstitutes the condition and need for dialogue and participation rather than specialism and private initiative in all levels of social experience." Thus this secular prophet warned us about the coming of the dialogue homily and the ever on-going effort to increase participation, even by down-grading the role of the remote, "visual" celebrant if necessary.

McLuhan's rather rosy picture of the dawning age of the global village should not be surprising. He was, as each of us is, a product of his times. (Even his relentless use of the word "men" and masculine pronouns dates his work as pre-women's movement.) His was an optimistic time for media analysis. As he looked to the future, communications satellites were just beginning to tie the world together with instantaneous relays. Television and telephone transmissions could reach any point on the globe. The paradigmatic event, of course, was the funeral of John F. Kennedy in 1963, when the world seemed bound together in mourning through television. By then virtually every household in the United States "had television," and instructional television had invaded many of the classrooms, promising an end to the drudgery of learning and perennial shortages of teachers. Families viewed television together. The set was called the "electronic hearth," and magazine writers praised the new "togetherness." The evening news was making civil rights an American issue, as a few years later it would make Vietnam the world's first television war. It was believed that the nightly newscast was turning the American people against not only that war but against all wars. It was a cheery time for media futurologists.

Things did not turn out as predicted, however. In a very few years the happy promise of the global village fell apart. Mass communication, as it penetrated the inner cities of the United States in the 1960's and the third world in the next decade brought a sense not of participation but of exclusion. The image of the good life, available so readily to middle-class Americans on the gray-blue screen, was not accessible to everyone, and the result was outrage and violence. Murder on the streets became as insignificant as murder on the screen; heavy viewers became sociopaths. Instead of a new generation searching for "participation and dialogue" the 1970's brought the "me-decade," with the solitary jogger monitoring his heartbeat and fiber intake in private rather than sharing feelings in "small-group discussions."

Clearly, something went wrong with the prophecy, but what or how? Why are the media apparently desensitizing us to the needs of the rest of the world when we had expected them to heighten our sensitivities? If Marshall McLuhan were alive today, he would have to revise his projections on the basis of new data and new trends, and for him that always meant beginning with the technology of communication. In fact, he can be faulted for focusing too narrowly on this area to the exclusion of other social and historical factors. However, since the "global village" is his creation, it is only fair to retain his methodology.

In McLuhan's time, every development in communications technology pointed toward greater unification, but in the last 10 years every development has led to greater fragmentation of the world-audience. Equipment is an obvious example. First the transistor made radios cheap, portable and accessible to everyone in every environment. Stereo radios and cassette decks increased the volume, thereby ending conversation. Radio listening has become an essentially private experience. No longer do people gather around the radio, but each person creates a private acoustical shell. Finally, the new lightweight headphones isolate the individual from his surrounding environment completely. Watch a group of the new wired listeners standing elbow-to-elbow on the corner waiting for the light to change, each following the beat of his own drummer, with street noise and fellow listeners effectively filtered out.

The Ayatollah Ruhollah Khomeini understood this during the worst days of the Iranian revolution. He did not have to block out information from communication satellites, rather he supplied his followers with tape decks and cassettes of his speeches. He may have been the first prophet to realize that mass communication, even from a satellite, is becoming obsolete. The future belongs to the tiny tape deck, with its private, personal message enhancing the importance of the individual listener.

When McLuhan was formulating his theories, the networks were at their peaks. One might complain about the types of programs American audiences were watching, but there is little doubt that "I Love Lucy" or "Laugh In" did provide a source of common, shared and unifying experience. Everyone knew Fred and Ethel, Ricky and Lucy and what it meant when someone received a "fickle finger of fate" award at the office.

In the last few years, the trend toward unifying television experience has been reversed. On both networks and on local nonaffiliated stations, advertisers pinpoint their target audiences for age, sex, earning power and geography. This segmenting of the audiences has developed even more drastically with the arrival of the cable with its capacity for 40, 80 or even 120 different channels. As of March 1982, 23.7 million households in the United States, that is 29 percent of all television homes, now have cable, and the industry is adding a quarter of a million new subscribers each month. There are separate channels for sports, music, drama, movies, public affairs, and even pornography. Every language group in the community has its own programming.

The cable, however, is still a medium for more affluent neighborhoods, where enough subscribers can pay the fees immediately and thus make the installation of the system profitable in the near future. For the present, at any rate, the poorer and less educated will remain with the networks, a fact that can be expected to influence programming decisions. In other words, network television will become even more vapid, and the quality material that is available will be on the cable, where the viewers can afford to pay for it.

Developments in over-the-air broadcast technology are also in the process of fragmenting the audience. The Federal Communications Commission is currently sifting through 6,500 applications—the number is expected to reach 12,000—for new low-power stations that can be received on a non-cable set. These will have a very limited broadcast range, and thus will serve a specific local community. The industry now speaks casually of a "narrow-cast" concept rather than broadcast, to indicate its desire to pinpoint particular target audiences for its advertisers.

The cassette and videodisc business is booming, and as the prices tumble further, the growth rate will accelerate. Rental libraries of videotapes are springing up in shopping malls around the country. Combining videotape and cable technologies, ABC has even devised a system for transmitting films and other specials over the cable at night to a cassette recorder with an automatic timer. For a fee, the owner can play the tape back through a special decoder. For people using these services, viewing television has become as private and idiosyncratic a pastime as reading a book. In fact, by year's end Sony will begin marketing a pocket-sized television set no bigger than a paperback romance novel. Its two-inch screen is mounted in a case an inch and a half deep, and it will have the same lightweight headphones Sony made famous on its Walkman portable radio/tape deck components. The private acoustical shell will become visual as well.

A similar trend has been going on in radio. With the opening of the FM spectrum, radio, too, has been segmenting its audience. Of the 8,000 stations now operating in the United States, nearly half are associated with some kind of network, if only for news, but even the networks— and there are now 30 of them operating in the country—have become directed at specific target audiences. Some have nothing but talk, and the music networks are directed to a particular type of listener.

There is more news on television, but the happy-talk format that most of the stations have adopted means that there is less time for information on most broadcasts. With deregulation, limits for news broadcasting on radio have been dropped, so many people will no longer have even the five minutes of headlines and weather that used to break up music schedules.

As a result of these developments, it follows that there is more information around, but fewer informed people. As the media audiences become more fragmented, communicators spend more time talking to like-minded people, or at least those with similar interests. A church professional, for example, is likely to be inundated by information about the third world, while the congregation he or she deals with is likely to remain disinterested or apathetic simply because of a lack of effective information. The exchange of news releases among interested parties has become not only overwhelming but incestuous.

The growth of neoconservative groups, even within religious congregations whose leaders are vocally liberal, is not a product of hardening of hearts or callousness or perversity but a lack of effective communication. Religious elites are talking to one another, and their congregations hear little of the conversation. If these elites issue a call for mobilization on behalf of a specific social program, they cannot presume that their congregations are informed or interested, even though the topic might be belabored to the point of cliché in the communications networks the church professionals are tuned into.

If the media are now leading us to greater fragmentation rather than unity, the liturgical renewal might have to stop to reassess its assumptions and goals. Many of the current reforms were put in during the 1960's with the presumption that worshiping congregations actually wanted, as McLuhan said, "participation and dialogue"—or at least would want it once they became accustomed to it. Perhaps now that the global village has been fragmented into condominiums of privacy, worshippers now want their own sense of the sacred. Congregational singing and the kiss of peace may be as alien to the sensitivities of the 1980's as benediction of the Blessed Sacrament was to the sensitivities of the 1960's.

The churches then might be faced with a problem in trying to transfer the wisdom of the 1960's into strategies of the 1980's. Should we then give up the goals of social involvement and worshiping community? Of course not. The Gospel has clearly mandated a mission "to all nations" and "to feed the hungry." We would, however, be wise to admit that the concept of the global village, which appeared so clear in the 1960's, never did materialize. Any strategies that take it for granted then run the risk of serious frustration. Steps to inform, to raise the consciousness or to build community cannot be omitted. If they are, the gap between church professionals and their congregations will widen, as the church people overload one another with information and the people they serve drift further away, into other concerns and other information networks.

Three centuries before Marshall McLuhan, John Donne wrote: "No man is an island." If he could see youngsters standing mesmerized in front of a videogame screen, he just might want to give that sentence a second thought. Despite the information explosion, people are becoming more and more "islands." The global village may soon become the global archipelago, with isolated tribesmen speaking in peculiar languages only to one another. If, on the other hand, people realize that they are living on a tiny island, they should have enough sense to build canoes to reach those other islands. Without that awareness, the world's loftiest projects, even evangelization itself, will remain a collection of photocopied notes, duplicated by the hundreds and written in a peculiar language understood only by the like-minded.

60 · THE SECOND AMERICAN REVOLUTION

BY BENJAMIN BARBER

The deregulation of broadcasting and the rise of cable television will change broadcasting from a national to a specialized medium, writes Benjamin Barber. Unless we plan policies to change the direction, he writes, "the electronic road to a national democratic neighborhood may be detoured down back alleys that terminate suddenly in the anarchic privatism of Babel, or in a world of Big Brothers. . . ." Barber is professor of political science at Rutgers University and author of novels as well as scholarly works. This article is reprinted from *Channels of Communications*, February/March 1982.

Democracy was conceived in an unwired world, one without telephones, computers, or television. When Alexis de Tocqueville visited America in the 1830s, he marveled at its "spirit of liberty," which, he concluded, arose directly out of vigorous civic activity, municipal self-government, and face-to-face interaction. Then, as now, democracy meant government by consent, and consent depended upon consensus and thus upon effective communication. In a society innocent of electronics, communications meant reading local newspapers, forming voluntary associations, developing public schools, and exploiting the American propensity for endless talk.

Democracy survives, but de Tocqueville's simpler world of self-governing townships has vanished. The community of citizens governing themselves face to face has given way to the mass society, and live talk has been replaced by telecommunications. Once a nation of talkers, we have turned into a nation of watchers—once doers, we have become viewers—and the effect on our democracy has been profound. The average American watches television between six and seven hours a day; he votes just once a year, if that. Indeed, only one of every two Americans votes in Presidential elections.

Although every schoolchild knows that television is the national pastime and politics is only one feature of its coverage, not even university professors have thought very much about the medium's long-term impact on democracy. Yet we have already passed through one major age of telecommunications technology, and we now stand on the threshold of a second. This may be our last opportunity to turn the technology of the new age into a servant of an old political idea: democracy. Democracy will have a difficult time surviving under the best of circumstances; with television as its adversary, it seems almost sure to perish.

The first age of television—from its pre-war inception through the 1970s—was characterized by the scarcity of air-waves available for television transmission. This so-called spectrum scarcity gave us a system in which three mammoth national networks monopolized public communication, the government regulated in the name of the public interest, and viewers came to perceive themselves as passive spectators willing to leave programming decisions to network executives and their corporate sponsors.

The effects of this first age of television on America's political culture were mixed. But in one clear sense, network television's homogenized programming benefited democracy: By offering the country the semblance of a national culture and national political norms, it provided a consensus indispensable to national unity. Occasionally this was a direct result of network attitudes—as in the fifties with integration, the sixties with Vietnam, or the seventies with Watergate. But more often, the television consensus was informal and indirect. National debates such as the Kennedy-Nixon exchanges, national media personalities such as Ed Sullivan, Johnny Carson, and Walter Cronkite, and such national rituals as the Kennedy funeral, the moon walk, and the mourning for Martin Luther King—all these bestowed upon the country a legacy of national symbols and myths that cut across our divisive regions, sects, interest groups, parties, races, ethnic communities, and political constituencies.

In a nation as fragmented and pluralistic as ours, where from the very beginning—in the Federalist Papers—the "specter of faction" loomed as the greatest peril, television has offered perhaps the only truly common vision we can have. If there is an American melting pot, it is fired nowadays primarily by electronic means. How else than in front of the communal fires of television could Americans have mourned together their fallen leaders? If *Roots* had not been screened in prime time on eight consecutive evenings, would the meaning of being black in America ever have touched so many non-black Americans? *Roots* is a celebration not only of being black but of being American. Network television, both at its best and its worst—*Roots* and *Holocaust* as much as *General Hospital* and *Family Feud*— has helped us to subscribe to common values and to identify with a single national community. It is difficult to imagine the "Kennedy Generation," the "Sixties," Watergate, the Woodstock Generation, or even the Moral Majority, in the absence of national television. Who we are in common is what we see in common.

One aspect of this television consensus has been corrosive both to democracy and liberty, however. The dominion of a few media giants over scarce public airwaves has centralized control over information and entertainment. Democracy thrives on dissent, deviance, political heterogeneity, and individuality; network television catalyzes uniformity and homogeneity. Move a program too far off center as measured by the mass audience, and plummeting Nielsen ratings will chase sponsors away. Whether the media's middling vision is seen as the victory of bad taste (as the intellectuals claim), or of an Eastern liberal elite (as Spiro Agnew used to insist), or of crass secular materialism (as the Moral Majority asserts), or of the corporate establishment (as the Left believes), there can be little doubt that it is a safe and complacent vision that offers little hospitality to alternative perspectives. A common vision may also be a homogenized, plasticized, and intolerant vision, one that distorts America's defining pluralism by imposing uniform stereotypes on a heterogeneous people.

To the extent the networks succeed in making Americans think in common, they may destroy in us the capacity to think independently. The great American television consensus of the last thirty years dismissed the aspirations of both religion and socialism (thus the hostility fundamentalists and leftists show the media today). In place of genuine American archetypes, it gave us watery stereotypes: Archie Bunker, your friendly neighborhood racist, who wouldn't do any man real harm; Sanford and Son, who proved that black folks, aside from being a bit more hip, are just like every one else: Mary Tyler Moore, who could gently mock the patriarchal world without ever truly challenging it.

There were tough-but-generous cops, misguided revolutionaries, reformed junkies, urbane preachers, and decent bigots—but no vicious detectives or legitimate terrorists or victorious punks or unbending Christians or despicable hypocrites. From the safety of the center, all differences were reduced to matters of style, while the difficult choices and grim polarities of real moral and political life were ignored. The first age of television gave us unity but exacted the price of uniformity.

Disturbing as these dilemmas are, they now belong to history. For we stand, prepared or not, on the threshold of a second television age. This new age, with its own innovative technologies, promises to revolutionize our habits as viewers, as consumers, and ultimately, as citizens.

Although cable television itself relies on a technology as old as communication by wire, the convergence of a group of new technologies has made possible an entirely new system of telecommunications, one that offers us two-way and multiple-channel cable television, satellite distribution, video discs, video cameras and recorders, and access to remote computers and data banks. These technologies will bring into our homes a vastly expanded range of news and entertainment programming, diverse information services, consumer and financial transaction services, public-access programming, security systems, and television referenda. Twenty-eight percent of American homes now receive some kind of cable service; that number will double by the end of the decade. Already in some places people are using interactive television to relax, look, talk, vote, play, shop, inform themselves, express opinions, secure their homes, and go to school. State-of-the-art systems like Columbus, Ohio's QUBE will be installed in all the major cities now being franchised. The prospect of a "wired society" is quite real.

What will be the likely effects of this new era of telecommunications on American democracy? How will it compare to the first, now seemingly primitive era? What sort of questions ought to be put to the new industry by the federal government, the municipal franchisers, and the public at large?

At present, the government seems disposed to put the new technologies into the hands of an unencumbered private sector. The Federal Communications Commission has consistently argued that cable's multiple channels make spectrum scarcity—and the regulations that issue from it—obsolete. The Supreme Court in 1979 ruled that the FCC is not justified in requiring cable companies to provide public access. And Congress seems inclined to let "market forces" shape the development of modern telecommunications. Consequently, America is crossing the threshold of the new television age without reflection or planning; few seem aware, or concerned, that the new technologies may profoundly affect the nature of our public life and thus the character of our democracy. Yet present tendencies suggest the emergence of one of three distinct scenarios, each with far-reaching political consequences. We might call these scenarios "The New Tower of Babel," "The Corporate Big Brother," and "The Electronic Town Meeting."

The New Tower of Babel   From the perspective of the viewer, at least, the new technologies would appear to decentralize television. In a cable system with fifty or a hundred channels, the responsibility for selecting services and programming shifts from the supplier to to the consumer. The passive spectator of homogenized network fare is replaced by the active viewer, who creates his own information and entertainment programming by choosing among the hundreds of local and national program services, pre-recorded discs and tapes, and the various services two-way cable makes available.

But a political price is paid for this new activism among viewers and the apparent decentralization of television: Where television once united the nation, it will now fragment it. Those it once brought together it will now keep apart. In place of broadcasting comes the new ideal of "narrowcasting," in which each special audience is systematically typed, located, and supplied with its own special programming. Each group, each class, each race, and each religious sect can have its own programs, and even its own mini-network, specially tailored to its distinct characteristics, views, and needs. The critical communication *between* groups that is essential to the forging of a national culture and public vision will vanish; in its place will come a new form of communication *within* groups, where people need talk only to themselves and their clones.

This fragmentation is already well underway. Among the proliferating new program services available today are a Hispanic network, several Christian fundamentalist networks, a black network, and a number of highbrow culture networks. The U.S. Chamber of Commerce recently announced plans for the American Business Network, a private satellite television system. "BizNet" will enable the business community to organize and to communicate more effectively—with itself.

In the New Tower of Babel, all this programming diversity and special-interest narrowcasting replaces communication with group narcissism. The tube now becomes a mirror showing us only ourselves, relentlessly screening out any images that do not suit our own special prejudices and group norms. Fundamentalists no longer have to confront Carl Sagan in the course of a day's television viewing. No longer do special-interest groups have to filter their particular concerns through a national medium and adjust their message to a pluralistic nation. Faction—the scourge of democracy feared by its critics from James Madison to Walter Lippmann—is given the support of technology; compromise, mutualism, and empathy—indispensable to effective democratic consensus—are robbed of their national medium. Every parochial voice gets a hearing (though only before the already converted), and the public as a whole is left with no voice. No global village, but a Tower of Babel: a hundred chattering mouths bereft of any common language.

The Corporate Big Brother The Tower of Babel may be a suitable metaphor for the heterogeneity and pluralism of the new media as they appear to the consumer; but the viewer's perspective is partial, and probably illusory. To examine modern telecommunications at the supplier end is to wonder whether Big Brother may prove to be the more apt metaphor for television's second age.

As abundant in number as these new channels and program services seem, they are rapidly falling under conglomerate control. The potential for leviathan profits from the new industries is drawing the attention of the communications giants. A few entrepreneurial upstarts —such as Ted Turner—may remain on the scene for a while, but they almost certainly will be absorbed or conquered. Diversity at one end of the cable may mask monopoly at the other.

If this picture of a few corporate elites playing the role of Big Brother under the camouflage of pluralistic special-interest programming seems exaggerated, it should be recalled that cable is a capital-intensive industry. The extraordinary costs of wiring America for cable or leasing transponder space on satellites suggest that only the most powerful corporations are in a position to sustain long-term interests in the cable industry.

Among these powerful corporations will be the networks, which are already actively moving into cable programming. ABC, in partnership with Westinghouse, will launch two cable news services to compete with Ted Turner's Cable News Network, a property in which CBS has expressed interest. Westinghouse's own position in cable is formidable: Not only does the company have several other program services on its drawing boards, but it will have enough transponders (fourteen) and cable subscribers (1.6 million, through its subsidiary, Teleprompter) to guarantee some success. And now that the government has lifted restrictions on AT&T, that company will also be in a commanding position. Even without its local subsidiaries, AT&T has research and development capabilities that could allow it to dominate videotex services.

Westinghouse, AT&T, Warner Communications, Time Inc., CBS, RCA, ABC: If all the new media are controlled by these few corporate interests, we cannot expect genuine political diversity or a truly free flow of information. Behind all those channels may eventually stand a single, prudent censor. Even if Big Brother is not watching us, we may find ourselves watching Big Brother.

And it does seem likely that if we are watching Big Brother, he will eventually begin to keep an eye on us. The very features of the new technology that make it versatile and exciting also make it frighteningly vulnerable to abuse. Warner Amex's QUBE system scans subscribers' homes every six seconds, recording what subscribers watch, their answers to poll questions, the temperature in their houses (for those who have signed up for energy management systems), and even (for subscribers who buy home security services) their comings and goings. Cable systems offering transaction services such as banking and shopping will accumulate detailed computer files on all subscribers. At present, there are no safeguards to prevent the abuse of such records, other than the good will of cable operators. (Responding to these concerns, Warner Amex issued in December a "Code of Privacy" under which the company promises to keep confidential all information it gathers on individual subscribers. The legal force of such promises remains to be tested.)

John Wicklein has elaborated on the dangers this new technology poses to privacy and liberty in *Electronic Nightmare: The New Communications and Freedom*. He argues that the new communications technology will give a few powerful corporations dangerous instruments of social and political control and, should democracy fail, of repression. Total television spells total control, and total control in the wrong hands spells totalitarianism. Indeed, can it be wise to place such information and power even in the "right" hands? Either way, the specter of Big Brother skulks in the shadows, just beyond the glowing tube. The scenario of the corporate Big Brother makes us pawns of a technology that controls us even as its versatility and diversity let us think we have mastered it.

Both this and the Tower of Babel scenario, for all their differences, are equally inimical to democracy. Babel and Big Brother alike subvert citizenship by denying the significance of viewers as public persons with national identities and public obligations.

The Tower of Babel subordinates commonality and public vision to personal choice, private preference, and individual interests. It transforms the most potent medium of public communication the world has known into an instrument of exclusively private concerns. Ironically, it *privatizes* us even as it imperils our privacy. It takes us seriously as consumers, spectators, clients, and buyers and sellers, but it ignores us as citizens. It services lust, religious zealotry, special interests, and individual needs efficiently and pluralistically: It helps us relax or play games, exercise or buy goods, pray or learn French; but it does not help us communicate or seek social justice or formulate common decisions.

Corporate Big Brothers are no less privatistic in their methods: They control by manipulating private wants and master by guiding private tastes. Their world, like Babel, is inhabited by atomized and alienated individuals seeking personal gratification in a society in which only individual wants and corporate profits count.

The Electronic Town Meeting Ten years ago, when he was an FCC commissioner, Nicholas Johnson said: "As never before, Americans need to talk to each other. We hunger to be in touch, to reaffirm our commitment to each other, to our humanity, to the continuity of hope and meaning in our lives. . . . The ultimate promise of cable is the rebuilding of a sense of community." The new television technology has at least the potential of becoming a remarkable new instrument of public communication and collective deliberation. From the ancient world to the American founding, the great enemy of democracy has been scale: the repressive effect of mass society on the communication and participation necessary to self-government. Television in its second age *can* be to the problem of scale what drugs were to disease: a miracle remedy. People can be brought together across time and place and be permitted to confront one another in a continuing process of mutual exploration, deliberation, debate, and decision-making.

What I have in mind has nothing to do with the instant polls and uninformed votes that have characterized the QUBE system's dalliance with politics and that politicians rightly fear. Voting without prior debate, polling without full-scale presentation of positions and facts, expressions of preference without a sense of the public context of choice, all do more to undermine democracy than to reinforce it.

But the true promise of interactive systems, public-access channels, and computer information-banks is that they can enhance knowledge as they enlarge participation. They can equalize by informing the poor as well as the rich and, by providing access to the powerless as well as the powerful, they can help to realize the ideal of an active and informed citizenry. But only if they are offered as a basic public utility at minimal cost to all Americans; otherwise, they will only increase the gap between rich and poor by dividing a single national constituency into two nations: one information-rich and able to participate and influence the national destiny more effectively than ever before, the other information-poor, relegated to still greater powerlessness.

Edwin Parker and Donald Dunn of Stanford University wrote in *Science* in 1972 that "the social goal of [cable television organized as a 'national information utility'] could be to provide all persons with equal opportunity of access to all available public information about society, government, opportunities, products, entertainment, knowledge and educational services." Today, equal opportunity may depend as much on equal information and equal access to communication as on economic equality; with cable television, this becomes a far more realistic aspiration.

In some places, the democratic capabilities of the new telecommunications technology have already been proven. In Reading, Pennsylvania, an experimental project sponsored by the National Science Foundation in 1976 (and developed by New York University) used the local cable system to establish an interactive communications network for the city's senior citizens. The elderly in Reading were able to create programming for themselves, and to hold their elected officials more accountable through a series of public meetings held on interactive cable television. Though this particular experiment has ended, cable's role in Reading's political system has not: Today all budget and community development hearings are conducted by two-way cable. Citizens can participate on-camera by visiting neighborhood centers equipped with television equipment; or they can ask questions from home by telephone. As a result, political participation increased dramatically. Reading's experience demonstrates the new technology's potential to create a more informed and active citizenry.

Perhaps the greatest promise lies with interactive systems like QUBE, which can link up thousands of citizens in an electronic town meeting where information and opinions can be exchanged, expert counsel called upon, and formal votes taken. In Columbus, Warner Amex hasn't seen fit to exploit this capability except as a toy: In amateur talent shows, citizens there can use their two-way cable "vote" to yank acts they don't like. Still, the potential exists.

The promise of the second age of television for democracy remains largely unexplored. Among the thousands of cable companies now serving more than twenty million homes, only a handful offer local political-access channels or services, and none have made service to public citizenship their principal product. Cable television is servicing every conceivable constituency in America save one: America's citizenry, the sovereign governing body responsible for the survival of our democratic republic.

Yet if in this conservative era of deregulation it is too much to hope for a national telecommunications service devoted to democratic and public uses of the new technology, it is surely not too much to call for a public debate on the future of American telecommunications. A number of years ago, former CBS News president Fred Friendly suggested America needed an "electronic bill of rights" to protect it from its pervasive new technology. Even more than a bill of rights, today we need an "electronic constitution"—a positive plan for the public use of a precious national resource on behalf of our nation's faltering democracy. Without such a plan, the electronic road to a national democratic neighborhood may be detoured down back alleys that terminate suddenly in the anarchic privatism of Babel, or in a world of corporate Big Brothers willing to share with us the profits won from destroying once and for all democracy's proud, public "spirit of liberty."

FOR FURTHER READING

Edward Cornish, *Communications Tomorrow: The Coming of the Information Society.* Bethesda, Md.: World Future Society, 1982.

Stuart M. Deluca, *Television's Transformation: The Next 25 Years.* San Diego, Calif.: Barnes, 1980.

Howard F. Didsbury, Jr., *Communications and the Future: Prospects, Promises, and Problems.* Bethesda, Md.: World Future Society, 1982.

Wilson P. Dizard, Jr., *The Coming Information Age: An Overview of Technology, Economics, and Politics,* second edition. New York: Longman, 1985.

Robert W. Haigh, George Gerbner and Richard B. Byrne, *Communications in the Twenty-First Century.* New York: Wiley, 1981.

Brenda Maddox, *Beyond Babel: New Directions in Communications.* Boston: Beacon Press, 1972.

Vincent Mosco, *Pushbutton Fantasies: Critical Perspectives on Videotext and Information Technology.* Norwood, N.J.: Ablex, 1982.

John Naisbitt, *Megatrends: Ten New Directions Transforming Our Lives.* New York: Warner Books, 1982.

Anthony Smith, *Goodbye Gutenberg: The Newspaper Revolution in the 1980s.* New York: Oxford University Press, 1980.

Alvin Toffler, *The Third Wave.* New York: Morrow, 1980.

INDEX